W9-BRN-113

VINTAGE: THE STORY OF WINE

HUGH JOHNSON

SIMON AND SCHUSTER
NEW YORK LONDON TORONTO SYDNEY TOKYO

Simon and Schuster
Simon & Schuster Building
Rockefeller Center
1230 Avenue of the Americas
New York, New York 10020

Copyright © 1989 Mitchell Beazley Publishers
Text © 1989 Hugh Johnson
Maps and Graphics © 1989 Mitchell Beazley Publishers

Edited and designed by
Mitchell Beazley International Limited,
Artists House, 14–15 Manette Street, London W1V 5LB

Simultaneously published in Great Britain by
Mitchell Beazley Publishers, London

Editors	Dian Taylor, Diane Pengelly
Art Editor	Paul Drayson
Illustrations	Pam Williams
Research	Helen Bettinson
Picture Research	Helen Bettinson, Milly Trowbridge
Index	Naomi Good
Production	Ted Timberlake
Managing Editor	Chris Foulkes
Senior Art Editor	Tim Foster

Typeset in Bembo by
Servis Filmsetting Ltd, Manchester, England
Colour reproduction by Scantrans Pte Ltd, Singapore
Printed in West Germany by
Mohndruck GumbH, Gütersloh

10 9 8 7 6 5 4 3 2 1

Library of Congress Cataloging in Publication Data

Johnson, Hugh.
    Vintage: the story of wine / Hugh Johnson.
        p.   cm.
    Bibliography: p.
    Includes index.
        ISBN 0–671–68702–6
        1. Wine and wine making—History.   I. Title.
TP549.J63   1989
641.2′2′09—dc20   89–33928
                                                CIP

CONTENTS

PRINCIPAL MAPS

FOREWORD

Farmer and artist, drudge and dreamer, hedonist and masochist, alchemist and accountant – the winegrower is all these things, and has been since the Flood.

The more I have learned about wine in the course of a quarter of a century of enjoyment, the more I have realized that it weaves in with human history from its very beginnings as few, if any, other products do. Textiles, pottery, bread . . . there are other objects of daily use that we can also trace back to the Stone Age. Yet wine alone is charged with sacramental meaning, with healing powers; indeed with a life of its own.

Why is wine so special? Partly because for most of its history, and mankind's, it has been his one source of comfort and courage, his only medicine and antiseptic, his one recourse to renew his tired spirits and lift him above his weary, saddened self. Wine was the foremost of luxuries to millennia of mankind.

Yet at the same time wine is unpredictable, and hence its value variable; so variable, in fact, that no two seasons nor two vineyards will ever give identical results.

It was the convention, when I began to read and write about wine, to provide each famous growth with a little flourish of history. This one was the favourite of Charlemagne; that of Henri IV, and the other the wine that cured poor Louis XIV of the ague. Classical scholars in particular were fond of referring to the apparently great wines of the ancients, yet never quite explained why their idea of fine wine and ours never matched. I remember thinking how little these anecdotes added to my enjoyment and understanding of what I was drinking, and in my first book, *Wine*, gave them rather short shrift. It was the taste of this mysterious, infinitely varied, infinitely subtle and perpetually inspiring drink that captivated me as a writer, because, first of all, of its utter elusiveness to words.

Words were not the ideal instrument, either, for exploring the relationships between vineyards adjacent on a hillside or opposite each other across a valley: this was geography, and maps were needed. Once I had plotted a vineyard on a map, I found, not only was I able to remember where it was, but even flavours seemed to organize themselves around something so graphic and so demonstrably true.

Maps in their turn were not enough, I later found, to bring into focus the modern world of wine: its goals, its methods, its plant of vineyards and cellars — and above all its practitioners. An encyclopedia was the only way to answer the immediate questions wine-buyers ask – except for the recurring question, why?

To try to fathom the causes and origins of things is a different discipline. It requires reading on a scale I had never undertaken, and a system of enquiry that I had to try and learn. It asks for leaps of the imagination into ages whose traces are few, and places that have disappeared. It demands ruthlessness with rumour, but an ear for clues that ring true. In short it takes a historian – and that I do not pretend to be. That is why I have called this book *The Story of Wine*: it is my interpretation of its history, my attempt to place it in the context of its times, and to deduce why we have the vast variety of wines that we do – and why we don't have others.

Of course it is, before all else, a human story. It begins with the worship of wine as a supernatural being; the bringer of joy. It climbs to the heights of dramatic inspiration, and descends to the depths of fraud, drunkenness, betrayal and murder. It involves passionate spiritual convictions; none more so than the Islamic belief that wine is too great a blessing for this world. It visits the physician at his task of healing, the politician in the act of cheating, the monk in his cell and the sailor at sea.

Wine, one might say, gave man his first lessons in ecology. It was at the birth of biochemistry. It has urged man forward in knowledge, and at the same time degraded him in stupor.

Only 40 years ago wine was in the doldrums, battered by disease, war and poverty; profitless and depressed. Today there are more fine wines in the world, and in greater variety, than ever before in history. Wine is a vast international business, a cultural network that spans more than half the globe, an art form with followers in almost every country – and with a vocal minority of enemies.

All in all, wine is a force to be reckoned with: and never has it been more topical than today. The time is ripe, if ever it was, to see it in its historical perspective.

In acknowledging all those whose help has made this book possible the name that must go first is that of the late James Mitchell, my dear friend and the co-founder of Mitchell Beazley, who encouraged me to write it. Faced with the research for such a vast subject, I turned to a young Cambridge historian Helen Bettinson, who has been the most dogged and ingenious, dedicated and loyal partner that an author could hope for, during four years in the library, on location, and in tracking down illustrations from around the world.

The project was interrupted – if that is the word – by two years' work on a 13-part television documentary series which used the same material in an appropriately different way. *Vintage – A History of Wine*, was co-produced by Malone Gill Productions, W.G.B.H., the Boston Public Broadcasting Service, and Channel 4, London, and sponsored by the Banfi Charitable Foundation. To John and Harry Mariani, the benefactors of the Banfi Foundation, I offer a sincere tribute: they are the world's most dedicated and liberal lovers of wine.

To Michael Gill and Christopher Ralling, the series producers, I owe countless insights into our subject as well as thanks for their patient hand-rearing of a raw presenter. Everyone who worked on the series deserves my thanks here: television is close and gritty work, and I learned something from all of them.

My colleagues at Mitchell Beazley have had a less exciting but no less demanding job. They are tireless, and more indulgent than I deserve. Sadly my editor of many books, Di Taylor, fell ill during the project, having christened it in her inimitable style. But to Chris Foulkes and Diane Pengelly, who shepherded it through, to Paul Drayson who designed it, and to Jack Tresidder, the Publishing Director, I offer the thanks of a sincerely grateful author. And to my wife, Judy, those of a grateful husband.

PART I

The god-like properties of wine: murals in the Villa of Mysteries at Pompeii

CHAPTER 1

THE POWER TO BANISH CARE

It was not the subtle bouquet of wine, or a lingering aftertaste of violets and raspberries, that first caught the attention of our ancestors. It was, I'm afraid, its effect.

In a life that was nasty, brutish and short, those who first felt the effects of alcohol believed they were being given a preview of paradise. Their anxieties disappeared, their fears receded, ideas came more easily, lovers became more loving when they drank the magic juice. For a while they felt all-powerful, even felt themselves to be gods. Then they were sick, or passed out, and woke up with a horrible headache. But the feeling while it lasted was too good to resist another try – and the hangover, they found, was only a temporary disease. By drinking more slowly, you could enjoy the benefits without suffering the discomforts.

Wine provided the first experience of alcohol only for a privileged minority of the human race. For the great majority it was ale. Most of the earliest cities grew up in the grain- rather than grape-growing lands of the Near East: Mesopotamia and Egypt. Although ancient Egypt made strenuous efforts to grow good wine, only a minority had access to it.

But wine was always the choice of the privileged. Mesopotamia imported what it could not make itself. Why should this be? A simple and cynical answer is that wine is usually stronger than ale. It also kept longer, and (sometimes) improved with keeping. One can hardly state categorically that it always tasted better. All we can say for sure is that it was valued more highly.

Other foods and drinks had mind- (and body-) altering effects. Primitive people are acutely aware of poisons. But whatever spirit was in this drink, mysterious as the wind, was benevolent; was surely, indeed, divine. Wine, they found, had a power and value far greater than ale and quite unlike hallucinatory drugs. Its history pivots around this value.

WHAT IS WINE, AND WHAT ARE ITS EFFECTS? What has made men from the first recorded time distinguish between wines as they have done with no other food or drink? Why does wine have a history that involves drama and politics, religions and wars? And why, to the dismay of young men on first dates, do there have to be so many different kinds? Only history can explain.

The polite, conventional definition of wine is "the naturally fermented juice of fresh grapes". A more clinical one is an aqueous solution of ethanol with greater or lesser traces of sugars, acids, esters, acetates, lactates and other substances occurring in grape juice or derived from it by fermentation. It is the ethanol that produces the obvious effect. What is ethanol? A form of alcohol produced by the action of yeasts on sugar – in this case, grape sugar.

Ethanol is clinically described as a depressant, a confusing term because depression is not in the least what you feel. What it depresses ("inhibits" makes it clearer) is the central nervous system. The effect is sedation, the lifting of inhibitions, the dulling of pain. The feeling of well-being it brings may be illusory, but it is not something you swallow with your wine: your wine simply allows your natural feelings to manifest themselves.

What is true of wine is true of other alcoholic drinks – up to a point. Ethanol is the principal active component in them all. Its effects, though, are significantly modified by other components – in other words, the differences between wine and beer, or wine and distilled spirits. Little that is conclusive about these differences has yet been discovered by scientific experiment. We are talking about tiny traces of substances whose precise effect is very difficult to monitor through the complexities of human responses. But much that is clearly indicative has accumulated over centuries of usage.

WINE HAS CERTAIN PROPERTIES that mattered much more to our ancestors than to ourselves. For 2,000 years of medical and surgical history it was the universal and unique antiseptic. Wounds were bathed with it; water made safe to drink.

Medically, wine was indispensable until the later years of the 19th century. In the words of the Jewish Talmud, "Wherever wine is lacking, drugs become necessary." A contemporary (6th century BC) Indian medical text describes wine as the "invigorator of mind and body, antidote to sleeplessness, sorrow and fatigue . . . producer of hunger, happiness and digestion." Enlightened medical opinion today uses very similar terms about its specific clinical virtues, particularly in relation to heart disease. Even Muslim physicians, as we shall see in a later chapter, risked the wrath of Allah rather than do without their one sure help in treatment.

But wine had other virtues. The natural fermentation of the grape not only produces a drink that is about one-tenth to one-eighth alcohol, but its other constituents, acids and tannins in particular, make it brisk and refreshing, with a satisfying "cut" as it enters your mouth, and a lingering clean flavour that invites you to drink again. In the volume of its flavour, and the natural size of a swallow (half the size of a swallow of ale), it makes the perfect drink with food, adding its own seasoning, cutting the richness of fat, making meat seem more tender and washing down dry pulses and unleavened bread without distending the belly.

Because it lives so happily with food, and at the same time lowers inhibitions, it was recognized from earliest times as the sociable drink, able to turn a meal into a feast without stupefying (although stupefy it often did).

But even stupefied feasters were ready for more the next day. Wine is the most repeatable of mild narcotics without ill effects – at least in the short or medium term. Modern medicine knows that wine helps the assimilation of nutrients (proteins especially) in our food. Moderate wine drinkers found themselves better nourished, more confident and consequently often more capable than their fellows. It is no wonder that in many early societies the ruling classes decided that only they were worthy of such benefits and kept wine to themselves.

The catalogue of wine's virtues, and value to developing civilization, does not end there. Bulky though it is, and often perishable, it made the almost-perfect commodity for trade. It had immediate attraction (as soon as they felt its effects) for strangers who did not know it. The Greeks were able to trade wine for precious metals, the Romans for slaves, with a success that has a sinister echo in the activities of modern drug pushers – except that there is nothing remotely sinister about wine.

In this sense it is true to say that wine advanced the progress of civilization. It facilitated the contacts between distant cultures, providing the motive and means of trade, and bringing strangers together in high spirits and with open minds. Of course, it also carried the risk of abuse. Alcohol can be devastating to health. Yet if it had been widely and consistently abused it would not have been tolerated. Wine, unlike spirits, has long been considered the drink of moderation.

EVEN AT ITS MOST PRIMITIVE (perhaps especially at its most primitive) wine is subject to enormous variations – most of them, to start with, unlooked for. Climate is the first determining factor; then weather. The competence of the winemaker comes next; then the selection of the grape. Underlying these variables is the composition of the soil (cold and damp, or warm and dry) and its situation – flat or hilly, sunny or shaded. Almost as important as any of these is the expectation of the market: what the drinker demands is ultimately what the producer will produce.

As soon as wine became an object of trade, these variables will have started to affect its price. Consensus arrives surprisingly quickly. The wine the market judges better makes more profit. If the merchant and the maker work together and do the sensible thing, they reinvest the profit in making their wine more clearly better – and more distinctive.

It is easy to see this process happening in the modern marketplace. It is the standard formula by which reputations for quality are built. The key word is selection: of grape varieties, yes, but also of a "clone", a race of vines propagated from cuttings of the best plants in the vineyard. Then restraint in production: manuring with a light hand, pruning each plant carefully to produce only a moderate number of bunches, whose juice will have far more flavour than the fruit of an overladen vine.

In the ancient world such practices probably first developed in the sheltered economy of royal or priestly vineyards. It would have been the king's butler who commended a particular plant and told the vine dressers to propagate from it. But the principle has not changed. Selection of the best for each set of circumstances has given us, starting with one wild plant, the several thousand varieties of grapes which are, or have been, grown in the course of history. And each grape variety has given the possibility of a distinctive kind of wine.

TAKING THIS PANORAMIC VIEW, the discovery that must have done most to advance wine in the esteem of the rulers of the earth was the fact that it could improve with keeping – and not just improve, but at best turn into a substance with ethereal dimensions seeming to approach the sublime. Beaujolais Nouveau is all very well (and most ancient wine was something between this and vinegar). But once you have tasted an old vintage burgundy you know the difference between tinsel and gold. To be able to store wine, the best wine, until maturity performed this alchemy was the privilege of pharaohs.

It was wonderful enough that grape juice should develop an apparent soul of its own. That it should be capable, in the right circumstances, of transmuting its vigorous spirit into something of immeasurably greater worth made it a god-like gift for kings. If wine has a prestige unique among drinks, unique, indeed, among natural products, it stems from this fact and the connoisseurship it engenders.

How can a rare bottle of wine fetch the price of a great work of art? Can it, however perfect, smell more beautiful than a rose?

No, must surely be the honest answer. But what if, deep in the flushing velvet of its petals, the rose contained the power to banish care?

WHERE GRAPES WERE FIRST TRODDEN

I t is late October in the steep-sided valleys of Imeretia. A mist hides the slow windings of the Rioni, gorged with the noisy waters of Caucasian streams.

Jason put in to the river mouth with his *Argos* and called the river Phasis. The land he called Colchis – the land of the Golden Fleece. They used sheepskins to filter the specks of gold that shimmered in the river shallows.

At intervals all through the subtropical summer fogs have invaded the Black Sea coastline in the afternoons of hot still days, softening the air in the tree-choked gulleys where the streams run and shading the rambling grapevines from the burning sun. Grapevines are everywhere: in stream beds, thick as dragons climbing forest trees, flinging themselves over pergolas, through orchards and against the walls of every wooden balconied farmhouse.

Shaded by laurels among the vines beside the house each farmer keeps his marani – his wine cellar. It is a mystery: there is no sign of wine, of barrels or vats or jars. A series of little molehills in the well-trodden earth is the only clue.

The family brings the grapes here, in long conical baskets, and empties them into a hollowed-out log beside the fence. When the log is half full the farmer takes off his shoes and socks, carefully washes his feet with hot water from a bucket, then slowly and deliberately tramples the bunches until his feet feel no more resistance.

The molehills cover his wine jars, his kwevris, buried to their rims in the laurel-shaded ground. With a hoe he carefully opens one, chipping at the molehill until it reveals a solid plug of oak under the clay. Into the kwevri, freshly scoured with a mop made of corn husks, he ladles the crushed grapes until they almost reach the brim. They will ferment in there, in the cool of the earth, slowly at first, then eagerly, then very slowly, popping single bubbles through a crust of floating skins.

In the spring the wine is ladled out again, with a hollow gourd fixed on a pole, into another scoured-out kwevri, leaving the skins – a potential source of fiery tchatcha, the grappa of the Imeretians and their brother Georgians. Sealed up under its molehill, cool in the shaded marani, the wine will keep almost indefinitely. When the time comes to open it there is no need to send out invitations: the heady perfume

TRANSCAUCASIA

leaps from the freshly opened well. The neighbours come, bringing their wine cups: shallow pottery bowls that the ancient Greeks would recognize. And a long banquet begins, stately and full of toasting and old epic songs.

To the Georgians, as to ancient Greeks, the banquet (their word is keipi) is an art form in itself. For every keipi a tamada, a toastmaster, is chosen. While the food, simple or elaborate, is constantly replenished by the women of the house, the drinking is measured by the tamada. No one may touch his wine bowl until a toast is given, and the speeches that preface them are often long, poetic or witty or brave.

At a long keipi there may be 20 or more toasts, but they are so carefully spaced that no one becomes drunk. Tradition says that the Georgians have always lived under threat; they must be sober enough to defend themselves at any time. The Georgian custom is to drain the wine bowl, then throw away the last drops. They are the number of your enemies. It is important not to have too many, but without any how can you be a real man?

Little has changed in Imeretian custom since the time of Homer; and in the way wine is made, almost nothing since prehistoric times. A Greek or a Roman would call a kwevri a pithos or a dolium: the vessels in which the wine of the ancient world fermented. Transcaucasia, the land of the Georgians and Armenians, is one of the native countries of the wine-grape vine. This could be the place where grapes were first trodden, and man discovered the joys of wine.

Sir John Chardin was a French traveller and jeweller to both the English King Charles II and the Persian emperor.

In the account of his travels to Persia through Georgia which he published in 1686, Chardin wrote of Georgia: "There is no country where they drink more or better wine." His experience of Colchis shows how little has changed in 300 years, at least.

"They hollow the larger trunks of great trees, which they make use of instead of tubs. In these they bruise and squeeze the grapes, and then pour out the juice into great earthen jars, which they bury in their houses, or else hard by . . .. And when the vessel is full, they close it up with a wooden cover, then lay the earth upon it."

Chardin believed that the burial of the wine jars was to hide them from enemies. Georgia was then nominally under Muslim rule, notwithstanding daily transport of great quantities of wine into Media, Armenia and to Ispahan for the king's table.

WE CANNOT POINT PRECISELY TO THE PLACE AND TIME WHEN WINE WAS FIRST MADE any more than we can give credit to the inventor of the wheel. Human agency is no more essential to the principle of the one than the other. A rolling stone is a wheel of sorts; a fallen bunch of wild grapes becomes, partly and fleetingly, a sort of wine. We know of intelligent races (the Incas, for example) who never cottoned on to the wheel. But men and women who lived in the regions where vines grow wild could scarcely fail to notice that grapes (a seasonal part of their diet they must have looked forward to) go through a stage when their juice loses sweetness and gains strength.

Wine did not have to wait to be invented: it was there, wherever grapes were gathered and stored, even briefly, in a container that would hold their juice.

There have been grapes, and people to gather them, for more than two million years. It would be strange if the accident of wine never happened to primitive nomadic man. But before the last Ice Age there were people whose minds were far from primitive. Such high intelligence, such organization and aesthetic sense as the Cro-Magnon people had to paint the masterpieces of the Lascaux caves, in French forests where the vine still grows wild – although now an escape from vineyards –

The Romans called the Caucasus mountains "the end of all the earth". One pass, the Georgian Military Highway, follows the courses of the river Terek and the "black" Aragvi through wild ravines below snowy peaks. Fearful of what lay beyond in Asia, the Romans closed the narrowest gorge with a great wall of iron-shod timbers. It was in the fertile foothills of this range that the first cultivated vines seem to have been grown, and wine made.

suggests that wine could have been known to them, even if we have no evidence one way or the other.

Archaeologists accept accumulations of grape pips as evidence (of the likelihood at least) of winemaking. Excavations in Turkey (at Catal Hüyük, perhaps the first of all cities), at Damascus in Syria, Byblos in the Lebanon and in Jordan have produced grape pips from the Stone Age known as Neolithic B, about 8000BC. But the oldest pips of cultivated vines so far discovered and carbon dated – at least to the satisfaction of their finders – were found in Soviet Georgia, and belong to the period 7000–5000BC.

You can tell more from a pip than just how old it is. Certain characteristics of shape belong unmistakably to cultivated grapes, and the Soviet archaeologists are satisfied that they have evidence of the transition from wild vines to cultivated ones some time in the late Stone Age, about 5000BC. If they are right, they have found the earliest traces of viticulture, the skill of selecting and nurturing vines to improve the quality and quantity of their fruit.

THE WINE-GRAPE VINE is a member of a family of vigorous climbing woody plants with relations all over the northern hemisphere; about 40 of them close enough to be placed in the same botanical genus of *Vitis*.

Its specific name, *vinifera*, means wine-bearing. Cousins include *Vitis rupestris* (rock-loving), *Vitis riparia* (from river banks) and *Vitis aestivalis* (summer-fruiting), but none of them has the same ability to accumulate sugar in its grapes up to about one-third of their volume (making them among the sweetest of fruit), nor elements of fresh-tasting acidity to make their juice a clean and lively drink. The combination of these qualities belongs alone to *Vitis vinifera*, whose natural territory (since the Ice Ages, when it was drastically reduced) is a band of the temperate latitudes spreading westwards from the Persian shores of the Caspian Sea as far as western Europe.

The wild vine, like many plants (willows, poplars and most hollies are examples), carries either male or female flowers; only very rarely both on one plant. The female plants therefore can be expected to fruit – given the presence of a male nearby to provide the pollen. Males, roughly equal in number, will always be barren. The tiny minority of hermaphrodites (those which have both male and female flowers) will bear some grapes, but about half as many as the females.

The first people to have cultivated the vine would naturally have selected female plants as the fruitful ones and destroyed the barren males. Without the males, though, the females would have become barren too. The only plants that would fruit alone or together are the hermaphrodites. Trial and error, therefore, would in time lead to hermaphrodites alone being selected for cultivation. Their seedlings tend overwhelmingly to inherit the habit of bearing both male and female flowers. So eventually the cultivated vine becomes distinguished from the wild one by being consistently hermaphrodite.

Botanists have labelled the two as separate subspecies of *Vitis vinifera*: the wild one as *sylvestris* (woodland); the form resulting from man's selection as *sativa* (culivated). (Strictly, by botanical definition, *sativa* is a cultivar, or cultivated variety, not a subspecies.) The earliest grape pips found in Soviet Georgia can be identified as *Vitis vinifera* var. *sativa* – the basis of the argument that vines were cultivated, and wine presumably made, in the country south of the Caucasus mountains at least 7,000 years ago, and maybe long before that.

To put this era of human history in some sort of perspective, it was when advanced cultures, in Europe and the Near East, had changed from a nomadic to a settled way of life and started farming as well as hunting, when speech and language reached the point where "sustained conversation was possible and the invention of writing only a matter of time", when technology was moving from stone implements to copper ones, and just about the time when the first pottery was made, in the neighbourhood of the Caspian Sea.

It seems, from what faint traces we can see, that it was a peaceful time, which has left us images of fertility rather than power and conquest.

The kwevri is the other evidence of this very early date. In the museum of Tbilisi, the capital of Georgia, is a clay jar that they call a kwevri which archaeologists have dated as early as 5000 or even 6000 BC. In fact its squat, pot-bellied shape resembles even more the pithos of the Greeks and the Roman dolium than the more slender and amphora-like kwevris of today. But it even has, as decoration, a delta-shaped bunch of little knobs on each side of the wide mouth, which could be interpreted as a bunch of grapes.

The same museum contains some rather baffling objects, which, if they have been interpreted and dated correctly, are the oldest indication we have that wine (or rather the grapevine) was held in special regard; perhaps veneration, perhaps affection – although why not both? They are simply cuttings from a vine, about as long as your little finger, which have been given close-fitting silver sleeves, moulded around them so that the characteristic vine-bud shape shows through like a breast through a blouse. There is no mistaking what they are. The vine wood is perfectly preserved. What they are for is another matter. Apparently they were part of the accoutrements of a burial. The simplest conclusion is that the vine was given a precious setting to symbolize its worth; perhaps even to carry it over into the world of the dead where it could be planted and give pleasure again.

These unique objects were found in southern Georgia in Trialeti. Carbon dating puts them at 3000 BC – which was about the time that the rich cities of the Sumerians were developing in Mesopotamia far to the south.

The grapevine is a native of more southern regions, too. All it asks is moisture in the growing season, and a winter rest to make new buds. Persia had her own vines. Although Mesopotamia is vineless, the Zagros mountains curve south from the Caspian Sea down towards the Persian Gulf, providing just the kind of country the wild vine enjoys.

Botanists, perhaps in desperation with such a vagabond, have given names to several strains or subspecies. Vines from the Caucasus and Anatolia have been called *Vitis vinifera pontica*. According to one theory, this strain was distributed as far as Europe by the Phoenicians from what is now the Lebanon and is the ancestor of many of our white varieties of grapes. *Vitis vinifera orientalis* is a strain from the valley of the Jordan whose descendants in Europe (they say) include the Golden Chasselas – Germany's Gutedel and the Fendant of Switzerland.

The wine vine had symbolic, if not sacred, significance to the people of Georgia at least 5,000 years ago. Little cuttings of vine wood were encased in sleeves of silver and buried in tombs, perhaps so that the deceased could plant them again in another world.

Most historians are happy with the idea that Egypt received its first vines from the lands to the north, Canaan or Assyria (it is difficult to know what names to use when one is talking about such vast stretches of time, long before countries in the modern sense existed). But it is also possible that vines came to Egypt down the Nile from African highlands to the south in Nubia, or from the west, along the coast of North Africa (according to one set of legends the route taken by the race who became the Egyptians). In any case, the vines of the Nile valley are said to constitute another subspecies, *Vitis vinifera occidentalis*, a proposed ancestor for many of our red varieties of grape.

WHETHER THESE DIFFERENCES ARE REAL OR SUPPOSED IS ACADEMIC. What matters is the adaptability of the vine. No other plant has adapted itself so effectively to the enormous range of climates and latitudes where man has introduced it. It is one of the most variable of all domesticated plants. Its genes (it has an unusually large number) are readily reshuffled to produce a marginally different variety. But it is also remarkably prone to mutation in the plant itself. Suddenly a bud will develop as a branch with greater vigour, or leaves of a different size or shape, or even grapes of a different colour. The famous Muscat vine of enormous size at Hampton Court near London is an example of spectacular mutation.

Moving a plant to a different region, with a different climate, tends to encourage such mutations. All of which makes the genealogy of grape varieties a Sisyphean labour, and the confident tracing of their remote history an impossible one.

COMPARED WITH SUCH SHIFTING SANDS, legends have a reassuring solidity. There are plenty about where wine was first made – starting, of course, with Noah.

The ninth chapter of Genesis tells how, after Noah had disembarked the animals, he "began to be an husbandman, and he planted a vineyard: and he drank of the wine, and was drunken; and he was uncovered within his tent. And Ham, the father of Canaan, saw the nakedness of his father, and told his two brethren without."

Shem and Japhet, I need hardly remind you, took a garment, walked into Noah's tent backwards to avoid seeing what Ham had seen, covered the old man up and retired.

The repercussions of this rather ambiguous incident were out of all proportion. Noah cursed poor Ham, surely an innocent party, and doomed him to sire the inferior (Canaanite) section of the human race; "a servant of servants shall he be to his brethren". There are practising bigots who can persuade themselves that this is true, and behave accordingly.

To others the drunkenness of Noah constituted the Second Fall of Man. Adam's disgrace was the first. No sooner had God rid the earth of all the sons of Adam except the upright Noah and his family, than the chosen servant of the Lord fell for the first temptation to come his way: his own wine. Pope Julius II instructed Michelangelo to paint Noah's transgression on the ceiling of the Sistine Chapel above the part reserved for the laity (but in full view of his cardinals).

THEOLOGY APART, THERE ARE OTHER INTERESTING ASPECTS TO NOAH'S STORY. First, it was "the mountains of Ararat" where the Ark grounded. Ararat (in Turkish, Buyuk Agri) is the climax of the lesser Caucasian ranges that stretch in pleats and folds down between what is now Turkey and Armenia, a vast double-peaked cone, ice-capped and forbidding, that reaches 16,946 feet (Mont Blanc, the summit of the

---

FAR CATHAY

The civilization of China was well advanced in the Bronze Age, and some sort of wine was an important part of it. Inscriptions on oracle-bones from the Shang and Chou dynasties describe the religious rituals of the time, all of which involved wine. Wine drinking, moreover (in the words of the curator of the great National Palace Museum at Taipei), "has been a favoured pastime of heroic figures and poets since ancient times, and has contributed to the creation of countless masterpieces in the history of human culture".

China has native vines, but *Vitis vinifera* is not among them. The first import of the wine vine to China is well documented. It took place from Persia, in 128BC, when the Chinese general Chang Chien made a famous expedition and spent a year in Bactria. From Fergana, the country east of Samarkand, the general took seed of vines and alfalfa (the horse fodder of the Persians) back to the Chinese emperor. In Fergana, he reported, the wealthy stored grape wine in quantities up to 10,000 gallons, keeping it för several decades without risk of deterioration.

Foreign envoys in China later noted large plantations of both alfalfa and vines not far from the imperial palace. Chinese texts report that vines were abundant in Kashmir, and later in Syria (this was in late Roman times). But the Chinese (and now Japanese) word for a grape, budo, seems to have its roots in the original expedition to Persia. A late Persian word for grape is buda.

No distinction is made in ancient Chinese records between wine made of rice and wine made of grapes or other fruit, nor between wine and what we would call spirits. Some of the bronze vessels used for "heating" wine could have been making a very crude sort of spirit – an

---

Noah, according to the Book of Genesis, was the first winegrower. This 15th-century illumination from a French Book of Hours tells the whole story, from the disembarking of the animals (although from a barn, not a boat) to the planting of his vineyard and his overindulgence. "He drank of the wine, and was drunken; and he was uncovered within his tent."

alembic is not essential to the principle of distillation. Another method that was certainly known to the Chinese in the 7th century AD is that of freezing wine and removing the ice (which is water) from the alcohol. A 7th-century courtier, Meng Shen, wrote that there were two sorts of grape wine, one made by fermentation, with a delicate taste, the other produced by distilling by heat, with a stronger action. The second came from Gaochang on the road to Persia, recently taken by the T'ang emperor.

The development of the Silk Route across Central Asia introduced more and different varieties of vine to China. At various times the growing of vines had the most influential support of all, that of the emperor. K'an-hi, who was contemporaneous with Louis XIV, was a positive Thomas Jefferson of an emperor, experimenting with vines in different parts of his realms, finding that they did well in the north, but rapidly degenerated in the subtropical south. One can almost hear the voice of Jefferson in his declaration: "I would rather procure for my subjects a novel kind of fruit or grain, than build a hundred porcelain kilns."

A note from the 13th century is intriguing for several reasons. Grape wine in glass bottles was sent as tribute from Mohammedan countries to the Mongol Khan. It was an orange liquid, and each bottle contained ten small cups. It was said to be intoxicating – but it was also clearly very rare. Perhaps it was distilled.

Marco Polo's account of wine in China in the late 13th century sounds authoritative: "In Shan-si province grew many excellent vines, supplying a great deal of wine, and in all Cathay this is the only place where wine is produced. It is carried hence all over the country."

Alps, reaches 15,771 feet). A guide to eastern Anatolia says: "The mountain is dangerous: severe weather, ferocious sheepdogs, rock and ice slides, smugglers and outlaws can turn an adventure into a disaster." Many expeditions continue to search the summit for a large lifeboat. In 1951, a piece of wood found in a frozen lake was brought down in triumph.

The Bible thus supports the thesis that the general area of the Caucasus was the original home of wine – unless, of course, one asks the awkward question: where did Noah live before the Flood? Wherever he built the Ark he already had vineyards, and knew how to make wine. Vines, clearly, were among the Ark's cargo.

A crazy but entertaining speculation is that Noah was one of many refugees from the drowning of Atlantis. It is pointed out that Basque legend celebrates a hero called Ano, who is credited with bringing the vine (and agriculture in general) with him in a boat with an unknown port of registry. Basque seems to be one of the most ancient of Western languages, and "ano" is also a Basque word for wine.

Continuing the word game, the spinner of this yarn points out that Galicia has a similar legendary figure, called Noya, that the Sumerians of Mesopotamia told of a sort of merman called Oannes, and that Dionysus was nursed by his mother's sister Ino, a sea goddess. For that matter Dionysus' own name can be seen to embody the same two syllables, which also happen to form the Greek word for wine: oinos. (To which the Georgians, whose unique language is very much older than Greek, reply that their word for wine, ghvino, is the root of all the others.) It is a game any number can play.

MUCH MORE IMPOSING THAN ALL THIS SPECULATION (and much older than the Book of Genesis) is the Babylonian Epic of Gilgamesh, which in part tells the same story of a deluge. Gilgamesh is the oldest literary work known, from perhaps 1800BC, but treats, like all epics, of a much earlier time of heroes.

The 11th tablet of Gilgamesh contains the account of Upnapishtim, who seems to be the Babylonian version (and perhaps the original) of Noah. Upnapishtim also built an ark, filled it with animals (and treasure), sealed it with pitch like Noah, sent out three birds in succession over the floodwaters, and finally grounded on a mountain, where, like Noah, he pleased the nostrils of the gods with burnt offerings.

Upnapishtim does not go on to make wine. Winemaking is the theme of tablet ten, in which the hero, Gilgamesh, setting out in search of immortality, enters the realms of the sun, where he finds an enchanted vineyard whose wine (if he had been allowed to drink it) would have given him the immortality he sought.

> It bears rubies for fruit,
> Hung with grape clusters, lovely to look on.
> Lapis lazuli are its branches,
> It bears fruit, desirable to see. . . .

The divinity in charge was a goddess, Siduri. (In Babylon, as we shall see, women usually seem to have been in charge of the wine supplies.) But if, like the deluge story, and most legendary incidents, some remote historical event lies behind it, could it have recalled an expedition from vineless Mesopotamia to regions that were the source of wine, whether they were in western Syria (as some authorities on the text believe) or in the mountains to the north?

Wine is related to yet another deluge story, this time in Greek mythology. The spring festival of Dionysus in Athens had many meanings. Some of them, as we shall see, tempt one to relate it to the Christian Easter. But one was the commemoration of the great flood that Zeus visited on the evil primitive human race. Only one couple was allowed to survive. Their children included Orestheus, who in this legend planted the first vine; Amphictyon, whom Dionysus befriended and taught about wine; and their sister Hellen, the eldest, who left her name as the name of the Greek (Hellenic) race. It is not in the nature of myths to fit together tidily. But the echoes of the Mesopotamian story here, and the obvious attempts to Hellenize it, are more encouragement to think that behind this legend lies some remote strand of real memory.

Most quoted of all the legends about the discovery of wine is surely the Persian version. Jamsheed – there are many spellings – was a semi-mythical Persian king. Some legends about him seem to relate him to Noah: he is said to have saved the animals by building a great enclosure for them. To Omar Khayyam he represented heroic antiquity:

> They say the lion and the lizard keep
> The courts where Jamshid gloried and drank deep.

At his court, the story runs, grapes were kept in jars for eating out of season. A jar with a strange smell, in which the grapes were foaming, was set aside as unfit to eat, possibly poisonous. A damsel of the harem sought surcease from "nervous headaches" and tried to take her life with this reputed poison. Instead she found exhilaration and refreshing sleep.

Dutifully she told the king, whereupon "a quantity of wine was made, and Jamsheed and his court drank of the new beverage".

CHAPTER 3

THE PHARAOHS AND THEIR WINE

T he Egyptians were not the first to grow wine, but they were certainly the first we know of to record and celebrate the details of their winemaking in unambiguous paintings. Vintage time in ancient Egypt is an image no more remote to us than the medieval harvest in France depicted in tapestries and illuminations. What is hard to register is that the activities we can witness so clearly took place between 3,000 and 5,000 years ago; that the technology of winemaking had by then been thoroughly mastered. There were experts in Egypt who discriminated between qualities of wine as confidently and professionally as a sherry shipper or a Bordeaux broker of the 20th century.

Mesopotamian citizens of the same time were wine drinkers too, but they make a much more shadowy picture: we have no time-capsule tombs to bring their existence to life for us.

Mesopotamia is the land between the two great rivers, the Euphrates and the Tigris, that rise in the mountains south of the Caucasus and flow south to join the Persian Gulf. It is flat, hot and (until irrigated) arid; the very antithesis of natural vine country. The Sumerian race settled here from the north or east some time between 4000 and 3000 BC and founded the cities of Kish and, later, Ur. Kish has provided us with the earliest form of writing that we know: stylized pictures known as pictograms, drawn with a stylus on moist clay. Among them is a recognizable vine leaf. Ur, dating from about 3000BC, offers much clearer evidence of the enjoyment of what is presumably wine in a famous inlaid box known as the Standard of Ur, representing serried courtiers who appear to be toasting their ruler.

It can be argued that their drink was more probably beer in a land where wine was then rare and exotic. On the other hand, who would drink wine if not the courtiers in the royal presence?

THE CITIES OF MESOPOTAMIA KNEW WINE AND USED IT, but where did they get it from? In later times they tried growing it for themselves, but originally it must have been an import from a country where vine-growing was already well established. It could have been the hills to the east in Persia (if vines were grown there then we don't know), but the readiest answer is provided by the Greek historian Herodotus, respectfully known as "the father of history". Two and a half thousand years later he gave an account of the use of the Euphrates for shipping wine to the great city that succeeded Kish and Ur, Babylon.

"But the thing that, next to the city, seems most wonderful to me is this: the vessels that go down the river to Babylon are round and made all of skins. For they make ribs of the willows that grow in Armenia, above Babylon, and cover them with hides stretched over the ribs on the outside to serve as a bottom, making no distinction of stem or stern. The vessels thus made like shields they fill with reeds and use for carrying merchandise down the river, generally palm-wood casks of wine. Every one has an ass on board, and the larger ones more; for after they have arrived at Babylon and have disposed of their cargo, they sell the ribs of the boats and the reeds, then loading the hides on the asses, they return to Armenia by land, the river not being navigable upstream by reason of the rapid current. For that reason they build their boats of skins rather than timber; and when they have driven their asses back to Armenia, they build more boats of the same fashion."

There are several surprises in this wonderfully graphic account – not least that the vessels to hold the wine were not earthenware jars but barrels. The Romans are

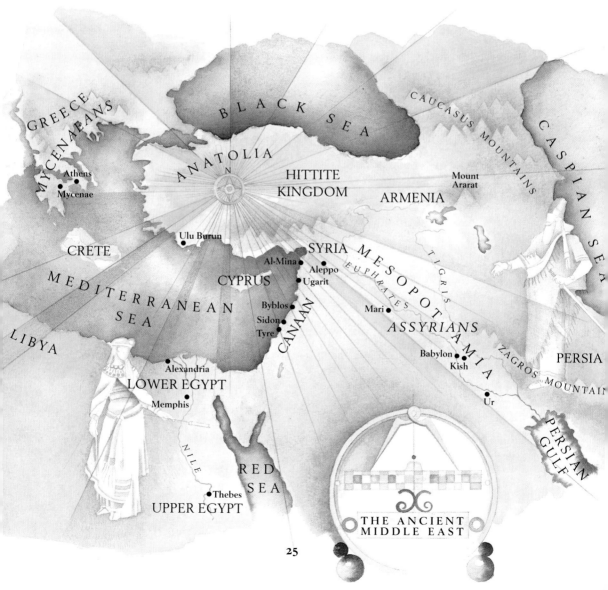

The Standard of Ur is the curious name given to a 5,000-year-old panel, inlaid with
semi-precious stones, now in the British Museum, that represents on one side peace
and on the other war. Peace is symbolized by seated courtiers raising their wine
cups to their ruler in the first known representation of wine drinking.

reputed to have learnt about barrels from the Gauls, and the Greeks not to have used
them at all. But Herodotus, a native of Halicarnassus in Asia Minor, then part of the
Persian Empire, speaks of wine casks as a matter of course. Can he be right, though,
about the wood being palm wood? Palm trunks are almost impossible to saw into
planks. Might they have burnt out the centre of a big log to make a hollow cylinder,
and found some way of sealing the ends? For that matter, if the wine came from
Armenia, where there are better trees, why use palms?

Armenia was not then the little land-locked country that it is today. It was the
whole region south of Georgia, now Eastern Anatolia, a part of Turkey – the region
where the Euphrates rises in the watershed of Mount Ararat.

But why the wine had to come all the way from Armenia is the question. The
Euphrates flows through Assyria, which had wine of its own. Was it perhaps not so
good as that from the mountains farther north? By Herodotus' time, wine had
grown for 2,000 years all around the eastern end of the Mediterranean, from
modern Turkey south through Syria (where Karkemish supplied Aleppo with a
famous wine), through Byblos in the Lebanon and south to Palestine – all this latter
part being then the land of Canaan. The Egyptians, proud enough of their own
wine, particularly prized the wines of the Canaanites.

Among the nations of the region were the mysterious Hittites, who for most of
the second millennium BC occupied the rich heart of Anatolia (rich both in crops and
in metals; it was the principal source of copper during the Bronze Age). If
enthusiasm for wine can be judged by the vessels created for serving and drinking it,
the Hittites score as highly as any ancient race. The artistry of their golden chalices
and rhytons (the hollow animal's head that served both as a beaker and for libations)
has never been bettered, even by the craftsmen of Athens in the 4th century BC.

No one need doubt that this part of the world can make good wine. The modern
Turks, halfhearted winemakers though they are (especially in this most Muslim part
of their country), maintain state vineyards at Elazig by the Euphrates, 200 miles
downstream from Ararat and at the very source of the river Tigris. The red wine
they produce, Buzbağ, is no miracle of finesse, but its potential is very clear; it is full
of vigorous flavour. In the Middle Ages the wines of Tyre and Sidon, in modern

Lebanon, were among the most expensive and sought-after in the world, and even today the Bekaa valley, east of Mount Lebanon, is the home of the celebrated Château Musar, a wild card among the world's great red wines.

TO FORM A CLEAR IDEA OF THE POLITICAL HISTORY OF THE MIDDLE EAST is hard enough even in our own times. To envisage the nations of 4,000 years ago, their culture, their migrations, beliefs and alliances is impossible. The landmarks are their achievements – if archaeologists happen to have stumbled on them.

Yet there is a sketchy picture to be drawn of the major powers around the eastern Mediterranean in the second millennium BC. A united Egypt dominated the south for most of these thousand years – the period known to Egyptologists as the Middle and New Kingdoms. The splendour and technical competence of the Egyptians made the deepest impression on all who came into contact with them. The island of Crete had a civilization comparable in refinement, if not in scale. We

DEATH OF A WINE SELLER

We have traces of legislation about wine from both of the two earliest books of laws that have come down to us: those of Hammurabi, the lord of Babylon from 1792-1750BC, and of the Hittites who brought his kingdom to an end.

Both are so specific that they can only be used as instances, but they paint a real picture. Hammurabi's code is generally fairly lenient in dealing with offenders over matters of trade. It is interesting to note that the three items relating to wine shops carry absurdly violent penalties: a little slip in accounting by the barmaid, and "they shall throw her in the water".

"If outlaws hatch a conspiracy in the house of a wine seller, and she" (note the gender) "do not arrest these outlaws and bring them to the palace, that wine seller shall be put to death."

And, most savagely, "If a priestess or a nun who is not resident in a convent open a wine shop or enter a wine shop for a drink, they shall burn that woman." The inference seems to be that wine sellers were expected to be women, but it was hardly because the calling was a humble one: it clearly carried considerable responsibility. The founder of the Fourth Dynasty of the Sumerian Kish, Queen Azag-Bau, is surprisingly described as "a female wine merchant".

The Hittite code of laws opens a new section at clause 101 under the heading "If a vine". Its clauses deal with every aspect of crops and plants, from stealing wood from a forest to allowing sheep to wander in a vineyard and eat the grapes. In each case the penalty is compensation and a fine. (Fines for slaves were normally half as much as for citizens.)

These laws at least make one thing certain: the wine in question was real wine, made from grapes. Mesopotamia's earliest wine may well have been made from dates; although there is a record of a "garden with vines" as early as 2900BC.

call it Minoan. From about 1500BC Greece was dominated by the Mycenaeans, who attacked and plundered Crete and ended the long and peaceful Minoan years.

Anatolia was the kingdom of the Hittites for the greater part of the period, at its peak extending as far east as Babylon. The eastern shore of the Mediterranean was the land of Canaan, separated from Egypt by the wilderness through which the Bible claims Moses led the children of Israel (in about 1200BC). North and east of Canaan lay Assyria, a great power that waxed and waned over an enormous period of time.

In Mesopotamia (roughly today's Iraq), the civilization of the Sumerians had given way to Semitic peoples from the west. Mari was their chief city, halfway down the Euphrates, until the great Emperor Hammurabi founded the fortunes of Babylon farther downstream (not far from modern Baghdad) in the 1790sBC. For both, the principal trade route was the Euphrates valley westwards towards Anatolia, their source of copper for making bronze. (The island of Cyprus, the other important source, takes its name from the metal it supplied.)

Where the second essential metal for making bronze, tin, came from remains an unanswered question. Unless some Anatolian mine existed and was exhausted, so that its traces are lost, the two possible candidates are Bohemia and Britain. No one knows how far back the tin mines of Cornwall were discovered.

There was a steady flow of trade and diplomacy between these powers. Long though the distances were, there was shipping on every river, the roads skirting the deserts (camels were not yet used to cross it) were busy, and the seaways of the Mediterranean provided a centre of exchange.

The empires surrounding the Mediterranean seem to have had remarkably little interest in asserting their power over its coastline. Their eyes were on the hinterland. Their strategy was to encourage the growth of independent ports of trade which they used as go-betweens, as politically neutral meeting points where merchants would not be frightened away by great castles and armies. Such ports were expected to pay tribute, but left in peace to make the money to pay it.

Ugarit (now Latakia in Syria) was probably the first of these ports, operated by the southern Canaanites, serving the Assyrian kingdom but not belonging to it. Al-Mina at the mouth of the river Orontes, now just in Turkey, was another, founded (although not until 900BC) by the Greeks as their point of contact with the world of the Euphrates. Later, and farther south, came Tyre and Sidon. This was the coast from which the Canaanites' successors, the Phoenicians, the most independent and ingenious of peoples (they invented the alphabet), set off to found a succession of similarly independent and unwarlike trading cities all around the Mediterranean and perhaps even beyond. Carthage in North Africa and Cádiz in southern Spain were among their outposts.

Eventually the great powers – above all the Greeks – developed naval forces to enlarge and protect their dominions. But the principle of the "port of trade" survived centuries of political change. Indeed, Alexander the Great, conqueror of the whole world we are speaking of, founded Alexandria as a neutral port at the mouth of the Nile, inhabited jointly by Greeks and Egyptians and Jews.

A vivid instance of the thriving and complex trade of the eastern Mediterranean came to light in 1987, when the wreck of a richly laden merchant ship was found at

The ancients employed their finest artists in the making of drinking vessels. This Hittite stag's head rhyton in solid silver was made in Anatolia between the 15th and 13th centuries BC. It probably served the double purpose of libations to the gods and refreshment for a priest. Even Benvenuto Cellini in the High Renaissance would not have been ashamed of its craftsmanship.

Ulu Burun, close to the southwest coast of Turkey, her whole cargo still intact. She seems to be a (possibly Canaanite) vessel that traded between Egypt, Canaan, Cyprus, the coast of Asia Minor, possibly Crete and Mycenaean southern Greece. When she sank in about 1400BC she was carrying great ingots of copper and smaller ingots of tin, stocks of the pottery for which the Mycenaeans were famous, pieces of blue glass, valuable arms and precious resins. She was also carrying wine.

WE KNOW EVERYTHING AND NOTHING ABOUT ANCIENT EGYPTIAN WINE. The available detail is almost overwhelming. It is most graphic in the tomb paintings of high officials whose business it was to supervise it, and more lowly craftsmen who so delighted in vines and their fruit that they decorated the ceilings of their tombs as arbours heavy-laden with grapes.

Luxor, the ancient capital Homer called "hundred-gated Thebes", at its height the greatest city in the world, is where most of the evidence is to be found. From Luxor the arid hills of the Sahara rise in golden crags across the Nile. It was here in the Western Desert that the pharaohs' mummies were entombed among treasure so fabulous that their own priests became tomb robbers even before their rock-cut vaults were sealed. Next to the Valley of the Kings, the most remote and desolate of cemeteries, lies the Valley of the Nobles, and a short distance across the desert the necropolis of the artists who worked, century after century, on carving and painting the walls that were to be seen only by the gods.

Royal tomb paintings are preoccupied with sacred matters. Bird- and beast-headed gods perform never-ending parades in a symbolic ballet that touches by its very meaninglessness. Real and descriptive incidents are the exception.

Some of the nobles' tombs, though, are filled with the activities that occupied their owners. Rekhmire, for example, was a high court official whose interests were encyclopedic. The walls of his tomb are a great catalogue of crafts, of foods, of gardens, of foreign races, of beasts and vehicles. What the Nubians or the Syrians wore, or how chairs were made or alabaster polished, is illustrated so accurately that nothing is left to the imagination. Winemaking is just one of the activities that make up a complete picture of Egyptian everyday life. The tomb of Nakht, another lofty bureaucrat, is more freely painted; apparently more for pleasure than information. But it, too, records every detail of the wine harvest, from grape-picking to the fermenting wine.

From these and other tombs it is not difficult to form an accurate picture. It covers a period of time half as long again as that from today back to the birth of Christ, and the passing of 33 dynasties of pharaohs. We know where wine was made and precisely how, how it was named, stored, served and drunk. What we don't know is what it tasted like.

It would not be difficult to reproduce the wines of ancient Egypt. What grape varieties to use would be the principal problem. But if we were to plant a vineyard in the Nile delta country on the antique model (which means in fertile silt, irrigated and manured with dung), train the vines as they did on a high pergola, tread the grapes and ferment their juice in clay jars, we would not expect wine of any quality. Certainly no wine of quality is made in modern Egypt. Yet to dismiss what people of such culture as the Egyptian aristocracy described as good, very good or excellent, took such trouble in making and pleasure in drinking, clearly cannot be right.

Already in some of the earliest pictures of winemaking there are signs of technical ingenuity which was not to be reproduced by any other civilization until modern times. Some of it is just applied common sense. Treading grapes in an open tank is trickier than it looks: to keep your footing in the deep slippery mass you need something to hold on to. Port treaders doing the same job in Portugal today hold on to each other, arms around neighbours' waists in a tight-linked chain. The Egyptians had a marvellously simple idea: bars across the treading floor just above

The art of glassmaking was developed to perfection by the Egyptians. This 18th-dynasty decanter in the form of a bunch of grapes is an extraordinary technical feat. The wine it contained may not have been up to quite the same standard.

head height. Workers steadied themselves as they trampled, like strap–hangers on an airport bus. Slightly later, Egyptian technology even anticipated the straps: workers are shown supporting themselves by short lengths of rope hanging from the rafters of a roof of reeds set up to shade them from the sun.

Another ingenious device they developed was the sack–press, in which the skins, after treading, still rich with valuable juice, are squeezed in a giant tourniquet which both recovers the juice and filters it. The Egyptian word for it is the same as that for wringing out the wash.

We can be sure the grapes they picked were fully ripe. Under the Egyptian sun they would have been honey-sweet. Most pictures show us black grapes. They also show us dark juice running from the press into the fermenting jars, which suggests (since treading alone extracts little colour from grape skins) that fermentation began in the trough where the grapes were trodden.

Not surprisingly, some paintings show the fermenting wine overflowing its jars: with very sweet juice and Egyptian autumn temperatures, the first fermentation would be as "tumultuous" as it is often called. We see no sign of filtration. Probably some sort of strainer held back the bigger particles of stalk and skin in the trough, but the fermenting wine must have included a fair amount of solid matter. After the first violent fermentation one might expect the wine to be racked, or transferred off its gross lees, to finish fermenting in a clean amphora. There are no pictures which show this being done. Siphoning would be the obvious

Tomb paintings from ancient Thebes might have been designed expressly to tell us the details of the Egyptian wine harvest. In this scene from the tomb of Kha'emwese the whole process is illustrated. Reading from right to left from the top, the grapes are picked from arbours (the vines are planted in raised troughs), a tally of the crop is taken, the grapes are trodden and a priest offers the juice to the gods (today he is called an oenologist and works in a laboratory). The wine is sealed in "Canaanite jars" for fermentation. The lowest level shows the wine being transported by boat along the Nile.

way to do it; the Egyptians used siphons, but not for this: apparently they just closed the original amphora with a rush bung completely covered with an immense clay capsule for the final stages of fermentation, leaving a small hole for the carbon dioxide to escape until all bubbling ceased, when the hole was plugged. While the clay of the capsule was still soft it was often stamped with the seal of the estate.

It is strange that, according to the pictures, they did not bury the jars as the Georgians bury their kwevris. None of the pictures shows any efforts at keeping the jars cool as they fermented – a fundamental precaution in a hot country, where the transition from juice to wine to vinegar can be disastrously quick. The final sealing with clay was undoubtedly as effective as any cork, but if the wine did keep well (or keep at all) it must have been due to its high alcohol content more than to hygienic making or inherent stability.

The fact that it was the regular practice to paint or stamp in the seal the year of the vintage, along with other details of the wine's provenance or purpose, is usually taken to mean that it was intended to be aged. The fact that relatively old wines were among the supplies left in royal tombs seems to bear this out.

On the face of it, though, freshness must have been the quality desired just as often as maturity. It seems reasonable to see the vintage date as a simple piece of information, just as it is today. For Beaujolais Nouveau the best vintage is the most recent; not so for vintage port. Perhaps the same thoughts went through the head of the "bearer of secrets in the wine-hall" – the title of the pharoah's palace manager.

How the Egyptians drank their wine is even better known to us than how they made it. Painting after painting expresses with brilliant vitality the pleasure they took in it. Scenes of feasting are sometimes serene, elegant, decorative, sometimes boisterous and licentious, but always painted with loving attention to the attitudes and relationships of the men and women involved. There are scenes so graphic, of girls gossiping, of dignified couples with their pets, of musicians and serving girls

GRAVE GOODS

When the tomb of the 19-year-old King Tutankhamun, who died in 1352BC, was opened by the great Egyptologist Howard Carter in 1922, he found among the treasures around the golden mummy the wine jars that were to accompany the royal spirit on its journey.

Twenty-six of the 36 amphoras were labelled, seven with the seal of the king's personal estates, and 16 with the name of the royal house of Aten; both "on the Western River" (the western arm of the Nile delta, always considered Egypt's best wine country).

Twenty-three of the wines came from three vintages: "year 4", "year 5" and "year 9". Whether these are the years of the king's reign, or whether they simply indicate the age of the wine, is unclear, but they show that top-quality wine was appreciated at a considerable age. One amphora is even dated "year 31" – which cannot refer to the king's short reign. The name of the chief vintner is recorded on every amphora except the three oldest. One chief vintner, Kha'y by name, made five of the wines of Tutankhamun's estate, but also one of the House of Aten, which suggests either that the royal officials ran both estates, or that Kha'y was such a gifted vintner that, like Professor Peynaud in Bordeaux today, he was responsible for several top estates at the same time.

Two wines (both labelled Sdh, which seems to mean new or fresh) are labelled "very good quality". The others are only described in any way if they are sweet (four out of the 26). By this analysis the most telling piece of information (apart from the vintage) on each label is the name of the chief vintner. What could be more realistic? Nothing matters more than the man who makes the wine.

(who are usually all but naked), that one feels like an eavesdropper on their perpetual partying.

Egyptians feasted in an atmosphere of brilliant colour, powerful perfumes (they put scented ointment on their heads which slowly melted and trickled down their braided hair and wigs), garlands of flowers and vine branches, lotus blooms and lotus buds. Sometimes they drank from wine cups, sometimes through straws directly from wine jars. Wine from different jars was sometimes siphoned into a fresh one, presumably to be blended. When wine was poured from an amphora it was often sieved (which confirms that solid matter was left in it after fermentation). There is not much evidence of self-restraint in these feasting scenes: ladies are occasionally sick, although nobody is seen under the table or being carried out.

The Greek writer Athenaeus believed that "among the Egyptians of ancient times, any kind of symposium was conducted with moderation. . . . They dined while seated, using the simplest and most healthful food and drinking only as much as would be sufficient to promote good cheer." But Victorian schoolmasters would have their pupils believe that all Greeks were sober, upright and honourable men.

The prestige of wine is clear from its ritual use as offerings to gods and to the dead. Beer was the everyday drink; it had no part in ritual. (Egypt's vineyards were never large. Wine consumption must always have been limited to the rich, and to the priesthood.)

The wine left in tombs, even from the earliest dynasties, is designated by origin, even if only vaguely. By 2470BC (the fifth dynasty), six different "appellations" were in use. Whether they signified distinctly different sorts of wine, or merely where they came from, we don't know. "Wine from Asia", an import, probably from Syria or Canaan, is also mentioned. Egyptian ships regularly visited Byblos in Canaan to buy timber. The famous cedars of Lebanon were one of Egypt's chief imports; palm trees are no better for building than they are for barrel-making.

The Egyptians buried their dead with food and drink for their survival into the afterlife, where they expected to entertain friends. This scene of feasting in a Theban tomb of 1500BC shows the kind of posthumous party they had to look forward to. Servants were informally dressed. The wine jars are clearly visible, wreathed with garlands to keep them cool.

By the time of the "New Kingdom", which came into being in 1550BC, and whose most famous monument is the tomb of Tutankhamun, the labelling of wine jars was almost as precise as, say, California labelling today – with the exception of the grape variety. It specified the year, the vineyard, the owner and the head vintner. The leading vineyards were on the "West River" (the western arm of the Nile delta), at Sile, Behbeit el-Hagar, Memphis and the oases – all in Lower Egypt. Wine-growing was not attempted, it seems, in Upper Egypt until the rule of the Greek-inspired Ptolemies from 300BC.

Insofar as the Egyptians ascribed wine to one particular god it was usually to Osiris, the god of life after death, who was also responsible for plant life. He was addressed as "lord of the wine at flooding" and "lord of carousing at the festival". Later Greek writers were apt to associate Osiris with Dionysus, the Greek wine god, but there is little evidence that he was held responsible in a direct way with wine and its effects on the spirit, as Dionysus was. Other gods are equally associated with wine. It is described as the sweat of Re (the sun god) and the tears of Horus, son of Osiris and the earth goddess Isis. "Horus-eye" could mean anything that was particularly treasured or valuable. "Green Horus-eye" and "white Horus-eye" are frequently mentioned in reference to wine.

VINEYARDS AS WELL AS WINE WERE DEDICATED TO DEITIES. The great pharaoh Ramses III, in the 11th century BC, recorded his gifts to Amun, the god of Thebes, and in a sense Egypt's national god. They included "vineyards without limit for you in the southern oasis and also in the northern oasis, and others in great number in the southern region . . . . I equipped them with vintners, with the captives of foreign lands and with canals from my digging . . . ." From the same period a letter has survived that gives a precise picture of the scale of operations on a fairly small delta wine estate:

"Another communication to my lord. I have arrived at Nay-Ramesse-miamun on the edge of Ptri-waters with my lord's scow and with two cattle-ferries belonging to the 'Mansion of Millions of Years of the King of Upper and Lower Egypt, Usikheperure-setpenre, in the House of Amun', and found that the vineyard keepers were 7 men, 4 lads, 4 old men, and 6 children, total 21 persons. For my lord's information, the whole of the wine which I found sealed up with the master of the vineyard-keepers Tjatroy was: 1,500 jars of wine, 50 jars of sdh-wine, 50 jars of Pwr-drink, 50 pdr-sacks of pomegranates, 50 pdr-sacks and 60 krht-baskets of grapes. I loaded them into the two cattle-ferries belonging to the 'Mansion of Millions of Years of the King of Upper and Lower Egypt', and sailed downstream from Pi-Ramesse-miamun, 'The great soul of Pre-Harakhti'. I handed them over to the controllers of the 'Mansion of Millions of Years of the King of Upper and Lower Egypt'. I have written to let my lord be cognizant."

The elements of this picture are still in place. The Nile slides majestically on among its palms. The shaduf raises water for the irrigation channels. The same brown faces smile and quick-footed donkeys run. White-winged feluccas are not precisely the boats that this accountant sailed in. But the Egypt of today matches its ancient records at so many points that only a little imagination is needed to visit the pharaonic world. It is a different matter with the world of the ancient Greeks.

CHAPTER 4

GREECE: THE WINE-DARK SEA

"The peoples of the Mediterranean began to emerge from barbarism when they learnt to cultivate the olive and the vine." It was Thucydides, the Greek historian, who wrote this at the end of the 5th century BC, when Athens had become the centre of the most cultivated and creative society the world had known.

Thucydides probably had no notion of when the process began to which he attached so much importance. It is still unclear. What seems to have happened is that about the time of the founding of Egypt (c. 3000BC), the precursors of the Greeks settled in four main areas around the Aegean: south and east-central Greece, the island of Crete, the Cycladic islands in the southern Aegean, and the northwest coast of Asia Minor. These are the places where most traces have been found of the earliest towns of the Aegean, with substantial public buildings and signs of overseas trade. They are also where vines and olives were being cultivated; two crops that added new dimensions to a primitive diet of corn and flesh, that could be grown on land too poor and rocky for grain, or grown in cornfields without reducing the corn crop: in both cases adding dramatically to the rations available, and hence to the potential population.

A rise in the population led directly to a more complex social system. A town is not a village; specialization begins; one man farms, another trades in his produce, a third becomes a lawyer to settle their disputes. Before long there is a need for administration, for ships' crews, for an army, and soon the force of personality brings out a leader, who establishes his family in a position of power.

Thucydides, I hasten to add, was not guilty of this glib sort of social history. But he was aware that oil and wine were powerful stimulants to trade; that trade led to the exchange of ideas, and that wine in particular brought a new dimension to social intercourse. Wine led naturally to festivities, to confidences, to a sense of occasion (which also had religious significance). The gold and silver drinking vessels that appeared in the Aegean at this time would hardly have been created for water. So wine feeds on its success, good wine fetches a premium, therefore more good wine is made. The better it is, the greater the demand, and the more stimulus for trade.

By the year 2000BC Crete had developed, partly through contact with Egypt, a rich, successful, cultivated and complex civilization based on a royal palace in which power and skills were concentrated. Writing had been invented, and the level of artistic accomplishment remains to this day a source of wonder.

By the year 1500BC Crete was superseded as the great power of the Aegean by Mycenae in southern Greece, whether by conquest or assimilation is not clearly known. The Mycenaeans were more aggressive than the Minoans of Crete, more active in trade and colonization. Their ships traded from Sicily in the west to Syria in the east (and of course with Egypt). It was the Mycenaeans, under their great leader Agamemnon, who with their neighbours the Spartans laid siege to Troy; the story told by Homer centuries later in epic verse.

Recent excavation has brought to light the wine cellar of one of the rulers of this era, King Nestor of Pylos, another city of the Peloponnese that took part in the Trojan war. Nestor's cellar had a capacity estimated at 6,000 litres in the big storage jars known as pithoi. The wine was delivered to the cellar in animal skins, which will have made their own contribution to its bouquet. Nonetheless, legend ascribes to Nestor the two-handled cup of pure gold which is one of the greatest treasures of the National Museum in Athens.

Homer, telling the story of the siege of Troy and the travels of Odysseus, the half-remembered epics of the Mycenaean era, gives us detailed information about at least some of the sources of its wine. He names the island of Lemnos in the Aegean as the supplier of wine for the Greek armies besieging Troy (it lies conveniently en route, 50 miles from the Trojan shore). Much-appreciated wine from Thrace to the north was also transshipped there. The Trojans' wine came from Phrygia, Troy's hinterland in Asia Minor. In the Peloponnese he names Epidaurus, famous for its colossal theatre, and Pedasos in Boeotia, in central Greece he mentions "Arne rich in vines" and on Euboea, the long island on the east coast, Histaia.

On his voyage Odysseus took wine from his own island, Ithaca, but also extra-high-strength wine he had extracted as a ransom from Maro, the priest of Apollo at Imarus in Thrace, the mainland to the north of the Aegean. The priest's Maronean "red wine, honey-sweet" was supposedly so strong that it was usually drunk diluted 1:20 with water.

Odysseus used this as his secret weapon. On the coast of Sicily the Cyclops Polyphemus, the one-eyed monster, captured him and devoured his companions. Odysseus offered him Maronean wine by way of a *digestif*. Polyphemus was accustomed to weak Sicilian wine – presumably made from unpruned wild grapes. Good Greek wine overwhelmed him. "Thrice in his folly he drank it to the lees", and sank into a deep sleep, in which Odysseus put out his single eye. The boulders that the blinded giant threw at the fleeing Odysseus are still to be seen, half-submerged, in the sea near Mount Etna.

Through Homer's *Iliad* the image of the "wine-dark sea" runs like a refrain. The poet's description of the shield of the hero Achilles has the ring of a favourite scene remembered: ". . . a vineyard laden with grapes . . . was beautifully wrought in gold, but the bunches themselves were black and the supporting poles showed up throughout in silver. All around it ran a ditch of blue enamel and outside that a fence of tin. The vineyard was approached by a single pathway for the pickers' use at

vintage time; and the delicious fruit was being carried off in baskets by merry lads
and girls, with whom there was a boy singing the lovely song of Linus in a treble
voice to the sweet music of his tuneful lyre. They all kept time with him and
followed the music and the words with dancing feet." It is a vision of vintage time,
of autumn's gilded haze, of labour and laughter that has never faded.

AN UNRECORDED CALAMITY STRUCK MYCENAE. A fierce race from the north (it is
supposed) laid waste to the Minoan-style palace culture of the Mycenaeans and their
allies in the century between 1200 and 1100BC. Dorians is the name given to these
invaders. All the empires of the Near East were shaken during this period and all
except Egypt fell. In Greece the art of writing was lost with the palace officials, and
Greece entered what historians call the Dark Age of dim memories, comparable
with the state of Europe after the fall of the Roman Empire one and a half thousand
years later.

The Greeks pursued the fantasy of maenads and satyrs, the followers of Dionysus, with gusto and obvious enjoyment in endless vase paintings, the main form in which Greek classical painting has survived. The painter Amasis of Athens decorated a black-figure amphora with this scene of satyrs at vintage time in about 540BC. One satyr harvests, one treads the grapes in a trough from which the juice runs straight into an almost-buried pithos for fermentation. Three more ithyphallic gentlemen are busy with cellar work.

To the Greeks of later years, Homer included, the age of Mycenae was the age of heroes, when the Olympians walked on earth. Certainly the ruins of Mycenae, built of stupendous blocks of stone, impose the idea of giants and superhuman forces.

Yet whatever people the new Greeks were, they had energy and intelligence to more than match their predecessors. Within two centuries the Aegean had again become a centre of creative activity. This perhaps was the age that Thucydides was talking of, when Greeks, including Mycenaean refugees, moved into the islands of the Aegean and across the sea to Asia Minor, turning the shores of Phrygia and Lydia, the former land of the Hittites, into "East Greece". They brought their characteristic vine-and-olive agriculture to every rocky spot, and with it the potential for civic life, commerce, and further colonization and conquest. Of this new era Athens, never entirely overrun by the Dorian invaders, became from the start the cultural and artistic leader.

At first Greece had to import its skills once again from the east. The art of fine metalwork was reintroduced, with iron now superseding bronze as the metal of the armourers. In the east, Phoenicia had taken the lead in both skills and exploration, founding her new cities far to the west at Carthage and Cádiz. From Phoenicia, via their new trading post in the east, Al-Mina, the Greeks adopted the new-coined alphabet. Written Greek, the language of Homer, was born in the 9th or 8th century BC. When the Olympic games were started in 776BC written records were kept. The idea of the palace and its administration returned. And with all this came the growth of population that once more intensified economic activity. Greece was ready to emulate the Phoenicians in voyages of exploration, and the founding of new cities outside the "Greek lake" that the Aegean had become.

THE EUBOEANS LED THE WAY. Euboea lies alongside Attica on the east coast of central Greece like a huge galley docked beside the mainland. Its citizens may have founded Al-Mina; perhaps it was here, from the Phoenicians, that they learnt to improve their ships for longer voyages. They went to Cyprus. They were the first to set up a colony in Italy, or rather off Italy, on the island of Ischia, just off the Etruscan shore, early in the 8th century. (The Etruscans themselves, mysterious in their origins, are said in legend to have been refugees from the fall of Troy.) By the middle of the century they had ventured onto the Italian mainland and founded Cumae, and had started the first Sicilian colony at Naxos (just south of Taormina) to defend the straits of Messina, between the toe of Italy and the football of Sicily.

The Euboeans also moved north on the Greek mainland, naming the three-pronged promontory of Chalcidice after their city of Chalcis. Parians from the island of Paros in the Cyclades settled in Thrace, famous for its horses, but were driven offshore, onto the island of Thasos, by its malaria. Thasos became so famous for its wine that Thasian coins all carried the head of the wine god and a bunch of grapes, rather as postage stamps advertise the local produce today.

The Euboeans were swiftly followed westwards by the Corinthians, who founded Syracuse in Sicily, the Rhodians, who also went to Sicily and founded Gela, the Achaeans from the northwest Peloponnese who settled on the fertile instep of Italy's boot and founded the city of Sybaris, so rich in its brief period of affluence that the word "sybaritic" is still in use today. Their second foundation Poseidonia (now Paestum) in Campania is famous for its three magnificent temples, almost unscathed by time.

The Spartans founded Tarentum, the modern Taranto, on the inside of the heel of Italy. The Rhodians founded Neapolis, whose modern name is Naples. Corinth extended its commonwealth north up the Adriatic to Corfu and Dalmatia. Athens went further and settled (or at least traded) in Lombardy, at the mouth of the river Po, where its colonists made contact with the Etruscans. Many of the colonies have misty origins, or were founded by more than one city or island. And very soon such thriving colonies as Syracuse had their own litters, so that Sicily and the toe of Italy were called "Magna Graecia" – greater Greece. They were also called Oenotria – the land of (staked) vines.

Various theories are in circulation about why the vines of Italy at this time were described as "staked" – presumably in contrast to Greece, where they were either grown in trees or prone on the ground. One is that Magna Graecia was colonized by a new kind of capitalist entrepreneur, whose farming methods were more intensive than the old ways; that a vineyard became for the first time a monoculture, tidily staked, and so presented a very different appearance.

Another is that traces were still evident in Italy of an earlier wave of Greeks – the Mycenaeans, who had travelled this way a thousand years before. It is certain that Mycenae did trade with Italy and its islands. Lipari, one of the little volcanic Aeolian islands just north of Sicily, was the source of obsidian; black volcanic rock that splits to a razor-sharp edge – far sharper than anything they could have made of bronze. If Mycenaeans knew that sea route and braved the steep grey rollers south of Italy, then perhaps the Minoans did before them . . . . But to these new colonists that was very ancient history, only dimly remembered in the legend of Odysseus.

TO THE SAME NEW ERA OF ENERGETIC SEARCHING FOR MORE LAND belongs the first Greek colonization of southern France, when the Phocaeans from Lydia in Asia Minor, under threat from the Persian invasion of their homeland, founded Massalia where Marseilles stands today, and also settled in Corsica.

Massalia was a masterstroke. Some say the Etruscans got there first, but whether they did or not, it gave the Phocaeans control of the route up the Rhône and across the heart of France to the tin mines of southern Britain. Their original route lay up the Saône, through Burgundy, then overland to the Seine where they established a point of contact at Mont Lassois, 100 miles southeast of Paris, and left spectacular relics. Another route lay down the Loire to the Atlantic.

By 500BC Massalia was making its own wine, and its own amphoras to export it. According to the Roman historian Justinius, "from the Greeks the Gauls learned a civilized way of life . . . to cultivate the vine and the olive. Their progress was so brilliant that it seemed as though Gaul had become part of Greece." A more modern historian points out that the first wine drunk in Burgundy was probably Greek wine from Marseilles (or indeed from Greece, shipped by the Etruscans). Again the question arises: had the Etruscans beaten the Greeks to it? There is no conclusive evidence, but the enthusiasm of the Gauls can be judged by the fact that within 200 years they had in turn overrun northern Italy, reached the youthful city of Rome, and performed the ever-popular ritual of sacking it.

CITIZENS OF MILETUS IN "EAST GREECE", or Asia Minor, seem to have been the first through the Bosphorus into the Black Sea, founding the trading posts of Sinope and Trapezus (modern Trebizond) on the south shore, and Phasis in Georgia – to them Colchis, the land of the Golden Fleece.

From Attica, Athens' neighbours the Megarans sailed as far north as they could go, reaching the Crimea and the mouth of the river Dniepr in the land of the

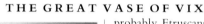

THE GREAT VASE OF VIX

Ideas about the connections between the world of the Greeks and the Celtic world of northern Europe were transformed in 1952 by the discovery, between Paris and Burgundy, of the most magnificent Greek vase that has ever been found. It lay in the tomb of a Burgundian princess at Vix, near the trading centre of Mont Lassois on the river Seine, where Phocaean Greeks, and probably Etruscans too, went for shipments of tin from the mines of Cornwall.

The vase, or crater, of Vix is a wine-mixing bowl in the finest bronze, standing seven feet high and with a capacity of 1,200 litres, or about 45 amphoras of wine. The princess died in about 600BC. One amphora of wine was traded at that time in Gaul for one slave. Almost more astonishing than the opulence implied is its carriage, either from southern Italy or Greece, either up the Rhône and Saône valleys or over Alpine passes. Expert opinion differs as to where it was made. Sparta is one theory, another is south-central Italy, where Etruscan and Greek cultures mixed. So huge and fragile an object must have been taken to pieces for transport, its great bronze shell cut up and then welded together again. But whether it travelled on pack animals over the Great Saint Bernard Pass or by ships and barge and wagon via Massalia, today Marseilles, its presence in the heart of France tells us that the Greeks had no monopoly of power even at the height of their colonizing period. It also tells us that the French loved their wine.

Scythians. These remote ancestors of the Russians were famous horsemen and archers (they were recruited, it is said, as policemen for Athens). The Scythian race originated in the region of Persia and was accomplished in fine metalwork. Their arms took them as far south as Palestine and as far east as Babylon. The Greeks introduced wine to Scythia, planting vines in the Crimea. The tomb of a Scythian chief of 500BC, found near the river Dniepr, was arranged with an amphora of Greek wine from Chios at his head and another at his feet, with a cup, dipper and strainer for him to help himself laid ready at his side. Of Scythia's own wine the Roman Ovid later said that you needed an axe to cut it. (A similar story is still told in Bulgaria; that their Mavrud can be carried in a handkerchief.)

WHAT CAN WE SAY ABOUT THE QUALITIES OF GREEK WINE? The Aegean islands were the main exporters, possibly because they were more prone to specialize. They lacked trees (except sometimes olives), and the wind forced them to grow their vines low against the stony soil, where the grapes would reach much greater ripeness than bunches hanging in rich swags between arching trees; the Arcadian picture of an idyllic vineyard.

Of the islands, Chios in the eastern Aegean, off the coast of Ionia in "East Greece", was the biggest exporter, and by most accounts had the best wine. It has been called the Bordeaux of ancient Greece. Its characteristic amphoras, easily identified by their design and the quality of their pottery, and usually stamped with the Chian emblem of a sphinx, an amphora and a bunch of grapes, have been found in almost every country where Greeks traded from the 7th century onwards. In 620BC a Greek trading town was established (with Egyptian permission) at Naucratis on the western branch of the Nile delta. From its very beginnings it imported Chian wine, as well as oil and silver, to trade for papyrus and Egyptian luxury goods. Chian wine jars have been found high up the Nile in Upper Egypt. They have also been found at Marseilles, in Tuscany, in Bulgaria, and in eastern Russia.

Equally famous was the wine of Lesbos, the large island due north of Chios, the home of the poetess Sappho (whose brother, it seems, combined the trades of wine merchant and procurer at Naucratis; a city famed for the "looks and easy virtue of its women"). Lesbian wine was highly rated under the island's name, but Lesbos may also have been a source (or *the* source) of Pramnian, the Greek equivalent of the rarest and most luscious of all wines, Tokay Essenczia. To make Essenczia the very ripest grapes are piled high until their own weight squeezes out thick drops of a sort of nectar. They are never pressed. So full of sugar is Essenczia that it ferments only very slightly, if at all. It remains a viscous honey-sweet fluid with legendary powers of revival in all situations where revival is desired.

Sweetness is praised in contemporary accounts of many Greek wines. Most often it was probably achieved in exactly the same way as the Cypriot Greeks make, and always have made, their Commandaria. The grapes are picked fully ripe, then laid out on straw mats (plastic today) in the vineyard for a week or so for the sun to really concentrate their sugar. A similar method is used in Spain at Jerez for sherry-making. Homer and his less famous successor, Hesiod, both describe the sun-drying of grapes in this manner. Surprisingly one writer, Archestratus, describes a Lesbian

The little island of Delos, in the very centre of the Aegean, was for centuries the hub of trade between the Greek mainland, Asia Minor, Egypt and the Greek colonies of Italy. The whole island was holy ground, sacred to Apollo, and during the first war with Persia it was used as the treasury of the confederacy of Greek cities. It has been uninhabited for nearly 2,000 years.

''THE CANAANITE JAR''

The standard wine container of the ancient world was the amphora, a clay vase with two handles, ranging in shape from the Don Quixote to the Sancho Panza, but generally rather like a root vegetable with a long neck. Its bottom end was either pointed like a root, or formed into a knob, but never flat. Size varied widely. Greek amphoras averaged about 40 litres, Roman ones about 26 litres – call it nearly three dozen modern wine bottles.

The amphora was an invention of the Canaanites, the forebears of the Phoenicians, who introduced it into Egypt before 1500BC. Up to that time Egyptian wine jars (used for fermenting and storage) had been of a similar shape, but without handles. The name (which is Greek) means something which can be carried by two; one on each side. So useful was the invention of a strong, inexpensive, disposable or reusable, easily lifted and stored container that amphoras were used for any substance that can be poured. Although wine was their usual contents, oil, grain, water, and the favourite seasoning of the Romans, the "garum" made of the fermented remains of fish, were often transported in amphoras.

Some ended their working life as funerary urns, a child's coffin, or even as roofing materials. Herodotus tells the story of how one Greek clan, the Phocaeans, even set an ambush with them. They dug a pit in a narrow mountain road, filled it with empty amphoras, then covered them with earth. When the enemy cavalry arrived the pit caved in and the horses were trapped.

A potter makes an amphora on his wheel in two or three sections; it is too big to turn all at once, and he cannot reach inside the neck to shape it. The sections are moulded together wet, then wine as having "its liquid locks thickly overgrown with white flower", which is a fair enough poetic description of the growth of the yeast called flor that sherry makers depend on for the special savour and longevity of their wine. One vase painting shows a long dipper, remarkably like a sherry-shipper's *venencia*, ideal for plunging through the scum of flor (in an amphora?) to extract a clear sample of wine.

Certainly the Greeks of Homer's time already recognized many different varieties of wine. Laertes, the father of Odysseus, whose vineyard was his pride and joy, boasted that he had 50 rows, each of a different vine, so that he had ripe grapes in a long procession from summer to late autumn.

The island of Thasos, off Thrace, was another quality producer, but of a (probably lighter) wine with a characteristic scent of apples. In Thasos today you may still see the gauging stone, pierced with holes, for measuring the standard sizes of Thasian amphoras. Mendean from Chalcidice and Magnesian from Thessaly on the northeastern mainland were also mentioned as good, although not as good as Bybline, which appears to have been a wine exported from Byblos in the Lebanon by the Phoenicians. Bybline remained a byword for quality into Roman times – and had its successors in the Lebanon in the Middle Ages: Tyre and Sidon.

Much lower down the scale were the bulk-producing islands of the Sporades, the southwestern corner of the Aegean. Koan from Kos, Knidian and Rhodian from Rhodes were the sort of wine used for army rations. Modern visitors to Rhodes will know that little has changed.

Were the ancient wines treated with resin to taste like modern Retsina? Certainly not, say some scholars, although others point to the pine cone that was part of the wine god's sceptre. The practice of adding pitch from pine trees was only mentioned in ancient Greece in connection with the already undrinkable wines of Galatia in Asia Minor. It seems to have been rare in Greece but common in Italy. On

---

the amphora is turned upside down and its original flat base pared down to a point (or knob). It seems curious to remove the base, but in practice it is much easier to lift and tip with its bottom forming a third handle.

Amphora stands (usually tripods) were common. In bars and cellars they were often leant against the wall. In ships, where hundreds were being carried, their points were dug into a bed of sand and their handles lashed together to hold them steady. Often their handles carried the stamp of their origins pressed in the clay. Well made amphoras of the right clay were perfectly impermeable. If necessary they were coated inside with wax or resin. Their mouths were bunged with cork where it was available and sealed with more wax or resin. (The Latin term for opening an amphora means, literally, to scrape the top.)

Properly sealed, an amphora was as airtight as a bottle, and like a very big bottle, kept good wine in good condition for an immensely long time. Without amphoras the ancient world would have had no knowledge of the splendour of matured wine.

To archaeologists, amphoras have unique value as evidence of ancient trading patterns. Each district, town or island had its own slightly different model, which developed over time. With the help of a computer, even a relatively small shard, a piece of neck or handle, can be accurately classified. Shards are virtually indestructable. So many millions of amphoras were made that even today in trading centres such as Delos, in the Aegean, entire beaches consist of nothing but a mixture of white marble from ruined monuments and the red sea-smoothed shards of broken wine containers.

the other hand, the Greeks did mix their wines – and in fact they rarely drank them straight. It was normal to add at least water (usually seawater), and the more formal the occasion and elaborate the food, the more spices and aromatics were added to the wine. The mixing was done in a vase of pottery or bronze called a crater, which could be of any size. The wine was scooped out with a dipper, a kythos, and drunk from a shallow, graceful, usually two-handled cup, a kylix.

THE GREEKS LOVED THEIR WINE AND RHAPSODIZED OVER IT, but reading them does not leave the impression that they were hard drinkers. Water in the wine had two obvious purposes: it stretched the supply of a commodity which may have been too expensive for some citizens, and it meant you could go on drinking longer. Their word "symposium" means nothing more or less than "drinking together".

The justification of its modern meaning, a learned conference, lies in the Greek practice of long after-dinner conversations between men over their wine. They

KOTTABOS

About the year 600BC some light-headed Sicilian colonist from Greece, leaning on his elbow at an after-dinner symposium, bet his friends that he could hit the lamp on top of its stand with the dregs in his shallow two-handled wine cup.

Whether he put out the lamp or not, it was just the sort of Drones-club idea that would catch on among the lighter element. Throwing bread rolls loses its magic after a while. The new game was baptized as kottabos, and a crafty bronze merchant designed a special stand, like a lampstand but with a tiny statuette on top with its arm held aloft. On the hand, precariously balanced, went a faintly concave bronze disc. Halfway up the stand he fixed a much larger bronze disc. The idea now was to dislodge the top disc, called the plastinx, so that it fell and hit the lower one, the manes, which when hit rang like a bell.

Kottabos became the rage. It spread back to Athens and Sparta, and for no less than 300 years, during the whole period of Athenian ascendency, it remained the fashionable after-dinner game. It is portrayed on countless Greek vases (the only graphic depiction of Greek domestic life we have) and the rules are known from literature.

The best illustration is on an Athenian wine cooler which shows four ladies of the town, whose names might be rendered Slinky, Wriggly, Couchy and Sexy. Slinky, naked on a couch, is flicking her wine cup with the index finger of her right hand. The caption by the cup reads, "I'm throwing this for you, Leagros." Other paintings show more decorous players in action, but leave no doubt at all how kottabos was played, nor how popular it was.

I have had a kottabos stand made, and practised assiduously. From personal experience I can say that it is not at all easy. The best trainers advise a very high arching shot, so that the wine falls onto the plastinx from above. But liquid does not dislodge bronze, however delicately balanced, easily. And it makes a terrible mess on the floor.

(An authentic game needs a dedicated young servant, who for economy wears nothing but a garland, to rebalance the plastinx and recharge the wine cups.)

reclined on couches, propped up on their elbows, a habit learned from the Assyrians in about 600BC, and an attitude then and now associated with nomadic peoples. The dining room was called the men's room and was appropriately plumbed. Women, if they were present, sat on the edge of the couch or on a chair. A symposium had a chairman in just the same way as Georgian banquets have a tamada, although his job was to stimulate the conversation rather than elaborate long toasts.

No one pretends that all Greeks were philosophers. Symposia came in all degrees of seriousness or laxity. It was common for flute girls and dancing girls to perform. But according to (the admittedly straitlaced) Plato: "Wherever men of gentle breeding and culture are gathered together at a symposium, you will see neither flute girls, nor harp girls; on the contrary they are quite capable of entertaining themselves without such nonsense and childishness, but with their own voices, talking and listening in turn, and always decently, even when they have drunk much wine."

Plato's views on the minimum drinking age are remarkably severe. "Boys under 18 shall not taste wine at all, for one should not conduct fire to fire. Wine in moderation may be tasted until one is 30 years old, but the young man should abstain entirely from drunkenness and excessive drinking. But when a man is entering his fortieth year . . . he may summon the other gods and particularly call upon Dionysus to join the old men's holy rite, and their mirth as well, which the god has given to men to lighten their burden – wine that is, the cure for the crabbedness of old age, whereby we may renew our youth and enjoy forgetfulness of despair." It is a sobering thought that to Plato old age began at 40.

Other authors took a different attitude. The playwright Aristophanes gives the orator Demosthenes this speech:

> Why look you now; 'tis when men drink they thrive,
> Grow wealthy, speed their business, win their suits,
> Make themselves happy, benefit their friends.

HIPPOCRATES, who was born on the island of Kos in about 460BC and lived, it is said, for nearly a century, is called the father of medicine. Wine played a part in almost every one of his recorded remedies. He used it for cooling fevers, as a diuretic, a general antiseptic, and to help convalescence. But he was completely specific, occasionally advising against any wine at all, and always recommending a particular wine for a particular case. The following passage does not make very attractive reading, but it shows how clearly and closely Hippocrates observed the human body and understood the chemistry by which, in this case, its bowels can be affected:

"Soft dark wines are moister; they are flatulent and pass better by stool . . . . Harsh white wines heat without drying, and they pass better by urine than by stool. New wines pass by stool better than other wines because they are nearer the must, and more nourishing . . . . Must causes wind, disturbs the bowels and empties them . . . ."

Of sweet – that is, partially fermented – wine he records "it causes less heaviness in the head than vinous [strong, fully fermented] wine, goes to the brain less, evacuates the bowels more than the other, but causes swelling of the spleen and liver . . . . As to white vinous wine . . . passing more readily into the bladder, being diuretic and laxative, it always is in many ways beneficial in acute diseases."

"Should you suspect, however," (he concludes), "in these diseases an overpowering heaviness of the head, or that the brain is affected, there must be total abstinence from wine . . . ."

Hippocrates also had strong views on how wine should be drunk: neither too warm nor too cold. The prolonged drinking of warm wine, he claimed, led to "imbecility", while the excessive use of very cold wine led to "convulsions, rigid spasms, mortifications, and chilling horrors, terminating in a fever".

Athenaeus, a Greek Egyptian from Naucratis in the 2nd century AD, is one of our most prolix sources of Greek wine lore. His work "The Deipnosophists", or The Learned Diners, is a great scrapbook of gossip and literary odds and ends loosely constructed around 24 famous scholars and lawyers (and including the great physician Galen). Several of them are the sort of pretentious gourmets we would describe today as "wine bores". But we are speaking of the age of Rome rather than classical Greece.

The most concise summarizing of Greek wine wisdom is ascribed to Eubulus, writing in about 375 BC: "Three bowls do I mix for the temperate: one to health, which they empty first, the second to love and pleasure, the third to sleep. When this bowl is drunk up, wise guests go home. The fourth bowl is ours no longer, but belongs to violence; the fifth to uproar, the sixth to drunken revel, the seventh to black eyes, the eighth is the policeman's, the ninth belongs to biliousness, and the tenth to madness and hurling the furniture."

It is remarkable with what consistency the figure of three drinks recurs throughout history as a moderate measure. We shall meet it repeatedly, until it leads to the modern size of a wine bottle – three glasses each for two people – and even to modern clinical views on a healthy regular diet of wine.

We can leave the conclusion to the wisest of all Greek philosophers, Socrates. "Wine", said Socrates, "moistens and tempers the spirits, and lulls the cares of the mind to rest . . . it revives our joys, and is oil to the dying flame of life. If we drink temperately, and small draughts at a time, the wine distills into our lungs like sweetest morning dew. . . . It is then the wine commits no rape upon our reason, but pleasantly invites us to agreeable mirth."

CHAPTER 5

DRINKING THE GOD

The Greeks had every reason to be enthusiastic about wine. It had provided the impetus for the economy of their strange country, half land, half sea. It gave them a pleasure they could find in no other form. But there was more to it than either business or pleasure; a mystical element that they expressed through their worship of the wine god, Dionysus.

Of course, wine was not alone in having a deity. All the elements, every concept, each crop, even a forest or a spring had its sponsoring senior god or junior guardian spirit. Zeus, the father of the gods, lived on Mount Olympus in Thessaly, surrounded by, and constantly intriguing and quarrelling with, 11 gods of cabinet rank, while a great civil service of gods milled about in complicated and frequently incestuous relationships, seducing hapless humans, causing accidents and interfering in battles, altogether more like a hippy colony than a responsible superior order of beings.

It is hard to know what weight to put on the word "worship" as between the Greeks and their gods. As all-powerful, unpredictable and often apparently spiteful characters they were best treated with respect. A sacrifice seemed a reasonable insurance policy. An enormous temple at huge expense was clearly something much more – not least an expression of national or civic pride.

Every effort was made to eavesdrop on the plans of the Olympians through the medium of oracles. The priests of such famous oracles as that of Apollo at Delphi became a very wealthy and influential class.

But the only personal relationships between men and Olympians belonged in the realm of mythology. Myths must sometimes have appeared to thinking Greeks to be handed out with the rations. This is where Dionysus was different. Dionysus was not a myth but a very palpable fact. You actually drank the god of wine, and having the god inside you took away care.

ONE MORNING IN MARCH IN THE YEAR 404BC, 14,000 of the people of Athens packed the huge theatre on the east flank of the Acropolis for the first day of drama of the annual Great Festival of Dionysus. The day before there had been sacrifices of bulls; so many of them that the stink of blood still filled the city, mingled with the sharper smell of wine. Most of the crowd were carrying wine skins, swaying as they swigged their "trimma", wine flavoured with an unknown formula of herbs, and joking that their wobbling goat skins were softer to sit on than the hard theatre benches.

Last into their seats in the huge amphitheatre were the senior magistrates of the city and the army commanders, and then the priests of Dionysus Eleutherus, the wine god from Eleusis on the road north to Thebes. They took stone thrones on the edge of the vast semicircular marble stage, where dancers were already weaving in elaborate patterns, chanting and beating tambourines. The women dancers wore only soft fawn skins, with wreaths of ivy, and carried long hollow stalks of wild fennel tipped with pine cones and wreathed with more ivy. The men jiggled about absurdly with preposterous leather phalluses flapping in front and long horse tails sticking from the back of their breeches. Each time one of these "satyrs" tried to catch one of the "maenads" she would scamper away, prodding him with her wand, her "thyrsis", the sceptre of the wine god and the symbol of his powers.

Legend says that Dionysus was kidnapped by Etruscan pirates on his way to Italy. He demonstrated his divinity by making a miraculous grapevine climb the mast, and turned the pirates into dolphins. The Athenian painter Exekias painted the scene on this famous kylix, the shallow two-handled wine cup of the Greeks, in about 550BC.

The contrasting masks of comedy and tragedy have symbolized the theatre since it evolved from the rites of Dionysus in the 5th century BC. In this Roman mosaic, comedy is a satyr's mask, tragedy a maenad's. All actors in the Greek theatre wore masks, whose stylized expressions were hypnotically effective and can be seen even from the back rows of an enormous theatre.

All this was entirely familiar to the Athenians. The various festivals of Dionysus went on at intervals throughout the winter, starting in December with the Country Dionysia in the villages, when the emphasis was more on the phallus and less on the wine god. He, after all, was symbolically dead. His body (in the form of grape clusters) had been dismembered and crushed at vintage time and now his vines stood bare and apparently lifeless. Only ivy remained as a wintry substitute, producing its hard little fruit in winter among its shiny but vine-shaped leaves. The word for the dance around a giant phallus was komos – the root of the word comedy.

Every second winter, though, a large crowd of women of all ages set off on a pilgrimage, taking the road via Eleusis and the sacred city of Thebes to the holy shrine of the oracle at Delphi. Delphi, sacred to Apollo for nine months of the year, became the shrine of Dionysus from December to February. His priestesses there were joined by housewives, maidens and grandmothers from all the cities around, who dressed as maenads and were sworn to secrecy. There were plenty of rumours about what went on. All agreed that the maenads went up into Mount Parnassus above Delphi and stayed there all night. In his *Antigone*, the playwright Sophocles describes the scene: "Surrounded by the light of torches, he stands high on the twin summits of Parnassus, while the Corycian nymphs dance around him as Bacchantes, and the waters of Castalia sound from the depths below. Up there in the snow and winter darkness Dionysus rules in the long night, while troops of maenads swarm around him, himself the choir leader for the dance of the stars and quick of hearing for every sound in the waste of the night."

This chilly picnic had many meanings. (The summit of Parnassus is at more than 8,000 feet, and there are very believable reports of snow storms cutting off the worshippers, of rescue parties and maenads suffering from frostbite, "their clothes frozen stiff as boards".) The simplest, perhaps, was to encourage the god to return from the dead. Greek historians said that it was a very ancient practice, kept up in their own times simply as an antique custom. Certainly the death and rebirth of a god, symbolizing the renewal of nature, is one of the oldest and most common of religious themes. But others, modern doctors among them, believe that "maenadism" really was mass hysteria. Maenads were always depicted with their heads thrown back: a clinical indication, they say. In this state, people commit acts they would normally shrink from: handling snakes, carrying fire or killing and eating raw flesh. There are other historical instances of dances turning to near-madness. Some point out that Greek womenfolk (respectable ones, that is) were virtual slaves to their men, and that permission to congregate for worship in the wilds was their unique psychological release.

One distinct possibility is that the secrets of the mountain involved taking drugs other than wine. The thyrsis itself can be seen as a symbol of drug-taking. The fennel stalk, known as a narthex, was what Greek herbalists stored their plants in to keep them fresh. The pine cone came from a tree whose resin, fermented, makes a powerful intoxicant (and was perhaps added to Greek wine, as unfermented resin is today). Some maenads wore coronets woven with the seed heads of the opium poppy. And the berries of the ivy are intoxicating even without fermentation.

Winter, moreover, is the season of mushrooms in Greece. The Indian god Soma, some of whose myths are so similar to those of Dionysus that they must have common roots, produces his narcotic effect through the common fungus *Amanita muscaria*, or fly agaric. The effect of fly agaric is to destroy inhibitions, lead to powerful sexual desire, induce hallucinations and finally lead to total lethargy.

Another fungus that was readily available, and was possibly used in the maenads' mysteries, is the parasite on barley and other grasses known as ergot. Its psychoactive alkaloids are better known today as LSD. We should remember that the Greeks rarely drank their wine unmixed. Even the "trimma" in the audience's wine skins was brewed with herbs. Syrian frankincense was another ingredient with narcotic properties. To sophisticated Greeks, at least in early times, it may be that wine more often meant one of a range of mildly narcotic cocktails.

DIONYSUS HAD A SECOND FESTIVAL, a perfectly unmysterious one, in February when it was time to open the fermenting jars and taste the new wine. This was the Anthesteria, the Flower Festival (from "anthos", a flower: an image wine lovers still use today in talking of the bouquet of a wine).

The Anthesteria took place at a shrine by the sea, far more ancient, they said, than the Eleutherian shrine. Water was mixed with the new wine before it was tasted, and an actor, masked and dressed as Dionysus, was carried up from the seaside in a boat on wheels – one of countless references to the god's arrival over the water from distant lands that crop up in every version of his convoluted mythology.

Drinking seems to have been the main attraction of the February festival, with amphora parties, competitions for the greatest and longest drink, and such side-shows as trying to sit on a bulging wine skin smeared with grease without falling off.

The Great (or City) Dionysia was the March meeting in Athens, based on the ancient Eleutherian cult but with far more ancient ancestry still. Back in Babylon the spring equinox, in March, was celebrated as the New Year. In that era the equinox coincided with the sun's entry into the constellation of Taurus. Bulls were ceremonially set to the plough. Babylon's chief god, Marduk, was represented as a bull. So, in many rites, was Dionysus.

By the 5th century BC the City Dionysia was adapted and expanded by the government into one of the main public events of the city calendar. It was a remarkable instance of authority bowing to popular demand. Far back into history, the cult of Dionysus had been regarded as disreputable or worse; an excuse for the underdogs in society, women and slaves, to kick over the traces. In the 6th century BC, this former minority cult suddenly became a force to be reckoned with. The shrewd tyrant Pisistrates, who ruled Athens from 546-527BC, recognized that the best way to control a popular movement is to make it official. If the Dionysiacs were going to dress up and dance in the streets, let them be organized into a popular spectacle. Thus the first of all theatres came to be built, in the heart of Athens, to accommodate and control an ancient rite that had acquired too much importance, and too many adherents, to be ignored.

THE PLAY THAT WON THE DAY in the competition of 404BC was a posthumous work. Its author, Euripides of Salamis, had died of old age in exile two years before, after a long and triumphant theatrical career. His last play, entitled *The Bacchae*, took one of the foreign names of the wine god, the name he was known by across the Aegean in Lydia, and told the story of his arrival in Greece at the city of Thebes in Boeotia, not far north of Athens.

Everyone in the theatre knew the story. The lives of gods and men in Greece were a tissue of legends, layer upon layer of them, often contradictory, usually with local variations. The more important the god, the more versions there were of his or her adventures. It is also certainly true that the more myths attached to a god, the older he or she was. Dionysus is larded with legend. He was born and re-born, of different parents in different places, again and again.

His Theban legend is best known, partly because of Euripides' play. But it is still hard to make intelligible. His father was Zeus; his mother the mortal Semele, daughter of Cadmus the king of Thebes. Semele, pregnant with Dionysus, dared to ask Zeus to show himself in glory. Reluctantly, he turned on his full voltage, Semele was fried alive, but the immortal infant in her womb was saved by Zeus, who opened his thigh and kept the foetus there until it was ready to be born. (Soma's story is very similar. He was born from the thigh of Indra, the Indian Zeus.)

The fate of Semele is a sort of prologue. *The Bacchae* starts years later when Dionysus returns to Thebes to bring it the gift of wine. He specifically says that he brings wine from the east: on the face of it a simple and true historical statement:

> From Lydia have I come and Phrygia
> The golden lands
> From sun-drenched plains in Persia
> From the walled cities of Baktria
> From the dreaded land of Media.
> And I have passed through the whole of happy Arabia
> And all of Asia Minor's coast. . . .

He appears in disguise, an effeminate youth rather than a god. Nobody in Thebes, he discovers, believes the story of his divine birth. Even Semele's sisters, the mother and aunts of the present king, Pentheus, believe she had a mere mortal lover. In god-like revenge, Dionysus drives the women mad, or as mad as the maenads who have followed him from Lydia and are now dancing in the hills.

The first half of the play makes the audience laugh. King Pentheus personifies indignant authority. How dare the women leave their household duties and go gallivanting on their own? He arrests Dionysus and believes he chains him up in the bull stables. But the god deludes him into chaining one of the bulls.

Suddenly the crowd that was laughing and drinking in the theatre is shaken by a stage earthquake. The royal palace is in ruins and Dionysus is free. Now the mood changes. Dionysus tempts the king to go and spy on the women, to watch "their obscene acts". Only by dressing up as a woman, the god argues, can he creep up on them. Is Pentheus deranged by lust, by anger – or by Dionysus' teasing? Watching the scene in which the king minces up the mountain in the equivalent of high heels, the audience is tense. Drunk, in the brilliant sunshine, with their eyes rivetted to the unblinking masks, strangely hypnotic, that the actors wear, they become intensely involved. We must remember that most of them could not read, and that drama was by no means an everyday experience. High emotions of rapture or rage come easily to such a crowd.

The farce grows fiercer and more ominous as Dionysus helps Pentheus into the topmost branches of a pine to watch the women. Then "Maidens", he cries, "I bring and offer up to you/the one who laughs at you/At me,/And at my secret rites./ Avenge yourselves on him."

All scenes of violent action in Greek drama happen off-stage and are reported by a messenger. What the messenger now tells freezes the blood. The women of Thebes, possessed by Dionysus, tear their king down from his tree, and led by his mother, rend him limb from limb. Agaue, his mother, finally wrenches off his head. They return to the city with no idea what they have done. Whatever effect the god has had upon their minds, they believe they have hunted and killed a mountain lion. Agaue shows her son's head to her father Cadmus and tells him to nail her trophy to the palace wall.

As Cadmus cries in horror, we must believe the audience cried too. As Agaue comes to her senses the sense of desolation is absolute. Dionysus alone remains unmoved. Gods punish men for disbelief.

WHAT ARE WE TO MAKE OF *The Bacchae*? It is one of the strangest of plays. Its poetry puts it on a level where literal meaning may be secondary, yet myth has meaning, and Dionysus is perfectly specific about where he comes from and why.

His purpose is to bring wine to Greece. He also brings a form of religion which threatens (and actually destroys) the state. But both are paradoxes. Wine, described as a blessing, apparently becomes a curse. And he is presented as a new god, while in reality he is among the oldest gods of all.

It is easy to read more into the maenads' rites and ravings than simply the effects of wine. Euripides implies what has already been suggested: that powerful narcotics were involved. Or we can simply interpret his meaning as the truism that wine is a blessing in moderation, and a curse in excess. "Balance" is a word Dionysus uses. He calls himself the Happy One. What is new about the god, and perhaps the crux of the play, is his direct relationship with wine. The old all-purpose god of growing things has become specific to the vine – and at the moment in history when the vine had become the economic motor of the expanding Greek empire.

HOW ANCIENT THEN IS DIONYSUS? He can be traced so far back that he first appears as the consort (or the child) of the earth-mother herself. He is probably the little figure in the most ancient representations (sometimes uncannily similar to the Virgin and Child) which go back at least 9,000 years, to Stone Age shrines in Catal Hüyük, the first of all known cities.

The first name we know of for this mother of creation is Kubaba, the name she was known by in Mesopotamia 3,000 years later. The Hittites worshipped her and her son Sabazius, whose annual death and rebirth is one of the many ancient premonitions of Easter. Her worship was practised by their western neighbours and successors, the Phrygians and Lydians of the west Aegean shore, as Kubil and Kybele. Kybele, in some accounts, was described as the mother of Dionysus. Lydia was also the land where the name Bacchus or Bakhos was first used for the young vegetation god.

To Orpheus, the mythical singer, long before the age of Homer, Dionysus (with the surname Zagreus) was a son of Zeus and Persephone, the goddess of death, who was torn apart and eaten by the Titans, a race of primitive giant men. In Orpheus' story, the goddess Athena saved Dionysus' heart, from which he was reborn – another resurrection story. (The clear parallel between this and the Egyptian story of Osiris, whose body was torn apart and scattered all over Egypt, then reassembled by Isis, explains why Osiris was identified with Dionysus by the Greeks.)

Orpheus himself was a follower of Dionysus. In his adventurous life he travelled as ship's musician with the Argonauts, saving them from the Sirens' seductive song, and visited the Underworld to bring back his wife Eurydice. But Orpheus suffered the same violent fate as Dionysus and Osiris: he was torn apart by Thracian maenads, apparently upset by his non-ecstatic behaviour.

THERE IS NO END TO THESE EARLY LEGENDS SURROUNDING DIONYSUS. He belongs firmly in the most ancient mythology, but strikingly not in the Olympian religion propounded by Homer, which is the "established" religion that, in *The Bacchae*, is represented by Pentheus and his beliefs.

The dozen relatively orderly Olympian divinities took up residence on Mount Olympus when Greece was subjugated by an invading race from the north in the middle of the second millennium BC. The "sky gods" were installed by the new Greeks, who made their capital at Mycenae (Indo-Europeans is the not very helpful handle given to the invaders by anthropologists), who had long been wanderers, not farmers but hunters, armed with bronze weapons, organized for violence, and led by men. They descended on a land which for perhaps 1,000 years had been just the opposite: agricultural and settled, unquarrelsome and unfrightened, whose towns had no walls and whose art no battle scenes. This was Minoan Crete. Their paintings, free, lifelike and loving depictions of birds, or flowers, or girls dancing or flying fish, are the world through undistracted eyes that love what they rest on.

Women ruled in this land, where strength was not at a premium – or at least had equal status with men. Its gods were like its people and its art; simple and earthy. What mattered most was fertility. In one form or other mother earth was the vital being, but her satellite spirits, too, her lovers or offspring, were linked to the functions of nature that meant good crops and easy living.

Was Minoan Crete really like this? Possibly, in the sense that it had no armies. In the Stone Age everyone had equal access to a weapon, so power was fragmented. It was when bronze took over that it became very clear who was in charge – and equally clear, to those who were not, that their old earth gods were kindlier to ordinary folk than the cruel sky gods of their conquerors.

Of all these gods, Dionysus was the most real and accessible. His appeal to the downtrodden is clear. He gives comfort and courage; courage to congregate and be noisy in a way that Apollo would not approve of at all.

Apollo was the official god of inspiration; ideally good-looking, moving only among the best people, promising order and security. "If his cult existed today . . . he might well be pictured in . . . a neat suit, a Brooks Brothers shirt, buttoned down of course, and a sincere tie. He was an organization man, with all the warmth of a State Street banker." It is scarcely surprising that Dionysus was the people's choice.

THE METAMORPHOSIS OF DIONYSUS from god of vegetation and fertility to god of wine took place gradually over perhaps 1,000 years. It did not stop there, but continued with more and more elaborate and mystic rites to embrace a whole system of beliefs about spirituality and the afterlife: an immediate forerunner of Christianity.

The wine god rose to prominence with the colonization of southern Italy from about 800BC. The first Greek city in Sicily was called Naxos, from the island where the god married Ariadne, and carried his effigy on its coins. His importance was

The springtime rites of the cult of Dionysus led directly to the building of the first of all theatres, on the eastern slope of the Athens Acropolis, in the 6th century BC. The first, a wooden theatre, held 14,000 spectators, and was replaced in 330BC by the surviving enormous bowl of creamy marble, with a capacity of 17,000. The Dionysus festival included four days of plays, competing for prizes and judged by the chief priests and magistrates.

confirmed by 582BC, when he was given three months of the year at Apollo's shrine at Delphi. A suggestion has been made that Delphi and the new colonies were more closely linked than might appear. Delphi is near Corinth, one of the principal colonizing cities. The oracle was well informed on where the best sites were to be found. A profitable arrangement grew up, involving trade, colonization and evangelism for the wine god. The wine trade has always been a desirable occupation. Here it carried an odour of sanctity as well.

During the 6th century BC his worship was officially accepted into the Greek Pantheon. His portrait, followers and attributes – maenads and satyrs, thyrsis and vines and ivy – became the most popular of all subjects for vase-painting. The most famous of these paintings, recalling a legend of his capture at sea by Etruscan pirates on the way to Italy, was painted by the master Exekias in 550BC. A place was even made for him among the 12 Olympians by the retirement of the modest Hestia, the goddess of the hearth. In 530BC Pisistratus sanctioned his rites in Athens and built his first theatre. *The Bacchae* was first performed in 404BC. A century later the present vast stone theatre, reaching right up the flank of the Acropolis, was built. Dionysus had an active following that outdid those of all the other gods.

It is not too difficult to account for the ascendancy of wine as a form of religion under the conditions of ancient Greece. The American historian and geographer Dan Stanislawski has written a convincing catalogue of its attractions: "Exaltation for the mystic; a sense of unity with the whole and of belonging for the disinherited; courage for the timid; peace for the troubled spirit; nepenthe for the tortured soul; aphrodisiac for the lover; surcease for the pain-wracked; anaesthetic for use in surgery; gaiety for the depressed. In addition to its mystical or personal appeal, wine offered pecuniary advantages: vines produce a crop with an ever-ready market. They produce a crop of relatively high value on a wide variety of surfaces and soils: on slopes so steep that almost no other crop can be cultivated and on virtually sterile rocks; thence through a gamut of soils to alluvium; and in a wide variety of climates. They do not demand irrigation. They yield a product that has international appeal and international markets (even in early times). The beverage produced is not only attractive but also healthy in lands of little and often polluted water. It is a persuasive beverage that makes lasting friendships. Once it is known, a permanent and probably increasing market is virtually guaranteed."

THE NATURE AND SCOPE OF THE GREEK WORLD CHANGED COMPLETELY in the late 4th century BC. The royal house of Greece's northern neighbour Macedonia, Philip and his son Alexander, ended the loose confederation of free city-states led by Athens and Sparta. Under Alexander, the Greeks became an irresistible force that carried before it all the ageing empires of the east. Anatolia, Assyria, Babylonia, Persia, Egypt fell. Alexander marched right to the frontiers of India and even over the Oxus into central Asia.

At his death this enormous, ungovernable realm split into three: Macedonia and Greece, Egypt under the Ptolemies, and a vast kingdom from Anatolia to India that took the name of its founder Seleucus. The influence of Greek thought was felt throughout the Middle East, as it already was in the rapidly expanding sphere of influence of Rome to the west. Yet within 200 years, by the middle of the first century BC, Rome had inherited, by conquest or secession, the entire Greek world, with the exception of Persia. The last to fall was Cleopatra's Egypt, in 31BC.

ROME WAS WARY AT FIRST of the powerful cult of Bacchus (the Romans knew Dionysus by his Lydian name). The Etruscans, whom they had not so long ago subsumed into the new Roman Italy, had had a similar god, who rejoiced in the name of Fufluns. The followers of Fufluns found Bacchus very much to their liking, and the two gods soon became one.

But the martial spirit of Rome in its republican days was not in tune with nature worship, or with personal enthusiasms of any kind. Bacchus' rites, the Bacchanalia, were a hole-and-corner affair where respectable citizens would never be seen. The state, like Pentheus in *The Bacchae*, was nervous and disapproving.

Matters came to a head in 186BC. The Bacchanalia were banned, on the evidence of a courtesan. The account of the historian Livy sounds suspiciously like the sort of accusation that was later levelled at the Christians. "There was not one form of vice alone, the promiscuous matings of free men and women, but perjured witnesses, forged seals and wills and evidence . . . likewise poisonings and murders of kindred, so that at times not even the bodies were found for burial." In the witchhunt that followed, some 7,000 people, all over Italy, were accused of conspiracy against the state. It is clear from the speech for the prosecution that the Roman establishment felt threatened by a popular movement that might undermine its stern and warlike values. Such people would never make Roman soldiers.

But Bacchus was not so easily dismissed. His cult continued to flourish in secret, fed by the doctrines of Orphism, the gospel according to Orpheus, which were effectively transforming cult into religion. By the first century BC he had outgrown the role of wine god and become a saviour figure, the god of the underworld with the power to grant an afterlife. His connection with the theatre remained, so that masks of the characters in famous plays were buried with the dead. He even acquired a military past, including a victorious expedition to India which identifies him with, of all people, Alexander the Great.

The ban on the Bacchanalia was lifted by Julius Caesar in response to popular pressure. The temper of Rome had changed with the enormous wealth of its empire. In the past, Bacchus had been the favourite god of the common man. Now he had followers among the rich and powerful. One of the most devoted of them was Mark Anthony, who saw himself, on Cleopatra's couch in Alexandria, as a new Dionysus. His austere rival Octavius, predictably enough, identified himself with Apollo.

THE INFLUENCE OF BACCHUS AND HIS CULT ON CHRISTIANITY, when it arrived in Rome, is beyond question. Orphism had already anticipated the concept of spiritual salvation, with Bacchus/Dionysus as the saviour. Returning from the dead was commonplace among the ancient gods. Eating the god's flesh was a familiar idea to the Orphics. And Bacchus' blood, of course, was wine.

Other active cults of the time also made their contributions to the new religion; in particular the worship of the sun god, Sol Invictus, that was popular in the Roman army. From this illuminating source the Christians borrowed the symbol of the halo and the date of Christmas, the rebirth of the sun on the shortest day of the year.

Like the followers of Bacchus, the Christians were at first persecuted, then tolerated, before they were fully accepted. In the 4th century the Emperor Constantine made Christianity the official religion of Rome and its Empire. By this time it was so confused with the old Bacchic cult that Constantine's daughter, building her mausoleum in the church of Santa Costanza, covered its ceiling with a mosaic of conventional Bacchic symbols, and herself appears on it wreathed in vines.

The Emperor Theodosius banned the old pagan cults in an edict of 392. The followers of Bacchus, now a small minority, adopted Christian symbols, just as the Christians had borrowed theirs. Bacchus wears a halo, and appears (as he did thousands of years before at Catal Hüyük) as an infant on his mother's knee.

Yet at the same time Christian theologians rediscovered Euripides' work, and were unable to ignore the clear parallels between *The Bacchae* and their gospels. Dionysus was the son of god and a mortal woman. He worked miracles and was persecuted. Euripides, they supposed, had been divinely inspired to prepare the way for Christianity. The Bishop of Constantinople, Gregory Nazianzos, wrote a three-part drama, *The Passion of Christ*, in which he borrowed, with acknowledgment, whole passages of *The Bacchae*.

HAS THE WINE GOD EVER BEEN SNUFFED OUT? His worship gradually dwindled, discouraged by the Christian authorities. An edict published at Constantinople in 692 strictly forbade women's public dancing ("the root of all evils and ruin"), chorus singing and mysteries; "ancient customs altogether alien to Christian life". It

DISGRACEFUL PRACTICES

Livy, whose instincts were conservative and sympathies with the authorities, tells of the skulduggery behind the ban on the Bacchanalia.

A Roman youth called Aebutius had a mistress called Hispala, a freed slave. Aebutius' stepfather, apparently trying to appropriate his inheritance, arranged for the young man to be initiated into the rites of Bacchus, thinking that membership of this disreputable cult would so damage his reputation that the courts would dismiss any claim he made.

Hispala learnt of the plan. (Abstinence from sexual intercourse was part of the initiation process.) Horrified, she told Aebutius that as a slave she had had to attend the Bacchanalia.

Initiates, she said, were led by the priests "to a place which would ring with howls and the song of a choir and the beatings of cymbals and drums, that the voice of the sufferer, when his virtue was violently attacked, might not be heard." She begged him "not to plunge into a situation where all disgraceful practices would

first have to be endured and then performed."

This was how the secrets came out. Aebutius fled his stepfather's house. Hispala was persuaded to give evidence to the consul Postumius. At first, she said, the Bacchanalia was a ritual for women and no men were admitted to it. Then a priestess from Campania had started to admit men. With "men mingling with women and the freedom of darkness added, no form of crime . . . was left untried. There were more lustful practices among men with one another than among women. If any of them were disinclined to endure abuse or reluctant to commit crime, they were sacrificed as victims. To consider nothing wrong . . . was the highest form of religious devotion among them."

Postumius was delighted with this information and called the extraordinary meeting of the Senate that outlawed the Bacchanalia. Hispala and Aebutius were both rewarded as informers with money and privileges which indicate that the Senate was also well pleased.

was forbidden to dress as the opposite sex or impersonate comic or tragic characters. It was also decreed that when wine growers tread the grapes, "nobody should invoke the name of the infamous Bacchus, and when wine is poured into casks, nobody should provoke laughter by actions which bear the imprint of lies and madness." The punishment was excommunication. Evidently the Bacchic rites still had their followers.

They exist still in much modified form. Velazquez painted Bacchus as a real being among the peasants of Castile. Rhinelanders dressing up as satyrs at a Weinfest may be self-conscious, but there is no ignoring the graven image that the Soviet Georgians have set up outside the Palace of New Ritual in their capital, Tbilisi. It is Dionysus, a modern bronze instantly recognizable as the Greek god. The Palace is where secular weddings are held. Georgia is one of the oldest Christian countries, yet its authorities choose the wine god as their symbol of celebration and blessing.

Sometimes his worship survives as a riotous note in a Christian ceremony. Each year on San Pedro's day at Haro in Rioja, his madness breaks out again. Thousands of people throng to Mass at dawn at a hillside chapel. The moment it is over a howl goes up from the crowd, and every man uses his wine skin to soak everybody in reach with pale red wine. The dancing churns up a mud of wine and earth under the olive trees.

There is no stage management here; no violence, either. But the Bacchae are there; a distant voice, a faint echo of the ecstasy that devastated Thebes.

Confusion between the old cult of Dionysus and the new cult of Christianity shows in this 5th-century mosaic from Paphos in Cyprus, in which the infant Dionysus is portrayed in a scene reminiscent of "The Adoration of the Magi". Instead of maenads and satyrs, he is surrounded by worshippers including Ambrosia and Nectar (divine Food and Drink) and old Tropheus the Provider.

CHAPTER 6

DE RE RUSTICA

Rome's monuments are all about us. Its language still rings in our ears. The private life of its poets and politicians is (or was to our great grandfathers a century ago) as familiar as that of the characters in much nearer history. Names, events, arguments, laws make up a relatively exact story. Yet ancient Rome is strangely elusive. It is no easier to touch and smell than the Egypt of a much more distant time. We know Egypt from its illustrations; Rome we know by its words, its monuments and its potsherds.

There is no shortage of Roman writing about wine. Horace, Ovid, Virgil – the greatest poets wrote about it, both in passing and in earnest. Pliny, the encyclopedic natural historian, is at his best on it; specialist agriculturalists (Cato, Varro, Graecinus, Columella) are calculating and exact; Galen, the great physician, is observant and precise.

There is no shortage of archaeology, either. The difference here is that scientific digging and scientific diving are new disciplines. The story handed down to us in writing is what it always was: teasingly rich in detail, always ambiguous in conclusion. Archaeology works in counterpoint with the written word; its conclusions computerized, its detail decidedly patchy. It throws light at odd angles on the great edifice of literature, and startles unexpected features from its august shadows.

WINE-GROWING ARRIVED IN A RUSH in southern Italy from Greece. There may have been earlier, Mycenaean, Greek settlements. But those we are sure about happened from 800BC onwards. The vine was the anchor the Greeks dug into the Sicilian and Italian shores. It took hold and so did they; within 300 years Syracuse in Sicily had outgrown Athens to be the most populous of all Greek cities.

Were there no vines in Italy before they came? Indeed there were, and winegrowers, too. The country just north of centre on the long boot shape of Italy, Tuscany today, was the land of the Etruscans. They in turn had probably come from the east, but we know little more. Asia Minor (even Troy) is one suggested origin. Phoenicia is another – but the Etruscan language seems closer to Greek. The Etruscans grew wine, making it and using it very much after the fashion of the Greeks, and traded with it, right up into Gaul beyond the Alps. They were almost certainly in Burgundy before the Greeks; selling wine, not growing it. They may have brought their vines with them from the east, had them from earlier Greek expeditions, or even found them in Italy. The wild vine was growing in the

The Etruscans, like the Egyptians, decorated their tombs with images of the
endless banquet they hoped for in the afterlife. This fresco in the "Leopard Tomb"
in Tarquinia shows another aspect of their social life: men reclined to feast, women
sat respectfully beside them. This was not Egyptian but Greek style.

peninsula prehistorically. Who first used it in Italy for wine has not emerged from
the night of time.

ROME WAS FOUNDED ON MILK, both in legend, where Romulus and Remus were
suckled by a wolf, and metaphorically in the unfrivolous attitudes of its early
citizens. To its north the Etruscans were enjoying themselves, as the decorations in
their tombs attest. We cannot read their language, but like the Egyptians they have
left a vivid testimony in paintings, sculpture, pottery, and above all bronzes.

Their vineyards reached up well into northern Italy; the earliest amphora yet
found with a cork stopper is Etruscan, of 600BC. In the south, the Greeks enjoyed the
land of staked vines. But vineyards were a low priority to the stern and martial
people who were steadily enlarging their dominion outwards from the centre of
Italy. Their womenfolk were forbidden wine; a husband finding his wife drinking
was at liberty to kill her for the offence (although it is hard to imagine that many
husbands would). Divorce on the same grounds was last recorded in 194BC.

The turning point in Roman attitudes was the long-drawn-out struggle with
the empire of Carthage in North Africa for control over the western Mediterranean. The three so-called Punic wars were fought between 264 and 146BC. The
Carthaginian general Hannibal crossed the Alps into Italy with his elephants in
218BC. His defeat, quickly followed by Roman victories over the Macedonians and
the Syrians, changed the mood of Rome. From 200BC, wine-growing began to
interest its increasingly worldly citizens; the security and wealth of empire brought
a market for luxuries which would have shocked the founding fathers.

The first author to write in detail about wine-growing was Cato, the very senator who had argued most passionately for the total destruction of Carthage. "Delenda est Carthago", Pliny quotes him as saying: "Carthage must be destroyed." In his eighties he set down, in *De Agri Cultura*, exactly how a country estate should be run – including cold-blooded calculations about how much slaves could do without dropping dead.

Romans were beginning to invest capital in farming enterprises with serious business intent, and wine-growing came top for profitability; partly because there were few commercial vineyards, and Rome had become a big city with a big thirst. Cato's textbook was, one might say, slavishly followed by new proprietors, many of them absentee landlords whose only concern was output. There was (and still is) a lack of sympathy between such speculators and country gentlemen, like the poets Horace and Virgil, whose love of the land (and care for their staff) might make their vineyards money-losers, but certainly resulted in better wine.

Ironically, the author whose farming manual was the most widely read was a long-dead Carthaginian, Mago. Mago had set down the Phoenician and Canaanite traditions of agriculture as perfected and practised in Carthage in 500BC. When Cato's wish came true, and Carthage was deleted from the map, Mago's ancient manual was the one book in all the city's libraries that the Romans rescued: Its 26 volumes were translated into Greek and Latin in 146BC – although they have since been lost; we know them only from quotations in other authors. More than any other work, it stimulated the growth of commercial wine-growing and the swallowing up of small estates by big ones. According to Pliny, by the time of the Emperor Nero, 200 years later, only six proprietors owned the whole of Roman North Africa.

Not only was Rome growing fast, but it was drawing in people of talent and cunning from all over its empire, and with them cosmopolitan tastes that led to a higher standard of living. A date that helps us pin down their progress is 171BC, when the first commercial bakery opened in Rome. The old Roman diet was porridge. Now Rome ate bread, it has been reasonably suggested, its thirst for wine was bound to increase. At the time, Rome was extending its control over the great Greek vineyards of southern Italy. They were boom years in the wine trade. It is no coincidence that the first mention of a Roman "first-growth", the top-quality wine of a particular vineyard, is in this era. The occasion was the miraculous "Opimian" vintage of 121BC (Opimius was the consul that year), and the vineyard in question was Falernum.

A century later, connoisseurs still drank (or thought they drank) Opimian Falernian. Its reputation might be likened, in modern times, to "Waterloo" port of the great vintage of 1815 – except that Falernian was the only great wine Rome had to talk about for many years.

Once the concept of a "first-growth", or "Grand Cru" (there is no precise Latin term), had been introduced, a clear division could grow up between wines produced for quality, and the great bulk where quantity was all that mattered. The Romans loved rarity. Rare fish fetched fantastic prices and fortunes were spent on dining tables made of the swirling burrs of aromatic "citron wood". Now wine joined the catalogue of conspicuous consumption.

At first it was Greek wines that headed the list, although whether they were better or because everything Greek was chic is not easy to say. Orientals, that is people from the eastern Mediterranean, brought Rome the luxuries and delicate crafts it lacked. Slaves from the east, from Asia Minor, Syria and Palestine, included expert vineyard hands and winemakers. Rome assimilated their skills, but meanwhile the mystique of imported wine remained.

BY THE END OF THE 1ST CENTURY BC, Romans of wealth and fashion had taken a liking to the Campanian coast, the Bay of Naples and the Surrentine peninsula, as a place to build villas with sea views and splendid gardens. Greek culture was still very much alive here in the south, and the wine from Greek vines was considered the best in Italy.

The vine in question was the Amineum. It made Falernian, and was to make all the wines rated "first-growths" in this first Golden Age of Italian wine. It is surprising to learn that all of them were white – until you also learn that they were all sweet. The taste of the Augustan age (Augustus reigned from 27BC to AD14) was for wine that was sweet and strong, and very often cooked in much the same way as madeira is today. Usually it was drunk diluted with warm water – even with seawater. Madeira and water, whether cold, warm or sea, is not exactly to your taste or mine. And yet there is no doubting the Romans' discrimination between one kind and another, or the technical refinement they put into making their best wines. Nor were they alone in appreciating them: the wine trade with Greece became a two-way affair, with ships passing at sea carrying Greek wine to Italy and vice versa.

By Augustus' time, the wine industry was established over the length of Italy. All the most famous wines came from between Rome and Sorrento, but the

THE GRANDS CRUS OF ROME

Falernian was the first Roman first-growth to be recognized. It was grown on the borders of Latium and Campania, where the Via Appia forks left and the Via Domiziana forks right towards Naples: a strategic site for an ambitious estate. The estate of Faustus made the best Falernian, "in consequence of the care taken in its cultivation", and possibly on account of its position on the mid-slope of the hill between the two other sectors, Caucinium above and "Falernum at the bottom". "It has three varieties, one dry, one sweet, and one a light wine" (in Latin, austerum, dulce, tenue).

Pliny is wholly believable until he makes an observation like his next: "It is the only wine that takes light when a flame is applied to it." Perhaps his meaning is that it was so alcoholic that it burnt when thrown on a fire. Certainly all authors agree on its high strength. In colour, when mature, it was amber or brown. The description of very old Falernian as bitter and impossible to drink neat brings to mind the sort of ancient

oloroso sherry that is only used for blending. To hold such concentrated wine in your mouth at all is almost painful.

The site of the Falernian vineyard today is between Rocco di Mondragone and Monte Massico. Massican wine was sometimes considered a first-growth equal with Falernian. Today the name Falernum is used for an unexceptional light amber wine by the Cenatiempo cellars of nearby Formia. They also make a dry red "Falerno".

Caecuban was reckoned to equal Falernian in the early Imperial years, despite the fact that it was grown (says Pliny) "in poplar woods on marshy ground" along the coast northwest of Falernum. Nero believed that treasure was buried there and dug up the area on the pretext of making a canal.

Pliny rated next, after Caecuban and Falernian, the wines of Alba, just south of Rome, "which are extremely sweet and occasionally dry". The Colli Albani region today includes the

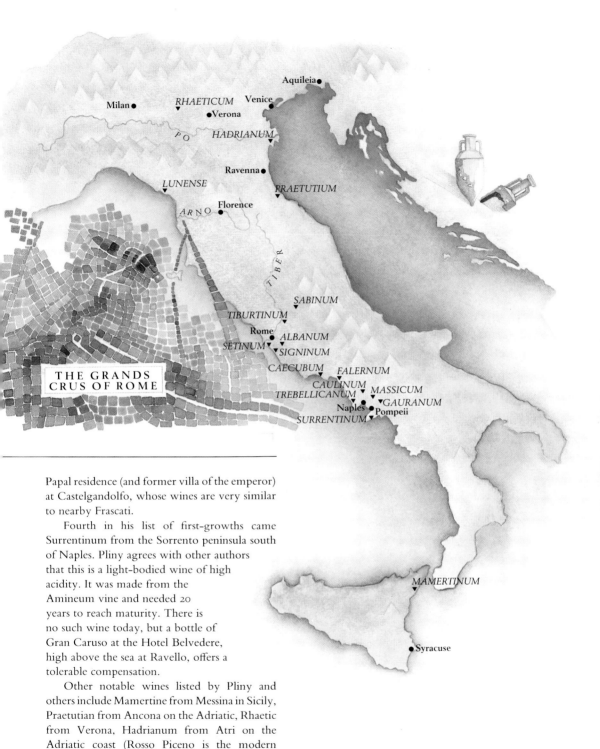

THE GRANDS
CRUS OF ROME

Papal residence (and former villa of the emperor)
at Castelgandolfo, whose wines are very similar
to nearby Frascati.

Fourth in his list of first-growths came
Surrentinum from the Sorrento peninsula south
of Naples. Pliny agrees with other authors
that this is a light-bodied wine of high
acidity. It was made from the
Amineum vine and needed 20
years to reach maturity. There is
no such wine today, but a bottle of
Gran Caruso at the Hotel Belvedere,
high above the sea at Ravello, offers a
tolerable compensation.

Other notable wines listed by Pliny and
others include Mamertine from Messina in Sicily,
Praetutian from Ancona on the Adriatic, Rhaetic
from Verona, Hadrianum from Atri on the
Adriatic coast (Rosso Piceno is the modern
wine), Luna from Tuscany and Genoa from
Liguria. In Campania, Pliny notes Trebellian
from Naples and Cauline from Capua.

production of the Adriatic coast was important (it exported to Dalmatia, Macedonia and Greece); the region of Aquileia (today's Venezia Giulia and Friuli) sent its wine east and north, using the river Sava to reach the Danube, and Pliny, our great source of information on all such matters, mentions notable wines in Liguria, Umbria, Emilia and Rhaetia (at Verona), besides old Greek colonial vineyards in Calabria and Apulia in the extreme south. If Tuscany is surprisingly missing from this list, it is because it was (as it still largely is) forest; the Via Chiantigiana north from Siena still seems to find it difficult to pick a way through the oak-clad hills.

One town, besides Rome, had a dominant position as a wine port, the Bordeaux of Roman Italy, producing and shipping vast quantities of all qualities of wine. It so happens that it is the one Roman town we can visit almost as though it still lived – Pompeii.

THERE ARE SOME 200 BARS STILL RECOGNIZABLE among the ruins of Pompeii. In one street near the public baths, eight line one block not 80 yards long. Outside one quite simple establishment you can still read the price list painted on the wall: wine on offer by the carafe, or cucumas (what today is known in Naples as a "cucumella"), at one, two or four "as" – call it a shilling.

> For one as you can drink wine,
> For two you can drink the best,
> For four you can drink Falernian.

The last price argues a pretty gullible public. Genuine Falernian, the wine of emperors, would certainly have cost more than four times the price of the house wine.

Inside, out of the glare of the street, one of these silent, dusty bars seems almost ready to resume business. Part of the ceiling is missing, giving a glimpse into the bedroom upstairs, where a bronze bedstead is perilously close to the edge of the floor. But an earthquake could have done more damage, and indeed did, only 17 years before the bar closed for good. Most of Pompeii had to be rebuilt in the year 63, after a serious shock that cost many lives, the roofs of most buildings – and almost all the wine of the 62 harvest.

The counter needs only a good scrub down to bring back the colour into the marble. Behind it in a rack lie a dozen amphoras, their bungs gone, as though a weekend's drinking had left the owner waiting for the morning's delivery. Two porters with a sling between them carried each amphora along the crowded narrow street, lifted it into the rack and took away the empty. That was the problem with amphoras: they weighed as much as the wine they contained – and 26 litres could be drunk up in an hour or two by a party from the baths across the street.

Gaius Plinius Secundus, whom we know as Pliny, a scholarly and sedate Roman grandee, a member of the court of the Emperor Vespasian, was more amused than scandalized by the Pompeians' famous thirst. He described their frantic efforts to work up what they considered a respectable one by "getting themselves boiled in hot baths and being carried out of the bathroom unconscious, while others are unable to wait to get to the table, no, not even to put on their clothes, but still naked and panting, they snatch up huge vessels as if to show off their strength, and pour

The streets of Pompeii are lined with bars and "thermopolia", snack bars open to the street where hot food was available at the counter at all hours. Wine was served in these bars, usually mixed with water, sometimes seawater. In cold weather its wine–and–water would be served hot.

down the whole of the contents, so as to bring them up again at once, and then drink another draught. And this they do a second and third time, as if they were born for the purpose of wasting wine, and as if it were impossible for liquor to be poured away unless by using the human body as a funnel."

Pompeii, with its mild winters, attracted retired expatriates from the colonies. Pliny himself, although only 55, had settled nearby in comfortable semi–retirement with the not very onerous command of the detachment of the navy in the Bay of Naples. There was plenty of time to spend in the baths and bars. The wine trade was brisk and profitable, exporting the powerful local growths, servicing the domestic market, and, it seems likely, importing popular wines from the colonies – especially those in eastern and southern Spain.

The study of amphoras is a branch of archaeology that can give remarkably precise information about trade. Certain forms of vessel, curves of the lip and shapes of handle can be deduced even from the small shards – of which so many millions survive that a computer can place most remnants in a recognized category.

A typical Pompeian amphora can be distinguished readily enough. What is less certain is its contents: the same form was sometimes used for wine, oil or corn. It was also, of course, often reused for the local produce of whatever province it reached.

Most conclusive is the stamp, usually on the top of a handle, of the original merchant whose wine it contained. Several Pompeian merchants were so famous on the export market that it seems possible that their stamps were sometimes forged far from home.

The man who probably did most to build the wine trade in Roman Pompeii was Marcus Porcius, who flourished in the last years of the Republic. His seals have been found in many parts of the western Roman world, but most often on the overland route from the Mediterranean to Bordeaux, via Narbonne and Toulouse. The family of the Porcii were prominent in business for several generations, but all the evidence suggests that it was Marcus who made its fortune. He seems, from inscriptions in the temple of Apollo, to have been the official responsible for building both the town's theatre and its amphitheatre.

Pompeii not only supplied Bordeaux; it seems in many ways to have foreshadowed what Bordeaux was eventually to be. There is a clear analogy between the Roman town, centre of the international wine trade, surrounded by splendid villas, and Bordeaux 1,700 years later, when its merchants began investing in wine-growing châteaux in Graves and the Médoc. Of 31 villas so far discovered in the countryside around Pompeii, 29 seem to have been wine producers. They were the châteaux of their day, their vineyards lapping their walls, their cellars full of maturing wine.

By far the greatest market for the wine of Campania – Pompeii and the surrounding province – was Rome itself. Its consumption grew and grew as wine became cheaper and millionaires distributed free wine when they sponsored games in the circus. The city had a porta vinaria, a wine-trade gate, on the inland, upstream side of the walls, for wine coming down the Tiber from Umbria and the Sabine hills where Horace farmed, and another on the side facing the sea and the port of Ostia. Today's Monte Testaccio, a hill near the Tiber 115 feet high and a thousand paces around, is nothing but broken amphoras from the downstream wine gate. And possibly as much as half of all that wine came by sea, in ships carrying 2,000-3,000 amphoras at a time, from Pompeii and the Campanian coast.

Pompeii was a town so imbued with the spirit of Bacchus that he appears again and again in the decoration and frescoes of its houses. Here he is dressed as a bunch of grapes, carrying his thyrsus or sceptre, standing on the slopes of Mount Vesuvius, which is covered with vines. Before its eruption the volcano apparently had a craggy peak.

POMPEII WAS DESTROYED IN AD79 by a massive eruption of Mount Vesuvius that laid waste the countryside for many miles around. Rome's principal source of wine went with it: the 78 vintage was destroyed; the 79 never made. The immediate consequence was a mad scramble to plant vines everywhere within reach of Rome. Cornfields became vineyards, the balance of supplies to the capital was seriously disrupted; established winegrowers, who benefited from the wine famine of 80 and the next few years by higher prices, soon found themselves instead in a glut of wine.

It seems likely that it was this situation that precipitated a famous edict of the Emperor Domitian. In AD92 he banned the planting of any new vineyards in Italy, and ordered the grubbing up of half the vines in Rome's overseas provinces. In a separate edict he also banned the planting of small vineyards (presumably by such as tavern keepers) within towns in Italy.

Domitian's edict has been the subject of endless scholarly debate. At first glance it looks like a measure to protect Italy's domestic wine industry from provincial competition, and to keep the price level up for the benefit of the sort of big winegrower who would be able to lobby the government. An equally valid theory is that there was real concern about the corn supply; vines were usurping the cornfields.

THE GREAT ERUPTION

The destruction of Pompeii is a story almost too well-known to bear re-telling – except for the fact that our best source of information about the wines of early Imperial Rome perished with the city.

We have met Pliny as naval commander in the region. His nephew, known as "the Younger Pliny", recounted what happened in letters to the historian Tacitus. In August AD79 his uncle was at Misenum, the naval port across the bay from Pompeii and Mount Vesuvius. "He had finished sunbathing, his cold plunge, and lunch, and was at work on his books" when "a cloud of extraordinary dimensions" was seen. "In appearance and shape it was like a tree – the umbrella pine would give the best idea of it." So grandiose a spectacle, his uncle decided, deserved close study. So he ordered a light galley to be made ready and set off towards it. By this time the alarm had been raised, boats were fleeing from the cloud, and "what he had begun in the spirit of a scientist, he carried on as a hero . . . keeping so calm and cool that he noted all the changing shapes of the phenomenon and dictated his observations to his secretary."

They landed at Stabiae, near Pompeii, where they went to a house, amid a thick shower of hot ash and cinders. From Vesuvius "great sheets of flame" were flashing out in more and more places. "My uncle, to relieve his companions'

fears, declared that these were merely fires in villas deserted by their peasants. Then he laid down and slept." Even for a Roman he was overdoing the sangfroid. The door of the room began to be blocked with ashes and the house was "swaying with repeated violent shocks". His companions woke him. It was daytime, but "blacker and thicker than ordinary night". They tied pillows over their heads with strips of linen and made for their galley.

But on the shore, with "the waves tumultuous and contrary", Pliny was overcome by the sulphurous fumes. He "struggled to his feet, leaning between two slaves; but immediately he fell down again." So died the author of the Natural History.

The eruption of 79 was ten times the size of that of Mount Saint Helens in 1980. It buried Pompeii under a layer of fine ash and coarser cinders more than 16 feet deep, and its neighbour Herculaneum to a depth of 65 feet. Apparently most of the inhabitants of Pompeii managed to escape the town – very few bodies have been found – but hundreds of Herculaneans were suffocated or drowned on the beach trying to get away. Yet items of cloth, delicate glass, even food, rope and straw survive where they were sheltered from the firestorm by buildings. They, and the skeletons, make up an almost complete record of the people and life of an ancient city.

Scholars have accused Domitian's government of strangling the infant wine industries of Gaul, Spain and the other provinces. There is very little evidence, though, that his edict, a political measure to placate big business and public concern about food prices at the same time, ever resulted in the uprooting of many provincial vines. It remained on the statute book for almost 200 years, until it was repealed by the Emperor Probus in 280. During that period, most of the principal vineyard regions of Gaul were either begun or steadily developed.

The writer who gives us most information about the actual mechanics and economics of Roman wine is Lucius Columella, a Spaniard from Cádiz. His comprehensive farming manual appeared in about AD65. Roman authors did not cast about for original titles. His book, like Mago's, is called *De Re Rustica*, or "On Country Matters".

Everything you could want to know about viticulture is in Columella, starting with the proposition that it can be the most profitable form of agriculture, and yet people lose fortunes at it. Why? Because it is fashionable and people rush into it without worrying about the soil, the situation, or whether they know what they are doing. They then neglect their pruning, ruin their vineyards with heavy crops that make miserable wine, and wonder what went wrong. Columella sets everything out in detail. His costings can be followed to the last vine stake and slave's breakfast. We learn from him that a good Roman vineyard produced about the same amount of wine per acre as a first-class French vineyard today (in French terms, 60 hectolitres per hectare: the Roman measure of surface was a jugera, equal to one quarter of a hectare. Production was measured by the notional whole cattle skin, a culleus, holding 20 amphoras, or about 500 litres. Three cullei per jugera = 60 hl/ha).

COLUMELLA RECOMMENDS A STAKED VINEYARD, with vines planted two paces apart each way, each tied to a chestnut stake the height of a man with withies of willow. This is more or less the method used, with variations, both on the Moselle and in Beaujolais today. (One man, he calculated, can cut and sharpen 100 stakes in a January day, plus ten before dawn and ten after dark by lamplight.) But staked vineyards were probably in the minority. Alternatives included everything from letting the vines trail along the ground, layering as they went (mice tended to eat the grapes), to training them up tall trees, a method still common in central and southern Italy. In between came every variation from "head-pruning" (French, en gobelet), which turns the vine into a small self-supporting pollard tree, to various forms of trellis, ranging from a simple T-bar to a full-scale pergola. The only element of a modern vineyard that was missing was wire.

Oddly, there was marked disagreement among authors about growing vines up trees. Earlier writers scarcely mention it; later ones go into great detail. To Pliny, slightly younger than Columella, it was the method that (in Campania) produced the finest wines of all, which by modern standards is certainly not the case. Poplars were recommended by some authors, elms by others (elms also provided cattle fodder, but at the cost of thinning their dense foliage, which overshaded the vines). Working up tall trees was left to casual labour; no prudent slave owner would risk a valuable asset on such a dangerous job. "A hired vintager", says Pliny, "expressly stipulated in his contract for the cost of a funeral and a grave."

Pliny's "Natural History" survived in edition after edition right into the Middle Ages. This fanciful portrait of the naturalist instructing a monarch is from a medieval copy in the Laurentian Library of the Medici family in Florence.

One advantage of arbusta, as they called their tree-clinging vines, might have been the effects of the tree roots in drying soil that inclined to be wet. The Romans understood very well the importance of drainage to vines, that slopes were preferable to level ground, and that stony ground is a positive advantage. Virgil even advised growers to "bury in the ground 30 stones or rough shells; for the water will glide between them . . . and invigorate the plants."

The first question for anyone planting a new vineyard was which grape variety to choose; colour, flavour, the size of the crop and its ability to age all depend on it. By the 1st century AD, varieties exercised Roman minds almost as much as they do Californians or Australians today. The best wines were still in the Greek tradition, and the Aminean vines (there were five kinds), whose wines Pliny describes as full-bodied and vigorous, improving with age, were unchallenged for quality. Only one other vine is mentioned as being close, the Nomentan, a hardier plant with "ruddy" wood, grown up the Tiber from Rome.

Vines from the overseas provinces, on the other hand, were being increasingly planted for greater fruitfulness. Of these the most promising were the Balisca and the Biturica, respectively (according to Columella) from Spain and Bordeaux. More of this in Chapter 8.

Some modern writers have claimed to recognize in one variety described as hardy and very fruitful, the Arcelaca or Argitis, no less a plant than the Riesling. It is hard to reconcile this with the judgment that its wine was cheap, common and had no keeping powers.

From the way Columella and Pliny categorize vines as being good in this or that district and not elsewhere, it seems that experimental planting was widely practised. Fashions in winemaking were changing, too.

THE ROMAN VINTAGE WAS CUT WITH A KNIFE LIKE A MINIATURE SICKLE, brought in baskets to the press-house and trodden in shallow tanks, like the lagars still used for port-making. The wine press was developed by the Romans up to the point where it remained almost until modern times: great beams were used for weight, capstans for adding pressure, and rope wound around the "cake" of pressed grapes to keep it in place.

Fermentation took place in earthenware dolia, like the Greek pithoi (and the Georgian kwevri), sunk up to their necks in the floor of the cellar. Dolia were also used for maturing wine and in later times for transporting it. As the seaborne wine trade grew, the amphora, weighing as much as its payload, gave place to the much more economical bulk of a dolium – even if the dolium could not be moved and had to be filled from wine skins. The archaeological evidence for wine shipments by sea becomes scarcer and scarcer after about AD250; only recently has it been realised that the reason is the gradual introduction of the much stronger and lighter barrel. Pieces of pottery are immortal, barrels usually disappear in time without trace.

The sweet tooth of the Romans meant that the vintage was left as late as possible. The poets Virgil and Martial both advised leaving the grapes on the vine until November, or until they were "stiff with frost". A Greek technique was to pick them slightly underripe (presumably to keep a relatively high acidity) and to leave them in the sun for three or four days to shrivel and concentrate their sugar. Another, a speciality of Crete, was to twist the stalks of the bunches and leave them on the vine to shrivel deprived of sap. Passum was the term for these wines concentrated by drying. In Italy today they are called passiti.

Reduction and concentration of the juice (the must) by boiling was another technique for making stronger and sweeter wine. Defrutum was the general term, although different degrees of reduction were called by different names. Defrutum was often used for blending with thin vintages. A third method for sweetening was simply to add honey – as much as $6\frac{1}{2}$lbs to 12 litres. The sticky result, called mulsum,

The luxurious villas of Pompeii and Herculaneum were provided with a triclinium, an outdoor dining room for use when the weather was not too hot or cold. The guests reclined on cushions on the gently sloping raised portions of the floor around three sides of a central table laden with food and wine – in this case probably rather good wine, since this was a wine merchant's house, the so-called House of Neptune, with a shop at the front.

was drunk as a gustatio, an apéritif, with the hors d'oeuvres. The Romans also knew how to make what they called "permanent must" (and the Germans today call Süssreserve). They prevented fermentation by submerging the amphoras in cold water (the sea or a well) and keeping them there until winter. This "semper mustum" was another way of sweetening wine that had fermented too dry for their liking.

PERHAPS THE CLOSEST WE CAN GET TO AN IDEA OF ROMAN TASTE at table is one of the spicy Oriental cuisines of today: Indian cooking without the curry, for example. Reading Roman recipes gives a strong impression that the seasoning was more important than the primary flavour. Powerfully savoury tastes; fermented fish sauce; garlic; and most of all assafoetida – a strange onion-smelling root that to modern sensibilities is a byword for nausea – were regularly combined with every sort of sweetening from raisins to honey, including a drench of the sweetest wine. Meat was regularly cooked and served with such fruit as apricots (an introduction from the Caucasus), and dishes of fig or plum sauce were used as all-purpose dips.

Pliny gives an alarming list of the flavourings that were added to make the forefathers of our vermouths. The whole class of wines cooked up with infusions or the maceration of herbs, spices, resin and other flavourings was often referred to as "Greek", since the Greeks rarely drank wine without seasoning. Adding seawater was a Greek idea that was followed in Pompeii (Pliny shrewdly advises that it be collected well out to sea).

Absinthe was a popular flavouring for a "Greek" wine; rose petals, violets, mint and pepper were others. The famous cookbook of Apicius gives a recipe for a "marvellous brew" involving resin, ground pepper, saffron, malobathre and grilled dates in a reduced mixture of wine and honey. Travellers often carried with them a flask of some such "conditum", perhaps just honey mixed with pepper, to drown the taste of the local wine along the way.

The "plebs", the lower classes, and the army often had to make do with less than wine; either with posca, which was vinegar mixed with water, or lorca, the thin and feeble brew made by soaking the pressed skins and stalks in water and fermenting the result. French peasants had to make do with the same until the last century – "piquette" they called it. The soldiers who crucified Christ gave him a sponge full of their vinegar ration.

It was the mark of fine wine with the Romans, as it is with us, that it improved with age. Horace, in one poem contemplating his end, seems more concerned about parting from his cellar of wonderful old wine than from his wife. Very sweet wines will usually keep well without turning to vinegar, but the Romans had no means of increasing their alcoholic strength to preserve them. No yeast will continue to ferment when the alcohol level reaches 15 or 16 percent of the wine. Distillation was unknown. This, then, was the strongest drink they knew. They made a clear distinction, though, between heavy sweet wines that they aged in the open air, "exposed to the sun, moon, rain and wind", and weaker wines that should be kept in jars sunk in the ground. The great Campanian wines came into the first category; like sherry and madeira they were intentionally oxidized – a process accelerated by changes of temperature. About these wines, Pliny anticipated a discovery of

17 centuries later: "With wines shipped over sea . . . the effect of the motion on vintages that can stand it is merely to double their previous maturity."

Another practice with the same aim in view – to speed oxidation and the symptoms of maturity – was the fumarium, a smoke chamber in which amphoras were stored above a hearth. The heat and the smoke both affected the wine. Apparently it eventually emerged with a smoky flavour and, curiously, paler in colour and sharper in acidity. Pliny and Columella give the impression that smoking was not something you do to first-growths.

PLINY ALSO NOTICED THAT THE THINNER A WINE IS, "THE MORE AROMA IT HAS". The taste of the Romans was to change, with their experience of more "thin" wines, from the north of Italy and from Gaul. The first Gallic wine arrived in Rome during Pliny's lifetime. A century later it accounted for one-third of all the amphoras found by archaeologists in their excavations at Ostia, the seaport of Rome.

Our best source of information about the wines of the second century is Galen, a Greek physician from Pergamon in Asia Minor, who became the personal doctor and advisor of the Emperor Marcus Aurelius. His name is still known to every doctor; his observations succeeded those of the great Hippocrates as the medical reference point which was not entirely superseded until the 19th century.

Galen studied for 12 years in Corinth and Alexandria before being appointed physician to the gladiators in Pergamon. Their diet as well as their wounds was his concern. He claimed that no gladiator died in his care, which sounds improbable, since almost his only recourse, faced with the most horrific wounds, was to bathe them in wine. Deep wounds gave him an opportunity to study anatomy and advance the technique of surgery.

The possibilities of pharmacy, the use of drugs and herbal medicines, were recognized, but the identities of plants were sadly in doubt, despite the work of Nero's Greek physician, Dioscorides, in finding and describing them. A conscientious doctor could not trust anyone but himself to collect the plants he wanted. Galen was both observant and methodical. It has been said of him that he transformed medicine from "a healing art to a healing science". His system of healing was "so well organized, so comprehensive, dogmatic and plausible, that it ruled European medicine almost until modern times".

In AD 169 Galen became the emperor's physician. An important part of his duties was to protect the imperial person from poisons. Concoctions of wine and drugs for this purpose were called theriacs. Superstitious faith in their ability to prevent illness and cure anything from a gumboil to the plague continued until the 18th century (the English "treacle" derives from theriac). The ancient King Mithridates, so legend has it, concocted a "mithridatum" theriac so efficacious that when in defeat he tried to poison himself nothing would kill him. Eventually a soldier obliged with his sword.

De Antidotis was the title of Galen's treatise on the subject. It contains a characteristically thorough and well-observed account of the wines drunk in Rome in his day, both Italian and Greek: how they should be judged, stored and aged. Falernian was still first choice. Galen's way of choosing the best was to start with wines 20 years old (which he expected to be "bitter") and then taste back through the vintages until he came to the oldest without a bitter aftertaste. He points out, though, that Falernian was so famous that it was often faked, and says that Surrentine, although harder and more austere, needing even longer to mature, equals it in quality.

The word "austere" continually enters Galen's descriptions of his choice of wines. Roman taste was clearly shifting away from the thick, sweet wines that had made Campania the most prestigious region. Galen and other doctors were recommending drier and lighter wines. The vineyards closer to Rome, dismissed in earlier times because their wine was "harsh" and acidic, are among Galen's favourites. Sabine and Tiburtine, from districts north of the capital on the Tiber, are promoted to first-growths. Setinum, from south of Rome, had made its name as the favourite of Augustus (the very opposite of a voluptuary). Another was Signine (which seems to have eclipsed the old first-growth Albanum). Galen describes these wines as "fluid but strong, and fairly astringent", and variably full-bodied or lighter. All of them, like the first-growths of previous generations, are white. It seems that red wine that was not expected to age remained the daily drink of taverns. The concept of full-bodied, tannic red wines, aged in barrel and then in bottle, was still in the distant future.

Although Galen mentions the wine of Etruria in passing, had tasted Hadrianum from the Adriatic, and approved of new and drier Campanian wines, Gauranum

THE GRAPE ARCHAEOLOGIST

The most respected winemaker in Campania today is Antonio Mastroberardino of Avellino, a town 20 miles inland from Vesuvius. Mastroberardino is a viticultural archaeologist. All his wines are made from grapes that were used in the region by the Romans, and two of them were reputed (in Pliny's account) to be imports from Greece in pre-Roman times. Their names, Greco and Aglianico (or Ellenico), both mean, simply, "Greek".

The highest rank among Greek vines, said Pliny, is given to the group called Aminea, whose wine has body and vigour and improves with age. The Greco is easily identified as Pliny's "twin sisters", the *Aminea gemina*, because its (white) bunches are always divided into two distinct parts. Its modern wine, Greco di Tufo, does indeed have body and vigour, although it is rarely given a chance to age today.

The Aglianico is not so easily identified in classical references, but makes the best modern red wine of Campania, Taurasi; wine with a firmness and depth of colour and flavour that outshines anything else from the south. The so-called Falernum of today is also made from Aglianico, in what is reputed to be the original area on the borders of Campania and Latium

north of Naples, but the modern product has no qualities that confirm, or even hint at, its past glory. (Pliny remarked that real Falernian vines were sometimes transplanted from the region, but "very quickly degenerated" everywhere else. Now the boot seems to be on the other foot.)

Mastroberardino also grows three grapes of identifiable Roman origin. The best is the rare Fiano, originally called Latino to distinguish it from the Greek varieties. "Fiano" is said to derive from "appianum" – although this name, which means attractive to bees, is given by Pliny to what seems to be the Moscadello of Tuscany. To confuse matters more, "musca", its Latin root, is a fly, not a bee. Fiano, in any case, is certainly not a Muscat vine but gives pale white wine with an aristocratic, even austere, firmness; Campania's best today.

The name of another white variety, the Coda di Volpe, or foxtail, suggests Pliny's Alopecis, "which resembles a fox's brush" – although to Pliny this was a table grape, not for wine. This and the Piedirosso ("red-stem") are still grown on Mount Vesuvius. Pliny certainly would not recognize the name their wine goes by today: Lacryma Christi. The Galilean was only 25 years old when Pliny was born.

and an Aminean from Naples, it is surprising that he does not recommend the Rhaetic of Verona and the Tirol, which back in Virgil's day had anticipated the vogue for drier wines, but then seems to have passed from favour. The district of Aquileia north of the Adriatic was also a major producer of lighter wines – but not, apparently, for the Roman market. And then, of course, there were the new wines arriving in Italy from Gaul.

It is frustrating not to be told more about these wines, whose characters must have been so different from the established taste of Rome. There is a conclusion to be drawn, though, from the fact that none of the first-growth regions of the ancient world would find a place in any such list in modern times.

AFTER GALEN we have no commentator on the progress of Roman taste in wine. The same first-growths apparently continued to fetch the highest prices. Imports from the provinces certainly increased, but there was room for all on the insatiable Roman market. With over one million inhabitants, Rome was by far the greatest city the Mediterranean world was to know until our own century. A hundred years ago even Naples, the most populous Mediterranean city of its time, had only half a million inhabitants.

Obviously most of the demand was for cheap wine, which was most easily brought by sea (unless it came down the river Tiber). Spain and Gaul obliged with huge amounts – although the increasing use of the wooden barrel means that we have no evidence to estimate how much. One effect of the growing provincial vineyards was that mass production became less profitable in the Italian regions that traditionally supplied Rome. A wine estate tended increasingly to become a gentleman's pastime – or even an emperor's; one emperor, Julian, is said to have planted a vineyard with his own hands and bequeathed it to a friend as the highest compliment he could pay him – "a modest souvenir of my gardening".

A positive disincentive to Italian growers was a tax in kind imposed on them from about AD250. They were obliged to deliver a proportion of their wine to Rome and other centres, for the rations of the army, and to supply the populace with subsidized drink. Only carriage was paid; not surprisingly, many winegrowers gave up.

It may have been partly to remedy this situation that in AD280 the Emperor Probus, whose principal concern in his short reign was to face the onslaught on the Empire of barbarians from the north, repealed the widely ignored edict of Domitian against the planting of vines. He even set the army to work to make new vineyards in Gaul and along the Danube (where, ironically, he was murdered in a vineyard). By now the decline of Rome had begun, the city's population was falling, and the future lay in the provinces of the Empire it had so spectacularly created.

CHAPTER 7

JEWISH LIFE AND CHRISTIAN RITUAL

"The various modes of worship, which prevailed in the Roman world, were all considered by the people as equally true; by the philosopher, as equally false, and by the magistrate, as equally useful."

This was Gibbon's cynical dismissal of Roman religion. He saw in it none of the fervour and mystery of ancient Greece: simply the opiate of the people.

Cults came and went; some of their own accord, some with a push from the magistrates. Educated Romans had read Livy's famous account (see Chapter 5) of the banning of the Bacchanalia. To them there must have been little to distinguish the early Christians – Jews, apparently, following what they called the cult of the Nazarene – from the followers of Bacchus.

There were enough parallels and points of contact to justify confusion. What they knew of Christian rites appeared little different from the Bacchanalia. Both were performed in secret (or at least private) and apparently involved a cannibalistic meal. The followers of Bacchus had claimed to be eating their god's flesh and drinking his blood. So did the Christians.

In principle the Roman state stood for freedom of worship under the emperor. Sometimes, though, it was useful to have a scapegoat. A mysterious new sect or secret society could be blamed for almost anything. Nero was the first to pick on the Christians, as his scapegoat for the great fire of Rome in AD64. But whenever the balance expressed by Gibbon was dangerously tilted, the authorities, however fair-minded, were inclined to take drastic action.

The "Younger" Pliny, nephew of the naturalist, was governor of the province of Bithynia-Pontus on the Black Sea under the Emperor Trajan. In AD114 he found himself under pressure to deal with the growing number of Christians. He reported his proceedings to the emperor and asked his advice over the ticklish problem. Christianity, he reported, had been spreading from the towns to the countryside. Temples had been "almost entirely deserted for a long time", although, thanks to his actions, "the sacred rites . . . are being performed again, and flesh of sacrificial animals is on sale everywhere, though up till recently scarcely anyone could be found to buy it."

His actions had been to summon persons accused of Christianity and require them to invoke the gods and make offerings to the emperor. If they refused, he had them executed, on the grounds that all political societies were banned. He tortured "two slave women, whom they call deaconesses", but "found nothing but a degenerate sort of cult carried to extravagant lengths." Stories of incest and cannibalism were unfounded. They ate "ordinary harmless food". Trajan replied: "You have followed the right course of procedure, my dear Pliny. These people must not be hunted out. . . ." He adds that anonymous denunciations "must play no part in any accusation. They create the worst sort of precedent and are quite out of keeping with the spirit of the age."

NOT ALL EMPERORS WERE TO BE AS REASONABLE. The game of cat and mouse continued for 200 years before Constantine capitulated to a consensus: by then Christians were more coherent and better organized than any of the alternative religions that invited his belief.

When the Romans first started to notice Christians they described them as obsessed with death. Some even took them to be a burial club, a mutual society to pay for funerals, because of their preoccupation with the afterlife and their insistence on burial rather than cremation. Their one distinctive feature, in Roman eyes, was that they were (or were assumed to be) Jews. Jews were constantly in trouble for putting their God before their emperor. In AD70, Israel had openly revolted and the Romans had sacked Jerusalem, destroying the Temple. But even now, to understand the Christian rites, we must see them in the context of Jesus' Jewish faith and upbringing.

Wine was no less important in Israel than it was in Greece; but there is no parallel between its meaning to a Jew and its meaning to a follower of Dionysus. In Israel the idea of a libation, or any sort of sacrifice in the Greek or Roman sense, was sacrilegious – indeed, the horror of the thought still lies behind the definition of what is "clean" and what is "defiled". To Greeks, wine was the bringer of liberation and ecstacy: drunkenness could be sacred. To Jews it was a blessing fraught with danger that had to be kept under strict rabbinical control.

For Moses' followers, the first sight of the Promised Land was a prodigious bunch of grapes. He sent spies into the land of Canaan, "And they came unto the brook of Eshcol, and cut down from thence a branch with one cluster of grapes, and they bare it between them upon a staff." The Israelites' interest in wine-growing is a continual theme of the prophets. Isaiah contains advice on planting a vineyard; Amos and Joel, Jeremiah and Ezekial, Zachariah and Nehemiah all use the vine as a symbol of a happy state. Indeed, in the whole of the Old Testament only the Book of Jonah has no reference to the vine or wine.

Joseph, when he interpreted the dreams of Pharoah's chief butler, talked as a man who had watched vines grow – and so did Jesus, when he called himself "the true vine". "Every bunch in me that beareth not fruit he taketh away; and every branch that beareth fruit, he purgeth it, that it may bring forth more fruit . . ." is a reasonable account of the process of pruning. "A householder", in one of his parables, "digged a wine-press" – an expression that remained mysterious to me until I found, near the Sea of Galilee, an ancient wine-press that had indeed been

The Talmud of the Jews is accompanied by anecdotes or parables called haggadahs to help explain the law. A 14th-century haggadah from southern France illustrates wine being used in the Passover. Wine is still an important part of Jewish ritual.

dug, in three separate pits at different levels, for treading the grapes, straining the must, and fermentation.

The book of laws known as the Babylonian Talmud contains an idea for distinguishing the terroir that I have only come across elsewhere in Burgundy: "The Hurites used to smell the smell of the earth, while the Hivites . . . they used to lick it like snakes." The Cistercian monks of Cîteaux, it is said, went so far as to taste the soil before deciding where to mark their vineyard boundaries.

Another Talmudic sentiment that is nowhere in Pliny or Columella I have heard in the mouth of a port-grower in the high Douro: "At the beginning, the product of the vine is trodden with mortal feet. Afterwards it is served at the table of kings."

JEWISH DEVOTION TO WINE runs right through their law and literature. It is the very essence of their civilization. There is a curious chapter in the Book of Jeremiah that sounds like a foreshadowing of Islam. The tribe of the Rechabites are bidden to drink wine and refuse. They have chosen, they say, to dwell in tents and abstain. Wine and the nomad, apparently, will never be friends. But to the Jews there is no communal, religious or family life without it. Jesus' first miracle, at Cana, was simply to make good the lack of wine as a necessity at a marriage feast. He ordered the servants to draw six pots of water from the well (which even now can still be seen in the crypt of the little Franciscan church now on the site). When it was poured out it was wine – and better wine than the apparently rather meagre supply that the bridegroom had provided.

Each Sabbath starts with an act of blessing, the kiddush, or "sanctification", chanted over a cup of wine which the whole family shares. Four cups of wine must be drunk at the Passover, two cups at weddings, and one at circumcisions. At a funeral, in ancient times, the "cup of consolation" offered to the bereaved was ten glasses of wine. When three or more men recite the grace after meals their leader pronounces the blessing over a cup of wine, which all present then sip. The law is wholly specific about these ritual uses. They introduce the joy of wine into each act of worship, but reject any Dionysiac idea that intoxication is a good thing in itself. In the words of one rabbi, wine "helps to open the heart to reasoning". Reason is the goal, not inspiration. The Sanhedrin, the High Court at Jerusalem, had a simple and grand test for drunkenness; whether the person affected is capable of addressing himself properly to a king. There is only one Talmudic injunction to take a Dionysiac view: on the feast of Purim, when the faithful should get too fuddled to distinguish between "Blessed be Mordecai" and "Cursed be Haman".

Lying behind the ancient rules is a much stricter injunction still that reveals the fundamental fear behind them all. More important than what you drink is who you drink it with. Jews should not accept wine from Gentiles. Such social intercourse may lead to intimacy, intimacy to intermarriage.

The rules defining a Jewish (or kosher) wine have the simple aim of ensuring (by strict rabbinical supervision) that no Gentile has tampered with it in any way. They are carried to extreme lengths. At the Quatzrin winery near the Golan Heights in northern Israel, a young worker dashed forward to prevent me from even brushing against the stainless-steel valve on a huge insulated vat. He steered me right away from the hose snaking across the floor; if I had touched either (or anywhere where the wine is or might be in transit), I could have defiled it. It would no longer be kosher. Even in the bottling room, even when the bottle was corked, I was not allowed to touch a bottle – until it was sealed with a capsule.

The harm that I might do, I was told, was to dedicate the wine to an idol; to perform a libation with it, in other words, even if only in my mind. The fact that this

A worker at the Quatzrin Winery near the Golan Heights in northern Israel observes strict rules under the supervision of a rabbi to prevent the wine from being defiled. A gentile may not go near it until it is bottled and sealed. Kosher methods include fining the wine with beaten egg-whites to clear the smallest particles from it; the same practice as is used for highest-quality wines worldwide.

sanction has survived long past the last hint of Baal worship confirms the underlying reason: a Gentile must be kept at a safe distance to ensure the integrity of the Jews. With a typically pragmatic touch, the law allows a Jew to drink wine that a Gentile has defiled with the intention of causing damage; this is in order to discourage other Gentiles from following suit.

Whatever the historic causes of Jewish law and custom in relation to wine, one point stands out strikingly. Its excessive use in Jewish communities is remarkably rare. Studies in the USA have shown that proportionately more Jews than other ethnic or religious segments of the population drink wine, beer or spirits, but proportionately fewer Jews are heavy drinkers or alcoholics. Looking for an explanation, researchers have fallen back on the fact that Jewish children from the earliest age are initiated into wine-drinking in their families, in a religious context, where drinking is always moderate.

THE EVOLUTION OF THE CHRISTIAN EUCHARIST was a gradual process composed of many elements. At first it was just a common meal in a tradition that was certainly Jewish, but was probably no less Roman. It was the natural thing to do when a club met, to share food and drink. Any Jew would do what Jesus had done; to bless the cup, either as kiddush or grace after a meal. How far the rites of the rival Orphic or Bacchanalian cult entered into the Christians' consciousness it is impossible to say; although there were probably converts who saw the apparent connection and were perhaps convinced by it.

St Paul's Epistle to the Corinthians provides the first reference to Christians remembering Christ's Last Supper as a formal observance: "For I have received of the Lord that which also I delivered unto you, That the Lord Jesus the same night in which he was betrayed took bread. And when he had given thanks, he broke it, and said Take, eat: this is my body, which is broken for you: do this in remembrance of me. After the same manner also he took the cup, when he had supped, saying This is the new testament of my blood: this do ye, as oft as you drink it, in remembrance of me." Paul wrote this before any of the gospels were compiled. St John's Gospel (chapter 6) on the other hand recounts how Jesus had already said, in the synagogue at Capernaum, "He that eateth my flesh, and drinketh my blood, dwelleth in me, and I in him." But: "Many therefore of his disciples, when they had heard this, said, this is a hard saying; who can hear it?" And: "From that time many of his disciples went back, and walked no more with him."

The symbolism of sacrifice in Christianity has never been easy to understand. It developed in a Greek, rather than a Jewish, tradition. (The New Testament was written in Greek, not Hebrew.) In pagan Greece it was a sacred act, to burn meat on an altar to feed the gods with its smoke, and then eat the meat. This sort of sacrifice could be described as a communal meal with a god. The very word for god in Greek, "theos", derives from the word for smoke. The same root, "thusia", is still preserved in the word enthusiasm, which thus means "filled with god". A similarly sacred act, going back thousands of years, was to drink blood, or blood mixed with wine, or wine as a symbol for blood. The Greek word "eucharistia" was used for such ceremonies when they were specifically formal acts of thanksgiving. Thus the Christians' word for their act of worship linked it directly to pagan sacrifices.

As soon as Greek thought touched Christ's teaching, it took on a meaning that was impossible for Jews to accept. Christ's sacrifice of himself was far too close in its symbolism, or in the symbolism that the church put on it, to the ancient pagan rites. The clearest connection was to the Orphic followers of the wine god. Originally, Dionysus had merely liberated the spirit. The Orphics turned him into a god who saved the spirit and could grant it eternal life. This was no different in concept from what the Christians taught.

The first account of the actual Christian practice after St Paul was written by St Justin to the far-from-sympathetic Emperor Marcus Aurelius in about 150, one of two apologia that he composed in the hope of protecting his fellow-Christians from persecution, without success. He himself was martyred at Rome in 165. ". . . at the end [of the gathering]", he wrote, "prayers being finished, bread, wine and water are brought; the person presiding prays and gives thanks as well as he is able." The water and wine were mixed by the deacons in a way that recalled certain Jewish rituals. Later, different Christian leaders were to offer different mystical interpretations: St Irenaeus that it symbolized the union of Christ's earthly and heavenly natures; St Cyprian that it represented the union of the believers with Christ – the view that eventually became orthodox, after more discussion.

A 15th-century German wood carving of the Last Supper is
full of earthy realism that would have appealed to the
persecuted Nazarenes hiding in the catacombs of Rome.

The image of these first celebrations of what was to become the Eucharist is preserved in wall paintings in the catacombs of Rome, where the persecuted Christians met in secret. In the catacomb of Priscilla, seven men and women are at a table set with a single cup, and plates with bread and fish. One of the figures is breaking bread. In another scene, more like a banquet, the six participants, sitting around a table with bread, fish and wine, and with an amphora beside them, are

The idea that wine, the blood of the grape, stood for Christ's own blood
is expressed in this Bavarian painting from about 1500. "Christ in the
Press" was a popular motive in the wine-growing regions of Germany
and Central Europe throughout the Middle Ages.

calling to their servants, whose names are Irene (Peace) and Agape (Love), for wine. One says, "Mix it for me"; another, "Give it to me warm."

By the 2nd century the Christians in Asia Minor had been able to build their first churches; by the 4th, when Constantine became a deathbed convert, the Eucharist had become the liturgy that remains with us to this day, although now interpreted in ways as different as a High Mass and the communal meal of a Baptist meeting.

The precise phrases of St Thomas Aquinas, the great Italian friar-philosopher of the 13th century, sum up the significance of wine in the Mass:

"The Sacrament of the Eucharist can only be performed with wine from the vine, for it is the will of Christ Jesus, Who chose wine when He ordained this Sacrament . . . and also because the wine of grapes is in some sort an image of the effect of the Sacrament. By this I mean spiritual joy, for it is written that wine makes glad the heart of man."

Armenians declined to water their wine, which led to disputes with the Greek church. In 1178 they tried to compromise; they would add water if the Greeks would desist from adding warm water. The Greeks refused, and eventually a neutral arbiter was found – a Muslim. He listened to both sides before observing that wine was an impure liquid forbidden by the Koran: the answer was pure water. Debates have continued about whether the wine should be red or white. In favour of red is the fact that it resembles blood; of white, that it does not stain the altar linen.

CHAPTER 8

A GREENER COUNTRY

No one disputes that France was to become the motherland of wine, but the circumstances of her insemination are a battleground between historians. In brief, there are those who believe what Roman writings, backed up by Roman remains, tell them, and those whose Gallic pride leads them to look much further back, and to claim that it was the forgotten predecessors of the Celts who established wine-growing in France. Some even argue that Stone-Age Frenchmen were vignerons. There are enough grape pips in a settlement site on Lake Geneva to indicate that the wild vine (certainly indigenous to France) was being exploited there 12,000 years ago or more.

Prehistory is turned on its head by this school of thought, which holds that civilization began in the west and spread its influence eastwards. According to this "Celtic" school, the achievements of the west are ignored because they were never written down; written records are the only reason why we credit the peoples of the east with discoveries and inventions made by others.

The Celts of Gaul were certainly an active and aggressive race. They dominated almost the whole of Europe north of the Alps in the time when Athens dominated Greece. They invaded Italy, occupied Lombardy (founding Milan) and reached Rome, settled briefly in Asia Minor, and in the aftermath of Alexander the Great they even penetrated his Macedonian kingdom, reaching as far as Delphi, and founded a settlement on the Danube at Belgrade.

There is no arguing with the fact that they appreciated wine. The evidence of the Vix Crater (see Chapter 4) of 600BC is conclusive. The ancient Gauls had extensive contacts with the Mediterranean wine world over a long period; they were a ready market for Greek and Etruscan wine; if the wine-vine was a native plant in France, then surely they must have made wine for themselves.

The Roman evidence says not. The account from the classics is that Greeks from Asia Minor, the Phocaeans, established the colony of Massalia (Marseilles) in 600BC, planted vines and traded with the natives. The Celts from the interior of Gaul had not even reached the south of France by this time: the inhabitants were Ligurians and Iberians, respectively from northern Italy and Spain.

The enormous success of Massalia was due to the natives' thirst for wine, but it is even doubted (by some authorities) that it had its own vineyards. Some say the

Greeks taught the natives to become adept at wine-growing, others that all "Massaliote" wine was imported from Greece or the Greek colonies in Sicily and southern Italy.

If there were vineyards in Celtic Gaul, they were not down on the Mediterranean coast, where the Gauls began to arrive in about the 5th century BC. They must have been in the interior, attached to such tribal settlements as Bourges, Chartres, Metz, Reims, Amiens, Troyes and Bibracte (of which more in a moment), growing native grapes (the climate would have excluded Mediterranean vines) and, moreover, subject to the disapproving looks of the Druids, who anticipated certain sects of Christianity in their moralistic stance towards wine. It is easier to believe the authors who say that France had no wine – and difficult otherwise to understand the enormous prices Gallic chieftains would pay for it. Diodorus Siculus, admittedly writing rather later, about the time of Christ, ensured himself fame with the statement that "Italian merchants, prompted by their usual cupidity, regard the Gauls' thirst for wine as a godsend. They take the wine to them by ship up the navigable rivers or by chariot overland and it fetches incredible prices: for one amphora of wine they receive one slave, thus exchanging the drink for the cupbearer."

MASSALIA BECAME PART OF THE YOUNG ROMAN EMPIRE in about 125BC, but continued to be regarded as a Greek town. The magnificence of the Roman buildings, monuments, theatres and aqueducts of Provence, in masonry as fine as any in the Empire and far ahead of anything in Gaul, is said to be due to the Greek tradition of craftsmanship in Massilia, as the Romans called it. Young Romans even came here to be educated in preference to making the longer trip to Athens.

The first true colony of the Romans in France was founded a few years later, along the coast to the west at Narbo, near the mouth of the river Aude. Narbo (Narbonne) became the capital of the province of Narbonensis, and indeed of the whole of what the Romans called Gallia Transalpina – Gaul across the Alps, the creation of the great pro-consul Domitius Ahenobarbus. Like all Rome's great

CELTS AND CASKS

The amphora was superseded for the transport of wine by the barrel in the course of the 3rd century AD; when, that is, the flow of wine from Rome to its northern colonies was reversed, and it was the Celtic races who began to furnish Italy.

The barrel as we know it was a Celtic invention: exactly as we know it, since hardly any changes have taken place in the art of the cooper, the barrel maker, for 2,000 years. Wood and metal were the Celts' favourite materials. So skilful were they with roof beams that some of the more ambitious of the stone vaults of Rome could not have been achieved without Celtic carpenters to make the templates. Iron wood-working tools have been found from the La Tène culture of Switzerland in the 5th century BC which would be familiar in a cooper's shop today. The earliest barrels even had iron hoops, which gave way to wooden encircling bands in Roman times, only to be reinstated in the barrels of the 17th century. The historic trend has been for barrels to become shorter and fatter – otherwise there has been almost no change.

The Romans soon realized the superiority of the light, resilient, rollable barrel over the cumbersome fragile amphora, particularly in cooler northern climates with high humidity. The one advantage of the amphora that the barrel did not possess was that it could not be made airtight. Wood "breathes"; wine cannot be "laid down" to mature for years in a barrel, as it can in an amphora.

ROME'S
WESTERN EMPIRE

colonial cities, it was based on veterans from the army (who did not have to be native Romans; army service conferred the coveted rights of citizenship on Roman and barbarian alike). It was the period after the destruction of Carthage when wine-growing was spreading like wildfire in Italy. Some of the soldiers would have been the sons of winegrowers and known all about vineyards. They planted the hill slopes near Narbonne, today's Corbières, Minervois and the Coteaux du Languedoc. These are the first extensive vineyards in France that we can be certain about. They provided the trading strength of a province that was to control all of France south of a line from the Spanish border to Geneva.

ROME'S WAR TO THE DEATH WITH THE CARTHAGINIANS had already given her another prize. With the defeat of Hannibal in 200BC, the coastal parts of Spain became the first two great overseas provinces of her Empire. The northern province, eventually extending right to the Atlantic, became Tarraconensis, based on what today is Tarragona. The southern province, modern Andalusia, was called Baetica, from the river Baetis, now the Guadalquivir, at whose mouth the town of Gades (Cádiz) had been founded a thousand years ago by the Phoenicians.

Wine was no stranger to these provinces. It was the Carthaginians' wine-growing skills, inherited from the Phoenicians, that had caused Cato's envious outcry, "Delenda est Carthago". Columella was a native of Cádiz. Wine from the coastal parts of Spain soon became commonplace in Rome. Pompeii traded with Tarragona, both buying and selling wine, which argues the quality of the Spanish product. Marcus Porcius, the millionaire merchant we met in Pompeii, had a wine estate here. Enormous quantities of Baetic wine reached Rome (the voyage normally only took a week). Most of it was described as ordinary, but one wine, Ceretanum, picked out by the poet Martial (who, although poor, had expensive tastes), was apparently highly regarded. If it came from Ceret, which seems probable, Martial was the first writer to write about sherry. The modern name of Ceret is Jerez de la Frontera.

The Phoenicians had not stayed on the seacoasts, but used the navigable rivers to go far inland. In Portugal (Lusitania to the Romans), they had sailed up the Tagus and the Douro (where Greek, although not Phoenician, coins have been found). In Spain they used the Baetis and the one considerable river of the Mediterranean coast,

IN A GLASS, LIGHTLY

Wine was first drunk from pottery, occasionally and ceremonially from gold, but by as early as the late Bronze Age, about 1500BC, also from glass.

The technique of firing a glassy or "vitreous" substance onto solid objects was discovered in about 4000BC. (On pottery it is called faience; on metal, enamel.) In about 1500BC the idea of a hollow glass vessel appeared – possibly in Egypt. It was made by dipping a cloth bag of sand into a crucible of molten glass, then modelling it by rolling it on a "marver", a flat stone bench, then when the glass had cooled, emptying out the sand. The technique was known all over the Near East until about 1200BC, then apparently lost in the first "Dark Age", to reemerge in the 8th century BC, with Egypt, Phoenicia and Syria as glassmaking centres, but also workshops in Italy and Celtic Europe.

The idea of glassblowing, instead of the sand-core method, originated in Syria in the 1st century BC. A blob of molten glass on the end of a metal tube was blown, probably into a mould at first, then freely into a bubble that could be "marvered" into shape,.

Glassblowing spread rapidly around the Roman Empire, with Syrian or Alexandrian craftsmen setting up workshops, especially in Italy, Gaul and the Rhineland – hence the similarity of styles wherever it was made. Roman glass beakers or tumblers survive in surprising numbers, appearing extremely frail because they are so light; their metal contains no lead. In fact they are quite resilient and rather like Bakelite in texture – now often with a lovely nacreous lustre.

Small bottles for scent are common; larger ones for wine rather rare. A superb example, made like a miniature amphora with two handles, is in the Cathedral Museum at Speyer on the Rhine. There is no real evidence, though, that Romans used glass wine bottles for storage. They were in practice only decanters for use on the table.

Glassmaking survived the fall of the Empire, with the Rhineland as a continuing centre. It tended to be concentrated in forested areas where there was plenty of fuel for the furnaces. Wine glasses, however, ramained objects of luxury until the 18th century.

the Iberus – to us the Ebro. They left traces up the Ebro as far as Alfaro in Rioja. The Roman legions went farther, and colonized what today is the wine region of the Rioja Alta. The towns of Calahorra, Cenicero and Logroño were all Roman veteran colonies (Cenicero means crematorium). In a field near the Ebro at Funes, no more antique or dramatic looking than any long-abandoned agricultural building, is the entire layout of one of the wine bodegas that must have dotted the region to supply the troops. Its sizeable cisterns, beside the four lagars for treading the grapes, indicate that it could produce and store as much as 75,000 litres, or nearly 3,000 amphoras of wine.

In the middle of the 1st century BC, the Gauls step from the twilight of illiterate barbarism, however gleaming with jewelled armour and ringing with battle cries, into the full light of history. It was their fortune to meet one of the greatest commanders and administrators of the ancient world, and one of its most lucid chroniclers – Julius Caesar. Domitius Ahenobarbus had already established Roman power in the south. Political contact had been made, and one powerful tribe of central Gaul, the Aedui, whose stronghold of Bibracte lay just to the west of what is today the Côte d'Or, seeking Roman help against its foes (and not averse to the luxuries of Roman life), had asked for and been given the title of Friend and Ally of the Roman people.

Rome soon realised the unstable nature of the tribal make-up of Gaul. Pillaging hordes of Teutons from the north hacked their way into what Rome was beginning to regard as its sphere of influence. Rome sent soldiers, who were three times thrashed. Rome and Gaul had common cause in beating off this invading savagery. The consul Marius then raised an army which defeated the Teuton, German and Swiss tribes, near Turin and at Aix-en-Provence. The tribes of Gaul were confused and divided as to whether to welcome or resist this formidable neighbour.

It was the custom of those times for armies in the field to be accompanied by a bazaar of traders, who sold accessories to the soldiers and bought their booty from them on the spot. Prisoners were auctioned there and then, and taken off to be sold at a good profit as slaves.

Constant fighting among the 60 tribes who divided Gaul assured that there was never a shortage of prisoners for sale. The currency most in demand by the conquering chieftains was wine. Wine was heavy, took time to transport, needed warehousing. Even before the Romans had subjugated Gaul, therefore, there was a wine-trade network, beginning with the Rhône Valley as the route from the Provincia Narbonensis northwards. When Caesar reached Chalon-sur-Saône, he found two Roman wine merchants already in business there.

Caesar's Gallic War was over in only seven years. It began with a call for help from the Aedui, involved marches all over France at amazing speed, sieges and even sea battles, included expeditions to Britain and Germany, and ended with the 60 tribes subdued, organized and paying tribute to Rome. One historian has described the whole episode as a gigantic slave raid. On the other hand, many of the Gauls were fatally tempted by the allurements of Mediterranean civilization – of which one of the greatest, to them, was wine. Caesar took note that a couple of northern tribes refused to be lured. Wine, they said, was a Roman trap. It dulled their fighting power. They might have noticed that it didn't dull the Romans'.

TRAP OR NOT, innumerable Gauls voluntarily joined the Roman army; the aristocracy sent their children to Rome; and the Romans were realistically generous in offering the privileges of citizenship, on certain conditions, to the conquered tribes. A Roman colony was a settlement by army veterans, but scarcely less dignity was accorded a town with "Latin rights"; the native aristocracy were made Roman magistrates with full Roman citizenship which their children inherited.

Under Augustus, Gaul entered an era of peaceful prosperity and varied industry it could never have imagined under the old tribal system. His great general Agrippa founded and fortified towns (often on the sites of old Gallic settlements) and drove the straight no-nonsense Roman roads through forests, over mountains and across rivers. The heart of Agrippa's road network was Lyons, where the waters of the Rhône, draining the Alps, merge with the broad slow-moving Saône that Caesar had described as "a great river of incredible tranquillity". Lyons was Roman Gaul's second capital, succeeding Narbonne in the south. It rapidly became the second-greatest wine port in the world, after Rome itself.

UP TO THIS TIME, the beginning of our era, there is no clear evidence of any vineyards in France north of the Mediterranean zone, defined by the Alpes-Maritimes in the east and the Cévennes in the west. The wine trade, though, was enormous – pouring up the narrow corridor of the Rhône Valley to reach central and northern France and Germany, and trundling by caravan, rather more laboriously, northwest up the valley of the Aude, which is not navigable much above Narbonne, through the lowland gap past what is now Toulouse, or over the shoulder of the Cévennes and down the rivers Tarn or Garonne to the west coast at Burdigala – Bordeaux.

Bordeaux, with its almost-perfect situation on the estuary of the Gironde, had customers in Ireland, Britain (a *negotiator Britannicus* was identified on the waterfront in the 1st century BC), around the north coast of France to Holland and even as far as the Baltic. Gallic seamen were not timid. We know from the Greek geographer Strabo, who made the first mention of "Burdigala" in the reign of Augustus, that it had no vines of its own. An "emporium" he called it; a store.

There were two rival routes north into Germany – where the garrison legions were an important market. One went down the river Moselle and one down the Rhine. Everything possible was done to avoid the cost of overland freight. The Romans even planned to dig a canal to link the Saône to the Moselle.

Underwater archaeology has told us more about the nature, the scale and the destination of the ancient wine trade than any other source. This wreck from the 1st century BC was found just off the south coast of France at Giens. Its cargo was wine in amphoras, probably from Pompeii and for sale in Gaul, where it would fetch enormous prices. Gaul's own vineyards at this time were insignificant.

Who were the customers in these unexpected northern markets? In Ireland the king's court was famous for its feasting. Britain had an active maritime trade, concentrated in Cornwall where the tin mines supported an unusually wealthy society. And of course there were thirsty Gauls at all stages in between.

The much-respected French historian Roger Dion has postulated a credible scenario for the advance of wine-growing north into central and western France from its suntrap in the Midi. It starts with the observant eyes of the Romans (or perhaps the earlier Greeks) scanning the hillside woods and scrubland for plants they knew. The vine, they knew, grew with the olive. In the Mediterranean zone, the oak is an evergreen plant; juniper, box, myrtle, thyme and countless herbs form the earth's prickly carpet. These are the conditions that made their vines welcome in the Midi and Provence; they were virtually in Italy still. The evergreen oaks gave them heart. They rode northward and found the evergreen aromatic flora extending almost to the top of the Cévennes, fronting the Mediterranean.

THEN THEY WERE OVER A CREST, and in a greener, more humid country, without olives, where the oaks shed their leaves, and there was more grass than herbs. Not vine country, surely. They had reached the northern limit of the zone they knew. Going up the Rhône, they had reached the steep scarps of hill we call Hermitage and the flood-scoured bluffs of the Côte Rôtie above Vienne. Their sharp incline towards the south gives these singular slopes a more Mediterranean vegetation than their surroundings.

Going over the shoulder of the Cévennes towards Bordeaux they had reached Gaillac in the country of the Ruteni, a tribe whose silver mines gave them wealth and the habit of trade. Dion believed Gaillac is where they thought vine country stopped. If they could make wine here, why cart it all the way up from the coast? Save the carriage and supply Bordeaux from the watershed above it, using the river Garonne. If this is what happened, Gaillac, in what became known as the High Country, was supplying Bordeaux with wine before it had a vineyard of its own. (Later generations in Bordeaux never entirely lost their jealousy of High Country wine, and did their best to suppress it.) To this day, Gaillac has vine varieties peculiar to itself: the Fer-Servadou, Ondenc, L'en de l'Elh, Duras (perhaps what Cato called the Duracina). Their wine is of no very special quality by today's standards. But why should this remote spot have ancient indigenous grapes unless it is a survivor from before the time that the great mainstream vineyards of Aquitaine began?

Bordeaux's first vineyards of its own must have been planted very soon after Strabo's visit – indeed, in the very generation when (in AD43) the Romans under Claudius conquered Britain. In 71, Pliny recorded not only the fact of vineyards in Bordeaux, but also what he knew about their grapes – which was not very much. He was confused by the fact that the same tribe, the Bituriges, had two settlements, one at Bordeaux and one at Bourges in central France (which certainly had no vines). And everybody has been confused since, because the Bituriges gave their own name (of Biturica) to the vines they planted, which were already well-known elsewhere under the name of Balisca.

The Balisca vine, we are told by Columella, was an excellent hardy and productive plant originally from Dyrrachium, a town on the Adriatic, since called

Durrazzo and now Durres. Today it is in the aloof little country of Albania; then it was part of Epirus, the northern Greek province with the highest reputation for its wine. I have not been able to trace the Balisca back to its homeland, but it is thought-provoking that this might be where the ancestral Cabernet vine came from, whose progeny includes the Cabernets Sauvignon and Franc, the Merlot and the Petit Verdot – all the red-grape varieties of Bordeaux. It is a long-held article of faith in Bordeaux (Adrien Valois believed it in 1675) that the very name Biturica has survived, corrupted to Vidure, a name still used locally for the Cabernet Sauvignon.

Certainly the Balisca was widely grown in Rome's Spanish provinces (where it was known as Cocolubis: even then the infuriating intricacies of synonymy were making life complicated). Roger Dion has an intriguing theory that the Roman Spanish vineyard that supplied vines to Bordeaux was none other than Rioja; principally on the grounds that this is where the Romans, following the river Ebro inland from the Mediterranean, planted vines nearest to the north coast of Spain – whence it is a very short sail to Bordeaux. In the 19th century we will see how Bordeaux repaid this ancient debt.

There is no question of there having been wild vines growing at Bordeaux already, waiting for the Bituriges or the Romans to domesticate them. In fact, Bordeaux is an unpromising site for any sort of agriculture except pasture. The site of the town was chosen for a port because a respectable bank of gravel fronts the river here on the outside of a wide crescent curve, with marshes or low alluvial land, subject to flooding, almost all around. It lies shortly above the confluence of the Garonne and the Dordogne, where the Garonne is still not too wide; but these are the thoughts of a trader looking for a safe and convenient haven, not a farmer.

It is rare, in fact, to find any ancient settlement in a place so unsuitable for growing its own food. Bordeaux's gravel is mean and hungry. It can only have been with a good deal of industry and recourse to manure that its first vines were persuaded to grow. The commercial argument was the overriding one. There was a well-established market for wine, and ships coming from the north to fetch it. If Bordeaux could supply the wine itself, without the expense and risk of bringing it down-river from Gaillac and beyond, all the profits would stay in Bordeaux. From its inception, Bordeaux was destined to be linked to the British Isles.

IT WAS A RATHER DIFFERENT STORY over on the other trade route, the Rhône Valley. The first great "emporium", going north, was a town of the powerful and (to the Romans) friendly tribe, the Allobroges, whose considerable territory extended from the east bank of the Rhône all the way east to the Alps at the lake of Geneva. The territory of Vienne includes the great granite outcrop called Hermitage, the broad Rhône swinging around its foot in a long left-hand bend that gives the hill the full benefit of the sunshine reflected off its waters. To plant vines here was not the calculated risk it was at Bordeaux; this was a bit of Mediterranean coast, ever-green oaks and all, conveniently shifted 150 miles inland. The same goes for the hills across the river from Vienne above Ampuis and Condrieu, on the west bank. The intelligence of the Allobroges is evident from the fact that their territorial boundary crossed the Rhône to include these sun-baked slopes – the Côte Rôtie.

The import of Italian wine into Gaul up the river Rhône was a strenuous business, with no alternative but to pull the barges up against the current, using gangs of slaves on a towpath. From the 3rd century AD the barrel had superseded the amphora in Gaul.

There was apparently no need to bring up vines from the Mediterranean to grow here. All the indications are that the vine they chose was already growing in their woods. The grapevine, always a variable plant, is most variable near the limits of its natural habitat. Perhaps a mutation produced a clearly superior vine that they baptized as Allobrogica. (Perhaps, on the other hand, they used the vine that Virgil had praised as producing Rhaetic wine in the Italian Alps.)

In any case its wine, sold at Vienne, had within 90 years of Virgil's death (as Pliny points out) become a challenger to the first-growths of Rome. It was particularly appreciated for its sharp flavour of pitch, or burnt resin, which seems a rather unreverential addition to a particularly fine wine. Some scholars are happy to think that the Allobrogica has become the Petite Syrah of the modern Rhône. Another suggestion is the Mondeuse of the Savoie Alps (a much underrated grape for forthright, fruity red). One of the synonyms of the Mondeuse is Grosse Syrah; another, which might link it with Rhaetic, is Refosco, a grape of northeastern Italy. There are also scholars who see in the Allobrogica the ancestor of the Pinot family, and hence of the red wine of Burgundy and Champagne.

The centre of gravity of Roman Gaul was Lyons, another 30 miles, or three days' hauling, for the gangs of slaves who pulled the barges upstream from Vienne. Lyons was the distribution centre for various routes northwards, and Gaul's greatest emporium. Northwards from Lyons, the wine was sent up the much easier Saône to Chalon, where its road journey began, either west towards the Loire or northwards by weary ways to the nearest point on the Seine, Meuse or Moselle. The troops manning the German frontier were fond of sweet southern wine; none of the austerum of the Alps for them. Amphoras of Andalusian sunshine were hauled by the hundred thousand to cheer their watches on the rainswept chain of forts they called the Limes, listening and waiting for the unpredictable Teuton raids.

After Chalon-sur-Saône, Agrippa's road runs northwest along the Saône for a few miles to Verdun at the confluence of the Doubs, then turns due north for Dijon. Most of this stretch can still be seen, sometimes as a minor road as straight as a spear, sometimes as a farm track, or just as a field boundary. Approaching Dijon, it converges with the line of hills to the west. Today you can clearly see their middle and lower slopes are covered with vines. Is this what the Romans saw? Nobody knows exactly when Burgundy's Côte d'Or was first planted, but there is less mystery about why.

ROME'S FIRST ALLIES AMONG THE GAULS were the Aedui, whose stronghold of Bibracte lies in the Morvan hills not very far to the west, behind the range of the Côte d'Or. Under Augustus, they abandoned Bibracte on its hilltop to found, with Imperial blessing and Roman help, the new city of Augustodunum, or Fort Augustus. Augustodunum has long since been shortened to Autun. In Roman days it was one of the principal cities of Gaul, but too high and cold to grow vines. On the other hand, its civitas (county would be the approximate modern equivalent) included and ended with the Côte d'Or; a magnificent opportunity for the Aedui to plant vineyards and make wine in, as it were, a shop window on the principal north-south artery. A river would have been better, they had to admit. The Côte d'Or, indeed, is the only great vineyard of ancient foundation without the benefit of a river at the door.

The first clear account we have of the Pagus Arebrignus, which the vine-growing Côte was then called, is in a plaintive address to the Emperor Constantine delivered when he visited Augustodunum in 312. The palmy days of the Empire were already past. The later years of the last century had seen catastrophic incursions deep into Gaul by barbarians from beyond the Rhine. Augustodunum was pillaged in 269 and 276 by Germans and Alamans. It was the fortuitous arrival of another tribe with gentler manners, the Burgundians from the Baltic, that helped restore the former Aeduan capital to its dignity and prepared it to meet its emperor. It also gave Burgundy its name.

The vineyards of the Côte, the orator told Constantine, although envied by all, are in a sorry state. They are not like those of Bordeaux which have limitless space to expand. They are squeezed in between the rocky hilltop and the marshy plain where frosts ruin the crop. In this narrow strip (which anyone who knows the Côte will recognize), the vines are so old, he said, that they are exhausted, and the soil cannot be worked because of the tangle of ancient vine roots. Also the main roads, even the great military road, were so potholed that half a load was enough to break a wagon. The bottom line, unsurprisingly, was that the loyal citizens were having difficulty with their taxes.

How old is old? How long had it taken the vineyard to reach the state described (allowing for hyperbole) by the worthy orator? It sounds as though the vines were cultivated on the system of provignage – not one recommended in the Roman textbooks – which consists of laying the trunk along the ground to form new roots by layering. Each year the new shoots and their fruit are supported above the ground by a temporary light stake. Provignage would account for a surface tangled with old roots – but in how long who can say?

Suppose the trouble started with the barbarian invasions, and the vineyard was well established before that, it seems reasonable to date the planting of the Côte d'Or in the first half of the 3rd century. The great city of Lyons went into decline at this time, although whether this was cause, effect or coincidence we don't know. Those who argue an earlier date point out that the town of Beaune was flourishing a century before that; even remains of pruning knives and effigies of Bacchus have been found. Amphoras stopped being delivered to Augustodunum in the 2nd century, which argues the use of barrels. It seems probable that they were barrels of the local wine.

WE ARE FRUSTRATED when we try to find precise starting dates for France's other vineyards, too. Their sites follow a clear logic: the nearness of an important town, almost always a river, and in every case, especially as we move north, a good steep hill. The Romans knew how cold air runs like water down slopes to form, like water, pools at the bottom. The pools are frost pockets, fatal to a good crop.

Certain prominent hilly outcrops in otherwise relatively flat country are known to have been among the first vineyards of the Gallo-Romans. The chalk hill of Sancerre, almost as much a landmark on the Loire as Hermitage on the Rhône, is a good example. Another is St-Pourçain-sur-Sioule, at the confluence of the rivers Allier and Sioule near the Roman road from Lyons to Bourges and the Loire. Auxerre, on the way north to Paris, is a probable Gallo-Roman vineyard, and Paris itself a certainty. The Emperor Julian, known as the Apostate, who rejected the Christianity of his predecessor Constantine and tried to return the Empire to the old true gods, stayed for two years at Lutetia, the little proto-Paris on the Ile-de-la-Cité, and enjoyed the wine grown on, presumably, the hill of Montmartre.

The mountain of Reims is another obvious candidate. Reims, the capital of Champagne, is hollow with chalk quarries cut by the Romans for building stone. The south slope of its "mountain", overlooking the river Marne, has all the qualifications. Although there seems to be no positive evidence of Gallo-Roman vineyards where champagne grows today, it would be surprising if they missed such an opportunity – and there was a villa at Sparnacus, Roman Epernay, which in the 5th century was occupied by the patron saint of Reims, St Rémi.

Most of these Gallic vineyards, with the probable exceptions of Bordeaux and the Rhône, were planted when the edict of Domitian, banning planting in the provinces, was still theoretically in force. We do not know whether they had special permission from Rome or (as seems more likely) local needs and desires overcame any scruples (and means of enforcement). There was, in any case, a convenient dodge available: any land owned by a Roman citizen could be described as "Roman" – and hence eligible for planting. Nonetheless, when the beleaguered Emperor Probus repealed the edict in 280 ("Citizens", he said, "plant vines and grow rich"), it gave a powerful new impetus to wine-growing. It seems likely that many of the vineyards of the Loire were planted in the 4th century. The Loire completed the process that had started with the Biturica in Bordeaux and the Allobrogica in the Rhône Valley – western and eastern grape varieties invaded the valley from their respective ends. Today along the Loire, the Cabernet lies down with the Pinot, and the Gamay of Burgundy with Bordeaux's Sauvignon Blanc.

THE TURBULENT TIMES OF THE LATER EMPIRE concentrated more power in the north than ever before. Successive emperors had added to the fence-and-ditch frontier line against the Germans, pushing it beyond the Rhine, so that at its greatest extent this great curtain between "civilization" and the barbarians ran for 342 miles and was manned by 25,000 soldiers, or one for every 24 paces of its length. Its name of the "Limes" was derived from a word for a track across country, but with its earthworks, watchtowers, fortresses and, for more than 100 miles, a ten-foot stone wall, it was perhaps Rome's greatest piece of military engineering. One stretch runs for 18 miles in a straight line without deviating by more than a single pace.

The barbarians saw their chance when the Empire was attacked on its distant eastern flank by the Persians. In 260, this bulwark was decisively breached by the Germans and Franks (who went on to sack such towns as Autun). Far from spelling the end for Roman power in the north, barbarian pressure intensified Imperial commitment. Cologne, and then Trier, was made an Imperial capital. Further Frankish raids followed, but in his short reign Probus put new heart into the Empire.

His successor, Diocletian, began a new chapter of firm administrative control, in which Trier, his Augusta Treverorum, was promoted to the capital of the Western Empire, and to hold sway over a region stretching from northern Britain to North Africa. The future Emperor Constantine was brought up at Trier. This was the period, in the 4th century, that gave the city palaces and baths on a scale that is still deeply impressive. Julian's generalship again routed the Germans at Strasbourg in 357 – this was during his residence in Paris. His successors, Valentinian and Gratian, reigned as emperors at Trier, Gratian being educated by the poet Ausonius from Bordeaux. Trier's hour of glory lasted until the end of the 4th century, when its powers passed to Arles in Provence. The insatiable Germans and Franks sacked it four times in the following 50 years.

The great black gate of Trier, still wonderfully preserved, was the end of the long Roman road north for thousands of Roman legionaries. Trier was Rome's northern capital, the seat of emperors and the centre of Roman wine-growing on the steep banks of the Moselle.

Roman officers at these distant outposts must have been at least as eager for a supply of wine as their friends at home. At the end of such a long journey, though, the price would have been high and the quality far from certain. The historian Tacitus tells us that the people of the country drank an inferior sort of beer. The prospects for vineyards in the darkness of the north must have seemed remote – unless, as seems perfectly possible, there were wild vines here, too. There are those who believe that the Riesling is a selection from a native German vine.

Probably Germany's first vineyards were planted in the same spirit as those of Bordeaux. Trier was a flourishing emporium for Imperial wine: what if vines could be made to grow on the steep forest slopes around? The three elements were present: city, river and hills. Only here the choice of hill made all the difference. A steep south-facing slope not only caught all the meagre warmth the sun provided; it sheltered vines from the north winds, rapidly drained off the excessive rainfall, and by tilting the surface at the sun's rays received them perpendicularly rather than low-angled and diffuse.

Trier was surrounded by suntrap vineyards hanging from improbable slopes, perhaps from as early as the 2nd century. Our evidence, when it comes, is of a long-established and flourishing vineyard scene in the second half of the 4th century; the scene described in a much-quoted poem by the Imperial tutor Ausonius.

The Moselle reminds Ausonius of his native Bordeaux, where grapevines are reflected in the river Garonne. He speaks of rich villas with smoking chimneys, of boatmen calling out insults to the workers among the vines, of the delicate fish playing in the river, and in a famous passage, of the hillsides mirrored in it:

> What colour paints the river shallows, when Hesperus
> Has brought the shades of evening.
> Moselle is dyed with the green of her hills; their tops quiver
> In the ripples, vine leaves tremble from afar
> And the grape clusters swell, even in the crystal stream.

Ausonius was one of the last Roman citizens to see the Moselle as a vision of peaceful fecundity. When he died in 391, the defences of the Empire needed only a determined push to bring them down. His grandson, on his own estate near Bordeaux, was reduced to a landless labourer by the invaders.

THERE REMAINS THE QUESTION OF ROMAN BRITAIN. The logical probability is that the Romans would certainly have planted vines, even in this misty outpost of their Empire. Enough grape pips have been found, in London, in Gloucestershire and Wiltshire, to suggest that wine was made. But proof is lacking, and we are left only with the certainty that Britain was a voracious market for imported wine. The cult of Bacchus had an eager British following: evidence has been found in 400 places, ranging from whole mosaic floors to marble statues to the sumptuous silver dish found at Mildenhall in Suffolk, which represents Bacchus supervising the journey of the spirit to paradise.

Excavations near Colchester, Britain's Roman capital, have identified at least 60 apparently different sorts of wine – or rather their containers. In the earlier years of Roman Britain they came principally from Italy and Spain, and included both

The cult of Bacchus was not limited to the Mediterranean parts of Rome's empire. This bronze bust of the wine god, apparently emerging from a bud, was found at Littlecote in Berkshire in 1985. There is evidence that Roman Britons were enthusiastic devotees of the Bacchic rites.

Falernian and Baetican. Later, the principal source of amphoras is the Rhine, with less evidence of wines from Bordeaux than the known history of Bordeaux would lead us to expect. But barrels rarely leave traces, and all the indications are that from the start the barrel was the standard container of Bordeaux.

TRIER IS A GOOD PLACE TO STUDY THE EFFECTS of the barbarian invasions. It bore the full brunt. Roman writings are bound to give us the view that the best you could hope for from a barbarian was a speedy death on a sharp sword. True, there were pillaging tribes whose attentions were always messy and usually terminal. But the Germans and the Franks and the Alamans were not only old foes of Trier, they were old neighbours, and undoubtedly customers for Trier's wine. Of all the misguided and forlorn attempts to stave off barbarian invasion, the most ill-conceived was an edict forbidding the sale of wine and oil across the frontiers. It was as good as an invitation to break down the door.

WATERY WAYS

The Rhine route was marginally more watery and less on rutted roads than the Moselle route; a good deal of wine even reached Britain this way. There was also a route from the Saône to the Seine and down to the English Channel, and another across to the Loire and west to the Atlantic. Calculations have shown that from the Mediterranean to England, the relative costs were in the following order, from cheapest to most expensive: by sea round Spain; by land to Bordeaux, then sea; via the Loire; via the Seine; via the Rhine; via the Moselle – and the last costing three times as much as the first. If this makes the German routes look absurdly costly, perhaps the explanation is that Britain bought the surplus from the German garrisons, or even conceivably that the amphoras were emptied of their original southern contents in Germany and sent on to Britain filled with lower-grade local German wine.

Having despatched Roman authority from the city, they are unlikely to have destroyed houses that would shelter them better than their own. Trier is, in fact, magnificently preserved; not only its immensely solid stone Porta Nigra, but the soaring brick walls of its baths and what is known as the Palace of Constantine have clearly not been put to the sack with any real conviction.

The same is true of the vineyards. The wisest move was to encourage the winegrowers, not to butcher them. There is no certainty about what happened as we enter the "Dark Ages", but patchy records show that life, at least in favoured places, went on as before, but without the Roman soldiers. Fortunatus, an occasional poet and Bishop of Poitiers in the 6th century, wrote of his delight in finding the Moselle just as Ausonius had described it two centuries before – at least as to its vineyards; he is not specific about the boatmen or fish. But every saint did not have the same experience. St Prosper, a hundred years before Fortunatus, wrote: "If the whole ocean had swept over Gaul, its receding waters could not have left it more devastated; the cattle have disappeared and the seeds of the fruits of the earth. No traces are left of the vines and olive trees . . . ."

GIBBON DESCRIBED ROME'S DECLINE AND FALL as "the triumph of barbarism and religion". The Age of Emperors was succeeded by the Age of Saints. Constantine had made the empire Christian, and established the Imperial capital at Constantinople. Rome had little power left. Franks, Vandals, Goths and Visigoths moved into an almost unresisting Europe – the Vandals eventually to command the western Mediterranean from North Africa, the Visigoths eventually to conquer Spain. The last legions of Rome made common cause with Franks and Visigoths against the fearsome menace of Attila and his reputed half a million Huns, checking him in a

---

ON THE GOVERNMENT OF GOD

The fate of Trier in the 5th century was vividly painted by the moralist Salvianus in his book *On the Government of God*. Even allowing for his view that the barbarian attacks on the Empire were God's retribution for its decadence, it seems that standards had slipped badly. . . .

". . . though they had already been ruined by the Barbarians, they now completed their own destruction. It is sad to tell what we saw there; honoured old men . . . making themselves slaves to appetite and lust . . . they reclined at feasts, forgetful of their honour, forgetting justice, forgetting their faith and the name they bore. They were the leaders of the state, gorged with food, dissolute from winebibbing, wild with shouting, giddy with revelry . . . . The wealthiest city of Gaul was taken by storm no less than four times . . . the very rulers of the city did not rise from their feasts when the enemy were actually entering the gates . . . all vices reigned at once – extravagance, drinking bouts, wantonness – all

the people revelled together. They drank, gamed, committed adultery. Old and honoured men waxed wanton at their feasts; men already almost too feeble to live proved mighty in their cups; men too weak to walk were strong in drinking . . . . Those whom the enemy had not killed when they pillaged the city were overwhelmed by disaster after the sack . . . . Some died lingering deaths from deep wounds, others were burned by the enemy's fires and suffered tortures even after the flames were extinguished . . . . There lay all about the torn and naked bodies of both sexes, a sight I myself endured. These were a pollution to the eyes of the city, as they lay there lacerated by birds and dogs. The stench of the dead brought pestilence on the living: death breathed out death . . . . What followed these calamities? The few men of rank who had survived destruction demanded of the emperors circuses as the sovereign remedy for a ruined city."

horrific shambles near Châlons (in Champagne) in 451. But now it was the Franks who controlled – and gave their name to – northern France. All that was left of the administration of the Empire was its church.

In a real sense the Church was a creation of ancient Rome, was organized in the Roman fashion, but had no army to rout, or troops to be pulled back to headquarters for a last-ditch stand. Its early bishops were members of the Romanized upper or learned classes of the provinces of the Empire. When Rome's temporal power was gone, those that survived continued as far as possible the Roman pattern of life in the vestments of priests or bishops.

Monks were something different. They opposed personal spirituality to the worldly wisdom of the Church. The monastic idea is said to have come to the hermit St Anthony in the Sinai desert in Egypt in about AD300. In the same generation his superior in Alexandria, St Athanasius – who is credited with the Creed – brought monasticism to Trier. Trier probably had the first monastery in Europe – established almost as soon as the Empire became Christian, almost as soon as the first monastery anywhere, and long before the sad scenes that Salvianus recounted with such masochistic relish.

But initially stronger than the scattered monastic brethren, whose ascendancy still lay in the future, was the well-tried hierarchical priestly system, organized in dioceses that were none other than Rome's old secular constituencies. Saintly bishops are credited with many miracles, but perhaps their greatest was the maintenance of organized agriculture (of which wine-growing was an important part) through the three centuries when it must have seemed that hell's legions were massing in the east, to bring yet another wave of sackings and pillage.

The great triumph of the Church in France took place in Reims in 496. The pagan Frankish king, Clovis, was baptized by a bishop whose name, Rémi, suggests that the tribe the Romans had found in Champagne five centuries earlier had been submerged rather than extinguished. We have already met St Rémi living in a Roman villa at Epernay and perhaps growing vines.

Many of the early bishops are associated in legend with wine-growing, starting with St Martin, a soft-hearted legionary from Hungary (the story goes that he divided his uniform cloak with a shivering beggar), who in 371 became Bishop of Tours. St Martin is credited with starting wine-growing in Touraine; also with the discovery of pruning, by watching a donkey – which is some measure of the dimness of the records of the fading Roman Empire. A later bishop of Tours, St Gregory, was also a great patron of the vine. St Germain, whose abbey lands in Paris occupied the left bank of the Seine, was born, wrote his chronicler, on a great wine estate in Burgundy. Another St Gregory, Bishop of Langres in eastern France, was not content with the wine supply of his episcopal lands and moved his seat to Dijon. St Ermelund planted a great vineyard near the mouth of the Loire, St Didier another at Cahors. Bishop Nicetius of Trier was patron of the winegrowers of the Moselle, and St Goar of the vineyards of the lower Rhine.

The bishops were soon rivalled by the growing power of the monasteries. They dominate the Middle Ages and we shall discuss them in their appropriate chapter. But all the struggles of the Franks are dwarfed in historical perspective by their great successor and first Holy Roman Emperor, Charlemagne.

CHAPTER 9

THE HOPE OF SOME DIVINER DRINK

The man who was to have the most profound effect of any individual on the history of wine was born as the Roman Empire finally disintegrated, far from any vineyards, in what is now Saudi Arabia.

Mohammed was born into one of the Middle Eastern cultures that from earliest times had been grateful for the gift of wine. If Arabian vintages can never have been other than unsubtle, wine, locally grown or imported from more fertile regions (Syria, Iraq or the Yemen), was part of the daily life of 6th-century Mecca.

Within ten years of his death in AD632, it was totally banned not only from Arabia but from every country which listened to his words, or which the armies of his followers had conquered. So vigorous was the thrust of Islam that its empire already included Egypt, Libya, Palestine, Syria, Mesopotamia and Armenia, besides the whole of Arabia. Within a century of his death, western North Africa, Spain and Portugal, Sicily, Corsica, Sardinia and Crete, and western Asia as far as Samarkand and the river Indus were ruled by his successors, the caliphs, first of Damascus, then of Baghdad.

Militarily it is possible to account for this startling conquest by referring to the vacuum left by the exhausted empires of Rome and Persia. Spiritually there is no question that Mohammed's one God, the God of Abraham, but stripped of his Jewish dogma and uncomplicated by Christian belief in incarnation, had and still has the vital appeal of an uncluttered faith. Islam is absolute submission and resignation to the will of Allah. Allah is compassionate; he is merciful, and his word, dictated by the angel Gabriel to his Prophet, promises Paradise after death in very specific and seductive terms.

Paradise is seen as a garden, watered by fountains and clear streams. In it the Righteous "may feed on such fruits as they desire". "Reclining upon soft couches they will gaze around them: and in their faces you shall mark the glow of joy. They shall drink of a pure wine, securely sealed, whose very dregs are musk; . . . a wine tempered with the water of Tasnim, a spring at which the favoured will refresh themselves. . . . And theirs shall be the dark-eyed houris, chaste as hidden pearls: a guerdon for their deeds."

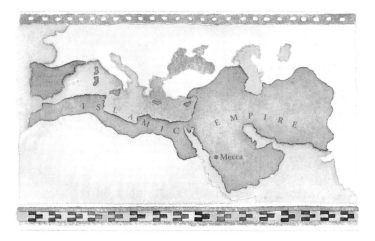

Two centuries after the Prophet's death, the Islamic Empire stretched from Afghanistan in the East to the Iberian peninsula in the West.

THE KORAN IS A BOOK OF GREAT POETRY AND WISDOM, but full of startling extremes. It is equally concerned with such scriptural matters as the story of Abraham, of Moses, of David and Solomon, and of the true nature of Jesus, with desert hygiene, with the touchy business of keeping a number of wives happy (Mohammed had nine), with general moral questions and others that are closer to etiquette. It enjoins charity, honest dealing, justice and care for the unfortunate – and also the cutting off of hands for theft. It ranges in tone from the avuncular to the apocalyptic.

Mohammed did not write. When Gabriel spoke to him he repeated what he had been told to his disciples, who committed it to memory. Later his revelations were written down, although not in any particular order. When an authorized version was compiled, some 15 years after his death, it was a jumble without sequence, and with many disputed meanings. It was accompanied, however, by a body of commentary that makes it possible to unravel which parts were revealed while the Prophet lived at Mecca, his birthplace, and which belong to the period of the hegira, the eight years when he and his disciples were in exile in the city of Medina, 300 miles to the northeast across the desert. This is how we know that the prohibition of wine in the Koran was the result of a change of heart – perhaps even a measure of desperation.

In one of the early verses, wine is part of a catalogue of the good things of the earth, with water, milk and honey. "We give you the fruits of the palm and the vine, from which you derive intoxicants and wholesome food." Its next mention is cautionary. "They will ask you concerning wine and gambling. Answer, in both there is great sin and also some things of use unto men: but their sinfulness is greater than their use." This revelation, we are told, was not considered as a prohibition. It is interesting to note that wine and gambling are linked – both in sin and in "usefulness". The usefulness of gambling is a matter the Koran does not explain. There followed a very reasonable admonition, similar to one in Jewish law: "Believers, do not approach your prayers when you are drunk, but wait till you can grasp the meaning of your words; nor when you are polluted – unless you are travelling the road – until you have washed yourselves."

The single verse on which the prohibition of wine is based was dictated, we are told, as a result of an incident in Medina when his disciples were drinking together after dinner. One of his Meccan followers began to recite an uncomplimentary poem about the tribe of Medina, whereupon one of his Medinite followers picked up the meat bone from the table and hit the ribald Meccan on the head. It was only a flesh wound, but Mohammed was distressed and asked the Almighty how to keep his disciples in order. The reply came, "Believers, wine and games of chance, idols and divining arrows, are abominations devised by Satan. Avoid them, so that you may prosper. Satan seeks to stir up enmity and hatred among you by means of wine and gambling, and to keep you from the remembrance of Allah and from your prayers. Will you not abstain from them?"

The believers' answer, according to Islamic scholars, was such a resounding yes that all the wine in Medina was immediately poured into the streets. Thus one of the principal characteristics of the Muslim way of life arose because of a quarrel (which may or may not have been drunken). It will immediately strike any observer of the Muslim world that Satan is not so easily foiled. The evil one does not need the help of wine and games of chance, nor of idols and divining arrows.

During his lifetime, Mohammed administered 40 lashes to those who violated his injunction against wine. (There was no prescribed penalty for gambling.) His successor, the Caliph Umar, made it 80, on the grounds that drunkenness "leads to obscene loquacity in which one calumniates the chastity of women". The Koran stipulates 80 lashes as the "hadd", the penalty, for the latter; therefore wine should have the same sanction. The penalty, you may note, is not for speeding: it is for driving the car at all.

Are we to imagine that moderate healthy winedrinking was unknown in 7th-century Arabia? Indeed, it was known, and widely practised, even among Mohammed's own followers, who justified their action with another Koranic verse: "No blame shall be attached to those that have embraced the faith and done

In 1986, Russia celebrated the 1,000th anniversary of its foundation by the Viking Prince Vladimir at Kiev. Although Vladimir's manners left something to be desired, he was a good king, worthy of his great country. For its proper dignity and the sake of their souls, he thought, the Russes should have a religion. He therefore sent to the Jews, to the Christian churches at Rome and Constantinople, and to the Mohammedans to inform him of their faiths.

First he was visited by the Bulgars, who professed the Mohammedan faith, and who (according to the "Russian Primary Chronicle", written by an 11th-century monk) thus addressed him:

"'Though you are a wise and prudent prince, you have no religion. Adopt our faith and revere Mahomet.' Vladimir enquired what was the nature of their religion. They replied that they believed in God, and that Mahomet instructed them to practise circumcision, to eat no pork, to drink no wine, and, after death, promised them complete fulfilment of their carnal desires. 'Mahomet', they asserted, 'will give each man 70 fair women. He may choose one fair one, and upon that woman will Mahomet confer the charms of them all, and she shall be his wife. Mahomet promises that one may satisfy every desire, but whoever is poor in this world will be no different in the next.' They also spoke other false things, which out of modesty may not be written down.

"Vladimir listened to them, for he was fond of women and indulgence, regarding which he heard with pleasure. But circumcision and abstinence from pork and wine were disagreeable to him. 'Drinking', said he, 'is the joy of the Russes. We cannot exist without that pleasure.'"

The silver wine vase (above)
from the Persia of the
Sassanids, old foes of Rome,
was made during the lifetime
of Mohammed. In 636 Arab
armies conquered Persia and
its wine was all poured away –
a scene repeated in Iran in 1979
(left), when the hotel cellars of
Teheran were sacked and their
stocks destroyed.

good works in regard to any food they have eaten, so long as they fear Allah, believe in him and do good works." Umar had them flogged.

Even the Prophet's favourite wife, Ayesha, quibbled with the injunction. "She quoted him as saying 'you may drink, but do not get drunk'." Mohammed, it is said, drank nabidh, a sort of wine made from dates. There was plenty of room here for ingenious sophistry. Was it indeed only wine that was forbidden, or intoxication? Did date wine count? How was wine to be defined? Before long the poets and courtiers at the Caliph's court were debating every hint of a more liberal interpretation of the law with the fervour of schoolchildren looking for a way around school rules. It has been said that the theological spirit of Islam was drowned in quibbling casuistry – and not only, of course, on the question of wine.

CERTAINLY IN THE 8TH CENTURY A SCHOOL OF ARABIAN BACCHIC POETRY GREW UP, in which wine became the focus of a romantic, rebellious philosophy. Prohibition took on quite a different aspect as Islam conquered lands whose wines had long been their pride and joy. It was one thing to give up the headache mixture of Arabia, quite another to throw away a cellar of treasured vintages from Syria or the Lebanon. The poems of such as Abū Nuwās are considered to be some of the finest in Arabic. They treat of wine and love in complex and elegant allusions that have some of the feeling of English metaphysical lyrics of the 17th century.

Much the most famous of the great poets who rebelled against Islamic domination of their heritage and their lives were the Persians: Firdausi in the 10th century, Omar Khayyam in the 11th, Sa'di in the 13th and Hafiz in the 14th.

No poet has ever made wine so much the hub of his universe as Omar Khayyam. His *Rubaiyat*, a long series of individual quatrains, were brilliantly linked by Edward Fitzgerald to form a single poem that sums up Omar's philosophy – Persian in its epicurean audacity; Muslim in its fatalistic resignation.

> You know, my Friends, how long since in my House
> For a new Marriage I did make Carouse:
>   Divorced old barren Reason from my Bed,
> And took the Daughter of the Vine to Spouse.
>
> The Grape that can with Logic absolute
> The Two-and-Seventy jarring Sects confute:
>   The subtle Alchemist that in a Trice
> Life's leaden Metal into Gold transmute.

To Omar, the promise of wine deferred until the afterlife is a sham:

> I sent my soul through the Invisible
> Some letter of that After-life to spell:
>   And after many days my Soul return'd
> And said "Behold, Myself am Heav'n and Hell.
>
> I must abjure the Balm of life? I must
> Scared by some After-reckoning ta'en on trust,
>   Or lured with Hope of some Diviner Drink
> When the frail cup is crumbled into Dust!

Omar Khayyam could, perhaps, be dismissed as a poet of little account in the history of Islam, were it not for the fact that he was also one of the greatest mathematicians and astronomers of the Middle Ages, who led the thought of his time in algebra, physics and geography, as well as calculating the most accurate calendar yet devised, with a measurably smaller margin of error than the Gregorian calendar of 500 years later, which is the one we use today.

Not in the *Rubaiyat*, but in J.C.E. Bowen's *Poems from the Persian*, is this exquisite stanza in a minor key:

> The winds that wanton in the vale
> Have suddenly grown colder;
> The errant clouds which by us sail
> Weep on the green hill's shoulder;
> But we, whatever griefs or fears
> Make other men repine,
> Will drink, in spite of April's tears,
> The red, the sun-warmed wine.

ARAB PHYSICIANS WERE THROWN INTO A QUANDARY by the prohibition of their principal medicine. The great Avicenna, in charge of the hospital in Baghdad a generation before Omar Khayyam was born, brought together much of the medical knowledge of the ancient Greeks, with pertinent observations of his own on the effects of wine in different persons under different conditions. His Rule 860 concludes with a thought that may possibly have some bearing on the success of prohibition in desert lands: "Wine is borne better in a cold country than in a hot one." Nor did the great doctor neglect the benefits of wine to his own person:

"If a problem was too difficult for me, I returned to the Mosque and prayed, invoking the Creator of all things until the gate that had been closed to me was opened and what had been complex became simple. Always, as night fell, I returned to my house, set the lamp before me and busied myself with reading and writing. If sleep overcame me or I felt the flesh growing weak, I had recourse to a beaker of wine, so my energies were restored."

A good summary, because an impartial one, was that written by Maimonides, a Jew from Córdoba in Spain who became personal doctor to the Sultan Saladin in the 12th century. "It is well known among physicians," he wrote, "that the best of the nourishing foods is one that the Muslim religion forbids, i.e. wine . . . . It is rapidly digested and helps to digest other foods. . . . The benefits of wine are many if it is taken in the proper amount, as it keeps the body in a healthy condition and cures many illnesses. But the knowledge of its consumption is hidden from the masses. What they want is to get drunk, and inebriety causes harm."

This contradiction between what was known to be good and what the Koran outlawed continued in a state of variable equilibrium for at least 1,200 years. Islam is not normally a proselytizing or coercive creed. By tolerating Jews and Christians within its boundaries it enabled the growing and distribution of wine to continue – subject to sanctions which produced a useful revenue in taxes.

As ALWAYS, IT WAS THE RULING CLASS THAT TOOK MOST LIBERTIES, both in drinking and in selling wine (or in having the right to sell wine) to others. Even caliphs – the highest rank of ruler – showed an unseemly desire to anticipate Paradise by giving parties in gardens that closely resembled the Promised Land of the Koran: not running streams nor soft couches, nor houris, nor fruit nor wine were wanting. We read of wine parties given in sumptuously decorated rooms. The Caliph Mutawakkil (846-861) was fond of the colour yellow, and caused a yellow room to be built in his palace. The floor was marquetry of sandalwood, the walls hung with yellow satin, the table decorations were melons and oranges, the fountain water was dyed with saffron, and the guests drank only yellow wine.

Upper-class wine parties commonly started in the morning (working people, who had a living to earn, drank at night if at all). A meal was offered first; wine-drinking came later, after the guests had washed, perfumed themselves and put on fine garments. They then formed a circle, sitting on seats or lying on cushions (young people had to stand). The first cup was taken in the right hand and drunk in one swallow, then given back to the servant who filled it for the next guest. Different wines were drunk in a prescribed order, while connoisseurs among the guests inhaled deep and discussed their bouquets.

THE HOPE OF SOME DIVINER DRINK

Some accounts of the wine parties of Baghdad bring to mind a Greek symposium: long discussions over many cups, often with musicians, the proceedings measured and ceremonial to slow down the effects of the wine. The participants gradually nodded off, for the party lasted at least one night, often two or three days, and occasionally, in literary circles, for as long as a month. Other records, though, tell of parties where stupefaction was the only object: opium was mixed with the wine, which was gobbled down without ceremony.

Only occasionally were specific wines mentioned, although we know that the Arabs recognized four colours: red, white, yellow and black. The Persians were fond of yellow wine; the Byzantines red. No great age is ever mentioned. New wine was cloudy, with little bouquet; one-year-old wine clear and ideal; older wine usually, we may imagine, spoiled, and considered less of a sin than sweet young wine. In principle, the sweeter the wine the more it was liked; it was common to add honey or spices, even drugs – and also water. The greatest luxury was snow from the mountains or ice from deep ice-houses. Specialist snow merchants could charge a fortune in summer. Sir John Chardin, travelling in Persia in the 17th century, records how the centrepiece of the Shah's magnificent touring tent was a golden basin full of snow and crystal ewers of ruby wine. There is a record of one Persian judge who went so far as to make a witness taste a cup of wine as evidence of his fitness to testify. Was the bouquet good or bad? Bad, the witness answered, to which the judge replied that he was either lying or else he had no sense of judgment; either way he was unfit to testify. The wine was fine.

FROM TIME TO TIME PUBLIC ATTITUDES CERTAINLY HARDENED. Tenth-century caliphs carried out a succession of measures to prevent winemaking, including throwing 5,000 jars of honey into the Nile, pulling up vineyards and burning raisins, and

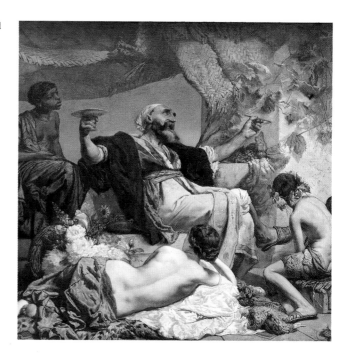

The poet Hafiz enraptured and scandalized 14th-century Persia with his sensuous and Bacchic verses. He was born and died at Shiraz, the most famous wine centre of the Muslim East.

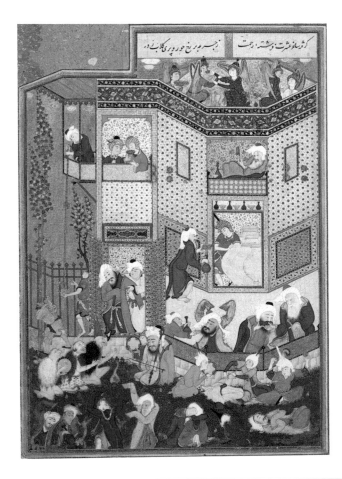

A Persian drinking party was portrayed almost in the manner of Hogarth by the famous painter Sultan Muhammed in 1527. Guests in the garden are capering about or passing out while an orchestra plays. Wine jars appear in the lower right-hand door and a jug is being hoisted aloft to more decorous drinkers on the balcony on the left. The roof is reserved for a private party: the angels themselves.

SHIRAZ

The Persian Gates is a romantic name given to the region of Fars where the Zagros mountains come closest to the Persian Gulf. The ancient trading city of Persepolis had passed away, but Shiraz had grown up to take its place; a name now given to one of the noblest of grapes. Shiraz, lying 5,000 feet above sea level, yet only 100 miles from the sea, had the essential combination of factors necessary to a successful vineyard: reasonable growing conditions and relatively good access to a market. It was, simply, the most convenient place in a difficult region.

Already in AD800, the Bacchic poet Abū Nuwās had written: "To the Persians, Paradise is called Khoullar" – a village in the mountains beside Shiraz. The region supplied Baghdad with wine under the caliphs. Then its export trade had dwindled, and little is heard until the 17th century when European merchants began calling and developed a thriving business shipping Shiraz wine to India. What is more remarkable is that by 1677 the wine was transported in bottles, wrapped in straw and packed in cases, to go swaying down to the Gulf Coast on mule back. There is scarcely any earlier instance of the regular use of bottles for shipping wine.

The business was still in full swing in the 19th century when a British doctor with the telegraph company, C.J. Wills, told how his friend and neighbour in Shiraz, the Mullah Hadji Ali Akbar, approached him with the proposition that they should make wine together in Dr Wills' house. "I cannot make wine in my house," said the Mullah. "I am a Mohammedan priest. But if I ask the Jews to make it for me things will be even worse, because the wine will be dreadful, and I am a connoisseur. If I make it at your house, Sahib, it will be first class and I will kill two birds with one stone. You and I will have good wine and there will be no scandal about it."

above all, raising the taxes on wine merchants. These very taxes, though, were the Jews' and Christians' insurance against their trade being prohibited altogether. It is recorded that on one occasion, feeling themselves threatened by the mood of the people, they volunteered to pay the caliph twice as much tax for his protection – which he granted.

No generalization holds good for all times and places, especially about a creed so open to interpretation as Islam, or an empire so shifting in its dynastic successions. The faith has grouped and regrouped again and again around new centres of energy and power. Yet from the start there have been schools of more liberal and more puritanical teaching. The Turks, arriving on the scene in the 13th century with the Mongol conquerors from Central Asia, were relatively late converts, fighting men who were not attracted by strict dogma. They embraced the liberal Hanafite rite which made the minimum fuss about prohibition, finding a simple way around it by discouraging wine but turning a blind eye to distilled spirits, which the Prophet had not mentioned. Arrack or raki, alcohol flavoured with aniseed, rapidly became their favourite drink (some say it entered Palestine with the Crusaders). In the Turkish Ottoman Empire, which by the 16th century controlled the Near East from the Adriatic to Iraq and Upper Egypt, raki was the essential element in masculine conviviality. One could say that the Ottoman sultans took the opposite view from Mohammed, believing that it was better to let citizens drink raki than "melancholy" coffee.

A 17th-century English traveller in Turkey wrote: "These men who drink only Water and Coffee, enter into discourse of State Matters, censure the actions and pass Characters on the Grandees and grand Officers. . . . And this was the reason why the great Vizier Kupruli put down the Coffee houses in Constantinople, and yet privileged the Taverns; because the first were melancholy places where Seditions were vented, where reflections were made on all occurences of State, and discontents published and aggravated; but Wine [here meaning all alcoholic drinks] raised the spirits of men to a gay humour, and would never operate those effects to endanger his condition, as the Councels which were contrived in the Assemblies of those who addicted themselves to a more melancholy liquor."

Yet established vineyard regions from ancient times had managed to survive with few exceptions while the controlling powers of Islam were Arab or Syrian or Persian. It was the Ottoman Empire that finally chased wine out of some of its oldest-established strongholds.

ON THE EVE OF OTTOMAN RULE, and indeed throughout the Middle Ages, vineyards implanted by the Greeks, the Phoenicians, the Romans, the Egyptians – all the most ancient civilizations – were still, however precariously, in existence.

Spain and Portugal never lost their vineyards on account of Islam. Wines of the eastern Mediterranean, of the Lebanon, Cyprus and Crete in particular, were much in demand in Europe throughout the Middle Ages. Algeria maintained a Roman wine tradition – although it was to supply the hard-drinking Barbary pirates of Algiers. Coptic Christians in Egypt continued to make wine. Persia proudly produced its vintages at Shiraz and in Bactria, not only for home consumption but to supply a considerable export market.

Remotest of all, and never apparently seriously threatened, were the vineyards of the High Indus Valley and Afghanistan. High in the Hindu Kush the Ismaeli sect nurtured vineyards, and vines lined the old route of the Silk Road through the Hounza Valley, north of Kasmir. Kafiristan, north of Kabul, supplied the court of the Sultan Babur, the founder of the Mogul Empire in 16th-century India, with his favourite wine.

How old these vineyards are no one can say. It is conceivable that they had an independent existence in prehistory; equally that they are the last memorials of Greek influence, the last echo of Alexander the Great. Only within the last century has winemaking as a way of life been extinguished in most of Afghanistan (it was reintroduced to Kabul in 1969) while the Hounzas, although nominally Muslim, continue cheerfully to ignore the Prophet's proscription.

The following tasting notes are almost a century out of date, but may be regarded as fairly accurate:

"The Hounza wine is not kept beyond a year, and stands underground in earthern jars. . . . It looks like cold weak tea with milk in it, and is not unpalatable, though sourish, tasting like Norman cider of the rough sort, and containing, I should say, about the same percentage of alcohol. For the benefit of travellers, I may mention that the vintage of Baltit is best. The Hum [ruler] has a cellar in the fort

The Muslim empire of the Moguls, descendants of the Mongol conquerors led by Tamerlane, rose to its full splendour in India in the time of Shakespeare. In elegance and refinement its court surpassed anything in contemporary Europe: the Taj Mahal was built in the decade that Louis XIV was born. In this painting of a young prince with his sage advisors in a garden, it is clear that wine was an acccepted part of courtly life.

there, where we discovered some jars of wine held in high estimation by Hounza connoisseurs." The tasting note is by E.F. Knight; the underground jars are surely cousins of the Imeretian kwevris we met in Chapter 2.

SUCH OUTLANDISH REGIONS never felt the lash of the Ottomans, but the vineyards of the eastern Mediterranean and its islands, survivors of a thousand years of coexistence with Islam, were much more hardly dealt with by the raki drinkers. As the Ottomans swept through the Levant, it almost ceased to be a useful source of wine for Europe. One exception was the lonely and precipitous ridge to the north of Crete which is all that remains of the great volcano of Santorini. The only value of this windswept rock to its Turkish masters was for any taxes they could extract from it, and the only possible crop on its raw volcanic rock is the vine.

Santorini's vines crouch low on its cliff like the nests of big seabirds braced against the gale. The island's wine, fermented in caves cut into its cliffs and manhandled down to ships waiting in the unfathomable water of its crater, became the staple Eucharistic wine of Turkey's greatest foe, Russia. Wines from Crete were similarly bought by Venetian merchants and traded north over the Alps to market in northeast Europe. One famous Levantine Jew of the 17th century, Joseph Nasi, bought a concession from the King of Poland to supply his kingdom with strong Cretan wine. What is certain is that the coffers of the Sublime Porte were at least as much a beneficiary as either winegrower or trader.

THERE ARE OTHER REASONS WHY WINE FADED even from its strongholds in the Middle East. The greatest is the decline in the wealth of the whole region, which never entirely recovered from the murderous onrush of the Mongol invasions of the 13th century. The horsemen from the Steppes destroyed villages and irrigation systems and drove the population from the countryside to the cities. Wars and epidemics further reduced the population, so that the great capital Baghdad, the home of 1.5 million people at its zenith, was reduced by the mid-19th century to a mere 60,000. An inevitable consequence of this decline was the departure of Jewish and Christian communities and traders, those who had kept the wine industry in being. As vineyards were abandoned, the price of wine rose and its consumption fell even further. For those who could no longer afford to buy wine, hashish became the affordable intoxicant.

PART II

The medieval winegrower's routine: a 15th-century fresco from Trento

CHAPTER 10

INHERITORS OF THE EMPIRE

The light at the end of the Dark Ages has a name – and it is Charlemagne. That, at least, is how he was seen, this steadfastly successful, ambitious but conservative ruler, by his contemporaries and the succeeding ages that credited him with every virtue, and most inventions.

Charlemagne succeeded his father, Pepin the Short, after two and a half centuries of Frankish rule extending over Belgium and northern France, then over most of France, Germany and Switzerland. Merovingian was the dynastic name of the kings succeeding Clovis to his throne in Paris. Clovis had been baptized; his successors continued nominally to support the old Roman church; but there was little unity or indeed Christianity in the Frankish kingdom. At one point the bishopric of Paris was openly bought by a Syrian merchant. Monasteries stood out – some of them – like good deeds in a naughty world. The men who created them tended to be either escapists, looking for refuge in their troubled times, or hell-fire preachers with short fuses doing their best on two fronts at once: against the cynically political Church and against the unrepentant paganism that Clovis' conversion had done little to dislodge.

In the darkest hours of the 5th and 6th centuries, even monasteries had become brigand lairs. Spirituality was displaced almost entirely from Europe, to find refuge among the Irish. Ireland was where the pre-Frankish Gallo-Roman culture of the Celts made its last stand, and the base from which it went out, inspired and inspiring, to reconvert Europe, hard-pressed by pagans within and without.

To the north, the Saxons were pugnaciously pagan; they had detached Britain from Christendom and piratically ranged the northern seas. St Columba went from Ireland to Iona, making Scotland, then Northumbria, a Christian missionary base. In the Mediterranean, it was Islamic Arab armies that raided the French and Italian coasts, conquered Spain and drove north as far as the Loire before being conclusively checked at Poitiers. The Frankish commander at Poitiers was Charles Martel. His son, Pepin the Short, established a united and determinedly Christian kingdom at Aachen in Germany. With him began the Carolingian dynasty. His son was Charlemagne.

Charlemagne added the whole of Germany to the Frankish crown, conquering the Saxons in the north and extending his borders eastwards from the Rhineland to include Bavaria, as well as south from the Alps to include Lombardy and Rome, and south beyond the Pyrenees to provide a "March", or buffer, against the Moors in Spain. This was the Holy Roman Empire, of which, on Christmas Day 800, the Pope crowned him emperor in Rome.

ROME WAS THE POPE'S HEADQUARTERS; IT WAS NOT CHARLEMAGNE'S. The great palace and chapel Charlemagne built at Aachen symbolized the shift in the centre of gravity of Europe from south to north. The 8th and early 9th centuries were a time of consolidation and relative prosperity in northern Europe. The Rhine, which had been both highway and frontier for the Romans, became the centre of activity for Charlemagne's empire. He built a palace near the river at Ingelheim, near Mainz, granted lands to nobles, bishops and monasteries and rights to settlements to hold markets and become towns.

An important motor in this Rhineland activity was the Frisians, the race of seamen from what is now Holland, who can be said to have initiated that country's

---

"SUMMA QUIES"

An example of the monk escaping into a Roman world of reason was the Italian St Benedict, founder of Monte Cassino and the (eventually enormous) Benedictine Order in 529. Benedict's motto was "summa quies" – utter peace. His desire for quiet reasonableness is perfectly expressed in the chapter of his Rule (the discipline of the Benedictine Order) concerning wine:

"Every man hath his proper gift from God, one after this manner, and another after that. It is therefore with some misgiving that we determine how much others should eat and drink. Nevertheless, keeping in view the needs of weaker brethren we believe that a hermina [about half a pint] of wine a day is sufficient for each. But those upon whom God bestows the gift of abstinence, should know that they shall have a special reward. . . .

"But when the circumstances of the place are such that the aforesaid measure cannot be had, but much less or even none at all, then let the monks who dwell there bless God and not murmur. Above all things do we give this admonition, that they abstain from murmuring."

An example of the precise opposite in a near contemporary was the Irish missionary St Columbanus, who arrived in Brittany in 591 and went on to found monasteries in Alsace, in the remote Vosges. Nothing could have been more rigorous or relentlessly austere than Columbanus' rule. His followers at his Abbey of Luxeuil – how inappropriately named – destroyed them-

selves with labour, and his relations with the royal house, notably with the Jezebel-like Queen Brunhild, were almost suicidally stormy. Perhaps he was saved by his Irish charm. There is a legend that as he and his monks were harvesting a field, an enormous thundercloud rolled up. Columbanus calmly posted a monk in each corner of the field and it rained everywhere except on the men of God and their crop.

An illuminating satire on a 13th-century Benedictine cellarer expresses a monk's opinion of the man who holds the keys – and uses a king-size tasting-cup while drawing the daily ration.

A bust in Aachen cathedral portrays the Charlemagne of legend: the ideal, active, benevolent, peace-bringing Emperor. This golden reliquary was made in 1349, five centuries after his reign. Throughout the Middle Ages the best of everything, vineyards included, tended to be ascribed to this monarch who knew the value of moderation.

energetic involvement in the wine trade. Their customers included not just the ports of the North Sea but the Hansa cities of the German Baltic, and indeed as far as Poland and Russia. Across the Channel in England, King Offa of Mercia opened a dialogue with Charlemagne which probably led to the first wine-for-wool trade with England since Roman times. The earliest post-Roman references to almost all the wine regions of Germany are found in the period between 650 and 850, the Carolingian era.

Charlemagne's energy was devoted as much to bureaucracy as to empire-building. The best-known legends about him that concern wine stress the ecologist. He observed, it is said, while passing by boat up the Rhine to Ingelheim, that the snow melted first on the steep apron of Johannisberg (or the even steeper scarp of the Rüdesheimer Berg, according to your informant). So he ordered that vines be planted there – and indeed it was during his reign (or, to be exact, three years after his death) that we know that the Rheingau had its first vineyards. In Burgundy they tell a very similar story about the hill of Corton, whose chalky upper slopes he gave to the Abbey of Saulieu in 775, and whose wine to this day is called Corton-Charlemagne. Burgundy has attached to the emperor the fairy story that he specified white grapes (in a red-wine district) because red wine stained his white beard.

It is less well-known that he laid down strict laws about hygiene in winemaking, including the revolutionary (and scarcely practicable) injunction that the grapes should not be trodden with the feet. With what other instrument? must have been the puzzled reaction. He also banned the storage of wine in animal skins, and gave winegrowers the right to hang out a green branch and sell direct to all comers. The right to do so survives, passed down by succeeding Holy Roman Emperors to the growers of Vienna. Every Heurige has its leafy bough – although, as the saying goes, good wine needs no bush.

Charlemagne's principal adviser was a priest from Yorkshire, one Alcuin, a lettered man of law and prolific writer. Alcuin returned to England for two years and sent this doleful letter to a friend at court. "But woe is me, oh man of God! The wine is gone from our wineskins and bitter beer rageth in our bellies. And because we have it not, do thou drink in our name and lead a joyful day; send to us for we have not wherewith to gladden us, and barely wherewith to strengthen."

Charlemagne himself could not write, but relied on his secretary and later biographer, a Frankish nobleman named Einhard (who afterwards served his successor, Louis the Debonnaire). Einhard gives us this picture of the abstemious emperor: "He was moderate in his eating and drinking, for he hated to see drunkenness in any man. All the same he could not go long without food, and he often used to complain that fasting made him ill. He rarely gave banquets and these only on high feast days, but then he would invite a great number of guests. His main meal of the day was served in four courses, in addition to the roast meat which his hunters used to bring in on spits and which he enjoyed more than any other food. During his meal he would listen to a public reading or some other entertainment. He was so sparing in his use of wine and every other beverage that he rarely drank more than 3 times [i.e. three cups] in the course of his dinner."

IN GREEK AND ROMAN TIMES it had been a matter of doubt whether grapes would grow at all outside their "natural" environment, a Mediterranean (or warmer) climate. The Romans had shown what you can do by planting on steep south slopes, and finding the right varieties of vine. Their Moselle was very light and low in alcohol by Italian standards, but they soon learned that the new "austere" taste had its points. At a strength of probably only seven or eight degrees, it was treated as the all-purpose drink. (It was certainly safer than water.) In winter it was heated in a kettle and drunk as we drink tea or coffee. Vineyard workers in Germany still often keep a kettle of wine on a fire of vine prunings on cold days. With a spoonful of sugar in a plastic cup, it has much to be said for it.

Occasionally, though, after a very sunny summer, the Romans must have found themselves drinking more gloriously juicy, sweet and fresh wine than anything Italy had ever made. Fermentation would be very slow in a German cellar in a cold autumn, and the wine in the barrels, gently fizzy and still sweet with unfermented sugar, must have sent them into raptures.

NOW THAT NORTHERN EUROPE WAS BEGINNING TO BUSTLE, much more wine was needed than a few privileged river bends could provide. Monasteries were springing up like snowdrops in January; each needed wine, and so did such towns as there were. Wine was needed in Britain, Ireland, by the Frisians of course, and across the north of France. Why did the old trade routes not operate to bring it from the south? What had happened to the shipping from Bordeaux, and the long trek up from the Rhône Valley and Burgundy?

The problem, in the case of Bordeaux, was probably pirates, or at least unfriendly heathens, who made the open seas too unsafe for business (but not for the Irish saints, who made the journey to the mouth of the Loire on many occasions, their ships returning with wine for Irish monasteries).

The short voyage across the English Channel or even up the North Sea was comparatively safe. At any rate, England's principal supplier at this time was Germany. German merchants kept houses in York, the ports of Boston and Lynn on the English east coast, and had a substantial headquarters at the Steelyard in London. French wine was shipped either down the Seine from Rouen, or down the little river Canche from the port of Quentowich – which was rediscovered in 1987 after disappearing for nearly a thousand years.

As for long-distance transport overland, the road from Burgundy had been almost impassable, we were told, in Constantine's time. By now it had probably disintegrated altogether.

The threat of heathen raiders was felt not only at sea and along the coast. In the 9th century, Viking plunderers reached and sacked both Paris and Orléans and virtually depopulated Normandy. In 867, the Chapter of St Martin at Tours on the Loire, a good 150 miles from the sea, appealed to King Charles the Bald for a vineyard site well inland and out of danger. He granted them land at Chablis on the river Yonne. Picture the satisfaction of the Brothers as they discovered not only that their wine was going to be better, but that the Yonne runs into the Seine, and the Seine means Paris. Chablis began to be a name in the capital (it was the only "vin de Bourgogne" that reached it) – although little Chablis was only a drop in the ocean compared with the vineyards that were already planted around the cathedral town of Auxerre on the same river.

Paris in the year 1000 was hardly yet a city at all, but the "Ile de France", the whole region of the Paris basin, was becoming the country's centre of religious, royal and commercial activity. It included the neighbouring towns of Chartres, Evreux, Melun, Senlis, St Denis, Compiègne, Beauvais. A little farther afield lay Rouen to the west, Orléans to the south, and to the northeast and east Soissons, Laon and Reims. Their combined consumption was an important quantity and growing fast, and through their merchants wine was flowing out northwards again to Flanders and Britain.

IF THE NORTH IN ITS NEW MOOD WAS TO HAVE ENOUGH WINE, it had to grow it, and as close as possible to its market. So vineyards were planted in places where a really ripe grape must have been a rare sight. The 9th century, for all its disruption, even saw a wave of planting in Belgium, where the river Meuse might be called a poor man's Moselle. Liège, Naumur, Brabant, Hainault, Antwerp were all wine-growing provinces in the early Middle Ages. The city of Louvain led the way, as the seat of

---

VINLAND

One of the most intriguing culs-de-sac of wine history is the story of Leif Ericson, the first recorded European discoverer of America. He landed somewhere in New England, perhaps at Cape Cod, having sailed from Iceland, around the year 1000.

His first impression was of a country smothered in grapevines, which is named, in the saga that records his voyage, Vinland the Good. Leif made at least two voyages and started a settlement, in which it is remotely possible that the first American wine was made. Had his exploits been better publicized the great continent, instead of taking its name from the obscure Florentine merchant Amerigo Vespucci, might have been named after the noblest of fruits.

A 16th-century Flemish prayer book illustrates the month of October with the arrival of the new vintage in the port of Antwerp. Merchants and their customers are tasting the wine, shipped while it had scarcely stopped fermenting. Flanders was the centre of wine distribution in northern Europe, with ships arriving from French, German, Spanish and Mediterranean ports, and waggons bringing barrels overland from Champagne and Burgundy.

the Dukes of Brabant (and later Burgundy). The eventual decline of the vineyards of Louvain corresponded precisely with the rise of the House of Burgundy and its Côte d'Or wines in the 15th century.

The true limit, it was found, to a realistic prospect of making drinkable wine was indeed the climate – although not in quite the predictable north-south sense. Northern France has a climate without great extremes, tempered (like Britain's) by the mild airs that accompany the Gulf Stream. The farther west, the more this Atlantic influence makes itself felt, but not, unfortunately, to the benefit of the sun-loving vine. Brittany has a balmy (if blowy) climate, but scarcely a single vine. The problem is the clouds that trawl eastwards up the Channel, following the north French coast and reaching inland to cover all of Brittany, and almost all of Normandy and Picardy.

Paris lies on the edge of this grey-green zone. Only a little farther east, the influence of the continent begins to be felt: winters are colder and summers hotter. Here the vineyards can edge north a little, profiting from the clearer skies. This is the Champagne region, today the northernmost under vines in France. Farther east still, the Moselle and Rhine are able to take profitable wine-growing as much as 80 miles farther north; by this point the climate is noticeably more extreme, influenced as much by the landmass to the east as by the great reservoir of grey skies to the west. All the vineyards that the Middle Ages planted north and west of this diagonal line have since disappeared – although some of them not until the 19th century. Yet those just south of it (Champagne, for example) produce some of the most highly prized wines of all. The vine, as we will often be reminded, does its best work at the very margins of where it is practicable to cultivate it.

The two centuries that followed the plundering raids of the Vikings, or Norsemen (once settled, they sounded much more respectable as Normans), saw a great acceleration of growth and trade in northern Europe. The population may have increased by 50 percent. Safer trade meant richer cities with more artisans to feed, which in turn demanded more farmland and a bigger population in the countryside.

As an emblem of this new prosperity, of the freedom of travel and a marketable surplus of goods, in the 1100s a pattern of regular fairs emerged, centred around the Ile de France, Flanders, and above all the towns of Troyes and Bar-sur-Aube in the open, unforested countryside of Champagne. Italian merchants even crossed the Alpine passes of Saint Bernard and Mont Cenis to trade in this marketplace. It was the first faint breath of a renaissance of the single Europe of ancient Rome.

SUDDENLY TO PLANT what must have been tens of thousands of acres of new vineyards around the towns and abbeys of newly prosperous northern Europe was a not-inconsiderable achievement. Vineyards – as Cato and Columella pointed out – need high investment, and skilled and intensive care. The last great planting had been under the slave system of the Romans. Who undertook this new great labour?

Much of the credit is given, probably rightly, to the monks. But in France, most of the land belonged to nobles who had given the king their support, in battle or otherwise. Royal thanks took the form of great tracts of what was often virtually wilderness: forest, marsh and mere, but not many fields, and not many peasants to take the part of slaves.

A solution was found in a new notion of partnership. A free labourer would offer a landowner to cultivate uncleared land in exchange for a share – either of the land itself, or more often of its crop. The system of "complant" as applied to vineyards meant that the worker, the "prendeur", owned the vines and the "bailleur" the soil. The period of contract was five years; long enough to establish a vineyard and judge its produce. Sometimes the partnership went on for generations, the bailleur receiving anything from one-third to two-thirds of the revenue. In other cases the bailleur bought out the prendeur – effectively paying him for five years' work. The system seems to have satisfied both parties, particularly in remoter districts where labourers were scarce. So much so that it still persists, in a modified form, now known as "metayage".

EARLY MEDIEVAL BRITAIN DRANK MORE GERMAN WINE THAN FRENCH; presumably because it was better – or at least better liked. (For that matter, speaking of white wines only, it still does.) Climatically, as we have seen, the Rhineland vineyards had the advantage over what were generically called the "vins de France" ("France" being limited to the Seine and its tributaries).

The expansion of the Rhineland vineyards (including those of Alsace) was even more rapid and impressive in the early Middle Ages than the boom in French planting. It was also more monastery-led. Two great Benedictine abbeys were founded in Charlemagne's reign that were to plant gigantically, not just along the Rhine, but in Franconia to the east, Alsace to the west, and Austria and Switzerland to the south. The names of Fulda (which is north of Frankfurt) and Lorsch (south of Mainz) appear in document after document as they spawned more and more abbeys and outlying dependencies. Fulda was founded by an Englishman, St Boniface, who is said to have stimulated the wine trade with England. It was due to them and scores of other monasteries that wine-growing villages multiplied along the Rhine from less than 40 in the 7th century to almost 400 two centuries later.

Working alongside the monasteries were the churches and cathedrals. Charlemagne followed the example of his predecessors in granting churches a tax (known as a "tithe", or tenth part, although it was usually between three and five percent) on all agricultural produce. A tithe of a peasant's haycrop was not so much use as a tithe of his wine, which could easily be turned into cash. Churches therefore gave villages every encouragement to plant vineyards, from technical help with terracing to celestial privileges for especially good results.

Pious legacies also swelled the Church's landholdings, frequently in the form of vineyards. It would be wrong, though, to paint too glowing a picture of benevolent clerics and respectful peasants. There were plenty of excuses for plucking such a fat fowl as the Church, and few were missed. When the 10th-century Archbishop Heinrich of Trier visited the great abbey of Lorsch, he found its cellars ransacked and dry.

The official encouragement given to winegrowers fostered a sense they already had of being a full notch up the social ladder from mere land workers. The

WANDERING SCHOLARS

Besides churches and monasteries, two other great medieval institutions derived much of their income from wine: hospitals and universities. The most famous wine-endowed hospital is the beautiful Hôtel-Dieu in Beaune, which dates from the later Middle Ages. But throughout Europe it was commonplace and logical for a hospital (which in its broadest meaning catered for the sick, the poor, and the traveller, student or pilgrim) to make wine both for use and for sale. The sick received an allowance which must have kept their whole families: 4.8 litres a day was the ration at one hospital on the Bodensee.

The University of Paris was the forerunner and model of similar foundations throughout Europe, which in the 13th century set a new fashion that could almost be called tourism. Students were given safe-conducts and exemptions from customs dues to encourage their travel to other seats of learning and the exchange of ideas.

(The "duty-free" idea appealed to merchants, too, who sent their clerks, who knew Latin and could write, on "study" trips disguised as students.)

The wandering scholars seem to have spent more time in taverns than lecture rooms. They formed a distinct subclass of society that was both learned and irresponsible, loosely attached to the Church but principally interested in wine, women and (ribald Latin) song. In a time when guilds controlled every calling, they called themselves the Order of Goliardi (from "gula", the Latin for gluttony). If anyone was knowledgeable about the different wines of different parts of Europe, it was probably these Rabelaisian wanderers. It was one of them who left us this memorable picture of an abbot:

> He would have his wine all times and
>   seasons
> Never did a day or night go by
> But it would find him, wine-soaked and
>   wavering,
> Even as a tree that the high winds sway.

(Translated by Helen Waddell: *Medieval Latin Lyrics*.)

6th-century Salic Law of the Franks put twice the price on the head of a wine-grower to that of a ploughman or cowherd if he were accidentally killed.

A great economic historian has pointed out that wine and wool were the two true luxuries of northern Europe in the Middle Ages. To be warm within and without was well-being indeed. Both were agricultural products that depended on skilled handling by the primary producer, which for wool was principally England. English wool was woven in Flanders. Trading in cloth and wine, Flanders soon became the banking centre of the north. Although town burghers could grow fat as vintners or clothiers, it was in everyone's interest that a fair proportion of the price be passed back to the supplier.

Hence the wine village, in Germany the "Winzerdorf", developed a special status, under the wing of mother Church (and positively saturated with saints' days) but businesslike and with a degree of independence that was unusual in feudal times. The Winzerdorf was usually walled like a tiny town, built beside the river road, with its own network of paths up into the terraced vineyards above. Little shrines and huts for watchmen were scattered among the vines. In the tiny square was a common hall and often a common cellar; the growers operated as what we would call a cooperative.

No great imagination is needed to picture such a place. They still exist by the score all along the Moselle and Rhine and their tributaries. Bernkastel on the Moselle is perhaps the finest – but it was granted town rights and a market in 1291. The tall and narrow half-timbered houses that huddle and confide over the steep streets may be more opulent, but their plan, and their attitudes, will have been much the same 700 years ago, and possibly 400 years before that. Another, and perhaps the most perfectly preserved of late-medieval wine towns, still entirely within its 15th-century gated walls, is Riquewihr in Alsace.

Riquewihr in Alsace, in the east-facing foothills of the Vosges mountains, is one of the most perfectly preserved of medieval wine villages, still earning its living entirely from vines on its surrounding slopes as it has done, invasions and wars permitting, for almost 1,000 years. So fruitful are its fields that a medieval poet wrote: "If the Rhine could not carry away the surplus of the vintage to the Friesians, the people of Alsace would drown in the bounty of their production." Many of the families making wine in Alsace today date their origins to the mid-17th century, soon after the utter destruction of the region in the Thirty Years' War.

What is reputedly Germany's oldest inhabited house is today a restaurant in the wine village of Winkel in the Rheingau. It was built in 1100 by the knightly family of Greiffenclau, who later built the moated and fortified tower of Schloss Vollrads in their vineyards a mile back from the Rhine. The position of the Rheingau was particularly privileged, even among wine districts. It passed from Charlemagne's successors partly into the hands of their Imperial abbeys of Fulda and Lorsch, but also to the archbishops of Mainz, just across the river. The power of the Church was such that when the archbishop founded a monastery (the first in the district) on the Bischofsberg – now Schloss Johannisberg – the count who held the temporal responsibility for the Rheingau under the emperor simply resigned, and sent his wife, his sister and his son into the new monastery.

The whole magnificent undulating landscape, sloping up to the Taunus forests and facing south over the broad silver waters of the Rhine, was now Church ruled, and its pious proprietors set about clearing its woods and planting vines so comprehensively that since 1226 there has been no more clearing or planting to do.

The Church's way of assuring hard work and good wine was to make even the lowly toilers in the vineyards free men with equal rights to townsmen. They could take their wine to market in Mainz and even carry arms. They were, you might say, wine-burghers, and the resulting esprit de corps can be tasted in the wines of the Rheingau to this day.

And whereas a town would have walls to define and defend its boundaries, the whole region of the Rheingau was encircled in the 11th century with a dense wall of planted trees, the Gebück. (The same idea was used by the Dutch to protect their colony at the Cape of Good Hope.) In places the Gebück was more than 100 yards wide and able to deter an army. The Swedes burst through it during the Thirty Years' War, but it was renewed and kept in being until the end of the 18th century.

MUCH THE GREATEST PART OF THIS SOARING WINE PRODUCTION, which reached right up the Rhine, through the Palatinate to Alsace and Baden, was destined for export. Alsace, although the last to be planted, was the biggest producer and exporter of the whole Rhineland. By 1400, 100 million litres a year went through the Strasbourg market, en route for all parts of Germany, the Hansa towns and England. The other great market of Alsace, Colmar, supplied huge quantities via Basel to Switzerland. The river-port towns prospered accordingly, both as merchants and producers. No potential vineyard was left unplanted. When Cologne, the chief of all the wine-trade cities, replaced its ancient battlements with a new curtain-wall 100 yards farther out, the intervening space was immediately filled with vines. (But of Cologne it was said, right up to the 18th century, that the water was poison.)

The town of Worms still contains, beside its Gothic Liebfrauenkirche, the vineyard that gave its name to the original Liebfraumilch. Würzburg in Franconia was described as being surrounded with vineyards "like a thick wreath". They are still there, the famous Leisten and Stein slopes that have produced wines of extraordinary power and plenitude for 900 years – although unfortunately today dominated by another and thicker wreath, of concrete tower blocks.

So besotted were the Franconians with their local wine (although not until 1665 did the noble Silvaner grape arrive from Austria to give it its modern quality) that

A public bathhouse in 15th-century Germany apparently combined the functions of a tavern with various other amenities. Bathing was evidently considered a daringly decadent pastime. Wine production and consumption rose to spectacular levels in late-medieval Germany.

they supported their prince-bishop in actually forbidding its export for fear of going thirsty, or having to import inferior stuff.

Other less chauvinistic wine towns formed free-trading partnerships (Frankfurt, for example, with Strasbourg) to their mutual benefit, and to avoid the ever-increasing tolls that almost every town imposed to cash in on the wine trade. In the 14th century there were 62 customs points on the German Rhine, and merchants were making laborious overland journeys to avoid them.

The pattern of supplies flowing down (and occasionally up) the great rivers of Europe, the rivalries between producing regions and trading towns, the complexity of tolls and customs add up to an economic epic that it would be beyond your patience and mine to pursue. On the Danube, for example, Vienna supplied Bohemia and Bavaria upstream with wines from Lower Austria, while resisting the import of Hungarian wines from farther down-river. Hungary therefore developed an overland trade to the north, to Poland and Silesia and even across the Baltic to Sweden (which were also supplied with German wines by Frisian and Jewish merchants working down the Rhine).

German documents of the times build up a picture of a great bubble expanding and expanding; of wine becoming the obsession of the German race. By the 16th century, noble households employed professional drinkers; Falstaffian characters whose job was to jest and swallow and belch and swallow again. The bubble is symbolized by the mighty "tuns" that were built to house the best vintages. The most famous of them, in Heidelberg, held 150 hogsheads, or 19,000 dozen bottles. An 18th-century Polish governor of Königstein took leave of his senses and ordered a tun of 25 times the capacity of the Great Tun of Heidelberg.

The bubble was to burst in the apocalyptic destruction of the Thirty Years' War. The Rhine would never again be such a river of wine. Sheer quantity eventually had to give place to quality. In this, as in so many stages of wine's history, the Church was in the lead.

CHAPTER 11

MAKING AND TASTING MEDIEVAL WINE

Whatever difficulty we may have in imagining the circumstances, the beliefs and superstitions, the dangers, the narrowness and what, to us, would be the privations of medieval life, we have a remarkably direct link, and real common ground, through the technology of winemaking. About the precise taste we can be less sure, chiefly because so much depends on grape varieties, and little is known for certain about which they used. Even some whose names match our own may have changed character in many centuries of cultivation. But the way wine was made in the Middle Ages persisted almost everywhere until at least the 18th century, and in some places has scarcely changed today. More, in most cases, has changed in the vineyard than the cellar: changes forced by the arrival of fatal but previously unknown diseases and pests of the vine in the 19th century.

A medieval vineyard was wherever possible planted by ploughing into deep furrows, then pushing in simple rootless cuttings, short canes of the last year's growth, with a small "heel" of older wood attached. In northern Europe the cuttings were put in a mere pace apart; the vines covered the soil in a dense carpet, with up to 20,000 vines to a hectare. In the south, where drought was a problem, the spacing was much wider: perhaps only 5,000 vines.

Unrooted cuttings were the cheapest way of planting, but there was small chance of them all "taking". Next year there would be gaps to be filled. The more expensive way was to grow roots on your cuttings in a nursery bed and transplant them with a tuft of roots, and a third way was to "layer" canes on growing vines by partially burying them, then separating these "marcottes" and planting them as soon as they had made roots of their own. Where "marcottage" was practicable, a new vineyard could be producing grapes within three or even two years. The same system, but without separating marcottes, and instead leaving the new plants in place to thicken up the vineyard, was called "provignage". It eventually produced a terrible tangle of roots and shoots, but it seems to have been the system used by the Romans on the Côte d'Or. Certainly it would explain their complaint to Constantine that the land had become choked with vines.

THE MOST FUNDAMENTAL DECISION, THEN AS NOW, was which variety of vine to plant. For most simple growers there would be little choice; but for preference they would plant several different kinds in a mixture as an insurance against the crop failing in any one of them. The textbook of French agriculture of 1600, Olivier de Serres' *Théâtre d'Agriculture*, recommends planting five or six. Each variety has its own peculiarities – particularly its time of flowering (and how reliably it flowers). But a vine that flowers late (and therefore has a better chance of fine flowering weather) also ripens late. Few ordinary growers would go around their vineyard harvesting at intervals to catch each variety at its ideal moment of ripeness. The ripest would add sugar, the least ripe acidity: the compromise was a reasonable one.

More important economically, and the cause of constant dispute between landlord and tenant, was the vigour and productiveness of the varieties. The 18th-century German author and traveller Goethe put the matter in a nutshell: "The rich want good wine, the poor plenty of wine." Even by the 13th century, in the Rhineland there was a clear distinction between "Hunnish wine" and "Frankish wine"; the latter at twice the price of the former. Today's terms would be bulk wine and fine wine. Eventually, in all the best vineyard sites the "Frankish" would prevail, but not without many generations of dispute – and not without backsliding either, even today. A classic case is the recent planting of the inferior Müller-Thurgau along the Moselle in place of the Riesling. Pruning, of course, was also vital in controlling the crop for quality: hard pruning was an uncomfortable sort of self-discipline, but without it the resulting heavy crop would never ripen properly, and after a few years the overcropped vine would die of exhaustion.

The mixed varieties in the vineyard might be either red or white. Although in the early Middle Ages white wine had the greater cachet, especially in northern

---

THE BATTLE OF THE WINES

The celebrated rivalry between the wines of France and the north, and stronger wines from the south, was the subject of at least two long poems. "La Bataille des Vins", by Henry d'Andeli, was written in 1224 and tells the story of a tasting organized by the king of France. More than 70 samples were sent for, from as far away as Cyprus and Spain as well as the Moselle, the Midi, Alsace, St-Emilion, Epernay and Beaune. Perhaps significantly, the king chose an English priest to be the unbiased and expert judge, and to say which wine: "Par sa bonté, par sa puissance, D'abreuver bien le roi de France." All the (identifiable) French wines judged are shown on the map opposite. The concentration in north and central France is the most striking feature.

After 150 lines of deliberation, in which he generally seems to favour the light white wines of the north, he eventually awards the prize to sweet Cyprus wine: "Qui resplendit comme une estoile"; ending with a commendably priestly line (such tastings didn't happen often): "Prenons tel vin que Dieu nous donne."

The second poem, "La Desputaison de Vin et de l'Iaue", was written about a hundred years later, when it seems that the lightness of northern wines was less in fashion. The true rivalry (leaving aside such totally different sorts of wine as that of Cyprus) was between the "vins de France" and the more powerful wines of Burgundy, then coming into their own. The prize in this case, though, goes to the mysterious St-Pourçain from the Loire, the favourite, says the poet, of both the pope and the king. Whatever peculiar quality won St-Pourçain such lofty patronage must always remain a mystery. Perhaps the secret was simply in the patronage. St-Pourçain-sur-Sioule is in the territory of the Bourbons, later to become the royal house. Judging by today's St-Pourçain, it would have been closer to "France" than Burgundy: a thin white wine, possibly with a slight sparkle.

vineyards, in most cases its colour was a secondary consideration. Presumably most ordinary wine was either pale red (in French, "clairet") or pink-tinged white.

The signal to begin the vintage (in French, the "ban de vendange") was given by the landlord. To pick before it was a punishable offence. Normally one week's notice was given, and watches were set in the vineyards to guard the ripening fruit. Only the landlord was exempt from the ban: an unfair advantage he was happy to enjoy. On the announcement, by drum, trumpet or bells, all hands set to picking. Twenty pickers, it was reckoned, could harvest a hectare of vines in a day.

THE BATTLE OF THE WINES

VERMANDOIS
MOSELLE
GATINAIS
ANJOU
ALSACE
AUNIS
PROVENCE

Laon
Beauvais • Clermont • Crouy
Soissons
Montmorency • Hautvillers • Reims
Meulan • Deuil Epernay
Argenteuil • Pierrefitte
Marly • Trilbardou • Châlons-sur-Marne
St-Yon • Étampes • Sézanne
Argences •
Samois
Rennes • Le Mans • Jargeau • Tonnerre
Orléans • Auxerre • Chablis
St-Bris • Vermenton
Orchaise • Vézelay
Tours • Lassay Sancerre
Montrichard • Savigny
Issoudun • Nevers • Beaune
Châteauroux •
Poitiers • Buzençais
• Chauvigny • St-Pourçain
La Rochelle Montmorillon
• St-Jean-d'Angély • Chambilly
• Taillebourg
Saintes • Angoulême
St-Emilion
Bordeaux
Moissac
Montpellier •
Béziers •
Carcassonne • Narbonne • Celebrated Wines
• Excommunicated Wines

An invited English priest in 1224 classed the wines as either "Celebrated" or "Excommunicated".

The standard work on wine-growing in the late Middle Ages was the *Liber Commodorum Ruralium* by Petrus de Crescentiis. This pruning scene is from a copy made for Edward IV of England.

ALL THE GRAPES WERE TRODDEN. It is surprising that France and Germany have scarcely any old stone treading tanks like the lagars of Spain and Portugal. The familiar medieval picture is of treading in a wooden trough or shallow vat. At this stage, white juice was strained from its skins and bucketed into barrels to ferment. But if the majority of grapes were red, and red wine was what was wanted, a deep vat was needed in which juice and skins could ferment together until the colour had been leached from the skins. Red winemaking was therefore a more elaborate operation. It could also involve risk. The obvious shortcut was to tread the grapes in the vat. Once they started to ferment as the vat filled, the carbon dioxide could suffocate the treaders – as parish records show that it not infrequently did.

A nice piece of judgment was needed as to whether to leave all or part of the stalks on the bunches. In a cold, wet vintage they simply diluted the wine; in a good year they gave it more astringent tannins and acidity: greater flavour and bite, in fact. They also made the skins much easier to press, if there was a press to be used.

Only large estates belonging to nobles or the Church had wine-presses in the Middle Ages. They were massive pieces of capital equipment, cumbersome structures built of the biggest trees from the nearby forest. Their only role was to extract an extra 15 or 20 percent of juice from white grapes, or wine after fermentation from red. The "vin de presse" that they produced was inferior in quality to the "vin de goutte" that ran free from the vat. Its only virtue was extra tannin (and in reds, extra colour), which in any case was scarcely a virtue in wines intended for immediate drinking. Good wine could be made very well without a press. Why, then, were they built? And why did tenants pay a proportion of their crop to use the landlord's press? The only answer is that the extra wine was worth the investment, despite the fact that, according to Olivier de Serres, it was unusual to

Above: Crescentiis' *Liber*
illustrates the racking of wine
by forcing it from one barrel
to another with a bellows.

Left: The 14th-century English
"Queen Mary" psalter leaves
few questions to be asked
about how the vintage was
trodden.

add it to the "vin de goutte". Normally it was sold separately, and more cheaply. He mentions the fact that it was blended in Anjou as an exception to the rule.

The principal change that was to come over winemaking during the 17th and 18th centuries was the goal of durability – for which press wine was needed. Annotations in an 1804 edition of the *Théâtre d'Agriculture* specify that press wine is an essential preservative if the aim is wine that will mature.

Once the wine was fermented, the grower's whole object was to sell it before it went sour. An ordinary grower could not afford to drink wine himself; for his family he made "piquette" by adding water to the waste skins. He probably had nowhere to keep it: wine cellars were for rich establishments and town merchants. It was well-known that leaky barrels, or barrels not topped up, could go off even on the way to market, particularly in a warm October. Thirsty carters were another common problem. A rule of thumb was that for an (admittedly large) shipment of 20 barrels on a road journey, one extra barrel should be sent for keeping the others topped up en route. The word is "ullage".

There was usually no time for "racking" the wine, the now-standard practice of transferring it from one barrel to another to leave its lees behind. The lees went with it. What practices were used if, as often happened, the wine arrived at the end of its journey in less-than-perfect condition we shall see in another chapter.

GIVEN THAT MEDIEVAL WINE WAS MADE IN A HURRY, often from a random mixture of grapes, with little or no knowledge of how to preserve it, it is surprising how much time was spent discussing it, and how much distinction was made between one wine region and another. The times, it seems, were far more preoccupied with wine than its quality can really have justified.

How was it judged? Most seriously, in the first place, by its supposed or alleged effect on the drinker's health. The first wine book ever to be printed was the *Liber de Vinis* of Arnaldus de Villanova, a physician who was probably Spanish or Catalan, but who taught medicine in the famous university of Montpellier in the south of France until his death, by drowning, in 1311. Unlike most medieval books, the *Liber de Vinis* was no rehash of the classics but a firsthand medical view of wine – perhaps the first since Galen's. Villanova is typically realistic about wine tasting: ". . . note that some wine dealers cheat . . . they make bitter and sour wines appear sweet by persuading the tasters to eat first licorice or nuts or old salty cheese. . . . Wine tasters can protect themselves against such doings by tasting wine in the morning after they have rinsed their mouths and eaten three or four bites of bread dipped in water, for whoever tries out a wine on a quite empty or on a quite full stomach will find his mouth and his tasting spoiled."

The book suggests cures for wines with bad smells or poor colour, and wines that have gone flat. It gives directions for racking from one barrel to another, and lists almost as many flavoured wines as Pliny as remedies for every sort of ailment, including ox-tongue wine (for healing the insane and demented) and rosemary wine, whose "marvellous qualities" include correcting the appetite, exhilarating the soul, rectifying the sinews, making the face beautiful and the hair grow. It also keeps you young and cleans your teeth. Yet just as you begin to suspect that the whole book is medieval mumbo jumbo there comes a passage of perfect good sense.

Arnaldus was a man of strong opinions. Among them was that the Second Coming of the Messiah would take place in 1378. It led to a long-running feud with the Dominicans, who burnt his book. The Friars also included in their number some

---

A WHIFF OF BRIMSTONE

A quiet revolution took place in Germany just over 500 years ago, in 1487, when a royal decree permitted the addition of sulphur to wine for the first time. It has often been asserted that this was an ancient practice. There are vague references in Homer and Pliny, but no document before 1487 stipulates how much, by what method, and why sulphur should be added.

The permitted amount was apparently 16.2 grams to 860 litres of wine, applied by soaking wood shavings in a mixture of powdered sulphur, herbs and incense and then burning them in the empty barrel before it was filled. It must have been known that sulphur has valuable properties in preserving wine, chiefly in killing microbes and protecting wine from the effects of oxygen, preventing spoilage and browning. (How this knowledge was acquired without royal permission is not recorded.)

From then on sulphur dioxide (which is pure sulphur burned in air) was regularly added to German wines, with immensely valuable results in keeping them fresh and allowing a slower maturing process. It has been said that before the advent of sulphuring the grape variety scarcely mattered, since all wines rapidly oxidized and thereafter smelt and tasted similar. The Germans, whose wines have little alcohol to preserve them and can contain enough sugar to make them unstable, perhaps needed sulphur more than other winemakers. Yet it is very surprising that the French did not officially allow its use until the 18th century – since when it has been used routinely, and often (especially in sweet white wines) seriously overused.

The original German permission was for only 18.8 milligrams per litre (or "parts per million"): an extraordinarily modest amount by today's standards, when amounts up to 250 ppm are not uncommon. The figure is so improbably low that one suspects a mistake in the records, or in their interpretation. At high modern concentrations (not, I hasten to add, found in fine wines) the smell is easily detectable as a slight stinging in the nostrils or throat (or a smell like a spent match), although it rapidly dissipates on contact with air.

---

experienced wine tasters, which for a mendicant order is perhaps surprising. One of them was Geoffrey of Waterford, who wrote this tasting note on "Vernache" or Vernaccia (a speciality of central Italy, although this is not mentioned): "Vernache wine is better" [than Greek or Cyprus, which "is perilous to drink in quantity"] "because its strength is tempered, it opens out sweetly as it comes into the mouth, greets the nostrils and comforts the brain, taking the palate softly but with force . . . ." It is not easy to describe the sensation of drinking a wine like Vernaccia, which is less a matter of aroma than texture, but Geoffrey, who included this in his *Secretum Secretorum* (a book that leant heavily on Aristotle), deserves our respect for trying.

Maturity was not a factor that medieval wine critics concerned themselves with, except as it affected the drinker's comfort. Drinking wine so new that it is still, in the French phrase, "trouble" can lead to severe collywobbles. If it was older than a year, the chances were that the wine was spoiled. The choice was distinctly limited.

Italy produced, in the late 13th century, the lineal descendant of Cato and Columella in a citizen of Bologna called Petrus de Crescentiis, whose *Liber Commodorum Ruralium*, completed in 1303, established him as the great agricultural writer of the Middle Ages. Crescentiis had strong views on the right age for wine. It should be neither new (first year) nor old, which suggests that he found one- or two-year-old wine best. His *Liber* was printed and reprinted for centuries (the memorable woodcuts of a later edition are still regularly commandeered for wine lists). Yet what he was expressing was only his understanding of the classics he closely followed, applied as well as he knew how to contemporary Italian wine. He was aware that oxidized or "maderized" smells of maturity added what we call "complexity", so he suggested rinsing out a barrel with old wine before filling it with new – a recipe for instant age which could produce instant vinegar.

The majority of critics held that it was better simply to wait until fermentation was finally finished and then drink up. The more northern (and weaker) the wine, the more important to drink it quickly. Taillevent, the famous chef to Philippe VI, began to look for stronger, more southern wine from Easter onwards. Burgundy of high quality could be expected to be drinkable at two years. The only known reference from the Middle Ages to any wine being especially good at as old as four years was, remarkably enough, the exceptional Chablis vintage of 1396.

Most original and precious of all the wine critics of the Middle Ages was a particularly harsh one, the Catalan author of an encyclopedia of morals named Francesc Eiximenis. His book was called *Lo Crestia*, "The Christian". He dedicated its third volume, called tersely *Terç*, to an immensely detailed discussion of the seven deadly sins. Under gluttony is found a complete cellar manual, treatise on drunkenness, book of table etiquette, observations on the benefits of moderate drinking, and conclusive evidence of the superiority of Catalan wines and customs. "Only the Catalan nation", he writes, "is an example to others in the way of tempered correct drinking." He is particularly censorious of the Italians, wine snobs, apparently, to a man, who "when they drink, do it in stages and small quantities at a time, examining and re-examining the wine just as physicians do with urine, and they taste it repeatedly, chewing it slowly between their teeth until they have drunk it all." Every wine writer should listen to the Catalan moralist: "Those

Soldiers in a 15th-century tavern in the Val d'Aosta have hung their armour on the wall. The Val d'Aosta was the well-travelled road from northern Italy up to the Great St Bernard Pass, the main route over the Alps to France, Switzerland and the north.

who dwell, think, and cogitate ceaselessly about wine, speaking, writing, following and moulding themselves to it, will suffer these consequences." I will spare you the list of consequences.

According to Eiximenis (who says, reasonably enough, that the French like white wines, Burgundians red, Germans aromatic, and the English beer), the English begin to drink before breakfast, and the Germans even get up in the night to drink. His own favourite wines are sweet and "Greek", from Cyprus, Crete and Mallorca. He prefers these even to the Spanish wines he mentions (two Catalan and two Castilian) and one Italian, Tribià – which may be Trebbiano. Most of his choices, he says, are white, sweet, aromatic and strong, which makes one commentator suspect that he hankered after Muscatel.

On the manner of drinking, Eiximenis is uniquely precise. "The drinker should hold the cup properly, with his hand, carrying it to his mouth and not the mouth to the cup. . . . Some never raise their elbow from the table while they drink . . . and appear . . . like pigs." Not that he was in favour of fancy table manners. Those who "hold the cup curiously with three fingers" are equally censured. The Italians are commended for providing individual cups for everyone, while the rest of Europe was apparently happy to pass the glass around.

On the qualities of an ideal wine, Eiximenis is just as precise. It should be pure, fresh, strong, odorous, fragrant, bubbly and effervescent. It should not be weak, insipid, unctuous, smoky, iron-y, subject to change, bitter, green, honey-like or have the flavour of the cask. With the exception of the last remark, he could be describing the ideal of not a few Australian winemakers.

Adding water was a subject that no writer of the time could avoid. Every man, Eiximenis very reasonably says, should know his own capacity, and should, if necessary, dilute his wine accordingly. Catalan wine (he must have been thinking of the inky Priorato) is so dense and strong that it quickly numbs the mind unless water is added. But the French, he says, if they could, would even shake off the water the vine collects when it rains.

CHAPTER 12

THE CLOISTER
AND THE PRESS

The links between wine and worship, whether through the ancient gods, the Jewish and Christian rites, or the initiatives of monasteries and bishops, recur so often in our story that the storyteller must keep challenging himself: was it really religion that called the tune again?

With the white monks of Cîteaux there can be no mistake. For 500 years the Benedictine black monks had been the one great order, found their secure and splendid place in the scheme of things and grown stout and perhaps a little short of breath. Their greatest abbey of all, greater even than their mother-house of Monte Cassino, was Cluny, in the hills near Mâcon in the heart of Burgundy.

Suddenly, in April 1112, in the same Saône valley, an extraordinary young zealot named Bernard de Fontaine raised the stakes. At the age of 21 he led a band of 30 well-connected youths into the tiny new monastery at Cîteaux, just north of Beaune, which had been founded only 14 years before. The founder was an unusually ascetic black monk called Robert de Molesmes. He had been succeeded by an English abbot, Etienne Harding.

Cîteaux was the diametric opposite of Cluny; a little farm in the forest with a tiny chapel – but a powerful sense of purpose. Part of it still stands, and has recaptured, through years of adversity, some of the feeling of holy austerity that originally set it apart. Its monks borrowed the name of Cîteaux, calling themselves Cistercians, and wearing white habits instead of black.

The novice Bernard pushed them to the limits. His followers lived by the strict rule of St Benedict, but with the fervour of revolutionaries.

With these educated and fanatical volunteers, the new Order took wing. Bernard's rule of expansion was rigid. Once a monastery had 60 monks, 12 of them must set out and found another one. Within three years Bernard had founded La Ferté, Pontigny, Morimond and the illustrious Clairvaux on the borders of Champagne, where he himself became abbot. So powerful was the appeal of Bernard and his white monks that in 1124 the dying Pope Calixtus II willed that his heart be buried at Cîteaux. Bernard launched a virulent attack on the luxury of Cluny, soon supported by the king, Louis VI. From then on, the records of the Cistercians become like a diary of the spiritual life of Europe's nobility. Even the Holy Roman Emperor sent ambassadors to ask for the Cistercians' prayers.

129

By the death (and canonization) of St Bernard in 1153, he and his colleagues had founded some 400 abbeys, and filled his own abbey of Clairvaux with 700 monks. A century later, there were almost 2,000 Cistercian monasteries and 1,400 nunneries across the length and breadth of Europe. Two of England's most famous and beautiful abbeys, Fountains and Rievaulx, are typical examples, built in remote countryside where the Brothers could lead a secluded agricultural life. But by the time the Order had reached this size, you will hear without surprise that it too was becoming a trifle stout and short of wind.

While St Bernard's influence was in full command the white monks were a formidable force. Their recruits were intelligent, even learned, young people, and like St Columbanus's Brothers of 500 years before they worked until they dropped. The life expectancy of a Cistercian in the 11th century was 28 years. Much of this work was labouring in their abbey's vineyards. They brought to wine-growing the zeal and perfectionism that St Bernard demanded in everything.

On Christmas day of the very year of their foundation the Cistercians had been given their first vineyard, by the Duke of Burgundy, in Meursault. The first Cistercians to buy vines were the monks of Pontigny, who bought land at Chablis from the Benedictines of Tours (the land they had been granted by the king in 867). One story has it that they were the first to plant Chardonnay vines in Chablis (where Chardonnay is still known by the name of Beaunois).

In 1110, Cîteaux was given some land on the Côte d'Or at Vougeot (the Vouge is the name of the stream that supplies the abbey) and set about acquiring more. Abbot Harding was not too proud to ask for it. The Abbey of St Germain des Prés in Paris was among the religious houses that gave at least some of their "friches"; the rough, uncultivated fringes of their land. The bargain was a sort of "complant": St Germain was to receive one barrel of 228 litres a year. More land was soon given, bought, rented or exchanged, in Corton, Beaune, Chambolle, Volnay, Fixin, Pommard, Vosne, Nuits . . . eventually in almost every commune of the Côte d'Or south to Meursault. But it seems that Cîteaux at an early stage set its heart on the nearest slope of the Côte, where the Vouge rises and where they could quarry building stone. It was this unspectacular site, a gradual bench from the level of the plain to halfway up the hill, that they made the laboratory of their pursuit of perfection: the Clos de Vougeot. Eventually, in the 1330s, they enclosed it with the great stone wall you see today.

IN 1100 THE VINEYARDS OF BURGUNDY WERE IN STAGNATION. They were outside the fashionable ambit of northern France and had nothing but a local market. Nothing was really known of their potential. But the Cistercians saw the vineyards of the Côte as their God-given challenge. It has been said that in their devotion they raised agricultural labour to an art form. To supplement their saintly but limited workforce, they recruited and trained hundreds of "layots", or lay brothers, who wore brown habits: another contribution to the quality of burgundy – their painstaking methods spread by example throughout the region.

The Cistercians set about reviving a neglected vineyard, or making a new one, by careful study of the best plants, by experimenting with pruning, by taking cuttings and grafting, by the most careful winemaking, and above all by tasting.

Cistercian monks still farm a diminutive remnant of the abbey lands of Citeaux, just north of Beaune, although no vineyard remains. The late-medieval cloisters in the rich Flemish style are half-ruined. The illuminated capital, below, is from one of Citeaux's own medieval manuscripts.

Their greatest contribution to wine was the concept of the "cru"; a homogeneous section of the vineyard whose wines year after year proved to have an identity of quality and flavour.

They observed that differences of colour, body, vigour and other qualities in the wine were remarkably constant from one patch to another. They made small batches of wine from separate plots, compared the scores of samples of tithe wines that came their way, and began to form a picture of the resources of the Côte: which parts made a more aromatic wine, which more robust and rough, which suffered most from frost, which needed picking early; a whole data bank of information. Then they started drawing lines on the map; even building walls around the fields that regularly produced a recognizable flavour.

They were certainly lucky with their choice of region. Not everywhere in France can you find an escarpment with the peculiarities of the Côte d'Or. Its long line of low hills, facing east across the plain of the Saône, is a complex geological fault where a chunk of the earth's surface has slipped vertically several hundred feet. The result is a layer cake of exposed rocks of different ages, all eroding and mingling to form varying cocktails of soil and subsoil according to the lie of the land.

A modern Burgundian winegrower has said she believes the Cistercians actually tasted the soil; they were so acute in their perception of its qualities and where it changed. The Professor of Geology at the University of Dijon describes them as geologists who used their noses and palates to find out the soil and subsoil structure of the region.

Their skill is measured by their success. They began the process by which the name of a "climat", a particular named vineyard, designates a certain style and value of wine. Other monasteries and churches were not slow to follow their lead. The word "clos" means an enclosure of vines under one ownership. (For arable land the word is "couture".) The Cistercian nuns of Notre Dame de Tart at Genlis established the Clos de Tart at Morey, the chapter of the cathedral at Langres (whose bishop had moved to Dijon for better wine) had a Clos du Chapitre and named their Clos de Bèze after their Abbey of Bèze down near the Saône, the cathedral of Autun made a clos at Corton, the chapter of St Denis at Vergy owned the Clos St Denis, the parish church at Santenay owned the Clos St Jean, while the Abbey of Cluny, which owned most of Gevrey-Chambertin and had actually built a castle there to stress the point, is remembered by the Clos Prieur and the Combe aux Moines.

It was this process that divided and subdivided the Côte d'Or into hundreds of separate climats. But it only explains a handful of their names. Where do such names as Montrachet or La Perrière or La Romanée come from? In most cases they are, in the untranslatable French term, "lieux-dits"; that is, places with names – names that may refer to their stoniness (La Perrière), a bare hill (Mont rachet), or (La Romanée) the tradition that there was a Roman vineyard on the site.

With the Cistercians such names began to provide a focus, and to mean something in terms of wine.

THE ENORMOUS SUCCESS OF THE CHURCH IN CULTIVATING THE CÔTE D'OR had interesting repercussions. The first was jealousy. Duke Hugh IV of Burgundy was particularly irritated by the continuing complacency of the Benedictines. (St Bernard had described them as "rising from the table with their veins swollen with wine and their heads on fire".) "These clerics", said the Duke, "are growing rich at the expense of the nobility. . . . It is time we saw some of those miracles which seem to have been rather thin on the ground recently."

There were many reasons why the Church was growing richer, of which good management was only one. A major contribution came from the Crusades. Eight generations of Crusaders set out to recapture the Holy Land between 1096 and 1290. Each parting knight had the same concern: to insure his soul against damnation if he should die in sin far from home. They bought indulgences, they endowed chantries, and they gave the monasteries endless parcels of land. No one knows for sure how much land Cîteaux owned in its heyday. Its fortunes began to decline in the 15th century. When it was secularized by the French Revolution it was down to its last 25,000 acres.

Most important of all, perhaps, for the fortunes of Burgundy, and of the Cistercians in particular, was the papal quarrel of 1308, when Pope Clement V, the former Archbishop of Bordeaux, set up a rival papacy to Rome in Avignon. The Avignon papacy lasted for 70 years – on the strength, some say, of the wines of Burgundy. Such pleasure did the Avignon popes take in the wine they knew as "Beaune" that in 1364 Urban V issued an edict, or "bull", forbidding the Abbot of Cîteaux to send any Beaune to Rome on pain of excommunication. They also found consolation in the vineyards they planted in the stone-strewn soil around the Pope's new château just north of Avignon: Châteauneuf-du-Pape.

AT THIS AUSPICIOUS MOMENT, when everything was going right for Burgundy, everything began to go wrong for its liege lord, the King of France. John II, known as The Genial, was captured by the Prince of Wales, the fearsome Black Prince, at the second famous battle of Poitiers and removed with due deference, but a prisoner of war nonetheless, to England. Negotiations followed that substituted his son Louis as surety. Back in Paris, in 1363, the King appointed another son, Philippe de Valois (who earned the name "the Bold" at Poitiers – at the age of 14), to the vacant dukedom of Burgundy.

He was unlucky in his sons. Louis, in London, jumped bail, leaving his father no choice but to go back to England, where the next year he died. Philippe regarded Burgundy not as a fiefdom from France but as his private kingdom, which he contrived to double in size by marrying the heiress to Flanders. With Flanders came Bruges, which was then the richest port in northern Europe. For four headstrong generations, the Valois dukes swaggered colourfully and lawlessly on France's eastern border. It was Burgundy's century of glory, and for a while it made the wine of Beaune the most famous in the world.

Philippe the Bold paid close attention to this important asset. Thanks to the popes, Beaune's reputation was already so high that in 1321 it had been used for the coronation of King Charles IV at Reims. But in 1348 and again in 1360 the Plague had terribly reduced the workforce, especially the Cistercians. Quantity was out of the question; Burgundy's policy had to be quality. (Having no river transport northwards, in any case, it always made sense for a barrel of burgundy to be worth more than the cost of carting it.) The Duke put his strategy brilliantly to the test at a conference at Bruges between England and the Pope. He offered his guests unlimited amounts of the finest white wines of France, but only a rare taste of the red wine of Beaune. His point was made – and after centuries of preference for white wines, red Beaune became the rage.

UP TO THIS TIME VERY LITTLE MENTION WAS MADE OF THE GRAPE VARIETY. The best in the northeast of France, according to reports from as far apart as Burgundy and Paris, was the Fromenteau or Beurot, now known as the Pinot Gris (and in Alsace as the Tokay d'Alsace). It has pale red berries which produce white, or faintly "grey", juice, and makes excellently "stiff", that is, full-bodied and even dense, but aromatic and delicate wine. But in Burgundy mention was sometimes also made of the "Noirien", which presumably was so-called because its wine was "black".

Philippe the Bold was well aware that the Noirien was essential for his red Beaune. In 1375 the name Pineau appears for the first time. The Duke himself has been credited with selecting a superior form of the Noirien and giving it this name (which may derive from pine cone, in reference to its small, tight bunches). It seems more likely that if anyone selected a new and superior grape it would be the Cistercians. In any case, the Duke took the first and most important step towards an eventual appellation contrôlée by specifying the Pineau and outlawing an upstart rival that had recently appeared, the Gamay.

The Gamay's appearance was mysterious and spectacular. It arrived from nowhere (or more likely as a mutation of the Noirien) in the village of Gamay, south of Beaune and one valley back in the hills from Meursault, some time in the 1360s. To the growers it seemed like a miracle; the Almighty was almost apologizing for the Black Death. The Gamay ripened two weeks earlier than the Pineau, was more hardy and reliable, and bore so much fruit that it needed a trellis to

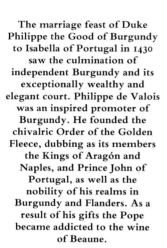

The marriage feast of Duke Philippe the Good of Burgundy to Isabella of Portugal in 1430 saw the culmination of independent Burgundy and its exceptionally wealthy and elegant court. Philippe de Valois was an inspired promoter of Burgundy. He founded the chivalric Order of the Golden Fleece, dubbing as its members the Kings of Aragón and Naples, and Prince John of Portugal, as well as the nobility of his realms in Burgundy and Flanders. As a result of his gifts the Pope became addicted to the wine of Beaune.

support it. One plant of Gamay gave up to four times as much wine as one of Pineau. What is more, the wine was darker and stronger.

What it did not have was the aristocratic elegance, the light texture and the glorious fragrance that made the world – or rather the worldly – hanker after Beaune. The Duke was enraged. In July 1395 he declared the Gamay an outlaw, "a very bad and disloyal plant", whose wine was "foul" – even "harmful to human beings". All plants must be destroyed before the following Easter. In the same decree he denounced the use of manure as fertilizer, saying that it gave the wines a bad taste and smell. His subjects did not take kindly to this decree. It caused an immediate shortage of wine, a slump in sales and the bankruptcies of leading citizens who had invested in this wonderful plant. Naturally, the growers stopped far short of pulling all the Gamay out.

The grandson of Philippe the Bold, Philippe the Good, was still issuing edicts against the Gamay 60 years later:

"It has been forbidden, time out of mind, to bring Gamay wines into Beaune. When new they flatter strangers with their sweetness" (the inference being that they disappoint them later). "The Dukes of Burgundy are known as the lords of the best wines in Christendom. We will maintain our reputation."

PHILIPPE THE GOOD BROUGHT THE REPUTATION OF BURGUNDY TO ITS HEIGHT. He insisted on the independence of his dukedom from France, siding with the English (and cynically selling them his prisoner, Joan of Arc, for 10,000 gold crowns). His court could be said to have staged its own renaissance, independent of the Italian renaissance of the same time. His Flemish court painters included two of the greatest artists of the Middle Ages, Jan van Eyck and Rogier van der Weyden. His Chancellor, Nicolas Rolin, founded the most famous of all hospitals, the Hospices de Beaune (where Van der Weyden's masterpiece, *The Last Judgment*, can still be seen). Philippe passed laws that brought Burgundy even closer to the concept of appellation contrôlée (although the term still lay five centuries in the future). He banned wine-growing from specified unsuitable land. Wine was the mainspring of the southern part of his Duchy; the raison d'être of Dijon and Beaune.

We cannot leave the Valois dukes without their appropriate coda. Pride led the next duke, Charles le Téméraire (Daredevil is a fair translation), to attempt the conquest of Alsace, Lorraine and Switzerland, to link them with Flanders and Burgundy and create a kingdom between France and the Holy Roman Empire as powerful as either. He was a great dresser and braggart, who covered himself with jewellery and is said to have invented military drill.

The combined Swiss, Alsatians, Austrians and Lorrainers decided that enough was enough. In the bitter winter of 1476, Charles laid siege to Nancy in Lorraine. Hundreds of his soldiers froze to death, rout followed, and the last Duke of Burgundy's body was found in a frozen stream, it is said, half-eaten by wolves.

THE CISTERCIAN ORDER WAS BURGUNDY-BORN, and as far as wine is concerned Burgundy is where it made its greatest mark. It would be wrong, though, to give the impression that wine was the only temporal preoccupation of the Order. It rapidly grew to resemble a modern multinational corporation, transcending national boundaries. It had every sort of agricultural investment from forestry to fish-breeding. Perhaps most profitable of all were its famous flocks of sheep, whose wool, coming particularly from England and Champagne, supplied the clothiers of Flanders and stimulated the great Champagne fairs.

Of the thousands of Cistercian monasteries that had vineyards, only one stands out in the history of wine with the same lustre as Cîteaux: the Abbey, or "Kloster",

---

ANCESTORS OF CHAMPAGNE

When the name Champagne was used in the Middle Ages it had nothing to do with wine. It was its great international cloth fairs that the region was famous for. They brought together merchants from all over Europe. So many Italians crossed the Great Saint Bernard Pass on their way to the fairs that extra lodgings had to be built for them.

The first references to the wine of the region of Reims and Epernay occur in the 9th century, and distinguish between the "vins de la montagne" (the "mountain" of Reims) and "vins de la rivière" (the river Marne at Epernay). Above the Marne stood the famous Benedictine Abbey of Hautvillers. The village of Aÿ nearby was rated highest for its (light red) wines; the king of France had vineyards there, and so, later, did the English royal house of Tudor. Its use in the coronation of the kings of France (from Clovis onwards) at Reims also gave the wine of Reims a special cachet, but its fate was usually to be drunk by the merchants and pilgrims, and all too frequently armies, that passed through the area.

The late 14th century saw a great expansion of the vineyards and the start of an export trade to Flanders and England. (Also perhaps to Bohemia, whose King Wenceslas, visiting Reims to confer with Charles VI in 1397 about the problem of two popes, got famously drunk.) The position of Champagne between the two parts of the Duchy of Burgundy did not encourage its progress in the 15th century; nor did the Wars of Religion that followed. Its rise to glory had to wait until the 17th century and the reign of Louis XIV.

of Eberbach, founded in the first great era of expansion in a typically tough Cistercian site: a forested valley in the hills of the Rheingau, on land granted by the Archbishop of Mainz. Its founders were Burgundians: 12 monks sent out by St Bernard from Clairvaux in 1136. Their dedication and efficiency had the usual result: within 30 years of its foundation it had a dozen satellites, and eventually became the centre of a monastic network with 200 establishments along the Rhine between Worms and Cologne. During the 12th and 13th centuries, Kloster Eberbach was the largest wine-growing establishment in the world.

Eberbach is the place to go both to see Cistercian splendour and to feel the pull of its asceticism. The great Abbey is completely hidden in a fold of the hills; a complex of cloisters, church, press-houses, dormitories and cellars that seems ready for a chanting file of white-robed figures to move in and set it all in motion again.

In fact it is not quite out of motion. Today it is the ceremonial headquarters of the State Domain of the Rheingau, and although its rows of giant wooden presses, not unlike the presses of an imaginary medieval newspaper, no longer open their great jaws, its lofty Gothic cellar is still full of wine. And above it on the hill, facing south towards the Rhine, its walled Steinberg, the Clos de Vougeot of Germany, is still planted with the Riesling vines that the monks planted – eventually.

At first they probably planted vines from Burgundy: Fromenteau and Noirien, perhaps. The Rheingau, like Burgundy, was only just finding itself as a wine region.

The Cistercian Abbey of Kloster Eberbach stands empty but almost
unaltered in its medieval splendour, the showplace of the Rhineland. The
vaulted hall now housing a magnificent collection of wine-presses was
formerly the refectory of the lay Brothers who worked in the vineyards
and the cellars.

The Burgundians may well have been surprised at how good their homegrown wine rapidly became. One can imagine them swapping notes with their Burgundian brothers, and soon discovering that nothing they could do in the Rheingau could make really satisfactory red wine.

Were it just for Mass and mealtimes, they might have settled for second-best. But Cistercians were entrepreneurs from tonsure to toe. Nothing could give them a cash income so quickly as wine of high quality. They tried white grapes, tried the steepest slopes, and found that the Rheingau was made for white wine.

Today the region is synonymous with the Riesling. Nobody is certain where it came from or whether it was the Cistercians who found it. The first documentary evidence we have is not until 1435, and then from Rüsselsheim on the Main, east of the Rheingau. There is, though, a direct link with Kloster Eberbach. Rüsselsheim was the castle of the Counts Katzenelbogen, and their family vault, an affair of typically chivalric panache, stands at the crossing of the Eberbach Abbey church.

Riesling or not, Eberbach wine set the standards for the region. From its own little harbour, or "hof", at Reichartshausen, the nearest point on the Rhine, the Abbey's three boats, the Bock, the Sau and the Pinth, relayed countless barrels to the Abbey's own gate and cellars in Cologne – passing all the customs posts with a duty-free smirk. As a measure of the importance of this trade to the Abbey, by 1500 its vines only covered 2.8 percent of its huge domain of 23,000 acres, yet they contributed three-quarters of its entire agricultural income.

The year 1500 is also the date of inauguration of the huge barrel, one of the first of its kind, which the Brothers built – not, you may think, in an excess of asceticism. It held 70,000 litres and was serenaded by the rhymer Vicentius Obsopaeus in some such words as these:

> The seven wonders of the world
> Have been increased by one.
> At Eberbach, as I've beheld,
> They've built a mighty tun.
> No, ocean is a better word,
> A sea of costly wine,
> And day and night it gushes forth
> Bacchus's drink divine.

Sad to say, the almost Babylonian high spirits engendered by the big barrel did nothing for community relations. In 1525 the peasantry stormed the cellars, drank the wine (or a good deal of it) and plundered the Abbey. But Abbeys, as we have seen, were accustomed to occasional unpleasantness. What mattered was that, by their readiness to experiment, their reinvestment in the land, and their ability to see things on a long time-scale, they slowly but surely moved the ratchet of quality up notch by notch.

CHAPTER 13

ENGLAND AND GASCONY: THE BIRTH OF CLARET

Every wine lover has an inkling of the fact that Bordeaux and England were almost literally married in the Middle Ages; an oil strike for Bordeaux and the start of the saga of claret that continues to this day. What had happened between its Roman budding and its medieval blossoming?

We left Bordeaux suffering the same sort of barbarian incursions as Trier, with the gentle phantom of Ausonius brooding over the dissolution of both these thriving Roman towns. In Bordeaux the unwelcome intruders were Goths, Vandals and Visigoths – and in short order; Goths arrived in 406, Vandals passed through in 408, and Visigoths came to stay in 414. To make matters worse, Bordeaux was on what the Romans had dubbed "the Saxon shore", by which they meant that no amount of patrolling could prevent the Saxon longboats from landing or their crews from helping themselves.

Gothic as they were, though, the new arrivals were not unimpressed by the old Gallo-Roman establishment. Not every move they made was a violent one. Having put the town to the torch as a matter of form, they sought out its leading families, intermarried with them, and were happy to take over their rational working of land and government. The Roman Emperor Honorius was content to acknowledge local Visigothic rulers. The old university professors of rhetoric and grammar were even given high rank at their court.

This extension of the Roman system was ended by the arrival of the Franks at the close of the 5th century. The 6th century is lost to us in a welter of Frankish princelings and Saxon earls. The 7th is complicated still further by the arrival of another cut-throat tribe, the Gascons, who came north from the mountainous headwaters of the river Ebro in Spain (just as, some historians believe, the Biturica grape had done six centuries before).

Loup, "Wolf", was the first duke to rule this new land of Gascony – whose frontiers were the Pyrenees to the south, and the mouth of the Gironde to the north. The Gascon era was interrupted by the advance of the Saracens, also from Spain. Duke Eudes of Gascony was killed in the defence of Bordeaux before the Muslims met their famous check at Poitiers. Now it was the turn of the Carolingian Franks.

Pepin the Short took Bordeaux in 763. The following year Charlemagne made his brief appearance in the city's history; although only to build a castle at Fronsac on the Dordogne as a marker for his southwestern ambitions. The Carolingians seem to have appointed Ducs des Gascons not so much "of" the Gascons as in charge of them. But it was not the Gascons they had to worry about; it was the latest and most devastating of the sea raiders, the Vikings. The city withstood three waves of Viking attack before it fell. The Carolingian duke was killed. Even then the Gascon leader – whose name, Sanche Sanchez, confirms his Spanish blood – struggled on, nursing the last glimmer of Roman Burdigala until nothing was left. The archbishop, Frotaire, left a totally devastated town in 870 and fled to Poitiers.

There is some evidence that wine-growing survived these centuries of changing management. The principal customers were Ireland and the western Celtic fringes of Britain. Eastern England imported wine by the shortest route, from northern France and the Rhine. But after 870 there is a silence of nearly 250 years.

WHILE THE ECONOMY OF THE NORTH GATHERED PACE in its burgeoning cities of the 10th and 11th centuries, Bordeaux remained a purely nominal seat of power. Gascony (or Guyenne) was now part of the larger Aquitaine, which stretched north as far as the river Loire and included Poitou. Bordeaux was dignified with an archbishop and a duke (now of Aquitaine), but was on nobody's route anywhere – except the pilgrim road to Compostella in northwest Spain.

The court of Duke Guillaume X in 1120 was famous for its elegance, its troubadours and chivalry – and for the Duke's beautiful daughter. But its economic motor was in the north, and this is where the Duke concentrated his ambitions. His western shore, including the islands of Ré and Oléron, was one of the principal European sources of salt, evaporated from the sea in lagoons – and this in an age when salt was almost the only preservative. He promoted, with enormous success, the new port of La Rochelle. La Rochelle was described as "vicum mirabile de novo constructum" – a wonderful new town. It attracted shipping from all the northern ports of Europe, and to add to its attractions its ambitious immigrant citizens planted vineyards. The area (now the Charentes) is sunny and relatively frost-free. By extensive use of the crop-sharing system of "complant" they made it a sea of vines, with the deliberate intention of undercutting the "vins de France" and the Rhine wines that everyone drank in northern Europe. They created a sort of medieval Muscadet (although it would have tasted closer to modern Gros Plant) – and no one went on south to pay more in Bordeaux.

IN ROME IN 1130 THERE WAS A DRESS REHEARSAL FOR THE ROW that later established the Pope in Avignon. Two rivals were both elected. Duke Guillaume and his appointee, the Archbishop of Bordeaux, backed the losing side. For his soul's sake, the Duke found himself on the road to Compostella, leaving behind, in the care of King Louis VI of France, his 17-year-old daughter Aliénor. The Duke died in Spain. As soon as he heard the news, King Louis sent his son and heir (who was only 16) to Bordeaux with a train of 500 knights to collect a bride and her enormous dowry: Aquitaine and Poitou; the southwestern third of France. They were married in the Cathedral of St-André in Bordeaux in July 1137.

Louis the Dauphin adored his young wife. He was also devoutly pious. But Aliénor was a girl of strong character, and not at that stage either particularly pious or in love. Her duchy was her first concern; to be Queen of France was secondary. Her husband appointed favourites to office in Bordeaux; she resisted every one. She quarrelled with his spiritual advisor, Abbot Suger of St-Denis, and had a running battle with Bernard of Clairvaux, who found her altogether too fine. Nonetheless, when Louis (now King) went on the second Crusade to the Holy Land she went with him – all the way overland; an immensely dangerous and tedious journey. (Acre in Palestine she found more to her liking than pious Paris.)

Back in Paris in 1151 the court received a visit of homage from the Duke of Normandy and his 18-year-old son, Henry Plantagenet. Aliénor, aged 29, compared the fiery youth with her religious husband, and decided on a change. Bernard of Clairvaux was consulted. Astonishingly, after 15 years of marriage (and two daughters) the King and Queen of France returned to Bordeaux to be ceremonially de-wed – on the grounds that they were cousins who should never have been married in the first place.

Eight weeks later Aliénor married Henry Plantagenet, Duke of Normandy and Count of Anjou. Two years after that, in 1154, he became King Henry II and she Queen Eleanor of England. The famous link was made.

THE FORTUNES OF BORDEAUX DID NOT CHANGE SUDDENLY. Eleanor followed her father in favouring La Rochelle. Her new husband was an Angevin, a man of Anjou on the Loire: his inclinations were also towards the northern part of their duchy. Unlike Louis, and although ten years his wife's junior, Henry did the real ruling. "When the King decides to travel", wrote his chaplain, "he starts at dawn, almost

THE VINE IN ENGLAND

The Domesday Book, William the Conqueror's acre-by-acre survey of his new English realm, gives us the first good information about the growing of wine (or at least grapes) in England. It mentions a total of 42 vineyards, including several in London and Westminster, the greatest concentration in Essex, east of London, and the northernmost at Ely, which the Normans called L'Isle des Vignes, much as their forebear Leif Ericson a century before had called America Vinland. Ely is an isolated hill in fen country, crowned with a cathedral already venerable before the Normans arrived; it is reasonable to believe that the Anglo-Saxons had been growing vines there for – who knows how long? Since the Romans?

England's vineyards were never extensive, but were an accepted accompaniment to any castle or monastery in the south. The royal Windsor Castle made its own wine in 1155. The Cistercian Abbey of Beaulieu near Southampton on the south coast naturally had a vineyard. It seems to have been the Archbishop of Canterbury who had most, but probably none were commercial, and no tasting notes have survived.

The acquisition of Bordeaux did not lead to any marked decline in English vine-growing – although it may have discouraged its extension. Nonetheless it spread through the Middle Ages, so that in 1509 there were 139 vineyards, of which 11 were owned by the Crown (on the head of Henry VIII), 67 by noblemen and 52 by the Church. "Theologicum" was the name given to the best (monastic) wine – whether generally or specifically is not known. At the dissolution of the monasteries in the 1530s their vineyards were appropriated by the local nobility. The antiquarian and headmaster of Westminster School, William Camden, travelled throughout the country to compile his survey *Brittania*, which appeared in 1586. His conclusion was that wine-growing had declined not due to the climate or the exhaustion of the soil, but to the sloth of the inhabitants.

without warning. Everyone is thrown into confusion. Men run about, urging the packhorses; chariots collide and all hell is let loose."

Eleanor bore him eight children, of whom four sons and three daughters survived. But she led a cloistered life among her troubadours at Poitiers and her nuns at the Abbey of Fontevrault, avoiding England, her masterful (and much-mistressed) husband, and his minister Thomas à Becket – another Suger, she may have thought, only a worldlier one. Trouble came when Henry divided his realm among their sons, crowning Henry, the eldest, King of England during his own lifetime, in the medieval manner, and the second, Richard, Duke of Aquitaine. Geoffrey, the third, married the heiress to the Duchy of Brittany. The old king left it to the new to provide for the youngest, John . . . in vain. The court called him Jean Sans Terre; the Anglo-Saxon peasantry, John Lackland.

Eleanor saw her chance to regain power, at least over her own duchy, and intrigued with her sons against their father. It was a messy business, plunging England and France into a dynastic war. Henry forgave his sons, but not her: she became a prisoner in England until he died, in 1189, a great but disillusioned king who must have felt about his sons as Lear did about his daughters.

The young Henry had meanwhile died, and Richard, his mother's favourite, inheriting both England and Aquitaine, released her and restored her to her French dominion. At last, in the 1190s, Bordeaux began to come into the picture. With its cathedral and ducal castle, it became King Richard's base in France. (Although from 1190 to 1192 he was away on the third Crusade, earning himself the surname of Coeur de Lion.) But La Rochelle still had favoured treatment. In 1190 the Queen-Duchess built it a new port, whose monumental walls still stand. New deep-draught freighters, known as cogs, were coming into use in northern ports, and needed

The ships that did the carrying in the wine fleets of the Middle Ages were called "cogs" or round ships. This 15th-century miniature of the King of France riding into the harbour at Sluys in Flanders shows how round and tub-like they were. Their capacity was measured in the number of "tuns", or wine barrels, they could carry: sometimes over 200 in a big cog, which needed a crew of 40 or more. Monarchs had a special interest in their wine ships, both as a principal source of revenue (through customs) and as the basis of their navies.

better anchorages and deeper wharves. Bordeaux began to complain bitterly that the royal favour continued to rain on the makers of down-market white wines around La Rochelle, while a great log-jam of old feudal dues and customs prevented its venerable wine industry from competing at all.

Royal favour was all-important. The wine the king drank today, everybody would drink tomorrow. It was Richard Coeur de Lion who first made Bordeaux his household wine, but since he lived almost constantly in France he can hardly be said to have popularized it in England.

When he was killed, besieging a Limousin castle, his mother manoeuvred her last surviving son onto the throne. (It is said she inspired the murder of her grandson Arthur, son of Geoffrey, the other main claimant to the crown.) John Lackland, therefore, was the King of England who first gave Bordeaux merchants a fair chance at the English market.

In 1203 at the Château de l'Ombrière, the seat of Plantagenet power in Bordeaux, he, with his mother presumably prompting him, accepted the arguments of Bordeaux's citizens that lower taxes would means higher revenues. Unblock our port, they said, and let our city prosper. John still drove a bargain. In exchange for vessels and support against the King of France from Bordeaux, Bayonne and Dax, the three ship-owning towns of Gascony, he exempted them from the principal tax on their exports, the so-called Grande Coutume, or Great Custom. Gascon merchants were at last to start coming to England.

At this point the 82-year-old dowager, the grand old ex-Queen of both France and England (Shakespeare rather sourly called her "a canker'd grandam"), died and was laid to rest beside her estranged husband at Fontevrault. Her last matriarchal act had been to cross the Pyrenees in winter to inspect her Spanish granddaughters.

LA ROCHELLE AND POITOU OBJECTED LOUDLY TO GASCONY'S NEW PRIVILEGE – so loudly that the next year the King was obliged to give them the same exemption. But the following year the intervention of yet another adventuring monarch gave Bordeaux a fortuitous advantage in royal favour. King Alphonse of Castile, who had married one of the daughters of Henry and Eleanor, another Aliénor, laid claim to Guyenne. The people of Bordeaux bravely resisted and survived a siege. King John's thanks this time took the form of an order for wine, and the acknowledgment of the first mayor of Bordeaux, one Pierre Lambert.

Another ten years and he was ordering a worthwhile quantity: 120 tonneaux of "Gascon wine" from Bristol. This was in 1215, the year when his troubles came to a head and he was forced by his nobles to sign the Magna Carta. Yet still there was jealous manoeuvring between Bordeaux and La Rochelle for the King's favour. What finally decided it against La Rochelle was not the acidity of its wine, but the disloyalty of its citizens.

In 1224 the King of France made a determined effort to chase the English out of Poitou and Guyenne. The mayor of Bordeaux had the pleasure of writing this magnificently smug letter to England: "We believe it right to tell you that the Château of Niort and the town of St-Jean d'Angely" (both in Poitou) "have given themselves up to the King of France, and that without constraint of force. The same King is at this moment before the walls of La Rochelle. As for ourselves, we are resolute to resist the enemies of the King of England and to keep our faith with him." The letter went on to say how they had pulled down houses to reinforce the walls of Bordeaux, all at their own expense. "We will defend Bordeaux, the town of our lord the King of England, whom we will never fail faithfully to serve, so long as life is left to us."

Sure enough, La Rochelle capitulated to the King of France. Its merchants had lost the English market. Perhaps they shrugged their shoulders. Flanders, Germany and the Baltic were still looking for cheap wine. But from this date Bordeaux took every advantage of its unique relationship with England. Its citizens pressed for, and in 1235 were given, the right to elect their own mayor in perpetuity (a right which Bristol had only acquired in 1217, and even London itself only in 1191).

THE QUANTITY OF WINE ENGLAND BOUGHT, and the speed with which Bordeaux was suddenly ready to supply it, suggests that huge vineyards had already been planted in the region in readiness. In fact it was not so. Bordeaux had started out in Roman times as an "emporium", and when her star rose in the 13th century was again more of a port than a producer. The area immediately around the city, especially the district of Graves to the south, was the principal vineyard of Bordeaux. There were also vineyards along the steep banks of the Garonne opposite the port (today the Premières Côtes), in Entre-Deux-Mers, between the Garonne and the Dordogne, and others along the estuary at Blaye. The Médoc had hardly any vines. The grand total was not very impressive.

It was the Aquitaine basin as a whole, reaching right up into the "high country" around, that supplied the bulk of England's needs. Most Gascon wine came down the Garonne from Gaillac (high up in the Tarn), Moissac and Agen, and, closer to home, St-Macaire, Langon and Barsac, or down the Dordogne from Bergerac and, although less important at first, St-Emilion. Cahors, high up the river Lot, was

THE MYSTERY OF VINTNERS

To be a wine merchant in Bordeaux in the Middle Ages had distinct advantages. Not only did the system of privileges known as the "police des vins" work in your favour, but wealthy and dependable Gascon merchants could also become Freemen of the City of London, and take advantage of reduced duties there too. To be a Freeman of both London and Bordeaux was a licence to print money – which is more or less what the grandest Gascons did, lending to the king in competition with the great Italian bankers.

Gascon merchants were, of course, subjects of the English king, who was ready to do almost anything to secure their loyalty against the French. Edward I was believed by Londoners to be especially partial to the Gascons. Much to the City's dismay, in 1302 he passed ordinances that exempted Gascons from the usual petty (but very expensive) regulations that applied to overseas merchants. He had good reason. Besides the throne, he had inherited his father's quite remarkable wine bill. This was his way of paying it.

The Gascons in London were even granted the right to establish their own association, the Merchant Wine Tonners of Gascoyne, later known as the Mystery of Vintners and in 1345 incorporated by royal charter as the Vintners' Company – one of the richest and most splendid livery companies throughout the Middle Ages. It still survives near its original site in the City, at Three Cranes Wharf by the Thames. A tablet on the wall of the present Hall records the "Feast of Five Kings" at Vintners Hall in 1363, when Sir Henry Picard gave a banquet to Hugh IV of Cyprus, Edward III, John the Genial of France (who was a prisoner in England), the King of Scotland and King Waldemar of Denmark.

France's finest medieval bridge, the Pont Valentré, was built over the river Lot at Cahors in 1308. Cahors was famous not only for its High Country wine but for the usurious bent of many of its merchants.

another provider of what were called generically High Country wines, to distinguish them from the produce of Bordeaux itself. In all probability they were often better, stronger wine than most of what Bordeaux made locally, and the Bordelais were correspondingly jealous of them and anxious to sell their own production first.

It is hard to exaggerate how important timing was. The wine Bordeaux sold, although certainly a degree fruitier, possibly a degree stronger, and probably a more pleasant and satisfying drink than the northern whites it began to supersede, was no less perishable. It was expected to turn sour within a year at most, and tasted best within a few months of the vintage. Year-old wine was halved in price as soon as the ships with the new vintage dropped anchor. In many cases it was simply thrown away.

All the politicking that went on over the privileges of this town or that turned on this simple fact. And Bordeaux, an ideal port lying between most of its rivals and the sea, was beautifully situated to send its wines to market before allowing its rivals to offer theirs. Gradually, during the course of the 13th and 14th centuries, the city arranged for itself a code of unfair practices guaranteeing its precedence over its neighbours and rivals – a system known as the "police des vins". It was tolerated by the kings of England chiefly because it simplified their tax collecting. When Bordeaux eventually became French again it was tolerated to prevent seditious backsliding by those who thought they had a better deal under the English.

Not that Bordeaux had suddenly become England's only supplier. Anjou wines were still in demand, being relatively ripe and sweet, and Rhine wines were perennially popular. The wines of Burgundy, which we have seen beginning to flourish at the very same time as those of Bordeaux, scarcely reached England. But the "vins de France" that used to flow in an acidic stream from Rouen were quite outclassed by the new Bordeaux. Moreover, from Bordeaux to Bristol, London, Southampton, Hull, Berwick or any of a hundred little ports around the coast was relatively convenient door-to-door transport. By the middle of the 13th century three-quarters of England's royal supplies were coming from Bordeaux – and by "royal" we should understand not just the King's table, but his households', the civil service, his gifts and favours, and indeed the supplies for his entire army. In 1282, Edward I ordered 600 tonneaux for his campaign against the Welsh.

BOTH SIDES TOOK ADVANTAGE OF THE NEW SITUATION. Hitherto useless royal lands in Bordeaux suddenly became valuable. King John and his successors, Henry III and Edward I, all sold, leased or granted land for the planting and building boom that swept the region. Such newly prosperous towns as Bergerac were soon petitioning for charters – which of course had their price. King Henry III built his own walled town to control the traffic on the river Dordogne: Libourne, founded in 1270 by the King's Seneschal, his chief officer in the region, Sir Roger de Leyburn. Libourne effectively took away the trade from neighbouring Fronsac and St-Emilion's little port of Pierrefitte. St-Emilion in any case grew more grain than grapes; it was a busy little town with many mouths to feed; a sharp contrast to the wild hillside where 400 years before St Emilianus had found his lonely hermitage.

The figures for the 1308 vintage show that Libourne exported nearly 11,000 tonneaux of wine, or 97,000 hectolitres. Most of it would have been grown in Bergerac. But this was only one-sixth of the massive volume that all Gascony exported that year – and the other five-sixths went through Bordeaux. It helps us to realize the size of the Bordeaux-England wine trade to read that the year before, 1307, King Edward II had ordered, for his wedding celebrations in London, 1,000 tonneaux of claret, which Edmund Penning-Rowsell has gleefully calculated to be 1,152,000 bottles. The Florentine bank that financed this huge purchase was the house of Frescobaldi, which we shall meet again.

In the first half of the 14th century we have complete records for seven years' exports. The annual average was 83,000 tonneaux, or 700,000 hectolitres; of which it has been calculated that the British Isles took almost half . . . to eke out among its population of perhaps five million. At a conservative estimate that was six bottles of claret for each man, woman and child.

To make this much wine, considering the much smaller yields of medieval vineyards than today's, it is estimated that the whole of Gascony must have had approximately its current modern total vineyard acreage, or about 100,000 hectares.

The French "tonneau" is the same as the English "tun" or "ton", a measure of wine described as "XII score and XII gallons" (i.e. 252 old – or American – gallons, or 900 litres). This size of cask is unmanageable, so it is broken down for shipping into two "pipes" or four "hogsheads" (now usually called "barriques") of 225 litres each. In modern terms, a tonneau equals 100 cases of a dozen (75cl) bottles of wine, a barrique 25 such cases.

In the Middle Ages all ships were gauged as to how many tons (of wine) they could carry. It was the practice in ancient times and is still in use today – although for bulk carrying a ship's "ton" is 100 cubic feet. A "metric tonne" is 1,000 kilograms weight. A hectolitre is 100 litres.

Today the same surface produces about three times as much wine. But only after World War II was this export figure reached again. In 1900, which you might well think was a good claret-drinking year, the total was about 12,000 hectolitres less than that of 1308.

IT WAS HARDLY LIKELY THAT IN THE LONG RUN France would allow the English king to rule a substantial part of its land. Already the French had recovered Poitou. The new French king, Philippe VI, was more determined. In 1338 he sided with the Scots against England and tried to stop the export of English wool to Flanders, the country's principal source of revenue. Edward III of England replied by claiming the French throne and, forming the first great fleet in English history – 200 ships, mostly wine freighters – off the Suffolk coast at Orwell, set out for France. At Sluys, just off Ostend, the English won the first battle of a war that lasted 115 years, and ended with the loss of all of Gascony.

The "Hundred Years' War" went on in fits and starts, mercilessly pursued by the Black Prince, interrupted by the Black Death; so black a chapter, indeed, that calmly to chronicle the commerce of one provincial city seems almost callous.

The flow of claret was never so great again as in the years before the war. For much of the time the High Country was in French hands. In the 1340s the French attacked and devastated many of the vineyards of the Dordogne and the Garonne. The king gave orders for all English and Gascon ships – which came, incidentally, from Bayonne, not from Bordeaux – to sail in convoy for safety. Froissart's *Chronicle* for 1372 describes the impressive sight of 200 ships standing as close-hauled as a cog could manage up the broad estuary of the Gironde. In that year the price of freight was 22 shillings a ton – compared with eight shillings in the years before the war.

The wine fleet convened twice a year, in October and February, to fetch the latest vintage. The east coast ships met first at Orwell, then sailing to the Isle of Wight met the Portsmouth fleet. With a favourable wind they could be in Bordeaux within a week. Waiting for the wind, though, could be a matter of months – in which case the wine must certainly have suffered. Often they had to shelter or revictual, usually at Port St-Mathieu on the western tip of Brittany where Brest stands today. They were provided with expensive passports by the Duke of Brittany. There were plenty of Breton pirates, however, who could not read.

Although the total quantity of Bordeaux wine fell, England needed a higher and higher proportion of it, as war with France in the north cut off the supplies of alternatives. In the 1390s, when a lengthy truce led to easier conditions, England still took 80 percent of Bordeaux's exports.

Some of the best wine available came from the estates of the archbishop, who grew a little red wine at Pessac in the Graves, and much more at Quinsac, ten miles up the Garonne. Bertrand de Goth, who later, as Pope Clement V, moved the papacy to Avignon, clearly saw his chance to capitalize on the boom. His Pessac estate, now known as Château Pape Clément, was planted in 1300, when exports were at their height. That year more than 900 ships cleared Bordeaux for England. It was only a small property, but it stands within a mile of the château where the next great Bordeaux boom was to be born 350 years later. The archbishop also grew white wine in the terraced vineyards of his villa across the river from the town, within sight of the cathedral, at Lormont – where no vines grow today.

How good even archiepiscopal wine could have been it is not easy to judge, although detailed records survive of how his estates were run. Bordeaux winemaking was no different in essence from the winemaking we have seen in Chapter 11, except that in Bordeaux presses were decidedly uncommon. It was a region of small producers, without lordly domains or great monasteries which would own a wine-press.

Many explanations have been put forward as to why the French word "clairet", anglicized as claret, is applied uniquely to Bordeaux. One, of course, is that during the 300 years of its Bordeaux dominion England learned it too well ever to forget it. Strangely, though, its use is not recorded in English, as opposed to French, before the 16th century. But from the outset it seems almost certain that very light red or rosé was the best wine (apart from white) that Bordeaux had to offer – or at least that it suited English taste, and the demands of the voyage to England.

Claret was made as a vin rosé is made today; or, more precisely, what the French call a "vin d'une nuit" – one that spends a single night in the vat. The grapes were trodden in the usual way, and the wine fermented at first in the vat on the skins – many of which in any case would have been white – but for no longer than 24 hours. Then the pale liquid was run off into barrels to ferment as clear juice. The wine left with the skins in the vat for longer became redder; it was known as "vin vermeilh" or "pinpin". It represented perhaps 15 percent of the crop, but like press-wine was considered too dark and harsh on its own. A little might be used to add some more colour or edge to claret; the rest was sold off for what little it was worth – when, of course, they made "piquette" with the skins alone.

It is tempting to compare claret, pale, light, highly swallowable, soft enough but with a refreshing "cut", to modern Beaujolais Nouveau. This must have been the general effect; although the flavour of Beaujolais is the pungent one of Gamay. Claret was presumably made with the ancestors of the Cabernets and the Merlot.

The end of the Hundred Years' War came in 1453. The later phase of the fighting, begun by the headstrong Henry V of England, had seen Normandy and most of the north of France retaken by the English, the heroic efforts of Joan of Arc, and an alliance between England and Burgundy that seemed to put France in a hopeless position.

The outcome was decided by Burgundy. It is too far-fetched, but amusing nonetheless, to say that it was Burgundy that severed Bordeaux from England. In 1435 Duke Philippe the Good changed sides (his reward was the province of Picardy) and the English, whose King Henry VI was a boy of 13, were put on the defensive. His courtiers, acting as regents, quarrelled constantly and bloodily. Affairs of state have rarely been in such a mess.

In 1438 the French entered Gascony and devastated the vineyards. A truce followed: on second thoughts this was part of France. The object was to throw the English out, not to destroy such a valuable asset. The French set about wooing the Gascons. England seemed neither able nor desperately anxious to keep its ancient possession. At home, civil war was breaking out between Yorkists and Lancastrians.

In Bordeaux a decade of prosperity followed, in which the pro-English archbishop, Pey Berland, did everything he could to coax English support. In 1451 the French closed in, taking the fortresses of Blaye and Bourg on the Gironde and Libourne (and St-Emilion) on the Dordogne. In June their commander, Dunois, took the peaceful surrender of Bordeaux itself.

But after 300 years the English made one last effort. The following autumn the venerable John Talbot, Earl of Shrewsbury, led a fleet up the Gironde and landed in the Médoc. The people of Bordeaux opened their gates to welcome "le Roi Talbot". He retook Libourne and Castillon with a mixed English and Gascon force and in July 1453 set out to meet the French, commanded this time by the King himself, just outside what is now called Castillon la Bataille. It is a tale still often told in Bordeaux that the aged Talbot, having once been released as a prisoner on the promise not to bear arms against France again, led the charge at Castillon (in his 80th year, say the true believers) without sword or lance. He and his son were both killed, and the French went on to accept the surrenders of Libourne and, in October, despite all the archbishop's efforts, Bordeaux.

Of course, what sounds like a great finale is nothing of the sort. Every year produces wine, and growers and merchants must go on living. The French gave the English six months to ship the 1453 vintage. They gave Gascons free leave to take themselves and their goods abroad. They grudgingly and selectively granted safe-conducts to English vessels coming for wine, while they invited Scots, Dutch, Flemish, Hanseatic and Spanish to come and buy freely, hoping to widen the narrow scope of the trade. (The Scots needed no encouraging; claret was already an important part of the victuals of that kingdom.) For a single year, they allowed the High Country wines free movement, but soon realized that if Bordeaux was to be kept loyal to France, the old oppressive restrictions had to stay.

Twenty years later, with finances pinching, the port was thrown open again to English and Gascon shipping. There were nervous moments in Bordeaux when as many as 7,000 Englishmen congregated there in the shipping season. But trade did not recover its old impetus. The vineyard area contracted, and shipments to

THE POLICE DES VINS

The privileges of Bordeaux, impudently established during English rule, were still effectively in place in the 18th century. Louis XVI's reforming Minister of Finance, Turgot, summed them up in a document that tells the whole unworthy story:

"Languedoc, Périgord, the county of Agen and Quercy; all the provinces linked by the multitude of rivers that join beneath the walls of Bordeaux, not only cannot sell their wines to the citizens of Bordeaux who may want to buy them; these provinces cannot even freely use the river highway that nature has provided to link them with foreign trade.

"The wines of Languedoc are not allowed down the Garonne before St Martin's day; they cannot be sold [in Bordeaux] before December 1st. And those of Périgord, Agen, Quercy and all the upper Garonne are barred from Bordeaux until Christmas.

"By this means the growers of the wines of the High Country are kept out of the market at its busiest season, when foreign merchants are obliged to hurry their purchases to get the wine home before ice closes their harbours. Nor are they allowed to store their wines in Bordeaux to sell them next season: no wine from outside the Bordeaux region can remain in the town after September 8th. The owner who cannot sell his wine before that date has the choice of distilling it

The final surrender of the city of Bordeaux to the French, after 300 years
of English rule, took place with due solemnity at the city gates in
October 1453.

England were down to 10,000 tons a year from the 13th-century peak of more than
80,000. Part of the reason was jealousy of continued Gascon privileges in England
which the English shippers did not like. France was also to become embroiled in its
bitter wars of religion, with Bordeaux a stronghold of Protestant dissent. Another,
and the most important, reason, was the growing number of attractive alternative
wines being offered by friendlier countries.

or taking it back up-river with him. By this
arrangement, the wines of Bordeaux have no
competition whatsoever between the vintage and
December 1st.

"Even in the low season between December
and the following September the trade in High
Country wines groans under multiple yokes.
They cannot be sold immediately on arrival; they
cannot be transshipped directly from one vessel
to another, either at Bordeaux or any other port
on the Garonne. They have to be unloaded and
taken ashore, and that not even in Bordeaux
itself, but in the suburbs, in specified parts of the
suburbs, and in special cellars separate from the
wines of Bordeaux.

"Wines from outside the region have to be
kept in barrels of a certain design, whose volume
is deliberately inconvenient for foreign trade.
These barrels, banded with fewer and more
feeble hoops, are less durable and less able to
withstand long voyages than the exclusive barriques of Bordeaux.

"The conduct of this set of rules, most artfully
devised to guarantee to the bourgeois of Bordeaux, the owners of the local vineyards, the
highest prices for their own wines, and to
disadvantage the growers of all the other southern provinces . . . is called, in this town, the *police
des vins* . . . and it has the full authority of the
Parlement."

CHAPTER 14

MERCHANTS OF VENICE

It is a fine November day in the Bay of Biscay – too fine for the wine fleet, almost 200 ships spread out from horizon to horizon. Their great square sails, gaudy with dragons and crosses and leopards, are hanging flaccid and useless. The master of the *Margery Cross*, a heavy cog or round ship from the port of Boston on the east coast of England, is looking out from the high sterncastle for any flurry on the oily swell that could mean a breeze.

He has 160 tuns of claret before and aft his great chunky mast. It has taken two weeks from Bordeaux to get this far; the weather is unseasonably warm; at this rate he could still be at sea come Christmas, the market past and the wine turning sour.

A dozen of the crew are throwing leather buckets over the sides and hauling them up to the yard to soak the sail, with the only effect that the *Margery Cross* wallows slightly more ponderously as each unhelpful roller lifts her port quarter and trundles on towards England. There is nothing else for his 40 mariners to do – and not much for them to eat either. He has his passport for Port St-Mathieu where there should be bread and meat, but until then the rations are bread and claret – and not very much bread.

His eyes follow a gull to the horizon astern. What is that? Three, no four, strange broad ships, very low in the water, their masts bare of any sail, but definitely coming clearer into view, closing the gap at an impossible speed. Once or twice a flash like a mirror in the sun breaks from the water low beside one of them. Oars! He has heard of the galleys that keep an uncanny, an impossible schedule between Genoa or Venice and Southampton. The merchants of Southampton had craftily convinced the king to give them a monopoly on importing Mediterranean wines, which did not endear them to the wine merchants of other English ports.

Now the crew have seen them too, and are crowding to the stern with their foul language and their fouler breath. The Winchelsea cog groaning as she rolls three chains off to starboard has suddenly come alive, with half her crew in the rigging, shaking their fists at the galleys, now clear to see, four in formation, with what seems like a thousand oars beating the water; four brown and gleaming birds flapping their wings.

Within the morning they have passed through the becalmed fleet, all agog at their mechanical propulsion. On each side were three banks of oars, 20 blades to each. The great lateen sails furled on the booms of the two masts pulled hard for most of the journey, but when the wind died the oarsmen, each one a small private trader with his bag beneath his bench, bent their backs to beat their famous schedule. The record passage had been made by a Venetian galley, from Otranto on the heel of Italy to Southampton on the Solent, in 31 days.

As they creamed through the fleet the archers on the decks of the galleys raised a cheer, then lifted their crossbows and sent a broadside of bolts high through the air, puncturing the impotent heraldry of the sails and here and there thudding with a shock into a mast. The arrogance of the Venetians was not to be borne.

GENOA, THEN VENICE, HAD BECOME THE POWERS OF THE MEDITERRANEAN. They were the link between the riches of the east and the mere money of northern Europe. What had woken the Italian cities from their long slumber had been the Crusades. The monarchs of the north and all their retinues had needed transport, and victualling, and to borrow huge sums of money. The first coastal city to awake was

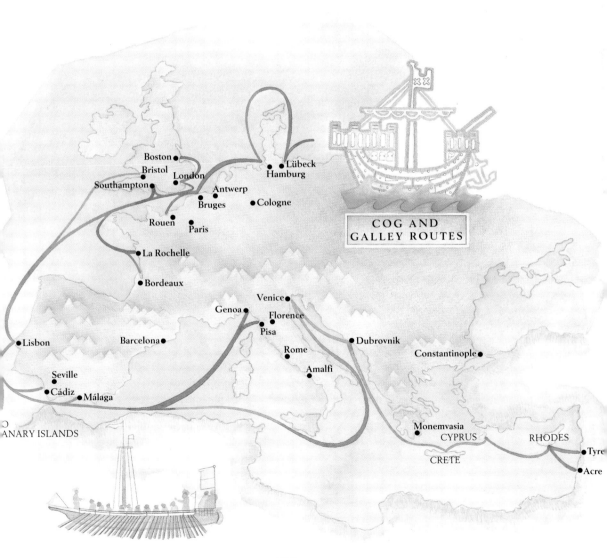

The war galleys of Venice returned in triumph to
the lagoon beside the Piazza San Marco to
salute the Doge, the elected ruler of "the Serene Republic",
after defeating a Turkish fleet.

Amalfi, across the Sorrento peninsula from the Bay of Naples, which Greeks and
Romans had so profitably occupied before the barbarians came. Amalfi was the
outpost of Byzantium in a Saracen lake – the whole Mediterranean – until the lake
almost swallowed it, literally, in a tidal wave.

Pisa in Tuscany was active too, and soon joined by Genoa in expeditions that
were as much like piracy on the Saracen shipping as legitimate trading expeditions.
They were beginning to perform the role of trading links, buying silks and spices in
the east and carrying eastwards such mundane things as grain, timber, salt and of
course woollen cloth in return. There was an extraordinary emphasis on wool. So
important was it to the growing wealth of Florence (and hence of Pisa) that the
house of Frescobaldi, operating as papal tax gatherers in England to finance the
Crusades, were eager to be paid in bales of wool rather than cash.

AMONG THESE ADOLESCENT RIVAL CITIES, VENICE had several great natural
advantages. It was (like Amalfi) historically part of the Eastern Roman Empire of
Constantinople. It had in the Adriatic what almost amounted to a private sea.
Strongholds on strategic islands were effective against pirates. Ragusa (now
Dubrovnik) was such a rich ally that to this day the term argosy, meaning a ship of
Ragusa, is a synonym for bounty. Above all Venice was on the highway to the Holy
Land, and uniquely able to act as travel agent, banker, and to provide any other
service that Crusaders or pilgrims needed.

HIGH ON THE LIST OF THE TRAVELLERS' NEEDS WAS WINE. They found it all along whichever route they took – for they were travelling through the countries of the Romans and the Greeks; rediscovering, in fact, the qualities of sweetness and strength that the ancients had so much appreciated, but that were unknown now in the north.

Falernian and the other Grands Crus of Rome were long since dead, but Greece and her islands, the Empire of Byzantium, had never entirely abandoned their traditions. The eastern Mediterranean was largely under Muslim control, but this had not stopped the making and selling of wine by Christians and Jews. The whole of the Levant, Syria, Lebanon, Palestine had wines to sell. Where Byblos had been a byword for excellence in ancient times, Tyre was now the name to conjure with. After the success of the first Crusade in establishing Christian kingdoms from Egypt to Armenia, the monastic orders moved in and planted vineyards with the same single-mindedness as they were doing at the same time in Burgundy and Germany. In the 10th century Byzantium had won back the islands of Cyprus and Candia, as Crete was then called, from the Saracens; both were excellent sources of wine, whose importance grew and grew throughout the Middle Ages.

At first there was not a great deal of discrimination between wines from these different sources. The term most generally used was Malmsey or Malvasia. The word is a corruption of Monemvasia, a Byzantine fortress town on the

CRUSADING

There were eight Crusades in all, whose avowed purpose was to liberate the Holy Land from the Infidel. From first to last was nearly 200 years. The only one that could really be called a success was the first (1097-99), which captured Jerusalem, Palestine and most of the Lebanon, a large part of Syria and the coastal part of Armenia.

All this territory had already been in Muslim hands for more than 400 years. Under the caliphs, pilgrims had been respected and well treated. The Koran venerated Christ. But in 1076 Jerusalem was taken by a new barbarian race which had overrun the caliphate of Baghdad: the Seljuk Turks. These were Tartars with a mere veneer of Islam. They were brutal to pilgrims, and evidently had no intention of limiting their conquests to the east.

Europe, in piety and alarm, took up the cross, the Normans to the fore, and retook Jerusalem with a barbarity that shook even the Seljuks. Five Christian kingdoms were set up in the Levant. Acre (or Akko) became the great Crusader fortress. For most of the 11th century the Holy Land was a magnet for pilgrims and sightseers. Monasteries (and new military orders of monks) were established. Vineyards inevitably followed. The second Crusade, in 1147, preached by St Bernard and followed by Louis VII of France and his Queen Aliénor, was prompted by a revival of Arab activity but proved both unnecessary and abortive.

In 1187 the greatest of Saracen sultans, Saladin, retook Jerusalem and all the Holy Land except the city of Tyre, prompting the third Crusade (1189-92). The King of France, the Holy Roman Emperor Frederick Barbarossa, the Duke of Austria and Richard Coeur de Lion joined in an impressive force. But misadventure, opportunism (Richard helped himself to Cyprus) and the brilliance of Saladin flouted them. They retook Acre but failed to take Jerusalem. Face was only saved by a treaty that allowed pilgrims free access to the Holy City – which the gentlemanly Saladin, in any case, was inclined to grant.

The fourth Crusade got no farther than Constantinople, which it incontinently sacked. The fifth was sidetracked to Egypt. The sixth reestablished Christian toeholds on the coast at Jaffa, Tripoli and Antioch. The seventh suffered a similar fate to the fifth.

The eighth Crusade, in 1270, saw the final victory of the Saracens. Acre, the last Crusader stronghold, fell in 1291, those of its inhabitants who could fleeing to Cyprus.

southwestern corner of the Peloponnese. It may have been a small producer; it was certainly a large supplier, giving its name to wines grown on the mainland, but mainly on Candia, and no doubt on such islands as Santorini in between.

Monemvasia also gave its name to the grape variety that produced them. The Malvasia, with many synonyms (in French it is Malvoisie) is alone with the Muscat (and all its synonyms) in having maintained its name and identity clearly throughout the centuries. With its big leaves and its slightly blushing fruit, giving dense and impressive wine, it is a character that stands out – and indeed one of the most venerable varieties we have. What is odd is that it should have picked up the name of a medieval port that made it famous, rather than carrying some reminder of its even remoter past.

In the Aegean the island of Chios resumed its role as a principal supplier, both growing its own and trading in wines from what in Dionysus' time was Phrygia, then a part of the fragmenting Byzantine Empire, and today is western Turkey. In 1261 Chios became a possession of Genoa, which gave it a market wherever the Genoese galleys traded.

In the Ionian Sea, Corfu, Zante and Cephalonia, all islands under Venetian dominance, made sweet wines of lesser quality that were sold as Romania, which was anglicized as Romaney or Rumney. Most highly prized were the Muscadels (as well as the Malmseys) of Candia. Muscadel, with its fresh grape flavour, was so sought after that plantations of Muscat vines were made in Roussillon in the south of France, in Spain and in Italy. Tuscany's lightweight version of Moscadello remained in favour throughout the Renaissance and greatly took the fancy of those followers in the path of the Crusades, English milords on the Grand Tour.

Tuscany also specialized in Vernaccia, which has been justly described as Italy's native Malvasia; its wine having the same soft texture and potential strength, although it was generally made less sweet. To the English, Vernaccia was known as

INSTRUCTIONS TO A PILGRIM

A 15th-century Italian priest, Santo Brasca, gave good advice to pilgrims for the Holy Land:

"In the first place, a man should undertake this voyage solely with the intention of visiting, contemplating and adoring the most Holy Mysteries, with great effusion of tears, in order that Jesus may graciously pardon his sins; and not with the intention of seeing the world, or from ambition, or to be able to boast 'I have been there', or 'I have seen that', in order to be exalted by his fellow men, as perhaps some do . . .

". . . he should carry with him two bags – one right full of patience, the other containing two hundred Venetian ducats, or at least one hundred and fifty . . .

". . . let him take with him a warm long upper garment to wear on the return journey, when it is cold; a good many shirts, so as to avoid lice and other unclean things as much as possible;

and also tablecloths, towels, sheets, pillow cases and such like.

". . . he should go to Venice, because from there he can take his passage more conveniently than from any other city in the world. Every year one galley is deputed solely for this service; and although he may find it cheaper to go on a sailing ship, he should on no account abandon the galley. He should make an agreement with the captain, who usually requires from fifty to sixty ducats. For this price he is obliged to provide the passage there and back, supply all food (except on land); pay for the riding animals in the Holy Land, and also pay all duties and tribute.

"In the Holy Land carry a cushion, and never leave the caravan of the pilgrims, and do not venture to argue about the faith with those Saracens, because it is a waste of time and productive of trouble."

The Aegean island of Santorini, or Thera, is the rim of a vast volcanic crater whose eruption in c. 1500BC destroyed a civilization closely related to that of nearby Minoan Crete. On its wind-scoured volcanic soil only vines will grow. When the Ottoman Turks took the island in 1579 they continued to encourage wine-growing despite their religion, being happy to collect taxes from a thriving industry. Santorini later became the principal supplier of Vinsanto for Mass to the Orthodox Church of Turkey's arch-enemy, Russia.

Vernage. French historians have confused it with Garnache (alias Garnacha or Grenache), one of Spain's most important varieties. The name of Garnache seems to have fallen out of use in 1500, at the same time as Alicante and Málaga, two ports on the Spanish coast not far from Granada, first appeared as the names of wines. (The Grenache grape is also called the Alicante, which seems to make that connection pretty clear.) Vernage, however, continued to be so described (and much appreciated) by Italians at least a century later. One Pope (a Frenchman) so doted on the Vernaccia grown in the precipitous Cinqueterre vineyards of the Liguria coast that he would have the eels for his supper, his favourite dish, drowned in the wine before he drowned them a second time with deep imbibing.

WHAT ALL THESE WINES HAD IN COMMON WAS MORE IMPORTANT than what distinguished them apart. In the Mediterranean sun their grapes reached a very high sugar content, which was encouraged by late harvesting, and often boosted by half-drying the bunches before they were trodden. Winemakers (if they could read) used the old textbooks; no doubt they practised both twisting the stems and piling the grapes on mats in the sun. The Cypriot method was described by Estienne de Lusignan in 1572. The grapes, he said, were ripe at the end of July, but were not picked until September. "When they have been gathered, they are put on the roofs of the houses, which are all flat, and remain there in the sun the space of three days, so that its ardour may consume whatever water may remain in them." The wine, in other words, was made from raisins.

Natural fermentation, especially if it was kept under control by burying the wine jars in the classical manner, could achieve as much as 17 degrees of alcohol from such sugar-rich must – almost twice the strength of the thin northern wines. There would often be unfermented sugar even at this strength. This combination of sweetness and a warm glow as it went down was strong drink indeed; the strongest anyone had tasted until the introduction of distilled spirits. And it had a yet more important quality. It would keep, and travel long distances, without turning sour. Its high alcohol content preserved it; even, under the right conditions, made it capable of maturing.

There is no question that it was considered a luxury, and would have been drunk exclusively by the rich: in the 14th century only three taverns out of nearly 400 in London were licensed to sell it retail. Wholesale, it was at least twice the price of claret. The most expensive price recorded was for a tun of Vernage: £10. In terms of prestige sweet wines came first; Rhine wine or "Rhenish" second. Claret was the everyday drink.

THE DOMINICAN FRIAR GEOFFREY OF WATERFORD was one of the earliest correspondents to bring back critical notes, in 1300. What he said, in a nutshell, was that the farther east you went, the stronger the wines became. In the Bataille des Vins in 1224, Cyprus (one of the easternmost) had won hands down – perhaps simply on grounds of strength. One question that remains a puzzle is that some pilgrims found Cyprus wine delicious; others, such as Pietro Casola, who wrote a detailed account of his pilgrimage in 1494, with copious advice for others, were evidently offered retsina, and did not like it.

Of Cyprus, Casola wrote: "Everything in that island pleased me except that they make the wine with resin and I could not drink it." Of the Peloponnese, where he visited a town near Monemvasia, he also reported: "The wines are made strong by the addition of resin during fermentation, which leaves a strange odour. They say the wines would not keep otherwise. That odour does not please me." One is inclined to suspect that there was local wine and export-quality wine; certainly nobody in London ever mentions Malmsey or Cyprus being resinated.

In the time of the Crusaders, Cyprus was considered in northern Europe to supply the finest wines in the world. Their sweetness and strength made them the ultimate luxury. The best was (and is) Commandaria, which took its name from a religious Crusading order that settled on the island. In effect it is raisin wine. The grapes in this ancient Commandaria press, still in use, are the traditional black Mavron.

Casola also visited Candia, where (with his delicate nose) he found the local custom of emptying all the chamber pots into the street at the sound of a bell exceptionally smelly and disgusting. Here, though, the wines were excellent – "malmseys and muscatels, not only in the city but also in the whole island, especially in a city called Rethemo". Sure enough, extra-quality Malmsey turned up in London under the name "Rotimo". The name of the port today is Rethimnon.

This was the wine the Genoese and Venetian galleys carried so profitably to England and Flanders: a luxury to compete for space on board with silks, spices, carpets, or the damask and steel of Damascus.

IN 1204 THE HOOLIGAN ELEMENT IN THE FOURTH CRUSADE had sacked Constantinople, and Venice, helping herself to the pickings of the broken Byzantine Empire, appropriated Candia. Opportunism was a Venetian speciality. Her power steadily grew through the strict and brilliant organization of her trade. At first Genoa had the upper hand; it was Genoa that pioneered long-distance bulk-carrying "carracks" of 1,000 tons or more. Venice then built even larger galleys. There were pitched galley battles with Genoa and Pisa (which can be seen in lurid detail on the walls of the Doge's palace). Venice came off best.

By land she took advantage, like other Italian cities, of the great Champagne fairs of the 13th century not just to trade but to set up a banking empire. When the fairs lost their momentum her ruling Signoria pioneered the eastern Alpine passes, the Brenner and the Saint Gotthard, giving her direct access overland to the Danube, and via the Rhine to the string of trading cities that culminated in Cologne, Bruges and London. By sea, her galleys and round ships steadily gained a monopoly of the route through the Strait of Gibraltar, stopping at Lisbon, then forging on to England and Flanders.

In the 15th century Venice extended her colonial dominion to Cyprus. After the fall of Acre, Cyprus had become the headquarters of two of the military orders of monks founded in the Holy Land: the Knights Templars and the Knights of St John, or Hospitallers (who had run the great 1,000-bed hospital at Acre). The Templars had departed, their great wealth appropriated by jealous princes – especially Philippe IV of France. The Hospitallers also moved on, to Rhodes, which they held for 200 years, but kept a Commandery, a sort of embattled priory, in Cyprus, where they continued to make the island's best wine; the intensely sweet Commandaria. The Commandaria vineyards are in the region of Pitsilia, reaching up above Limassol onto the Troodos mountains. Today the villages of Kalokhorio and Zoopiyi grow respectively the white Xynisteri and red Mavron; stunted vines in ashy and sandy soil that must have looked very much the same when the Venetians arrived.

Venice, of course, was the archetypal exploiting colonist. She planted so many cash crops, mainly sugar, cotton and vines, that the inhabitants had nowhere to grow their food and the population dwindled. Sugarcane in particular is a terrible robber of the soil, making it difficult to restore fields to a healthy system of rotation. When eventually the Ottoman Turks captured the island in 1572 the people rejoiced; at last they were allowed to grow what they wanted rather than what the Venetians wanted to sell.

The tough commercial system of Venice did not allow direct carrying, even by her own ships, from foreign port to foreign port. Everything had to come to Venice on the way. Specialist merchantmen, the largest for the longest voyages, went back and forth to Alexandria, Tripoli, the Black Sea, Cyprus, Flanders, Aigues-Mortes in the south of France. Venice was the entrepôt for it all; a unique mart that tied together east and west and north. It was a serious blow for her when in 1488 the Portuguese discovered the Cape of Good Hope. A direct sea route to the Indies meant that Venice's quasi-monopoly of oriental luxuries was over.

WHEN SHAKESPEARE WROTE *The Merchant of Venice* the subject was a familiar, if not a topical, one. England and Venice had conducted a long trade war about the shipping of Malmsey. The Venetians had seen an opportunity when England lost Bordeaux (it was the same year as the Turks took Constantinople) and without delay had sent the English king eight butts of the their finest wine. England took the bait. Malmsey became the rage. In 1472 a Venetian galley with more than 400 butts of sweet wine for England was taken by French pirates in the Channel. In 1480 the English royal Duke, George of Clarence, invited to choose the method of his execution for treason, chose, according to the Flemish contemporary historian Philippe de Commines, to be drowned in a butt of Malmsey.

For 25 years the Venetians charged 50 shillings for a butt of 130 gallons, and were prepared to be paid two-fifths of the value in cloth. Having created a strong demand, they then began to reduce the supply, sending fewer and smaller barrels, down to 108 gallons, charging more than three times as much and refusing cloth as part payment. The English reacted by sending their own ships into the Mediterranean: gingerly at first – not many English cogs had been that far since King Richard's crusading fleet. One of the first recorded voyages was that of the

THE SERENE REPUBLIC

Venice in the 15th and 16th centuries was the first great Mediterranean wine emporium since the Ostia of the Ancient Romans. Apart from importing Malmseys and other sweet wines from Candia, Greece and Cyprus for re-export, her merchants filled their waterside *maggazini* with wines from both shores of the Adriatic and Venice's own hinterland, made as strong as possible after the Greek model.

The traditions of winemaking in Dalmatia, Istria and their islands are probably a Venetian revival of ancient practice. Such wines as the Grk of Korčula, Vugava of Vis, Dingač and Postup of the Pelješac peninsula and the notoriously heady Prošek all involve sun-dried grapes.

Greek Malmsey vines were planted in Istria around Fiume (today Rijeka) beside the local Teran, which on the stark "karst" limestone of this coast gives powerful wines. Prošek is made of a grape called Marastina, which on the island of

Hvar makes the excellent strong Čara-Smokviča – apparently quite unrelated to the Prosecco that provides Venice's light dry sparkling wine, the "ombra" or "little shade" of Venetian cafés.

The blockade by the Turks of their eastern supplies stimulated the Venetians to develop the vineyards around Verona and on the volcanic Eugenean hills south of Padua, even nearer to home. Bardolino, Valpolicella and Soave are three regions that were encouraged to make high-alcohol wines by half-drying their grapes. The tradition persists in the powerful Recioto Amarone of Valpolicella and Soave.

A more lasting contribution of Venice to wine culture was the art of clear glassmaking (lost since the Romans) that the Serene Republic imported from Syria to its island of Murano in about 1300. By the 16th century, Venetian glass was affordable for admiring fine wines and began to be imitated all over Europe.

This mural in the Church of San Martino dei Buonomini in Florence
shows the deeds of compassion: giving food to the hungry and wine to
the thirsty. The wine appears to be being distributed directly from the
fermenting vat.

Anne of Bristol, whose master, Robert Sturmy, reached the Holy Land with her in
1446. Her fate was not one to encourage others; she was wrecked on Chios, where
she had gone for wine on the way home.

By the end of the century there were many more merchant venturers willing to
try – especially as Florence, seeing the chance to steal a march on Venice, opened her
port of Pisa to foreign vessels. Pisa had Vernage to sell. The noble houses of Antinori
and Frescobaldi, bankers and general traders in the Florentine style, drifted into the
wine business by such means; the Antinoris as early as the 1380s.

Venice became anxious and imposed a tax on Malmsey bought in Candia by
foreigners. England's King Henry VII retaliated in the obvious way by taxing
Malmsey arriving in England in Venetian ships. But there was fresh competition
now for Venice and her sweet wines: new Malmsey-style wines being made in Spain
and Portugal. Well might Antonio, in *The Merchant of Venice*, be "sad to think upon
his merchandise". He had, said Shylock, rubbing his hands, "an argosy bound to
Tripolis, another to the Indies . . . a third for Mexico, a fourth for England." Venice
and her competitors stood on the threshold of the New World.

CHAPTER 15

CASTILIAN CONQUEST

"The day is damp with dew and the cheek of the earth is covered with a down of grass. Thy friend invites thee to partake of the enjoyment of the two pots now cooking on the hearth, which give forth an excellent aroma, and of a jug of wine in this most beautiful place. More could he offer should he so desire, but it is not seemly that too much pomp should be displayed to a friend."

This invitation, charming in its mock modesty, was written by an Andalusian Arab of the Middle Ages. It invokes the spirit of Al-Andalus, the most civilized corner of Europe in the years of the Carolingian Emperors and the invasions of the Norsemen – and for many years after that. At a time when Paris was still a cluster of buildings on an island in the Seine, Córdoba, with 100,000 inhabitants, was the greatest city in western Europe – and not just in scale, but in cultivation and learning.

Córdoba was the pearl of the Arab world, which after its triumphant century of conquest had divided into three caliphates: Baghdad and Cairo in the east, Córdoba in the west. The climate of Al-Andalus, seductive enough today, must have been paradise to the desert dwellers, with its rivers and fertile soils, its matchless grazing, its snow-capped cordilleras and its palm-fringed coast. Andalus probably means "end of light" – the western land where the sun sets. Its inhabitants lived a life of unfanatical ease, as our host's gentle letter shows. Omar Khayyam would have been happy in his company.

THE FIRST THRUST OF THE ARAB INVASION had taken it right through Spain and into France, where it was turned back at Poitiers by Charles Martel. Christian Spain in the 9th century, the inheritance of the Visigoths from the Romans, was cornered in the northern seacoast kingdom of the Asturias, as different from Andalusia as Normandy is from Provence. The two Spains, indeed, are complementary. The south needs the dour products of the north just as the north desires the products of the south. But while northern and southern Europe found each other in the Middle Ages through their developing commerce, the two Spains had to meet through the bloody wars of the Reconquista.

It was the king of the Asturias who started to push south. In 844 King Remiro I was facing the Moors on the field of Clavijo, near Logroño in the Rioja, when there appeared a mysterious knight whose banner was a red cross. As he scattered the fleeing Moors, the Christians recognized him as St James the Apostle, known from his temper as the Thunderer. The apostle had preached in Spain, the story went, in Galicia in the northwest corner, and his bones had been buried there. Spain and the Reconquista had found a patron saint, and his shrine at Santiago de Compostella became almost as great a pilgrim goal as Jerusalem itself.

The Christian-Moorish frontier moved fitfully south from the 9th century on. The Moors had never occupied the north; there were never enough of them. Nor were there enough Christians to occupy whatever territory they won. The north was inhabited by a mixture of peoples: descendants of the Visigoths, of Roman and pre-Roman Iberians, Basques and Catalans. The south also had a mixed population; of many tribes of Arabs, of Syrians in Córdoba and Seville, Egyptians in the Algarve, of Berbers from Africa, and (probably in the majority) of pre-conquest

LAND OF THE
CATHOLIC KINGS

Spaniards who were converts to Islam, but still spoke their Latin-based language. Al-Andalus was richer as well as more populous than the north, but scarcely more cohesive; in such a vast, almost empty land, government tended to be by local rulers paying tribute to the caliph, rather than central control. The frontier was more or less dangerous, but no real campaigns were possible, or seemed worthwhile, until the 11th century.

The folk hero of this time is El Cid. His name is a corruption of El Seyd, "the Lord" – the light in which many of the Moors viewed such a formidable soldier of fortune. Fortune, more than faith, was the name of the game. The rules were simple: athletic and well-armoured Christians demanded protection money from local Muslim rulers. The protection package included trouble from other Muslims, too. These tributes in gold, known as "parias", were a practical way of earning from the wealthy south without invading it. Why interfere with such a majestic and successful civilization? Besides, what was the point of conquering territory if you had no followers to guard it or even to farm it?

BY THE TIME OF THE FIRST CRUSADE TO THE HOLY LAND the frontier ran almost across the middle of Spain. Portugal was Christian as far south as the river Tagus; Toledo became Christian in 1085; on the east coast the boundary was near Alicante. The Moors now took a more active interest in their frontier and called for Berber help from Africa. Both sides tensed, and military religious orders were founded by the Cistercians, the Templars and others for a Spanish Crusade. Still there was another century of intermittent conflict and colonization, with adventurers and settlers coexisting in uneasy partnership as they do on any frontier, before the monarchs of the north started a concerted invasion. Las Navas de Tolosa in 1212 was their set-piece victory. Ferdinand III of Castile and León was the king who took Córdoba in 1236, Murcia in 1243 and Seville in 1247. His cousin, Jaime I of Aragón, with a Catalan fleet from Barcelona took the Balearic Islands and, in 1238, Valencia. Cádiz fell in 1262. On the map Moorish Spain was reduced to the Kingdom of Granada – which was to remain Moorish for another two centuries.

The map is not necessarily an accurate guide. A town might fall, but its inhabitants did not change religion – nor even necessarily lose their property. There was often nobody to move in and claim it. In the case of Córdoba or Seville with their famous wealth there were plenty of takers. No fewer than 21 Genoese

---

A FRONTIER TOWN

The son of Ferdinand III of Castile and León was Alfonso X, known as "El Sabio", "the Wise". He busied himself colonizing western Andalusia, from Seville to Cádiz, where the mainly Moorish inhabitants were still resisting Christian government by a monarch as far away as Castile, closing the gates of such towns as Jerez and Arcos in the hope that the Christians would go home.

In 1264 a series of simultaneous planned revolts broke out. Ten cities joined in resisting the king. Jerez held out against him in a seige that lasted five months. His answer was to expel the inhabitants (who were allowed to go to Granada or Morocco) and find new ones from among his knights. There are landowners and sherry-makers today (the Valdespinos are an example) who can trace their families directly back to Alfonso's reconquistadors. Jerez became Jerez de la Frontera: for a century the frontier against the armies of Islam in the Kingdom of Granada, the scene of many scuffles and at least one more full-scale siege.

merchants set up shop in Seville, seeing its potential as the great port of the west. But in less glamorous areas there were often more houses than people, and their new royal masters had to make extravagant land grants – "latifundias" – to fighting men to persuade them to settle down. The vacuum also drew in many immigrants from France, England and Germany.

THE MOORS HAD NEVER BEEN SHORT OF WINE. Vineyards were plentiful in the south; it was a matter of conscience whether you took your refreshment in liquid or pill form. As the Reconquista gradually settled the rest of Spain, the planting of vines was a top priority. Wine was considered an absolute essential, a fundamental daily provision for all.

From the 10th century the Ebro valley, the plains of the Duero and the green hollows of Galicia were equally planted, and as the Christians controlled more land

The castle at Jerez de la Frontera was built by the Moors, then taken and re-embattled by the knights of King Alfonso of Castile in the 13th century. For a century it marked the frontier between Christian and Moorish Spain. The Moors of Valencia were meanwhile making their wine in great earthenware tinajas (these date from the 15th century), freely copied from the ancient Roman "dolia" which must still have survived in Andalusia.

The spiritual history of the Rioja since its brief occupation by the Moors can be read in the stones of San Millán de la Cogolla. Its ancient hillside church has Mozarabic columns and Visigothic tombs. In the fertile valley the great Benedictine monastery of Yuso sheltered pilgrims on the road to Santiago de Compostella: one of the well-travelled tracks led right through the Rioja.

farther south, and monasteries, many of them Cistercian with Burgundian connections, followed the reconquistadors, viticulture became inseparable from any settlement. A vineyard belt gave a green and welcoming look to the surroundings of every town and castle. To plant vines was to make a claim of permanence in holding the land, would certainly give pleasure and had been known to bring solid profit. Moreover, in many areas it was legally enjoined. In Galicia a peasant leasing land under a form of contract from a monastery was instructed to plant vines wherever they would grow, and where they would not to plant chestnuts – which would feed the pigs.

By the 13th century, all the inhabited parts of Spain grew wine except the mountainous extreme north, which therefore became a target for all winegrowers within reasonable range – which was surprisingly far. Rioja, Navarre, León, the Duero and the vineyards of Galicia all competed for this northern market.

The Duero probably made the best wine, because its main consumers were the citizens of the important cities of Castile: Burgos, Salamanca, and above all the capital, Valladolid. But fashions changed. In the 13th century it was Toro (and to a lesser extent Zamora) that had the great name – for its powerful dark red. Toro continued to be the drink of the dons of the great university of Salamanca for centuries; one draught was enough to make them forget their lectures. A little later it was the district of Rueda, south of Valladolid, that was in vogue.

Some of the earliest wine ordinances, dating from 1423 (renewed with modifications in 1592), set out in minute and tedious detail exactly what wine could be brought into the capital, in what quantity, when and by whom (viz, Ordenanza No. LX: "That not more than one day be taken in unloading wine", or No. XLVIII "Forbidding citizens of the town to negotiate with persons from outside so as to pretend that the wine originates inside"). And this despite the fact that Valladolid's own wine was notoriously bad, from low-lying, "dew-soaked" land, and that of its neighbour Cigales only marginally better.

For the best wine they went 30 miles south, to Medina del Campo – the site of international fairs that almost, it was said, rivalled the great fairs of Champagne. When Medina del Campo was at its zenith, in the reign of Charles V, its (white) wines were expected to age, cost twice as much at two years as at one and lasted up to ten. In 1607 the town had 478 bodegas, or winemaking establishments. The crops were tiny: only six hectolitres per hectare. Undoubtedly they were making very strong, concentrated wine capable of resisting bacterial attack and oxidizing gradually and harmlessly in its barrel – the term was "rancio": in fact a sort of primitive sherry.

Unfortunately, the cupidity of the Medinites led them to stretch their famous wine with low-strength "mostos" from outlying areas. Their reputation and prosperity passed on, in the 17th century – but not very far, to Nava del Rey, a few miles west. In due course Nava (whose pride and joy was a pit of the finest clay, perfect for fining its wine) was challenged by the towns of Rueda and La Seca – but we are approaching modern times: this was in the late 18th century.

Burgos drew most of its supplies from the Ribera del Duero, the region of Aranda and Peñafiel, whose wine was dark red, not particularly strong and not a good keeper – which will surprise anyone who knows the resounding reds of the region today. They include the legendary Vega Sicilia, a Gargantua of a wine, and such wines as Pesquera and Protos, which are seemingly ambitious for similar legends of their own.

THESE WERE NOT THE WINES THAT THE WORLD OUTSIDE SPAIN EVER MET – or very rarely. Some Rioja wine was exported via Bilbão or Santander. It was known as "Ryvere" (presumably from the river Ebro) and appreciated for its "sweetnesse". The first requirement for an export wine is a port, and those nearest busy sea-lanes were first in the running. Shipping between northern Europe and the Mediterranean put into northwestern harbours in Galicia, occasionally into the Portuguese Minho, into the estuary of the Tagus, and into the Bay of Cádiz or the estuary of the Guadalquivir, the river of Seville. The crusaders were occasional customers at the ports of Galicia and northern Portugal: it was the last place they could stop and load wine before sailing down the long Moorish coast of the peninsula, where they could hardly have expected a friendly reception.

As the Reconquista opened up the west coast farther south to Christian wine drinkers, references to Andalusian wines begin. In the 14th century the English poet

TENT

The name "Tent" is now extinct, but it applied to dark red wines from the coastal zone near Cádiz, especially from the town of Rota, from the Middle Ages right up until the middle years of the 19th century.

Tent (in Spanish, "tintilla" or "tinta di Rota") was described as "a rich wine, drank generally as a stomachic" – in other words, after dinner. In the 1830s it had about 13.3 degrees of alcohol; no more than many a modern red burgundy. In all probability the grapes were those known to the French as "teinturiers", whose juice is as red as their skin. Some compared it with the red wine of Alicante, but said it was darker and more mellow. It was certainly classed as the best red wine of Andalusia. Samuel Pepys had a small cask (a "runlet") of Tent in his cellar, and it appears on Victorian menus.

Why the wine and the name died I cannot tell. In being a completely English term for a dark red wine, "Tent" is directly comparable with, and complementary to, "claret". It would be pleasant to see it reintroduced for that general class of wine, such as Australian Shiraz, California Zinfandel, and indeed such dark Spanish reds as Duero (as opposed to paler Rioja) wines.

Chaucer described the wine of "Lepe" (a village near Huelva, between Jerez and the Algarve), "of which there riseth such fumositee" that after three draughts the drinker doesn't know whether he is at La Rochelle, Bordeaux, Lepe or home in bed. In fact he was talking about a remote ancestor of sherry. Any remaining idea that 14th-century Englishmen had hard heads should be dispelled by Chaucer's French contemporary, Froissart. He recounts how the archers sent by England's "king-maker", John of Gaunt, on their way to help King John I of Portugal against the Castilians, landed in Galicia. The best of the local wine there, Ribadavia, is not very different from the vinho verde of northern Portugal; light and acidic. Nonetheless, says Froissart, the Englishmen found it so "ardent" that they could scarcely drink it, and when they did, they were helpless for two days afterwards.

They evidently came back for more, because Ribadavia became one of the most-exported Spanish wines. Closeness to Compostella must have helped; at the height of its popularity the pilgrimage there counted up to two million foot-sloggers a year, each in his long cape and broad-brimmed hat with scallop shells. By the 16th century the restrictions on what might or might not be sold as Ribadavia at the port of La Coruña were so strict as almost to amount to an appellation contrôlée. English merchants, it is said, helped with their knowledge of shipping, and introduced the use of sulphur. Then, as so often with medieval, and particularly Spanish, wines, a change in the political tide made the customers move on. In this case it was the cooling of Anglo-Spanish, and warming of Anglo-Portuguese relations in Queen Elizabeth's reign that made merchants sail a little farther south, to the Minho, and buy their (not very different) wine at Viana do Castelo.

A third wine that emerged on the northern market in the 1380s as a result of ships calling at Lisbon was the long-defunct Osoye. Although there is some confusion between variant spellings of both Auxerre and Alsace, there is no doubt that 14th-century Osoye was a sweet wine from Azoia, a harbour just south of the Tagus near Setúbal (now famous for its Muscatel) where fishing boats put in for salt

SOUTH OF THE TAGUS

Portugal has such ideal conditions for wine-growing, and the northern part of the country is so thickly planted with vines, that it seems an anomaly that the southern one-third of the country, the Alentejo or land beyond the river Tagus, has almost no wine-growing tradition.

In both ancient times and during the Moorish occupation this was wine country, but the wars of the reconquista were particularly fierce in the Alentejo, and the constant capture and recapture of the land over a long period left it destitute and depopulated. The first King of Portugal, Alfonso Henriques, gave every encouragement to the Cistercians to bring their agricultural skills and in 1153 granted them an enormous estate at Alco-baça, north of Lisbon, which eventually became the largest of Cistercian monasteries, controlling an area of 360 square miles. The austerity of St

Bernard was soon forgotten in the magnificence of an establishment with up to 900 monks, and with a refectory and kitchen described (in 1774) as "the most distinguished temple of gluttony in Europe". It was the very success of the north that starved the south of resources, particularly after the Black Death decimated the population and again when the Age of Discoveries emptied the countryside of farmers.

Royal grants of land in the Alentejo were on a huge scale, and to fighting men who were more inclined to cattle-ranching and hunting than laborious viticulture. Large areas were left as wild forest (with valuable cork oaks) for hunting. Grain was the crop that Portugal needed most; so the Alentejo was left vineless. Where vines have been planted since, the wines have shown as much potential for quality as any in the country.

to preserve their catch. Perhaps Osoye was even a Muscatel, with vines replanted from the Levant (Genoese galleys called at Lisbon) and the real forerunner of Setúbal. Its appearance is contemporary with the first mention of planting Muscat vines (by the Bishop of Avignon) in France.

A fourth newcomer, also from Portugal, was Bastardo or Bastard. Since there is still a Bastardo grape grown in Portugal (and used in making port) it is just possible that we are talking about a "varietal" wine. That was not the opinion of earlier writers, who said that it was a "mungrell" made of wine and honey as a cheaper substitute for Muscadel. As it was sold either white or brown, this seems more likely than the varietal theory. That it was a down-market drink is pretty certain. When Shakespeare's Prince Hal said "Your brown Bastard is your only drink", I am sure he put on a cockney accent.

IN MANY CENTURIES OF FRIENDSHIP BETWEEN PORTUGAL AND ENGLAND no single relationship has had such lasting repercussions as the marriage of John of Gaunt's daughter, Philippa of Lancaster, and King John I in 1387. Their fifth son, Prince Henry, nicknamed the Navigator, was the visionary whose dreams discovered the New World.

When he was born in 1394, Venice was building her near-monopoly of oriental trade. In 1415 (while England's Henry V was invading France at Agincourt) he took part in a naval expedition to Ceuta in Morocco that smoked out the Barbary pirates there and made safe the Strait of Gibraltar, at least for a while. But the Prince's obsession was what might be over the Atlantic horizon. He talked to mariners of all nations, studied astronomy and naval architecture, collected the "ruttiers" (from the French "routiers") which medieval ships' pilots compiled as their personal guides to the seas, and developed the art of navigation by compass and sextant. At Sagres, the rocky southwest tip of Portugal (and Europe), he started a sort of maritime university. Its graduates were the boldest and most successful navigators of all time.

During his lifetime he was directly responsible only for Portugal's discovery of Madeira and the Azores, and for voyages far down the coast of Africa. After his death a succession of great Portuguese sailors – Dias, da Gama, Cabral – took their long three-masted caravels, the most advanced ships of their time and the first to be able to tack to windward, around the Cape of Good Hope (1488), to India (1498), up the Persian Gulf, to Siam and China (1540) and westwards to Brazil.

In their discoveries they were in competition with the Spaniards, who had discovered the Canary Islands and were also looking for a passage to the Indies. The Genoese Christopher Columbus (a protegé of Vasco da Gama, and whose wife was Portuguese) tried first in Lisbon for sponsorship for his voyage westward. But the Portuguese were thinking south and turned him down. He found his backing from King Ferdinand and Queen Isabella of Castile, and sailed from Seville. In 1494, two years after his discovery of America, the Portuguese and Spanish divided the world by treaty into Portuguese east and Spanish west. The line they drew gave all America to Spain – except Brazil. Had the Portuguese already discovered it, and kept it secret? But in its determination to have the east for its own, the Portuguese nation was exhausting itself. Its countryside was depopulated as farmers went to the coast, to sea and to the new colonies. In half a century the population halved from two million to one million.

It seems extraordinary that no sooner had the Reconquista given the Spanish and Portuguese more land at home than they could use, their frontier spirit drew them overseas to perilous lands from which most of them never returned.

WITH HINDSIGHT, SPAIN'S GREATEST AGE, THE 16TH CENTURY, SEEMS SUICIDAL. It started with the discovery of America and the final conquest of Granada from the Moors. In the same year the Holy Inquisition expelled all Jews from Spain; brains and manpower that could well have been invaluable and that certainly helped her enemies. Moors and Protestants were persecuted. Pure proud Catholic Castilians were to rule the world. But there were simply not enough of them. Armies and navies (and priests) were needed to exploit Mexico and Peru. Then a great dynastic lurch in Europe gave Charles, the Hapsburg heir to the Spanish throne, the Netherlands and almost the whole of Italy to rule. Three years later he was elected Holy Roman Emperor as Charles V and became responsible for Germany and Austria as well.

For 40 years Charles struggled with this superhuman task, before retiring exhausted to a monastery. The Holy Roman Empire he bequeathed to his brother Ferdinand. His son, Philip II, was perhaps the only person in history who could or would have undertaken to run Spain and its Empire from his lonely desk. In the Escorial his candle burned into the small hours every night as he annotated papers on matters great and small from lands he possessed but had never seen.

The Americas, apparently such priceless assets, he discovered were nothing of the kind. All the silver bullion of Mexico and Peru made up only about one-sixth of his revenue – scarcely enough to pay the interest on the loans he negotiated with (usually Genoese) bankers. What subsidized this huge Castilian octopus was nothing more or less than the poor Castilians themselves, paying higher and higher taxes. No wonder they planted Castile almost solid with vineyards; they needed every maravedi they could earn to keep troops (and, of course, priests) in the Netherlands, Sicily, Peru . . . and at the same time to face a continuing onslaught from the East; the advancing crescent of the Ottoman Turks.

Towards the end of Philip's reign the bullion supply looked up. New mines at Potosi in Peru and Zacatecas in Mexico came into full and spectacular production. The treasure galleons of the 1580s and 1590s carried four times as much as when he came to the throne. But Philip's ambitions were never limited by his resources. In 1580 he swallowed Portugal and its empire (and another deluge of paperwork). Portugal was to remain under Spanish rule for 60 years, bringing with it more problems.

THE NEW WORLD PROVED DISAPPOINTING FROM ANOTHER POINT OF VIEW. An acquiescent colony is supposed to deliver cheap raw materials and provide a market for manufactured goods. At first this is what happened. Ships laden with wheat and wine sailed in regular fleets to Vera Cruz in Mexico and to the various miserable, feverish harbours on the isthmus of Panama that served to supply Peru. There was also Manila in the Philippines. Prices rose sharply as treasure came back. In Andalusia (which had most direct dealings with America), in the 40 years after the

The galleons of Spain's annual treasure fleet (this is the *Santa Trinidad*)
took 70 days to sail from Cádiz to Panama, their rendezvous with the
Pacific fleet bringing silver from Peru.

conquest of Mexico the price of wheat doubled and the price of wine went up eight
times. One westbound fleet carried 150,000 casks of Andalusian wine.

But it soon became clear that the wine and oil the colonies were supposed to be
buying could not survive the voyage. Seventy-five days in the tropics (the length of
a good passage to Mexico) turned oil rancid and wine to vinegar. From the start the
conquistadors had taken vines with them. Cortés had commanded every landholder
in Mexico to plant a plot of vines. By the mid-16th century, although Mexico was
no great vineyard, the high southern coastal valleys of Peru, Trujillo, Pisco, Ica and
Nazca were producing so much wine (from plants brought from Andalusia, with
black slave labour) that they were supplying not only Lima and Potosí but the new
colony of Chile, as well as Colombia, Venezuela, Central America and Mexico.
Many of these Peruvian wine estates were Jesuit-owned. Intercolonial trade cut out
the mother country, which protested but could do very little. There was even a
trans-Pacific trade in Chinese goods for silver and wine between Manila and Mexico
and Peru.

Santiago in Chile was founded by Pedro de Valdivia in 1541, less than ten years
after the conquest of Peru and 20 after Cortés had taken Mexico. Wine-growing
could not have better conditions than the beautifully cultivated and irrigated fields
of the dispossessed Indians. If it was slower to catch on than in Peru it was because
food, not wine, was needed for export to the slave-labour force in the Peruvian
mines. Nonetheless, our first sighting of "the pirate Drake" is in December 1578,
when he seized a ship bound from Chile to Lima containing 1,770 bulging wine
skins; a retail rehearsal for his wholesale looting in Andalusia nine years later.

CHAPTER 16

"GOOD STORE OF FERTILE SHERRIS"

Sanlúcar de Barrameda is a fishing village and part-time resort, justly renowned for the delectable prawns that its beach-front cafés grill and serve right on the sandy foreshore. The tawny water before you is the Guadalquivir, where its estuary broadens to the sea. Looking half-left you have the open Atlantic in full view. Farther left, out of sight down the coast, is the fortress-port of Cádiz. To your right, 70 winding miles upstream, is the city of Seville, a busy port despite its distance from the ocean and the shifting shoals in its approach: it is beyond the reach of the worst southwesterly gales – and of pirates.

Up behind you, overlooking the little town from a low hill, is the long white palacio of the Dukes of Medina Sidonia, the feudal owners of Sanlúcar. And just in front, where the small boys are pushing bright-sailed dinghies through the surf, is where Columbus left to discover America, followed from the same spot 30 years later by Magellan's five small ships, the first ever to sail around the world.

Sanlúcar was the Cape Canaveral of the 16th century. The great voyages were planned and discussed at Sagres, in Genoa, in Lisbon and Madrid. The caravels were built and fitted out in Seville and Cádiz. But the final push of the mariner's bare foot on his homeland was on Sanlúcar beach.

MAGELLAN'S STORES

The complete costings of Ferdinand Magellan's fleet for his expedition around the world in 1519-21 have been preserved and reveal some striking aspects of his priorities. He took five ships, the largest, the *San Antonio*, of 120 tons, the smallest, the *Santiago*, of 75.

The *San Antonio* cost 330,000 maravedis, the old Spanish unit of currency, and all five ships 1.3 million. The wages of the 237 crewmen for four months were calculated at 1.154 million (an average of 1,217 maravedis per man per month). Cannon, shot, powder, armour, muskets, swords and all armaments for the fleet came to a total of 566,684 maravedis. "Vino de Jerez" for the fleet, including the cost of hiring one Juan Nicolas to travel from Seville to Jerez to choose the wine and arrange for its transport, came to 594,790 maravedis.

Thus Magellan spent more on sherry than on armaments. The expedition was the first to successfully circumnavigate the globe, although Magellan himself died on the way. He discovered the Strait of Magellan as a route around South America almost a century before an expedition rounded Cape Horn, and was the first to reveal the Pacific as the greatest ocean. But of the five ships only one returned, and of the 237 men only 18 saw Sanlúcar beach again.

NOTHING YOU HAVE EVER TASTED is as savoury as these prawns with this narrow tulip of pale amber wine. You are drinking manzanilla, the dry sherry of the surrounding vineyards, matured in the old stone bodegas that cluster close to the beach. It is the exact contemporary, in its inception, of the great voyages of discovery. It was even born to put to sea, for the name it was known by was sack, or "saca": export goods.

AT THE CLOSE OF THE 15TH CENTURY the Venetian monopoly of the sweet-wine trade in the eastern Mediterranean was in trouble. Constantinople had fallen to the Turks in the same year as England had lost Bordeaux to the French. 1453 was also the year Gutenberg in Mainz set up the first printing press, and Leonardo da Vinci celebrated his first birthday. Some have called it the end of the Middle Ages; some the birth of the Renaissance (although the Medici, in full swing glorifying Florence, would not agree to that). It certainly signalled the final snuffing out of the "Roman" Empire of the eastern Mediterranean and turned people's thoughts towards the west, where the open Atlantic beckoned.

The Spanish seized the opportunity with both hands. Venice could no longer guarantee its trade with the Orient. The sweet-wine supply for all of Europe was in the balance. England, what is more, had lost its prime source of all wine. Northern ships, particularly the English, had been making more voyages to the Levant. Entice them to Andalusia and they would forget the Mediterranean. Seville, Cádiz, Sanlúcar and Jerez, just inland, could become the world's great source of luxury wine, strong enough for long-distance travel. The Spanish even called their wine Romania or Rumney; a frank admission that it was Greek wine they were imitating and whose market they wanted.

THE DUKE OF MEDINA SIDONIA TOOK THE INITIATIVE. In 1491 he abolished taxes on the export of wine from Sanlúcar in both Spanish and foreign ships. In 1517 he gave English merchants preferential status: eight houses in the town, the right to bear arms by day or night, and even the site for their own church (which still stands, dedicated to St George). He also took steps to distinguish clearly between Bastards, which were second-rate wines, and Rumneys and sacks, which had to be

A 16th-century German woodcut gives a fleeting (and probably imaginary) view of the harbour of Sanlúcar in Tudor times. It is an illustration from the memoirs of one Jerome Coler of Nuremberg, who sailed from Sanlúcar on his way to Venezuela in 1533.

individually gauged, and kept in stores with two locks. Although the English name sack does not appear in any document before 1530, its Spanish root, saca, was common. An English version simply means that it was becoming a familiar name in England.

This was the honeymoon period. Henry VIII of England married the daughter of Spain's Catholic monarchs, Catherine of Aragón. England joined the "Holy League" with Spain against France (partly in the hope of regaining Bordeaux). But life for everybody in Spain was being made tense by the severity of the Inquisition. In Rome "The Holy Office" reacted to heresies with draconian measures. They were nothing compared with the witch-hunt against heretics instituted by Queen Isabella. The name of her Grand Inquisitor, the Dominican Torquemada, can still provoke a shudder. It certainly did for Englishmen in Spain when their sovereign, married to her daughter for 18 years, demanded a divorce from the Pope because he had fallen in love with the beautiful Anne Boleyn. In 1533 he married Anne bigamously and was immediately excommunicated. In 1534, by the Act of Supremacy, he severed the Church in England from Rome and made himself its head. The next year he started dismantling England's 616 monasteries, hanging many of their abbots and distributing their wealth and lands among his henchmen – perhaps the greatest and most wanton destruction ever done in England. Could anything be more heretical (or more insulting to Spain)?

English merchants soon heard from the Inquisition. The case of one Thomas Pery, who had lived in Andalusia for years, is particularly well documented. One evening, while he was "brushing some cloths", a priest and several other Spaniards entered his warehouse. They pointed to a big bronze bell and asked Pery: "What a good Christian is your King of England to put down the monasteries and to take away their bells?" Did Pery, the priest asked, approve of what his sovereign had done?

Stoutly Pery said that it was not his business what the King did but he was sure he was not a heretic. Two days later he was in the town of Lepe (where Chaucer's wine had come from) buying 100 pipes of Bastard from the Duke of Bejar, when he was seized and thrown into prison in leg-irons. Ten days later he was examined and some of his goods confiscated. The Duke, to do him justice, stood bail for him for a week for 2,000 ducats. But at the end of the week Pery manfully presented himself at the castle of Triana, the Inquisition headquarters in Seville, where he was kept in a verminous cell, with frequent interrogations, for three months and then most unpleasantly (he later gave full details) tortured.

His sentence, when it came, was only six months in the prison of "perpetwe", the loss of all his goods, and the threat of burning at the stake if he offended again. Many merchants managed to keep a low profile or be protected by their Spanish trading partners (in 1541, 60 English ships arrived as a fleet to load wine in Andalusia), but some in other parts of Spain they were actually burned.

It was in this atmosphere of tension, but yet with good business to be done, that in 1545 a young merchant of Southampton, Robert Reneger, who normally carried grain to Spain (and perhaps South America) and imported wine and woad – for dyeing – found his trade falling off and, like many English seamen of his day and later, armed his ship as a privateer. This was legitimate. England was at war with

France. But the prize he took in March 1545 was not a Frenchman. He seized and looted a Spanish treasure galleon, inbound from the Indies. In London he was welcomed as a hero. The Spanish reaction was to impound English ships and property in Sanlúcar, Seville and other ports.

Now the English were blooded. Trade with Spain was seizing up. Many merchants, even those who had been in Spain for a generation, turned privateer or, less politely, pirate. There was a formal peace when England's Queen Mary, the daughter of Henry VIII and Catherine of Aragón, much against the will of her people, married King Philip of Spain. Her short reign introduced the Inquisition to England and created 300 English martyrs. When she died, her half-sister, Anne Boleyn's daughter, became Queen Elizabeth I – and England's still half-amateur navy, nurtured by her father, became the terror of the Spanish seas.

An old book on the history of Jerez tells a story which certainly bears repeating, although there is no independent evidence of its truth. "The celebrated seaman Drake . . . was at first strongly attached to Spain, and established himself in business in Jerez, where he lived for some years and was apparently well content; but he quarrelled with a Jerezano called Melgarejo, who went so far as to strike him in public. This so infuriated Drake that he left the town, and from then onwards his open hostility towards Spain knew no bounds. Had this not happened, it is possible that Drake might not have left the country and his name would not have gone down to history." Had it happened, on the other hand, it is hard to imagine Drake not striking him back.

It is remarkable how much wine got through despite these inconveniences – and how hard the poor Dukes of Medina Sidonia kept trying to sweeten their best customers and worst enemies. In 1566 the Duke again extended special privileges to the English at Sanlúcar. In this period, no less than 40,000 of the 60,000 butts of wine made annually in the region were reaching England and the Netherlands; along with up to 2,000 beautiful foals from some of the best bloodstock in Europe, one of the Arabs' many bequests to Spain.

Nor was the Jerez area the only source of what was now generally known as "sack". The Spanish, having exterminated the Guanches, the aboriginal inhabitants of the Canary Islands (who may have been a race of Cro-Magnon age) in the 1490s, planted their volcanic soil with vines from Crete. "Canary sack" was almost as popular in London and Antwerp as "sherry" or "sheris" sack ("sherry" being the

---

If sweet wines were one commodity that northern Europe wanted from the Levant at almost any price, a more important one was cane sugar. Honey, the medieval sweetener, had risen in price with the decline in the number of monasteries, which had needed mountains of beeswax for their candles.

As with Malmsey vines, the Spanish and Portuguese took cuttings of sugarcane with them to their new colonies, the West Indies, Madeira, Brazil. To labour in the cane fields of America they took slaves from West Africa. All classes of Africans from the Gold Coast, Guinea and the Congo were kidnapped or bought into slavery. In 1550, Portuguese Brazil had five sugar plantations; in the 1620s, 350 – at which point the Dutch moved in and took over both ends of the business.

The success of sugar in Brazil soon ruined the sugar planters of Madeira. The island began to specialize in Malmsey wine. By 1580, English merchants were calling at Funchal, the island's capital, and madeira was added to the kinds of "sack" available in England.

English attempt at "Jerez"). Málaga, in the former kingdom of Granada, took to using the name sack (also sometimes "Mountain") for what it once sold as Garnache. Raisins, another Moorish inheritance, were its other speciality. And from 1537 Malmsey vines (but much more sugarcane) had been successfully planted on the new Portuguese colony of Madeira. When Cyprus fell to the Turks in 1571, its wine was scarcely missed.

BY THE 1580S, THOUGH, THE TEMPER OF THE SPANISH BULL, constantly baited by the English bulldog, was not to be soothed by mere commerce. Philip II gave orders for an invasion of England. Cádiz now had the world's greatest naval dockyard, and it was there in 1587 that a large part of the Armada for England was being prepared when Sir Francis Drake paid his most famous visit.

Already he was so well known on the coast of Spain that mothers would say to their children, "Mira que viene el Draque" – "Look out, Drake is coming". This time he came with a fleet 24 strong, scattered the squadron of galleys that guarded the entrance to Cádiz, and sailed straight in.

The outer and inner harbours were crammed with shipping in various degrees of helplessness; without sails, without ammunition or without crews. In Drake's own terse words: ". . . among the rest, 32 ships of exceeding great burden, laden, or to be laden, with provision and prepared to furnish the King's navy, intended with all speed against England; the which, when we had boarded and thereout furnished our ships with such provision as we thought sufficient, we burned." The work took two days and nights. Many small ships fled through the shoals to nearby Puerto de Santa Maria, but among the galleons destroyed was the 1,400-ton flagship of the Admiral of the Armada, the Marques de Santa Cruz, who shortly after died, it is said, of a broken heart. Philip replaced him as commander with the unfortunate, seasick, anglophile Duke of Medina Sidonia. Had Spain no other noblemen?

Among the extensive loot that Drake's fleet took away, having found time to load four prize ships as packhorses, was his most celebrated trophy – or at least the one with which his exploit was most celebrated when he brought it home. Two thousand nine hundred butts of sack had been waiting on the shore for loading.

Little of Elizabethan London has survived, but the one remaining wing of the 17th-century George Inn at Southwark is typical of the galleried hostelries where Shakespeare and his characters went for refreshment. The Elizabethan theatre itself was a development of the inn yard with its galleries. The George was only a stone's throw from Shakespeare's Globe Theatre.

There can hardly have been a tavern in England that year and for years afterwards whose sack was not advertised as "authentic Cádiz".

WE HAVE THE PERFECT WAY OF TASTING THE FLAVOUR OF THE TIME. In 1597 Sir John Falstaff first heaved himself onto the stage; the preposterous parasite, the chuckling cutpurse, the arrant knave, coward, liar and most lovable character Shakespeare ever created. Sir John lived at The Boar's Head Tavern in Eastcheap in the City, on credit for which he had no surety but his spectacular effrontery – egged on by Prince Hal, the future Henry V. Hal introduces him: "Thou art so fat-witted with drinking of old sack, and unbuttoning thee after supper, and sleeping upon benches after noon . . . ."

Sack is Falstaff's constant drinking. (Although on Good Friday "he sold himself to the Devil for a cup of Madeira and a cold capon's leg", and Doll Tearsheet, a close acquaintance, declares that "there's a whole merchant's venture of Bordeaux stuff in him".) His supper bill, found in his pocket (but never, you can be sure, paid) itemizes his consumption: a capon; sauce; sack, two gallons; anchovies and sack after supper; bread. Cost of sack (and anchovies) 8 shillings and twopence; cost of supper, 2 shillings and sixpence halfpenny.

Sack is sometimes sweetened with sugar, served with a piece of toast in it, or (to Falstaff's disgust) whipped up with eggs: "I'll have no pullet-sperm in my brewage". All this, though, is but a preamble to the fat knight's considered opinion, delivered not at The Boar's Head but upon a Yorkshire battlefield:

"A good sherris-sack hath a two-fold operation in it. It ascends me into the brain, dries me there all the foolish and crudy vapours which environ it, makes it apprehensive, quick, forgetive, full of nimble, fiery, and delectable shapes, which delivered o'er the voice, the tongue, which is the birth, becomes excellent wit. The second property of your excellent sherris is the warming of the blood, which before (cold and settled) left the liver white and pale, which is the badge of pusillanimity and cowardice, but the sherris warms it and makes it course from the inwards to the parts extreme. It illumineth the face, which as a beacon gives warning to all the rest of this little kingdom, man, to arm. And then the vital commoners, and inland petty spirits, muster me all to their captain, the heart; who, great and puffed up with this retinue, doth any deed of courage; and this valour comes of sherris. So that skill in the weapon is nothing without sack (for that sets it a-work), and learning a mere hoard of gold kept by a devil, till sack commences it and sets it in act and use . . . . If I had a thousand sons, the first humane principle I would teach them should be, to forswear thin potations, and to addict themselves to sack."

Not all Tudor seamen were as fond of wine as Drake. For a contrary view from another famous seaman, and a most unlucky gentleman, listen to Sir Walter Ralegh:

"Take especial care that thou delight not in wine, for there never was any man that came to honour or preferment that loved it; for it transformeth a man into a beast, decayeth the health, poisoneth the breath, destroyeth the natural heat, brings a man's stomach to an artifical heat, deformeth the face, rotteth the teeth, and to conclude, maketh a man contemptible, soon old, and despised of all wise and worthy men, hated in thy servants, in thyself and companions, for it is a bewitching and infectious vice."

"If I had a thousand sons", said Sir John Falstaff, "the first humane principle I would teach them, would be to forswear thin potations and addict themselves to sack." The Victorian actor-manager Sir Herbert Beerbohm Tree is seen here as Falstaff in *The Merry Wives of Windsor* with the great star of the day, Ellen Terry (left), and Mrs Kendal.

By thin potations he meant, of course, all the light wines of the north, whether Gascon or Rhenish. He expressed, in fact, the taste for strong wines that is supposed to be peculiarly English. Not that his sack was strong by modern standards. It was not a fortified wine. If vintage port had existed in Falstaff's day, he would probably have relegated the sack he knew to the category of "thin potations".

At a maximum natural alcoholic strength of 16 degrees or so, Elizabethan sack would have had something of the character and "weight" of a present-day montilla – Córdoba's local variant on the theme, which is still locally drunk at its natural strength (although fortified a little for export).

The conditions for producing good sherry were all present in the 16th century. What grapes they grew is not certain, but local opinion today is that the best modern grape for dry sherry, the Listan or Palomino, was probably present in a minority in the vineyard, and the Pedro Ximénez, the grape used for dark, sweet wine, was certainly there. They also grew Malmsey, maybe Muscatel, and such lesser varieties as Torrontes which are still used elsewhere in Spain.

The best sherry today comes from a belt of chalk soil west of (and close to) Jerez. The earliest vineyards were on sandy soil nearer the coast, whose wine is not so fine – except in the immediate neighbourhood of Sanlúcar. But ageing sack was not part of the plan, so differences that are obvious today were unimportant: the goal was freshness and strength. Probably the wine started to grow "flor", the peculiar floating white yeast that gives modern "fino" its essential character. But flor needs time and encouragement, so it can have had little effect. Sack was what is classed today as an "oloroso" – the word means pungent – which by definition means that it needed years to develop great character; years that it never got. It was also normally and naturally dry – hence the addition of sugar at The Boar's Head. Perhaps ancient Roman techniques of boiling down the must were sometimes used to sweeten it – but it was usually Canary sack that was qualified by the word sweet.

The development of high-quality sherry, carefully matured, started soon after, and not in Jerez but in Bristol. By 1634 the wine that was sold as "Bristol Milk" must surely have been softened, if not by time, at least by the vintner's art.

CHAPTER 17

THE BEVERAGE REVOLUTION

The age of Shakespeare is a good time to pause and scan the horizon. In the story of wine (and much else) it is one of history's hinges. In wine it saw the last of the age of innocence (innocence of knowledge, that is, not of malpractice).

We have seen wine advancing and diversifying, not as a result of greater knowledge, but rather of the diligent application of the simplest of formulae. Up to now the range has been limited to light wines that made refreshing drinks but quickly spoiled, and stronger wines that were valued more highly both for their strength and relative durability. The market was uncritical and connoisseurship (despite such attempts as the "Battle of Wines") had little more stimulus than a literary critic at a station bookstall.

Wine up to this time has been an essential part of diet, with only beer as an alternative. From this time on it begins to be discretionary, the choice gets wider, and wine has to justify itself by being more than just readily available. The French philosopher Michel de Montaigne seems to sum up for the age of innocence in his essay "On Drunkenness": "If you make your pleasure depend on drinking good wine, you condemn yourself to the pain of sometimes drinking bad wine. We must have a less exacting and freer taste. To be a good drinker, one must not have so delicate a palate."

Yet this passage from William Harrison's *Description of England*, written in 1586, gives the distinct impression that the perennial figure of the wine snob had already made his appearance, and that what he was looking for was the strongest wine he could get: "The kind of meat which is obtained with most difficulty (and cost) is commonly taken for the most delicate, and thereupon each guest will soonest desire to feed . . . . These forget not to use the like excess in wine", of which there is not "anywhere with more store of all sorts than in England . . . . Neither do I mean this of small wines only, as Claret, White, Red, French, etc; which amount to about 56 sorts . . . but also of the 30 kinds of Italian, Grecian, Spanish, Canarian etc; whereof Vernage, Cate Pument, Raspis, Muscadell, Romnie, Bastard Lire, Oseie, Capricke, Clareie and Malmsey, are not least of all accounted, because of their strength and value. For as I have said in meat, so the stronger the wine is, the more it is desired."

SIR JOHN HARINGTON WAS THE SORT OF MAN WHO TODAY would belong to all the best dining clubs and keep a good cellar. He was a courtier, a godson of Queen Elizabeth, a lawyer, a part-time diplomat, author and "wit", with England's best education (at Eton and King's College, Cambridge, the two royal foundations of King Henry VI). At the latter establishment he is credited with the invention of the water closet, although perhaps only because he wrote a Rabelaisian satire on what was then called the "jakes". He also translated into rather bumpy English verse the "Regimen Sanitatis Salernitatum", the synopsis of medical knowledge compiled in the 11th century at the famous Medical School of Salerno and still regarded by doctors, five centuries later, as the next thing to Holy Writ.

Harington's advice on wine-buying is sound, indeed thirst-provoking:

> Choose wine you mean shall serve you all the year,
> Well-favoured, tasting well, and coloured clear.
> Five qualities there are, wine's praise advancing,
> Strong, Beautiful, and Fragrant, cool and dancing.

More specifically, he says,

> White Muscadel, and Candia wine, and Greek
> Do make man's wits and bodies grosse and fat . . . .

His little joke about Canary wine and madeira is that they make you lean – on a stick, to hold you up. Then comes his much-quoted couplet:

> Wine, women, baths, by art or nature warm,
> Used or abused, do men much good or harm.

It emerges, from much more bad rhyming which I will spare you, that Harington shared with his contemporaries a deep mistrust of water (Andrew Boorde, in his "Dietary" of the 1550s, warned, "Water is not wholesome sole by itself, for an Englishman"). It had long been empirically established that wine or beer was much safer than the polluted water supplies of the time.

The Governance of Good Health, attributed to the great Dutch scholar Erasmus in 1530, contains this advice: "Wine and other drinks be the most profitable medicines and pleasant repast, nothing hurtful moderately taken . . . . It is therefore convenient that every day we [make a habit of putting] one or two glasses of water into our wine, both to delay the fume of the wine and to make our bodies lighter, and also in case need should constrain us, by this use without danger we may learn to drink water." Which is a roundabout way of describing the process of immunization. Erasmus's publisher's blurb contained this sinister ambiguity: "Thou wilt repent that this book came not sooner to thy hand."

IN 1613 SHAKESPEARE, HAVING WRITTEN HIS LAST PLAY, *The Tempest*, retired to a new house outside London at Battersea. In the same year at the opposite side of London in Islington, a village on a hill overlooking the City, a revolutionary project was completed. The New River, an aqueduct 38 miles long, the project of a Welshman called Hugh Myddelton, brought fresh water in abundant supply into London for the first time.

Sir Henry Unton was Queen Elizabeth's envoy to King Henri IV in Paris.
His banquets epitomized Tudor English manners at their most polished.
No glasses or goblets are to be seen on the table. They were brought from
the cup-board when called for, drained, and taken back. The cup-bearer
had strict instructions not to use the same cup for wine and beer.

Fresh water helped to remove the most basic of reasons for drinking wine –
simply to quench thirst safely. Now suddenly there was a host of reasons not to. In
the course of the 17th century we move from a Europe that was almost perpetually
under the sedation of alcohol to one that had a whole range of both sedatives and
stimulants to choose from. The politics and religious convictions of the time did not
exactly encourage winedrinking. Nor did they encourage winemakers to improve
their quality or enlarge their repertoire. The troubles of the first half of the 17th
century included the cataclysmic Thirty Years' War, which almost closed down
Germany altogether, religious wars in France, the growth of the Puritan movement
(the *Mayflower* sailed in 1620), persistent new taxation and new laws restricting the
freedom of shipping. Wine also met a succession of formidable new rivals that each
in turn stole the limelight as the social drink of the day.

Of these the first in time was aqua vitae, or distilled spirits. Their invention has
been credited to the Chinese, the Persians and the Arabs – whose words alcohol and
alembic certainly seem to implicate them. The Medical School of Salerno seems to
have understood distillation in the 12th century, and Arnaldus da Villanova, the
sage of Montpellier (whose education was in Moorish Spain) cited aqua vitae –
among many other things – as a panacea. By 1485 an illustration (from Salerno) of
distilling apparatus shows it well advanced and on an almost industrial scale. But the
acceptance of spirits as a drink in their own right, or even as a useful addition to
wine, was extremely slow in coming – presumably because, the principle being
imperfectly understood, some highly noxious forms of "vinum ardens", or
"burning wine", were produced. Germany seems to have been the first place in
Europe where aqua vitae caught on. Fernand Braudel quotes a Nuremberg doctor

of the 1490s who wrote: "In view of the fact that everyone at present has got into the habit of drinking aqua vitae it is necessary to remember the quantity that one can permit oneself to drink if one wishes to behave like a gentleman."

The 16th century saw the very slow advance of distillation, with the Germans still apparently unusual in considering spirits a drink rather than a medicine. Alsace was soon involved in "burning" its excess wine (the word "brandy" comes from "Gebrandt [burnt] wein"). But the real industrialization and commercialization of spirits had to wait for the ingenious Dutch in the 17th century. It was the ever-increasing Dutch fleet from the end of the 16th century that found the first great outlet for distilled wine or fermented grain – whichever was cheaper. It was ideal for long voyages, took up little space, kept perfectly, and worked wonders on the natives at the far end.

Tobacco, in being narcotic and sedative, cannot be left out of the equation. By Shakespeare's time its use was widespread. It was either smoked, chewed or (rather later) sniffed as snuff. In its effects it could be seen as a rival to wine and beer; in practice it was more often a complement.

Beer itself had become more of a challenge to wine in Shakespeare's lifetime, again thanks to the Dutch. Ale, as drunk in most northern countries, was a very mild-flavoured drink. The Dutch added the aroma and bitterness of hops, as Andrew Boorde reported in 1542: "Beer is made of malt, and hops, and water; it is a natural drink for a Dutchman. And now of late days it is much used in England to the detriment of many Englishmen." Not all, though, by any means. The controversy between ale and beer was still going strong a century later. In 1645, James Howell could write: "since Beer hath hopp'd in among us, Ale is thought to be much adulterated." John Taylor, the eccentric "water poet", a Gloucestershire countryman turned Thames bargeman who diverted all London with his antics and rhymes (he invented a very sinkable brown-paper boat) was still, in 1651, of the view that: "Beer is a Dutch boorish liquor, a thing not known in England, till of late days an Alien to our Nation, till such times as Hops and Heresies came amongst us, it is a sawcy intruder in this Land."

BY TAYLOR'S TIME THE SAUCY INTRUDERS WERE COMING THICK AND FAST. Chocolate had been brought to Spain as long ago as 1504 from its home in Mexico. Cortés had found that the Aztecs valued the cocoa bean so highly that they used it as currency. The alarmingly stimulating drink of Montezuma's banquets was brewed from cocoa, vanilla, maize, herbs and spices (including chillis) and fermented, so that it combined the effects of caffeine and alcohol, not to mention red-hot peppers, in one potation – which even Falstaff could hardly have described as "thin".

The secret of "xocoatl" was guarded by the Spanish, who added sugar and concocted a recipe we would recognize as chocolate. Not until the 1600s did cakes of chocolate paste made in Madrid reach Italy and Flanders. Cocoa beans were so little understood that in the 1640s when "English and Hollanders" took a good prize at sea, a (Spanish) ship laden with cocoa, "in anger and wrath we have hurled overboard this good commodity, not regarding the worth of it". Chocolate became the fashion in France in 1660 when Louis XIV married the Spanish princess Maria Theresa. It was regarded as something between a drink and a medicine, and inspired one of the gossip Madame de Sevigné's most delicious stories: "The marquise de Coëtlogon took so much chocolate, being pregnant last year, that she was brought to bed of a little boy as black as the devil". London first met it in June 1657, "In Bishopsgate Street, in Queen's Head Alley, at a Frenchman's house" where "is an excellent West Indian drink called chocolate to be sold, where you may have it at any time, and also unmade at reasonable rates".

BY THIS TIME LONDON WAS JUST GETTING USED TO COFFEE HOUSES. While chocolate came from the New World, coffee came from the very old, the East, which still provided the most luxurious articles of commerce. Its origins are in Ethiopia, but it was first traded at Mocha near Aden in the Red Sea, in the 15th century, and from there spread quickly through the Arab world – a cause of profound Islamic debate, because its effects, although opposite to those of wine, were obviously distinctly mind-altering. Some rulers declared that the Koran prohibited it: that it was, in fact, a sort of wine. Others claimed that Mohammed himself had been given it to keep him awake during his long sessions with the angel Gabriel.

European travellers started to meet coffee in the East in the 16th century. Turkish Constantinople had scores of coffee houses. A Greek at Oxford introduced it to the diarist John Evelyn in 1637, and it was in Oxford that one Jacob opened England's first coffee house in 1650. Within a few years Londoners had taken to the idea like bees to lavender. The old taverns must have left something to be desired for their clientele to change their habits with such alacrity. It is true that coffee was cheap: coffee houses were nicknamed "penny universities" because a penny was all it cost to drink a cup and stay as long as you liked, reading the newspaper provided by the management and debating its contents. The novelty of drinks that were not alcoholic was a powerful attraction; and so no doubt was the effect of the coffee.

A catalogue of coffee houses, and the groups who gathered in them, would show almost every shade of political sentiment, of literary taste, and even of commercial activity in London in the later years of the 17th century. Will's in Bow

---

So overwhelmingly popular did coffee houses become in London that in 1675, with positively theatrical irony, the King issued a proclamation almost identical in sentiment, and not very different in wording, from the edict of the "great vizier Kupruli" in Constantinople that we read in Chapter 9:

"Whereas it is most apparent that the multitude of Coffee Houses of late years set up and kept within this Kingdom . . . and the great resort of idle and disaffected persons to them, have produced very evil and dangerous effects, as well for that many Tradesmen and others do herein misspend much of their time which might and probably would be employed in and about their lawful calling and affairs, but also for that in such houses, divers false, malicious and scandalous reports are devised and spread abroad to the defamation of his Majesty's Government, and to the disturbance of the peace and quiet of this Realm, his Majesty hath thought fit and necessary that the said Coffee Houses be (for the future) put down and suppressed and doth strictly charge and command all manner of Persons, that they or any of them do not presume from and after the tenth day of January next ensuing, to keep any Public Coffee House, or to utter or sell by retail in his or her or their house or houses (to be spent or consumed within the same) any Coffee, Chocolate, Sherbett or Tea as they will answer the contrary at their utmost peril."

In the event, the King first postponed and then cancelled his hasty attempt at coercing his people. It had, of course, the effect of making the coffee-house keepers persons of some consequence.

The London coffee houses of the 1690s were the focus of every sort of fashionable, literary and business life. Tradition says that the word "tip" was coined here, from the initials TIP (To Insure Promptness) on a collecting box at the counter.

Street, Covent Garden, was the smartest literary resort, where the great poet Dryden held court; Man's at Charing Cross was for fashionable beaux; Child's, near St Paul's Cathedral, was full of clergymen; the St James's was the meeting place of the Whig Party; and White's in St James's Street was chock-full of aristocrats. Jonathan's in the City was where stockbrokers met; and Lloyd's, first in Tower Street, then Lombard Street, the most famous of all, was from 1688 the place where ship owners and ship masters met.

Edward Lloyd, the owner, took the imaginative step of publishing his own paper, *Lloyd's News*, whose first issue appeared in 1696. It established his coffee house as the centre of marine mercantile life. When goods from prize ships were to be auctioned, we read in the *London Gazette* that Lloyd's became the auction room. (Its first sale, in 1703, was of "a parcel of Turkey coffee".) Up to 1804, when the insurance business of Lloyd's involved whole convoys of ships, it still retained the pretence of being a mere coffee house and referred to its employees as "waiters".

Lloyd's was exceptional in evolving from casual meeting place to world-famous business enterprise. The coffee houses of the fashionable parish of St James's had very

Coffee received a fortuitous boost in publicity, especially in France, from the outcome of the 1683 Siege of Vienna by the Turks – their final attempt at adding Austria to their Empire, that then included Hungary. Louis XIV notoriously did nothing to help his Christian fellow-monarch, the Emperor Leopold I, ward off the Muslim invasion. But with the help of the Polish hero Jan Sobieski, the Austrians and their allies routed the Turks, capturing their baggage and a small mountain of coffee.

Distributed around the capitals of Europe, Vienna's Turkish coffee had something of the effect of Drake's sack from Cádiz.

different progeny. From them emerged that most characteristic London upper-class institution, the gentlemen's club. Of the clubs still extant, White's, Brooks's and Boodles, all in St James's Street, are the direct or indirect descendants of coffee houses. Needless to say, wine soon made up its lost ground, and very much more port and claret than coffee was being drunk in clubs in the 18th century.

COFFEE WAS INTRODUCED TO FASHIONABLE PARIS by a Turkish ambassador in 1669. Parisians delighted in the oriental chic of the new drink and bought their first cups from the brass trays of turbanned Armenians who brewed it on little stoves in the streets. One of them opened a stall in the market of St Germain des Prés in 1672, without conspicuous success: he moved on to London. But a Sicilian who had worked for him, one Procopio Coltelli, tried again with more determination. The coffee house he opened in 1686, on a lavish scale, under the name Procope, had mirrored walls and chandeliers and carpets, and served not only coffee but food and wine; it was, in fact, the prototype of the Paris café. Procope is still in business, in the rue des Fossés St Germain, making the not untenable claim that it is the oldest restaurant in Paris.

In France the coffee house still survives: the café as a national institution has scarcely altered since it caught on in the 18th century (Paris soon had 600 or more). England, its fashionable clubs apart, turned back to something much closer to its traditional taverns. The severely named "public house", dealing mostly in beer, was the revenge of the powerful brewers on their apostate customers – who in any case were much more taken by the latest of the exotic stimulants to make its mark: tea.

Again we have the Dutch to thank. In the early years of the 17th century they made a successful grab for Indonesia and the trade with the Spice Islands. The Portuguese and English who stood in their way were summarily dealt with. In Bantam, their first trading post at the western end of Java, they learned the Chinese habit of drinking tea, and were soon importing not just the leaves but the necessary paraphernalia, pots and cups, to Amsterdam. Unlike coffee, tea first appeared as an expensive luxury. The diarist Samuel Pepys had his first cup, in a coffee house, in September 1660. The price came down when the rival Dutch and English East India Companies began carrying tea in quantity around the turn of the 18th century, but by then the new craze was for Holland's latest contribution to the range of new beverages thronging the market: gin.

In England the evils of gin, and its eventual conquest by tea, were matters of deep concern in the 18th century. Meanwhile, in the 17th, the vintners had plenty to worry about. It was time to devise new wines that could compete with such novel patterns of consumption. Happily for them, there were still such conservatives about as Francesco Redi:

Cups of chocolate, aye, or tea,
Are not medicines made for me.
I would sooner take to poison,
Than a single cup set eyes on
Of that bitter and guilty stuff ye
Talk of by the name of Coffee.

Let the Arabs and the Turks
Count it 'mongst their cruel works:
Foe of mankind, black and turbid . . .
. . . if the Mussulman in Asia
Doats on a beverage so unseemly,
I differ from the man extremely.

183

CHAPTER 18

WAGGONERS
OF THE SEA

If Shakespeare had written his plays half
a century later, they might well have included *The Merchant of Amsterdam* and *The Two Gentlemen of Haarlem*, and Romeo and Juliet might have found their ecstasy on a balcony in Leyden or Delft. Such was the extent to which the Netherlands seized the initiative in Europe in the first half of the 17th century. It was the Dutch, rather than the Italians, the Spanish or the French, who taught Europe the meaning of commercial power and translated it into cultural conquest.

The story is astonishing, because for more than a century the Dutch had been mere vassals of the Spanish, an unimportant, resourceless peasant outpost of Spain's great Empire whose few flat fields could not even support its population, but which relied on its fishermen for food. Under the leadership of William the Silent, Prince of Orange in Provence and Nassau in Germany, and his two sons Maurice and Frederick-Henry, the seven northern provinces of what is now the Netherlands united against Spain and the Inquisition and harried them out of the country.

In the process they separated from the rich provinces of Flanders (the future Belgium) but so far overtook them in commercial power that almost overnight Amsterdam became a far richer city than Antwerp, which had been Europe's greatest port for a century. In 1609 the Dutch simply occupied and closed the mouth of Antwerp's river, the Scheldt, and blocked off its trade. The wealth and talent of the southern provinces poured northwards to join this revolutionary new society based on religious tolerance and sheer hard work; 100,000 families moved from Flanders to the United Provinces (as they were called) between 1560 and 1610.

By 1650 the Dutch had the greatest merchant fleet the world had ever seen, with some 10,000 ships, despite the fact that up to 1648 they had been at war with Spain for 80 years with only one 12-year truce. In 1639 Spain had sent a great Armada, as it had against England half a century before; the Dutch Admiral Tromp destroyed it off the coast of Kent. Not only were they "the waggoners of the seas", but they peopled them with corsairs able to teach the Barbary pirates lessons in ferocity. If there was lucrative smuggling to be done the Dutch were there, too.

With ruthless vigour the United Provinces established colonies in the East and West Indies, in North America, in Ceylon and at the Cape of Good Hope, discovered Tasmania and New Zealand, fought in the Thirty Years' War in

Germany and twice against England, and repelled an invasion by Louis XIV, all within the space of one lifetime.

We saw in the last chapter how Dutch commercial enterprise introduced so many new stimulants and narcotics to Europe that wine almost fell by the wayside. But as the dominant trading nation, with far more ships than any other, they also called the tune in the growing and distribution of wine. Nor let it be thought that the Dutch led coldly efficient lives on their quarterdecks and in their counting houses. They were famous for their guzzling of food, drink and preposterous amounts of tobacco, for their passion for rare flowers, their joy in every sensual delight (expressed in matchless paintings of objects for their own sake) and their zeal in pursuing every known science, but especially those of navigation and war.

On their capacity for drink, the baffled English ambassador, Sir William Temple, hazarded: "The qualities in their air may incline them to drinking. For though the use or excess of drinking may destroy men's abilities who live in better climates, yet on the other side, it may improve men's parts and abilities in dull air, and may be necessary to thaw and move the frozen or unactive spirits of the brain" – a most ingenious excuse. "Gentlemen of the Netherlands", wrote a French visitor, "have so many rules and ceremonies for getting drunk that I am repelled as much by the discipline as by the excess."

HOLLAND, LIKE VENICE, MADE ITS FORTUNE by importing and exporting the same goods. Transit trade was the livelihood of Amsterdam, which grew rich by linking the Baltic with the Mediterranean and the Indies (despite such formidable obstacles as a harbour approach so shallow that big freighters had to be piggybacked over the shoals by pumped-out lighters lashed alongside). Temple observed: "Never any country traded so much, and consumed so little . . . . They are the great masters of Indian spices, and Persian silks; but wear plain woollen, and feed upon their own fish and roots." Of all these wares, only one remained behind in goodly quantities in the stomachs of the merchants: wine, for which Rotterdam was the chief port. Rhine

Hard drinking was endemic in 17th-century Holland, despite the frantic industriousness of the people. Women drank almost as much as men. The English ambassador reported how young girls drank beer all day until "their inflated appearance was matched by a look of helpless stupidity that never left them". Taverns ranged from gloomy hovels to positive mansions with marble floors and stained-glass windows where you could eat sumptuously and listen to a concert. Some settings were more dubious, such as the one in this painting by Jan Steen.

wine was the most convenient; Rotterdam lies at the mouth of the Rhine. White wine, preferably sweet, was also very much to the Dutch taste; they did not share England's passion for claret. But the Rhineland was so devastated by the Thirty Years' War in the first half of the 17th century, and the Palatinate by Louis XIV in the second half, that Germany had little wine (and perhaps none of quality) left to export. It was in the 17th century that wine as Germany's national drink was largely replaced by beer.

The Dutch bought from every source, even from Spain, although they were at war. Their tasters were sighted sniffing around the old kingdom of Aragón, just over the Pyrenees from France. The overland route to Spain was as familiar as the sea-lanes. In Venice's old monopoly, the eastern Mediterranean, they were able to make special arrangements with the Turks for supplies of Greek wine (as they did for supplies of tulip bulbs, another Turkish speciality and Dutch passion). The Turks, recently beaten by the Spanish and Venetians at the sea battle of Lepanto, were delighted at this chance to insult both enemies at once. Cretan Malmsey was also bought in Lisbon, from the Portuguese, who had apparently anticipated the discovery of later colonists that strong wines can benefit from sea travel: the Portuguese took their Malmsey from Crete to the Indies and back as ballast.

For the bulk supplies they needed to furnish all their northern clients and top up their taverns, the Dutch turned to the great well of wine represented by the west coast of France and its hinterland, from Nantes at the mouth of the Loire south to Bordeaux and Bayonne. The old annual wine-fleet idea was out of date: they wanted a constant flow. As far as they were concerned, all the elaborate traditions and privileges, the pecking order of ports, the "police des vins" at Bordeaux, were worse than out of date. Where they could get away with it they ignored them (they did not apply to distilled wine). In several cases they married into local families to qualify for privileges. But principally they concentrated on such areas as the Dordogne where there were no rules to get in the way.

They were welcomed at first at Bordeaux, both as buyers of wine on a bigger scale than the English had been for centuries and also as skilled drainage engineers, with the experience of their polders, who could drain the marshy land along the rivers. But whereas the English only looked for traditional light red claret, the Dutch wanted things done differently. They bought huge quantities of white wine, the sweeter the better, and even huger quantities of ordinary wine suitable for distilling into brandy. (Prunes were another crop they gobbled up, and made the region of Agen famous. They were the best anti-scurvy precaution they could find for their long-distance freighters to the East Indies, a 300-day journey.) Brandy was routinely added to the drinking water on board ship to make it both safer and more palatable. As for red wine, the Dutch liked it dark and strong. Cahors in the High Country was their ideal. By planting the "palus", the newly drained alluvial land along Bordeaux's rivers, they achieved (at least in the better vintages) what they were looking for, a wine that was the antithesis of claret.

Their preferences and buying power soon persuaded farmers to switch from red grapes to white, not only in Bergerac up the Dordogne but even in Bordeaux's own backyard, in Sauternes. The Dutch brought with them (presumably from the

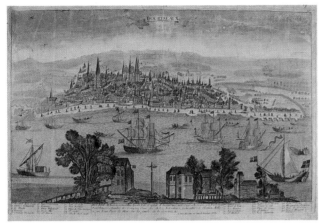

Bordeaux in the 17th century, seen here from across the river Garonne, was a walled medieval city. For most of the century the Dutch were the dominant force in its trade. Owning three-quarters of all the ships in Europe, they could dictate what wine was produced, at what price. Their chief interest was cheap white wine.

Rhineland) a trick that would stabilize sweet wines and prevent them finishing their fermentation on the way to the customer. It was the sulphur (alias "brimstone") candle, or wick dipped in sulphur and burned in the barrel before it was filled. Formerly it had been possible to stabilize sweet wines up to a point, but only very laboriously by repeated racking from one barrel to another, and by shipping in cold weather. The Dutch were not so finicky, and were perfectly prepared to add sugar and indeed spirits before they re-exported the wine onwards from Rotterdam.

The French were not slow to adopt the sulphur technique, at first calling the candles "allumettes hollandaises"; later "mèches soufrées" (the English word "match" comes from "mèche"). It is doubtful, judging by the report of a Scottish traveller in France in 1665–7, whether, having learned the trick, they observed much restraint in using it. Sir John Lauder, Lord Fountainhall, wrote: "There comes no wine out of France to foreign country, save that which they brimstone a little, otherwise it could not keep on the sea, but it would spoil. It's true the wine works much of it out again, yet this makes that wine much more unwholesome and heady than that we drink in the country where it grows at hand. We [in Scotland] have very strict laws against the adulterating of wines, and I have heard the English confess that they wished they had the like . . . ."

The mastery of water, whether on land or at sea, was the cornerstone of Dutch life. As Barbara Tuchman wrote in *The First Salute*: "In a stupendous feat of labour and engineering, a nation succeeded in creating land for itself to live on, doing by the hand of man what only God had done before."

Dutch shipping was as original as the Dutch landscape. Baltic timber was their material. They designed light ships built with standard parts, not strong enough for armaments but cheap to build (half the price of English ships) and very economical to man. Simplified rigging meant that a 200-ton "flute", as such traders were called, needed a crew of no more than ten, whereas an English ship of the same size needed up to 30 men.

Every ship's master returning from abroad had to file a report with the Admiralty on any news he had learned while away. Like the Romans, the Dutch realised the importance of communications. They invented newspapers, and created a regular postal service which had no parallel. Mail went by land and sea: from Amsterdam to Paris a letter took four days. In key cities the Dutch kept resident agents whose sole task was to communicate useful information back to Holland. Amsterdam had the first Stock Exchange which regularly published the prices of stocks. And to pay for all this, the Dutch paid taxes that horrified their competitors.

THE DUTCH SOON BEGAN TO IDENTIFY THE AREAS that could produce fairly sweet wines by delaying the harvest until the grapes were as ripe as possible, and others where exceptional conditions of soil and climate could give them really sweet "vins liquoreux"; the equivalent of modern Sauternes. There is no specific mention of waiting for the grapes to rot under the influence of *Botrytis cinerea*, the so-called "noble mould", until much later; the late 18th century (the period when its effects were also "discovered" in the Rheingau). But it is hard to believe that the sweet wines of Bergerac and Sauternes, and also of Anjou, which the Dutch bought at a premium, were not at least partially achieved through the action of botrytis.

ORDINARY WINE SUPPLIES FOR DISTILLING WERE NO PROBLEM, but for economy and efficiency the Dutch looked for areas where the second necessary element was also plentiful: timber to fuel their stills and build their barrels. Armagnac was a forest region with no proud wine tradition. True, it was not on a convenient river, but distilling reduced the volume to be transported to a mere one-sixth or one-eighth. Furthermore, in these backwoods there was no bourgeoisie to haggle over the price. Armagnac's "brandewijn" was taken by waggon to the nearest little rivers, the Adour and the Midouze, which took it to the sea at the port of Bayonne.

The country of the Charente, north of Bordeaux, also had everything the Dutch wanted. For centuries the coastline south of La Rochelle had been one of Europe's chief suppliers of salt, and rich in grain. Vines here took second place. But the hinterland, between Saintes and Angoulême, was also already familiar to the Dutch. Angoulême had clear streams where in the 16th century the Flemings had established papermills to make "Holland paper", and the district known as the Borderies, just north of the river Charente from the little town of Cognac, was a source of sweet white wines that were later to enjoy a considerable vogue.

The chalky "champagne" slopes south and east of Cognac were available for huge harvests of distilling wine, with no shortage of firewood for the stills. Perhaps their wine could have been good for drinking, but that was not what the Dutch wanted. They were making fortunes in distilling, whether of undrinkable beer at Schiedam near Rotterdam, or of scarcely drinkable wine up and down the French coast. They were also doing well selling Swedish copper (Sweden was Europe's foremost supplier of metals) to the French to build stills, then buying back their brandy. It was a matter of sheer chance that the light wines of the Charente produced a brandy with relatively little of the unpleasant taste of crude spirits that normally needed disguising, as Dutch gin was with juniper berries.

What turned the corner for cognac, and raised it from being just another spirit to a liqueur of world renown, was the interest of the English and the Irish, who insisted on much more painstaking methods of distilling, and ageing of the spirit in oak barrels. The first advertisement for the sale of "Old Cognac Brandies" was in the *London Gazette* of the early 1700s.

ANOTHER GREAT SOURCE OF WINE THAT THE DUTCH DID NOT NEGLECT was along the river Loire. Angers and Tours were surrounded with vineyards growing the ancient and excellent Pineau de la Loire, usually known today as the Chenin Blanc, whose wine has great keeping qualities, and in sunny autumns can also become distinctly sweet. The Dutch were too canny to involve themselves in the stately traditions of commerce in privileged cities such as Angers. They went instead to a district nearby which could be persuaded to produce cut-price Anjou wine; the valley of the little river Layon. Here, it must be said, they left behind them a goodly inheritance.

High-quality sweet wines were the only ones it was worth shipping down the Loire from Touraine and Anjou, because at the border of Brittany, at the little port of Ingrandes, there were high duties to be paid. Dutch commercial logic therefore identified the vineyards below Ingrandes as the place for more cheap wine (which in any case the increasingly cloudy maritime climate suggests). So here it was the Muscadet and the Gros Plant, low-grade, bulk-producing vines, that they encouraged. It seems their purses of guilders could persuade the poor French farmers to jump through hoops.

The biggest source of cheap wine and cheap brandy of all, however, they failed to tap to much effect. They had watched (and helped) with mounting interest as the extraordinary project of the Canal des Deux Mers arrived at completion. This Herculean feat of engineering, a winding waterway linking the Mediterranean at Sète with the Garonne and thence with Bordeaux, and climbing hills in ladders of locks in the process (the Ecluses de Fonseranes at Béziers is a chain of nine locks rising 25 metres in less than one kilometre) was completed in 1681. One can imagine the excitement in the Languedoc as the growers thought the Atlantic was about to be opened to them. They had reckoned without Bordeaux and its "police des vins". Throughout the 18th century, only five percent of Languedoc's wines and spirits were exported through the new canal. Even the Dutch had to sail around Spain and through the Straits of Gibraltar to fetch them direct from Sète.

THE WORM BEGAN TO TURN IN THE 1650s. This frantic commercial activity was all very well, but first the English, then the French, became increasingly jealous. During the 1640s, England had been too preoccupied with its civil war to compete.

"COGNIACKE"

It was the Dutch who first persuaded the winegrowers of Cognac to distil their wines, but the British take credit for recognizing and encouraging its potential for quality. In 1638 an English traveller, Lewes Roberts, mentioned "a small wine called Rotchell, but more properly Cogniacke". Cognac was still therefore providing the thin wines shipped from La Rochelle.

The first mention in England of "cogniack brandy" appeared in the *London Gazette* in 1678. During the 18th century prices between cognac and other brandies, between young and old cognac, and between cognac from the inland chalky "Champagne" district and vineyards nearer the coast, continued to widen.

Why cognac in particular? Most wines when distilled in simple stills needed boiling up again and again to get rid of foul-tasting (and headache-making) "congeners". Any good flavour was destroyed with the bad. Cognac alone became palatable after only two distillations, which allowed it to keep at least some of its original winey character. Ageing it in oak barrels added another – and a little sugar probably helped, too.

With England and France rarely at peace, smuggling became a considerable industry. Brandy is far less bulky than wine: ideal for small boats and midnight coves. The island of Jersey was a smugglers' headquarters. From Jersey came Jean Martell in 1715 to settle in Cognac. In 1723 another merchant house was established, in the neighbouring town of Jarnac, by Ranson and Delamain. Forty years later they were joined by the English firm of Hine. Then in 1765 the Irishman Richard Hennessy moved shop from Bordeaux to Cognac.

The Dutchman's favourite drink remained the light, aromatic, long-lived wine of the Rhineland, drunk from a capacious glass with a knobbly trunk known as a Roemer. Pieter Claesz painted this quintessential Dutch meal: herring, bread and Rhine wine, during a Thirty Years' War that devastated the vineyards of Germany.

In 1650 Oliver Cromwell, reigning as republican dictator between the unfortunate King Charles I and his son Charles II, passed the Navigation Ordinance, which was intended to prohibit the use of third-country (i.e. Dutch) ships between English and foreign ports. (Of every six ships leaving English ports, it was said, five were Dutch.) In 1652 Cromwell declared war on the Netherlands, a war in which the English captured some 1,500 Dutch ships, enough to double the size of their own comparatively puny merchant fleet. (Three years later, with admirable impartiality, the English seized Jamaica from Spain, the Netherlands' old foe.) In 1664 Charles II started a second Dutch war with much less success. The Great Plague and the Great Fire of London paralysed him. The Dutch fleet, emulating Drake, sailed into Chatham harbour and burnt the English fleet. The score may be said to have been evened, though, by the English acquisition of New Amsterdam, which they renamed New York.

Meanwhile, Louis XIV's Minister of Finance, Colbert, resolved that France should have a navy worthy of her power. The merchants of Nantes and Bordeaux were among many who were telling him that the Dutch shipping monopoly was insufferable and their methods of business less than respectful. Colbert found that France had indeed miserably few ships. His estimate (in 1669) was that Europe's total merchant fleet consisted of some 20,000 vessels, of which 15,000–16,000 were Dutch, 3,000–4,000 were English, and 500–600 French. With wonderful deliberateness and foresight he ordered the planting of great oak forests in the Limousin and Tronçais to build French fighting ships far into the future; oaks whose timber now flavours some of the finest of all wines. A few of Colbert's original trees still stand as titanic memorials to his faith in wooden walls. From oaks of older planting, he rapidly built a fleet and by 1672 was ready for a Dutch war on France's account.

The Dutch, of course, took their custom elsewhere, at least for the duration, and went prospecting anew in Spain and Portugal. It was a day of rejoicing for Jerez and Málaga, Alicante and the Canary Islands, Lisbon and even (once more) the isles of Greece. By 1675 Dutch prospecting had led them to open yet another new chapter in the history of wine: they bought a small quantity of a potent red from the hills of the Douro in Portugal at its river-mouth port, Oporto.

CHAPTER 19

JUG AND BOTTLE

Up to the advent of the adulterating Dutch with their aqua vitae and their sulphur matches, the chief concern of every wine merchant was to get the goods off his hands as quickly as possible. It was like playing pass-the-parcel. A barrel of wine was perishable goods, with a sell-by date approaching perilously fast.

With such rare exceptions as the merchants of Venice, who dealt in strong wines, and the abbots or prince-bishops of the Rhine, who possessed cold cellars and enormous casks, the first axiom of everyone making or dealing in wine was to ship it quick. There is more mention of ships than of cellars in the foregoing chapters. The merchant's role was simply that of a carrier loading at the producing end and distributing the moment he docked. What the French call the "élevage" of wine – its "upbringing" in cellars where it is carefully aged and sometimes blended – scarcely existed. If the product did not keep, there was no call for complicated commercial organization. In the Middle Ages, vinegar merchants in France were more organized than wine merchants; their product could be stored, blended and distributed on demand.

Why did wine so rapidly turn to vinegar? Because several of the bacteria it contains, but in particular one called *Acetobacter aceti*, only need a supply of oxygen to multiply catastrophically. Acetic acid, or vinegar, is the result. As with all biochemical reactions, the lower the temperature the slower the process; hence the virtue of cold Rhineland cellars. The virtue of giant barrels was simply that a greater volume of liquid has a smaller proportionate surface area, therefore less contact between the *Acetobacter* and its food supply.

A high alcohol content is also protective; the bacteria are less nimbly reproductive under its influence. Sulphur dioxide equally inhibits their sex life. These scientific facts were unknown, but their empirical results were what the Dutch so profitably exploited when they burnt their sulphur matches and added their brandewijn. Still, however, they were handling wine in bulk, selling it by the barrel, unwittingly giving it every opportunity for contact with air. The Germans in their cellars, again empirically, knew better: they took whatever steps were necessary to keep their storage tanks (barrels is scarcely the word for such monsters) full to the brim. When they drew wine off, they straightaway topped them up from smaller barrels of similar wine. If there was nothing suitable at hand, they even dropped stones (well washed in wine) into the bunghole to displace the air and keep the "Fuder" full.

REVOLUTION CAME WITH THE BOTTLE, AND A SECURE MEANS OF SEALING IT. This was the great contribution of the 17th century to the story of wine: bottles and corks. Without them the quality of wine could advance – but its capacity to age could not. Nobody knew, or had known since the Romans, what transformations can take place when good wine is sealed away from the air for long periods of time. We are talking not just of a pleasanter or smoother taste, but a different dimension of taste altogether. A little science is needed to explain this felicitous phenomenon.

Wine in bottle, securely corked, has no access to the air, nor the air to it. The bottle contains a small amount of oxygen, as it does of carbon dioxide. Both these gases are soluble, are present when the wine is bottled, and thus find their way into the bottle with the wine. But at that point their amount is fixed. The wine may be swarming with microbes and bacteria. But if they need oxygen to reproduce (as they do), the amount of reproduction they are capable of is limited by the tiny amount of oxygen in the bottle. All the life processes of the organisms that make up the flavour and aroma of wine are slowed down to a crawl in a sealed bottle: slower still if the bottle is kept in a cool place.

There are other biochemical reactions going on, too, which are also competing for oxygen as their fuel. Pigments, tannins, acids, hundreds of natural organic compounds are inherently unstable. They will combine and recombine to form new compounds. Some reactions can take place anaerobically – without, that is, any supply of air. Most need the presence of oxygen to rearrange their chemical structure. So the wine in the bottle is in what is called a "reductive" state: any change reduces the possibility of further change by using up the oxygen supply.

Very fine tuning indeed is what happens under these circumstances. It takes a wine with good inherent qualities: good balance, for example, between its components of acidity, tannins and sugar (closer to 500 than 400 different natural components have been identified in wine). Given this inbuilt structure, though, the fine tuning can merit the happy description of a "chemical symphony".

ALL THIS WAS NOT EVEN A GLEAM IN THE EYE OF THE BOTTLE MAKERS of the 16th century. Bottles were only made for the convenience of bringing wine to table from its barrel. They varied widely in strength and elegance – from leather "jacks" to stoneware jugs to very beautiful flagons of clear glass. Glass was one of the more expensive materials, and also the most fragile. Its snob appeal was pointed out by William Harrison in 1586 in his *Description of England*: "It is a world to see in these our days wherein gold and silver abound, how that our gentility, as loathing these metals (because of the plenty) do now generally choose rather the Venice glasses . . . ."

For those who could not afford glass, the most popular substitute was a form of salt-glazed stoneware originally made in the Rhineland. (It was glazed by throwing handfuls of common salt into the kiln during firing. The salt reacted with minerals in the clay to produce a glassy, mottled, usually greyish or brownish surface.) For a long period these were made in a single pot-bellied pattern and decorated with a grotesque mask below the lip; a hideous face supposed to be that of a much-hated Italian cardinal who bitterly opposed the reformed Protestant church. His name, and the name of the jugs, was Bellarmine.

Left: The glass wine bottle (being blown here in the original manner at the glassworks of Jamestown, Virginia – America's first factory) superseded its predecessor early in the 17th century. The stoneware "Bellarmine", right, produced in Germany with the mask of a well-loathed cardinal, was its immediate forerunner.

The fragility of glass bottles made in the Italian fashion (when most glass technology came from Italy) was overcome by jacketing them in straw or wicker or leather. The still-familiar Tuscan "fiasco" dates from the 14th or 15th century. A more elaborate version, the "cantinflora", had a curving spout and a pocket in the side for ice to cool the wine. Flanders, France, Germany and the Netherlands were all great producers of glass. The Dutch had the very practical idea of blowing bottles into square-sectioned moulds, which packed well in cases (or "cellars", as they were called) without wasting space. The pattern still exists in the Dutch gin bottle: why it was never a success for wine is not very clear. But as very few of these 17th-century bottles survive, they were presumably very fragile.

Workaday bottles were made of pewter, tin, even wood – presenting the problem that you could never see if they were thoroughly clean. But while all glass was blown thin it was bound to remain a luxury, and indeed no separate bottle works existed: bottles were made at the same glass houses as drinking glasses and window glass.

Nevertheless, the demand rose so much in the early 17th century (there was also a surge of imports to England of Bellarmines from the Rhine) that the Crown became concerned about the destruction of woodlands to fire the innumerable furnaces. The result was a proclamation from King James I "to provide that matters of superfluity do not devour matters of necessity and defence; understanding that of late years the waste of wood and timber hath been exceeding great and intolerable by the glass houses . . . as it were the lesser evil to reduce the times unto the ancient manner of drinking in Stone[ware] and of lattice-windows, than to suffer the loss of such a treasure . . . . Therefore we do . . . straightly ordain, that . . . no person . . . shall melt, make or cause to be melted or made, any . . . Glasses whatsoever with timber or wood, within this our Kingdom . . . ."

So it was to be stoneware jugs and windows made of little pieces of glass in lead "lattices" unless the glassworks changed their fuel. In those days the king offered monopolies in manufacture – naturally for a very substantial fee. The monopolist who bought all the rights to make glass in coal furnaces was Sir Robert Mansell, who in the 1620s made his headquarters near England's best-known coalmines, at Newcastle-upon-Tyne in the northeast. He was allowed to sublet his monopoly to others, though, and thus coal-fired glass houses sprang up in many parts of the country. It was found that the higher temperatures of coal fires made stronger glass, if not so white as the Venetian style.

At this stage the history of bottle-making, as everything else in England, becomes confused by the troubles of the royal house of Stuart, culminating in the civil war of 1642-9. All the evidence, though, points to an extraordinary courtier, author, alchemist and even part-time pirate called Sir Kenelm Digby as the inventor of the revolutionary successor to Mansell's still relatively frail bottles. Some time in the 1630s, and possibly at Newnham-on-Severn in Gloucestershire, close by the collieries of the forest of Dean, Digby started making bottles that were much thicker, heavier, stronger and darker – and also cheaper – than any known before.

They were globular in shape, a simple bubble, with a high tapering neck ending in a "collar" or "string-rim" for tying down a stopper. They held about a quart, or quarter of a gallon (which, confusingly, is almost the measure the French at that time called a "pinte"). The bottom had a deep "kick-up" or "punt" where the blowpipe had been attached, which made them very stable standing up. Digby had apparently found a way of making his coal furnace even hotter, using a wind tunnel, to melt a glass mixture with more sand and less potash and lime. The "metal" was darkened to brown or dark olive-green or almost black by the coal fumes, but this was seen as a sign of strength (and was to have the unforeseen advantage of protecting the contents from the light). Digby was shortly afterwards imprisoned as a Royalist and Roman Catholic, and others claimed to have invented his process. But in 1662 Parliament decided it was indeed his invention. He was the father of the modern wine bottle. His technique was not used in Holland until about 1670, and in France not until 1709 (when the bottles were described as "in the English fashion"). It now remained to equip them with the perfect stopper.

DIGRESSION

The career of Sir Kenelm Digby (1603–65) merits a digression, although it can hardly be called an important part of the story of wine. He epitomized the cultivated, enquiring, versatile and also hardy, even foolhardy, 17th-century English gentleman. His father was executed for his part in the Gunpowder Plot to blow up the King in Parliament in 1605. He travelled restlessly through boyhood, learning every language and every science (including the occult arts and alchemy) that he could.

At 17 Digby left Oxford for Paris, although deeply in love with a famous beauty, Venetia Stanley. In France he met Marie de Medici, the Queen-Mother, who made immodest advances: to escape he spread a report of his own death and sailed to Italy.

He eventually returned to England and married Miss Stanley (who had meanwhile become a mother by another gentleman). They were extremely happy, but his restlessness moved him to an extraordinary buccaneering expedition. At the age of 24 he took two well-armed ships and turned pirate, capturing Flemish, Spanish and Dutch ships in the Mediterranean before making a Drake-like raid on a harbour full of French and Venetian ships at Scanderoon in the Aegean. Having devastated this port, he turned to archaeology and went excavating for antiquities on Delos and other Greek islands.

Lady Digby died in 1633 and left him desolate: this was when he took to experimenting and presumably invented his new kind of wine bottle. His further adventures are all in keeping: trouble and glory were consistently both at hand, yet he studied (among many things) the physiology of plants and was apparently the first to observe the importance of oxygen to vegetation. He left a reputation as a charmer, a scallywag and a sage, and writings on everything from religion to recipes. Such was the 17th century. Sic transit . . . .

How to plug bottles of whatever sort was a very old problem. The Romans had used corks, but their use had been forgotten. Looking at medieval paintings one sees twists of cloth being used, or cloth being tied over the top. Leather was also used, and sometimes covered with sealing wax. Corks began to be mentioned in the middle of the 16th century. By the time Shakespeare wrote *As You Like It* (between 1598 and 1600), they were well enough known for Rosalind to say: "I pray thee take thy cork out of thy mouth, that I may drink thy tidings."

It has often been suggested, and may well be true, that cork became known to the thousands of pilgrims who tramped across northern Spain to Santiago de Compostella. On the other hand, the cork forests grow in the south of Spain and Portugal, not the north, and the south had frequent direct communications by sea, so corks were more likely to have been introduced to the rest of Europe from the south – if they were in use there.

It seems that the marriage of cork and bottle, at least in England, took place by degrees over the first half of the 17th century. Sir Kenelm, an inveterate experimenter, was not entirely won over. In *The Closet Opened* he recorded all sorts of recipes for mead and methegelin – strong drinks made by fermenting honey. Sometimes he advised corks; sometimes "ground stoppels of glass". He appears at one point to have been experimenting with sparkling white methegelin, because his recipe concluded: "If you will drink it presently, put it in the bottles, and rub the corks with yeast, that it may touch it, and it will be ready in three or four days to drink" – or, one imagines, to explode, as the yeast started a second fermentation in the bottle.

Stoppers of ground glass made to fit the bottle neck snugly held their own for a remarkably long time. It is clear from Worlidge's *Treatise of Cider*, published in 1676, that great care was needed in choosing good corks, "much liquor being absolutely spoiled through the only defect of the cork. Therefore are glass stoppels to be preferred . . . ." – at the cost of no small trouble, since each one had to be ground to fit a particular bottle, using emery powder and oil. The "stoppel" was then tied to the bottle by a piece of packthread around a "button" on top, because of course it would fit only the bottle it was ground for. As late as 1825, the ultimate luxury bottle stopper was still, at least in some eyes, a ground-glass one. Beautiful handmade bottles, "bouchée a l'émeri" (that is, with glass stoppers ground with emery), were used for some of the wine of Château Lafite in 1820 and 1825. It was (wrongly) believed that cork allowed air to reach the wine and spoil it: in reality the problem was probably just poor-quality cork giving the wine a "corky" taste. Eventually, glass stoppers were abandoned because they were usually impossible to extract without breaking the bottle.

Cider, beer and homemade wines were what the 17th-century householder chiefly bottled. Bottling by wine merchants only began at the very end of the century. In 1609, Sir Hugh Plat's *Delights for Ladies* advised keeping beer in barrel 10 or 12 days before bottling it (presumably in stoneware bottles), "making your corks very fit for the bottles, and stop them close." He added: "The reason why bottle-ale is both so windy and muddy, thundering and smoking upon the opening" is because it is usually bottled too soon, while there is still yeast working in it. By 1676, when Worlidge wrote his *Treatise of Cider*, all the elements were in place for modern-style bottling. Having chosen good corks, says Worlidge, steep them in scalding water and "they will comply better with the mouth of the bottle, than if forc'd in dry; also the moisture of the cork doth advantage it in detaining the spirits."

"Therefore", he goes on, "is laying the bottle sideways to be commended, not only for preserving the corks moist, but for that the air that remains in the bottle is on the side of the bottle from which it can neither expire" (i.e. escape) "nor can new be admitted, the liquor being against the cork. Some place their bottles on a frame with their noses downward for that end" – not a good idea, says Worlidge, because (as any visitor to a Champagne house knows) any sediment then rests on the cork, and "you are sure to have it in the first glass." His ideal cellar is one with a "cool refrigerating spring" which will keep cider "until it be come to the strength even of Canary itself." Seventeenth-century cellars still exist equipped with shelves with holes to take the "noses" of upside-down bottles. Others used a bed of sand for the same purpose. What is clear is that by this time the principle of "binning" liquors in corked bottles to age them was well understood.

Only two facilities remained to be invented: a corkscrew so that the cork could be driven right in, not left half-out like a stopper, and a cylindrical bottle that could be binned on its side, not ostrich-fashion. The second evolved gradually over the first half of the 18th century. The first remains a teasing mystery.

The first mention of a corkscrew in print is rather later than you might expect: 1681. It was described (by one N. Grew) as "a steel worm used for the drawing of corks out of bottles." "Steel worms" had been in use for at least half a century for drawing bullets and wadding from firearms that had (rather unnervingly) failed to fire. When did imagination, provoked by thirst, make the connection with bottles? No one knows. But the word corkscrew was not coined until 1720. The original of the essential implement was called a "bottlescrew".

Perhaps the earliest written account of a bottlescrew was published in 1700 in *The London Spy*, an odd record of London manners and modes by a tavern keeper called Ned Ward, a staunch advocate of claret and the Tories. The book pretends to

THE PERFECT STOPPER

Cork is the thick outer bark of the cork oak, *Quercus suber*, a slow-growing evergreen tree which has evolved this spongy substance for protection and insulation, particularly against fire. The world supply of cork is concentrated in the western Mediterranean and the neighbouring Atlantic coasts. Portugal, above all, furnishes half of the total, and almost all of the top-grade cork for use in wine bottles. The records of the oldest surviving cork-importing firm, William Rankin and Sons, go back to 1813 when they bought 8,000 acres of forest in the Alentejo for £1,800. Visits to the cork forests of Portugal even as recently as 1860 were extremely difficult and uncomfortable, and the outcome hard to predict. There must have been very many more poor corks a century ago.

"The Corkmaker" is one of the famous series of engravings made for the *Encyclopaedia* projected by Denis Diderot in the 1750s as a French version of the original *Cyclopaedia* of Ephraim Chambers. Diderot illustrated the precise mechanism of all the trades and crafts of 18th-century France (of which cork-making was one of the newest). 120 years later (below), little had changed, as a young corkmaker in Spain demonstrates.

What makes cork so ideal for sealing wine? Its lightness, its cleanness, and the fact that it is available in vast quantities are all important. It is almost impermeable. It is smooth, yet it stays put in the neck of the bottle. It is unaffected by temperature. It rarely rots. Most important of all it is uniquely elastic. Corking machines are based on this simple principle: you can squeeze a cork enough to slip it easily into the bottle and it will immediately spring out to fill the neck without a cranny to spare. As for its life span, it very slowly goes brittle and crumbly, over a period of between 20 and 50 years. Immaculately run cellars (some of the great Bordeaux châteaux, for example) recork their stocks of old wines every 25 years or so, and one or two even send experts to recork their old wines in customers' cellars.

But many corks stay around for half a century.

Today the bark is cut into sheets from mature trees every nine or ten years in mid-summer. The sheets are stacked to dry for three months, then boiled in vats with fungicides. After several more months' storage in a dark, cold cellar, the corks are cut as plugs from the thickness of the bark.

The longest and best-quality corks are graded for the best wine. Dust and scraps from the process are agglomerated to make cheap corks. For specialized use by champagne makers, extra-large corks are made of three layers glued together. A normal wine cork is 24mm in diameter, compressed into an 18mm neck. For champagne a 31mm cork is compressed into a 17.5mm neck, with the upper third protruding in the characteristic bulging mushroom shape.

be the tale of a countryman being shown the sights of London by a cockney friend. They enjoy the entertainments of the town at all levels; some of them richly indecorous. On this occasion he describes a dinner with two country parsons and a Quaker. It becomes clear that the bottlescrew was already an object in common use.

"At last we came to a good-looking . . . bottle of claret, which at least held half a pint extraordinary, but the cork was drove in so far that there was no opening it without a bottlescrew. Several attempted with their thumbs to remove the stubborn obstacle, but no one could effect the difficult undertaking; upon which the donor of the feast: 'What, is nobody amongst us so provident a toper as to carry a bottlescrew about him?' . . . . The oldest and wisest of the parsons, having observed the copious dimensions of the bottle and well knowing by experience that sound corking is always an advantage to good liquor, says, 'I believe I may have a little engine in my pocket that may unlock the difficulty', and fumbling in his pockets, after he had picked out a common prayer-book, an old comb-case full of notes, a two-penny nutmeg grater, and made a great move of such kind worldly necessaries, at last he came to the matter, and out he brings a bottlescrew, which provoked not a little laughter throughout the whole company.

"'Methinks, friend', says the Quaker, 'that a common prayer-book and a bottlescrew are improper companions, not fit to lodge in the pocket together. Why doest thou not make thy breeches afford them separate compartments?' To which the parson made answer: 'Since devotion gives comfort to the soul and wine in moderation preserves the health of the body, why not a book that instructs in the one and an instrument that makes way for the other, allowed as well as the soul and body to bear one another company?'"

PART III

Eighteenth-century luxury: a banquet at the Palazzo Nani in Venice

CHAPTER 20

BORDEAUX REBORN

There have been few times in European history when the rivalries of nations were more blatantly, petulantly, one could almost say childishly displayed than the closing years of the 17th century. Whatever irked a monarch was a pretext to go to war. Underlying the major themes of dynastic successions, rival religions and the Divine Right of Kings, meaty matters that did eventually determine the modern constitutions of nations, ran a dialogue of bickering and jealousy about trade and tariffs and whose ships should carry what that kept international relations in ferment at every level.

The three nations most involved were France, Holland and England, in a web of intrigue and treachery that reflects little credit on anyone. For a large part of his reign, England's King Charles II was secretly in the pay of Louis XIV; money that he accepted shamelessly to give him independence of his parliament. Louis, prodded by his minister Colbert, became so envious of Dutch commercial prosperity that he treacherously invaded the Netherlands. Spain, and the question of whether its empire should pass into French or Austrian hands or be divided, remained the motive (or excuse) for acts of aggression – eventually leading to 11 years of something close to world war, in which France and Spain fought Britain allied to the Austrian Empire. The net outcome of the War of the Spanish Succession was to humble Louis XIV and make Britain the leading European power.

WE HAVE SEEN REPEATEDLY THROUGHOUT OUR STORY how politics shape trade, and trade fashions the wine it wants from wherever it is forced to buy. At this juncture, politics pushed trade about until it grew almost dizzy. But at the same time trade had found a new impetus and new resilience: the wine trade in particular was supplying new classes of customers that encouraged it to diversify.

The days of the petulant sovereigns were the last gestures of medieval-style monarchy. In France everything still centred around the Court: only the king could set a fashion. But England and Holland were no longer overawed by Majesty. The last English king to pretend to absolute power, James II, was firmly shown the door.

The Glorious Revolution of 1688 wedded Dutch and English interests. Charles II's niece Mary married Prince William of Orange, who became William III of England. From now on it was not the king, but ever more independent and opulent grandees who spent the money and set the tone. It is no coincidence that in England, at least, a single generation saw the birth of modern party politics and of great private cellars of the world's best wines.

On April 10th, 1663 (a full three weeks since his last renewal of his fervent vow to abstain from wine entirely), Samuel Pepys, then aged 30, spent an evening drinking at the Royall Oak Tavern in Lombard Street in the City of London with Alexander Brome, an attorney, an editor and a poet of sorts, a merry companion "if he be not a little conceited". Next day in his peculiar coded diary Pepys wrote the most momentous tasting note in the history of Bordeaux. "Drank", he wrote, "a sort of French wine, called Ho Bryan, that hath a good and most particular taste that I ever met with." Pepys, no great connoisseur but a man who liked to be up with the fashion, was the first to record a completely new kind of wine, and that within a few years of its invention. What is more, he characterized it perfectly in that one word, "particular". What he had tasted was Haut-Brion, the first wine from Bordeaux ever to be sold under the name of the estate where it was made; the prototype of every château wine from that day to this.

For 16 centuries England had been buying the majority of its wine from Bordeaux. But it had always been a simple bulk commodity, better or less good according to its freshness, the season, and the competence and honesty of the traders involved. Suddenly, faced with competing new drinks and the impudent thrift of the Dutch, Bordeaux's most dynamic citizen, the first president of the regional parliament, had taken the initiative. In 1660 he started marketing (the modern term seems quite appropriate) the wine of his estate as a distinct brand (another term as yet uncoined) at a substantial premium. And he directed his campaign not at the Dutch, the biggest buyers of the time, but deliberately at Bordeaux's most loyal and oldest market: London.

The Pontac family had been in the ascendant for well over a century. They were landowners and lawyers, not aristocracy but self-confident members of the rising class of merchants, descended from artisans and heading for titles of nobility. Already in 1505 an Arnaud de Pontac had risen through the classic formula of exporting wine and importing cloth to become mayor of Bordeaux.

The Pontac pattern was to be followed time and again in the following centuries. Trade bought land; land brought power – but the acquisitive instinct did not fade in the new landed proprietors as it had in the old aristocracy they were eventually to replace.

In 1660 the Pontac in power was another Arnaud. He had reached the very top: the whole region of Bordeaux, Guyenne, circulated around its Parlement, and as President his revenue and style of life were almost regal. His town house, with four domes, was the grandest of the city's mansions. Only slightly humbler, and infinitely more important to our story, was his ancestral country house an hour's ride to the south: the stone-built château of Haut-Brion, sited by his great-grandfather on the meanest patch of gravel in the region that took its name from its parched and stony soil – the Graves.

Experience had shown that the arid, gritty soil was as good for vines as it was poor for anything else. The Archbishop's estate close by had been admired in centuries past. Not until the second Arnaud, though, did anyone see fit to capitalize on the fact.

As though to underline the novelty of his move, in 1647 a committee had sat to

The name of Pontac was synonymous with the best wine of Bordeaux in the reign of Louis XIV. Arnaud de Pontac, lawyer and landowner, staked his family name on his claret, and the name of his country estate, Haut-Brion (opposite) on his top-quality wine. It was the first wine to be known by anything approaching a brand name, and Haut-Brion was, in time, the first of Bordeaux's "first growths".

establish prices for the different wines of Bordeaux; a sort of distant foreshadowing of the celebrated classification of 1855. The scale of prices is a direct reflection of the formidable new Dutch influence. In 1635 the Dutch had become allies of the French. By 1647 they were calling the tune in the affairs of Bordeaux. Hence a price scale that put their favourite white Sauternes at the top. Dark "palus" wines, made from Petit Verdot grapes, many of them on the Bec d'Ambès, the drained marshes at the confluence of the Dordogne and Garonne, came close behind. But the scale made no distinction of the best sources of "claret". It trailed the coarse "palus" wines in price. And not a single estate is mentioned by name. This was the situation that inspired Arnaud de Pontac to carve out a new sort of market.

What was new about the "Ho-Bryan" that Pepys and Brome found "most particular" – apart from its name? We can only suppose that de Pontac's standards of winemaking were as elevated as his social position. He could afford to be a perfectionist. He could charge for his name; he could limit his crop to gain more flavour and strength; he could reject mouldy grapes and less successful barrels. He presumably possessed a press and may possibly have judged it a good idea to use a little press-wine to "stiffen" his claret and give it more colour and character. Extra time in the vat is a probability. Pontac is described in several references as deep in colour. He could use new barrels for all his wines if he chose, and see to it that the barrels were kept topped right up to the bung. All these practices became standard in the 18th century on prosperous estates setting out to make their reputations. Up to de Pontac's time they were rare or non-existent.

There is no evidence that he was concerned about specific grape varieties, nor that he was aware that older vines make tastier wine. Although it was certainly unusual to have a large block of specialized vineyard, the best conclusion seems to be that Arnaud's real innovation was marketing. He made Haut-Brion his "first-growth"; then, like that other prince of the vine three centuries later, Philippe de Rothschild, he lent his family name to the wine of his other properties, of which, unexpectedly, the principal was the estate of de Pez, in St-Estèphe, far to the north in the then largely undeveloped Médoc, reachable only by river. His Médoc wine

(some also came from Le Taillan, just north of the city) he sold simply as "Pontac". With the two brands he attacked the London market – and with perfect timing.

In 1660 the English had restored a monarch to their throne and ended a decade of Puritan Commonwealth rule. The king had already shown his mettle in his continental exile. Charles II ran a far racier court than Louis XIV. The lighter-minded element at Versailles noted the fact and followed him to London. It is easy to follow Pontac's reasoning; although London just then was not quite the rollicking capital he evidently hoped. In 1665 the Great Plague killed between 70,000 and 100,000 of its inhabitants. The following year, as though to cauterize the wound, the Great Fire laid waste 400 acres of the City. That was the very year that de Pontac sent his son François-Auguste to open a tavern more luxurious than any seen before in England (or possibly even in France), under the sign of "Pontack's Head". It was a roaring success. It stood just behind the Old Bailey, and seems to have remained in business for more than a century, until it was demolished in 1780. Pontack's Head has been called London's first restaurant. Its prices were extremely high: dinner could cost two guineas. Haut-Brion sold for seven shillings a bottle (when two shillings was a normal price for good wine). Pontac and Haut-Brion were also sold retail, to a clientele of London's aristocracy and fashionable men of letters.

THE ENGLISH PHILOSOPHER JOHN LOCKE, DURING HIS FIVE-YEAR STAY IN FRANCE, was intrigued enough to pay a visit to see the apparently unique vineyard that could produce such a "particular" taste. When he arrived at Haut-Brion, on May 14th, 1677, he inspected the vineyard and found it on a little hillock facing west, whose soil "is nothing but pure white sand, mixed with a little gravel. One would imagine it scarce fit to bear anything". As for the price of the wine, he blamed his fellow-countrymen: "A tun of the best wine at Bordeaux, which is that of Médoc or Pontac, is worth . . . 80 or 100 crowns. For this the English may thank their own folly, for, whereas some years since the same wine was sold for 50 or 60 crowns per tun, the fashionable sending over orders to have the best wine sent to them at any rate, they have, by striving who should get it, brought it to that price."

Locke's mention of the Médoc is surprising, since his pilgrimage was to Haut-Brion in the Graves, on the opposite side of town. Vines in the Médoc then were few and scattered. Some, however, did belong to the Pontacs. This is the earliest evidence that the district name (as opposed to the family name) carried any weight.

PONTAC'S INITIATIVE HAD BEEN DAZZLING; ITS PROSPECTS HIGHLY ENCOURAGING. It almost proved premature nonetheless. In 1679 a tariff squabble led the English government to ban French wines altogether. Colbert took advantage of the distress in Bordeaux to try to abolish its "police des vins". In 1682 Arnaud de Pontac died, leaving a messy succession involving lawsuits and resulting in divided ownership – so often the curse of French estates. The English market reopened to a flood of claret in 1685 (in 1687 more barrels were shipped than in any year between the 14th and the 20th centuries) – only to be slammed shut again three years later by the Glorious Revolution and the arrival of William III, whose whole thrust was anti-French.

To make matters worse, the years 1692–95 saw four catastrophic vintages in a row. Bordeaux was even (for one year) forced to admit Languedoc wine via the Canal des Deux Mers to fulfil her depleted order book and supply Paris (where, too, the harvest had failed) and the naval arsenals at La Rochelle and Brest, where the French navy, bottled up by the British blockade, was presumably consoling itself at table. The accounts of Haut-Brion for these years show such wine as there was being sold off either to the navy or to the hostelries of Bordeaux. There was a similar tale of woe at Château Latour, just emerging from the anonymity of the Médoc. Its owner, the Marquis Daulède, sold no wine at all in the four years up to 1693.

William III's war dragged on until 1697, causing almost as much complaint in London as in Bordeaux. In 1691, the frustrated English thirst for claret found its laureate in a doggerel writer called Richard Ames. His "Search after Claret" is a long tavern-crawl; its object "a Bottle of good Old Dry Orthodox Claret". Even:

> At Puntack's the famous french ord'nary, where
> Luxurious eating is never thought dear,
> We expected to meet with a glass of that same
> Wine, which carries the master's own name;
> But his vaults could not yield us a drop of that tipple . . . .

(I'll spare you the final rhyme). Instead of claret, the taverns could only offer him port or madeira.

There was immense relief on both sides in 1697 when William III and Louis XIV signed a treaty – considerably tempered for Ames and his friends by the fact that the English government then charged duty on French wines at more than double the rate charged on Spanish and Portuguese. After a decade of doing without claret, with an ever-greater range of alternatives being offered at lower prices (and not just wines, but spirits, coffee, tea and the rest), it is a wonder that the English persisted in their old affection at all. Most, of course, did not. The great change, remarkably foreseen by Arnaud de Pontac, was that claret in England had become a luxury wine, and a status symbol for a new breed of political potentate.

The shipping figures for the port of Bordeaux in the year 1699–1700 tell the story. Of 86,000 tonneaux loaded in the port, less than 2,000 were (officially) destined for England, a similar number for Ireland (where Dublin was already a considerable city, and the population of the country almost half that of England), and 1,000 for Scotland. Of the rest, more than a half (but mainly white wine) was loaded for Holland, the Baltic and northern Germany, especially Hamburg, and not much less (mainly red) for Brittany and French north-coast ports. How much of this was destined for smuggling to England there is no knowing, although a certain suspicion must rest on the tiny Ile d'Yeu off the French coast, which supplied a very large number of small boats and whose inhabitants (if they drank what they imported) were getting through something like 200 litres of claret a head a year.

The volume of English imports scarcely rose in the few years of peace before the next war, but their cost did. Buying the best wines, with prohibitive duties, Englishmen were paying between six and ten times as much for their Bordeaux as the Dutch (and three times as much for port). At that rate it is not surprising that the few remaining English claret lovers were only interested in the very best wines.

UP TO THIS POINT, THE MEDOC HAS ONLY HAD A PASSING MENTION. By its very nature it is cut off: a long tongue of forested and marshy land running north from Bordeaux between the Gironde estuary and the ocean, with dunes of sand (the world's highest) on the ocean side, and not dissimilar "dunes" of gravel deposited over many millennia along its river shore. Where it narrows at its northern end (the "Bas-Médoc") was so marshy that the northernmost Roman settlement was an island (to them Noviomagus; today "Brion") three miles west of St-Estèphe, where they cultivated oysters. Not until the Dutch "dessiccateurs" were given drainage concessions there in the early 17th century did the fertile fields of today begin to emerge from the swamps.

"Sauvage et solitaire", wild and lonely, was the description given to the whole of the Médoc in the 16th entury. Fortresses going back to the Hundred Years' War dotted the length of the Gironde, but there was no road: communication was by boat between the little harbours and jetties of Macau, Margaux, St-Julien, Pauillac, St-Estèphe and points between. Only the villages nearest Bordeaux, Blanquefort and Le Taillan, had some direct commercial activity, selling wine in taverns in town. Most landowners were absentees, deriving scant rents from scattered hamlets

The draining of marshland to make vineyards and potential vineyards in the Médoc and elsewhere in Gascony was only a small part of the extraordinary Dutch civil-engineering business in the 17th century.

In 1599, King Henri IV gave a concession to a contractor based in Brabant in Flanders to drain all the marshland of France. From his name, Humphrey Bradley, he appears to have been an Englishman. It was a comprehensive concession: Bradley was to arrange everything from finance to who should do the digging.

A landowner applied to Bradley, who put him in touch with a Dutch company of drainers, or "dessiccateurs". The landlord had to make over his land to the contractors to give them authority. They in turn took all the financial risk, and when the work was done kept the larger share of the drained land but paid the owner rent. After two years' residence in France, a Dutchman could become naturalized French without paying the customary tax.

Bradley was adept at interesting influential people, and the vicinity of Bordeaux was soon drained; the main evidence today being the deep ditches, or "jalles", that run down to the river. As time went on the drainers gained status and the right to start manufacturing on their land. Not surprisingly, a number of them stayed and invested their profits in the wine business.

Amsterdam cartographer Jocondus Hondius' map shows the route up the river
Gironde to Bordeaux from the sea, with the Médoc in the foreground. When it was
drawn, in about 1629, the Dutch were by far the biggest buyers of Bordeaux's wine.

in the forest. Where there were vines, they were part of a mixed subsistence
agriculture. In 1572 the domaine of Lafite was divided among some 60 tenants, who
mainly grew wheat.

Nonetheless, it was only a few years after the Pontacs started work on their
Graves estate that a handful of Bordeaux lawyers and "parlementaires" had a similar
idea about the Médoc. The old aristocracy was not unwilling to sell its rights over
such marginal fragments. The name of the game was consolidation. What is
immediately striking is that the first estates to be consolidated remain the first-
growths to this day. It must have been very clear to these ambitious investors that
the best vineyard land was, like Haut-Brion, the most unpromising-looking gravel,
which, particularly in the Médoc, is found on the highest of the low swellings of the
land (they scarcely merit the name of hills) designated by the names "Lafite",
"Lamotte" – and also "Brion".

In the 1570s, one Pierre de Lestonnac began assembling small parcels of land
around "Lamothe-Margaux", the future Château Margaux. In the same years the
Pontacs were acquiring properties in St-Estèphe, Le Taillan and the Bas-Médoc.
Best documented of all is the enterprise of Arnaud de Mullet, who by 1595 had
become proprietor of the estate of Latour de St-Mambert – known to future
generations simply as Latour. His son Denis was to absorb all the micro-properties
of tenants, buy more adjoining land, and by the 1650s complete the transformation
from a feudal patchwork to an estate in the modern sense, run by a salaried manager
or "régisseur". At the same time he planted vines where wheat had grown before,
taking advantage of his right as a privileged citizen of Bordeaux to send his wine up-
river to the city by gabare (the shallow-draft Bordeaux barge) to be sold on the
Bordeaux market.

There is no doubt that agriculturally the new nobility of Bordeaux had profited by the example of the Dutch (as well as by their engineering). When the Dutch put in their new vineyards in the dark earth of the palus beside the river it is was in the tidy polder style; the vines all of one kind, in straight rows so that oxen could pull a plough between them. Old Bordeaux vineyards had been planted "en foule" – the French for higgledy-piggledy – propagated by layering and workable only laboriously with a spade.

When Denis died the Latour estate was inherited by the family of Daulède de Lestonnac, already proprietors of Château Margaux and in due course to succeed to a share of Haut-Brion. To an extraordinary extent it was one family, or rather one close-knit and interrelated group of local politicians, which founded and developed the whole concept of the Bordeaux "château" – and the first-growth one at that.

THE BREATHING SPACE BETWEEN THE TREATY OF 1697 and the outbreak of the next and more widespread war was too brief to allow a serious new initiative by the first-growths in England. London was being provisioned by Spain and Portugal – and also by Tuscany, whose "Florence", bottled in flasks and packed in wicker hampers, was a fashionable alternative to an all-Iberian diet. The principal change when war started again was the exclusion of the (now enemy) Spanish wines – to the glee of the Portuguese.

The English were to grow more and more accustomed to drinking white wine from Lisbon and red wine from Oporto, not to mention madeira and even "Fayall" from the Azores: every Portuguese flavour, in fact. A little relief came down the Rhine in the form of Rhenish, or via the merchants of Amsterdam, who managed, even at the height of the war, between 1705–09, to negotiate passports for their ships into Bordeaux. But for top-quality claret and other French wines, the only recourse was the harvest from privateers operating under all colours in the western approaches and the English Channel.

The record of sales of "prize wines" – wines captured at sea by privateers, to be sold by auction in the coffee houses of London, Bristol or Plymouth – gives a fascinating insight into the progress of the first-growths, their recognition by the British public and the prices they fetched. It also poses a question with no apparent answer: what were these precious goods doing at all in the narrow waters infested with sea robbers that separated France from England?

In 1703, the year war broke out, one of the first prizes to be brought in was the good ship *Prophet Daniel*, laden with white wines from Bordeaux and the High Country and also with claret, unspecified. The white wines fetched £8 a tun; the claret £25. The *Golden Pearl of Stettin* (evidently a Baltic ship) carried a similar cargo, but with claret of widely different qualities that fetched between £8 and £60 a tun. Other ships captured were carrying Spanish wines, sherry, sack, Canary and Málaga.

By 1705 prizes had been brought into port with cargoes of Loire wines and brandies as well as the usual barrels from Bordeaux, the High Country and divers parts of Spain. But in May 1705 began a sequence of substantial auctions of "first-growth" claret. In the first auction there were 200 barrels of Haut-Brion and Pontac (sold two barrels at a time), a month later 230 barrels of Haut-Brion and "Margose"

(Château Margaux now had the same proprietor as Haut-Brion), and only two weeks after that the cargo of the *St-Jean-Baptiste*: 288 barrels of Pontac, Margaux and Haut-Brion. The prices fetched were about £60 a tun.

It is very hard not to smell a rat in this sudden apparition, on the high seas, of a quantity of one proprietor's wines that must have represented his entire production. Not many years earlier the harvest at Haut-Brion filled 50-odd barrels. Even with the production of de Pez and his other properties 718 barrels is a remarkable amount. What prudent proprietor would have loaded it all in three ships at the same time? Where were they going? And who had bought the wine? Was it a mad merchant of Amsterdam taking the risk?

Various suspicions cross my mind. First, it seems probable, if not obvious, that the Pontacs and Daulèdes were making a calculated assault once more on the London market: their only serious market, war or no war. Second, since the privateer received a large proportion of the price (the government getting the rest, with a fee to the coffee-house owner), is it just possible that the privateer was under charter to the château owners? Nobody could afford to lose his entire crop to the enemy year after year (which is more or less what happened). The simplest explanation is that a private arrangement brought the auction price, less some fairly hefty commissions, back to Bordeaux.

First-growth tastes were not the only ones catered for. In 1706 the Breton ship *Mary of Oléron* was taken with a cargo of palus wine. Perhaps she was heading for Holland. The same year Sauternes turned up for the first time, under its village

---

THE WINE-BREWER'S TRIAL

Smuggling and privateering were by no means the only way of relieving the wine shortage during times of war. In 1709 Joseph Addison reported in *The Tatler* on the (imaginary) trial of the "wine brewers" – "a certain fraternity of chymical operators, who work underground in holes, taverns and dark retirements, to conceal their mysteries from the eyes and observations of mankind". These enterprising professional adulterators could "squeeze Bourdeaux out of a sloe, and draw Champagne from an Apple".

The fabrication of false wines was viewed with alarm as they were believed (with some justification, one imagines) harmful to consumers. One wine brewer had even been heard to boast that with one tun of so-called "claret", "he should give the gout to a dozen of the healthfullest men in the city, provided that their constitutions were prepared for it by wealth and idleness". A group of wine brewers was asked to bring their ingredients and utensils into the court and to show their art. One Tom Tintoret claimed to be the greatest master of colouring in London. This he proved by the addition, drop by drop, of some red colouring into water. First he made

some beautiful pale Burgundy, then a perfect Languedoc, passing to a florid Hermitage, ending with a very deep Pontack. The judge was so impressed that he offered to find him a job with a scarlet-dyer of his acquaintance.

Then came the turn of the famous Harry Sippet, who offered to prepare any wine the judge might care to drink. When the judge asked for claret he dropped some inky juice into a glass of white wine. Having decided against trying it for himself, the judge's eye fell upon a suitable taster: his cat. After only one sip "it flung her . . . into freakish tricks, quite contrary to her usual gravity" and "in less than a quarter of an hour she fell into convulsions".

The judge was so incensed by this torture that he called the wine brewers no better than assassins or murderers, then asked them not to poison any of his friends. As for his own health, "I am resolved hereafter to be very careful in my liquors, and have agreed with a friend of mine in the army, upon their next march, to secure me two hogsheads of the very best stomach-wine in the cellars of Versailles, for the good of lucubrations, and the comfort of my old age."

This was the clientele the first-growth proprietors had in their sights: the nobility and gentry of England. The brothers Clarke "taking wine with other gentlemen" were painted by Gawen Hamilton in London in the 1730s.

names of Bommes and Preignac, decribed as "pure and strong" – not, at this stage, sweet. An enormous amount of brandy was regularly captured. To cope with these random quantities, new wine merchants set up shop; this was more than the simple old vintage-by-vintage trade could handle.

However the system worked, it encouraged the owners of Bordeaux's two other "first-growths" to follow suit. In May 1707, "an entire parcel of New French Clarets" was offered at Brewer's Key, near the Tower of London, "being of the growths of Lafite, Margaux and Latour". They were the new season's wines, shipped without racking on their "gross lees". In the same week the cargo of the *Liberté* was auctioned: 200 barrels of Haut-Brion. Who can doubt that it was all a cosy arrangement? If the only way to your market was to steal your own goods, what harm was done?

BY THE LATER STAGES OF THE WAR, it must have become clear to proprietors in the Médoc that the peace would bring them a fortune. At last the Dutch star was falling in Bordeaux. After 1709 no passports were issued to Dutch ships and the price of their favourite white and palus wines fell, while the English appetite for "new French claret" from the Médoc promised a golden future. Tasting notes described with relish these splendid clarets, better than anything known before, not just as "particular", Pepys-fashion, but as "bright, deep, fresh and neat".

When in 1709 a terrible winter froze northern Europe, killing large numbers of the Bordeaux vines, the need to replant to be ready for the end of the war seized the Médoc and started what contemporaries described as "a fury of planting". In the next 20 years the Médoc we know today was born.

CHAPTER 21

THE FIRST PERFECTIONIST

Of all the world's great wines, only one is popularly credited with an inventor. The wine is champagne, and the man held responsible a Benedictine monk, Dom Pierre Pérignon, the treasurer of the Abbey of Hautvillers, which has overlooked the river Marne from its vine-covered slope since the time of the ascetic St Columbanus. Hautvillers was founded in 650 in the spirit of Columbanus, to be a place of untiring work and prayer. Its fame, as well as its holiness, was ensured by the possession of what were believed to be the remains of the body of St Helena, the mother of the Emperor Constantine. But since the archives of the Abbey disappeared in the French Revolution neither allegation, the relics or the invention, is any longer capable of proof or disproof.

Many different claims have been made about good Father Pérignon. The easiest to dismiss is that champagne suddenly became sparkling in his cellars. Many legends about him, such as the idea that he was blind, that he was the first to use corks, that he said "I am drinking stars", or that he could unfailingly name a precise vineyard by tasting a single grape of its production, seem to have been inspired by the fantasies of the last treasurer of the Abbey, Dom Grossard, who was obliged to leave when the Revolution closed it down. It may be argued that Grossard had had access to the lost archives (although nobody before him had told these stories), but it seems more likely that he simply liked to embroider the already lofty reputation of his predecessor. For Pérignon seems to have become almost the patron saint of Champagne within his own lifetime. It is intriguing that we can only surmise the reason why.

When Dom Pérignon was appointed treasurer of Hautvillers in 1668, at the age of 29, the Abbey was just finding its feet again after a catastrophic 30 years of continual wars and military occupations. The position of Champagne on the map, at one of Europe's great crossroads, has made it perpetually prone to the tramp of armies since the beginning of history, as well as making it a natural centre for commerce: witness its pan-European fairs of the Middle Ages. The Hundred Years' War repeatedly devastated parts of the region. Then in 1560 Hautvillers was destroyed in the Wars of Religion and its monks retired to Reims for 40 years. When they rebuilt and reoccupied the Abbey, a brief generation of peace was to pass

The name of the cellar-master Dom Pérignon, shown in a stained glass window
from Epernay, has been successfully exploited to sell champagne for generations.
On these slopes overlooking the river Marne he perfected its luxurious flavour.

before the marches and countermarches of the Thirty Years' War again turned
Champagne into a great military parade ground. The civil wars of the "Fronde"
brought years of occupation by mercenaries up to 1659. Whichever side they were
on, they were equally destructive. The troops of Marshal Turenne drank 600 barrels
of wine at Hautvillers alone. "It is not dogs that the King sends to guard his flock,
but wolves", wrote a miserable citizen of Reims.

In the 1660s the people of Champagne had not seen the last of armies, although
the battles were over for a while. Louis XIV's wars in the Netherlands and Germany
kept troops continuously camped in or marching through the region. But however
frustrating and menacing they were, this was the period when champagne made its
great leap into prominence; a feat greater and more far-reaching even than the
activities of the de Pontacs in Bordeaux in the very same years.

IN A SENSE CHAMPAGNE WAS ONLY RECOVERING LOST GROUND. It had been
acknowledged in Paris in the 15th century that the wines of Aÿ (originally
considered among the "vins de France", rather than coming from a distinct region)
were of exceptional quality. In the early 16th century, King François I was glad to
call himself "Roi d'Aÿ et de Gonesse" – Gonesse was the place reputed to produce
the finest flour for white bread in the north of France. The name of Aÿ came to be
used as shorthand for the whole district, just as "Beaune" was used for Burgundy.
The same wines were alternatively known as "vins de la rivière": wines, that is,
from the north bank of the Marne opposite Epernay. The vineyards here slope
steeply up to the "mountain" that separates the Marne valley from the district of
Reims. "Mountain" is a slight exaggeration for this substantial flat-topped hill,
crowned with a forest of beech, but "vins de la montagne" was the term for the less
highly esteemed production of the vineyards on its gentle northern slope.

In the later years of the 16th century the wines of the mountain also found a
powerful advocate at court: Pierre Brulart, a privy councillor of King Henry III, a
Parisian who had married the heiress of a great estate at Sillery, near Reims, with
vineyards on its southern flank at Verzenay, Mailly and Ludes. Their son Nicholas
became Chancellor of France under the great and benevolent Henry IV, the king

who will always be remembered for desiring that every Sunday every peasant in France should be able to have a "poule au pot". Nicholas's son was ennobled in 1621 by Louis XIII as Marquis de Sillery, and Sillery was to remain one of the great wine names of the world for nearly two centuries.

THE ABBEY THAT RECRUITED DOM PÉRIGNON AS ITS TREASURER had already set its sights on developing its wine business. The Brularts were an example of what could be done, and since the Wars of Religion St Helena was no longer the pilgrim-puller she had been. In 1661 the Abbot commissioned a great new vaulted cellar. Hautvillers possessed a modest 25 acres of vineyards of its own, but was paid tithes of grapes from villages around; most notably Aÿ and Avenay. The payment of these tithes was a matter for endless wrangling that raises the most fundamental question about the wine of the region at the time. We know that it was not sparkling. We know they were growing black grapes, the Pinot Noir among them. But was the wine red or white, or something in between?

The debate arose over tithes because they were collected in kind, in the vineyards, during the vintage. Small barrels called "trentins" were distributed, and had to be filled with grapes packed tight by treading. In the case of Aÿ, the Abbey had the right to one barrel in 11. The citizens objected that if they trod their grapes into the trentins the juice would be stained red by the skins. It ruined their chance of making their best wine, which was white. They would prefer to pay in wine (or cash) when the wine was made.

The question of red or white was crucial because the region had deliberately set out to compete with Burgundy as far back as the days of the Valois Dukes. It was probably then, in the 15th century, that Pinot Noir was planted. And red was what was wanted. Reims was on the road followed by Flemish wine merchants travelling to Beaune; they were glad to be offered a cheaper alternative with a similar flavour and after a shorter journey. Their wines did not quite achieve the "moelleux", the richness, of burgundy, but their colour could be (and was) deepened with elderberries.

Why then did the people of Aÿ want to make white? Because experience showed that if their red could never be truly first class, their best attempts at white wine could. This was presumably even more true of the Brularts' wine at Sillery, which does not have the advantage of a south slope to ripen its Pinot Noir. White wine made from white grapes had nothing like the same flavour and, they found, quickly turned "yellow". What they actually made was a very pale wine, varying with the vintage from claret colour to "gris" (grey), a slightly darkened white, but more often "oeil de perdrix" (partridge eye), a shade of delicate pink caused by the white juice having brief contact with the red skins. Hence the fuss about the trentins for the tithes. And hence, it seems probable, the first success of Dom Pérignon. He organized the harvesting in such a way as to achieve truly white wine, and at the same time studied the best vineyards, the best timing, the best techniques, and the best way of preserving the wine to make it as aromatic as possible, silky in texture and long in flavour.

The golden rules of winemaking that were established in Dom Pérignon's time, presumably by him, were set out in 1718, three years after his death, by the very precise Canon Godinot. First, use only Pinot Noir. The vineyards of the region also contained Pinot Meunier, Pinot Gris (or Fromenteau), Pinot Blanc (or Morillon), Chasselas and perhaps Chardonnay. Dom Pérignon did not approve of white grapes partly because they increased a latent tendency in the wine to referment.

Second, prune the vines hard so that they grow no higher than three feet and produce a small crop.

Third, harvest with every precaution so that the grapes are kept intact, on their stalks, and as cool as possible. Work early in the morning. Choose showery days in hot weather. And reject any grapes that are broken or even bruised. Small grapes are better than big ones. Lay out wicker trays in the vineyard and pick over the crop for rotten grapes, leaves or anything undesirable. Even lay a damp cloth over the grapes in the sun. They must be kept fresh at all costs. If possible have the press house nearby so that you can carry the harvest in by hand, but if animals are essential, choose mules: they are less excitable than horses. Failing mules, donkeys.

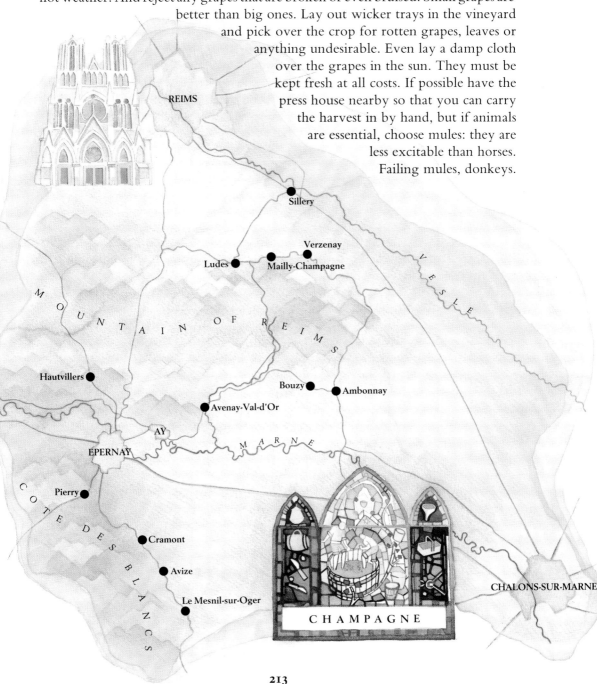

Fourth, on no account tread the grapes or allow any maceration of the skins in the juice. An efficient and fast-working press is essential (peasants, therefore, stood no chance of making this kind of wine). The press must be used repeatedly and briefly, and the juice from each pressing kept apart. The first, the "vin de goutte", runs with the mere weight of laying on the wooden beams. Its wine alone is too delicate; it lacks body. The next two pressings, the first and second tailles or "cuts" (because the cake of grapes must be cut up and replaced in the press) are of good quality. The fourth, the "vin de taille" is rarely acceptable, and any further "cuts" are "vins de pressoir", but this time distinctly coloured and of no use to the perfectionist cellarmaster. The press-house workers were completely exhausted by the quick-fire work, day after day for three weeks or more. That was part of the price for extraordinarily fine wine.

ALL REPORTS AGREE THAT DOM PERIGNON STUDIED HIS RAW MATERIALS with the minutest care. It is true that he tasted his grapes. It was his habit to pick them in the evening and leave them all night by his open window before tasting them in the morning. Perhaps a very slight concentration of flavour took place overnight. He was a man of very abstemious habits. A newspaper reported after his death that "this monk, whom one would expect to be a gourmet, never drank wine and lived almost entirely on cheese and fruit". Could this explain the delicacy of his palate?

The blending of wines was a regular practice, but Pérignon, it is said, blended the grapes from different vineyards before they even went into the press. He had three press houses at his disposal, and grapes from many different plots. It was his discovery that carefully judged proportions of grapes from a number of different vineyards, according to their ripeness and the distinctive flavours derived from their soils, made a better and more consistent wine than lots pressed individually. It is the exact opposite of the philosophy of Cîteaux, whose monks strove to distinguish and differentiate, letting the soil show through the Pinot Noir. At its simplest it could be explained as an attempt to guarantee quality and consistency, which makes it sound almost suspiciously like the public-relations patter of a modern Champagne house.

The more one learns about Dom Pérignon, the harder it is to decide exactly what he did to make his Abbey's wines as valuable as their invoices show that they were. In 1700 the "most excellent" wines of the region sold for 500 livres a cask, but those of Hautvillers (and also of another Abbey, St-Pierre-aux-Monts at Pierry, whose treasurer, Dom Oudart, was a friend and colleague of Dom Pérignon's) sold for 800 to 900 livres. So famous was Pérignon by this time that Parisians took him to be a village like Aÿ or an abbey like Hautvillers, and looked for his name on the map. But the most impressive evidence of the advance of champagne in his lifetime is the fact that in 1706 it was reported that "a recent traveller had drunk champagne in Siam and Surinam". Such travels would have been impossible without the mastery of bottling. We should look in the cellar as well as the vineyard and the press house to see what advances the famous monk was making.

His region's wine presented one great problem to Pérignon. It had an inherent instability: a tendency to stop fermenting as the cold weather closed in in autumn, then start again with rising temperatures in spring. This did no harm while the wine was still in cask in the cellar, but Pérignon was not enamoured of the cask. He found it "tired" his wines and they lost all their famous aroma, unless they were bottled as soon as possible. Pérignon used intensive cellar-work to prepare them. The abbé Pluche, who seems to have known his methods, wrote in 1744, "Lees and air are the two plagues of wine". To rid the wine of all lees needed repeated rackings into clean barrels, with the attendant risk of exposing the wine to too much air. The answer was laborious: as many as 12 successive rackings by the method that allowed the least splashing and contact with air, by forcing the wine from one cask to another with a bellows providing pressure from the top.

The lighter and greener the wine, experience showed, the more subject it was to fizzing in the spring. White-grape wine was fizziest; one of the reasons why Pérignon used only black grapes. But black-grape wine, made with his precautions, also lasted and matured for far longer. "Formerly the wine of Aÿ lasted hardly a year", wrote the abbé Pluche, "but since white grapes have not been used in the wines of Champagne, those of the mountain of Reims keep for eight to ten years, and those of the Marne easily go five or six."

IN ENGLAND, CELLAR WORK WAS NOT SO METICULOUS. A treatise under the title "The Mysterie of Vintners" was presented to the newly formed Royal Society in 1662. Its subtitle tells all: "A Brief Discourse concerning the various sicknesses of wines, and their respective remedies, at this day commonly used". A wine merchant was a wine doctor. Among the remedies were beetroot for colouring pale claret, elderflowers, lavender, cinnamon, cloves, ginger . . . . To preserve Rhenish must, the author tells us, the Dutch "rub the insides of the vessel with cheese". More alarmingly, "country vintners feed their fretting wine with raw beef", and most off-putting, "herrings roes preserve any stum [that is, muted or stopped] wine". These are the practices of honest vintners. "Many other ways there are of adulterating wines, daily practised in this our (otherwise well-governed) City."

Many wines are mentioned by name. Champagne is not among them. But one sentence is momentous in our story: "Our wine-coopers of later times use vast quantities of Sugar and molasses to all sorts of wines, to make them drink brisk and sparkling." In the very next year, 1663, the satirist Samuel Butler, in his "Hudibras", makes the first English mention of "brisk Champagne". Champagne was not a normal part of the repertoire of the English wine trade. But it was already known in London, and coming into fashion, three years after Charles II took the throne (and five years before Dom Pérignon moved to Hautvillers). And there is an implication (although less than evidence) that it was rather fizzy. By 1676 it was specifically described, on stage, as "sparkling".

WE KNOW WHO WAS RESPONSIBLE for the prompt modishness of champagne in London at a time when

It was the whim of the Sun King to be portrayed in classical guises. Any less likely Bacchus than this vain puritan is difficult to imagine.

it was still a rarefied taste in Paris. It was the Marquis de St-Evremond, a soldier, courtier and irrepressible satirist who had been threatened with a third sojourn in the Bastille for a malicious letter he had written about Cardinal Mazarin, Louis XIV's prime minister. In Paris, St-Evremond and his friends were known as Epicureans, or laughingly as the Ordre des Coteaux because they would drink nothing but "Coteaux d'Aÿ", "Coteaux d'Hautvillers" or "Coteaux d'Avenay".

In London St-Evremond made himself the unofficial agent of champagne, with immediate effect. In 1664 the Earl of Bedford ordered three tonneaux of Sillery for his palace at Woburn. Buckingham, Arlington, all the grandees of the day took to the new taste. With it they ordered bottles and corks: the new strong bottle invented by Sir Kenelm Digby. Unlike the vintners, they probably did not "use vast quantities of Sugar and molasses". But they did find their champagne, bottled on arrival, was perceptibly fizzy, if not downright frothing, when they opened it months, perhaps even years, later. What is more, to the disgust of St-Evremond, they were delighted with the fizz, and rapidly noticed its uninhibiting effect. The old Epicure was as repelled by bubbles in his favourite wine as we would be by bubbles in our claret. Dom Pérignon was fully in agreement. It was his life's work to prevent champagne having bubbles, and make a white wine the court would prefer to red burgundy.

Needless to say, the bubbles won. It took much longer in France. Paris was already in love with the glorious white wine whose "perfume so embalms the senses that it could raise one from the dead". In 1674 champagne was "so frantically fashionable that all other wines scarcely passed, in smart circles, as more than 'vinasse'", or as we might say, plonk. Louis XIV had simply never drunk anything else. He was a great conservative. He never tried coffee or chocolate or tea, or spirits, until in 1695 his all-powerful physician Fagon put him onto a mixture of old ("usé") burgundy and water. The Burgundians were no doubt delighted, but by this time champagne was permanently established.

Louis XIV gave the signal for the start of regular commerce in champagne in 1691. He created the office of "courtier-commissionnaire", giving (for a hefty price) the right to set prices, arrange purchases and take commissions, although not actually to buy and sell. This essential activity was still done by personal contact or at an open market: buying to hold stock was not unknown, but it was illegal. It was also illegal to sell or transport champagne in anything but barrels. A trade in sparkling champagne was therefore strictly speaking impossible. Admittedly wine was delivered in bottles by, among others, Dom Pérignon. He wrote in 1694: "I gave" (he does not say sold) "26 bottles of wine, the best in the world." It was also impossible up to this time for another reason: France did not have bottles strong enough to take any pressure. Her glassworks were still wood-fired. There were many experiments with different shapes, from globes to pears, and English glass blowers went to work at Ste-Menehould, the nearest glasshouse. But the problem remained until the 1730s: if champagne became really "mousseux", the bottle would probably burst.

The precise Canon Godinot gives us the best indication of when the fashion changed. In 1718 he wrote, "for more than 20 years French taste has preferred vin mousseux". To reconcile the state of taste and the lack of bottles is a problem. The solution, perhaps, is that "mousseux" is a relative term. Given only the natural tendency to referment (and no English-style addition of sugar), wine bottled in March (the full moon was preferred, when high atmospheric pressure helps to keep the wine "tranquil" and clear) would be variably fizzy, but probably most often in the condition known today as "crémant" with just enough gas to pop the cork.

An English play of 1698, about the date Godinot indicates, seems to confirm the state of sparkle. The play is *Love and a Bottle* by the Dubliner George Farquhar. Club, the valet of the fashionable Mr Mockmode, pours out his champagne. "See how it puns and quibbles in the glass", he says: a marvellously apt image for the jostling of random bubbles in a crémant wine, less apt for the racing streamers of bubbles in a fully sparkling one. The French used various terms for this slightly foamy wine: "sablant", "pétillant" or "mousseux" all meant the same thing.

BY THE TIME DOM PÉRIGNON WAS 60, fashion was demanding more and more of the sparkling wine he had spent his career trying to avoid. Nobody knew more about it than he – his experience of cellar work would have been invaluable whether you wanted bubbles or not. He certainly knew, for example, that the cooler the vintage and the lighter and more acidic the wine, the less fully it fermented in autumn; therefore the more potential it had for sparkling the following year. White wines from white grapes were lighter and more prone to referment, so a proportion of them was increasingly added. At first the desire for sparkle led makers into overdoing the under-ripeness. The Epernay landowner and one of the first champagne merchants, Bertin de Rocheret, described one champagne in about 1700 as "green and hard as a dog, dry as the devil". "Montagne" wines were rarely used: the famous Sillery remained "vin gris", and utterly tranquil, until the early 19th century; the champagne of old-fashioned, unfrivolous connoisseurs. Increasingly, the best white-grape wines came from certain villages on the hills south of Epernay: Cramant, Avize, Le Mesnil were recognized for qualities of their own.

A most important factor, increasingly so with sparkling wines, was good cellarage. Deep cellars with unchanging temperatures could make all the difference between bottles bursting or not. The subsoil (and indeed the soil) of Champagne is solid chalk. "Spreading the butter of vegetation on the dry bread of chalk", is how one writer describes agriculture in the region. Chalk, happily, is the ideal material for excavating deep, capacious cellars with little risk of collapse. It is said that Dom Ruinart, another religious colleague of Dom Pérignon's, made the momentous discovery, under the city of Reims itself, of gigantic funnel-shaped chalk quarries

---

The continuing distaste of French connoisseurs for sparkling champagne appears in this note on Avize, the principal white-grape-growing village, in 1744, by Bertin de Rocheret, the first celebrated champagne merchant.

"Avize is quite a considerable town, enormously enlarged over the last 12 or 15 years by the frantic invention of sparkling wine. It was still poor in 1710 ... their vineyards, almost all planted with white-grape vines, only produced a little wine with a harsh taste and with one of the lowest reputations of the region, selling for 25 or 30 livres the barrel ... but since the mania for 'saute-bouchon', this abominable drink, made even more disagreeable by intolerable acidity, sells for up to 300 livres; also Avize has broken out in so many fancy press houses that you would not recognize it."

dug by the Romans for building stone and long since forgotten. Ruinart's nephew Nicolas founded what is considered the oldest surviving Champagne "house", using these "crayères", in 1729. In 1716 an even more familiar name had made its appearance: Claude Moët, a grower of Epernay, bought himself the recently created office of a courtier-commissionnaire. Now that champagne-making was becoming so complicated, involving capital to buy and bottle wine, the development of a specialized manufacturing side to the business was inevitable.

STILL THE FIZZINESS OR OTHERWISE OF THE WINE REMAINED A HIT–AND–MISS AFFAIR, and the sufficient strength of the bottles extremely uncertain. So much so that once an order was placed the risk of "casse", of bottles bursting, was borne by the purchaser. Depending largely on the vintage, anything between 20 percent and 90 percent of the bottles exploded. It was the height of folly to walk through a champagne cellar without an iron mask to protect your face from flying glass.

By 1735 the business was well-enough established for a royal ordinance to dictate the shape, size and weight of champagne bottles, the size of cork they should use (an inch and a half long) and the way they should be tied down with strong pack thread to the collar of the bottle. Since pressure was unpredictable, all champagnes, whether sparkling or not, were lashed down in the same way.

There remained the question of sediment. Any refermentation produces a residue of dead yeast cells, which are trapped in the bottle and will look unsightly in the glass. Modern champagne-making, which involves adding both sugar and yeast to achieve a high degree of sparkle, produces so much sediment that removing it is an essential part of the process. But when there was only a little yeast left naturally in the wine the sediment was usually tolerable. Early 18th-century champagne glasses, elegant conical "flutes", were often made with a dimpled surface to hide any slight sediment in the wine. In years when the sediment was substantial there was nothing for it but the uncertain and wasteful process of "dépotage", or decanting the wine into another bottle, losing a great deal of the precious gas en route. The modern system of "remuage", indeed the whole process understood by the term méthode champenoise, was not to begin for almost another hundred years. Throughout the 18th century the majority of champagne remained still wine (and much of it red). It was only a minority of light-minded customers (and rich ones, too) who became addicted to the "saute-bouchon".

JUST HOW LIGHT-MINDED IS MADE REMARKABLY CLEAR in the memoirs of the Regency that followed the death of Louis XIV in 1715. The later years of the Sun King's reign had been less than brilliant. Although Paris was enjoying an economic boom, life at Versailles was austere and boring. The Regent, Philippe d'Orléans, held a very different court at the Palais Royal. He surrounded himself with ladies of high rank and no morals at all, and the "roués", who were defined as "men of the world, who have neither virtue nor principles, but who make their vices seductive, even ennobling them with elegance and wit". Philippe himself coined the term roué; they were so wicked, he said, they deserved to be broken on the wheel.

The nightly "petits soupers" at the Palais Royal deserved all the scandalized gossip that surrounded them. The Duc de Richelieu laid all the blame on the

The Oyster Lunch is the title of this painting of the 1720s by Jean François de Troy, but all eyes are on the flying champagne cork: the "saute-bouchon". Sparkling champagne became the rage of high society in Paris under the Regency of Philippe d'Orleans, whose nightly parties at the Palais Royal were very much less decorous than this.

fashionable wine: "The orgies never started until everyone was in that state of joy that champagne brings". The games were led by the Regent himself, who liked to see his mistresses (including the Duchesse de Berry, his own daughter) perform tableaux as Greek goddesses, although less modestly dressed. The candles were taken away to give free reign to the emotions provoked by champagne. Sometimes the host would wait until the darkness was full of sighs and then throw open a cupboard full of lighted candles to illuminate the luxurious scene.

No other wine, no other drink, had ever created, by its special qualities, a whole mood that almost amounted to a way of life. We can speculate about what those qualities were, but it seems likely that we would recognize them. The perfectionism preached by the Abbey treasurer had given the world its first wine of unmistakable, irresistible quality: a model that all other wines with pretentions to excellence would have to emulate.

If the Regency in Paris became over-excited by champagne, Londoners were no less so. They simply expressed their excitement in a different way. *The Connoisseur* of June 6th, 1754, reported:

"Some bloods being in company with a celebrated fille de joye, one of them pulled off her shoe, and in excess of galantry filled it with champagne, and drank it off to her health. In this delicious draught he was immediately pledged by the rest, and then, to carry the compliment still further, he ordered the shoe itself to be dressed and served up for Supper. The cook set himself seriously to work upon it: he pulled the upper part (which was of damask) into fine shreds, and tossed it up in ragout; minced the sole; cut the wooden heel into very thin slices, fried them in batter, and placed them round the dish for garnish. The company, you may be sure, testified their affection for the lady by eating very heartily of this exquisite impromptu: and as this transaction happened just after the French king had taken a cobbler's daughter [a Miss Murphy] for his mistress, Tom Pierce (who has the stile as well as art of a French cook) in his bill politely called it, in honour of her name, De Soulier à la Murphy."

CHAPTER 22

ANYTHING BUT PORT

If champagne, and the "new French clarets" of the Bordeaux parlementarians, were wines created specifically for a growing class of rich and more or less discriminating customers, port, which shares their birth date almost precisely, was just as precisely the opposite. It was a makeshift, wished on the English by their politicians. Two elements entered their calculations: an embargo on imports from enemy France, and the brazen intention of taking advantage of an old ally. There were few scruples in the way England imposed herself upon the luckless Portuguese. The port-wine trade is a happy ending to a story with a fairly discreditable start.

PORTUGAL IN THE 15TH AND 16TH CENTURIES had flung herself into overseas exploration and expansion with utter recklessness. The feats of her navigators, without any precedent, had gone to the nation's head. This tiny people had fanned out across the world from Greenland to Goa, from China to Brazil. In doing so they had almost shut up shop at home. Their own fields were left untilled while their menfolk sailed away to bring back the exotic produce of any number of new worlds. When in 1580 the King of Portugal died in battle in a typically harebrained expedition against the Moors in Morocco, the cold-blooded Philip II of Spain annexed his neighbour's realms. Portugal's imperial revenues became the revenues of Madrid. Philip launched his armada against England, Portugal's ally, from Lisbon. The "captivity" of Portugal by Spain lasted for 60 years.

England and Holland both used the opportunity and the excuse to buccaneer into her overseas possessions. The Dutch took Formosa and with it most of her China trade; Cochin and Negapatam and with them her position in India; Malacca and her Malaysian colony. The English merely interfered in India and Brazil.

At the same time England introduced her own goods into the domestic vacuum in Portugal, so that when freedom from Spain finally came, with the Battle of Montijo in 1644, her relations with England were distinctly one-sided and rather too close for comfort. Portugal was at risk of becoming an English colony. To make matters worse, Portugal supported the losing Royalist side in England's Civil War. Cromwell, the victor, took advantage of the fact to consolidate England's advantages in a treaty. England was to have access to Portugal's markets both at home and (most importantly) in Brazil. As a sop certain Portuguese goods, some textiles for example, were to be protected from the overwhelming English competition. These terms, agreed in 1654, were reaffirmed when England's King Charles II married the Portuguese Catherine of Braganza in 1662. As an additional dowry Charles received Bombay, Tangier and the port of Galle in Ceylon. The English were so well established in Portugal, with so many privileges, that when they quarrelled with France it is no wonder they came to Portugal for wine. It was already almost as though they were buying it from themselves.

IN THE 1660S THERE WERE THREE ESTABLISHED ENGLISH TRADING HEADQUARTERS in Portugal: the feitorias, or factories, at Lisbon, Oporto, and Viana in the Minho, the northernmost province. The English firm of Hunt, Roope was founded in 1654 to conduct a typical trading operation, in this case a triangular one between Portugal, London and Newfoundland. From England they sailed to Newfoundland to catch or buy cod. Bacalhau, dried cod, is Portugal's staple diet. They docked in Viana with cod and exchanged it for red Minho wine, which they took to England, returning with English cloth. For the cloth they took more wine, which they sometimes then carried to Newfoundland. Some wine was even sold at a premium in London as "returned from Newfoundland" – suggesting a surprising durability. Black slaves were also traded at Viana for wine.

Viana began to lose its importance to Oporto as trade with the bigger city grew, and as Viana's harbour started to silt up. The sandbar at the mouth of the Douro was also a problem, but more traffic and a narrower entrance here made it easier to keep open. The wine country was still considered to be the Minho, north of Oporto up the coast, with a preference for the wines of Monção on the border with Spanish Galicia. Monção grows a better grape variety, the white Alvarinho (some said it was introduced by the English from Greece). It is trained low, not up trees, and makes a stronger, more stable wine than the usual Minho lightweight.

The Minho is intensely fertile, densely populated and highly cultivated country where the vine has to take its chance with every sort of agriculture, and is consequently grown overhead, out of the way, up tall trees in the ancient Roman fashion or (more recently) on high pergolas. Today the quality of its wine: freshness, not to say sharpness, is appreciated and taken advantage of as "vinho verde". The familiar white exported version, though, is a mere polite parody of the original. In the 17th century Minho wine was considered a just-passable alternative to claret. Then, as now, the great majority of the region's produce was full-coloured red, light in body but with an alarmingly acidic "bite" and considerable astringence. At an old tavern in Braga only 20 years ago, it was served from the barrel standing in the corner of the one smoky room that served for kitchen, dining room and cellar. It was a deep mulberry colour, frothing slightly, and left an equally deep stain on its white pottery jug. With the primitive grill of sardines and meat, and vegetables in highly flavoured oil, its rasping fruity flavour was perfectly appropriate ... but claret it was not.

IT WAS THE DUTCH, BY A FEW YEARS, WHO FIRST STARTED BUYING WINE AT OPORTO from up the river Douro. Holland's war with France in 1672 sent her Bordeaux

The steep and savage landscape of the upper valley of the river Douro had to be reconstructed mile by mile with terraces to support the vines to make port. Today it resembles a life-size map, as its stone terraces hug every winding hill. To spite the French was the original motive for all this expenditure of energy. Yet within a generation port was the English passion, and claret was all but forgotten.

ships farther afield. They bought white wine in Jerez and Lisbon, and red in Oporto. In 1675 they had gone as far inland as Lamego, on the western fringe of what is now the port country. The monastery at Lamego had a reputation for good wine from its vineyards still higher up the river, reputedly at a remote spot in the upper reaches called Pinhão. There is no word of the Dutch on that occasion making the arduous journey all the way to the upper Douro. At that stage nobody had considered how that high country, different in every way from the well-rained-on coast, could be a source of wine of powerful character with immense potential. Once past the 4,600-foot Serra do Marão the climate changes suddenly, the Atlantic cloud cover stops, and the bare hills of slaty schist crowding around the river have a challenging majesty. But it is a world where nothing useful grows without strenuous exertions. Schist has to be brutalized into becoming soil. It is a savage country where workable land has to be created from scratch, starting with gunpowder.

ANXIOUS TO KEEP A DOMINANT POSITION IN PORTUGAL – above all for the sale of English cloth – London's "Portugal merchants" sent a memorandum to Parliament in 1677 urging it to strike a deal by reducing excise on Portuguese wines. Events rapidly overtook them. The next year England went to war with France and blockaded French ports. In the instant shortage, her wine trade needed no urging to scour Portugal for whatever was on offer. But strange to say, apart from the Minho and the Lisbon wines they already knew, there was nothing of export quality – or even close – to be found. Wine-growing was not part of a Portuguese nobleman's interests, nor was the merchant class involved. It has been suggested that the reason was the amount of Morisco blood in Portugal's upper classes. Her energetic relations with Asia, Africa and Brazil had certainly resulted in a darker-skinned race than her Spanish neighbours. For whatever reason, there was almost no such thing as a good-quality wine ready to be bought. What casks there were were rotten, and most wine reeked of the goat skins in which it had been transported from the insanitary lagar where it had been trodden. If foreigners wanted steady supplies of tolerable wine they would have to organize it for themselves – which is what the English, Scottish and Dutch "factors" set about doing.

In the first year of war with France, merchants managed to find about 400 pipes of wine in Oporto to ship to London. The pipe is the standard Portuguese measure: a barrel holding 522 litres, or more than two Bordeaux barrels. As the war went on quantities seem to have risen spectacularly: to nearly 17,000 pipes in 1683. But it is certain that much of this was French wine using rapidly constructed Portuguese barrels to disguise it from the English customs. The first genuine Oporto wine in England was known as "portoport". Nobody seems to have had anything to say in its favour, and when peace with France came in 1686 Portuguese shipments slumped, while claret shipments soared to heights not seen since the Middle Ages.

AS THE 18TH CENTURY BEGAN, the political orientation of the European powers was uncertain. Portugal flirted with Louis XIV and even Spain for a year or two, which made England and Holland nervous. Lisbon as a hostile port would be a serious threat to their Atlantic and Mediterranean shipping. England's King William III sent an experienced diplomat (and cloth merchant), John Methuen, to treat with the Portuguese in conjunction with the Dutch.

Methuen proved persuasive on both the political and commercial fronts. On his own initiative he undertook that if certain restrictions on the import of English cloth to Portugal were lifted, he would guarantee that Portuguese wine could enter England at a maximum duty of two-thirds what was charged on French wine. Why the Portuguese accepted such a hollow concession is not immediately easy to see. Since 1697 Portuguese wine had enjoyed the lowest duty of any wine landing in England: £22 a tun against £53 for French (which in any case was now under embargo altogether). And there was no guarantee that all wine duties would not be raised. Indeed they were, within a year. Much of the credit for lobbying the Portuguese Court goes to Methuen's son Sir Paul, who persuaded the great landowners of Lisbon, unenthusiastic as they were about wine, that a golden future lay in supplying the discriminating English. One wonders whether perhaps he murmured the magic name of Pontac. The Methuen Treaty was signed in 1703. Portugal allied herself with England and Holland against France and Spain at the same time. The plan was for the allies to invade Spain through Portugal. The Treaty is usually cited as the symbolic starting-gun for the port-wine trade. It was more than symbolic: England's new sovereign, Queen Anne, placed an order for ten pipes of port, eight red, two white – presumably for her thirsty husband Prince George of Denmark rather than herself. (Nor did she scruple to order substantial quantities of French wine from Holland, which had no embargo, at the same time.)

MEANWHILE, THE RESIDENT FACTORS IN NORTHERN PORTUGAL (AND ALSO SPAIN) had been prospecting for the best wines to see them through the coming war. To anticipate more problems between England and France needed no second sight. Galicia was canvassed as the likeliest producer of a claret substitute, with Monção close behind. When the War of the Spanish Succession broke out in 1702, a number of English merchants were also prospecting up the Douro as far as the tributary river Corgo, near Peso da Régua, where the steep Upper Douro hills begin in earnest.

The first authentic account of an Englishman buying and exporting Upper Douro wine is of one Thomas Woodmass of Kettering, who had an eventful journey. On his way from Liverpool to Viana his brig was captured by a French privateer, then recaptured by an English one. Riding from Viana down the coast to Oporto he was captured by brigands, and again rescued. In Oporto the English consul, John Lee, told him that there was no problem trading with farmers, but that he should beware of large landowners, the church and government officials, who were jealous of the English trying to start their own wine industry. It turned out to be a prophetic warning.

When Woodmass rode up the Douro valley he was not the only English prospector about; indeed he avoided his fellow-countrymen so as not to give away what he was discovering. Among the others was probably Peter Bearsley, whose firm, after almost 300 years and no less than 19 changes of name, now trades as Taylor, Fladgate and Yeatman.

One must respect the doggedness of these pioneers. Not only were travelling conditions appalling, with no roads and only a scattering of flea-infested taverns, but the wine they were investigating was almost undrinkable, crudely trodden, fermented on its stalks until it became dry, tannic and harsh, and then offered in resin-treated goat skins. The only wine they could drink with any pleasure was made in the monasteries, the best by Jesuits, and was bought and sold in England as "priest-port". Anything so powerful tasting as portoport, it was felt, must have medicinal qualities. A "stomachic" was how physicians described this overblown, under-refined wine.

SOMEHOW, IN THE DECADE THAT FOLLOWED, THE INFANT PORT TRADE managed to revolutionize the production of the Douro valley. Principally it must have been a matter of hygiene; stopping the use of skins and organizing new barrels to be

---

BARCOS RABELOS

Today the Douro is a sequence of lagoons between hydroelectric dams, placid except for the water-skiing families of the port shippers, but up until the 1960s much of the journey down-river could still be made by barco. With 30 or 40 pipes of port piled high on board, the unwieldy ship cruised quietly enough along calm stretches of water, then became agitated as soon as one of the many rapids approached. In the mounting clamour of river over rocks, with high stone banks closing in to form a gorge, the oarsmen took a deep swig from a big wooden bottle, then almost delicately directed the accelerating vessel towards the main channel, while the helmsman, perched high on a rickety bridge astern to look out for rocks ahead, shouted directions. With a sense of huge weight effortlessly propelled, the boat plunged quivering down the white-water sluice, sheets of spume flying from the bow, then settled calmly among the whirling eddies, while the helmsman set her prow straight for the next "cachão".

For the first two and a half centuries of its existence the only way port wine could be brought down from its mountain vineyards was piled on the decks of ships that came directly from the ancient world. The white-water journey called for nerve and sinew. This early 20th century photograph shows the water low and the river in its placid summer mood.

available to bring the wine down-river. The river journey in itself was a daunting adventure. The "barcos rabelos" that plied the Douro were loosely based, it is said, on the ships of the Phoenicians who had settled the coast 3,000 years before: beamy open boats with two high sharp ends, a single mast and sail, a steering oar lashed on the stern to starboard, and five or six great oars for the crew to row with, standing up on the foredeck.

In the 1700s the wine they carried was natural-strength table wine, but the natural strength, from such rocky vineyards, where the summer temperature is torrid, was extremely high: regularly 14 or 15 degrees. It soon became the custom to add a little brandy after fermentation was finished. Whether this was to improve the flavour or as an insurance policy against the ills that might attend a crudely made wine is not certain: probably both. But whatever attentions they gave the wine began to pay off. Richard Ames, the claret lover, had written in 1693:

> Mark how it smells, methinks a real pain
> Is by its odour thrown upon my brain.
> I've tasted it – 'tis spiritless and flat . . . .

and concluded,

> . . . fetch us a pint of any sort,
> Navarre, Galicia; anything but port

However, a merchant in 1712 could advertise: "Red port, red Lisbon, deep, strong, fresh and of excellent flavour . . . the new Lisbon at 6 shillings, the neat port at 5s 6d a gallon."

To find a truly objective tasting note at any time in the early years of 18th-century England is almost impossible. Wines became so much the symbols of political sympathies that they are praised or vilified on political grounds alone. To the Tories, the party whose heart lay with the old order, even with the exiled royal House of Stuart, claret was a rallying cry. To the Scots in particular, whose "auld alliance" with France was fondly remembered long after Scotland's official union with England in 1704 – from henceforth we may speak of "the British" – claret spelt freedom. This sad little ditty tells the story:

> Firm and erect the Highland chieftain stood,
> Sweet was his mutton and his claret good.
> "Thou shalt drink port", the English statesman cried;
> He drank the poison, and his spirit died.

Even the English had to be persuaded with propagandist jingles that it was a patriotic duty to deny yourself French wine:

> Be sometimes to your country true,
> Have once the public good in view;
> Bravely despise champagne at court
> And choose to dine at home with port.

Today we can be objective about the table wine of the Douro, which was what the first port wine in England was, and declare that it has nothing whatever to be ashamed of. Since the 1980s there has been a move among port shippers to sell a little of the wine they have always enjoyed themselves as a daily mealtime drink, and it has been found delicious: intensely fruity, rather soft and dense – the antithesis of claret, but a very good wine notwithstanding.

AFTER THEIR INITIAL HESITATION, the British (but more particularly the English) took to port with a vengeance. No doubt, once bottled, it improved with age as well as acquaintance. The first 30 years of the 18th century saw unprecedented expansion in the upper Douro. The Methuen Treaty had, as it turned out, devastated the Portuguese textile industry. Shepherds and weavers were unemployed, labour was cheap, and farmers undertook monumental vineyard-building programmes. The word building is no exaggeration. To see the upper Douro today, an entirely man-made landscape, where terrace upon terrace reaches from horizon to horizon, it is almost impossible to believe that in 1700 it was nothing but stark, scrubby schist. Infinite pains built the fortress-like walls that hold the soil in place on the mountainsides; infinite pains are still needed to cultivate them, and to lug out the entire vintage in baskets shoulder-high where not even a mule can go.

THE BRITISH AT LAST HAD A SOURCE OF THE STRONG WINE they had always hankered after, almost entirely under their control. Their methods of control were none too delicate: a farmer's daughter, it was said, was often the price he had to pay for striking a reasonable bargain. The shippers built warehouses, or "lodges", to handle the huge quantities of wine at Vila Nova de Gaia, on the south bank of the Douro near its mouth, facing the steep bluff on which Oporto stands from a gentler and more manageable slope. In 1727 the British shippers formed themselves into an association, largely to be able to browbeat the growers and keep down their prices. But Portugal was, for once, thriving. Gold and diamonds pouring in from Brazil made the government feel able to cope with even the domineering British.

It soon occurred to the less scrupulous vintners that it was altogether too much trouble to go mountaineering up the Douro, and that something they could pass off as port to a gullible public could be concocted out of almost any wine, so long as the result was thick and fiery. The vintner's trade had rarely had a conscience about adulteration. Brandy was not the only thing that began to be added. Deep colour was provided by elderberries; the fiery flavour the English began to crave by adding dried pimentos. The merchants' greed eventually had the inevitable result. The fashionable drink was denounced by envious brewers and distillers – and by honest vintners, too. In the 1730s the price of port began to falter; in the 1750s it began seriously to slide.

Self-righteously the British shippers in Oporto wrote a letter blaming their woes entirely on their suppliers, whom they accused of growing inferior wine in the wrong places, not treading it long enough, adding too much brandy of inferior quality too soon, and using elderberries for colour. The growers' commissioners threw back similar accusations in the face of the British. There was a degree of right on both sides: both seem to have an idea of an ideal port wine which scarcely, at that time, existed.

Neither had made the discovery that for brandy to really stabilize the wine and make it sweet, as well as strong, it must be added halfway through fermentation and in substantial quantities. Adding small amounts merely postponed the end of

EXCEEDING THE LIMITS

The English merchants' complaint about the quality of the wine was met by a well-phrased retort from the port-growers' commissioners: "The English merchants knew that the first-rate wine of the feitoria had become excellent; but they wished to exceed the limits which nature had assigned it, and that, when drunk, it should feel like liquid fire in the stomach; that it should burn like inflamed gunpowder; that it should have the tint of ink; that it should be like the sugar of Brazil in sweetness, and like the spices of India in aromatic flavour. They began by recommending, by way of secret, that it was proper to dash it with brandy in the fermentation, to give it strength, and with elderberrries . . . to give it colour . . . ."

According to the Marques de Pombal, the complaints of the port growers were well-founded: ". . . the English at Oporto had ended by entirely ruining the important vines of the Douro, and their produce; that they had reduced the price of wine . . . and thereby rendered the expense of cultivation greater than the value of the produce; and even then they refused to become purchasers without two years' credit; that the low price did not even suffice to pay the necessary hoeing of the land, which in consequence was becoming gradually abandoned by its owners; that all the principal families of that district found themselves reduced to the lowest

Sebastiao de Carvalho, Marques de Pombal, was the Portuguese minister who reconstructed earthquake-stricken Lisbon and faced up to the high-handed British merchants.

degree of poverty, so much so indeed, that they had been obliged to sell or pawn the spoons or forks with which they eat; that this general and extreme poverty had caused the continual prostitution of the daughters of the wine growers and proprietors, who hoped by those means to facilitate the advantageous disposal of their wines, unmindful of the public scandal and high offence against God that sprung from such conduct."

The city of Oporto looks today much as it did in the 18th century, rising in tiers on
the steep north bank of the Douro. This view is from Vila Nova de Gaia, the
suburb entirely given over to the storage of port.

fermentation and virtually guaranteed murky and unstable wine. The shippers were
right in thinking the vineyards could have been better, too. Vines had not yet been
planted around the highest reaches of the river, where the wine was eventually to be
the very richest and most high-flavoured of all. But in the 1750s river traffic stopped
at the Valeira gorge; a fall too rapid even for the barcos rabelos. Above the gorge
(which was later to play a tragic part in our story) the schistous mountains stretched
moonlike, still waiting for the vine.

THE ARGUMENT MIGHT HAVE DRAGGED ON INTERMINABLY, had not Portugal been
struck, in 1755, by a devastating calamity. Lisbon in all its prosperity was almost
totally destroyed by an earthquake that killed 40,000 people. Perhaps for the first
time in history the international community reacted with sympathy and sent relief
supplies. The hero of the hour was the King's chief minister, Sebastião de Carvalho
– who was later created Marques de Pombal. This intelligent and dedicated patriot
soon achieved almost dictatorial powers. To finance the rebuilding of the capital, he
conceived of a series of monopolistic trading companies. The following year he
established the General Company of Agriculture of the Wines of the Upper Douro,
and seized effective control of the port trade.

THE DOURO WINE COMPANY, AS IT WAS SOON CALLED FOR SHORT, had sweeping
powers. Its charter obliged it to control all exports of port, to reserve 10,000 pipes a
year for export to Brazil (to be sold for gold), and to demarcate the vineyards in
which port could be grown in two quality zones: ''ramo'' for domestic and
Brazilian consumption, and ''feitoria'' for the better wines to go to Britain and
northern Europe. It controlled the quantities produced, fixed maximum and

228

minimum prices, and arbitrated in all disputes. In 1761 it also acquired the monopoly of the sale of brandy for fortifying the wines. Whether this improved the quality of the brandy is hard to say, but it must have inclined the Company to encourage its use. The only exception to its export monopoly was that British firms could ship wines, once they had been passed by the Company's tasters as being of "feitoria" quality, to Britain. Foreigners could become shareholders in (but not officers of) the Company.

The British, of course, were furious. From virtual monopolists themselves they were now reduced to mere middlemen who were told what they could buy and at what price, and where they could sell it. Accommodation had to be found, though, because buyer and seller still depended on each other. Indeed, in 1762 Portugal had to cope with another Spanish invasion – which she could only repel with the help of British arms. It soon became known whom, and how much, to bribe; but bribes added to the cost of the wine.

There is no doubt that Pombal intended to improve quality as well as to break the British stranglehold. He ordered and enforced the uprooting of all elderberry trees in northern Portugal. He also strictly limited the use of manure in "feitoria" vineyards. But it was in delimiting the best wine-growing areas that he was positively visionary. By choosing only the schistous soil (and avoiding the granite outcrops in the area) he foreshadowed the whole notion of controlled appellations. Port-growers today bear out his judgment. If you are buying a vineyard, they say, go to see it by moonlight. The quartz in granite soil glints under the moon; true schist is unreflecting black. You will be able to taste the difference in the wine.

Pombal's stated reason was that vines should not grow where corn could be planted; an argument that increased the quantity of food and the quality of wine at a stroke. The destiny of the high wilderness of the Douro was to be wine. In acting as he did he made Oporto the specialist wine port and obliged Lisbon to diversify. As for his own splendid estate, just west of Lisbon at Carcavelos, it was said to grow some of the best red wine in Portugal, so it could do no harm to sell it, if the price was right, as port.

PORT WAS NOT YET BY ANY MEANS A WINE OF REFINEMENT. In 1763 James Boswell, Dr Johnson's biographer, wrote: "A bottle of thick English port is a very heavy and very inflammatory dose. I felt it last time that I drank it for several days, and this morning it was boiling in my veins." But the best must already have had the potential to mature into an excellent drink. Strength cannot have been its only commendation to Englishmen who could afford to drink any wine they wanted. As the 18th century progressed so did the Englishman's cellar, full of bottles quietly metamorphosing into plenitude.

CHAPTER 23

TOKAY ESSENCE

The same war that forced the British to accept Portuguese wines as their destiny was responsible for the promotion of another wine, scarcely less novel and not at all less noble, at the extreme other end of Europe. In 1703, the year of the Methuen Treaty, Ferenc Rákóczi, the Prince of Transylvania and a Protestant, took up arms against the (Catholic) Austrian occupation of his native Hungary. Louis XIV saw his intervention as a useful distraction. His enemy the Emperor of Austria would be obliged to keep a guard on his back door as well as his front. The Sun King was also extremely impressed by the present of wine that arrived from Rákóczi's estates: a wine that already had a reputation in eastern Europe, but had never before reached Paris. Its name (slightly simplified from the Hungarian) was Tokay.

Eastern Europe has been absent from our story for many centuries, appearing only now and again as the Greeks, then the Romans, colonized the more accessible parts of its Celtic tribal lands, as the successive hordes of Huns, Vandals and Goths streamed out of the Steppes, or as their successors, the Tartars, then the Turks, invaded and established themselves closer and closer to the heart of Europe. This tide was only finally turned back in 1683, when the Turks' last siege of Vienna was brusquely overturned (and their coffee supplies circulated around Europe's capitals). It was noteworthy that Louis XIV did nothing to discourage the Turks from bothering his Imperial rival. Rákóczi appeared on cue to fulfil the same useful role.

THE LONG SILENCE HAS NOT MEANT THAT WINE–GROWING FELL INTO DISUSE. It is doubtful whether at any time since the Greeks introduced it via the Black Sea (if that is what happened) the valley of the Danube has been without wine. Many centuries later it was while he was zealously planting vineyards in Pannonia that the Roman Emperor Probus met his end. The Greeks had approached from the southeast up the Danube and its tributary the Tisza; the Romans from the west across the Pannonian plain, leaving their legacy of vines around the inland sea of Lake Balaton, at Peć, Villány and Szekszárd, in Lower Austria and Moravia. Their legacy, it is said, goes so far as to make wine presses part of western Hungarian tradition, while across the Danube in the east the grapes were simply trodden, Greek style.

Neither Attila and his Huns, nor the Avars who succeeded them (to be crushed in due course by Charlemagne), nor the Magyars who founded the Hungarian nation had any motive in destroying the amenity of vineyards. The inevitable Charlemagne legend runs that he was enthused by Avar wine, and took vines with him back to Germany. King Stephen I Christianized the Magyars in the 10th century. A great monument of bronze in Budapest helps us to picture these impressive horsemen, their florid moustachios suggesting the spirit of the cowboy under the exterior of a Viking. With the Magyars came a Bulgar tribe from the Volga called the Kaliz, respected for their agriculture and way with vines.

The church played its usual role in the Middle Ages in propagating and stabilizing wine-growing, encouraged by such enlightened monarchs as Bela IV, who imported Italians and Flemings skilled in wine, and the famous wine lover King Matthias Corvinus, whose realm stretched (briefly) from Bohemia to the Carpathians. Matthias (who reigned 1458–90) is a favourite subject of Hungarian storytelling, appearing rather like the benevolent Henri IV of France. All his people, he said, should have wine, and winegrowers were people to be respected.

Like their contemporaries in the wine villages of the Rhineland, serfs who worked conscientiously with their vines acquired privileges. Hill vineyards were distinguished from flat ones, for sound empirical reasons, and the communities that established them became remarkably democratic, with rights of inheritance, and privileged access to the market, matched by duties of loyalty, service and attendance at assemblies to check the quality of their wine. Vineyards were surrounded by hedges that clearly defined privileged areas. These were surprisingly early moves in the direction of controlled quality. The results were that such communities as Sopron, Somló, Eger and Debrö built reputations that went far beyond Hungary, to her natural market in northern lands with no wine of their own. Poland, Russia, Sweden and the Baltic countries all looked to Hungary for more potent and flavoursome wine than (for example) the north of France could provide. Summers are hot in Hungary. Its continental climate is tempered by the influence of the

The last of many attempts by the Turkish Ottoman empire to conquer Austria and enter Europe was the siege of Vienna by Kara Mustafa in 1683. He was defeated with the help of Polish knights who took home a keen interest in the wines of Tokay.

Mediterranean. The Hungarian hill regions could provide wine halfway between the light wines of the north and the expensive Malmseys of the old Greek world.

This promising scenario was disastrously interrupted in 1526 by the Ottoman Turks under Suleiman I, who destroyed the Hungarian knights at the Battle of Mohács on the Danube. For 160 years the Turks were to occupy the greater part of Hungary. Wine-growing was not entirely suppressed (the Turks were content to collect taxes, and not exactly allergic to wine themselves), but its high morale was at an end in most of the country. The exceptions were along the northern borders, where Eger's famous resistance to a siege by Ali Pasha earned its wine the name of Bull's Blood, and where the hills of Tokaji-Hegyalja, rising from the banks of the Tisza and the Bodrog, presented the invaders with no obviously desirable prize. The worst threat here was Turkish slave raids: Hungarians fetched good prices in the market at Istanbul.

THE VERY EARLY HISTORY OF THIS SINGULAR REGION IS LITTLE KNOWN. If the Celts grew wine they would very probably have chosen these steeply swelling, well drained, south-facing hills. If the Greeks, following the Tisza up from the Danube, arrived here they would have done the same. The Romans crossed the Danube to establish their colony of Dacia in the 2nd century – another possible starting point. What is reported is that King Bela invited Italians here in the 13th century and that they brought with them their favourite vine, the mysteriously named Furmint, which, together with the more succulently flavoured Hárslevelü and a little Muscat, composes the modern wine of Tokay.

Whatever wine they made in such a naturally favoured site was surely above average, but it had no special importance until the Turkish invasion, when it became one of the few potential sources of revenue for the beleaguered Hungarians. In the 16th century their commercial instincts were tempered by mistrust, and a curious situation arose in which they tried to persuade the Poles to come and buy from them, while the Poles refused to budge unless the Hungarians brought their wares to Poland. In times of active warfare with the Turks the Hungarians refused to sell any wine at all, lest their fighting men should go thirsty. The Polish answer (or part of it) was to employ "Szkoci"; itinerant Scotsmen who acted as agents, buying wine for them in Hungary, in Moldavia to the east across the Carpathian mountains, even in Greece. Moldavia was the source of a now-forgotten wine, at one time a rival to Tokay: the powerful "green" Cotnari. The old Polish capital of Kraków was the centre of the wine trade, slowly giving place to Warsaw at the end of the 16th century. For both sides, Jews and Greeks (as well as Scotsmen) acted as go-betweens.

It is tempting to find some connection between the Furmint of Tokay and the not dissimilarly named Froment, or Fromenteau, alias the Pinot Gris, which is known locally in Alsace as the Tokay d'Alsace. In reality the grapes are very different; the Pinot Gris a pink grape with juice low in acidity, the Furmint pale gold, with strikingly acidic juice. Moreover, the Pinot Gris is well-known in Hungary under the name of Szürkebarat, or "Greyfriar".

One tenuous connection between Alsace and Tokay is that the Austrian court was apparently addicted to Alsace wines until the peremptory annexation of Alsace by its enemy Louis XIV in 1683, when it in turn appropriated estates in the Tokay hills.

**The source of Tokay is a remote province
between the River Tisza and the Carpathians.**

THE RÁKÓCZI FAMILY MAKES ITS APPEARANCE IN THE STORY IN 1617, when it acquired the estate of Sárospatak and started a long campaign to monopolize the wines of the region. Thirty years later the old castle of Tokaji itself became theirs. It was surely not coincidental that only three years later their overseer delayed the vintage, on the pretext of an expected Turkish attack. So legend explains the discovery of the noble mould, *Botrytis cinerea*, which shrivelled the grapes, softened their skins, and led to the most luscious wine anyone had ever tasted. If this account is true, it antedates the similar story of its discovery in Germany, in the Rheingau, by 120 years.

The Turks did attack in 1678, and pillaged the region. It was their last fling: five years later they were routed at Vienna, with enthusiastic help from the King of Poland, and in 1686 lost Budapest. The Hapsburg Empire had them on the run. By this time the growers in Tokaji-Hegyalja had started digging small-bore tunnels, unique in the world's repertoire of wine cellars, deep into the volcanic rock of their hills. The tunnels are too low for a man to stand upright (let alone swing a scimitar). Lining one wall is a row of little barrels, known as gönci from the carpenters' village of Gönc. The wine ageing in them is not topped up, but allowed to oxidize gradually under a film of yeast, less vigorous (at least in these cold cellars) than the white flor of Jerez, but playing a similar role in subtly altering the flavour.

This was the wine that Ferenc Rákóczi used as his diplomatic weapon in trying to save Hungary, now free of Turks, from being similarly overrun by Austrians. He failed; Austria and its allies (England included) won the war, and the Hapsburgs began their colonialist rule of the long-suffering Hungarians.

Tokay was much the finest wine of the Hapsburg Empire, which stretched from Dalmatia to Poland. So the Emperors appropriated its best vineyards, and used it, as the Dukes of Burgundy had used their Beaune, for impressing and ingratiating foreign monarchs. Peter the Great of Russia and Frederick I of Prussia both rapidly became addicts. The Tsars set up a Commission for Hungarian Wines at St Petersburg to ensure regular supplies, leased vineyards (the Emperors banned foreigners from buying them) and took vines to the Crimea to try making their own Tokay. What did not go to Vienna, Moscow, St Petersburg, Warsaw, Berlin or Prague was snapped up by the grandees of Britain, the Netherlands and France. The world had no wine to compare with it for sweetness – except perhaps a truly

233

Tokay, the original of all wines made from "nobly rotten" grapes, is fermented and aged in half-size casks in tunnel-like cellars. It was destined for the courts of eastern and northern Europe. Russia's appreciation is made manifest in the façade of this 18th-century merchant's house in Zagorsk, near Moscow.

exceptional cask in some prince-bishop's cellar of the Rhine. Port was still "blackstrap" while Tokay was a wonderfully perfumed syrup.

THE PRECISE METHOD OF MAKING TOKAY, and the way in which its sweetness and intensity are determined and measured, are still unique in the world of wine. They seem to relate more closely to Pliny's way of describing different degrees of concentrated sweetness in a Falernian than any current winemaking techniques. The most fabled liquor of all is (or was) Tokay Essenczia or Essence. Essence is made only of the syrupy drops squeezed from a tub of grapes, if grapes is the word for the perished mass, half raisin, half fungus, by their own weight alone.

These first drops have a sugar content so high that they preserve themselves against fermentation. In cool conditions they remain simply grape juice of incredible sticky sweetness and overwhelming flavour, pouring as slowly as treacle and by no means transparently clear. They are a blending ingredient, rather than a drink. Their very scarcity, though, as well as their searing sweetness, makes them a legendary luxury. Tsars and archdukes were pleased to believe that failing powers of almost any kind could be restored by this elixir. There are countless stories of inert noblemen and enormously senior men of religion springing from their beds – or

The wild claims about the restorative powers of Tokay went on right into the 20th century, and at an address as respectable as London's St James's St. This is what Messrs Berry Bros and Rudd were prepared to say in 1933: "A medical man, and a friend, who had sneered at the suggestion to try this wine in a case of extreme illness, actually put a little in a man's mouth . . . when he really had come to the conclusion he had passed away. My friend told me afterwards that the effect was like an electric shock – the old gentleman is alive today, and believe me, this is no fairy tale."

alternatively into them – as a drop touched their lips, and of octogenarians becoming fathers of large families.

To make more of a drink of such a sticky fluid, it is my belief that the merchants often added brandy. It would help to discourage any feeble effort of the Essence at fermentation and give the patient (drinker is scarcely the word) even more of an impression of fortifying power. I should add that this has been strenuously denied by officials and experts, but was stated as an unsurprising fact by the cellarmaster of the State Cellars in Sátoraljaúhely, the headquarters of Tokay today.

THE TOKAY THAT WAS TRADED AS WINE, RATHER THAN AN IMPERIAL ELIXIR, was what is known in Hungarian as Aszú, and in German as Ausbruch. The original procedure was to wait until the Essence had oozed from the shrivelled grapes, then pour the juice of the remaining grapes over this "Aszú dough" and tread them together. The must of this first treading fermented to produce Aszú. A second treading of the same "dough" with more juice of normally ripe grapes gave the second-quality wine, known as Maslas. Between the two in quality, although not so clearly defined, came a wine known as Forditas. The Tokay known as Imperial and drunk ("at table", it is said, although with what food it is hard to imagine) by the Emperors in Vienna was the Aszú blended with a measure of the Essence.

Today the richness of the wine is regulated by formula. It consists of a stated number of measures (tubs called puttonyos) of the must of the fully concentrated "Aszú" grapes displacing the contents of a barrel of "normal" juice. The maximum number of puttonyos is six, resulting in an intensely sweet wine with almost limitless ageing potential. A very little of the Imperial-style wine is still sold, as "Aszú Essenczia".

In specially favoured years all the late-picked "Aszú" grapes would be "nobly rotten". The situation of the hills above the two converging rivers, the Bodrog and the Tisza, is conducive to autumn mists, just as the Garonne and the little river Ciron dispense their moisture–laden air around Sauternes and Barsac with the same effect. In other years, with steadily sunny autumns and no mists, the grapes are more raisined than rotten; there is less Essenczia and a less luscious flavour in the Aszú.

THE CENTRE OF SUCH CONNOISSEURSHIP THROUGHOUT THE 18TH CENTURY WAS WARSAW. The famous merchant house of Fukier there maintained a cellar of every vintage since, it is said, 1606, the bottles always kept standing up, their corks renewed every six years. Tokay was always in demand, despite the jealousy of the Hapsburgs, who decreed that for every barrel of noble Hungarian wine exported, a barrel of their relatively pedestrian Austrian wine must be sold as well.

But these are the mere incidentals: the meaning of Tokay in the story of wine is simple and strong. Another and better kind of wine could just invent itself, given a very peculiar set of natural conditions – and the help of a princely patron. A wine so striking would have political consequences. And the world, or more accurately the worldly, would beat a path to its cellar door.

CHAPTER 24

GROOT CONSTANTIA

In 1816, an apparently omniscient Frenchman named André Jullien published a work of breathtaking breadth and boldness, leaving far behind every book that had ever attempted to catalogue the wines of the world. He called it *Topographie de Tous les Vignobles Connus* – the topography (it should really be translated as "whereabouts") of all known vineyards. He might well have added "and unknown" to his title: his researches discovered pockets of wine-growing in corners of Asia, Africa, America and eastern Europe, on islands in the ocean and in passes of the Hindu Kush, where nobody would expect any such thing. He recorded the soil, the grape varieties, the quantity produced, often the price, and generally some snippet of information, even about the most obscure vineyards. The pleasantly named Gracieuse, for example, must surely be worth looking for. Jullien tells us that it is an island in the Azores whose wine is so poor that most of it is distilled.

Most remarkable of all Jullien's undertakings, perhaps, is his bold-as-brass classification of almost every wine in the world into one of five categories of quality. Few, it is true, were likely to take issue with him on whether the Cossack productions of Ekaterinoslav or those of General Bekelof in the outskirts of Astrakhan rightly belonged in class four or five. He was more exposed, though, when he described the wine of Constantia at the Cape of Good Hope as "among the finest liqueur wines of the world, ranking immediately after that of Tokay". This was the generally accepted view of his time, reflected in the alarming prices Constantia fetched in Europe.

Stranger still is the fact that Constantia and Tokay rose to eminence at almost exactly the same time; that the first wine of the New World to be acknowledged great is yet another product of the era that gave us sparkling champagne, first-growth claret, Tokay and the first fumblings of port. Perhaps Constantia was only a first fumbling, too, in the 17th century. But Constantia is the more remarkable in demonstrating how even in a savage and backward environment, infinite pains can procure excellence. Also how when the pains stop, so does the quality.

THE PORTUGUESE NAVIGATORS WHO DISCOVERED THE CAPE OF GOOD HOPE found nothing to interest them in this empty land, sparsely inhabited by savages. They were looking for cities rich in spices, and sailed on for India. The same is true of the early Dutch seamen, who did no more than fill their water casks from the Fresh River in Table Bay, pick bundles of wild sorrel to ward off scurvy, and set sail again for the Indies. It was when their trading port of Batavia in Java started to merit regular fleets that a settlement at the Cape became a logical, if not specially promising, step. In 1652 Johan van Riebeeck set up the first permanent victualling station for his masters in the Dutch East India Company, a fort and a farm. He wrote to the 17 directors for vine cuttings, which they sent in 1654. The Company had taken the trouble to fetch cuttings from the Rhineland and sew them up in damp little packets of sailcloth. Too damp, in all probability; they did not take root.

The next year's batch, assembled from Germany, France, Spain and Bohemia, was more successful. The first vintage was pressed in the Cape in 1659: 15 litres from French Muscadel grapes. The "Hanepoot Spanish" were "not yet ripe". Hanepoot, or sometimes Hanepop, is a Cape Dutch word (whose origins are perhaps best left obscure) for the most ancient of Muscat grapes, the Muscat of Alexandria, brought from the eastern Mediterranean as the mainstay of Málaga and also planted in the Canary Islands. The Canary Islands may have been a staging post for some of the vines that eventually found their way to South Africa and later Australia.

But the development of a wine industry was no part of the Company's plans for its possession at the Cape. Rice to feed the slaves was more important. The Company has been described as "that most profitable blend of unblushing piracy and commercialized Protestantism". It only allowed a few chosen and hopefully sober ex-servants, released from service to become Free Burghers and farm on their own behalf, to make and sell wine locally. Anyone else who hoped to earn from wine-growing had to send his produce all the way to Batavia. Gradually the Dutch factors in the Indies realized that their best hope of drinkable wine was to encourage the Cape to make it, and arranged for a winemaker from Alsace, a press and a cooper to make barrels on the Company's farm of Rustenburg. Twenty-five years after van Riebeeck's settlement there were still only 189 European settlers (including 117 children) and 191 slaves.

THE MAN WHO BROUGHT PROSPERITY AND CIVILIZED LIFE (AT LEAST FOR HIMSELF) to the Cape was the Company's new Commander in 1679, Simon van der Stel. Van der Stel was born on an East Indiaman in the Indian Ocean. While he was a child he saw his father murdered in Ceylon and his mother (reputedly a half-caste) die in Batavia, but returned to Amsterdam to join the army, fight the English and the French, and become a valued officer in the East India Company. He was 40 when he was sent to the Cape as Commander. Among his recruits he took with him a French winegrower. He founded the new settlement of Stellenbosch in a lovely wooded valley a few miles inland and in 1685 contrived to be granted (against the law and custom of the Company) an estate at the back of Table Mountain; a big estate, in fact exactly the size of the whole of Amsterdam at the time and about 15 times as much as a normal land grant. He named it Constantia, perhaps after one of the Company's ships, or possibly in honour of a quality he admired. The legend that it was named after his wife is false. She was called Johanna, and stayed behind in Amsterdam, never to see her husband or children again.

The Cape has a perfect climate for fine wine, but few of the early Dutch settlers had the temperament necessary to make it. It was the governor Simon Van der Stel who founded what became the first-growth of the new colonial world.

Van der Stel developed Constantia with extraordinary speed into an almost princely estate. He planted avenues of European oaks to break the force of the destructive southeast gales, leading through the glittering clusters of the native silver-trees to a substantial mansion. In his extravagant gardens he planted every sort of fruit tree, but lavished most care on his vineyards. The first tasting note came back from Batavia in 1692: "The wine from Constantia is of a much higher quality than any sent out so far, but obviously only available in small quantities". By 1705 (when Count Rákóczi was sending his Tokay to Louis XIV), F. Valentijn, in his *Description of the Cape of Good Hope*, could write: "The lovely red Constantia wine . . . need not yield place in strength and charm to the best Persian wine or to the Italian Lachryma Christi, and in addition this estate has also an exceptionally good, in fact the best, Steenwyn and Krystalwyn, so divine and enchanting in taste, that only a truly fine palate could distinguish it from the best Tosca . . . ."

The comparison with Persian wine is teasing. Other references infer that Persian vines were taken to the Cape. Were they from Shiraz? The Steen grape is the Chenin Blanc, imported from the Loire valley and the favourite grape of the Cape today, but what Krystalwyn was is a matter for conjecture . . . as indeed is the identity of the "best Tosca".

There are just enough glimpses of Constantia in those early days to show what perfectionism went into its winemaking. A visitor in 1710 reported, "I saw the wine-pressing house with all the casks . . . their woodwork and all equipment is scrubbed white and clean". Van der Stel planted many varieties of vine, often under confusing names. "White French", for example, was the Spanish variety Palomino, used for making sherry, "Green Grape" was Sémillon, and nobody knows what "Pontac" was – although one may imagine it came from Bordeaux. It seems that he also planted Steen. But his fame was to come from Muscat varieties.

The genealogy of the Muscat subfamily of grapes is far from simple. Van der Stel's Spanish Hanepoot was the white Muscat of Alexandria. His "Frontignac" was the Muscat à Petits Grains, the finest but also the most variable of the clan, at least in colour, ranging from white to a warm brown. Since he sold both white and red Muscat wines, he may have also used (if only for colour) the only really dark-coloured Muscat, the Muscat Hamburg, which is a low-grade wine grape, however delicious it is to bite into. Alternatively, he may have blended his red dessert wine using a non-Muscat red variety. In any case his white was very good, but it was red Constantia, less powerfully aromatic but wonderfully mellow and harmonious, that became so famous. When aged it was described as a rich topaz colour – which suggests that it may never have been a deep red even when young.

SUCH WAS THE FIRST FLOWERING OF CONSTANTIA – AND IT WAS BRIEF. The Governor, as he was to become in 1691, retired in 1699 and his seemingly loathsome son Willem Adriaan inherited the post. He was recalled to Holland in disgrace, and when Simon died in 1712 his little empire was divided. Two of the three parts had vineyards: Groot and Klein (Great and Little) Constantia. It was Klein Constantia, under its new master, Johannes Colijn, that took up the challenge of making the Cape's one outstanding wine.

Colijn was evidently a good businessman. He sold his wine to the Company regularly to make sure that the Dutch market was made aware of it. He charged twice as much for the red wine as for the white, and seems to have been able to stretch his supplies by buying wine from his neighbours. In 1733 Groot Constantia once more came on the market and he was able to unite the properties. When he died in 1743 the ownership became complicated, but the two Constantias were perceived as being one wine estate again, and remained so, although with a somewhat dimmer reputation, for his widow's lifetime.

Passing travellers have left us every detail of the winemaking process in the 1740s, from which it is clear that the Dutch technique of sulphuring was used, but very carefully, to stop the wine from fermenting to dryness. Once it had stopped, the wine was carefully racked as many times as necessary. A German visitor described how they judged whether fermentation had stopped by "listening at the bunghole for the moment when the wine no longer makes a noise; for as long as it is not entirely quiet, there is an irritation in the barrel as though it contained crabs".

Two famous Swedish botanical collectors both recorded their views: Sparrman in 1772 and Thunberg, on his way to Japan, the following year. Sparrman was convinced that the quality of Constantia was all a question of the soil of "certain particular vineyards" (a very French view) while Thunberg believed that it was the

---

If any proof were needed of how seriously Europe – even the French – took Constantia it is here, in this paragraph from the famous *Description générale et particulière du duché de Bourgogne*:

"The plants of the celebrated vine of the Cape [of Good Hope] have been planted in Beaune and its neighbourhood. What is strange is that this plant has only succeeded at the Cape; everywhere else it has degenerated. The Dauphin and the Prince de Conti asked M. Brunet of Paris why the wine of the plants they had procured were so inferior to those of Beaune. He replied that they had not been able to ship with the plants the soil and the sunshine."

The cellar building of the Groot Constantia estate is the high-point of
the cool, white-painted style of architecture known as Cape Dutch. Its
gable was ornamented in 1790 with a Bacchic relief of a quality worthy
of Bordeaux.

situation, not the soil, that made all the difference, and that other equally good
situations (and wines) existed.

What really mattered, of course, was neither, but the man in charge. In the 1770s
this became clear when Groot Constantia was sold, in a very run-down condition,
to a rich middle-aged landowner, Hendrik Cloete of Stellenbosch, who "possessed
about one hundred slaves, and enjoyed every comfort obtainable in the country".
Cloete replanted the vineyards and in 1790 built the new cellar which is the best
example of the Cape Dutch architecture of its day. The farmers of the Cape had
developed a homely style of building of enormous charm, characterized by a gable
in the middle of a long wall of the building over the door. The purpose of this gable
was to protect the doorway from burning thatch if the house caught fire. Long
hooked poles were used to pull the thatch off, so the exit had to be kept clear. At
Groot Constantia, the businesslike gable was made the frame for a masterpiece of
Bacchic baroque sculpture. It represents Ganymede, the cupbearer of Jupiter, astride
an eagle surrounded by classical Bacchantes cavorting against a background of oval
barrels and drapery – all in the dazzling white of every Cape farmhouse.

Hendrik Cloete used his 100 slaves to extraordinary purpose. In his pursuit of
perfection he stationed them among the vines so that if an insect dared to land on one
of his grapes it was instantly removed. His wine was acknowledged magnificent,
but his business sense, unfortunately, was less so. In 1793 he made the fatal mistake of
signing a perpetual contract with the Company to sell them 60 casks of his best wine
every year at a fixed price – with no allowance for inflation. He did not live to reap

the whirlwind. It was his son Hendrik, who took over the management in 1794, who had to face the problem – compounded with another and more immediate one: the invading British.

IN 1795 THE BRITISH LANDED AT THE CAPE and rapidly overwhelmed the slight Dutch forces at the Battle of Muizenberg, almost within sight of Constantia. Hendrik Cloete commanded the Stellenbosch Burgher Cavalry. But there was scarcely a fight.

Under the British there was no interference with the peaceful farming life of the Cape settlers; just a new set of bureaucrats to deal with – and a much-augmented stream of sightseers. The languid tones of the British upper class can be heard loud and clear in their memoirs. Robert Percival was, I fear, typical: he did not even trouble to find out Hendrik Cloete's name. "The farm which produces this richly flavoured wine belongs to a Dutchman, Mynheer Pluter, and has long been in his family . . . ." Not entirely surprisingly, Percival did not find "Pluter" in a good humour. He and his friends simply tipped the Constantia slaves and were shown all over the estate – including a wine tasting.

At least Percival appreciated the wine. "Its exquisite flavour", he wrote, "is chiefly to be attributed to the great care taken in the rearing, dressing and encouragement of the vines . . . and not suffering the leaves, stalks and unripe fruit to be mixed in the press as done by the other Dutch farmers." "A couple of glasses", he added, "are quite as much as one would wish to drink at a time."

British possession of the Cape was confirmed in 1814. It had not apparently occurred to them that this addition to the Empire could provide an answer to the problem that started with the loss of Bordeaux 350 years before; the need for a wine supply firmly in British hands. Nelson had pointed out that it was a vital victualling station. He called it an "immense tavern".

At first all they were interested in was the famous Constantia. Having promised the inhabitants freedom from "the monopolies and oppressions which have been hitherto exercised by the East India Company . . . . Everyone may buy from whom he will, sell to whom he will", the British commander, Sir Henry Craig, discovered

LADY ANNE'S VISIT

An altogether more sensitive account of Constantia comes from Lady Anne Barnard, the wife of the secretary to the Governor: "Mynheer Cloete took us into the wine-press hall; where the whole of our party made wry faces at the idea of drinking wine that had been pressed from the grapes by three pairs of black feet; but the certainty that the fermentation would carry off every polluted article settled that objection with me. What struck me most was the beautiful antique forms, perpetually changing and perpetually graceful, of the three bronze figures, half-naked, who were dancing in the wine-press and beating the drum (as it were) with their feet to some other instrument in perfect time. Of these presses there were four, with three slaves each. Into the first the grapes were tossed in large quantities, and the slaves danced on them softly, the wine running out from a hole at the bottom of the barrel, pure and clear – this was done to slow music. A quicker and stronger measure began when the same grapes were danced on over again. The third process gone through was that of passing the pulp and skins through a sieve, and this produced the richest wine of the three; but the different sorts were ultimately mixed together by Mynheer Cloete, who told us it has been the practice of his forefathers to keep them separate and sell them at different prices, but he found the wine was improved by mixing."

to his glee the agreement Cloete's father had made with the Company, and promptly forgot all fine sentiments about oppression. Disregarding Cloete's protests, he left the new Governor, Lord Macartney, to enforce the letter of the unfortunate contract, keeping enough barrels of each vintage, bought at a knockdown price, to give the British high officials at the Cape a wonderful perquisite to which they had not a shadow of right, and sending the bulk to England "to be at his Majesty's disposal".

Under the impossible circumstances, with the virtual confiscation of a large part of his production, it is a great tribute to Cloete that he kept up his standards as long as he did. It is true that Constantia was now world famous. Napoleon, exiled on St-Helena, was known to have enjoyed it. King Louis-Philippe of France in due course joined the appreciation society. But the British government not only starved the goose that laid the golden eggs; it removed the workforce that made such luxury possible. In 1799 Macartney's secretary, Barrow, was writing memoranda about trading wine for slaves with America, "a trade that seems susceptible of very considerable augmentation". Thirty-five years later slavery was proscribed in all British dominions and the Royal Navy used to blockade slave-trade ports. A British army captain at the Cape made a very pertinent observation, even if Constantia was the exception that proved the rule: "Among the terrible reactions produced by the slave trade", he wrote, "none is perhaps more merited or more evident than the dissoluteness of morals and ferocity of disposition which it creates among people who are concerned with it." The standard of wine farming at the Cape was generally lamentable. "The defects in the Cape wine proceed from the avarice of the planter on the one hand and his extreme indolence on the other", wrote Barrow.

A hasty step by the British government was to make it worse. Suddenly alive to the fact that a British possession could supply cheap wine, it reduced the duty on its import to one-third of that on Portuguese wines. By creating a virtually open market for any sort of rubbish, it pre-empted any move by South Africa to capitalize on Constantia's reputation. Constantia alone held its standards for as long as it could, under the dogged Cloete. Having encouraged cheap winemaking, the British then changed their minds and (in 1841) raised the tarriffs, so that South Africa's cut-price wines were hopelessly uncompetitive in Britain.

The end of the story of Constantia was sad but inevitable. In 1859 the fatal vine mildew oidium appeared at the Cape. In 1861 Britain removed its tariff barrier against French wines. In 1866 phylloxera struck.

For all practical purposes, Constantia is as extinct as Falernian. Groot Constantia is a national monument; its vineyards a state wine farm whose wine, although good in the modern style, does not attempt to reproduce the famous dessert wine of the 18th century. So what was it like? In 1970 I was privileged to drink a glass of the 1830 vintage from the London cellar of the publisher George Rainbird. The wine was in an English pint bottle of the period, sealed with wax over the cork. It was in beautiful condition: extremely soft, pale amber in colour, with odours of balsam and, I thought, a trace of orange. It was still sweet, mouth-filling and exceptionally harmonious, with a flavour that seemed to combine a tang of citrus and a smoky richness. The only wine I have tasted that it resembled was a Málaga of about the same period from the Duke of Wellington's estate of Molino del Rey, which shared these smoky-orange aromas and soft richness. Neither had any trace of the very recognizable Muscat flavour – which is not to say they never did.

CHAPTER 25

ISLAND OF THE IMMORTALS

Great wines are made by their markets. It is an axiom you can apply at any stage of history. Of course they are not made without good grapes and a tolerable climate; still less without investment and diligence. Only one wine, though, has gained its place in history by the brutal way it has been treated. The masochist is madeira. If it had remained in its beautiful island home, or merely been shipped the few hundred miles to Europe, its unique qualities would never have emerged. But its fate was to suffer the tropics, and conditions that destroyed its competitors. Madeira became what it is (or rather has been), the longest-living, most pungent and luxurious, yet most vigorous and energizing of wines, because its market lay across oceans, even across the equator – and by some miracle it had the constitution to survive.

Madeira is the largest of a group of islands 400 miles into the Atlantic off the coast of Morocco; the nearest of the Atlantic archipelagos that had been dimly known to the ancients as the Isles of the Blest, and perhaps given rise to the legend of Atlantis. Who knows what ancient seamen, like Ulysses, set out beyond the Pillars of Hercules, the Straits of Gibraltar, "to sail beyond the sunset", and never returned?

The Canary Islands were the first to be rediscovered in the 14th-century Age of Exploration, probably by the inquisitive Genoese following the coast of Africa southward. None seem to have returned, though, from a course due westward straight out into the Atlantic, until in about 1345 a cog from Bristol was blown off its course for the Mediterranean, and after 13 days of tempest made a landfall on an unknown island. The story is full of pathos. The cog belonged to a Bristol merchant-venturer, Robert à Machin, who was eloping with the daughter of a nobleman above his station. Both died on the island and were buried on the beach where a village now stands bearing a Portuguese version of his name, Machico.

When the crew set sail again eastward they were captured by Moorish pirates and the cog, *La Welyfare*, was taken into Tangier. There, in the prison, they met a captive Spanish pilot, Juan de Morales of Seville, and told him their story. Morales was ransomed, but on his way home captured once more, this time by the Portuguese captain Juan Gonçalves, known as Zarco, the one-eyed. Zarco was one of the skippers trained by Prince Henry the Navigator – hardened scourges of the Moors ("unemployed Crusaders", they have been called).

Two years later, in 1418, Zarco, together with the Genoese pilot Perestrello, in turn found himself blown off course en route for West Africa, and landed on an island that they supposed to be Machin's discovery. From it, on the southwest horizon, they watched a dark cloud like "vapours rising from the mouth of hell". The experienced Genoese knew it must be a considerable island, and stayed with his ship while Zarco returned to Portugal to report to Prince Henry. The Prince gave him men and stores. In July 1420 they landed on an island of magnificent mountains that Perestrello named in Italian Lolegname, the Island of Woods, and the Portuguese just "Wood": Madeira.

THE GENOESE, AND THE SPANISH, HAVING DISCOVERED THE CANARY ISLANDS, had to conquer them before they could colonize them. Their native inhabitants, although still living in the Stone Age, put up a resistance that was not finally crushed until almost the end of the 15th century.

Madeira had no inhabitants. From the shoreline to the top of its 6,000-foot crags it was one dense forest. Under its characteristic cloud its climate was quite different from that of the Saharan coast only 400 miles away; almost equally warm but never short of rainfall and immensely fertile.

Prince Henry gave command of the island to Zarco, and ordered it colonized with sugar cane and vines from Crete. For revenue, no crop could be expected to equal the luxurious produce of the eastern Mediterranean, then falling more and

Madeira towers out of the Atlantic off the North African coast with some of the highest sea-cliffs in the world. It was discovered uninhabited, one enormous primeval forest, but was quickly turned by the Portuguese into the world's biggest producer of sugar. Wine took over as its principal export when Brazil and its slave-labour undercut Madeira's sugar industry.

more under Turkish control. To clear the land for planting the settlers started bushfires, which tradition says burned for seven years, laying waste the rich indigenous forest but leaving an enriching covering of wood ash. Sugarcane was the great success. The previous sources of sugar for Europe had been Sicily, the eastern Mediterranean, North Africa and a little in Andalusia and the Algarve, but everywhere it was a luxury. It grew so well on Madeira that between 1470 and 1500 the European price of sugar halved. At the start of the 16th century, Madeira was the world's greatest sugar producer. As early as 1456 records also show that Madeira wine was imported into England.

AT THE SAME TIME, BUT WITH LESS STRIKING RESULTS, Portugal was colonizing the Azores, far out in the Atlantic on the latitude of Lisbon, and the Cape Verde Islands, far south of the Canaries on the latitude of Senegal and, across the Atlantic, the West Indies. The Azores proved the least profitable: wine was growable there, grain did well, but the prevailing winds made the islands awkward to reach, and they are a notorious centre of high barometric pressure, which means no wind at all. The Cape Verde Islands were too hot and dry for the vine, but useful for cotton.

Of all the Atlantic islands, the first whose wine found a ready market and made a name were the Canaries. Canary sack, modelled by the Spanish on sherry sack and malaga, was well-established in England by the middle of the 16th century. Shakespeare's most vivid tasting note concerns Canary: "A marvellous searching wine; and it perfumes the blood ere one can say 'what's this?'" It seems to have been, in general, sweeter than sherry sack and more like malaga, mostly of the Malmsey grape, although that known as Vidonia, from Tenerife, was a relatively dry and high-acid wine that aged well – Vidonia is another name for the Verdelho grape of Madeira. Canary remained popular in northern Europe throughout the 17th and most of the 18th centuries, reaching its peak in England in the 1660s. James Howell, the author of the *Familiar Letters*, in one of which he gossips about every drink he has ever tasted, or heard of, had the highest opinion of it. Canary wines, he wrote, "are accounted the richest, the most firm, the best-bodied and lastingst." "French wines", he added, "may be said but to pickle meat in the stomach, but this is the wine that digests." If Howell is right, it was more in fashion in the 1630s than sherry or malaga, which "well mingled, pass for Canaries in most taverns, more often than Canary itself." In the end, though, it did not have the quality or the staying power of madeira.

MADEIRA OWED ITS RISE TO FAME partly to its peculiar natural constitution, the result of the island's soil and climate, but more particularly because of its position on the Atlantic shipping lanes. In several ways it has been the Americas that have shaped madeira's fortune. The first was that sugar plantations in Brazil produced better (and, with slave labour, cheaper) sugar. In the 1570s the island found that wine was a more profitable crop. But Madeira's style of wine, even from the best Malmsey grapes, was light and acid (especially by sack lovers' standards). Falstaff washed down his cold capon's leg with it: he did not compose an ode to it.

The second was the development of plantations by the English in North America and the West Indies. The plantation of Virginia was begun in 1607, of

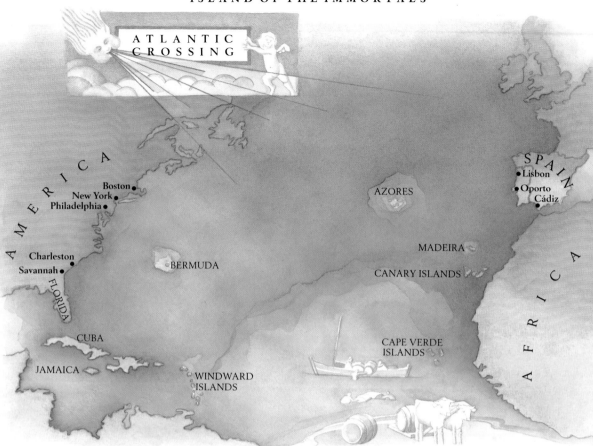

Massachusetts Bay in 1629, of Maryland in 1632. The Leeward Islands and Barbados became British in the 1630s. Oliver Cromwell took Jamaica from Spain in 1655. South Carolina was settled in 1663. By the reign of Charles II there was a widespread demand for wine along the North American seaboard and south into the West Indies. King Charles confirmed Cromwell's Navigation Ordinance, designed to give the monopoly of shipping goods from Europe to the colonies to English ships alone. Colonial ships therefore had to go to England for everything they needed.

But Charles made one exception: Madeira. Some say it was out of respect for his Portuguese Queen; others that Madeira is more truly Africa than Europe. It could hardly have been an oversight. Almost every west-bound ship for the Americas stopped there in any case, if only to fill its water casks. It was a question of winds. The prevailing winds make the westerly passage a penance in the north Atlantic. The natural sea-lane lies south down the coast of Portugal until you meet the northeasterly trade winds at about the 30th degree of latitude, between Madeira and the Canaries. A direct run westward then takes you to Bermuda and Charleston or Savannah, but the prevailing winds on the North American coast are southerly, making the run up to more northern ports a simple matter. Thus almost every ship, whether British or American, put in to the open harbour, the "roads" at Funchal, the capital of Madeira, and loaded wine for the crossing.

An early witness to the effect was Christopher Jefferson, in 1676, whose ship, on its way to St Kitts in the Windward Islands, was chased into Funchal roads by a

Turkish privateeer and nearly came to grief. The drenched Jefferson was revived by the "restorative and anti-rheumatic virtues of old Madeira" (it is surprising that the wine he was given was old) and discovered, when he arrived in the West Indies, that "there is no commodity better in these parts than Madeira wines. They are so generally and so plentifully drunk, being the only strong drink that is natural here, except brandy and rum, which are too hot." Young Jefferson put his finger straight on the great virtue of madeira in a hot climate: it not only remains in good condition, but it retains a vital freshness, a little bite of acidity that makes it a refreshing drink when "brandy and rum are too hot". At this stage most madeira was still an ordinary beverage wine, made in September, racked in December or January and shipped out as soon as possible to be drunk within the year.

THE SHIPPING CONDITIONS WERE TOTALLY PRIMITIVE. There was no jetty or quay, and the hogsheads, or "pipes", of wine were rolled into the sea, to be pushed and pulled by swimmers to the ships lying off the pounding beach. Yet in December 1697, William Bolton, an English merchant at Funchal, recorded that within 17 days 11 ships had loaded wine, ten of them British and bound for the American plantations. Eight of the ships (three for Jamaica, two for Boston, and one each for Barbados, Antigua and Nevis) between them took on 695 pipes; about 100,000 gallons of wine.

A distinction was made between the regular beverage wines and Malmseys, which were grown only in the best sites and probably represented about four percent of the total. The Malmsey grape was in a class apart for rich wines. For dry, the Sercial emerged as much the finest. Legend had it – quite wrongly – that it was really the same grape as the Riesling. André Jullien made the comparison between Sercial and Rhine wines, on the grounds that they were the two longest-lived white wines in the world. Between the best sweet and the best dry came the Bual or Bagoual grape, good for medium-rich wines, and the Verdelho (alias Vidonia) for medium and milder ones. Very good wines were also made from Muscat and a grape called Terrantez (now an extreme rarity). Ordinary wines were made from the Tinta. They were extremely astringent and were recommended for treating dysentery – which gave them a steady market in the tropics.

It was originally Malmseys that the Funchal merchants began to store and age on the island, to sell at much higher prices. They had no cool cellarage, so kept their pipes in the open air or in the lofts of their "lodges", where although the wine oxidized (the French say "maderized") and turned brown, the high temperatures seemed to do the flavour nothing but good.

Arriving at their destination the pipes were commonly syphoned off into great glass demijohns or carboys, protected with wicker casing, where they lay in high summer temperatures with no protection from oxygen. All this maltreatment did was to make them smoother and more pungent. The parallel with Falernian is remarkable; one feels that Pliny would shrug his shoulders and say, "of course".

MADEIRA IN THE 17TH CENTURY WAS CHRONICALLY SHORT OF FOOD, especially after 1640 when Portugal was once more at war with Spain (and hence with the granary of the Canaries). The Azores had plenty of grain, but the Lisbon government directed it to its latter-day Crusaders, its garrison in Morocco, leaving Madeira to fend for itself – which it did by making foreign ships, calling for wine, turn aside for a wearisome voyage to the Azores and back (often returning empty-handed). As soon as the North American plantations had grain to spare, therefore, Madeira welcomed a two-way trade that was profitable for both. New England in particular sent grain and maize. "In return, Madeira had little to offer but wines, wines, and more wines" – wines that, it is said, "softened the rigidities" of Puritanism and made the inhabitants of New England seaport towns altogether more human.

Old England, meanwhile, despite its sworn brotherhood with Portugal, for a long time remained faithful to Canary. What awakened interest in madeira back in London was the information of how good it had become in America. The great botanist Sir Joseph Banks, sailing with Captain Cook to Australia on HMS *Endeavour*, left a graphic but not exactly flattering picture of Madeira in 1768: "When first approached from seaward the island has a very beautiful appearance, the sides of the hills being entirely covered with vineyards almost as high as the eye can distinguish. This gives a constant appearance of verdure, although at this time nothing but the vines remain green, the grass and herbs being completely burnt up, except near the rills by which the vines are watered and under the shade of the vines themselves.

"The people here in general seem to be as idle, or rather uninformed, a set, as I ever yet saw; all their instruments, even those with which their wine, the only genuine article of trade in the island, is made, are perfectly simple and unimproved. In making the wine the grapes are put into a square wooden vessel ... into which the servants get (having taken off their stockings and jackets), and with their feet and elbows squeeze out as much of the juice as they can; the stalks, etc, are then collected, tied together with a rope, and put under a square piece of wood which is pressed down by a lever, to the other end of which is fastened a stone that may be raised up at pleasure by a screw. By this means and this only they make their wine, and by this probably Noah made his when he had newly planted his first vineyard after the general destruction of mankind and their arts, although it is not impossible he might have used a better, if he remembered the methods he had seen before the flood."

Cook bought more than 3,000 gallons of wine on the island for the 94 crewmen and scientists on the *Endeavour*. Brandy was added to this wine to help preserve it for a voyage that lasted two and a half years.

FROM ABOUT THIS TIME THE LEDGERS OF THE MERCHANT HOUSES OF MADEIRA (increasingly in English ownership) begin to record another excellent market for their wine: the new British possessions in India. (Portugal's Indian feitorias had undoubtedly used a steady supply since they were founded in the 15th century.) The island was equally en route for an East Indiaman as it was for a ship plying to America. By the start of the 19th century almost half the island's shipments were crossing the equator, rounding the Cape, crossing the equator again, and having the same refreshing effect in the East Indies as the West. The records of Cossart, Gordon and Co., one of the oldest firms on the island, record exactly which wine went to each of the many British regimental messes in such Imperial bastions as Meerut, Bangalore, Secunderabad, Rawal Pindee and Lucknow.

MADEIRA'S YOUNG WINES BEFORE THEIR ADVENTURES BEGIN are surprisingly light and unimpressive, except for their noticeable edge of acidity. For these long voyages the wines were undoubtedly fortified with spirits; "two bucketfuls of brandy a pipe" sounds very much like the practice with mid-18th-century port. The dessert qualities, made of Malmsey, Bual or sometimes Verdelho grapes, were also often sweetened with "vinho de surdo": a mixture of unfermented must and brandy. The extra strength helped their already uncanny stability; the extra sweetness simply made them taste even more luxurious on the verandah at the end of the voyage.

If one voyage across the Atlantic (or the equator) was good for the wine, two, it was argued, must be better. It certainly turned out so. By the second half of the 18th century, orders were arriving from London for pipes to be loaded on ships outward-bound for the West (or even the East) Indies, to be treated as ballast on board and to return with the ship to Europe.

Barrels of extra size and strength were built to be stowed in the bilges of an East Indiaman, whose voyage from Funchal to Bombay and back to London would take at least half a year. Why these wines, constantly in motion in stifling heat, the barrels often submerged in foetid bilgewater, did not turn out undrinkable is a mystery. On the contrary, they developed softness and depth of flavour, while never losing their piquant liveliness that made people think of them almost as eccentric but much-loved old friends. Even more eccentric was the method of ageing them in bottles buried in a pit of horse manure for six months, which Jullien reports. What quality this was expected to add is hard to imagine. With any other author one would suspect a hoax.

NOWHERE WERE THE IDIOSYNCRASIES OF MADEIRA MORE LOVINGLY STUDIED than in East Coast America. Savannah, Georgia, which happens to be on exactly the same latitude as Funchal, was famous in the first half of the 19th century for its madeira

---

VINTAGE MADEIRA

It is possible to be categorical about the astonishing quality of madeiras up to 150 years old and more because such wines still exist in a few collectors' cellars. In 1988 a bottle of 1838 Malmsey was drunk at a dinner in Savannah, Georgia – where there is still a Madeira Club – and overtopped in quality a succession of five other excellent vintages, the youngest of them 80 years old. It proved the point that the constitution of this wine is unlike all others.

Vintage madeiras, like vintage ports, were only made in particularly successful years when the quality of the wine was well above average. The bulk was, and is, aged in something similar to the Spanish solera system – if it was aged at all before leaving the island. Traditionally the island's merchants sold their wines under the grape variety name and their own names only: these were a sufficient guide to quality and style.

Occasionally the name of one of the best-situated villages of the island (e.g. Campanario, Câmara de Lobos – both on the sheltered south side) was mentioned.

Disasters that hit Madeira's vineyards late in the 19th century almost put a stop to the trade in top-quality and vintage wines. Shortage led to high prices and a falling off of demand, followed by Prohibition in the United States; another blow to the island. Shippers have concentrated their attention in this century on the Scandinavian market for fine wines, and the French for low-quality cooking wines from inferior vine varieties introduced after phylloxera. Unaccountably, the British have all but forgotten madeira in favour of port and sherry. It comes as news to most people to learn that such vintages as 1920, 1934 and 1954 are still (although in tiny quantities) available commercially.

Savannah, Georgia, was famous for its heirloom madeiras. At the Owens-Thomas
house a 19th-century cellar-full is still in place, hand-written labels telling the story
of each wine. The bottles were kept upright: the wine apparently took no harm.

cellars, and particularly for the wines of a merchant named William Neyle
Habersham. The Habersham mansion in the handsome seaport town contained,
over the ballroom, a solarium, accessible only through his dressing-room, where he
apparently aged and blended the wines he sold for fabulous prices. One Habersham
speciality was Rainwater, a pale blend of Verdelho wine whose name is the subject
of various legends – some of them obvious. Whether because of the appeal of its
name, or a singular softness in the mouth, Rainwater became a firm American
favourite.

The first name that was usually given to a madeira when it was decanted into
carboys in a Savannah cellar was that of the ship that carried it; the most famous
being not a merchantman at all, but the US Navy frigate *Constitution*, built as an
escort to shepherd American ships through waters infested with Algerian pirates.
The wine she brought home in 1802 was considered a great treasure. Something
about the marriage of a wine and a ship had enormous romantic appeal. Lovingly
handwritten labels recall the *Juno, Comet, Hurricane, Catherine Banks, Southern
Cross*, the famous clipper *Red Jacket*, and even the ship that took madeira all the way
to Japan and back with Commodore Perry in 1852, the *Susquehanna*.

Often the ship's name was followed by that of the buyer of the wine, then even
of succeeding generations who in due course inherited the heirloom, so that its label
became almost like the flyleaf of a family Bible. Sometimes the style of wine –
"Malmsey", "Rainwater" – was mentioned; sometimes not. One jereboam in the
cellars of the Owens-Thomas house in Savannah bears the simple legend "Miss
Wright's Delight".

THE TROUBLE AND EXPENSE OF SHIPPING BARRELS BACK AND FORTH ACROSS THE OCEANS
inevitably led in the end to an industrial shortcut. If long periods at high
temperatures were what was required, they could be provided more simply than by
travelling halfway around the world. In 1794 Funchal saw its first "estufa", a lodge
equipped with a huge stove that circulated hot water to provide tropical heat. The

pipes of wine are stacked high and left in this stifling atmosphere for months on end. There is no nautical motion, no smelly bilgewater.

Originally, "estufa" wines were thought to be inferior to ones that had travelled the oceans. In 1832 Jullien wrote that "wines aged in a stove never rise to the heights of a vinho da roda. When one of these is 30 or 40 years old it has formed a thick crust inside its bottle; it is white and clear as water; its perfume is so powerful when the bottle is opened that persons with delicate nerves can be quite alarmed by it." But such glorious wines have been made by the stove method over the last two centuries that even nostalgia can find nothing to complain about. Estufa Malmseys over a century old are as full of vigour and sumptuous flavour as ever, and seem only to improve however long they are kept. No drink, no foodstuff of any kind, one might almost say no living thing, shares the apparent immortality of old vintage madeira.

The practice of vinhos da roda did not entirely die out until World War I. But long before that time, the island had suffered from the vine diseases that threatened all the world's vineyards in the 19th century, and from which they have not entirely recovered to this day.

A MADEIRA PARTY

Nothing so vividly recreates the atmosphere in which madeira came to its full flowering in early 19th-century America as a little book by Silas Weir Mitchell, a famous Philadelphia physician, called simply *A Madeira Party*.

Mitchell set the scene "early in the second quarter of the century" in Philadelphia, and described the dining-room: "Silver candlesticks lighted a table laid for four, and their light fell on buff and gold Nankin china, glass and glistening plate. A negro servant well on in years, dark as the mahogany he loved to polish, with fine contrast of very white hair . . . considered for a moment the table and the setting . . . . With a smile of satisfaction he turned to inspect a row of decanters on the mantel . . . ."

The four dined on terrapin and canvasback duck before they came to the discussion of four venerable wines. Their conversation tells us much about madeira folklore. "The English officers during the French war [in America]", we learn, "found our Madeira so good that they took the taste back to England."

"And yet", said Chestnut, "Madeira is never good in England. Is it the climate, or that they don't know how to keep it?"

"Both, both", returned Wilmington, "they bottle all wines, and that is simply fatal. Madeira was never meant to be retailed. It improves in its own society, as greatness is apt to do."

LE GRAND THÉATRE

Bordeaux began the 18th century as a town still surrounded by its medieval walls. By the time of the Revolution in 1789, it was the most handsome modern city in France and the country's greatest port. It had added to its ancient wine trade in quantity and revolutionized it in quality. More dramatically, perhaps, it had become the country's principal point of contact with its colonies: half of all colonial trade, above all West Indian trade, passed through Bordeaux's famous crescent-moon-shaped harbour. To celebrate its worldly success, in the 1780s its citizens built Le Grand Théâtre, symbolically upstaging the Gothic cathedral, the heart of the old town, with something more in keeping with the spirit of the times; the most magnificent theatre built in Europe since the Romans.

THE THEATRE, CROWNING THE HILL RISING FROM THE PORT, with its spectacular peristyle of Corinthian columns and arcades down each side, was the climax of half a century of perpetual building activity that had made the town like one great mason's yard. When the Royal architect Jacques Gabriel arrived in 1729, summoned by the Intendant, the King's deputy in the province, he wrote: "I will swear, Monseigneur, that I have never seen such a fine prospect and such a grand spectacle as this port; it demands some great work, which posterity will find worthy of commendation. I shall stay here for as long as it takes to draw up the plans."

Few waterfronts on earth can compare with the palatial Place Royale that became the frontispiece of Bordeaux in the 1740s. For 50 years the city spent its great trading income on transforming itself from a medieval town to France's most perfect modern city. Behind the classical façades of the Quai des Chartrons (right) lies the source of much of its wealth: the long barns or "chais" that house the wines from the surrounding country.

It took much longer than he ever expected. He found the citizens extremely loath to do away with the walls that gave them their identity and privileges (and at whose gates they gained a very useful income came from taxes). His first great project was to open the town to the river in a magnificent three-sided square, the Place Royale, richer than the Place Vendôme in Paris, its buildings sumptuous with sculpture by the master-sculptors of Versailles, Verbeckt and Van der Woort. He died before it was even started, a dozen years later, with his son in charge.

The succeeding Intendant, Louis-Urban Aubert, Marquis de Tourny, arriving in 1743, was shocked to find Bordeaux still "a muddle of ugly houses without symmetry or convenience, among which wander narrow streets with never a right-angle." He immediately banned all new buildings until he had personally approved the plans.

Under Tourny the pace quickened. The town was seriously inconvenienced, to say the least, by the massive fortress, the Château Trompette, built by Charles VII against its northern wall in the 15th century to encourage loyalty to France after the defeat of the English. Louis XIV had modernized and enlarged this great excrescence (today its size can be judged by the vast emptiness of the Place des Quinconces that stands on its site). All the merchants who were not citizens of Bordeaux, which included almost all the growing class of wine traders, coming from Holland, England, Germany, Ireland and Scandinavia, had to make their base on the far side of the fortress, downstream from the city and completely removed from it; almost as a separate town. This was palus land, partly covered in vines and named after an old Carthusian monastery in its midst, the Chartrons.

Tourny commissioned Gabriel Junior to link the two with boulevards around the Château, and had the wonderfully dreamy idea of a public garden of extraordinary elegance to be the meeting place between them, "where merchants, often having occasion to meet, would strike many more bargains; it is a sort of second stock exchange; an evening one". Guards were to be kept at the gates so that the "petit peuple" would not venture in. There were only second-rate vineyards on the site when Gabriel moved in in 1746, to play with ideas that he afterwards put to use for the Place de la Concorde in Paris and the Petit Trianon at Versailles.

BY THE 1780S, COURSE UPON COURSE OF CREAMY STONE HAD RISEN along a two-mile stretch of the muddy banks of the Garonne above the crowded shipping with its chaos of cordage and the bullock sleds with their dead weight of barrels groaning down to the tide. The streets and squares, in a consensus so perfect that one hand might have designed the whole, stretch back half a mile from the river. Perhaps no other city has ever caught the spirit of its own flowering so completely in its architecture, so that even the dwindling houses of the "petit peuple", moving away from the centre, built of the same stone, share the same sense of proportion, beguiling not by ornament but by harmony.

What had produced this flowering? Civic pride, diligence, and a strong itch for gold. The Parlement where de Pontac had presided continued to produce a race of lawyers, the *noblesse de robe*, whose wits and ambitions made short work of the old *noblesse d'épée*, families whose inheritance ran back to deeds of knightly valour, but liked to hunt their land, rather than farm it. Their property was fractioned by feudal custom. Some was share-cropped on the various intricate systems of metayage or bourdieux derived from the "complant" of the Middle Ages; very little was rationally managed. Alongside and overlapping with the parlementaires were the risk-taking merchants, the négociants who freighted ships for the booming West Indies; with luck a much more profitable pastime even than waiting for Dutchmen to come and haggle over the latest vintage.

TEN YEARS INTO THE 18TH CENTURY, losing the war of the Spanish Succession made Frenchmen look forward rather than back to the fading glories of the Sun King. The vineyards of all of France had been devastated by a winter in which temperatures plunged to −17.5°C in Marseilles. It was time to get going, on the farm and on the ocean that the French, inimitably, call "le grand large". In the 17th century "America", for France, had meant Newfoundland and the (very profitable) cod fisheries. But already during the war, wafts of spicy breezes had been coming in from France's new plantations in the Antilles. During the war, two ships a month

THE CHARTRONS

Foreign merchants in Bordeaux were obliged to stay outside the old city and develop a northern suburb of their own, just downstream from the menacing Château Trompette. The Quai des Chartrons took its name from the Carthusian monastery there, and its merchant class soon became a distinct and influential body, referred to as the Chartronnais.

They were viewed with mixed feelings by the Bordeaux bourgeoisie. Winegrowers accustomed to selling via brokers to visiting merchants could see snags in a new class of substantial traders holding stocks on their doorstep.

Foreigners operated as both brokers and négociants; the brokers travelling from property to property, the négociants commuting from Bordeaux to their native ports. Most started as general merchants. The oldest firm is that of Beyerman, founded from Rotterdam in 1620. Several of the most famous were Irish, including the celebrated broker Abraham Lawton from Cork, who in the 1740s had 2,500 accounts, and the exceptionally successful Tom Barton, whose family is still Franco-Irish after nearly 300 years in Bordeaux. Barton, still referred to by his descendants as "French Tom", set up in Bordeaux with perfect timing in 1715, when first-growths had become the height of English and Irish fashion and peace had at last broken out. He became much the biggest buyer of first-growths, buying a great estate in Tipperary and marrying his daughters to English noblemen. In 1821 his descendants bought the magnificent Château Langoa, in which they still live.

had been arriving with sugar and spices. Bordeaux did well by re-exporting them to northern ports on the Dutch ships that had negotiated passports to come to the city to buy wine.

Before the war it had been the port of Nantes that dominated the new traffic with the sugar plantation in the Windward Islands, dealing mainly in raw sugar and the slaves needed to cultivate it. Now Bordeaux had a sugar refinery, and overtook Nantes in trading with the richest and fastest-growing colony of all, Saint-Domingue (or Haiti). In 1714 the port saw 7,000 tons of sugar arrive from Haiti; in 1742, the year the wall came down to start the Place Royale, the figure was more than 40,000 tons. The plantations had gone too fast, in fact: the 1730s saw a glut of sugar and its price fall from the luxury level to something for the common man. In mid-century an even more profitable commodity made Haiti a goldmine: coffee. Together, by the 1770s, sugar and coffee planters were importing slaves into Haiti at the startling rate of 36,000 a year. By the French Revolution there were half a million. It is small wonder that two years later Haiti had a revolution of its own.

The 1770s saw the fastest growth of colonial trade in Bordeaux, with ships from the Indies (East and West) arriving at the rate of five a week, and turning round, as one observer put it, "without careening or anything". Bordeaux was in a unique position among French ports to profit fully by all this shipping: its own produce was wanted everywhere. Wine was the main export, but the hinterland (which Bordeaux's citizens, mindful of their taxes, liked to describe to the government as "maigre et infertil") provided bountiful grain, eaux-de-vie, the ever-popular plums of the Agenais, hemp for cordage, sailcloth (another speciality of Agen), and such necessaries for the colonies as stoves and mills (and also stills). Every part of inland France crowded to the great March fair in the city to find exporters for its produce: linen from Brittany, cotton fabrics from Normandy and silks from Lyons. Bordeaux had learnt a good deal about re-exporting from its Dutch friends as well. Ireland was an excellent market for wine: in turn it provided first-class salt beef, which found a ready market in the West Indies.

A list of Chartronnais names gives an idea of their origins. Nathaniel Johnston came from Ulster; Lynch was another highly successful Irishman. Such names as Sandilands, Jernon, Knox and Cope, Power, Chalmers, Fennwick, Bonfield, Sullivan, Ferguson, Horish, Bethmann, Schroder and Schÿler, MacCarthy, Halford, Sichel, Thomson, O'Brien, Coppinger and Kressman represents a spread over northern Europe, with a strong stress on Britain and Ireland. One German family, Cruse, became the epitome of everything Chartronnais. But even the French elements of which de Luze, Dolor, Eschenauer (from Alsace), Calvet (from the Rhône) are examples, acquired an almost Anglo-Saxon air. Their intermarriages produced a closed society which lasted until the 1970s.

"French Tom" Barton from Ireland became the greatest buyer of first-growth claret.

FRENCH COMMERCE HAD HAD AN UNLOOKED-FOR BONUS FROM LOUIS XIV when he effectively expelled all France's most talented and productive Protestants by repealing the Edict of Nantes (by which the wise Henri IV had given freedom of religion to his people) in 1685. Bordeaux stood to gain as much as anywhere when its Huguenots took flight, largely to Holland, and many of them to set up as merchants in Hamburg. Quite early in the century, Hamburg overtook Amsterdam as Bordeaux's biggest market in northern Europe (even if the majority of the freighters were still the Dutch sea-waggons).

More and more, Bordeaux looked to Germany, and beyond to the Baltic, for a two-way trade that was both profitable and essential. Ships that left Bordeaux with wine returned with barrel staves of Baltic oak, the best wood in the world for the casks that were needed for high-quality wine. Polish, Pomeranian and East Prussian oak forests produce close-grained timber that gives a less obvious flavour to the wine than French-grown oak, while still providing enough tannin. The fussy English, paying whatever it cost to buy their first-growths, their Latour, Lafite, Margaux and Haut-Brion, specified Stettin oak as best of all. Hamburg merchants provided timber of all grades (including much that went into the floors and the delicate *boiseries* of Bordeaux's new mansions), and gratifyingly took a massive amount of coffee, as well as claret, on the homeward voyage.

IN POINT OF TIME, THE FAMOUS "FURY OF PLANTING" STRUCK BORDEAUX before the "colonial fever". The lead had been so daringly and successfully given by the first-growths at the end of the 17th century that they were to prove uncatchable. They had, quite simply, secured the best sites in the Médoc, buying up and planting the three places where the gravel soil was coarsest, best drained and warmest, and it was to the Médoc that parlementaires and merchants rushed to emulate them. One of the first was an ambitious merchant called Pierre de Rauzan, who acted as manager of the Latour estate between 1679 and 1693, and profited by its example and his position to buy up as much of the neighbouring land as he could on his own behalf. By 1690 he had assembled some 50 acres of good vineyard land (not yet all planted), which passed by the marriage of his daughter Thérèse to Jacques François de Pichon, seigneur de Longueville, becoming the basis of the great Pichon-Longueville estate. Professor Pijassou of the University of Bordeaux points out, in his great work on the Médoc, that "the vineyard of Pichon is a little less well situated than the first-growth [Latour]; the pebbles there are a little smaller, the proportion of sand greater, the pattern of slopes more gentle; finally, the area of the vineyard was smaller". These factors meant that, in the firmly held belief of Bordeaux's experts from that day to this, the wine could never be quite as good. De Rauzan was then operating in the other part of the Médoc that was acknowledged supreme; as close as he could get to Château Margaux. He was able to bequeath to Thérèse's three brothers about 60 acres of vines "around the house called Gassies". This one man laid the foundations for what today are four "second-growths": Châteaux Pichon-Longueville, Pichon-Lalande, Rauzan-Gassies and Rausan-Ségla.

AT A VERY EARLY STAGE, IN 1638, ANOTHER MERCHANT, MONSIEUR MOYTIÉ, had started a similar process of assembling little parcels of land on the hillock just south of Latour, across the stream that divides the parish of St-Julien from Pauillac. He named his gravel "dune" Mont-Moytié. A century later it was bought by another President of the Parlement, Monsieur Léoville. At this stage it was possibly the largest vineyard in the Médoc. Today it is three, all second-growths, distinguished by the names of subsequent owners: Châteaux Léoville-Las-Cases, Léoville-Barton and Léoville-Poyferré.

Among the other estates whose owners and approximate extents are recorded from the first half of the 18th century are those of the parlementaire the Marquis de Brazier, who owned the medieval fortress of Lamarque and in 1757 built Château Beychevelle by the river at St-Julien: certainly the most monumental and architecturally sophisticated of all Médoc wine properties. He also owned the "Poujaux" estate at Moulis, with a total of 150 acres of vines.

The Avocat de Gorsse was another lawyer whose name lives on in various versions in smaller properties north of Margaux, but whose original Château de Gorce (he spelt as badly as Shakespeare) is now the second-growth Brane-Cantenac. Another was Counsellor Malescot who had 60 acres in Margaux; another Counsellor de Castelnau, who owned the beautiful medieval moated Château d'Issan with 20 acres of vines. In 1723 Issan became one of the first properties besides the first-growths to be sold by name in London.

THESE RELATIVELY SMALL ACREAGES DO NOT IN THEMSELVES SOUND EXACTLY LIKE A "fury of planting", but we must remember that they were being repeated all over what had never been dedicated vine-growing land before, and that similar things were happening in all the other country districts around Bordeaux. In 1744 the

THE PRINCE DES VIGNES

Of all the grandees of the Bordeaux parlement, none can be compared with the President Nicolas-Alexandre, Marquis de Ségur (1697-1755), who in the first half of the 18th century owned the two first-growths of Lafite and Latour, plus Mouton (now first-growth), the great estate of Calon-Ségur in St-Estèphe and other properties in the Médoc and Graves. Louis XV dubbed him the Prince des Vignes, after being told that the (apparently diamond) buttons of his coat were the precious stones of his vineyard, cut and polished. Ségur's income from Lafite and Latour alone was estimated at 100,000 livres a year, of which 60 percent was profit. He complained to the Intendant de Tourny that 1744 was a bad vintage and that his taxes should be reduced. The official reckoning was an income of 272,000 livres, with expenses of 34,000.

While most talk of this exceptionally prosperous man concentrates on his income, it should be remembered that it was he who drew the definite boundaries between the land of Lafite and the neighbouring Mouton, thus creating two profoundly different styles of wine. He undoubtedly ran his estates with great zeal and gave their reputations the solid foundation that has never foundered. Latour belonged to his descendants until 1963, and his family is still represented among the directors of the Société Civile de Château Latour.

Intendant's subdelegate estimated that "half of his jurisdiction" was planted as vineyard, nine-tenths of it belonging to the wealthy bourgeois and nobility of Bordeaux. By this time the government had been concerned for nearly 50 years (since the 1690s) that more vines would mean less corn. The phrase "fureur de planter" was coined by the Intendant Boucher as early as 1724. "For ten leagues around Bordeaux", he said, "you see nothing but vines. The same mania has taken hold on the rest of the province." His solution, though, showed that a great deal of the planting was on palus and former corn lands, and that he was aware of the value of the new estates on gravel sites. "All the vines planted since 1709" (the year of the great frost) "must be ripped out, in all the high country and in the Bordeaux district, except those in the graves of the Médoc, Graves of Bordeaux" (the modern Graves), "and the Côtes" – in other words, the traditional vineyard land plus the best sites of the Médoc.

OTHER EVIDENCE MAKES IT CLEAR THAT PARIS SAW TOO MANY VINES as a national problem. In the 1720s France seemed to be going vine-mad; prices fell, the common people spent all their time in bars ("cabarets") drinking wine from tankards. In 1725, Boucher's ban became legally enforceable in Bordeaux. In 1731 it was royally decreed that no more vines should be planted anywhere in France without the King's express permission. For an objective point of view on the ban it is interesting to read Adam Smith, the Scottish philosopher and economist, who wrote, in *The Wealth of Nations*: "The pretence of this order was the scarcity of corn and pasture, and the superabundance of wine", while the real cause was "the anxiety of the proprietors of the old vineyards to prevent the planting of new ones."

Those who objected to the ban, in Bordeaux at least, had an eloquent spokesman. Charles de Secondat, Baron de Montesquieu, the inheritor of the magnificent moated castle of La Brède just south of Bordeaux, had just written his first book expressing his liberal political views in the form of letters from an imaginary Persian visitor to France. Montesquieu's name was known throughout the country. He challenged Boucher in a forthright manifesto for market forces and free trade. He could, he said, buy 24 acres of waste land (admittedly near Haut-

HEREDITY OR ENVIRONMENT?

Adam Smith also questioned the reasons why some vineyards are "better", and more valuable, than others, and came to an interesting conclusion.

"The vine is more affected by the difference of soils than any other fruit tree. From some it derives a flavour which no culture or management can equal, it is supposed, upon any other. This flavour, real or imaginary, is sometimes peculiar to the produce of a few vineyards; sometimes it extends through the greater part of a small district, and sometimes through a considerable part of a large province." (The Côte d'Or would be an example of the first, Bordeaux closer to the last.)

For such wines, he goes on to say, demand always exceeds supply: therefore they fetch a high price. On the other hand they do not cost that much more to cultivate, so their profits will be higher. "For though such vineyards are in general more carefully cultivated than most others", he concludes, "the high price of the wine seems to be not so much the effect as the cause of this careful cultivation. In so valuable a produce the loss occasioned by negligence is so great as to force even the most careless to [pay] attention."

To what extent a first-growth depends on its position, and to what extent on its cultivation, is almost like the debate between heredity and environment.

Brion) for 60 livres, turn them into vineyard and sell them for 400,000. (He already owned about 3,500 acres.) Why interrupt the new planting which is bringing in so much good foreign business? Why send the business away to the profit of the Portuguese?

In the event, it seems that Boucher was not even supported by his own deputies; Pontet, for example, who built the beautiful château in St-Julien which is now called Langoa. Venal officials sold planting permissions. The decree was renewed several times, but when de Tourny took over from Boucher as Intendant he was faced with the same determination to plant and be damned. By the 1760s the government had given way.

WINEMAKING METHODS, AT LEAST IN THE NEW ESTATES, HAD BEGUN TO STABILIZE BY THE 1760s. At last it is clear just how the wine was made as well as how it was bought and sold. The Scots family Johnston had settled in Bordeaux in 1734 and prospered as négociants (later they became château owners; today, still prospering, they are wine brokers). A notebook dated 1765 records the Johnston technique for judging vintages and properties and buying and shipping at the best moments. It is interesting that Mr Johnston did not turn up his nose at peasants' wines, so long as he could rescue them from the peasants' keeping before they had ruined them. He thus explained the vociferous opposition of the big landowners to a road being built up the Médoc from Bordeaux; an argument that raged from 1730 to 1750. They did not want négociants discovering small growers' wines for themselves, when they were in all likelihood buying them cheap for topping up their own barrels. The bourgeois had access to the *gabares* that plied the river, carrying wine from their jetties up to the merchants on the Quai des Chartrons. A visit from a broker or merchant on horseback was welcome, but not a waggon going from chai to chai.

Johnston's notes on tasting show what he was looking for: body, flavour, good colour, cleanness in taste, no taste of rot or greenness. His instructions are most precise about sniffing at the bunghole of each cask to detect any taint of rot; about the use of the "Dutch (sulphur) match" to disinfect casks – he was the first to describe this – and about avoiding contact with air while racking. He also describes what became known as the "travail à l'anglaise": the blending or "cutting" of pure light wines with darker, more full-bodied or harsher ones to suit the customers' taste.

There is a strange contradiction here which has never found a clear explanation. On the one hand we have every indication that the proprietors of the first-growths and their imitators were doing everything in their power to make the best possible wines, modifying their techniques as they learned and pouring back money into the land. Their expertise (or that of their managers) grew steadily. Towards the end of the century the managers of Lafite, Latour and Margaux were well-known and highly respected in their own right. They were acutely aware of their better and less good patches of soil and of the problem of drainage – even stony slopes needed help from artificial drains. They believed in renewing the vigour of the soil, and dug up common lands wholesale to cart in fresh topsoil, to the extreme chagrin of the locals. Nothing was too much trouble.

On the other hand we have the merchants, who bought and sold their wine, making potent brews with it that must have changed its nature altogether.

Johnston's recipe involved strong Spanish reds, Alicante or Benicarlo, sometimes Rivesaltes from the Midi, often dark palus wine from over the river, and occasionally Cahors or Hermitage, not just mixed with Lafite or Latour, but actually made to re-ferment with it. To start the fermentation they used a bucket of "stum" (juice whose fermentation has never been allowed to start, by dint of sulphur and/or eau-de-vie). So what was sold at very high prices as first-growth claret in the mid-18th century was often a brew-up, with as much as one-third of the total coming from outside the region (or even from outside France).

As WITNESS TO THE FACT THAT THE GROWERS WERE DOING THEIR UTMOST, they regularly sacrificed a substantial amount of their potential income by down-grading large parts of their crop to "second wine". It is commonly believed today that the notion of the "grand vin" of a château as a top selection, with a second wine at half the price or less, is a recent invention. (It has certainly come back into fashion in the last 20 years.) In fact it was a regular practice with the first-growths from the start – and for good reason: vintages were extremely irregular in quality and quantity, there were no means of countering rotting grapes except by sorting them out and throwing them away, and perhaps most of all because they had a muddle of vine varieties, including many white ones. Even "new French claret", improved though it was, was still in some senses "claret" in the old meaning of the word, with white grapes in it, picked early (almost always in September) and given a short fermentation, a week at the most, which would rarely have made deep-coloured or full-bodied wine. Château Lafite regularly had nine or ten degrees of alcohol, instead of the 12 we expect today. These are reasons why the merchants of the Chartrons intervened; to give their customers, the English especially, something more full-blooded; something closer to their favourite Portuguese wine, while still keeping the flavour of Bordeaux.

It was not until about the time of the Revolution and the Napoleonic wars that such celebrated *régisseurs*, or managers, as Domenger, who saw Lafite and Latour through the Revolution, and his successors at Lafite (Goudal) and Latour (Poitevin and Lamothe) became absolute masters of their vineyards and their wines. Lamothe

BERLON OF MARGAUX

There was one famous régisseur of an earlier era: the manager of Château Margaux in the first years of the 18th century, whose name was Berlon. Although he is rather a shadowy figure, he has been described as the Dom Pérignon of the Médoc. Certainly the evidence shows him to have been a great perfectionist.

Like Dom Pérignon he did not record his methods, but they were written down apparently after his death. The most striking revelations are that Château Margaux made white wines ("chiefly of Sauvignon") separately from, and after, its red, and blended the two in the proportion of three barriques of white to a vat (equal to 28 barriques) of red. Berlon would pick white grapes in the dewy morning, but wait until red ones were dried by the sun before starting to pick.

Each vat was started with a "pied de cuve" of very ripe grapes to provoke its fermentation. Four grades of wine were made: Grand Vin, Second Vin, workers' wine and Vin de Provision for the personal use of the owner, whose favourite was a wine between red and rosé from the two best corners of the estate.

Berlon knew exactly which his best plots were, and evidently used scrupulous care in all his operations.

was an ex-ship's captain who had seen every ocean before he settled, aged 53, in Bordeaux and threw all his energies into running Latour. His predecessors had been weeding out the white vines bit by bit. Lamothe went much further. He found out how to cut the tops off white vines and graft on red ones, and he is the first on record in the Médoc to have named the Cabernet as the best grape of all, and planted it massively. "All the Cabernet", he wrote to his employer, "which is the best variety, has gone into the Grand Vin." He also observed (although he was probably not the first) that older vines produced better wine.

It seems very late in the day to be talking about vine varieties in Bordeaux for the first time. The fact is that up to now they had been given very little thought. The old-established parts of the region had a mixture of dozens. At Cadillac, up the Garonne, in 1796 a priest of great intelligence, the abbé Bellet, had listed 18 black varieties and 20 white. The Dutch had been very selective in choosing only the Verdot for their palus plantings. Because the Médoc was a new vineyard its repertoire was relatively limited: about four black varieties and four white. These included Grand and Petit Vidure, alias Carmenet or Cabernet (Vidure means "vigne dure": the Cabernet has very hard wood). Lafite was largely planted with Malbec (alias Noir de Pressac) and Verdot, but had a minority of vines from Hermitage on the Rhône, which were presumably Petite Sirah. Latour was largely Malbec and Cabernet. There is no mention of any Merlot, by a recognizable name, in the Médoc, and only a little Cabernet Franc, or Bouchet.

In all of France the first person to tackle the great chaos of vine varieties seriously only started in the 1780s. In 1600, Olivier de Serres, in his magisterial *Théâtre d'Agriculture*, had been content with saying that the muscat was known "by all nations", and that the 1,000 other varieties (or however many there were) were "a closed book". It was the abbé Rozier, author of the *Dictionnaire Universelle d'Agriculture*, who began comparative plantings near Béziers in the Languedoc. He ran out of money, but the idea was taken up by the new Intendant at Bordeaux, Dupré de St Maur. St Maur tried to use his fellow-intendants in other provinces as correspondents to collect samples. At least a start had been made.

It is also time to cross the river. It is hard to imagine that up to this time and well into the 19th century, the only contact between Bordeaux and the greater part of its territory, across the Garonne, was by boat. A bridge was the next project in line – after the theatre. The plans were laid in 1782 by Dupré de St Maur; the Revolution intervened; Napoleon ordered it built in 1810 as an important shortcut in hurrying troops to Spain; finally it was constructed between 1815 and 1822, with money raised by the millionaire shipowner Stuttenberg and the wine merchant Guestier.

The town of Libourne, east of Bordeaux across two rivers, the Garonne and the Dordogne – a 20-mile ride through the area that takes its name from them, Entre-Deux-Mers – was an important target of the Dutch commercial invasion of the 17th century. Libourne itself had palus wines that the Dutch bought, but acted mainly as the exit port for their huge purchases of white wines up the Dordogne at Bergerac. St-Emilion, Pomerol and Fronsac, the three regions of potentially high quality grouped around Libourne, the Dutch more or less ignored.

The wines of Pomerol began to make their reputation in the 18th century. At that time it was still a region of mixed farming unlike the strict monoculture of vines that cover its plateau today. Château Rouget is one of its few substantial 18th-century houses; when it was built Pomerol was known as much for white wine as for red.

There were a number of reasons why little happened here until the mid-18th century. One was the presence of the Church and religious institutions as landowners (which they were not in the Médoc). The Cathedral Chapter of Bordeaux had a strong hold over St-Emilion, and much of Pomerol belonged to the (formerly Crusader) Knights Hospitallers. Instead of feudal micro-properties, the land-holding was in the less vulnerable (to developers) form of share-cropping. In the case of Fronsac, which largely belonged to the Ducs de Richelieu, their feudal tenants were not encouraged to grow vines.

From the shipping point of view, Libourne had a major disadvantage. Until 1728 it had no port registrar who was authorized to clear cargos for export, so any ship loading there had to make a great detour back up the Garonne to Bordeaux for clearance. The War of the Spanish Succession was a help here. Navy supply officers buying wine for the fleet simply ignored the regulations and commissioned the merchants of Libourne who sold them salt to find them wine as well. The 1730s saw the arrival of Amsterdam and Rotterdam freighters of 100 tons and more. Then in 1740 the winter was cold enough to kill many vines. Like the winter of 1709 in the Médoc it stimulated replanting, which usually meant better planting, and even a certain selectivity over varieties. The Libourne region seems to have been ahead of its time in concentrating on the best grapes. The 1740s were the starting point, when Libourne merchants took the initiative and began looking for markets, less in Holland than in Brittany, along the north coast of France, and in Flanders. The English aristocracy with their Médoc fixation were beyond them. To an extraordinary extent the pattern of trade that was set up in those early years continues to this day. St-Emilion and Pomerol are better known and loved in the north of France and Belgium than they are in England.

LIBOURNE BECAME A LITTLE LESS REMOTE FROM BORDEAUX when the Intendant de Tourny built a road across Entre-Deux-Mers. From the 1760s we have detailed reports of everything going on in the region. It is clear that the top of the St-Emilion Côtes, the hill around the old town, was already taking the strange form that we see today, with deep stone quarries cut into the hill just below the surface, leaving pillars of the limestone rock to support vineyards hanging as it were in midair above them. The vineyards (many of them walled) of Châteaux Belair, Canon, Berliquet, Clos Fourtet, Magdelaine and Ausone date from about this time.

PROFESSOR ENJALBERT OF BORDEAUX HAS DELVED INTO MEMOIRS, official reports and notaries' papers that give some remarkably detailed information. In 1750, what is now Château Tropchaud (then Trochau) in Pomerol was inherited in a decrepit state by the remarkable Monsieur Fontémoing. He wrote that he proposed to dig drains, pull up the old vines, and plant "Bouchet, Noir de Pressac" (Cabernet Franc and Malbec) "and Cabernet". He was also doing away with the white varieties, notwithstanding that Pomerol had a reputation for good white wines where the soil is clay. (In Burgundy, too, Chardonnay is planted where there is most clay.)

Elsewhere in Pomerol, within the next two decades, the little estates of Trotanoy, La Conseillante (so the charismatic Madame Conseillan called her property), Nenin, Gazin, Beauregard, Vieux Château Certan and the Arnaud family at Petrus make their appearance under direct ownership as opposed to share-cropping – presumably with similar planting plans to those of Trochau.

Between Pomerol and St-Emilion on the plateau stood the one really big estate in the area: Figeac, with a history going back to the Romans and an enterprising owner, Vital de Carle. Over the period between about 1730 and the end of the century, Vital, followed by his son Elie, took the whole estate "in hand", cleared woodland and planted at least 75 acres of vineyard. The imposing château was rebuilt by Elie's nephew Jacques, a soldier who commanded the garrisons at Dunkerque and Boulogne – coincidentally the very heart of the main market for St-Emilion wines.

THE WINES OF FRONSAC WERE HELD IN EQUAL ESTEEM WITH THE BEST OF ST-EMILION. Indeed, the whole of the 1783 harvest of the eminent Monsieur Boyer's Château Canon at St-Michel de Fronsac was reserved for the court of the Dauphin at Versailles. There is a wonderfully confusing legend surrounding the name of Canon (confusing partly because there are two properties with the name in Fronsac and one, of great renown, in St-Emilion). Fronsac lies just downstream from Libourne on the Dordogne, where the north bank is a steep escarpment – marvellously situated for vines. The story goes that the navy ships anchored in the river used to test their artillery on this huge firing range – hence "canon". Canon in St-Emilion, on the other hand, was called St-Martin until it was bought in 1670 by a prosperous privateer named Jacques Kanon from (you will have guessed) Dunkerque. Kanon built himself the gentleman-privateer's residence that still stands, replanted the vineyard, built the vat room and chais, freed his negro slave and in ten years was off again, this time to Haiti, selling his property to the principal Libourne merchant, Raymond Fontémoing. It is tempting to draw a comparison between Fontémoing, the most celebrated citizen of Libourne in his day and the present négociant emperor of the region, Jean-Pierre Moueix, the great revitalizer of Libourne.

THE REGION OF BORDEAUX whose 18th-century history is still least clearly understood is Sauternes and its neighbouring communes, the gentle green and yellow hills lying back from the west bank of the Garonne about 25 miles before the river reaches the clutter of shipping and clamour of the town. Sauternes is a relatively modern term for a region that used to be known by the names of its different centres: Langon, Barsac, Sauternes, Preignac, Bommes . . . . There is no mystery about the fact that they sold a good deal of more or less sweet wine to the Dutch in the 17th century. But it has been the convention in the past to regard the great characteristic of Sauternes, the fact that it is best when made from rotten grapes, as a development of the mid-19th century. It is difficult to understand this when Tokay had been famous for this very fact since the end of the 17th century.

Much has been made of the fact that in the 1830s the proprietor of an estate close to the great Château Yquem, Château La Tour Blanche, was a Monsieur Focke from the Rhineland, who supposedly introduced the technique of waiting for *Botrytis cinerea* to shrivel the grapes to make, in effect, a Bordeaux Auslese. Yet there is plenty of detailed evidence that a century before M Focke's time the white grapes of the region (which also grew red) were sometimes harvested as late as the end of November. The abbé Bellet, whom we have met counting grape varieties in Cadillac, over the Garonne from Sauternes, kept an account of every vintage in Cadillac between 1717 and 1736. He confirms that the Sémillon was an important grape in the vineyards. By October, in the conditions of the Garonne valley (but particularly in Sauternes), the Sémillon is almost always attacked to a great or less extent by the botrytis mould.

What is hard to discern, at least in reading the abbé's vintage notes, is whether the mould was viewed as noble or the opposite. He speaks of going around the vineyard several times selecting either the rotten or the ripe but not rotten grapes. But he is silent on whether the mouldy ones were used or rejected. The general inference is the latter. He even mentions that in "Italy and Provence" grapes for sweet wine are over-ripened by twisting their stems and leaving them on the vine, which suggests that sun-dried, raisin-like grapes were the most highly prized.

There is no question that sweetness was the goal. It may have been achieved partly by the Dutch trick of adding "stum". One vintage had so much sugar, the abbé records, that they used no less than 12 sulphur matches in a barrel but still could not prevent the fermentation (in order to make stum). Nine were usually enough.

Nicolas Bidet, in his *Traité sur la . . . Culture de la Vigne* of 1759, confirms that "Barsac, Preignac and Langon" wines were not just sweet; when they were harvested late their sweetness was "mingled with strength and vigour", and they matured for many years to even greater perfection. Bidet also confirms (speaking of Entre-Deux-Mers) that they harvested at intervals repeatedly, "only cutting the grapes that are very ripe".

One theory that has its advocates is that nobody wanted to admit that they made their wine from rotten grapes. This might have been true of the priesthood, for sweet wine was the holy wine of the Sacrament. There is a strong hint in the first printed description of Sauternes, by another priest, the abbé Baurein, in 1786, that the place has a secret, and that "if the silence, into which they retreat, does damage to our project" (which is to describe the parish) "it is of greater benefit to . . . those who are determined to keep it." If this oracular remark does not mean that Sauternes has something to hide, it is hard to make head or tail of it.

THE ACKNOWLEDGED FIRST-GROWTH OF THE SAUTERNES REGION IS CHÂTEAU YQUEM. It has stood as a fortress (now a very friendly looking one) at the highest point in the parish since the 12th century, when it was an English stronghold. In the 16th century it became the property of the family of Sauvage d'Yquem, whose eventual sole inheritor, Françoise-Josephine, married the young Comte Louis-Amedée de Lur Saluces in 1785. Poor Louis-Amedée, a colonel, fell off his horse on manoeuvres only three years later and died, but the Lur Saluces family still presides at Yquem. We should be able to discover the secret from them. Tantalizingly, the archives of the château, possibly the most complete of any in Bordeaux, have never yet been thoroughly investigated. So we must be content with an educated guess.

Alexandre, the present Comte de Lur Saluces, has pointed out that all white wines in the 18th century and before were made as sweet as nature allowed. The modern notion of a "crisp" dry wine would have been regarded as a very thin potation. The same applied in the Graves (which was largely planted with white varieties), in Entre-Deux-Mers, in Cadillac, and in Sauternes and its district. All picked their grapes as late and as ripe as possible. The difference was in the natural conditions. Where autumn mists were prevalent, botrytis was a regular occurrence. There can be no doubt about the sweetness of rotten grapes: you have only to lick your fingers. In Sauternes more than anywhere, a golden autumn day is followed by

Alone among first-growths Château Yquem wears the outward semblence of ancient power; it dominates the valley of the Garonne from the highest point in Sauternes. But its wine came to prominence only in the 18th century, and world renown was not achieved until the middle years of the 19th.

a rising river mist. Its wine was always likely to be sweeter than that of Graves.

The real question is when did the market make it worthwhile to make Tokay-style wine only from the rotten grapes? To pick in repeated "tries", selecting, waiting, and selecting again, is a very long and costly undertaking. Tokay had been developed as a princely promotion and found a market in Imperial courts. But the customers for such an exotic and expensive wine only appeared in Bordeaux (and apparently in Paris) in the years leading up to the Revolution.

THE MOST FAMOUS CUSTOMER WAS THOMAS JEFFERSON. In 1784, at the age of 41, he was dispatched (as a Commissioner, then Minister) by the new government of the United States to France – not without considerable distaste. "I would go to hell for my country" was his reaction; and his journals in France make clear that he found its government diabolical. He was a laconic, not to say terse, journalist. You meet almost nobody and see few sights in his daily chronicle; just statistics, details of the land and its produce, a panorama of more or less starving peasantry, and damning reflections on the regime that was about to pass away.

Among the few moments of (moderate) enthusiasm are when, in his two excursions through France and Italy in 1787 and 1788, he reaches a wine region. Jefferson was eager to learn about wine-growing; first in order to introduce it to America, but also to supply himself with the best wines he could buy.

In Bordeaux he quickly informed himself about the red first-growths. He also listed a dozen "second" and "third" growths. "Of white wines", he recorded, "those made in the canton of Grave are most esteemed at Bordeaux." He listed as best Pontac (a former de Pontac property), St-Brise (then a de Pontac property) and the Benedictine abbey "De Carbonius" (now Château Carbonnieux).

"Those made in the 3 parishes next above Grave and more esteemed at Paris", he continued, "are 1. Sauterne. The best crop belongs to M. Diquem at Bordeaux, or to M. de Salus his son-in-law." He then listed "2. Prignac" and "3. Barsac". "Sauterne is the pleasantest . . . and all [are] stronger than Grave" – surely if he had tasted the wines "sweeter" is the word he would have used. When he did taste the Yquem he had bought, back in Paris, and later at home in America, he was moved to write: "This [Yquem] proves a most excellent wine, and seems to have hit the palate of the Americans more than any wine I have ever seen in France." To Louis-Amedée (Jefferson did not know he had been killed) he wrote from Philadelphia: "The white wine of Sauterne, of your growth . . . was so well received by the Americans who tasted it that I do not doubt it will conform generally to the taste of my compatriots. Now that I am established here I have persuaded our President, General Washington, to try a sample. He asks for thirty dozen [bottles], sir, and I ask you for ten dozen for myself . . . ."

JEFFERSON VISITED BORDEAUX AT THE CULMINATION OF ITS 18TH-CENTURY EXPANSION – and on the eve of Revolution. All was bustle. England was buying wine in greater quantities than for many years. There were no starving peasants here; not even the tension of class conflict that was evident on the streets of Paris. On its thronging quays nobody would have believed that the hour of the guillotine was at hand. The Grand Théâtre was finished. But so was the play.

CHAPTER 27

MAPPING THE COTE

If your hot-air balloon were to land you on the hill of Corton, or in the vineyards of Volnay or Chambertin, on a spring day 250 years ago, you would know exactly where you were – supposing, that is, that those hillsides are familiar to you now. You would rub your eyes at the strange dense tangle of vines without wires putting out green shoots around you. (The villagers would rub their eyes, too: the Montgolfier brothers, inventors of the "Aerostat", had not yet produced their first model.) You would be surprised to see the panorama of vines broken up with so many hedges and walls. But fundamentally, from the church spire in the cleft of the hills at Volnay to the beret of woodland on the brow of Corton, you would be looking at the same vineyards as today. And when you found your way to a cellar you would be offered, in your silver tastevin, a not very different wine. The rising mint-fresh scent of the Pinot Noir would tell you that this was indeed the Côte d'Or. The scent above all is the clue. In the words of Claude Arnoux, the priest who wrote *La Situation de la Bourgogne* in 1728, the wines of Burgundy have "sweet vapours". They are drunk "in two ways, through the nose and through the mouth, either at the same time or separately".

BURGUNDY HAD NO EXPERIENCE LIKE THE BOOMTIME OF 18TH CENTURY BORDEAUX. No new wines were invented, no new districts planted. The Bordeaux picture is all expansion and creation; the Burgundy one of evolving tastes and techniques, of new market forces, and overall of slowly progressing definition: a more precise notion of the character, style and value of the wine from each corner of the Côte.

Burgundy, of course, is not just the Côte d'Or, and the balloon trip over the northern and southern extremes of the sprawling region would be much more confusing. In the north, in "Lower Burgundy", where Chablis is now the only substantial vineyard area, your eye would travel over miles and miles of rolling vine and orchard country, interspersed with woods: perhaps 100,000 acres of vines in the region of Auxerre and Tonnerre (Chablis included) whose produce, red and white, was destined for the daily drinking of Paris.

Drifting south, following what is now the Autoroute du Soleil, the same concentration of vines continued, with breaks, all the way down to Dijon. Châtillon-sur-Seine and Pouilly-en-Auxois were wine centres; Avallon had a winepress set up permanently in the town square for the use of small growers who had no access to any other. At Dijon, where the distinctive ridge of the Côte d'Or begins, the vineyards crowded round the town, then followed the ridge south, spreading out a mile or more into the plain at Gevrey, failing to reach the sprawling abbeys of Cîteaux and Mezières, hugging the hill at Beaune, invading the little valleys behind the ridge at Auxey near Meursault, and continuing over the natural gap at Chagny into more mixed cultivation through Mercurey, Rully and the villages down to Chalon-sur-Saône.

On this spring-time journey the Saône is in spate, a river two miles wide; a great silver sash across the plain. Beyond, the distant hills of the Jura, still in Burgundy, are dappled, among their forests and pastures, with the yellow-green of the young vine-leaves around Arbois, Château-Chalon and Poligny.

South again, you gaze down at the great grey rooves of the abbey of Cluny. The hills east of Mâcon, strange ramps rising to sudden precipitous drops like the dwindling rollers of a distant storm, are intensely and variously cultivated. Thomas Jefferson, riding through, said "this is the richest country I ever beheld . . . they have a method of mixing beautifully the culture of vines, trees and corn". Others compared the Mâconnais to Provence; even to Tuscany with its "cultiva promiscua".

Finally, before leaving Burgundy and sailing over the grey-gold city of Lyon, clustered round the confluence of the Saône and the Rhône, we pass the softly-contoured mountains of the Beaujolais. The slopes are more densely planted with vines: the tall plants of Gamay surround every village on the lower ground and reach up in patches here and there into the chestnut woods above. This and the hills of Mâcon are the newest parts of the Burgundy vineyard; a creation, largely, of the 17th century. From end to end of Burgundy, from the borders of Champagne to the gates of Lyon, the vine has rarely been out of sight for long.

READING THE WRITINGS OF THE TIME OF OUR BALLOON-TRIP the feeling of familiarity is just as striking. The vocabulary is different; simpler, less metaphorical than today's, but this helps to emphasise the unchanging basics. The 18th-century commentators (most of them priests: if anyone doubts the continuing influence of the church on wine-making, these oenological abbots clinch the point) were the first to find words for the distinguishing styles of wines from each parish, and for the most highly-regarded individual vineyards. But there is a strong sense, in reading them, that they were simply writing down what had long been known and passed on by tradition. The difference between Volnay and Pommard, or Chambertin and Nuits, was not a discovery of the 18th century; it went back to the Valois dukes of the 15th century, and before them to the pioneering monasteries and churches. An ancient practice is slowly being revealed in all its depth of experience, and all the variety of local customs that have been built up over 500 years of doing the same things in the same place. "Terroir" is the almost mystical burgundian word for the unchanging unity made up of the soil, the situation, and every facet of the vine's environment. It is terroir that interprets Pinot Noir, or Pinot Noir that interprets terroir: either way, intimately linked, the two together are the key to the variety of the Côte d'Or.

THE 16TH AND 17TH CENTURIES HAD NOT BEEN WITHOUT CHANGES. One was the introduction of good white wines; another the increased demand for common wines, which means that Gamay had invaded the Côte d'Or over the dead body of

A balloonist's eye view of the Côte d'Or clearly shows how narrow is its famous ribbon of vineyards. The Côtes were first mapped (below) by Claude Arnoux in 1728. Rivers play a disproportionate part in his composition, and the gentle Côtes are drawn more as a range of mountains, but the wine-centres are clearly marked, allowing for a certain licence in their spelling.

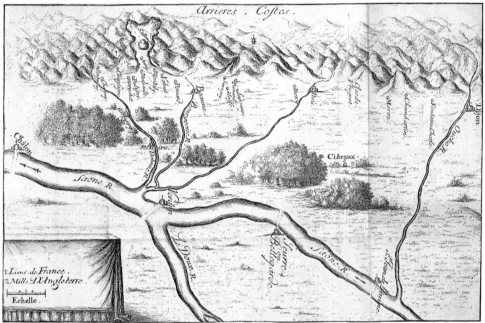

Duke Philippe, and the vineyard had strayed down from the Côte to invade the plain. The old domaine of the Dukes themselves had declined. And in the 17th century the Church started selling lands to the bourgeoisie of Dijon.

Dijon, like Bordeaux, had its Parlement, and at about the same time, the early 1600s, its lawyers began to look lustfully at the prestigious vineyards on their doorstep. Unlike the Bordeaux parlementaires, they could not start by assembling the scrappy tenancies on unexploited land. Instead, they offered the abbots and the Cathedral chapters what sounded like generous terms for their vineyards: money up-front, and a proportion of the wine till kingdom come. The Abbey of St-Vivant sold la Romanée at Vosne in 1631, the Cathedral at Langres sold the Clos de Bèze in 1651, and the Cistercians of Cîteaux sold their land in Corton in 1660 and their Clos de la Perrière at Fixin near Dijon in 1662. In 1660 the Chapter of Saulieu sold their famous legacy from the great emperor, the Corton vineyard of Charlemagne.

Partly, perhaps, because of the investment of Dijon's money, for most of the 17th century the "vins de Dijon", those, that is, from the northern end of the Côte de Nuits, were the most fashionable. Chambertin and the Clos de Bèze, which lie side by side only an hour's ride from the city, were considered the best. Their wines were uncompromisingly red. Later in the century Volnay in the Côte de Beaune became highly fashionable, but for a very different sort of wine, very pale in colour, almost the oeil de perdrix of Champagne, known as vin paillé (paille is straw) because the grapes were pressed between layers of straw to help the juice drain out quickly. They were "vins non-cuvés"; they went straight to the press, it seems without any treading, and without spending any time fermenting in the cuve, or vat, with their skins. "You only leave, you only *can* leave the grapes of this terroir a short time in the vat" said Arnoux. "if they are left there a moment longer than necessary, the wine will lose its delicacy and smell of the bunch or the stem to which the grapes are attached". Volnay of the time was also made with a high proportion of Fromenteau, or Pinot Gris; a grape with very little red pigment in its skin.

During this period, then, while Champagne was rising in reputation, having started by imitating burgundy with wines as red as possible, Burgundy (or at least Volnay) was returning the compliment by producing something not dissimilar to the vins gris of the mountain of Reims. Volnay was a "primeur" wine, "premier potable" – or the first to be drunk after the vintage. "This slope produces the finest, the liveliest, and the most delicate wine of Burgundy. . . . The finest comes from a part of the vineyard called Champan." This is a note from Arnoux in 1728; Volnay had not changed its style. Still as late as 1775 Volnay was being described as "the finest, the lightest, the first to drink".

MUCH WAS WRITTEN ABOUT THE RIVALRY BETWEEN BURGUNDY AND CHAMPAGNE. When Louis XIV was advised by his physician Fagon to drink mature "Nuys", or Nuits St-Georges, it was considered a great propaganda coup for Burgundy. That the wine was recommended on medical grounds is completely consistent with convictions that go back to the Middle Ages, when Savigny (next door to Beaune) was described as "nourissant, théologique, morbifuge" – a hard phrase to translate, but literally meaning "nourishing, theological, and apt to chase out illness". "Easy to digest" was a compliment paid by Erasmus to the wine of Beaune. How much, though, should we read into the fact that Fagon did not specify the light "primeur" wines of Volnay and the Côte de Beaune, those closest in style to Champagne, but Nuits, whose wine seems always to have been considered (and still is) a vin de garde; a wine to keep (even if only, in those days, three or four years instead of one)?

Burgundy in the 18th century, it seems, was in several different states of transition at once. The two parts of the Côte, the Côte de Nuits running from Dijon to Nuits St-Georges, and the Côte de Beaune, from Corton south to Santenay, had quite different traditions. The Côte de Beaune was in several ways less advanced. It had fewer specific "crus": substantial plots with one owner. The name "Clos" occurs much less often here than in the Côte de Nuits.

Vineyards in the Côte de Beaune were still overcrowded in immemorial fashion with a jumble of plants increased haphazardly by provignage, or layering. When vines are layered they are constantly making new roots near the surface; their wine therefore tends to have more of the quality of young vines than old: it is lighter, less deep and forceful in flavour. Since the wine was traditionally intended for drinking early, no great trouble was made to select the best grapes, or keep apart the grapes from the best plots. Claude Arnoux made this point forcibly: "those who want to make excellent wines only put in the vat the grapes from a single vineyard; but almost all the private owners (of the Côte de Beaune), having plots of vines in different sections, mix the grapes together so that the strong prevails over the weak, the good corrects the less good, in a word in order to make as many and big vats as possible".

The exceptions to this were the vineyards in Meursault and Puligny (and some in Volnay and Chassagne) that had begun to specialize in fine white wines. Their emergence had been one of the principal changes of the 17th century. Montrachet, the most celebrated white wine vineyard of Burgundy, was first mentioned by name about 1600. By the early 18th century Montrachet, and to a lesser degree Meursault, were recognised as white wines at least on a par with the long-established Chablis of Lower Burgundy. "Mulsault" (sic) was "as fine and clear as spring-water", but "Morachet" (sic), which was in the noble ownership of the family of Clermont-Montoison, "possesses a vein of soil that makes its terroir unique of its kind. It produces the most original and the most delicious white wine of France". No Côte Rôtie, says Arnoux, no muscat of Frontignan equals it. Montrachet must be ordered a year in advance because there is so little and it is so sought after. "This wine has qualities of which neither the Latin tongue nor the French can express the sweetness; I have drunk it at six and seven years old. Words fail me to express its delicacy and excellence". A high proportion of it was made of Chardonnay grapes. They had long been called "Beaunois" at Chablis, and in 1511 the abbey of St-Germain-des-Prés in Paris had asked for Chardonnay cuttings. There was probably Fromenteau, Pinot Blanc and perhaps Aligoté in the vineyard too.

Ironically Montrachet and Meursault, Puligny and part of Chassagne next door had been forced into their speciality against their inclination by the combination of hard limestone and heavy clay in their soil. Good as their white wines were, they were a long time catching up with the prices of their neighbours' reds, and the people of these villages lived in relative poverty in the 18th century. Jefferson's note

ARTHUR YOUNG

The English agricultural writer and reformer Arthur Young toured France at exactly the same time as Thomas Jefferson and continued his detailed survey of the country even among the perils of the Revolution, when it was uncertain who was in control of each town. Here, with his usual sang-froid, he arrives at the Côte d'Or:

"August 2nd. . . . To Beaune; a range of hills to the right under vines, and a flat plain to the left, all open and too naked. At the little insignificant town of Nuys [Nuits-St-Georges] forty men mount guard every day, and a large corps at Beaune. I am provided with a passport from the mayor of Dijon, and a flaming cockade of the tiers-état, and therefore hope to avoid difficulties; though the reports of the riots of the peasants are so formidable, that it seems impossible to travel in safety. Stop at Nuits for intelligence concerning the vineyards of this country, so famous in France, and indeed in all Europe; and examine the Clos de Vougeot, of 100 journaux, walled in, and belonging to a convent of Bernardine monks. When are we to find these fellows choosing badly? The spots they appropriate show what a righteous attention they give to things of the spirit."

runs: "At Pommard and Voulenay (sic) I observed them eating good wheat bread; at Meursault, rye. I asked the reason for the difference. They told me that the white wines fail in quality much oftener than the red, and remain on hand. The farmer therefore cannot afford to feed his labourers so well. At Meursault only white wines are made, because there is too much stone for the red. On such slight circumstances depends the condition of man!"

IN THE CÔTE DE NUITS THE NOTION OF THE "CRU" was further advanced. Its red wines were and are generally more full-bodied and less easy to drink "en primeur". How much of this is due to the influence of the monks, bishops and noblemen who had traditionally concentrated their efforts here is hard to judge, but it seems that selectivity was more part of the local tradition than in the Côte de Beaune. The vineyards were generally less overcrowded and by now planted with cuttings rather than layers; hence more deep-rooting. Increasingly, in the 18th century, owners of the most prestigious crus selected their best grapes to make separate cuvées; the best vat being called the "tête de cuvée". To make the most of its distinctive character was the object, which led to more treading and longer fermentation with the skins before pressing, which in turn made the wine darker and more tannic, needing longer ageing.

A PHRASE BOOK

Claude Arnoux (1695-1770) was a priest from Beaune who moved to London to teach Latin and French, and as a sideline to sell the wines of his native Burgundy. His "Situation de la Bourgogne" of 1728 is not only a most clear and concise account of the wines of the time and how they were made; it must also be the first attempt at direct sales by putting English customers in touch with Beaune commissionaires.

Arnoux also published an Anglo-French phrase book intended, he wrote, to be wittier and more up-to-date than the existing kind. Several chapters, such as a gentleman being dressed by his valet or how to address a perruque-maker, are hilarious. These selections from the chapter (dated 1761) "Upon Buying Liquors" provide a fascinating glimpse of the developing vocabulary of wine tasting at the time when connoisseurship was beginning to spread from the small circle of the aristocracy to the bourgeois buyers of phrase books. Coincidentally, the first cellar book was published in London in the same year.

A – Have you any good wine in your cellar?

B – I don't believe there is any better in London. Will you give yourself the trouble to come down?

A – With all my heart. Let us taste some of your best Port, Burgundy and Champaign.

B – Will you have any white wine? Pale wine between white and red, or carnation colour (du vin paillet, du vin gris, du vin couleur oeil de perdrix). Claret, red wine (du vin clairet, du vin rouge)... that is excellent, exquisite wine. Wine that hath body (qui a du corps). Brisk wine (qui a du montant). A smooth palatable wine (du vin coulant et aisé à boire). Luscious wine (qui a de la liqueur). Wine of the first and second pressing (du vin de la première et de la seconde cuvée). Wine that will bear water.

A – Have you not also coarse wine, small weak wine, not ripe (N'avez-vous point aussi de gros vin, de petit vin, de vin foible, verd)? Rough hard wine, heady wine, wine that gets into the head (de vin dur, fumeux et violent, de vrai casse tête). Wine of an ill twang, pall'd or dead wine (de vin gâté, de vin éventé ou sent l'event). Adulterated wine (frélaté)?

B – Sir, you must know I sell none of those drugs.

A – Don't you see I am disposed to be waggish, come, let me taste your wines . . . . This is the cask I pitch upon; let me mark it, and this . . . . Here fill them up before me, and let me mark it over the bung, that nobody may meddle with it.

B – Do you distrust me, sir? However, you shall be obeyed.

A – I beg your pardon. You wine merchants are good honest sort of people, but your men are not to be depended upon.

By the 1780s the abbé Rozier, the most influential of the text-book writers, was advocating, where necessary, adding honey to the juice to raise the sugar, and hence the alcohol content. In 1763 the abbé Teinturier (whose name, coincidentally, means a grape with red juice as well as a red skin) accused "foreigners" – Flemings, Germans and northern Frenchmen – of wanting their burgundy as dark and heavy as possible. They were on the road to perdition. When Chaptal, Napoleon's Minister of the Interior, recommended adding sugar to beef up the wine, the modern misconception of burgundy as a high-alcohol, dense, dark-coloured wine was conceived – to be born in due time and to subvert the whole character and reputation of the region.

Meanwhile the curious situation had arisen that the Côte de Nuits deliberately kept a proportion of white grapes in its vineyards to soften the increasing tendency of its wine to deep colour and initial hardness of flavour, while the Côte de Beaune did precisely the opposite. As the 18th century progressed it cut down on the light grapes to make its red wine more positively red – although Volnay seems to have been the exception. Up to the mid-19th century the Côte de Nuits still made white wines, from vineyards scattered about among the red. There was, for example, white Chambertin. But no parish or cru dedicated itself to white wine because none had to, and in the end virtually all the land was turned over to Pinot Noir.

Bit by bit the practice of the Côte de Nuits, of deliberately selecting "têtes de cuvée" within their Clos, gave its best wines the edge, both in individuality and their ability to age for long periods. Long maturing revealed yet more qualities: from the lovely but relatively simple aroma of Pinot Noir, piercing and fresh, one of the most mouth-watering of smells, the mature wine conjured bouquets of unimagined sublety and depth. The process fed on itself. The more care you took, the more arrestingly individual the wine would be, and the longer it would live to cover itself with glory.

I am speaking of course of the most ambitious crus, usually those with noble or priestly owners, but increasingly also the properties of Dijon parlementaires and merchants, where no trouble was too much. The most famous clos of all was the Romanée clos of the Prince de Conti. Everyone had to renew their soil on the slopes when it was washed away or when it lost its fertility. Manuring was done very gingerly, lest it affect the flavour. The best way was to bring in new soil altogether as top-dressing. In 1749 La Romanée-Conti was "refreshed" with hundreds of waggon-loads of chopped-up turf from the hills behind, the Arrières-Côtes. The church, seeing how much improved were some of the vineyards it had sold a century before, made vain attempts to buy them back. The new owner of the Clos de Bèze, Monsieur Jobart, was accused of not sending good enough wine to the Chapter at Langres. Probably the wine was much better than a century previously: what pained the church was the rise in value of the land it had sold.

THE FIRST OFFICIAL CLASSIFICATION OF THE COTE D'OR was not undertaken until 1861, by Dr Jules Lavalle for the Comité d'Agriculture de Beaune, for the Paris Exposition Universelle the next year – stimulated no doubt by the success of Bordeaux's classification for a similar event in 1855. It revealed how far ahead the ambitions of the Côte de Nuits had taken it. The "têtes de cuvée" were far more numerous in the Côte de Nuits than in the Côte de Beaune – and even then the owners of the Côte de Nuits felt hard done by. Eventually têtes de cuvée became exalted to the status of "Grands Crus" by the new laws of Appellation d'Origine Controlée in the 1930s. The process of perfecting the wine-making had become, as it were, part of the official geography. There were 20-odd Grands Crus among the red wines of the Côte de Nuits, and only one, Corton, in the Côte de Beaune. The Côte de Beaune on the other hand had the only Grand Cru white wines.

There will always be an argument over whether the soil (in all its variety) is inherently superior for Pinot Noir in the Côte de Nuits; whether with the same traditions and motivation the Côte de Beaune could have selected "têtes de cuvée" that would match the Grand Crus. It will never be answered because the pattern is set. The historical moment is past when considerable parcels of vineyard could be acquired and experimented with. The different crus of Burgundy have existed since the end of the 18th century not just as physical facts (now enshrined in law), but as metaphysical facts in the consumer's mind. If they did not correspond to reality and fulfil expectations they would crumble away. One need look no further than the Clos de Vougeot, the first, biggest and most famous of all crus, for proof.

Its Cistercian creators gradually assembled their great clos and eventually farmed it as a single unit, all 120 acres of it. They made their tête de cuvée selections according to the vintage. Generally the wine from highest on the hill was best; in certain vintages the wine from the middle had either better or complementary qualities; sometimes the wine from the bottom by the road rose above the middling, and was judged to have something to offer to the cuvée. The philosophy was expressed by the famous abbé Teinturier: "We need (grapes that are) cooked, roasted, and green; even this last is necessary; it improves in the cuve by fermenting with the others; it is this that brings liveliness to the wine." Even Arnoux, having been so damning about the mixing of all sorts to make as much as possible, says "the mère goutte (the juice that runs before pressing) is the lightest, the most delicate, and the least coloured; that from the first pressing is richer; and that which comes from the second and third pressing is harder, redder and sharper; so that the three kinds, being united, produce a wine which is better, more durable and darker coloured".

All these possibilities of creative selectivity were available to the owner of a considerable cru; the Clos de Vougeot being the great example. But since 1889 it has been sold off in so many little lots that there are now about 80 growers who can claim to own parts of the Clos de Vougeot. It is a true homogeneous Grand Cru no longer – or one only in name. Some wonderful wines are made in it, but the name of the Cru is meaningless without the name of the maker of the wine.

TO TALK OF SUCH FRAGMENTATION, WHILE VITALLY RELEVANT TODAY, is to look well beyond the 18th century. It is a process that started with the French Revolution, when the lands of the Church and the aristocracy were confiscated and sold by auction as "Biens Nationaux". (Among the officers whose task it was to tell the abbot of Cîteaux that all the abbey's lands – the Clos de Vougeot and another 24,000-odd acres – were being appropriated by the state was Napoleon Bonaparte.)

The fate of the Clos de Vougeot was typical of the chaos of the time and the big business machinations that soon took over. It was auctioned in 1791 as national

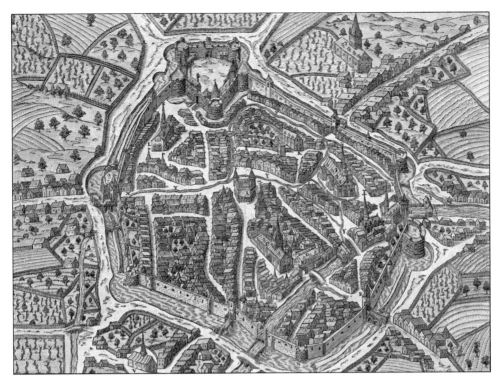

This "True Portrait of the Town of Beaune" shows it in 1575 still enclosed within its moat and medieval walls. Although the moat is now dry, and much of the château at the centre top demolished, the town today is still much the same.

property, but the highest bidder never paid. There was no alternative but to ask the abbey's last cellarer, a popular monk called Dom Lambert Goblet, to continue his good work in the name of the nation – which he did so conscientiously that he was voted a special reward. Two Paris bankers – so much for Egalité – then each bought half the Clos. (One of them was soon in jail.) In 1818 its was reunited, nominally in the hand of another banker, Victor Ouvrard, who promptly gave it to his 19-year-old cousin Julien-Jules. In reality the money came from the young man's father, Gabriel-Julien Ouvrard, one of the great arms-dealers of the Napoleonic wars and Bonaparte's personal banker, who is said to have financed the Battle of Waterloo. He had apparently been piqued that another client of his had bought Château Lafite. (Among Ouvrard's other accomplishments were four illegitimate children by Madame Tallien, the aristocratic wife of the Revolutionary gauleiter of Bordeaux.)

The young Ouvrard was a worthy proprietor. He came to live nearby and not only became Mayor, but manager of several other great crus – including La Romanée-Conti, whose wine was made, under him, at the Clos de Vougeot. When he died in 1861 the Clos de Vougeot was divided among his sister Betsy's four children (all titled aristocrats), who put it up for sale in lots. This time Baron Thénard saved it (the great fear was that the British would buy it), only to sell it back to the Ouvrard descendants. They put it on the market again in 1887. Again the sale was a flop: it was held in the hunting season and the likeliest buyer, M. de Vilaine, was too busy hunting to turn up. At last, in 1889, a century after the Revolution (and with phylloxera beginning seriously to damage the vines) it was bought by 15 négociants of Beaune, Dijon and Nuits and its progressive fragmentation began.

If the Clos de Vougeot took much longer than most crus to be broken up, the Revolution eventually had its way. The centuries of effort that had been put into making coherent crus out of the wayward terroirs of the Côtes was to be dismantled bit by bit, so that today it is a rare vineyard that has one owner, and most are divided several times – with that much less chance of assembling the ultimate tête de cuvée.

AS FOR WHO DRANK BURGUNDY IN THE 18TH CENTURY, and how they got it, there was, if not a revolution, at least a considerable augmentation of the clientele in the middle of the century. Beaune, as we noted as far back as the Romans, always suffered from transport problems. It is the one great wine centre not well served by a river. Its wines had to be valuable to be worth the enormously high cost (and risk) of ox-cart transport over abysmal roads for weeks on end.

In 1700 the clientele was what it had always been: Dijon, south by the Saône from Chalon to Lyons and the Rhône, north overland to Flanders, faithful to the memory of the Dukes, and in small quantity and with much effort, up to Auxerre by road to join the barge-fleet of the Yonne to Paris.

In the 1690s and 1709 the terrible winters damaged the Côtes badly, but largely spared the Rhône and the new vineyards of Beaujolais. Beaune was suddenly pinched by competition it had not experienced before; the wines of the Rhône reached Paris in quantity (and indeed Beaune, where their strength suggested possibilities for blending).

A legend lives on to commemorate the efforts of this era. A wine-grower of enormous physique, one Pierre Brosse of Charnay, determined to find a Paris market for Mâcon wine. He set off for Versailles with his ox-cart loaded with barrels, which after weeks on the road he parked as close to the Palace as he could get. He then went to Mass in the Palace chapel (Versailles was always more or less open to the public), where the King was puzzled by a man apparently standing while everyone was kneeling. He naturally called for this giant visitor after the service, whereupon Brosse, in rich patois, told of his journey and gave the King a sample. Orders (the legend has it) were quick to follow. . . .

MASTERS OF WINE

From the 15th century Beaune took the defence of its reputation very seriously. The office of courtier-gourmet was reformed in 1607 along the strictest lines. Entry into the profession was by examination, almost the equivalent of the present-day Master of Wine. In 1615 there were six courtier-gourmets in Beaune. Their tasting-test might include the same wine twice in different cups: a trick still used. A courtier was obliged to live within the town walls, and could not buy wine on his own behalf or for absent merchants without a special authorisation. He had to taste every barrel himself before presenting any wine for the town's official brand and date on its barrel: the "marque". He had to present a complete register of his activities to the authorities twice a month.

By the late 17th century commissionaires were authorised to represent buyers and gradually superseded courtiers. They were described by Claude Arnoux as "connoisseurs who from distant times and from father to son have personal experience of all the cuvées, who know the vineyards, the clos, and all the good cellars". They carried out the equivalent of laboratory analysis by filtering wines through paper to examine its lees. If they charged more than their authorised commission the penalty was hanging.

SEVERAL DEVELOPMENTS IN MID-CENTURY GREATLY ALTERED THE PICTURE. One was a long-overdue road-improving effort, led by the reforming Minister Turgot, that made the way to Auxerre much quicker and reduced the journey-time to Flanders to two weeks. The cost of freight dropped from about twice the value of the wine to (for fine wine) one-fifth. In 1776 Turgot also abolished a whole cat's cradle of legal limitations on the free movement of wine around France.

Another trend was connected. It was the branching out of the long-established cloth trade of eastern France with Flanders. Among the first to combine cloth trading with dealing in burgundy was Michel Bouchard, a merchant from the Dauphiné in south-east France, who regularly passed through Beaune to buy textiles in Liège or Antwerp or Bruges. In the 1730s he invested in wine at Beaune on the way north and made good profits, and did the same with his textiles back in Beaune. The house of Bouchard Père et Fils that he founded still has the evidence: a vellum book full of cloth samples at the front, and a wine-list (the other way up) at the back. The houses of Champy, Poulet and Chanson are three other négociants in Beaune with similar dates of foundation that still survive.

The ancient way of buying and selling wine through officials called courtiers-gourmets was strictly controlled by the municipality. There were very strict limits to what they could do – which was fundamentally to check the quality of each barrel, and introduce a prospective buyer to its owner. They acted only for sellers, but were not allowed to solicit buyers or buy for themselves. In the 17th century the function of broker on the buyer's behalf became important: the role of commissionaire slowly supplanted the old courtiers-gourmets. By the 18th century the commissionaires were becoming merchants – and even holding stocks. There was great benefit (as well as obvious risk) for growers and customers in having stock-holding merchants at hand. By investing in young wines and taking them into their own cellars they could give them the "after-care" that good wine needs; new barrels, racking, and maturing until it is ready to drink. In response, growers were more ready to take pains to make vigorous wines to repay keeping. By the 1780s mature burgundy was for sale in bottles, ready to travel in wicker hampers to the lucky few who could afford it all over Europe.

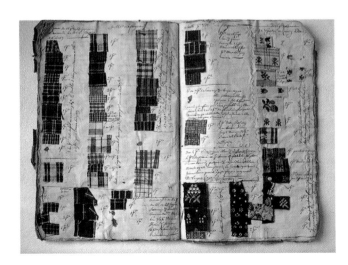

A travelling textile-merchant's sample book was transformed, in the 1730s, into his price-list of wines from Burgundy. Michel Bouchard was one of the first to set up as a wine-merchant in Beaune, taking over from the ancient statutory functions of "courtiers" and "commissionaires". Holding stocks of wine to mature and blend was a complete departure from tradition. By giving both growers and customers assurance it encouraged the making of better and longer-lasting wines.

CHAPTER 28

PARIS CABARET

If the great fortress of the Bastille, stormed and sacked on July 14th 1789, will always stand as the symbolic start of the French Revolution, a much less spectacular, indeed a fairly squalid, little event that took place three nights before has at least an equal claim to be considered the first shot in the battle.

Late in the evening of July 11th, two prosperous reprobates named Monnier and Darbon led a party that set fire to a barrier, la Barrière Blanche, that blocked the street called the Chaussée d'Antin just before the corner of the Rue St-Lazare. The following day a larger crowd did the same to similar gates across the roads leading into Paris from the villages of Montmartre, Monceaux and Clichy, to the northwest, and the day after, the 13th, to the barriers of the Faubourg St-Martin and Faubourg St-Antoine to the north and east.

All these barriers were key points in a customs wall that entirely surrounded Paris: the city's primitive and ill-conceived means of taxing the consumption of goods being brought within its limits, above all, of wine. A tax called the *droit d'entrée*, dating back more than 400 years and frequently increased, had led to the situation in which the most basic wine cost three times as much inside Paris as immediately outside it – to the common people. The nobility and the bourgeoisie were privileged to bring in whatever they pleased. The most obvious consequence was that the city was surrounded, just outside the customs zone, with drinking places known as *guinguettes* – pleasure-gardens is a pretty euphemism. There were at least two in the rue St-Lazare immediately opposite the Barrière Blanche: la Belle Chopine and la Grande Pinte (both names mean very large mugs of wine). But all the villages of the suburbs lived almost by this trade alone: as resorts where Parisians flocked daily to get drunk on cheap wine, and as bases for smugglers who did a roaring trade avoiding the barriers by various ingenious devices. The village of Passy, it was said, had no other commerce "but that of the mouth".

Monnier, the hero of the Barrière Blanche, was such a smuggler. In fact it is rather puzzling that he led the destruction of the customs posts that indirectly provided his income. It seems that he was set on making a quick killing. At three in the morning of July 12th he was seen in the driving seat of a waggon piled with barrels heading through the barrier for his warehouse in town. The next day it was two groaning carts into the seedy area known as La Petite Pologne (Little Poland) just below the hill of Montmartre. Before destroying each barrier it seems he did a deal with the nearest wine merchant and had his waggons ready.

His steady income before these events had come from more ingenious (if scarcely subtle) smuggling activities. In the rue de la Pepinière, which ran along the city boundary, he had set up a "machine" for throwing bulging wineskins over the wall. He sold the wine at bargain rates (by city standards) in his two bars ("cabarets") in town. It is not known whether he was party to the remarkable underground pipeline of "taffeta gommé" – some sort of waterproofed linen – that ran for "over 400 fathoms", or 800 yards, from near the village of Monceaux into the city. A hot-air balloon, or "Montgolfier", was also occasionally used.

Monnier and his kind (there were scores, if not hundreds, of similar smugglers) made their fortunes. Opinions were divided on their credentials as revolutionaries. After the fall of the Bastille their "brigandage" was described as "an insult to the Revolution". It was a hollow triumph that brought an immediate crisis to the city: most of its revenue came from the "droits d'entrée"; without it there was no money to run the hospitals and what few public services there were (or to pay the innumerable bureaucrats). The King (who was still, however uncertainly, in charge) recruited 600 new guards for the customs posts. The smugglers were the first to volunteer. In 1791 the "droit" was abolished: Paris went bankrupt. In 1798 a similar system was introduced under another name. But meanwhile in the full fervour of revolution, an official memoir of 1795 made the claim that: "It is by the destruction of these barriers that the dawn of liberty first shone on the people of Paris. It was from this moment that they first felt themselves freed of the shackles which had weighed upon them. The overthrow of the barriers and that of the Bastille are two facts linked together in the annals of the Revolution; they will be inseparable."

WHAT PARIS DRANK WAS NATURALLY OF INTEREST not just to the Parisians but to aspiring vineyard areas over a large part of France. From the Middle Ages there had been a clear distinction between the "bourgeoisie" and the common people, and the

At the time of the Revolution, L'Etoile was a barrier at the city limits where wine was heavily taxed. The first stirrings of the Revolution were the destruction of these customs barriers and the rejoicing represented by this contemporary print.

predictable contrast that Goethe had summed up: "the rich want good wine; the poor a lot of wine".

When cities were small the bourgeoisie had their own vineyards on the outskirts, both to guarantee supplies and as a status symbol. To have a "closerie" of your own with a full-time vigneron in charge was très snob. It was also profitable; the bourgeois could sell his surplus wine from his house in town without paying tax. He even grew vines in his town garden on trellises: the acid "jus de la treille" supplied the servants. As towns grew (so argues Roger Dion, whose work has provided much of the matter for this chapter) so did the demand for common wine. Trade offered the bourgeois the choice of different, often better, wine from other regions. But every commoner saw wine as his right. Few were without bourgeois contacts of some kind (in 1719, a quarter of Paris's population were domestic servants). And the bigger the town, the less drinkable the water.

The result was a steady growth in wine-growing by and for the common people as near to town as possible. The bourgeois did not like it: such coarse wines spoiled the good name of the area. But the process was inexorable. The reign of Henri IV accelerated it: he encouraged the growth of towns (especially Paris, which he had first to besiege, then woo into surrender: he even called a truce in his siege in 1594 to let the Parisians out to pick their grapes at vintage time).

It seems an extraordinary contradiction that at the same time laws were passed that forbade the entry into the town, for sale in taverns and "cabarets", of any wine from within 20 leagues (55 miles, or 88 kilometres) of the walls – except, of course, that grown by the bourgeoisie. Two developments that flowed from this were the suburban ring of guinguettes, where the populace flocked to refresh themselves, and a 20 league cordon in which there was no commercial incentive to make good wine. It stretched, for example, up the river Marne into the Champagne region. The Marne valley was an example of how the temptation of a quick sale of bulk wine could overcome the pride of a community. Château Thierry, immediately outside the cordon, made cheap wines for the cabaret trade. Yet a few leagues farther on, Epernay, Aÿ and Hautvillers were making some of the finest wines of France.

THE LONG-TERM RESULT OF THIS BIZARRE EXERCISE IN TAX GATHERING was the downfall of three great vineyard areas whose wines used to be well made from good grape varieties. Orléans was the first to go. Admittedly it was pushed. In the 16th century Orléans wine was high in royal favour; indeed reckoned the equal of Beaune, and enjoyed a wide market through Paris to the north – even to England. It had one of the best highways in France for access to Paris; since 1577 paved along its whole length. Henry IV, however, who is supposed to have said: "Paris is worth a Mass" and turned Catholic to gain the capital, did not hesitate to switch to Parisian wines (or "vins de France" as they were still called). His volte-face, playing on the jealousy between Paris and the (naturally better) vineyards along the Loire between Orléans and Blois, was a cynical act. He allowed his personal doctors to publish statements that the wines of Paris were health-giving, not "filling the head with acrid vapours" as Orléans wines did. Admittedly, due to the 20 league rule, there were undoubtedly some revolting wines coming from Orléans. But there were also aristocratic growths of high renown.

In 1606 the royal doctor Du Chesne absolutely banned Orléans wine from the royal table. The effect was almost as though the Department of Health declared that all wine from Calais (let me not libel a real wine region) was carcinogenic. Orléans as a quality wine region – which it certainly had been – was dead. When, only 40 years later, the Canal de Briare, one of the many improving schemes of the great Huguenot engineer and minister Sully, was opened to link the Loire and the Seine, it simply provided an easier route for cut-price bulk Orléans wine to stock the "cabarets" of Paris. To this day the name of Orléans is known not for wine, its ancient pride, but as the capital of French vinegar.

Auxerre and the huge vineyards of Lower Burgundy were the next to suffer in reputation and decline in value as their fatal privilege took hold. Being the first recourse of the capital for cheap wine inevitably ruined their name. The 20-league rule sent them the wholesalers or the tavern keepers whose only interest was price. In the 17th century, taverns multiplied in towns where they had formerly been for

---

THE DEEP SOUTH

France's oldest, and now by far its largest, wine region seems to have had little part to play in this sad act of the national story. On the contrary, the Languedoc never ceased to increase its acreage from the reign of Louis XIV on, when the far-seeing Colbert planned for it the new port of Sète, which was opened in 1670, and the Canal des Deux Mers, which linked Sète with Toulouse and Bordeaux a dozen years later. We have seen how the citizens of Bordeaux did not exactly encourage wines even from their own hinterland, still less from the distant Midi, to issue via their jealously guarded port. But Sète found other channels of distribution: the Rhône valley to Lyons and Switzerland; the considerable market patronized especially by the English at Livorno (or "Leghorn") in Tuscany; Genoa for Piemonte; even Germany and Russia.

The Languedoc had few quality products to distribute, the most notable being being the sweet Muscats of Frontignan, Mireval and Lunel, although Montpellier, a city of ancient culture, was proud of the red wine of a village in the hills just to the north, St-Georges-d'Orques, and the fizzy Blanquette de Limoux, from the hills to the west near Carcassonne, made itself an early reputation that even reached Paris. But here, too, the fury of planting took hold after the winter of 1709, and every peasant set about improving his lot by invading stony and uncultivated marginal lands. Instead of banning more planting here, as in the 1730s they did in Bordeaux and most of France, the Intendants declared it was the only way the people could pay their taxes. It seems that a remarkable proportion of the revenue was spent on the roads. Arthur Young was astonished by them. England, he said, had never imagined such highways, where even little bumps were levelled out.

The great business of the Languedoc was brandy. (It is interesting that it was at Montpellier that Arnaldus da Villanova had perhaps introduced the still into France.) Brandy had the great advantage of relatively small bulk to transport and found a ready market with the quartermasters of armies and navies. It was much used by northern European merchants for strengthening and disguising low-grade wine. A second distillation, it was discovered, made a better spirit at higher strength and lower volume which became known as trois-six (three-six).

The vast majority of Languedoc wines were white, from such neutral grapes as the Clairette and the Picpoul. But their very success inevitably led to them invading the corn lands. "Vines grow marvellously there", said the Intendant in 1776. "They give huge crops; but it is easy to tell that the wines are coarse, inferior in quality and rapidly spoil." At this stage they were still in polyculture with fruit, vegetables and grain. It was, ironically, the huge demand for brandy caused by Napoleon's wars that encouraged the bourgeoisie to move in and industrialize the production. Sixty-five thousand new acres of vines were planted between 1791 and 1808. After the wars the demand for cheap wine for France's towns rose again – but still in 1821, two-thirds of Languedoc's wine was distilled. As we shall see, the ever-growing, low-quality vineyard was eventually to suffer utter disaster.

travellers only. The humble citizens had not been allowed to drink in them; they were supposed to be hard at work. Taverns were regarded as the best way to part travellers from their money. In Auxerre, certain noble and priestly growths held their heads high for a while: curiously enough, the best-known "clos" was called La Migraine. Chablis did not give in – perhaps because it was well beyond 20 leagues out. But by the 18th century a grape called the Gouais, all juice, no taste, had vulgarized most of Lower Burgundy and invaded the vineyards of Paris.

Paris was the last to go. The killing winter of 1709 is blamed for much of the decline in quality, here and elsewhere. The total replanting that was needed was done not with the high-quality grapes that some, at least, of the suburban vineyards grew (Chardonnay, Pinot Noir and Fromenteau among them). Growers seized the chance to plant the "disloyal" bulk-producing Gamay. Paris had several important wine-villages on its outskirts – all to the west, along the windings of the Seine from the Bois de Boulogne to the royal palace of St-Germain-en-Laye. The total area was 60,000 acres of vines. The biggest was Argenteuil, which in 1788 provided more than 5,000 barrels for the capital. What the wine tasted like is better left unimagined.

PARIS GREW MIGHTILY IN THE 18TH CENTURY. Its population rose by almost a quarter between 1720 and 1789 and its demand for wine with it. It was always the magnet for inland wine regions with any practicable means of access to it – even those as far away as Beaujolais. Beaujolais is one of the success stories of the period. Its serious development started in the 17th century, growing Gamay on the outskirts of Lyon, the second city of France. Lower Beaujolais, nearest to Lyon, was a land of peasants living relatively well on tiny plots. But Upper Beaujolais looked more ambitiously northwards to Paris. Its wine was of the fair medium quality that the bourgeoisie were glad to buy. And surprisingly, it is only a matter of 30-odd miles to the west over good stony roads to the little port of Pouilly-sous-Charlieu on the Loire. The Loire flows northwards from there all the way to the new Canal de Briare, and so Beaujolais was only two or three days by waggon from a water route all the way to Paris –– a cheaper and easier route, although longer in miles, than from either Mâcon or the Côte d'Or. The development of the crus of Upper Beaujolais was done in a

BORDER PROVINCE

Alsace was utterly devastated in the first half of the 17th century by the Thirty Years' War – in 1650 it was almost an empty land, open to resettlement from the Alps, Lorraine and the north. Now in French hands, its wines were cut off from their traditional export route down the Rhine through Germany. Switzerland and its own cities of Strasbourg and Colmar were to be its principal markets for a century. Its monastic vineyards continued, however, and it is striking how many of the family firms in business there today were founded in the terrible 17th century: Hugel, Humbrecht, Kuehn, Dopff, Trimbach.

Religion as well as the perpetual tension between French and German divided the land.

Ribeauvillé for example was a Catholic village, while its neighbour Riquewihr, whose overlord was the Duke of Württemberg, was Protestant. (In 1752 Voltaire, then chamberlain to the King of Prussia, lent the spendthrift Duke so much money that Riquewihr was mortgaged to him and he moved to Colmar nearby, intending to build a château. But his money was not repaid and the château remained unbuilt.)

Under more settled conditions in the 18th century the Riesling grape was introduced, perhaps from the Rheingau. Alsace began to revive; to become, during Napoleon's wars, a scene of bustle and prosperity for the first time in nearly two hundred years.

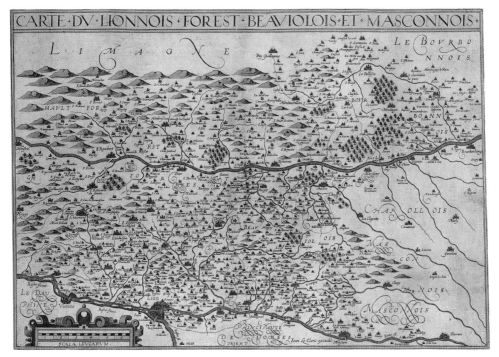

Turning a map on its side can put geography in a new light. Beaujolais and the Mâconnais lie between the river Sâone (bottom) and Loire (centre). A short journey to the Loire, and, via canals, to the great marketplace of Paris.

business-like manner with finance from Lyon. Being well outside the 20-league band was exactly the right stimulus. Quality could be made to pay.

The same conditions stimulated, although in much smaller quantities and at a higher price, the wines of the ancient vineyards of the northern Rhône: the extremely fine wines of Côte Rôtie and Condrieu from their cliff-hanging vineyards near Vienne. The road to the Loire is a little longer and steeper here, winding up to the north of St-Etienne. But these were high-value wines, whether for aristocratic tables or for "coupage", blending with baser matter to give an unusually tasty drink. Hermitage had to come even further, but for the power and character of these southern wines merchants were quite willing to pay the price. In Paris's wine repertoire of the 18th century, Hermitage and Côte-Rôtie, Beaune and Champagne were the best wines that arrived, by devious ways, down the Seine. Very little came up the river. Paris was not a sea-port, and the flavours of Bordeaux were only familiar in the circles that were curious to try the best of everything.

REQUIEM

In his last letter, the night before he went to the guillotine, King Louis XVI compared himself with a vine (and noted that the Revolutionary Robespierre drank water).

"At Versailles I lived in outrageous luxury. But today I praise you, O Lord, that I end my reign as did the wise kings of antiquity, before a simple glass of wine, in my modest room in the Tower of the Temple . . . . I am with the priest, who, at this moment, is mixing wine and water in preparation for this union of God and the fruit of the vine, when wine is God, and God, wine; the very opposite of my enemies; the most savage of them drink water . . . . I am no longer king but a poor man, cut off from my own, from my children, like a vine without its shoots."

CHAPTER 29

CABINET WINE

Perhaps the oldest bottle of wine that anyone has ever drunk (and enjoyed) was opened in London in 1961 when it was 421 years old. It was a Steinwein; wine, that is, from the steep vineyard called Stein that looks down on Würzburg on the river Main, the baroque capital city of Franconia. Its provenance was impeccable. 1540 (24 years before the birth of Shakespeare) was a freak vintage, a legend. The summer was so hot that the Rhine dried up; you could walk across; wine was cheaper than water; according to some slightly confused accounts there were two distinct grape-harvests. Certainly some extraordinarily sweet wine was made from over-ripe grapes.

It was the custom in Germany to celebrate famous vintages with huge casks. The cask that is known to have held this particular wine is not especially big – or perhaps replaced a bigger one as the treasured wine was used up. The usual system was to keep a commemorative cask topped up with fresh wine of comparable quality: the smallness of this one could be taken to suggest that worthy wines to replenish it – or worthy occasions for drinking it – were rare. It still lies in the cellars of the Residenz of the Prince-Bishops of Würzburg – cellars almost as lofty and dramatic as the salons of the stupendous palace above. Its contents are thought to have been bottled in the late 17th century, in other words as soon as bottles and corks became available. The last remaining bottles were kept in the cellar of King Ludwig of Bavaria (Franconia is the northern part of Bavaria) in the 19th century. Eventually they were auctioned, and the London wine-merchant Ehrmann bought them.

What was it like, this pre-Shakespearean wine? The expectations of our little group of tasters were not high. Its opening was preceded by two much younger bottles from the same cellar: a Rüdesheimer 1857 and a Schloss Johannisberger 1820. Both had completely perished. They were utterly dead: they actually smelt of corruption. But the Steinwein of 1540 was still alive. Nothing has ever demonstrated to me so clearly that wine is indeed a living organism, and that this brown, madeira-like fluid still held the active principles of the life that had been conceived in it by the sun of that distant summer. It even hinted, though it is hard to say how, of its German origins. For perhaps two mouthfuls we sipped a substance that had lived for over four centuries, before the exposure to air killed it. It gave up the ghost and became vinegar in our glasses.

It was a moving event in any case to drink history like this. What made it all the more moving was to have experienced a physical link with the golden age of German wine. The early 16th century was the climax of Germany's success as the

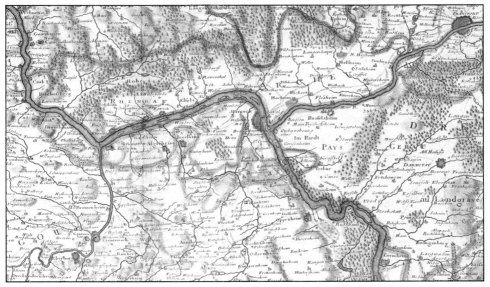

The Rheingau lies at the heart of the wine-growing Rhineland, shown in this 18th century map just west of the confluence with the river Main. Schloss Johannisberg lies close to the Rhine; Kloster Eberbach in the wooded Taunus hills.

producer of the most, and the best, wine of northern Europe. In England Rhenish (the English term for Rhine, and hence all German, wine) was a luxury almost as great as Malmsey, when claret was an everyday drink. The Rhine was then Europe's greatest wine highway, with thousands of cask-laden barges moving in all directions through a river-system bristling with customs posts. Huge quantities went both up and down the Rhine from Alsace, down the Main from Franconia to the Rhine, down the Mosel, the Nahe and the Neckar to the Rhine, and from the Neckar to the city of Ulm and down the Danube.

There is some evidence that the late 15th and early 16th centuries witnessed a period of exceptionally warm weather that made wine-growing possible and profitable in parts of Germany where it has since become impossible or marginal. The stories that come down from that age of huge harvests make clear that they were guzzled with almost incredible gusto. In the 15th century Germans were drinking over 120 litres of wine a head a year. The allowance for a patient in hospital (also for a doctor) was seven litres a day. It is said that teetotalism ruled out any chance of preferment in the priesthood. The Bishop of Strasbourg in the 1590s, Johann von Manersheid, founded a drinking club for religious nobles called "Vom Horn". The horn which its members had to drink at a draught contained four litres. Perhaps it is not surprising that the Bishop joined the angels at the age of thirty-three. But quantity was not the only god: this is also the period in which the first unequivocal references are found to the Riesling; the grape that was eventually to ennoble German wine.

In 1577 the first German edition of the Latin treatise of Hieronymus Bock said "Riesling grows on the Mosel, the Rhine and in the region of Worms".

ALL THIS BUSTLE AND GULPING BEGAN TO SLOW DOWN about the middle of the 16th century. Various reasons have been suggested. One is that the wine-trade overreached itself, overpricing good wine and doctoring bad. Another that the countless towns on the rivers asserting their rights and increasing their tolls on barge-traffic made many wines uncompetitive. Certainly there was more competition at the mouth of the Rhine where exports left for England, and in the cities of north Germany. Flanders, as part of the Duchy of Burgundy, had been no friend to German wines, and the growing trade of the Hansa cities of north Germany with France and the Mediterrancean presented Rhine wines with rivals even at home. Growers also had to contend with deteriorating weather.

Starting in the second quarter of the 17th century, and continuing until about 1715, the behaviour of the sun went through a cycle known to science as the "Maunder Minimum". There were no sunspots, and the consequent changes in the Earth's upper atmosphere resulted in the coldest weather recorded in the past 1,000 years. The miserable harvests of the 1690s in France and the famous freeze of 1709 were all part of the pattern.

CUMULATIVE THESE CAUSES MAY HAVE BEEN, BUT THE THIRTY YEARS' WAR dwarfed them all. The political and religious reasons for the war do not concern us, neither do the details of its intricate and murderous campaigns. Enough to say that from 1618 to 1648 Germany was the vortex of a pitiless struggle that drew in the forces of all her neighbours. Spaniards, Swedes, Poles, French, Danes, Swiss, Austrians, Bohemians, Bavarians, Hungarians, Dutch and even Russians all behaved in the usual manner of soldiery, so that in 1648 many German cities, and most property, had been destroyed or badly damaged. Vineyards, press-houses, cellars and boats – all the capital equipment of the wine industry – were gone; and so were great numbers of the people.

The country, now divided into a series of more or less despotic states and starving cities, tried to raise revenue from a wine-trade that scarcely existed – except in the hands of the Dutch and French. Alsace, the region with much the greatest production, having been occupied and laid waste by Swedes, was in French hands and had lost its German market. Nor did the French want the competition of its wine. Switzerland was almost its only outlet.

FROM THIS CATASTROPHIC POSITION THE CHURCH, aided by the nobility, with a zeal that reminds one of the 13th century, began to reconstruct the wine industry of a broken Germany.

When a massive replanting of vineyards is needed, history repeatedly shows us that the easiest and most prolific vines are planted first, however poor their produce. Any sort of wine will sell, and there is no money in the bank to allow for the inevitably slow build-up to quality. There was another disincentive to the common man to plant the best grapes, which without exception give smaller crops than coarser sorts: he had to pay taxes in kind, which meant a proportion of his crop, either as tithes to the church or the equivalent to a landlord.

Against this background the abbeys went into battle for the Riesling. Its exact origin is unknown, its early history obscure. But the quality of this grape was never in doubt. It is hardy against all weathers; it ripens late (very late for the traditionally early harvest of a northern country). But in ripening it does something no other grape quite manages: it achieves exceptional sweetness while maintaining a high degree of (extremely tasty) acidity. Both sweetness and acidity preserve it. When they are concentrated in a small crop the wine maintains its balance of intense and yet transparent flavours for improbable periods of time. When Thomas Jefferson (he went to Germany too) stayed at the Great Red House Hotel in Frankfurt the list of the wines offered – not just by the bottle, but by the barrel – went back from 1783 to 1726.

No-one surely would have pretended that the casks contained these vintages unmixed. The custom was clearly to operate a sort of "solera" system by topping up. It cannot have been at random, though, if they were to charge (as they did) three and a half times as much for the oldest wines as the youngest. The list at the Great Red House offered a choice from five districts; four from the Rheingau (Hochheim, Rüdesheim, Johannisberg and Marcobrunn – the last a celebrated vineyard of Erbach rather than a district) and one, a blend, from the Rhine-side vineyards at Nierstein, Laubenheim and Bodenheim, just south of Mainz in Rheinhessen. In those days the baffling intricacies of a 20th-century German wine list were still undreamt of.

ONCE THE QUALITIES OF THE RIESLING WERE KNOWN the devout mind could scarcely trifle with alternatives. In 1672 the abbot of St Clara in Mainz, with vineyards in the Rheingau, gave instructions that his vines (then mainly red) vines should be replaced with "Rissling-holz", and the same year the Bishop of Speyer specified Riesling for his vineyards at Deidesheim in the Palatinate. The great Benedictine abbey of St Maximin at Trier, which in the Middle Ages had owned vineyards in 74 different places along the Mosel and its tributaries the Saar and the Ruwer, started a

This engraving of the huge "tun" at Konigstein, built in 1725 with a dance-floor on top, boasts that its capacity was even greater than that of its more famous brother at Heidelberg.

programme of clearing forests around Trier to compensate for the more distant vineyards that it had lost. In 1695 its Abbot Wittman had planted over 100,000 new vines which will certainly have been principally Riesling. The superlative Ruwer vineyard of Maximin Grünhaus, today one of the best in Germany, is witness to the extinct abbey and its perfectionist standards.

Most famously, in 1716 the Prince-Abbot Constantin of the Imperial abbey of Fulda, Charlemagne's creation in the northern part of Hesse, bought what was left of the old Benedictine monastery of Johannisberg in the Rheingau, ruined in the "Great War", rebuilt it more or less as the mansion you see today, and completely replanted its splendid southern slopes to the Rhine exclusively with Riesling vines, at the rate of over 200,000 plants a year over five years. Interestingly, many of the plants came from Flörsheim, just across the river Main from Rüsselsheim, the home of the counts Katzenelenbogen. Their 15th-century records include the first mention of the Riesling in literature.

KLOSTER EBERBACH WAS THE HEADQUARTERS OF THE SWEDISH KING Gustavus Adolphus in the war. Its cellars had been drunk dry by Swedish and Hessian troops, but its buildings survived, and so, apparently, did its famous vineyard, the Steinberg. The Cistercians, like the Benedictines, planted Riesling, and in the 1760s built the high protective wall that gives the vineyard a superficial resemblance to its Burgundian cousin, the Clos de Vougeot.

Of all the great religious authorities the only ones not to insist on more and more Riesling were the Prince-Bishops of Würzburg and their Franconian peers. Riesling is not the right grape for Franconia. The heavy, often limey, soil and the more extreme climate further east were better suited to the earlier-ripening Sylvaner, originally from Austria, the source of wines of a presence and potency that seem perfectly to fit their almost stiflingly baroque environment.

Toward the end of the 18th century the potentate of the Mosel, the Prince Elector (and Archbishop) Clemenz Wenceslaus of Trier, became perfectly categorical. You have seven years, he told his flock, to replace all your vines with Riesling. They were almost the last seven years of the ancien régime in Germany.

THE RECORDS OF THE 18TH CENTURY SHOW NOT ONLY THE RECOGNITION that in most parts of Germany on good vineyard soils Riesling has no peer. They reveal the gradual discovery of its greatest qualities and the techniques for achieving them. The recovering economy and population in themselves had several beneficial effects

OLD BROWN HOCK

No wine region has so consistently stressed the necessity to age its wines as Germany. Early in the 16th century, Olivier de Serres explained to his French public that in the Rhineland a bridegroom customarily gave his bride wine from the year of her birth – undoubtedly old by French standards. The account books of Frau Rat, mother of the great poet Goethe, show that in 1794 she had five "Stück" – casks – of old wine in her cellar: two from 1706, one from 1719 and two from 1726, and she reckoned the oldest to be best. Undoubtedly they had been "refreshed" as time went by, but their capacity to improve as well as just endure is something that the modern age has quite long forgotten. It is the folly of the 20th century to expect fine German wines to show their qualities young. They need as long as claret – and decanting helps them, too.

There was little that was modest or retiring about Karl-Philip von Grieffenclau, the Prince-Bishop of Würzburg who commissioned Giovanni Battista Tiepolo from Venice to decorate the staircase of his Residenz. The stairs continue down to cellars as imposing in their way as the huge baroque place above. But whereas the palace is now a museum, the cellars brim with the great Franconian wines of the State Domain of Bavaria.

on the country's wine. One was the increased demand for food, which filled the fertile lands with corn and put the vines back where they belonged; on the steep and stony hillsides. Another was the growing ability of customers to pay for quality and the whole population's enhanced sense of security, that allowed Germany's cold damp cellars to fill up and work their slow-motion metamorphosis on wines that cannot be hurried.

It almost goes without saying that the most looked-for characteristic of all German wine was sweetness – or if not sweetness, strength. A good vintage was one that provided this naturally. Failing ripe grapes, the ways of artfully assisting nature had hardly changed since Roman times. Boiling the must to reduce its volume and increase the ratio of sugar was one. Drying the grapes in the sun to make what the French call a vin de paille was another. The use of sulphur, the "Dutch match," was routine by this period to prevent the wines from fermenting completely dry: it also partly accounted for the very long time wines were kept in cask – until its obvious smell and taste had worn off. One should not underestimate the importance of Germany's very cold cellars, either, in preventing the fermentation from ever finally consuming all the wine's natural sugar.

Another, and tragic, legacy from ancient Rome was sweetening the wine, especially in unripe sour vintages, with lead. It was not until 1696 that a methodical and perspicacious doctor, Eberhard Gockel of Ulm, discovered that lead was a deadly poison that had claimed countless victims and caused endless agony since Pliny and his contemporaries had advocated its use.

BETTER WEATHER IN THE 18TH CENTURY COINCIDED with the spread of the Riesling. Its grapes showed their qualities in continuing to ripen into sunny October days to make mouth-watering, naturally sweet, wines. This was the context for the inception of the so-called Cabinet cellar: a cabinet in the sense of a receptacle for precious objects, or a cellar for the use of the dignitaries who formed a cabinet in the political sense. The precise semantics of the term have been debated ad nauseam by adherents to one view or the other. Who used it first and precisely what they meant by it is a matter we can safely leave to discussion by the supporters of Schloss Johannisberg on the one hand and those of Kloster Eberbach on the other: the Benedictines versus the Cistercians.

What is significant is the increasingly selective approach of their cellar-masters

CONTAINS LEAD

Chronic lead-poisoning has often been cited as one of the causes of the decline of ancient Rome. Lead cisterns and water-pipes are usually blamed. Still scarcely acknowledged, though, is the effect of the Roman practice of concentrating grape-juice into a syrup (called sapa, or defrutum) by boiling it over a slow fire. In Pliny's words, "leaden and not bronze vessels should be used". Columella agreed.

Where the Greeks used resin to preserve their wines from spoiling, the Romans discovered that lead also gave them a sweet taste and succulent texture. It preserved them because lead ions have a drastically inhibitory effect on enzyme growth and hence on all living organisms. Lead ointment, for example, was widely and sometimes effectively used before antibiotics were discovered for the treatment of wounds: no bacteria could survive it. (Occasional external use may be beneficial: regular face-painting with white lead as a cosmetic in the 18th century undoubtedly killed many.)

Early in the 17th century a French physician accurately described the acute symptoms of lead poisoning under the name of Colica Pictonum, or the cholic of Poitou, where it was endemic: all wine-drinkers suffered from it, because all Poitou wine was then treated with what was known as "litharge", a lead oxide, to sweeten it and mask its acidity, making it more like the expensive Loire wines.

A description of the symptoms is almost too much to read. They include unbearable gripes, fever, complete constipation, jaundice, the loss of control of extremities ("hand and foot drop"), loss of speech, blindness, insanity, paralysis – and, mercifully, death. It was noted that epidemics were commonest after cold years and bad vintages (when most lead was used for sweetening); yet nobody connected the two. A late 18th-century English cookery book, Townsend's The Universal Cook, included "a pound of melted lead in fair water" in a standard wine-making recipe, and the disease was so prevalent in the west of England, where farmers hung lead weights in barrels of cider to sweeten them, that it was known as the Devonshire cholic. It seems probable that at least some of the gout that afflicted 18th-century port drinkers was in reality mild lead-poisoning, and it is certain that moonshine-drinkers who use soldered car-radiators as condensers often contract the disease.

Dr Gockel's discovery took place in Ulm, one of Germany's greatest wine-trading cities, at the time when bad vintage had followed bad vintage all over Europe, and the wines of the Neckar, Ulm's stock-in-trade, were undrinkably sour without the addition of "litharge". Gockel gave credit to Samuel Stockhausen, who in 1656 published his findings on mortality among workers in lead-mines and described very similar symptoms. He proved his theory on himself, however, by sampling the wine that was poisoning his monastic patients and experiencing some of the pains. Yet despite his work, its acceptance by the Duke of Württemberg and a ducal edict of severe penalties for using lead in wine, the embarrassing truth was successfully suppressed by wine-merchants for many years. It was not until the mid-18th century that most states passed laws prohibiting it. In France as late as 1884 lead musket-balls were reportedly used for sweetening wine. Even in the 1980s the same effect was being sought by Austrian growers who sought to increase the sweetness and value of their wine by adding (relatively harmless) glycol.

at vintage time. They kept the best grapes for the cabinet wine. They can hardly have been unaware of the incidence of the noble rot – the German term is Edelfäule. A famous vintage was made from rotten grapes in the low-lying Burgenland in Austria as far back as 1526. Tokay owed its great reputation entirely to the late-harvesting of rotten grapes. We can even pin it to the Rheingau: in 1687 a Dutch scientist, van Leeuwenhoek, one of the inventors of the microscope, drew the fungus *Botrytis cinerea* which he saw on Rheingau grapes and claimed that he himself had found it in no other vineyards.

There are records of single casks of outstanding quality at intervals through the 18th century. In 1753 in the Steinberg one was made entirely from rotten grapes; in 1760 fifteen were made from rotten and very ripe grapes together and pronounced of "delicate" quality. The Rheingau poses a similar question to Sauternes: was there a real reluctance to use rotten grapes to make sweet wine, or was it just something nobody liked to admit?

IN GERMANY HISTORY IS MADE CHARACTERISTICALLY TIDY. 1775 was the first official "spätlese", or late-gathered, vintage. Schloss Johannisberg was the place. The manager was Mr J.M. Engert from Dittingheim on the Tauber. And his age was 47. Yet the account of this famous harvest makes it all sound like a miraculous mistake.

Permission to pick was always given by the owner – in this case the abbot of Fulda. Directions were sent by courier. Judging his time (Fulda was seven days' ride) Mr Engert sent word to the abbot that the grapes were ripe, and seeing the weather,

The legendary first late-gathered vintage of the Rhine, the Spätlese of Johannisberg of 1775, fermented in this Benedictine cellar under what were then abbey buildings. In an adjacent cellar the family of the Metternichs, inheritors of the estate, keep a musuem of bottled wines from the estate going back to 1748.

in danger of rot. For a reason never explained, the courier took so long on the road that by the time he came back with the order to pick, all the neighbouring properties had finished, and Johannisberg had a vineyard full of rotten grapes.

THE NEXT SCENE IS THE CELLAR, THE FOLLOWING FEBRUARY. Johann Engert, a puzzled man, is tasting. "The new wine", he reports, "is mostly still cloudy and has stopped fermenting with a spicy sweetness. We are hoping for something extraordinary!"

Scene three, same place, April 10th: "this 1775 wine is so extraordinary that from the eight tasters no word was heard other than – I have never had such a wine in my mouth before!"

STAGE-MANAGED OR NOT, THE SPÄTLESE HAD BEEN BORN. Not Spätlese in the modern sense, which means normally ripe grapes with a good concentration of sugar, but Spätlese as a concept: the harvest delayed until, rot or no rot, the wine could be expected to be naturally sweet. With remarkable alacrity the government at Mainz took it up. In 1788 it enjoined each community to choose its own harvest date, but to bear in mind that only fully ripe or nobly rotten grapes could make the finest wines.

Thus in almost their last year of office the father abbots of the Rhine relinquished the secrets of their cabinets (if that is what they were) and set the pattern for a great Rhenish flowering in the 19th century, when Ausleses and Beerenausleses, Trockenbeeren- and Edelbeerenausleses were to bloom. In the 1790s the Rhineland was occupied by the Revolutionary French, and Eberbach and Fulda, like Cîteaux and Cluny, were taken from their monks for ever.

VOLLRADS

Although it was the Church that had the highest profile most consistently throughout the centuries of German wine-growing, a number of noble families have a lineage almost as long. Longest of all is the Greiffenclau family, now represented by the 29th in line to a title first mentioned in 1100.

The Greiffenclaus had estates in several parts of the Rhineland, but were mainly resident in Franconia until the 17th century, when they rebuilt the 14th century Schloss Vollrads, a mile from the Rhine at Winkel in the Rheingau. Their earliest residence, now known as the Graue Haus in the town of Winkel, is said to be the oldest inhabited house in Germany and is now a tavern.

The 17th-century castle ast Vollrads was still built for defence: a tall tower surrounded by a moat. It proved too tight a fit for Georg Philip von Greiffenclau who in 1680, with 26 children to house, added the bulk of the present Schloss.

One of his successors, Karl-Philip, became the Prince-Bishop of Würzburg who glorified his colossal Residenz with one of the world's most extravagant essays in the baroque: the staircase ceiling painted by Tiepolo to represent the four continents (and his princely patron).

The fertility of Georg Philip was not, unfortunately, repeated by his descendants and in 1847 the male line died out; but the last daughter married the Silesian Count Matuschka. The Matuschka-Greiffenclaus have been more active in Rheingau wine-growing than their ancestors. Richard, the father of the present Count, was the doyen of German wine-growing in his generation and was largely responsible for the rapid recovery of the industry after the Second World War. Erwein, the 29th Count, is Germany's most prominent wine-ambassador of the 1980s.

CHAPTER 30

THREE-BOTTLE MEN

$\mathbf{I}$f the principal glory of wine, and what distinguishes it from all other drinks and foods, is the endless variety of its qualities and flavours, then that variety was first appreciated and celebrated, albeit by a small minority of plutocrats, in the England of the first King George. What happened in the stately mansions of the great, serene in their deer parks, may not seem very relevant to the wider population. But it certainly made its impact in the vineyards of the world, which vyed for the patronage of this unique class of discriminating, unbiased and infinitely wealthy connoisseurs.

Drinks had become a talking point in England in the 17th century, to the grandfathers and fathers of the first Georgian generation. They had seen chocolate and coffee arrive, tea become fashionable, gin, rum and cognac become more or less drinkable, and Monsieur de Pontac target them with his new French claret.

England had emerged from the War of the Spanish Succession as the most powerful nation in Europe, militarily supreme on land and sea, hungry for empire and anxious to be cultured. Where in the 17th century her art and architecture were sometimes as naïve as they were wonderfully vigorous, the noblemen and gentlemen of 18th century England set out to educate themselves; to travel abroad, to collect and follow the finest classical models. Young men were sent with tutors on the Grand Tour, spending months or even years in contemplation (and not infrequently dissipation) in Rome, Athens, Florence, Naples . . . everywhere where antiquity was in propinquity with fashion.

At home, they developed, in the course of the 18th century, an aesthetic of such suave elegance, so understated, so harmonious and trim, that to this day it remains the most admired production of English taste. A "jardin anglais" is one that apes, however misguidedly, the classic 1750s line of "Capability" Brown. The rough edges of this society were all too obvious, but the gloss it put on its vigour, on the vitality and inventiveness that produced the Industrial Revolution, set the continuing standard for sophisticated wealth right round the world.

A CATHOLIC TASTE IN WINE WAS ONE OF THE HALLMARKS of this new English breeding. It was always a prerogative of the wealthy (the government saw to that in high taxation), but to some degree it permeated at least through the gentry and professional classes. Even at very earthy levels English taverns liked to pretend they kept a range of Portuguese, Spanish, Italian and French wines, even if, as a French visitor, Monsieur Grosley, reported in 1765, they were often really home-made.

"Three-bottle men" were mere beginners at meetings of "The Brilliants", a club
in Covent Garden whose only rules were the minimum number of bottles every
member had to drink. In Rowlandson's print of the club in session in 1798 a bowl
of punch is being brought to refresh the members.

The red wine in one tavern was made of aloes and blackberries with turnip juice;
"port" was turnip juice fermented with "wild fruit beer" and a small (one hopes)
addition of lead oxide. As for the white wine, he adds (exaggerating, to be sure) that
it was mostly made in England by such enthusiasts as Mr Hamilton of Cobham,
who actually grew grapes. Six weeks in England was perhaps not enough to give M.
Grosley the total picture. The best bottle he drank, he said, was one of Mâcon that a
surgeon had brought back with him from France and that they shared on the Dover
coach. To be even-handed he did add that he would have fared no better in France,
outside of wine country. French excise duties were so high that genuine wines were
commonly adulterated with the cheapest available.

Others were more complimentary about English efforts at home-made wine.
The Swedish botanist Kalm (the shrub Kalmia, America's "calico bush",
commemorates him) said that his landlady in Gravesend in 1748 used Smyrna raisins
in her wine-making to such an effect that it was frequently confused with fine
madeira. A.D. Francis, the historian of the English wine trade, relates that Lord
Palmerston's grandfather, Lord Pembroke, always told his guests: "I cannot answer
for my champagne and claret, as I only have the word of my wine merchant that it is
good, but I can answer for my port-wine. I made it myself".

THE COMMONWEALTH PERIOD IN THE MIDDLE OF THE 17TH century had sent English
royalists abroad in large numbers and the Restoration of King Charles II had
brought them back with tastes for every sort of drink. England was not a wine-
producing nation (a situation Mr Hamilton and others did their best to remedy) but

it had always been predominantly a trading one. To promote and satisfy all these new demands a new race of wine-merchants came into being, several of them Huguenots chased either from Flanders by the Spanish or from France by Louis XIV. Such families as the Houblons (Houblon is the French for hops) made their mark not only in the wine-trade (James Houblon was the wine-merchant of the Duke of Bedford, among many other noblemen) but throughout European business. James Houblon's brother, Sir John, became Lord Mayor of London and in 1694 the first Governor of the newly-founded Bank of England.

Of men of letters travelling through wine country Thomas Jefferson is perhaps the most-quoted; but he was by no means the first. The diarist and friend of Charles II, John Evelyn, went so far as to tread his own grapes in Italy, at Padua, and produced what he was pleased to call "an incomparable liquor". Joseph Addison, one of England's first great periodical journalists, in his *Remarks on Several Parts of Italy* made the soundest of observations on the value of good cool natural cellars. The Scottish novelist and journalist Tobias Smollett ("Smelfungus" to his critics) was as fascinated by fermentation as John Locke had been on his tour to Haut-Brion. Another Scot, the poet James Thomson, taking a broader view of the Italian landscape, remarked (with only too much truth) that "the condition of Italian vineyards reflects the corruption and oppressive politics of the nation". The author of *Tom Jones*, Henry Fielding, made his comment on Portuguese wine when he went to stay in Lisbon – by taking his claret with him. To do justice to both port and Fielding, however, he may not have been feeling very well. He died in Lisbon in 1754, the year before the great earthquake.

CLEARLY WHAT FASCINATED MOST OF THESE WRITERS (Fielding apart) was the chance to taste "liquors" not available at home, where the wine list, up to the end of the 17th century at least, was still extremely limited. For political reasons French wines were usually unobtainable or very expensive. Claret was something to hanker after (except in Scotland, where it was almost, it seems, something to bath in, so liberally did the Scottish treat themselves). As far south as Yorkshire in England arrangements could be made to be supplied with claret from Edinburgh's port, Leith on the Firth of Forth.

HIGHLAND WINE

The love and use of wine, and claret in particular, was not restricted to Edinburgh, or indeed the Lowlands of Scotland. Early in the 17th century the King (James VI of Scotland and I of England) set up a Commission to "civilize and improve" the remote Western Isles. To reduce wine consumption was a major part of its work. In the words of the standard work on wine-drinking in Scotland, which is well-named *Knee-Deep in Claret*:

"The 1616 Legislation defined how much wine could be used annually in the households of island chieftains. Smaller chiefs such as the MacKinnons of Skye, Maclean of Coll, and Maclaine of Lochbuie in Mull were restricted to one tun or four hogsheads. Those of a higher rank such as Clan Ranald were permitted three tuns or twelve hogsheads, while chiefs of even greater standing – Macleod of Dunvegan, Maclean of Duart, Donald Gorm of Sleat – were allowed four tuns each for their household's annual use. One can only wonder what the 'normal' ration of wine was in these households, if a restricted supply was set at four tuns annually. At a constant rate of consumption this would be equivalent to up to 10 litres of wine per day."

Rhenish, England's other ancient favourite, was in its time of troubles. Imports to England never dried up completely, but the wine was expensive and probably not very good. Even the fact of German kings on the English throne only made "hock" and "moselle" (Rhenish was becoming an archaic term) a necessity at court: not in a tavern or in a gentleman's cellar. Italian wines, unless imported privately, and with extravagant care, had the reputation of arriving in poor condition or not keeping. Overwhelmingly it was from Spain and Portugal that England drew its regular supplies – and as travellers found, the wines shipped to England were made for the purpose. They were not the wines the inhabitants drank at home.

It is hard to resist quoting the voluble reverend James Howell, although his *Familiar Letters* on everything potable was written as early as 1634. "Now in Spain," he writes, "so in all other Wine-Countries one cannot pass a day's journey, but he will find a differing race of Wine. Those kinds that our merchants carry over, are those only that grow upon the Sea-side, as Malaga, Sheries, Tents, and Aliganto: of this last, there's little that comes over right, therefore the vintners have Tent (which is a name for all wines in Spain, except white) to supply the place of it." Spain's best wine of all, says Howell, is St Martin, "which is near the court" (ie near Madrid). "There is a gentle kind of white wine grows among the mountains of Galitia but not of body enough to bear the sea, call'd Ribadavia." Portugal Howell dismissed: it "affords no wine worth the transporting."

Others would disagree about Portugal, particularly about Lisbon, but we only have to examine Samuel Pepys's cellar, thirty years later, to see that little had changed: "I have two tierces (a third of a pipe; rather more than a barrel) of Claret, two quarter casks of Canary, and a smaller vessel of sack; a vessel of Tent, another of Malaga, and another of white wine, all in my wine cellar together." It was a lavish cellar indeed (for which he thanked God) – especially for a man who had solemnly forsworn wine. But take away the claret (England and France were not often at peace) and all the other wines, barring perhaps the white, were Spanish. As between Canary, sack, Tent and Malaga one could hardly imagine a less interesting variety. Pepys himself must have found it so: he tried blending and didn't like that either.

CANARY

In order of price and quality, in Pepys's time and for another forty years, Canary probably led Malaga, and Malaga led (sherry) sack. The Canary Islands having the warmest climate, their wine was naturally the richest and strongest. All southern Spain tried to copy it for export; Malaga, less hidebound by tradition than Jerez and Sanlucar, did the best job.

The Pedro Ximénez was the favourite Andalusian grape. It makes the strong brown wine of Malaga, the strong but lighter wine of Montilla and Lucena, inland near Cordoba, and sherry in the sack style (ie strong and brown, but not fragrant or fine).

Andalusians did not drink sherry sack: they preferred pale young wine approaching what is now called fino, and drank it with water or ice.

Canary lost its supremacy not only because it was successfully imitated, but because its thinly-populated islands were a poor market for exports. Not needing cloth, they had to be paid in cash. Mainland Spain, in contrast, could even buy merchants' goods with silver bullion. Overtaken in Europe by Malaga, Canary tried the American market. But preferential treatment of madeira by the British government applied in America too. About 1720 the Boston customs would "usually pass consignments of Canary up to 50 or 60 tuns provided they were declared as madeira". The Islands, however, did not give up, and the Napoleonic wars saw (at least a brief) revival of their wine trade.

Up to the second half to the 17th century Venice maintained a virtual monopoly of the making of fine drinking glasses. Those made (usually by Venetians) elsewhere were known as "façon de Venise", or in the Venetian style. In the 1670s an Englishman, George Ravenscroft, experimented with the addition of lead oxide (the same "litharge" which sweetened and poisoned wine) to his molten material and developed a heavier, stronger, more lustrous glass than ever before. English lead crystal could not be blown or worked into such fine and intricate detail as Venetian glass. It lent itself perfectly, though, to the bold forms of English baroque, and rang with a unique bell-like sound.

EVEN AT A LORDLY LEVEL THINGS WERE SCARCELY MORE THRILLING in the 1660s. The red-brick Jacobean palace of the Cecil family, Earls (now Marquesses) of Salisbury, a short ride north of London, has in its archives the wine-bills of every age since Queen Elizabeth's. Those of the 1660s are startlingly simple. Lord Salisbury and his guests (including the king) apparently drank either Canary or white wine, some from Langon (close to Sauternes) and some from "my lord Bristol", logged in as "Paries wine"; in all probability something that John Hervey, the first Earl of Bristol, had tasted and approved in Paris, rather than something grown there. Could it have been Chablis? The Duke of Bedford in 1661 recorded buying "Shably" – the first mention of this oldest of white burgundies by name in England.

"High Countrie wine" appears in an earlier account, and in 1670 Lord Salisbury bought a hogshead of Burgundy for £17 (the Langon white had cost him £6). Rhenish, "Muscadine" and sack are mentioned; then in 1677 "six gallons of Haut Brion wine", and a very expensive hogshead of "Tournane alias Hermitage wine" for £20. Tournon is the town on the Rhône where Hermitage is grown; whether the wine was white or red is not mentioned, but white Hermitage for a long time held a reputation as one of France's two or three greatest white wines, with a greater capacity for ageing than any. The duties on such French wines (even the best) were commonly double the value of the wine. When the Duke of Bedford bought some Haut-Brion in 1671 two hogsheads cost him £4 in Bordeaux: the customs and other charges brought the total bill to over £15.

Leafing through the old bills it is clear to see how the aristocratic taste-buds were aroused in the last years of the 17th century. The fourth Earl of Salisbury, who was politically naïve to say the least, had spent several years in the Tower of London; his wine bills show extra charges for delivery to his cell. The fifth Earl ran up enormous bills with Thwaites, his wine merchant. To analyse his consumption would be a labour of love: in essence his bills simply show that fashion required (or at least suggested) a vastly wider range of wines as the 18th century approached.

A brief extract from the Salisbury accounts also shows the relative prices of the popular wines in the 1690s. All the prices are in shillings and pence per gallon. They can at least be used to put the wines in order of prestige.

Canary and Palme	8s 0d per gallon
Sherry	6s 8d
Young Hock	6s 8d
Florence	6s 0d
Calcavella	6s 0d
Port	4s 8d
Pontack	4s 8d
White wine	4s 0d

In 1692 the Earl, for the first time, bought a considerable quantity of champagne – though it was not called that. All wine accounts of the time show that it was the common practice in noble households (when buying direct from abroad, rather than through an English merchant) to share shipments with friends: in this case he bought half a consignment of six barrels of wine under the names of their respective "river" and "mountain" vineyards: Hautvillers, Sillery (spelt "Cellary") and "Espernay". The wine travelled north from Champagne via Brussels (where customs dues had to be paid) and on into Holland (the ship sailed from The Hague). With the barrels the Earl bought 150 new bottles (which cost £1 for fifty) and sufficient corks, so he clearly had some of the wine bottled on arrival in the cellars at Hatfield.

ENGLISH VINEYARDS

Hatfield House was unusual among great houses of the 17th century in having a vineyard of its own; four walled acres of sloping land down to the river Lee, planted by the Salisbury's celebrated gardener, John Tradescant, about 1610. Tradescant went to Flanders to buy some vines, and 30,000 were sent by the French ambassador. Some were grown against walls for dessert grapes; others "vineyard-fashion" for the making of wine. 50 years later Pepys recorded visiting The Vineyard, but not whether the vines were still there. It is perhaps unlikely, because William Hughes, author of *The Compleat Vineyard* of 1670 (an extremely practical manual) makes no mention of it. "There are now in Kent", he says, "and other places in this nation, such vineyards and wall-vines as produce great store of excellent good wine." With duties on imports rising to the highest level they had ever seen, there was every incentive to grow your own. Hughes was an optimist, but the climate was bad then and getting worse, not to recover until the second quarter of the 18th century.

Two English vineyards of the mid-18th century were famous in their time. Both were in Surrey, south of London: Westbrook, planted by James Oglethorp about 1730, and Painshill, the most famous of all, the pride and joy of the Hon. Charles Hamilton at Cobham near Guildford.

Oglethorp was the great dreamer who founded the American plantation of Georgia. Savannah still boasts his warlike statue. Part of his rationale for the colony was that it should (like the Cape Colony later) make England independent of Europe for its wine. Surrey was a more practicable idea: his wine there was said to be "like Rhenish".

As for Painshill, Hamilton created a picturesque garden around an articifial lake, giddy with follies, and a spectacular island grotto, glittering with felspar. His vineyard sloped down to the north shore of the lake and may have been as large as five acres, planted with Pinot Meunier and Auvernat vines. Red was his first attempt – and a total flop. His great success was sparkling wine, which to his amazement "had a finer flavour than the best Champaign I ever tasted". A French visitor (M. Grosley) took a different view: that it was dark grey in colour, and tasted of vinegar and verjuice with a strong flavour of the soil.

JOHN HERVEY, LATER THE FIRST EARL OF BRISTOL, cast his net wider than Lord Salisbury. The accounts of his cellar at Ickworth Lodge, his "seat" in Suffolk, from about 1690 to 1740, start with the usual emphasis on Spain. He was fond of Lucena – today's Montilla – and Galicia. Despite James Howell's belief that Ribadavia from Galicia was too "gentle" to "bear the sea" it appeared under many variant names (Robdavie, Rubbadavie) in many cellars in about 1700. There was also a suspicious number of purchases of "Navarre" during wars with France. (Navarre is the Spanish province closest to the French border and Bordeaux.)

As though with premonition of the war that started in 1703, Hervey laid in no less than four hogsheads of Haut-Brion the previous year. (When he bought Margaux in the middle of the war it cost him twice the price.) He had wine sent in bottles, packed in chests, from Florence (this was the standard way with Tuscan wine) and, unusually, from Avignon: this is a very early bottling of Châteauneuf-du-Pape.

Not until 1710, seven years after the Methuen Treaty, did he record his first purchase of "Portugal wine". "Red-port" he called it in 1714, and in 1716 "Port-wine" – although as late as 1730 there is an entry in the ledger for "Methuen-wine": the treaty must still have been firmly in people's minds.

When peace was made with France Lord Bristol bought "Burgundy for dear wife" and experimented with white Condrieu from the Rhône. In 1719 he bought Meursault for the first time, spelling its name "Muljo"; then La Tour claret, La Fitte Claret, and several times "Côte Rôty". There was a growing fashion for Rhône wines, despite the difficulty of bringing these from the very heart of France. We do not know whether they were transported down the Rhône and via the Mediterranean, or down the Loire (or possibly via Paris and Rouen). The significant thing is that they were good enough, and different enough, to send for by whatever laborious means.

GRANDEST OF THE GRANDEES, AND MOST DISCRIMINATING IN HIS TASTE FOR WINE, was James Brydges, who held the supremely lucrative post of Paymaster-General to the Forces in the Duke of Marlborough's wars. A percentage of every private's pay and every naval rating's meagre stipend stuck to the Paymaster's fingers and went to embellish "the most magnificent house in England", Defoe's description of Canons, his long-since demolished palace at Edgware just north of London. If Brydges is remembered for anything today, it is for his employment of Handel as the "Kapellmeister" of his private choir. Handel's "Chandos anthems" were written when his employer was created Duke of Chandos in 1719.

During the war with France his military sponsors were so fiercely pursuing, Brydges took full advantage of the passports to France negotiated by the Dutch and bought all his wine in Rotterdam and The Hague. All the wines we have mentioned so far in this chapter were included, with many interesting, and a few mysterious, additions. We also have the advantage of Brydges' own graphic tasting-notes on a few of his wines.

Like Lord Bristol he was an enthusiast for Hermitage, and in 1711 bought white as well as red for the first time. One French wine that was drunk at Canons but was evidently rare was "Capbreton". It was a claret-like wine from sandy seaside

Silver decanter labels, or "bottle tickets", became part of the paraphernalia of English wine-drinking in the 1730s, and reached their peak as a minor art form in about 1800. They hang from a silver chain around the neck of a decanter. "Mountain" was the name by which Malaga was known, Calcavella is Lisbon's luscious Carcavelos.

vineyards in the Landes in southwest France, just north of the port of Bayonne (which saw a great deal of Dutch trade as the harbour for Armagnac, and was a busy entrepôt at times when it was politic to disguise French wines as Spanish). Brydges thought highly of his Rancio of Navarre, which was also shipped from Bayonne – along with, for some unfathomable reason, Rhenish. "Rancio" is a taste much appreciated in Spain and the French provinces near the Pyrenees: the nutty tang of deliberate oxidation over several years. In 1736 Brydges described it as "a noble strong-bodied wine. I have had some 20 years in the cellar here (at Canons) and it is grown to be a strong racy wine, the sweetness all gone." Tokay from Breslau in the south of Poland he shipped via Holland. For valuable wines he had learned an ingenious way of preventing pilfering en route: he had them bottled in Holland, then packed the bottles back into a hogshead "canvas't over" for the journey.

After the war the number of hogsheads of French wine arriving at Canons suggests non-stop entertaining on the most lavish scale. In 1716 he bought no less than 50 hogsheads of Hermitage at £60 each: a stupendous amount of a top growth for any cellar. But Brydges' taste was becoming more and more demanding and catholic at the same time. His Canary had to be the finest "Palme", from Tenerife, a light yellow wine with a scent of pineapple; his French repertoire extended to Montrachet, Pommard, "Bone" and Nuits, as well as the first-growth clarets, the best Rhône wines and even something called "Kill-priest" from the Dauphiné: "tho' light in the mouth, the strongest French wine I have ever tasted".

LESS CONVENTIONALLY, BRYDGES WAS A CONNOISSEUR of Italian wines, which he bought mainly through the British consul at Livorno, or "Leghorn". Tuscany and Sicily were his chief sources. He bought Tuscan red Montepulciano and white Verdea and the inevitable "chests of Florence", but principally the Moscadellos or Muscatines that were a speciality of Montalcino in Tuscany, Montefiasconi near Rome, Calabria, and Syracuse in Sicily. From Sicily he also bought "red dry Syracuse, strong-bodied and fine-flavoured, not sweet or luscious, but very rich . . . it does not fill the mouth as Monte Pulciano, and has a better body and taste than Syracuse Serragosa". What he meant by "Serragosa" is hard to determine, since Zaragoza is a town in Spain.

Like the merchants of ancient Pompeii, his friends in Leghorn dealt in Greek wine as well. There is a very antique ring about the Zante and Cephalonia, not to mention the Chios (once spelt "Chaos") that joined the more modish barrels rolling into the Canons cellars. Not until 1722 did the Duke buy any port or madeira. He considered champagne (both "green" and red) "a very ticklish purchase". Yet in

1736 he paid a high price for red Constantia from the Cape of Good Hope and had his merchant in Southampton on the look-out for madeira that had been to the West Indies and back. Nor did he turn his back on Rhenish, but in the 1730s bought such old vintages as 1666, 1684 and 1696.

The cellar of Canons was a prodigy for its time; the hobby of a multi-millionaire. It shows better than any the resources available in the early 18th century. England's most famous contemporary cellar, though, was more conventional. Sir Robert Walpole was the son of a Norfolk squire who rose by ruthlessness and charm to become the most powerful man of his age: in fact, if not precisely in title, Britain's first Prime Minister.

Norfolk's port of King's Lynn was second only to London as the principal wine port of England in 1700. Its hinterland was where England's political power-base lay: the rich agricultural counties of East Anglia and the East Midlands, counties such as Norfolk and Northampton which have more massive mansions than the Loire has châteaux, hunting country where hard riding and hard drinking were the accepted way of life. Lynn even had its own recognisable style of port, lighter than "the heavy London cut". Travellers agreed that in an East Midlands tavern, at Leicester, Grantham or Biggleswade, you were more likely to get good port than elsewhere in the country.

On his ancestral acres at Houghton, just south of Lynn, Walpole built himself a Palladian palace as grand as any in England, from 1731 the scene of his "Norfolk

Sir Robert Walpole's dining room at Houghton Hall in Norfolk reflects in every detail of its decoration its builder's devotion to the vine. Walpole bought his first-growth clarets four hogsheads at a time.

Congresses", when he entertained his political colleagues and his neighbours. The Earl of Bristol (almost a neighbour) reported to the Prince of Wales that the party was "up to the chin in beef, venison, geese, turkeys etc, and generally over the chin in claret, strong beer or punch".

Claret was Walpole's favourite wine. Walpole, one feels, was the model Englishman the proprietors of the Bordeaux first-growths had in mind. He bought his Château Margaux four hogsheads at a time, regularly every three months a hogshead of Lafite, and always had some Pontac in his cellar – not to be kept for long; he evidently drank his claret brisk and young, unlike "old burgundy" which be bought in chests of bottles, at a considerably higher price.

There was port, of course, in the Houghton cellar, but it was definitely second choice to claret. Sir Robert seems to have preferred the more expensive white Lisbon, which he bought in massive quantities. He did not trouble with sack or sherry, and canary was going out of fashion. He bought champagne and Rhenish (6 dozen "Hoghmer of the year 1706" is a very specific reference, both to vintage and to vineyard: Hoghmer is Norfolk spelling for Hochheimer). By no means to be forgotten was the Houghton Hall strong beer, which was brought up to the dining room by pipes from the cellar with taps on the front of the marble serving tables.

Walpole's attitude to the laws of the land was typical enough of his time, but still alarming to find in the highest of public servants. During the war of the Spanish Succession he plotted with his friend Josiah Burchett, who was secretary to the Admiralty (Walpole was then on the Admiralty Council) to smuggle a large quantity of claret, burgundy and champagne from Holland – actually using an official Admiralty launch under the customs-officers' noses. In Lynn his smuggling was less successful: one shipment was impounded. On another occasion an employee "with the help of brandy secured all the officers" while the casks were sent out to Houghton by waggon. Such peccadillos as declaring French wine as Portuguese in order to pay the lower duty were standard practice.

WINE AND PORT WERE ALMOST SYNONYMOUS to most of the population throughout the 18th century. Portuguese wines accounted for about three-quarters of the total imports of Great Britain. With one voice the people complained, with another they called for more. Certainly their consumption, of a wine frequently described as "fiery", as "blackstrap", as "boiling in the blood", was heroic. "Athletes of liquor" is how one historian has described the squires, the parsons, the officers and university dons who were to be found, night after night, drinking themselves under the table. So common was the term "three-bottle man", meaning one who regularly drank three bottles of port at a sitting (or more likely during the course of the day) that to provoke comment greater efforts were needed.

Dufferin, Blayney and Panmure were three noblemen who were celebrated as "six-bottle men" – though not, I imagine, on very many occasions. Asked if he had drunk three bottles one evening without assistance, one peer reputedly denied the charge. "No Sir", he said, "I had the assistance of a bottle of madeira".

Part of the explanation lies in the size of the bottles. Wine was normally bottled in either pints or quarts. The pint (about two-thirds of a modern bottle) was presumably the standard measure of consumption, which reduces a three-bottle

The 18th century saw the wine-bottle evolve from its original role as a decanter to a storage vessel in which wine could be "laid down" on its side, its cork kept moist, gradually to reach maturity.

1708   1739   1753   1793

man to (a mere) two. There may also have been considerable lees which would be left in the bottle. As to the strength of the wine, it began the 18th century as high-strength table wine, but was dosed with more and more brandy as the years went on. Yet far from deterring its drinkers, extra strength coincided with still higher consumption.

THE EXPLANATION PROBABLY LIES IN THE MATURING STATE OF THE WINE. It was during the third quarter of the 18th century that the wine bottle was re-designed to lie snugly horizontal on a shelf. Its shape had been evolving for over a century from an onion to a mallet; now quite suddenly it became a cylinder with a relatively short neck; close to the ideal shape for stacking.

Before the 18th century the cellar of a house (if it had one) was identical in function with the cellar of an inn. Barrels (in England they would generally be of cider and beer) stayed in them until they were emptied, by daily drawing off. Mansions at first, then rapidly smaller town-houses, manors and farms, adapted

THE ENGLISH SPIRIT

The drink of the English poor was spirits: notoriously gin. In the 1720s there was abundance of grain. The government, always mindful of the farmers' interests, allowed freedom of distillation – with results which are only too well known from Hogarth's harrowing etchings. There were more town-dwellers than ever before; they took their miserable wages straight to the gin-shops. Gin was the epidemic of the poor until a providential failure in the grain crop in 1759 made the government change its policy.

When the affluent drank spirits it was usually in the form of punch or toddy: hot, diluted with water, fruit-juice and often tea. Rum or arrack,

the Turkish spirit, was usually the base. It was an essentially sociable custom with the steaming punch-bowl as the focus of the party.

It has often been pondered why England does not have a native spirit, as Ireland and Scotland have their whiskies. Usquebaugh, as whisky was called, moved into fashionable circles at about this time – and was by no means cheap.

England, did have an incipient spirit of its own until it acquired a Dutch king in William III. West Country cyder would have made England the equivalent of Normandy's Calvados. But King William discouraged it to give the Dutch a market for their invention – gin.

their cellars for storing the new bottles. The standard arrangement was open shelving of brick, stone or slate, often vaulted, in "bins" that held 25 dozen bottles: the contents of a hogshead. To buy a pipe of port (enough to fill two bins) became almost a convention among country gentlemen with plenty of room in their cellars. Usually the merchant would send two men to bottle the wine in the customer's cellar and lay it down in the bins.

Even the three-bottle man, at this rate, would soon find himself drinking port that had been in its bottle for a year or two, and notice how it "crusted" the side of its bottle with a dark, clinging film, while the wine itself changed colour from almost black to glowing ruby, and its fieriness gave place to a lingering glow.

DEMOCRATIZATION OF THE WINE-CELLAR IN ENGLAND – that is from the aristocracy to the middle classes – may be said to date from the 1760s, when for the first time a London bookseller thought it worthwhile to issue a cellar-record book. (It went into at least three editions.) The bookseller was Robert Dodsley, of Pall Mall, who had been responsible for Samuel Johnson's great Dictionary. "The Cellar-Book, or Butler's Assistant, in keeping a Regular Account of his Liquors," is prefaced by remarks on its "usefulness. . . . to any gentleman, who has a stock of liquors in his cellar, and is willing to know how it is expended . . . and the method proposed is so easy, that any common servant may keep the account".

Most telling, and the surest evidence we can have of the wines to be expected in a gentleman's cellar a century after Pepys, is the printed specimen page in the book suggesting its probable contents. These are the numbers of bottles: Ale 235; Cyder 60; Port 400; Claret 48; White-wine 85; Sack 4; Madeira 29; Champagne 19; Burgundy 48; Brandy 4; Rum 18; and Arrack (the spirit much used for punch) 34. Almost twice as much port, in other words, as all the other wines in the cellar combined.

PART IV

Victorian technology: modern winemaking in the Médoc in the 1860s

CHAPTER 31

REVOLUTION
AND AFTER

The glinting wedge-shaped dead-weight
of the guillotine in its fatal drop is such a powerful symbol of the end of the old
regime, not just in France but in all of continental Europe, that it is tempting to think
of a new world in new hands at the start of the 19th century.

The wars that followed, as Napoleon came close to turning Europe into a
French Empire, and the Mediterranean into a French lake, obscure with battle-
smoke the petty affairs of the next 20 years. When the smoke clears, it is a surprise to
see so much that is familiar still in place; incredible that one-and-a-half million
Frenchmen have been led off to more or less glorious deaths and France continues to
function; vintage after vintage picked, trodden and consumed.

There are the bottles still in their bins at Château Lafite: none for the fateful year
of 1793 when the owner, Président Pichard, was taken to the guillotine, but there
are bottles marked 1797, the year Bonaparte chased the Austrians out of Italy; and
1799, when having declared that "this little Europe is too small for me", he
abandoned his attempt to take the Ottoman Empire as well, left his army in Egypt
and scuttled back to France. The bottle of 1803 marks the return to war after 30
months of fitful peace; that of 1811 a superlative vintage and the retreat from
Portugal of Marshal Masséna, "l'enfant chéri de la Victoire".

In the Peninsula the chaos of war raged around the two principal wine-
exporting centres, Oporto and Jerez, and to a lesser extent Malaga. Both Oporto
and Cádiz were besieged, and yet their trade continued. The fighting spared their
vineyards. The war in Portugal, where the Duke of Wellington and the best part of
the British army was deeply engaged for three years, was to make a whole
generation of British officers proudly familiar with every shade of Portuguese wine
– as well as the port they knew so well already. Their entertainment in Oporto alone
was enough to addict them to its liquor for life.

WARTIME PRODUCES BYZANTINE PATTERNS OF INTRIGUE between partners in trade
who depend on each other – whatever the policies of their governments. Bonaparte
attempted to impose a "Continental System" of blockading trade between Britain
and all European ports. It failed, because such trade was as essential to the French as it
was to their newly-conquered vassals. He was forced to issue licences of exemption

to merchants, but they were widely abused and circumvented. The French army was even said to be dressed in Yorkshire broadcloth. The Emperor tried to avoid buying manufactured goods from the enemy, but was glad of the market for each wine harvest. His only preference was that as much as possible was smuggled past the British customs to deprive his enemy's government of useful income.

The British government, for its part, was glad to have French brandy, as it saved the corn supply for making bread rather than gin. There was also the thriving re-export business to consider. Of nearly 5,000 tuns of brandy imported into England from France in 1808, over half was sold on to Sweden and the Baltic, which were under French blockade. That year and the following England's docks were said to be choked with thousands of tuns of French and Spanish wines en route for third countries. There was a kind of tacit agreement even at the height of hostilities that France would manage Europe's internal trade, while Britain would be the waggoner of the sea.

WAR SERVES TO FORGE OR REINFORCE PERSONAL TIES. Foreign merchants forced to evacuate a town had no option but to trust a native rival with their business. Mr Barton of Bordeaux, for example, placed his entire business in the hands of M. Guestier (and did so again, 150 years later, in the Second World War). Seldom were any such trusts betrayed.

The art of conveniently changing nationality was perfected by British residents in Spain, who might suddenly become Irish and Catholic according to the fortunes of the war and the level of Spanish resistance to the French.

The officers' messes of the British crown, lavish with toasts, downed considerable quantities of port – or anything else locally obtainable. In this mess at St James's, champagne and port were the late eighteenth-century favourites.

Loyal Souls ;— or — a peep into the Mefs Room at S.t James's.

Madeira, and also the Canary Islands and the Cape, benefited when after the Battle of Trafalgar in 1805 the Royal Navy held the seas undisputed, and could guarantee access to these regions. Madeira was even garrisoned with British troops, which reinforced the reputation of its wines in Britain. Outbreaks of yellow fever at Cádiz, on the other hand, did little for the trade in Spanish wine.

British control of the sea also loosened the bonds between Spain and her South American colonies. Instead of trading with South America through middlemen in Cádiz, English merchants started to go direct – making contacts that were soon to wean these oppressed dominions from their mother country.

MARSALA

When the smoke of battle cleared, a single new recruit had joined the international wine-list: Marsala from Sicily. The manufacture of this new wine was a pre-war idea, the venture of an Englishman from Liverpool named John Woodhouse. It had occurred to him in the 1770s that Sicily, poverty-stricken and misruled by the notorious Naples branch of the Bourbon family, had once been the source of famous Greek wines (even as recently as the Duke of Chandos' time) and could be so again. He went to Malaga to learn how "Mountain" was made, then organized his

This splendid "dipping-bottle", for serving half gallon of Marsala at a time from an open barrel, was painted with Lord Nelson's portrait and his great victory at Trafalgar.

own version in the vineyards of western Sicily, with Marsala as his headquarters.

Liverpool lapped up his invention. Fame, though, came through his contacts with Nelson's Mediterranean fleet. Before his victory at the Battle of the Nile in 1798 Nelson had stocked his battleships with Woodhouse's strong brown wine in place of rum. After it, in the most disreputable episode in his career, he helped the King of Naples escape from the French to the safety of Sicily and Palermo. His reward from the King was the Dukedom of Bronte, a village on Mount Etna. Emma Hamilton, the wife of the British ambassador in Naples, also famously rewarded him.

It was whilst they were living à trois in Palermo that Sicily effectively became a British colony – indeed at one time the Queen became so hard-pressed for cash she offered to sell it to Britain for £6 million. The presence of 17,000 British soldiers and investment from London brought great prosperity. By 1812 there were 30 British Consuls and Vice-consuls overseeing the investment. The fashionable salons of Palermo even developed a snobbish affectation of speaking Sicilian with an English accent.

The Marsala shippers were at the forefront of this mini-boom. Nelson ordered 500 pipes or some 50,000 gallons of Woodhouses's Marsala "to be delivered to our ships at Malta". On this foundation was built one of the great wine fortunes of the 19th century, as the related Ingham and Whitaker families overtook John Woodhouse as the lords of this curious English colony in Mafia-country. The secret of Ingham's eventual millions was the American market: he reinvested his American profits in the new-fangled railroads. In 1860 he owned 40% of the New York Central Railroad stock and vast amounts of real estate in New York City.

THE SINGLE GREATEST CHANGE THAT THE REVOLUTION IN FRANCE, and Napoleon elsewhere, made to the ancien régime of wine was to dispossess the monasteries and the Church of their enormous holdings. New aristocrats (or at least new money) soon filled the shoes of the unfortunates who lost their heads, but the divorce of church and land was a radical and permanent change. We have seen how it affected Burgundy. Bordeaux was never very clerical country. Germany was the place where it most directly affected the most famous estates.

The Mosel was the first German district to fall to France; to a sans-culotte army of revolutionaries who must have appeared to the citizens of Trier as savage, and as formidable, as the Franks of 1400 years before. From 1795 for 18 years, the Mosel, as well as Alsace, the Palatinate and all the west bank of the Rhine, was in French hands. Unlike their Frankish forebears, though, the revolutionaries brought with them a legal system, an administrative machine and a very different method of taxation from the old feudal dues. Princes and Electors, the despots of each German mini-state, were stripped of power and place.

It was Napoleon himself who in 1803 summoned the Diet, or Council, of Ratisbon, or Regensburg, and instructed the assembled lords of the church to declare themselves absent. On the Moselle, the most church-dominated of the German regions, France thus seized a quarter of all the vineyards, and very much more than a quarter of the best. As "Biens Nationaux" they were sold (or sometimes

---

CORSICA

Corsica, the island birthplace of Napoleon, has a long and honourable history of wine-growing, more in the Italian tradition than the French. In the early Middle Ages it was subject to Pisa in Tuscany; in 1284 the Genoese, whose own hinterland is limited by the Maritime Alps, defeated Pisa and subsequently ruled the island for nearly 500 years. Its most appreciated wines were made in the "Greek style" on the limestone promontory of Cap Corse; strong sweet or dry malmseys capable of considerable quality. James Boswell, visiting the island during its brief period of independence between Genoese and French rule during the 18th century, compared these wines to Malaga or Frontignan. Today the Malvoisie and Vermentino grapes make distinguished strong dry white wines in the Cape, but in derisory quantities.

Between 1755 and 1795 Corsica struggled for independence under Pascal Paoli, and attracted the admiration and support of such French liberals as Rousseau and British ones as James Boswell. As "Générale de la Nation" Paoli had created the first state to have a constitution and be ruled by its people. Ironically, although it was from a Corsican wine-growing family that France found its greatest national leader, while Napoleon was in France in 1794 Paoli joined forces with England in an Anglo-Corsican kingdom to free Corsica from France. It ended sadly with his exile to London.

Napoleon did little for his native island, and its indigenous wine-growing was drowned in a flood of cheaper wine from France. During the 19th century efforts were made to revive Corsican traditions and prosperity. The excellent native red grape, the Sciacarello, was planted, and cellars dug at Vizzavona on the highest point on the railway line that links Ajaccio, the capital, with Bastia on the opposite coast. The cool mountain conditions are said to have produced wines of high quality. (It was at the railway station at Vizzavona that the most famous of Corsican bandits, Antonio Bella Coscia, gave himself up to the law at the age of 75, to live for 20 years in peaceful retirement.)

Phylloxera and depopulation put paid to the hopes of famous Corsican wine for a century. It was once more almost drowned in vin ordinaire as "pied-noirs", refugees from Algeria, planted its eastern plains in the 1950s and 1960s. At last, in the 1970s, its true revival began, and very good wines are now made on Cap Corse, at Patrimonio, and around the capital, Ajaccio.

Tom. I. p. 193. *Pl. XII.*

Le Corinthe blanc.

Chaptal's *Traite sur La Vigne* is the forerunner of today's wine primers, with its paintings of grapes – this is Corinthe Blanc, used at the time for sweet wines in the Midi – and diagrams of a "highly efficient mechanized press" which, Chaptal enthused, needed only two operators instead of the normal 10. One turned the handle, his mate shovelled away the *marc.*

leased) to those who could afford them. It was high time, according to some, for business motives to replace the privileges of the past. Was there such a clear advantage in the dispossession of the Cistercians from Kloster Eberbach to make room for the Duke of Nassau? In practical terms, no. On the contrary, to dismiss such an elite of experienced technicians and connoisseurs was the height of folly. But in philosophical terms it had been a foregone conclusion for half a century.

Napoleon was the agent, merely, of the Enlightenment, answering the call of rationalists already in their graves. Montesquieu would have nodded; Rousseau shrugged his shoulders; Voltaire smiled his benevolent and enigmatic smile.

IN THE FIELD OF PRACTICAL SCIENCE, AS OPPOSED TO PHILOSOPHY, one figure dominates the world that Napoleon fashioned; that of his Minister of the Interior, Jean-Antoine Chaptal. France's greatest scientist, Lavoisier, was one of those whose head the guillotine removed. Chaptal was also a chemist, ten years younger than Lavoisier, and a man with an immensely practical (and patriotic) mind. Today his name is known to the world of wine for one thing only. Chaptalization means adding sugar to the juice to increase the alcoholic content of the wine. But Chaptal deserves a place among the immortal names in wine's long history. His *Traité sur La Vigne* (he wrote Book II himself – the rest is a compilation under his direction) went far beyond the efforts of previous writers. It is the first general treatise which we can properly call modern – in the sense of not looking back to the classics for justification, but starting with the evidence of recent (that is 18th-century) science.

What he had to deal with was a present crisis – of overproduction, of falling standards, of fabrication, and of plain incompetence – in France's greatest industry

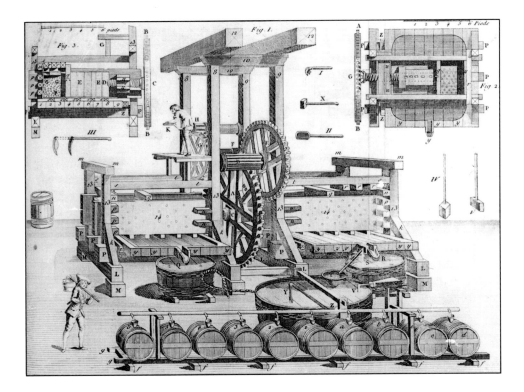

of all. "How is it then", he wrote, "that a great number of French wines, famous in former times, are fallen into discredit? Why is their quality so mediocre, while those from other districts acquire or maintain a well-deserved reputation? Only a little thought is needed to see that it is not the situation, the climate or the soil that is to blame: the fault lies with careless cultivation, with the repetition of unthinking routine, with ignorance or forgetfulness." Above all, "with the preference for the grapes that give the maximum of vulgar juice over those that produce the best quality."

Not that Chaptal was the first to identify the problems. On the one hand there were such archaic laws as the 20-league rule and systems of taxation that encouraged bad wine. On the other, a great increase in population had made the Gamay mentality endemic outside the most commercially-privileged regions. Worst of all, though not exactly freely admitted so soon after the Revolution, was the total anarchy in the planting of new vineyards on any farmland anywhere in France. That was the meaning to most peasants of the great word Liberté.

One of Balzac's characters, barely a generation after Chaptal, enunciated all too clearly the cynic's view: " The bourgeois – I mean monsieur le marquis, monsieur le comte, monsieur this that and the other, claim that I make junk instead of wine. What use is education? You figure out what it means. Listen: these gentlemen harvest seven, sometimes eight barrels to the acre, and sell them at 60 francs apiece, which makes at the most 400 francs an acre in a good year. Me, I harvest 20 barrels and sell them at 30 francs, total 600 francs. So who's the ninny? Quality, quality! What use is quality to me? They can keep their quality, the marquises and all. For me, quality is cash."

THERE HAD BEEN 30-ODD BOOKS IN THE PAST 50 YEARS adding to the evidence. Most were the well-meant treatises of oenological abbots, full of detailed observation but less than comprehensive, and authoritative only in local information. This was in itself one of the problems: each writer thought that his experience could be applied to wine-growing everywhere.

A reputed exception was the abbé Rozier. Chaptal even dedicated his book to him as the author of the *Dictionnaire d'Agriculture*. In the Languedoc where Rozier lived he was widely regarded as a crackpot for his experiments: to do anything that was not the local custom was considered almost like dabbling in the occult. Arthur Young, in Bezier in 1787, called to see the eccentric priest, only to be told that he had left two years before. "I was sorry", he wrote, "to hear, at the table d'hôte, much ridicule thrown upon the abbé Rozier's husbandry, that it had 'beaucoup de fantaisie but rien de solide . . .' it is not in the nature of countrymen, that anybody should come among them who can presume with impunity to think for themselves."

Two years later Young caught up with Rozier in Lyon. He was left with doubts of his own. "I made one or two efforts toward a little practical conversation: but he flew from that centre in such eccentric radii of science, that the vanity of the attempt was obvious in the moment. . . . Monsieur l'abbé Rozier is, however, a man of considerable knowledge, though no farmer."

CHAPTAL WAS NOT A FARMER EITHER, BUT HE WAS A SCIENTIST with a most practical bent. A discovery to him was of interest only if it could be put to immediate use. In

A LA MODE

Chaptal also encouraged the revival of the reputation of Olivier de Serres, the philosophical farmer whose *Théatre d'Agriculture* of 1600, the only French classic on the subject, had long been forgotten – and indeed suppressed. De Serres, a protestant, had lived through the Wars of Religion, and dedicated his book to the reforming King Henri IV, who invited him to introduce the silk industry to France.

Up to 1675 *Le Théatre* went through 20 editions. But to be protestant was dangerous under Louis XIV; worse, to be agricultural was deeply unfashionable. The attitude of the age was well represented by Le Nôtre, who created the dream landscape of Versailles. The thought of a vine, a cow, a cornfield – of anything useful or productive – obtruding on the view appalled him. Hunting, not agriculture, was the pastime of a nobleman. The Royal eye must see nothing but forests; the forests, of course, trimmed into allées of preposterous length, and dignifed with marble nymphs and water-jets of ostentatious uselessness. Nor did 18th century France appreciate de Serres – although England's Arthur Young went on pilgrimage to his Provençal estate. It took the revolutionary age to see the value of his protestant pragmatism – and even to compare him with Virgil and the spirit of Augustan Rome.

several fields of manufacture he freed France from dependence on her neighbours. He organised the mass production of gunpowder. His name will always be associated with sugar because he developed its extraction from beet.

Called to Paris from the University of Montpellier, he was soon propounding the politics of manufacturing. France, he said, had always seen industry as a mere tax cow to be milked, when in reality it was the whole basis of public prosperity. In the breadth of his vision and his eye for detail there had been noone like him since Colbert, the great minister of Louis XIV. In Paris he built the wings of the Tuileries and the quays of the Seine. Wherever he went with Napoleon he dragged the Emperor into factories to see where France's wealth originated.

IF A WELL-USED COPY OF THE *TRAITE SUR LA VIGNE*, its buff leather faded and scuffed, is to be found in almost every château's library, and in every house where wine-growing has been of concern for generations, it is because the chemist who set out the principles, as far as they were known, never lost sight of the particulars.

"It is for chemistry to make known," his preface reads, "the laws of fermentation; to unscramble the different effects of soil, climate, situation and cultivation; to discover the reasons why wines change; in a word, to direct and master all the operations of oenology, and to refer them back to the fixed and general principles." But it is his discussion of the given factors of nature, different in every vineyard, and how, intimately but emphatically, they communicate themselves into each wine, that is at the heart of France's whole wine theology.

AFTER THE SCIENTIST, THERE FOLLOWED THE ENCYCLOPEDIST: André Jullien, whom we have already met classifying Constantia, and collating statistics about every wine region under the sun. There seems to be a quantum leap here: from the tentative investigation, the humility of a scientist, to confident pronouncements that smack more of the journalist – or at least the professional deeply engaged in the wine trade. Only 15 years separate them: Chaptal's *Traité* in 1801, Jullien's *Topographie* in 1816 – yet in comparison Chaptal sounds like the summing up of the 18th century, Jullien like the 19th century already in full unblushing cry.

Topographie de Tous les Vignobles Connus is the foundation-stone of modern writing about wine. This is its modest introduction: "We possess several good books on the culture of the vine and on the best procedures to follow in winemaking; but none, to my knowledge, deals with the characteristics which distinguish between them the wines of different vineyards, and still less with the nuance of quality which is often noticed in the produce of adjacent crus, which , being so close together, it would seem ought to resemble each other exactly. I have tried to fill this gap and to gather together in my book all the details likely to interest the owners of vineyards, as well as persons anxious to keep a good cellar."

The author's methodical approach, his definition of his terms, his deliberate categorizing of each wine in relation to its neighbours all have a familiar ring: they have been imitated so many times. Jullien was a wholesale wine merchant in Paris who, according to the great bibliophile André Simon, was born in 1766 and who travelled widely and regularly around the wine regions of France. "He made it a practice to write down everything that interested him" – like Jefferson or Young.

"Later on in life he undertook to visit most of the vine-growing districts of Europe, and even passed into Asia". His *Topographie*, says Simon, "is of the highest interest, because most of the information it contains is completely original". Also because his practised palate had a worthy partner in his analytic and descriptive powers.

There were five editions of *Topographie* over no less than 50 years, the last two "corrected and augmented by C.E. Jullien", who was probably the son of the industrious wine-merchant. There has never been such an ambitious and original undertaking in its field. Each edition covers more ground, with constant updating of details, of prices, of quantities, even of rates of duty in importing countries – all of which meant correspondence from Paris to every part of the world.

In this, above all, lies the originality and enduring influence of Jullien's work – perhaps more outside France than within it. He puts France firmly first, naturally enough, but unlike many later French writers, takes the whole world into account. "What distinguishes the wines of France from those of other countries is their astonishing variety", he writes. Nobody could deny that this still holds true. Beyond that, however, and the loving care with which he enumerates them, he feels free to range around the world making comparisons, without the slightest chauvinism, in a way that few Frenchmen have ever done.

WRITING ABOUT WINE FROM THE CONSUMER'S POINT OF VIEW had in the past been almost a branch of medicine; sometimes practised with great wit and skill (as for example by Andrew Boorde) even when specific information was lacking. Boorde's 16th-century contemporary, the Italian physician Andrea Bacci, was also much quoted, in a more poetic vein. Such writing was to become the speciality of the English, for the simple reason that English wealth, at the top of the social ladder, had accumulated the most varied cellars of top-quality wines on earth. Despite an overwhelming preponderance of Portuguese and Spanish wines in the taverns, English minds were open – which even Jullien admitted was never the case in France.

"The Bordelais", he wrote (in his one other book, the *Manuel du Sommelier*), "find the wines of Burgundy too heady . . . the burgundian accuses Bordeaux wine of being tart and cold; both scorn Rhine wines because of their sharp taste, and those of Spain and other southern contries because they are sweet."

THE FIRST ENGLISHMAN TO OFFER A MORE AMBITIOUS SURVEY was, indeed, a doctor: Sir Edward Barry, who in 1775 published *Observations, Historical, Critical and Medical, on the Wines of the Ancients and the Analogy between them and Modern Wines*. The book is a magnificent production, but it is awkwardly stuck in the mould of classical education, reverentially believing that ancient wine, like ancient architecture, was of a quality that could only be humbly imitated. "Modern" wines form a mere appendix to the information on the ancients. More awkwardly still, Sir Edward contrives a lengthy commercial for the curative powers of the waters of Bath Spa, in which he was no doubt professionally interested.

A slight attempt at a more realistic treatment was made by a London wine-merchant, Robert Shannon, in 1805. Such writers, though, lived before the age of quotation marks. We are given to believe that what we are reading is Shannon's own poetic appreciation of, for example, burgundy, when in reality the text is lifted word for word from (the admittedly highly quotable) Claude Arnoux.

The mould of precedent has always proved hard to break. Even 50 years after Barry's book, a Scottish doctor thought to base a history of ancient and modern wines on Barry's work – only to find it so full of absurdities that he had to start again. Alexander Henderson was a much more original writer , and seems to have had more first-hand experience both of vineyard country and of tasting. He touches most aptly on the perennial wine writer's problem of finding words to convey flavours. "To tell us that it is penetrant, volatile, transient, and so forth, is nothing to the purpose; and the only satisfactory and intelligible way the description can be given . . . is by a comparison with some other known sensation of taste, regarding which all men are agreed." Yet still, 24 years into the 19th century, he devotes almost as many pages to the extinct wines of Greece and Rome as to the actual productions of his day.

VERY MUCH MORE TO THE POINT, AND INDEED ALMOST THE ENGLISH EQUIVALENT of Jullien (though with a chapter borrowed, without acknowledgement, straight from Chaptal) is the *History and Description of Modern Wines* by Cyrus Redding. Redding, a journalist born in Cornwall who lived some years in Paris, can truly be called the first of many hundreds in English to catalogue and compare the wines of the modern world. His History was published in 1833. In André Simon's words "no other book written in English on the subject of wines has ever been more popular nor so copiously copied from by later writers." To compare his book with Jullien's in point of style is hardly fair. The Frenchman is a wine-merchant with a genius for

Cyrus Redding's cynical chapter entitled *On the Adulteration and Sophistication of Wines* recalls a fraud practised on King George IV. His companions secretly drank the best from the royal cellar and had hurriedly to concoct a substitute when the king called for that very wine to be served the next day. From a surviving specimen bottle, a "wine brewer" was able to concoct a stand-in and "the princely hilarity was disturbed by no discovery of this fictitious potation, and the manufacturer was thought a very clever fellow by his friends".

analysis, organization and measured judgement, working to a formula, while Redding is a writer whose curiosity and enthusiasm lead him up byways of anecdote, and onto mountain-tops of speculation, as well as through crowded lanes of local practice and down avenues of statistics.

Being a journalist he is angry and quite specific about abuse and adulteration. "The clumsy attempts at wine brewing made a century ago", he says, "would be scorned by a modern adept". But, he observes, it is the fault of the British themselves if they are fooled, because they will drink port and fiery wines which are easily imitated – and because they import them already so dosed with brandy that if they met a genuine example they would not recognize it. Redding laments that even "the delicious sherries of Spain" must be strengthened for British consumption. "For England no wine will do without brandy. An attempt to fabricate Romanée-Conti would never answer, because the fineness, delicacy and perfume of the wine are not to be copied."

Above all, Redding is a genuine companion whose honest opinions and sympathies shine through his book. He recalls in his introduction the disastrous cold and rainy vintage of 1816 (the year that Jullien was first published). Redding – an English traveller to the marrow – "was shooting in vineyards, where even in November the fruit hung neglected. . . . I witnessed the disappointment of the laborious vine cultivator. . . . The vintage is immemorially an ancient jubilee, of which, when, as is rarely the case, there is no joyous celebration, the toil of the labourer becomes doubly onerous, the bosoms generally cheerful are oppressed, and the gripe of poverty clutches its toil-worn victims with redoubled violence." Despite the passage of more than 150 years, *Modern Wine* remains a volume to carry with you to the vineyards.

BUT EVEN BEFORE REDDING WAS PUBLISHED A NEW BREED OF WRITER was on the prowl: the investigator from the New World. What Thomas Jefferson had been in the almost dilettante spirit of the 18th century, James Busby, visiting Europe from Australia in 1825, was in the practical and pragmatic spirit of a colonial; determined to bootstrap his extremely raw young country into the proper appreciation of nature's great gift.

CHAPTER 32

BODEGAS AND LODGES

The retreat of Napoleon's army from Spain left one wine-merchant devastated. Juan Carlos Haurie, the leading sherry shipper of his day, was in deep trouble. Although he was born in Andalusia, his family was French, and he had supported the French invasion of Spain, collaborating fully with the occupying forces of Marshal Soult in Jerez. He had considered it an honour to provision the troops, which meant commandeering the food and wine supplies of his neighbours, and even exacting taxes from the Jerezanos to pay for their enemies' keep.

Jerez was occupied from 1810 to 1812, while the British supported the Spanish in holding nearby Cádiz. Cádiz prospered while Jerez starved. In 1812, harried by Wellington in Spain and stretched by their invasion of Russia, the French withdrew, leaving poor Haurie unpaid, ruined, his entire fortune lost in paying compensation.

The Haurie story, though, neither begins nor ends with this incident. The firm he inherited was probably the first to encompass the whole business of growing, making, ageing and shipping sherry in the modern sense, and went on, after his bankruptcy and under a new name, to become one of the greatest in the world of wine.

AFTER ITS WELL-PUBLICIZED LAUNCH IN TUDOR TIMES, sherry sack had become a staple wine for northern Europe. Throughout the 17th century it flowed freely, not earning the extravagant praise that Falstaff had heaped upon it, perhaps, but an indispensable part of any cellar. Its principal rival was Canary sack, which was generally considered sweeter and better. The Canary Islands, though, were less profitable to trade with than mainland Spain. In Spain a merchant bringing "rags" (even then the cloth-trade was known by this disrespectful term) could take his pick between wine and silver bullion (not to mention horses) in exchange. Sanlúcar, Cádiz, and the growing Puerto de Santa Maria, serving Jerez, were much-visited ports – especially by the ubiquitous Dutch.

Then came the War of the Spanish Succession as the 18th century opened. The Methuen Treaty diverted English traders to Portugal and Madeira. The Dutch trade fell away. There was little business going on in the sherry country. Orange trees, for the newly fashionable orangeries of northern Europe, were a more profitable crop. Sack, whether from Jerez or the Canaries, slumped in sales – except to its captive market in South America. But from Brazil Portugal was now receiving gold bullion, which gave her yet another advantage over Spain.

Only one Spanish port reacted with energy to the challenge: Málaga, which rebuilt its harbour, reduced its duties to well below those imposed on sherry from Seville, and succeeded in making its sweet "Mountain" wines, grown in the hills behind the port, the fashionable form of sack in the middle years of the 18th century.

IN JEREZ APATHY WAS COMPOUNDED by protectionist regulations. One factor not to be ignored was the church. The Carthusian monks and Dominican friars in Jerez were the only holders of large stocks of wine (no doubt some of it both old and excellent). And as a consumer of new wines the church must have been the biggest single customer. Seville cathedral alone had 24 altars celebrating 400 masses each day – for which it needed an annual total of 2,500 tuns of wine.

The church was naturally well represented on the "Gremio", the guild of wine growers that controlled the trade, its prices, and decreed who could hold stocks. Growers might stock their wine, but merchants were severely limited in the amount they could buy and hold. It was precisely the opposite arrangement to the way the port trade operated, where the growers were isolated inland, far up the perilous Douro, and stock-holding merchants were essential at Oporto. Here the growers were all around the town, with as much access to the market as the merchants. It was the Gremio's policy to keep the merchants in their place.

NOT ENTIRELY DISCOURAGED BY THE LACK OF TRADE, or seeing it perhaps as an opportunity (or just liking the climate of Andalusia), a trickle of foreign merchants continued to set up shop beside the very few Spanish houses. (J.M. Rivero, founded in 1650, is the oldest firm, and its mark C.Z. perhaps the oldest brand-name of any wine.) As in Bordeaux at the same time, the Irish were particularly active – some of them Catholic refugees from the British persecution of the 17th century, some from the Irish weather. Timothy O'Neale was in the first category. He married into a local family and began to trade in 1724. Patrick Murphy was quite possibly in the second; he arrived about the same time, a farmer who became a grape-grower, but was hampered by poor health. It was Murphy who induced his French-born merchant neighbour, Jean Haurie, into the sherry business – and it was Haurie who challenged the Gremio for the right to both grow his wine, stock it until it was mature, and ship it to his customers himself.

In 1772 he won a crucial court case: the Haurie bodega (Murphy had died and left him the business) became the first to control its wine at every stage of its production. It was probably from this time that sherry began to gain what today is called market-share. The years between this and Napoleon's invasion – despite yet another war with England – saw several new bodegas founded, mostly by Scots, English or Irishmen. Sir James Duff was a Scot. He bought his first wine from Haurie, and was British consul in Cádiz throughout the Peninsula War. James Gordon was another Scotsman. William Garvey came from Waterford in Ireland; Thomas Osborne from Devonshire. At the same time the companies of Averys and

The room in which Tio Pepe was created. Don Manuel Maria Gonzales
founded the firm of Gonzales Byass in the 1830s. Since his death in 1887
his tasting room has been preserved exactly as he left it, his sample
bottles now dried up among the dust and cobwebs of 100 years.

Harveys were founded in Bristol, the most famous remaining names in a tradition
that was already old: of holding the stocks which the Gremio disallowed and doing
the blending at the consuming end. Meanwhile Jean Haurie died, and five nephews
inherited his business, the biggest in Jerez. One was the unfortunate Don Juan
Carlos. Another was Don Pedro Domecq.

The structure of the sherry industry was now in place. How did the wine it sold
differ from the sack of previous centuries?

THE FIRST DIFFERENCE MAY SIMPLY HAVE BEEN ITS AGE. After half a century of a flat
market, those wines with the quality and "structure" to age (which were those from
the chalk soils, called albarizas, mainly towards the north and west of Jerez and
towards Sanlúcar) will have become concentrated, nutty-flavoured; capable of
giving a smack of mature quality even to young wines blended with them. It is the
nature of sherry to oxidize gracefully (and also peacefully, in a silent stately
chamber, without the frantic tourism, motion and extremes of heat that madeira
demanded). Yet with time and gradual evaporation it can achieve madeira-like
potency, both of flavour and alcohol.

THE CHARACTERISTIC SYSTEM FOR AGEING SHERRY, in what is now known as a solera,
probably started as a result of sluggish sales. "Fractional blending" is the modern
term. Whatever you draw off from a barrel you replace with a similar but younger
wine. It was not an invention of Jerez, but a development of the system of topping

319

up that we have seen in the Rhineland, and might occur naturally in any cellar where the wines keep well, and customers like to a buy a consistent wine, without great fluctuations from year to year.

But the regular use of the solera revealed to the Jerezanos aspects of their wine that they had scarcely known about. Far from all having the simple character of sack, in aging it became several different sorts of wine. The nose, it came to be said, told all. Some of the young wines, of better quality and not too strong, were apt to develop a floating white scum in the barrel which gave them extra fragrance. It was a yeast (this they did not know) which they christened "flor", or flower.

The preference of the export market was for a strong sweet style, which could easily be made by simply leaving standard wines, liberally dosed with brandy, for not very long in their great boat-shaped "butts". No flor grew; there was too much alcohol. Here the solera was used simply for consistency of flavour. The name coined for the best of this kind of sherry was "oloroso", or pungent. But 90% of it was second-grade wine, known as "raya", which had been given the Jerezano version of the "travail à l'anglaise".

An English doctor called Thudichum went to Jerez in 1871 to study first-hand, and in great depth, the way the favourite English drink was made. He reported back in a series of lectures to the Royal Society of Arts in 1873. At the beginning of Lecture Two he did not mince his words: "Many a sherry-drinker has heard the oft-repeated tale, that in the south the grapes were so sweet . . . that the muste made from them . . . remains sweet . . . even after fermentation produced the ordinary quantity of alcohol. This tale is often made to justify or explain the sweet taste of sherry, and the large amounts of distilled spirits which is added to it. For, say those who spread this tale, if spirits were not added to this sweet liquorous wine, it would not keep during transit, and the vicissitudes of being kept in private houses it would again ferment and spoil."

Having measured the "muste-weights", and so the natural strengths, of countless sherries for himself, he went on to say "that the assertion so frequently made to screen the true nature of sugared and brandied wines is untrue. Sherry wine is never sweet except when it is expressly and intentionally sweetened by makers and exporters. Sherry is so sweetened, and coloured, and brandied, in order to cover the natural defects of the taste; and no sherry of any claim to quality is ever coloured or sugared, because the maker knows very well that pale, dry wine, with the least possible amount of alcohol, is far more valuable than the cooked and drugged, coloured, sweet and hot liquids".

The locals, of course, knew which was best. The Andalusian taste was just the opposite: it was for pale young wine with a lively tang, at its best from the Listan, or Palomino, grape, even picked slightly underripe. Unaged, this was the Vin du Pays of the district, "preferred to all other wines by people of all ranks". To produce this racy drink consistently the solera had to be refreshed with new wines much more often – which provoked, it was discovered, a much more abundant growth of the fragrant "flor". By keeping barrels only perhaps seven-eighths full, with plenty of "head-space", it was found that the crust of flor on the best quality wines would grow several inches thick – protecting the wines from oxidation as effectively as a cork in a bottle. What the frequent refreshment did was to provide the nutrients, the proteins that the flor needed to flourish. "Fino" was the name given to this delicate style. In its lightest and most extreme form, made from grapes shaded from the sun, it was even compared with the freshness of an apple: "manzana". Manzanilla or "little apple wine" – there are various theories about how this name came about – is the speciality of Sanlúcar, of bodegas air-conditioned by the breezes off the sea. Fino was sold dry (while export wine was always sweetened with cooked must). It was also sold at close to its natural strength, of about 15% alcohol.

THERE WERE OTHER POSSIBILITIES TOO. In the good old days (as some must have thought) before the Gremio was formed to protect the growers of Jerez, wine from the inland regions of Montilla and Lucena was brought down to Jerez, either for blending or for passing off as sherry. (The practice only finally stopped well into the 20th century.)

The style of that wine was soft and nutty, the produce of the Pedro Ximenez grape, ripened in the hottest grape-growing area of Spain. With age it oxidizes into a different scale of fragrances and flavours – and gains perceptibly in alcoholic strength. The effect could be achieved, they found, by taking wine with fino inclinations, but refreshing its solera less frequently, so that the growth of flor was less abundant, and over a period of years a gradual oxidation and concentration took over, making it something between fino and oloroso. "Amontillado" was the term they coined for it: sherry in the style of well-aged Montilla. At its natural best it could be sublime. But again, what was exported as amontillado was usually a blend of cheap "rayas", smothered with brandy and sugar.

THESE WERE THE DEVELOPMENTS, OR SOME OF THEM, THAT SPRANG from the liberation of the shippers to hold stocks for as long as they liked – whether of their own wines or wines they had bought. Their art was to fashion them in the ways that customers in different countries wanted. Up to that time any such fashioning had had to be done in the customer's own cellars abroad. (Bristol Milk was the first famous example: a sweetened oloroso aged to singular smoothness in the cool cellars of Bristol. Perhaps its name derived from the local practice of fining the wine with milk.) After the Napoleonic wars the tastes of their foreign markets were well understood by the shippers in Jerez, both Spanish and above all British, who built enormous warehouses to hold their ever more varied stocks, improving at the same time with ingenuity and age. No building built to house wine can be compared with the great church-like barns that began to fill Jerez: nave upon nave of white-washed arches soaring over the grave geometry of countless grey oak butts. By the end of the century there were to be almost a thousand such bodegas in the district. When it was pointed out to them that digging cellars would help the wine to keep, the Jerezanos shrugged. Sherry became what it is by enduring hot days and cool nights.

THE UNFORTUNATE HAURIE HAD BACKED THE WRONG HORSE. The best hope a Spanish wine would ever have in France would be to be blended (even sherry was sometimes used for the "travail à l'anglaise"). 200 years later the French still remain in ignorance of one of the world's great apéritifs, preferring, of all things, sweet port before a meal. The wars over, though, all obstacles to trade with Britain were out of

The Domecq family stare confidently from this local artist's portrait. Their palace, grouped around a courtyard, typifies the cool Jerez architecture of Moorish inspiration. The great resting-places for the soleras (far right) are a later flowering of the same architectural style.

the way – and Haurie's cousin Pedro had been to school in England. Did it need a Franco-Spaniard to make the running, with so many British merchants in Jerez? It needed a man who could move in the right circles, and this was almost the definition of Don Pedro Domecq Lembeye.

The Australian James Busby visited Don Pedro in 1831. He found him on the best of Haurie's old estates at Macharnudo, a chalk hill of blinding whiteness four miles north of Jerez. "Mr Dumeque", Busby wrote, "is a gentleman of French extraction and speaks English fluently. We found him under the verandah of his wine cellar, and having mentioned the object of our visit, he undertook, with great readiness, to give us all the information we should ask. He . . . explained his proceedings in the manner of a man who was thoroughly acquainted with his subject, and had not been accustomed to follow blindly the practices he had found established. . . . It was evident, on entering the enclosure, that the vines were treated with greater care than any we had examined. The mother branches were better balanced and supported from the ground and were regularly pruned; and not a weed or blade of grass was to be seen among them."

Nor were there any flies on Domecq's partners, Mr Ruskin and Mr Telford, who rapidly and dramatically increased the company's English sales. Mr Ruskin confirmed James Busby's opinion: although Don Pedro "lived chiefly in Paris, rarely visiting his Spanish estate", he had "perfect knowledge of the proper process of its cultivation, and authority over his labourers almost like a chief's over his clan".

THE STORY OF JEREZ IN THE 19TH CENTURY is very much a matter of clans. Those who could envisage and organize manufacture on a very big scale grew prodigiously,

married their children to those of their business associates or rivals, and grew more prodigiously still. The name Gonzales (with Domecq, the greatest name of all) first appeared in the annals of Jerez in 1795, when a dashing young member of the Royal Bodyguard (who dashed, rumour had it, just a whisker too close to a Royal body) was made Administrator of the King's extremely profitable salt monopoly at Sanlúcar; so profitable that bandits made regular visits. The combination of soldier and courtier was Don José Antonio Gonzales y Rodriguez, who married before long the most eligible of the beauties of the region, a Doña Angel. Having fathered five sons, Don José died young. It was his youngest boy, Manuel Maria, who in 1835 started the firm now called Gonzales Byass.

BY THE 1830S JEREZ WAS A BOOM TOWN, by some accounts the richest city in Spain, a city of discreetly palatial houses around Moorish-style courtyards and cathedral-like bodegas, many of them built with South American fortunes. In 1816 Argentina had followed the example of the United States in declaring Independence; in 1818 Chile, and in 1821 Mexico. "Many gentlemen of substantial means", wrote Manuel

---

COINCIDENCE

Two of the immortals of English literature, separated in time by 500 years, were both the sons of men who sold Andalusian wine.

Geoffrey Chaucer, the first great poet in English, who died in 1400, was the son of the vintner John Chaucer, who imported wine into Southampton from Lepe, just west of the sherry region.

John Ruskin, the Victorian art critic, essayist and philanthropist, who died in 1900, was the son of John James Ruskin, the active partner in London of Ruskin, Domecq and Telford.

Gonzales Gordon, "returned from South America, on account of the Revolutions there". At that moment they could hardly have invested more shrewdly than in this remote, still outwardly backward provincial town, their vineyards within view from the walls, their wines stacked visibly and pungently around them, and with a direct line to the richest wine-importing country in the world. In 1827 the export route almost became Spain's first railway line: George Stephenson, the pioneer of the railway, accepted an invitation to come and lay out a track to Puerto de Santa Maria. It was not built until 1854 – but even then it was only the third railway in Spain.

The export figures speak for themselves. In 1810 Jerez exported some 10,000 butts; by 1840 more than double the amount; by the 1860s, double the amount again, and in 1873, the record year, over 68,000 butts. Over 90% of the sherry exported went to Britain (some, it is true, to be re-exported from the cellars of Bristol). In 1864, at the height of the British craze for sherry, it accounted for no less than 43% of the nation's total wine imports. From this moment, as we shall see, the Free Trade movement started to allow French wines to catch up again.

We must not think that sherry-drinking was confined, as it is today, to a polite couple of glasses before a meal and perhaps one or two of a sweet wine afterwards. The apéritif, as Byron bitterly complained, had still not been invented; he spoke of the "black half hour before dinner". Thomas Love Peacock, the English novelist who lovingly recorded the table-talk of squires, of nouveaux riches, of the clergy and the eccentrics of his day, in 1843 (at Headlong Hall) regaled them with "a cold saddle of mutton and a bottle of sherry". And still in 1915, whatever its value as evidence, the poet Rupert Brooke could write:

"With ham and sherry, they'll meet to bury
The lordliest lass of earth".

WHAT, IN THE MEANWHILE, HAD HAPPENED TO PORT? Were the British adding this tide of sherry to their already formidable national intake of strong wines from Portugal? At the end of the Napoleonic wars port (and all Portuguese wines) surged back into fashion with the returning heroes. The ratio of Portuguese wine to Spanish was in the order of three to one. (Even of Cape wine it was briefly two to one.) But as the 19th century adopted manners less robust than the 18th, wine-drinking figures lagged rapidly behind the increasing population.

In 1790 (according to Cyrus Redding) the British drank one gallon of wine (most of it strong) per head each year. By 1840 they drank only half as much. The fact can be accounted for in many ways. Spirits, beer, tea and coffee all became popular. Perhaps just as important was an increasing standard of living that offered a greater range of comforts to the middle class than a mere fiery glassful.

And this was the age of chapel building; a puritan religious revival that for the first time promoted the idea of Temperance. Port, in particular, carried with it associations with three-bottle men that sherry, the newcomer, was innocent of. There was a significant moment in the 1820s, when the pages of the Royal household, up to then issued with a bottle of port a day, found it replaced by a bottle of sherry. In 1837 the Victorian age began. The 1840s saw sherry draw level with port; in 1859 sherry overtook.

PORT HAD STARTED THE CENTURY HOLDING ALL THE CARDS. Perhaps one of the reasons why it was so successfully challenged was that it was still, well over a century after Pombal had tried to define it, perpetually in a crisis of identity. Even in 1877, on a visit to the port country, the English journalist Henry Vizetelly complained: "There are almost as many styles of port wine as shades of ribbon in a haberdasher's shop".

Before the Peninsula War this was perhaps partly accounted for by the poor communications between the shippers and the distant growers, and the fact that the Douro Wine Company was an unwanted intermediary in every transaction. But in the 19th century the shippers began to buy quintas, or farms, up the Douro, and become makers of some of their wine themselves. More fundamentally, it was because the climate of the Upper Douro is almost as wayward as that of, say, Bordeaux. Unlike the Andalusian seaside, where every season is not unlike the last, different vintages in different valleys high above the river Corgo sent down wines varying from mulberry-coloured monsters to quite pale insipid fluids.

The effect of adding brandy to the first was to make what we now think of as a Vintage port; a wine of huge but rugged character that needs many years to mature in bottle. The same amount of brandy added to the second produced nothing but the inflammatory sort of dose James Boswell so bitterly condemned: all fire and no flavour.

The solera system had almost by chance presented Jerez with various but consistent personalities for its different wines. Customers could pick and choose from a known range of samples – and indeed blend their own brands, which is what

The Battle of Oporto in 1809 left the city in the hands of the British. Wellington's forces, having liberated the Factory House from the French, dined there often until the tide of war removed them into Spain in 1812.

they increasingly came to do. Port was just finding its way, and ageing its wines more in wood before selling them, when a single superlative vintage pushed it towards a conclusion. 1820 was the year: a magnificent summer and ports of such natural "generosity", so rich, sweet and fruity, that they could not be improved. Unfortunately it created a demand that could not be satisfied. The only way in succeeding years to try to match the 1820 was by increasing the contentious dosage of brandy.

PORTUGAL MEANWHILE WAS THROWN INTO A SERIES OF REVOLUTIONS and civil wars. 1820 saw the first: a nationalist movement aimed once more at reducing the influence of the British. The commander of the Portuguese army was still General Lord Charles Beresford, who had led it against the French, and the English had even permeated Portuguese politics. Other convulsions that followed were more often, in Rose Macaulay's words, "the proclamation of noble and infatuated constitutions" – but nonetheless fatal for those who stood in their way. Here was another difference betweeen Jerez and Oporto. In Jerez integration of expatriates with the community was complete; in Oporto the British lived in an enclave in the shadow of the Factory House, maintaining "their calm British annoyance" through civil strife and insurrection. Very few spoke Portuguese; nearly all played cricket.

IN 1852 EVEN THE MOST PHLEGMATIC RAISED AN EYEBROW: the Upper Douro itself was seized by the "Miguelites", the followers of the would-be dictator Dom Miguel. Oporto was held by his brother and rival Dom Pedro, the former Emperor of Brazil. In due course Dom Miguel laid siege to the town and occupied the wine lodges across the river. There followed 18 months of extreme discomfort, in which

---

THE FACTORY HOUSE

The living symbol of the historical British presence in Oporto is the stately stone building of 1790 known officially as the British Association, but universally referred to as the Factory House. It is a masterpiece of 18th-century English understatement in architecture: almost a Palladian English country house, in fact, except that it stands on a rusticated arcade of seven bays, and in the busiest part of Oporto.

Inside, its pillared entrance hall, monumental staircase, ballroom, drawing room, library and map room have the same understated opulence and seem designed more for comfortable private life than for commerce. Indeed it feels as though the most urgent business transacted there was the regular luncheon and dinners. They had a unique feature: the drawing room and the dessert room, placed end to end, are equipped so that the guests can move on to an identical table in another room to drink their port undistracted by the smell of food. For the same reason the original kitchen (still perfectly preserved) is on the top floor of the building.

The original function of a "factory" or "feitoria" for foreign merchants was abandoned shortly after the building was finished. In 1814 it became simply a private club rather after the manner of those in London, but jealously guarded by the established port-shippers against incursions by parvenues, fish-merchants and others. At the frequent formal balls of the 19th century it was decreed: "no Portuguese officer under the rank of Field Officer can be invited".

Today members, still all of them port-shippers and most of them British, meet weekly for Wednesday lunch, except during the vintage. The time-honoured ritual of passing the decanter to the left is observed. A glass of Tawny port is followed by a vintage wine whose identity only the chairman knows – and a modest wager (the oldest English custom of all) is placed on which vintage, and which shippers, it turns out to be.

the exploits of a motley mercenary army, largely from Glasgow, loom large in local folklore. There was more than alarm when the Miguelites blew up the stores of the Douro Wine Company, the great brandy depot: the flames threatened everybody's port. Happily a British warship, stationed in the river, as Britain's prime minister Palmerston said, to "see fair play", landed a fire-fighting force that prevented a general conflagration, but had to watch as 27,000 pipes "of boiling port" made their muddy way down to the Douro. 27,000 pipes was approximately one year's exports to England.

THE FINAL THROES OF PORT'S STRUGGLE FOR IDENTITY were still to come. They were precipitated by a young man who arrived from England, at the age of 22, just in time to become one of the minor heroes of the siege; crossing the river by night to stand guard in the lodges of his family's firm, Offley Forrester & Co.

Joseph James Forrester was a polymath and a dreamer, a good farmer, a tolerable businessman, a talented artist and portraitist, and a scientist and cartographer of genius. He rapidly made himself fluent in Portuguese and known to all classes, from the aristocracy of Oporto to the peasantry of the Upper Douro, where he spent months on foot, in the wildest country, surveying for his masterpiece: his maps.

One of these maps charts the whole river from the Spanish border to the sea, another, whose detailed draughtsmanship makes it a work of art, the wine country, which he grew to know better than any man. In the 1850s, when the deadly vine fungus Oidium reached the Douro (as it was to reach most of Europe) Forrester's study of its nature and possible cure was well in advance of his time.

The Portuguese title of Baron was just one of many honours showered on Joseph Forrester by governments all over Europe.

Baron Forrester's accusations against the Douro Wine Company included the charge that their tasters failed to smell the wine when judging it, relying only on the prejudice that the darker the wine was, the better.

Ten years, or a little more, of watching port grown, fermented and prepared for shipping convinced Forrester that the accepted methods were destroying its potential. He, more than anyone, should have known what he was talking about. He owned the Quinta Boa Vista, high up the river, and signed himself "Douro Farmer and British Merchant". In 1844 he published a pamphlet whose title, *A Word or Two about Port Wine* is a masterpiece of understatement. In essence, he repeated the accusations that had been tossed back and forth a century before: that brandy and elderberry juice were ruining port, which should be, and always had been (this is certainly not true) a "natural" wine, without fortification.

If no brandy was used, what was the Douro Wine Company for? Its monopoly of brandy was its trump card – and may have been, to do the Miguelites justice, the reason why they blew up its stores. As to the quality of its brandy, that was another matter. Redding (writing before Forrester) described it as "execrable . . . distilled from figs and raisins of which no other use can be made. They even once tried to make it from locust pods. . . ."

As to the potential of the Douro to make excellent natural wine he was right: there is no longer any doubt. That there was general use of elderberries again was also true (though not, perhaps, of very great importance).

But Forrester was completely wrong about English taste – which was, when all is said and done, the sole arbiter of what is or is not good port. He was so disingenuous as to believe that "my countrymen do not desire . . . wine full of brandy; they prefer wines the most pure, and the least inebriative possible". Would that it were so. It is not impossible that taste will change; that one day the "light" wines of the Douro will replace its dessert wines in public favour. But not in Forrester's lifetime; nor, I believe, in mine.

FORRESTER FOUGHT A PASSIONATE CAMPAIGN, but lost it with good grace. He did not alter the nature of port; probably he reduced its adulteration. He lived in the heyday of the industry, when it was not too difficult to forgive: demand was steady, and a series of excellent vintages, maturing in bottle to ever more delicate fragrance, was proving that blackstrap was not the only outcome of adding brandy to the wine.

By the 1840s something akin to the pattern of port today was being developed. Charles Dickens, in 1844, made the first reference in literature to "tawny"; port

---

THE PORT SHIPPERS' SECRET

Just what fine wine unfortified port (or rather the table wine of the Upper Douro) can be is well-known to port shippers, but until recently has been treated almost as a secret.

The British journalist Henry Vizetelly was given some to taste at the famous Quinta do Noval in 1877, and he certainly liked it very much: ". . . by combining a certain roundness with a subdued astringency [it] participated somewhat of the character of both Burgundy and Bordeaux. It certainly possessed none of the characteristics of port".

The distinguished Portuguese firm of Ferreira have long made a small amount of a wine of outstanding quality called Barca Velha, or familiarly by the diminutive of Ferreira, as "Ferreirinha". There is, however, nothing diminutive about the wine.

More recently the Quinta do Cotto has produced excellent deep-coloured table wine of quite remarkable smoothness, and Noval is once again among the Quintas which are actively experimenting with a wine which poetic justice should call, simply, "Forrester".

---

wine made lighter, faded in colour and with its fruity taste transmuted by ageing for a decade or more in barrel. Even the shippers' names, or most of them, are familiar to us now, and the quintas that they built, higher and higher in the canyons of the Douro, became the setting for a social life that a contemporary tea-planter would have recognized.

This is where Forrester, fittingly, met his end. Famous and respected, in the prime of middle age, he set out with two of the aristocrats of the Upper Douro, owners of many farms and terraced hills, from the Fladgates' Quinta de Vargellas to sail down-river to Pinhao. He had decorated his famous map with the beauty spots of the river. One of them was the Cachão de Valeira: the deep gorge that up to the 18th century was the limit of navigation. Even today, with the Douro dammed and placid, it is a haunting spot, between smooth granite walls that rise sheer from the water. In May 1862 the river was in spate; the pinnace hit a rock. Donna Antonia Ferreira and Baroness Fladgate floated to safety on their crinolines. Forrester's body was never found.

EXHAUSTING LABOUR

The scene described in the lagar of the Quinta do Seixo, where the 1877 vintage was being trodden, sounds like a painting by Goya . . . "The treaders, with their white breeches well tucked up . . . form three separate rows of ten men each . . . and, placing their arms on each other's shoulders, commence work by raising and lowering their feet . . . varying this, after a time, with songs and shoutings in order to keep the weaker and the lazier ones up to the work, which is quite as irksome and monotonous as either treadmill or prison crank, which tender-hearted philanthropists regard with so much horror . . . . Taking part with them in the treading is a little band of musicians, with drum, fife, fiddle, and guitar, who strike up a lively tune. Occasionally, too, nips of brandy are served out and the overseers present cigarettes all round, whereupon the treaders vary their monotonous movements with a brisker measure."

The first treading goes on for 18 hours; after a break the second treading starts. "By this time, the grapes are pretty well crushed, and walking over the pips and stalks, strewn at the bottom of the lagar, becomes something like the pilgrimages of old when the devout trudged wearily along, with hard peas packed between the soles of their feet and the soles of their shoes. The lagariros . . . move slowly about in their mauve-coloured mucilaginous bath in a listless kind of way . . . . The fiddle strikes up anew, the drum sounds . . . and the overseers drowsily upbraid. But all to no purpose. Music has lost its inspiration and authority its terrors, and the men, dead beat, raise one purple leg languidly after the other."

Only a small minority of (the best quality) port is trodden today; and by whole families together in a scene more like a barn-dance than a treadmill.

CHAPTER 33

METHODE CHAMPENOISE

The sun rising over Champagne on the tenth of September 1815 found something more stirring to illuminate than the usual placid dewy vines, their leaves yellowing and their grapes turning gold for the approaching vintage.

On the plain south of Epernay, where the first light had touched the little hill of Mont Aimé among the eastern slopes by the village of Vertus, a seemingly endless army was assembling from bivouacs in all the villages around. The light of dawn flashed on the cuirasses of hussars and glowed on the bearskins of great-coated grenadiers. It gleamed on the flanks of Cossack ponies and gilded the long barrels of muskets and field artillery. Marching files of infantry half a mile long broke to make way for cavalry squadrons at the trot, kicking up the chalk, their harness slapping and jingling, their officers standing in their stirrups, straining to find their place in what seemed the biggest battle-plan Europe had ever seen.

At seven o'clock, the gigantic muster was in order. Seven Russian army corps, almost 300,000 fighting men, formed phalanx after phalanx as far as the eye could see. At eight, a mounted procession climbed the Mont Aimé, whose top had been levelled for the occasion. Alexander I, the Tsar of Russia, was flanked by the Emperor of Austria and the King of Prussia, the Prince Royal of Bavaria, the Prince of Wrede and the Duke of Wellington.

The Tsar raised his hand, and the seven corps launched into a series of yet more intricate manoeuvres, eventually to form a colossal square. The monarchs, the generals and their staff descended from the mount, and deep in thought rode slowly along the ranks of whiskered Russians. They had been invited to inspect the contemporary equivalent of Russia's strategic ballistic missiles – and in the heart of France.

THE CREDIT FOR THIS EXTRAORDINARY PIECE OF POWER-PLAY goes largely to France's representative at the Congress of Vienna, which had been in session since Napoleon's abdication the previous year to decide on the future of France and the territories she had conquered. He was Charles-Maurice de Talleyrand-Perigord, Prince of Benevento, universally and respectfully known as Talleyrand. Before the Revolution he had been Bishop of Autun. No twist in the deadly complexities of revolutionary politics had wrong-footed him, and now, in his 60s, "cynical and voluptuary", he was the embodiment of French diplomacy. For infantry at Vienna he brought France's greatest chef, Antoine Carême. Champagne provided his artillery.

As for the political significance of this greatest of military parades, it stemmed from the Tsar's discomfort (Talleyrand and Carême helping him to think clearly) at seeing his two great military neighbours, Prussia and Austria, set on dismembering a defeated France. Three months after the Battle of Waterloo their intention was to reduce France to a minor power. Russia (and each other) would then be their only considerable rivals. Russia's interest lay in keeping France as a power to be reckoned with at the far end of Europe, to give the Austrians and Prussians a second front to worry about. Thus the Tsar and the newly-restored King of France, Louis XVIII (Louis XVII was lost and never found), had common cause. The show of strength on the fields of Champagne took place with French consent. It was a strange outcome to Napoleon's invasion of Russia three years earlier. And politics apart, it was the greatest public relations event that any wine region would ever see.

BUT THE STORY IS MORE COMPLEX, AND MIGHT BE STARTED ANYWHERE back in the 18th century, where such pioneers as Moët, Ruinart, Roederer and Heidsieck were wooing crowned heads, building on the brilliant debut of champagne at the courts of London and Paris.

The adoption of champagne by monarch after monarch in the 18th century is the folklore of the industry which made public relations into an art form. How Frederick Wilhelm of Prussia commissioned the Academy of Berlin to discover why the wine sparkled, but balked at giving them a single bottle to experiment on; how Catherine the Great in Russia fortified her young officer friends; how Louis XVI consoled himself before the guillotine, and how Napoleon encouraged the

On his last visit to Epernay, the embattled Napoleon decorated Jean-Rémy Moët with his own cross of the Legion of Honour. Days later the Russians arrived, and soon the Emperor was in Elba. Imperial favour was no bar to Moët's social advance: in 1815 he entertained every Allied prince and general from the Tsar to Blucher, and in peace-time he became supplier to every European court.

Napoleon's visits to Epernay were so frequent that Jean-Rémy Moët built two
guest houses for the use of the emperor and his entourage. The gardens and
orangery – designed by the miniaturist Jean-Baptiste Isabey – still survive.

intimacy of the Mayor of Epernay, Jean-Rémy Moët, who built a species of private
tavern for the Emperor and his family to stay in on their frequent visits to Epernay:
an essential staging post (they found) between Paris and any activity on the Austrian
and Prussian fronts.

SINCE ITS LAUNCH OVER A CENTURY BEFORE, Champagne had pursued three different
careers at least: as one of France's most celebrated still white wines (largely in the
form of Sillery) for the conservative gourmand; as an honourable red alternative to
one of the lighter sorts of burgundy, and in its sparkling form as the wine of the
sinfully rich and richly sinful. But the region really made its bread and butter (and
not very much butter) from oceans of cheap red wine. At the start of the 19th
century red wine was 90% of its production; by 1850 it had still only been reduced
to two-thirds.

   While the reputation of sparkling champagne had grown, and the demand now
reached several hundred thousand bottles a year, its technology had not. A large part

SILLERY

The wines of the pioneer Brulart family's estate at
Verzenay and other villages near Reims were
always called Sillery, and the name was synonymous with the top quality of still champagne
throughout the second half of the 18th century.

   The last Brulart in direct line was the
Maréchale d'Estrées, a masterly lady of formidable determination who made divine wine and
treated her peasants like convicts. Her brilliant
blend of Pinot Noir and Fromenteau (Pinot Gris)
was the royal favourite, and became known
simply as Vin de la Maréchale. After her little-
regretted death in 1785 her estate and fabulous

stock of wine was inherited by a distant cousin,
the Comte de Genlis, who took the title of
Marquis de Sillery. His wife, Madame de Genlis,
was the best-known blue-stocking of her age, and
an important educational reformer. Alas, the new
marquis paid for the sins of the old Maréchale
under the guillotine and Sillery was sacked.

   Madame de Genlis became almost a private
tutor to Napoleon, but the Brulart vineyards
were sold to M Moët and M Ruinart. The name
Sillery continued in use throughout the 19th
century, but the last time this great wine was
made was in 1814.

The Château de Sillery, home of the Brularts and the infamous Moréchale d'Estrées, survived the fury of the revolutionary mob, but not the shelling of the First World War.

of the fun (thought those frivolous times) was in cutting the string that held down the cork, and sprinkling the filles de joie with the expensive mousse. Ageing courtiers in particular found irresistible symbolism in the explosion of froth. They were still often disappointed by bottles with very little gas, or with a few big bubbles that were horribly described as *yeux de crapauds* – toads' eyes – or by various ailments of unstable wine that produced the effect of a slimy worm in the bottle, or just a thick and murky fluid. Meanwhile a depressingly large proportion of the bottles continued to explode in the cellars.

There was no shortage of potential customers, for anyone who had drunk a good bottle, as M. Moët and his colleagues found, was hooked for life. The only catch was that they had to be very rich; the laborious and uncertain manufacture was extremely expensive. If sparkling champagne was ever to become a universal wine, that could be packed off abroad with confidence and in industrial quantities, many technical problems still needed to be solved.

IN ALL OF HISTORY ONLY ONE WOMAN IS KNOWN AS "THE WIDOW", without qualification. If it is true that the perfectionism of Dom Pérignon earned for champagne a unique place as the wine of princes and palaces throughout Europe, it is no less true that Nicole-Barbe Clicquot-Ponsardin, widowed with a baby daughter in 1805 at the age of 27, found the way to make it the celebratory wine of the entire world.

The Russians, with their unerring taste for the most effective liquor, were her improbable allies in her enterprise. Not her countrymen (though many were her rivals) nor the British, whose bilious national taste for brandied wine only gave way to champagne later in the century. In Russia she conquered a wider market for her sparkling wine than champagne had ever known. In order to supply it she was obliged to industrialize its manufacture. The firm her husband started was a little country practice; as a widow she transformed its yellow label into the most widely-recognized on earth.

The veuve Clicqout as a relatively young woman in an early daguerreotype. Widowed at 27, she ran the firm until her death at 89.

THE REVOLUTION HAD BEEN A DISTRESSING INTERLUDE for an industry that catered for the very heads the guillotine removed. One merchant of Champagne, it is said, saved several heads, including his own, by deleting the titles of each of his customers and writing the word Citizen instead. Napoleon's wars caused the removal of all ready cash from the scene in France, before it was exacted for the Imperial levies. To export was the answer, but elaborate blockading and counter-blockading had made trade between European ports uncertain, to say the least. Representatives of the Champagne houses followed the armies, vulture-like, to quench the victors' thirsts while the bodies were counted. But there was a limit to the amount of expansion that could be based on celebrating the Imperial victories, and after 1811 their number started steeply to decline.

The widow Clicquot was fortunate in having a salesman of genius; a Mr Bohne that her husband had met in Bâle. He first tried England, without much success, then took his wares to Russia, Prussia and Austria. One of his letters, written from St Petersburg in 1806, epitomizes the rivalries involved: "The Tsarina is with child. If it is a Prince, gallons of champagne will be drunk all over this vast country. Do not mention it, or all our rivals will be here at once."

Napoleon's invasion of Russia in 1811 was the turning point. Many had misgivings about the distance and difficulty of the Emperor's most ambitious enterprise. Not all: a legend says that Charles-Henri Heidsieck arrived in Moscow on horse-back, his order book at the ready, several weeks before the Imperial army.

But in 1812 at Borodino, just outside Moscow, it was the pessimists who were proved right. The Russians and their deadly allies, Generals Janvier and Février, turned what had appeared to be the relentless tide. The retreat from Moscow was an ice-bound shambles that left the Emperor with no alternative but to hurry home and raise the new forces he now needed for the defence of France.

Henry Vizetelly made an acid comment on the Russians' conversion to champagne: "From this influx of sparkling wine into the frozen empire of the Tsar the acceptance of civilisation, of rather superficial character, it is true, may be said to date. Had Peter the Great only preferred champagne to corn-brandy, the country would have been Europeanised long ago".

NAPOLEON'S LAST DEFENSIVE BATTLES BEFORE HIS ABDICATION brought the Russian and the Prussian armies in force to Champagne. The region had suffered as a camp and crossroads in many wars, but for three weeks in the early spring of 1814 it was the bearpit in which the retreating Emperor fought and won skirmish after skirmish with generalship as brilliant as he had ever displayed. In the words of Victor Hugo, he "wrote with the local names of Champagne the last pages of his prodigious poem: Arcis-sur-Aube, Châlons, Reims, Champaubert, Sézanne, Vertus, Méry, La Fère, Montmirail. So many combats; so many victories".

He had no forces left, though, to face the massing allies marching inexorably west. Reims and Epernay fell to the Russians and the Prussians, The day before Epernay fell, taking his leave of his loyal friend Jean-Rémy Moët, the Emperor pinned on his breast his own cross of the Légion d'Honneur, then left for Paris and his abdication.

THE RUSSIANS UNDOUBTEDLY HAD THE BEST OF THE OCCUPATION, and the French, though terrified of the Cossacks and Kalmucks, found that the pillage might have been worse. As it happened the Russian commander in Reims was one of St Petersburg's most polished officers; Prince Sergei Alexandrovich Wolkonski. The Prussians, no doubt envious of the Russian billet, proposed to enter Reims and extract tribute and supplies. "I have received orders from the Tsar", wrote back Wolkonski, "not to exact any requisitions from this town. As for your insolent threat of sending troops to Reims, I have plenty of Cossacks here to receive them."

If the legends are true, requisitions did not need to be extracted. They were carried up willingly from, amongst others, the cellars of the far-sighted Widow Clicquot. "Today they drink", were her somewhat tight-lipped words, "Tomorrow they will pay".

Nor did she hesitate for a moment before putting her maxim into effect. She ignored the fact that the borders of Russia were still officially closed to French goods. The occupying forces left in May 1814. By the beginning of June, scarcely giving them time to reach home, she had a ship chartered, a 75-ton Dutch "flute", the Sweers Gebroeders, loaded with Mr Bohne and as much champagne as it could carry (and that the Russians had left undrunk), and sailing for the Baltic. 1811, the year of Halley's comet, had been a wonderful vintage. She sent as much as she had. The ship reached Koenigsberg (today's Kaliningrad) on July 3rd, to find that French goods were no longer excluded. Bohne had the field to himself. There was not another voyageur from Champagne within 500 miles.

"It is with infinite satisfaction", wrote Mr Bohne, "that I have examined the samples. Spring water is infinitely less limpid than they are. Everyone is agog at the idea of tasting them." The Tsar himself had arrived back in Koenigsberg; even the Imperial door was not closed to Mr Bohne. "You see", he wrote again to the widow in Reims, "what authority one has when one has good merchandise to provide. I had only to let drop the number of my hotel room, and a queue formed outside my door."

ONE OF THE REASONS WHY THE RUSSIANS SO DOTED on what they called "Klikofskoe" was that the widow made it extremely sweet. Before dispatching her bottles she removed the sediment – an essential operation – and filled its place (even as much as a third of the bottle) with a syrupy mixture of wine, sugar and brandy. The Asti Spumante of today, though lower in alcohol and with its distinctive muscat flavour, perhaps comes nearer than any modern champagne to the taste the Russians loved.

As to the limpidity that gave Mr Bohne so much satisfaction, there is little doubt that the art of clearing the wine of sediment was the great Clicquot contribution to the technology of champagne – arrived at, so the legend goes, by the nightly vigils of the widow, lantern in hand; the very Florence Nightingale of the cellar.

IN THE FIRST YEARS OF THE 19TH CENTURY SEDIMENT was an increasing problem. The more sparkling the wine was required to be, the more sugar was added to produce more fermentation in the bottle and – providing the bottle withstood the pressure – the more dead yeast cells would result. That they were yeast cells was unknown: the deposit was referred to as the "marc" – as though grape-skins had mysteriously survived the pressing, the first fermentation in the barrel, the racking and the bottling, and had somehow reappeared in the bottled wine.

To remove this "marc" it had to be collected. The standard way was by periodically picking the bottle up, giving it either a sharp tap or a rousing shake, and then putting it back in its pile. The intention was to concentrate the sediment in as narrow a compass as possible along the lower side of the bottle, so that at the next stage, dépotage, or decanting into another bottle, the maximum of clear wine could be poured out before the sediment started to move and cloud it. Every bottle, in other words, required as delicate a decanting operation as an old bottle of burgundy. It goes without saying that at least half the pressure of gas was lost in the process. It was not the widow herself, but one of her employees, Antoine de Muller, devised a

The production line of champagne, as described by Vizetelly: disgorging, liquering, corking, stringing and wiring. Despite the advent of machinery, making champagne was and remains a labour-intensive business.

better method. If the bottle was kept with the cork downwards the "marc" could be persuaded to collect, not along the side of the bottle, but on the cork. Then when the cork was removed the sediment would fly out first, and there would be no need to decant the rest of the wine and lose half its fizz. It could simply be topped up with "liqueur" and equipped with a new cork.

The precise evolution of the idea is unknown. De Muller came to work for the widow in 1810. In a letter of January 1816, writing from Avize, he referred to bottles "on the table", and explains his observation that a more compact marc is formed if the bottle is not moved too much. Folklore joins in here, suggesting that the Clicquot kitchen table was taken down to the cellar and pierced with holes to take the necks of the bottles; at first vertically, then, with the refinement of practice, at an oblique angle.

Certainly it was on some such table that the first modern-style "remuage" took place. The new technique was to wait until the "marc" had come to rest on the side of the bottle, then put it in a hole in the table, and at frequent intervals lift it half out of the hole, give it a sharp shake, and drop it back in. The jerk against the table gave the sediment another impulsion towards the cork. Up to 1821 the firm of Clicquot was the only one practising this technique and had managed to keep it a secret. It was in 1821 that the widow was joined by a German partner, Edouard Werlé from the Rhineland, who in due course took over the running of the establishment. It remains, though, a teasing possibility that the bottles of "comet" wine that so excited Mr Bohne by their limpidity in 1814 were the first fruits of de Muller's labours, and hence the first that might be called "modern" bottles of champagne.

CHAMPAGNE BECAME AN INDUSTRY ONCE THE SECRET OF REMUAGE was known. It could be organized on a production- line scale in a way that decanting never could. In the 1820s alone four famous houses began to trade: Irroy, Joseph Perrier, Mumm and Bollinger. In 1826 a clerk from Clicquot took the technique to Heilbronn on the Neckar in Württemberg. In the same year the first sparkling-wine house opened in Burgundy – to make, of all unlikely things, sparkling red Nuits St Georges. Before the middle of the century Pommery & Greno, Deutz & Geldermann, Krug and Pol Roger had all founded houses in Reims or Epernay. Five out of these ten familiar names of long-established champagne-makers, like Mr Werlé of Clicquot, came from Germany.

From a total sales figure for sparkling champagne at the end of the 18th century of something like 300,000 bottles, by 1853 the total had reached 20 millions. As in the sherry business, which was growing at almost the same rate at the same time (both Reims and Jerez, by coincidence, acquired a railway link the same year: 1854)

Once the technology of making sparkling wine was mastered, Germany and Burgundy were quick to adopt it. By 1830 it was in use for white burgundy, mainly of Buxy near Mercurey, which fizzed well enough to break plenty of bottles, but did not keep its mousse for years like champagne. Wine made from red grapes did better, and soon red burgundy was being put through the "méthode champenoise". Nuits-St-Georges became the centre of the industry, which enjoyed a vogue among Paris dandies, and which at one point went so far as to make a sparkling Romanée-Conti (but spoilt it, it was said, by blending in some Chablis).

there seemed to be no limit to the money to be made. Sherry and champagne shared a new concept in the wine industry; the elaboration of wines by manufacturing methods that require time and capital tied up in stocks which are beyond the reach of almost any farmer. In Champagne particularly the industrialist found it easy to dominate his supplier; he could refuse to buy grapes until they were in danger of becoming worthless and the farmer grew desperate. Nor were there any workable regulations to prevent him buying grapes outside the region, which was not then defined in any meaningful way by law. There were many cowboys in the trade, and much appalling wine sold as champagne to a gullible newly-prosperous public. It was easily masked behind a heavy dosage of sweet liqueur: the concept of dry champagne had yet to be invented.

MEANWHILE, FROM THE MAKER'S POINT OF VIEW, BY FAR the most serious problem remained the dreaded explosions below ground as the unpredictable pressure shattered the unreliable bottles. 1828 was a disastrous year: 80% of the bottles burst. The unanswered question was how to estimate the sugar needed for the second fermentation to produce the right amount of gas, other than simply by tasting. Another unknown was not even suspected: how much yeast the wine contained. A year of serious "casse" was probably a year in which the yeast was more active than usual – but no one yet knew that yeasts were involved in fermentation at all.

1836 saw the first of the problems at least partly solved. A chemist named François from Châlons-sur-Marne invented the sucre-oenométre; an instrument for measuring the sugar content. With its help the number of breakages was gradually reduced until, in 1866, André Jullien could report that the average was only 15 or 20 per cent. It was still extremely unwise to go into a champagne cellar, at least in spring, without a wire mask to protect your face.

All bottles arriving from the glass companies were suspect. According to Cyrus Redding, recording every detail in about 1830, the custom was to clink them together smartly in pairs when they were delivered. Any that broke at the first clink were charged to the glassmaker; any of irregular shape or with obvious faults were set aside for bottling red wine.

Fifty years later, England's most thorough, and most entertaining, chronicler of champagne, Henry Vizetelly, told the same story, adding in a footnote the mysterious circumstance that champagne bottles, it was believed, could never be re-used, because the pressure weakened the glass. Of a batch of 3,000 bottles used a second time as an experiment, "only 15 or 16 resisted the pressure". His scriptural reference about new wine in old bottles inclines one to take the whole notion with a pinch of salt.

Vizetelly's book, *A History of Champagne*, published in London and New York in 1882, with 350 engravings ranging from works of art to diagrams to cartoons, marked a new departure in publications about wine: the popular illustrated wine book – but with no less scholarship than his forerunners.

"Good champagne does not rain down from the clouds", he writes, "or gush from the rocks, but is the result of incessant labour, patient skill, minute precaution, and careful observation. . . . The special character of champagne is that its manufacture only commences where that of other wines ordinarily ends."

The enormous crayeres –
Roman chalk quarries –
beneath Reims were
increasingly used for the
storage and "elaboration" of
champagne in the nineteenth
century. Later the caves were
to serve as shelters during the
1,000 days of bombardment
the city endured from 1914 to
1918.

His description of that manufacture in progress brings home the fact that champagne is a product of the Industrial Revolution. "What with the incessant thud of the corking machines, the continual rolling of iron-wheeled trucks over the concrete floor, the rattling and creaking of the machinery working the lifts, the occasional sharp report of a bursting bottle, and the loudly-shouted orders of the foremen, who display the national partiality for making a noise to perfection, the din becomes at times all but unbearable. The number of bottles filled in the course of the day naturally varies, still Messrs Moët & Chandon reckon that during the month of June a daily average of 100,000 are taken in the morning from the stacks in the salle de rinçage, washed, dried, filled, corked, wired, lowered into the cellars, and carefully arranged in symmetrical order. This represents a total of two and a half million bottles during that month alone."

IT WAS THE PROCEEDS OF THE INDUSTRIAL REVOLUTION, supporting the affluence of a middle class unknown before in history, that allowed the once-exclusive luxury of the aristocracy to break out at balls, picnics and parties all over the world. As early as 1828 the English had adopted champagne as the drink of the turf: the first Champagne Stakes were run that year.

Not many years later we are informed that champagne was commonly packed for Russia in hampers of sixty bottles, but for China in hampers of 120. They were Herculean coolies in those days.

THE LAST DEVELOPMENT THAT WAS NEEDED TO BRING THE CHAMPAGNE OF HISTORY into its modern context was its drying-out from the Sauternes-like sweetness which made it a dessert wine – at least in the widow's time – to something that could be drunk with any food, or in the new-fangled role (the word first appeared in 1894) of an apéritif.

In mid-century the degree of syrupy liqueur added to the wine varied from country to country of its destination, but all were very sweet. Measured in grams of sugar per litre for France it was about 165; for Germany a little more; for Scandinavia as much as 200; while Russians would drink anything from 250 to 330 – which would have made an actress's slipper very sticky indeed. The United States had a rather drier taste than France, (from 110-165 grams), while England, eccentrically, required only 22-66 grams; that is 2-6% of "liqueur d'expédition". For comparison, the figures today for sweet champagne may rise as high as 50 grams, for "dry" as high as 35; Brut has up to 15 grams, while true or "ultra" brut has no liqueur added at all.

The manner of drinking champagne in the 1840s and 50s partly accounts for its overwhelming sweetness. The "coupe" glass with its wide and shallow bowl was invented in about 1840 (although the public relations machine has long since attributed its shape to the bosom of Marie-Antoinette). The wine served in it was "frappé" – whose best translation, perhaps, would be "knocked cold": it was almost as much a sorbet as a drink. It was also frequently tinted with what was euphemistically called "vin de Fismes": our old friend elderberry juice.

THE CREDIT FOR THINKING DRY GOES TO A LONDON WINE MERCHANT named Burnes, who in 1848 tasted the excellent Perrier-Joüet vintage of 1846 in its natural unsweetened state. His reasoning was that the English were already only too well supplied with sticky drinks for dessert; that champagne would never oust port, but that (its price apart) it would be a wonderful drink to go with dinner if it tasted winey rather than sugary. It was also, to borrow Jullien's marvellous phrase, more "susceptible d'être bu à haute dose sans incommoder". Shipped completely without sweetening it caused more shock than pleasure, but from the 1850s on house after house in Champagne started shipping somewhat drier wines to England. 1865 was an excellent vintage: both Ayala and Bollinger scored hits with the Prince of Wales when they shipped it unsweetened – or almost. Even the house of Clicquot sold a "dry" 1857, but waited respectfully until 1869, after the death of the widow, before shipping a "perfectly dry wine", or Brut. 1874 was the outstandingly fine vintage that made the practice general – at least for the English market: to this day in France the preference is for a medium-dry version.

The legend that the champagne "coupe", the shallow bowl on a stem, was modelled on the bosom of Marie-Antoinette is not entirely without foundation. The Sèvres porcelain factory did take a cast from this august model and produced four detailed white bowls that were mounted on elaborate bases of three goat's heads to adorn the Queen's Dairy Temple at the Château de Rambouillet near Versailles. The dairy still exists; as does one of the four "coupes".

The wide, shallow shape of the bowl, however, was never intended for champagne, and cannot be compared with the tall "flute" glass for revealing the quality of the wine.

Having to produce unsweetened wine was salutary for the champagne industry. Sweetness is a mask for many faults; dry wine put the producers on their mettle. Few were substantial vineyard owners in relation to their enormous demand for grapes, so they were forced to buy a higher proportion of their raw materials from the villages of the "river", "mountain" and the Côte des Blancs that produced the best quality. Dry champagne, it might be said, was the spur to the proper reward of the growers of the best grapes. Those in such famous villages as Aÿ, Hautvillers, Verzenay, Bouzy, Avize and Vertus had always made a relatively good living, but the competition among the producers now led to a serious classification by quality of the villages of the entire region.

IT IS FITTING TO LEAVE CHAMPAGNE ONCE MORE TO THE TRAMP OF MARCHING FEET that has always been the refrain to its story. In 1866 the widow died at the age of 89, having lived her later years in a state of superfluous pomp which expressed only too well the self-satisfaction of the Champenois. Her Château de Boursault, over-looking the valley of the Marne, might have been the place Byron had in mind when he wrote "wealth had done wonders; taste not much". In 1869 the Prussians were back, Champagne was a battlefield again, and the pain and ignominy of two years of enemy occupation settled once more over the region.

The winter siege of Paris by the Prussians in 1870 provides a gastronomic footnote. There was no food in the city, but plenty of wine. The menu for Christmas Day at the famous restaurant Voisin proposed (I had better leave it in the decent obscurity of the original tongue) "chat flanqué de rats, accompagné d'un Bollinger frappé".

CHAPTER 34

JOHN BULL'S VINEYARD

"In a climate so favourable, the cultivation of the vine may be carried to any degree of perfection, and should no other article of commerce divert the settlers from this point, the wines of New South Wales may perhaps hereafter be sought with avidity and become an indispensable part of European tables".

These words were written by Captain Arthur Phillip of the Royal Navy, the first Governor of the new penal colony on the east coast of Australia, on September 28th 1788, within nine months of his landing his small force and the 700 convicts they were to guard on the shores of Sydney Harbour. Suiting his action to his words, on the banks of what is now Farm Cove, he planted the vine cuttings he had brought with him from home.

Unfortunately, many articles were to divert the settlers. They were to found fortunes with sheep, and ruin themselves with rum; to spend 20 years in a sometimes cruelly disciplined, more often chaotic, and almost perpetually drunken state before anything resembling civilization was to take root in the colony. When it did, it was a sad caricature of the motherland that had disowned her unfortunates. The privileges

---

THE FIRST TOAST

Captain Cook had sent the expedition to the wrong address. Distracted, perhaps, by the botanising enthusiasm of his scientist passengers Sir Joseph Banks and Carl Solander, the First Fleet headed for what they had agreed to call Botany Bay, a wide open beach with no shelter, no anchorage for the ships, and no water supply – but convenient for laying out Banks's botanical specimens. The First Fleet stayed in Botany Bay for a week while Captain Phillip went north up the coast to explore an inlet Cook had named Port Jackson, but not investigated. To their joy they found it everything Botany Bay was not. They were just about to set sail to take the fleet to this new anchorage when to their alarm they saw two French warships beating towards them.

Hurriedly they hoisted a flagpole, ran up the Union flag, claimed the land for King George III and drank a toast. If this was the first toast drunk in Australia it was probably not the first wine. Lieutenant Gidley King had offered some to two Aborigines who greeted their arrival. They spat it out, but there is no reason to think that the lieutenant wasted the rest of the bottle.

Port Jackson turned out to be "the finest harbour in the world" – lacking nothing but an Opera House. So dense was the vegetation running down to the limpid water of its many branching arms that "each man stepped from the boat literally into a wood". Phillip renamed their chosen settlement Sydney Cove, after the Minister who had despatched the fleet.

of the military guards of the convicts, the New South Wales Corps, were so cynically exploited that they rapidly became known as the Rum Corps. By monopolising the supply of the only liquor available, rum from Bengal, they cornered the accepted currency and were able to use convicts as slaves on the land that was given to them as of right.

Governor Phillip was right about the potential of Australian wine – but wrong in his timing by almost two hundred years. The chronicle of those two centuries, and why the process was so slow, is the story of wine in Australia.

NOT SURPRISINGLY IT WAS THE PAYMASTER OF THE RUM CORPS who first procured himself a comfortable, and immensely profitable, billet. He was John Macarthur, the son of a Plymouth corset-maker, characterised by Robert Hughes, the great historian of the convict years, as "a choleric man with a rage for gentility, who saw plots and insults everywhere and was as touchy as a Sicilian." Macarthur was the black comedy version of the Duke of Chandos; a man who revelled in the riches his ruthlessness brought him – not the least of which was his wine.

Macarthur's (and his wife's, for she was a leading actor in all this) principal part in the making of New South Wales was their grazing and breeding of the greatest number of the colony's best sheep. With the devil's luck, he was sent home to England for court-martial for wounding an officer in a duel – and arrived at the very moment when, for two brief years, Napoleon's "Continental System" was pinching. It was depriving the booming English textile industry, the first great success of the Industrial Revolution, of its raw material from Spain and the grazing lands of eastern Germany. Macarthur arrived with samples of Australian wool in his pocket, contrived to be acquitted at his court martial, and was back in New South Wales in 1805 with a gift of several of the king's own prize Merino sheep and a special grant of 2,000 acres of the best grazing land in the colony to raise them on. The land, which he renamed Camden Park after the Treasury Minister who presented it to him, lies 40 miles south of Sydney along the Nepean river. Its former name of Cowpastures arose, it is said, because in the first years of the colony its herd

John MacArthur's descendants still live at Camden Park, the imposing white-painted mansion he built inland from Sydney, and bottles of his wine still lie in the cellars.

of cattle had escaped, causing great consternation and much beating about the bush. When it was finally found it was in a bovine paradise of long grass among millennial gum trees along a gentle river.

This was where Macarthur made his home, bred his sheep, and more germane to our story, planted his vineyard. Eventually his mansion, which would look more in place in Sussex or Hampshire, stood in 60,000 acres of Macarthur land, including enough vineyard to merit a substantial (now ruined) stone-built winery with half a dozen capacious vats. In 1815 he took two of his sons to France to visit vineyards and collect cuttings, and did the same at Madeira and the Cape on the way home. Records of his production are scant, (although it is known that he kept a nursery and sold vines), but the medals they won are not, and nor, amazingly, were unopened bottles when I visited his descendant in his almost unchanged house in 1988. The undated bottle that we tasted (which might have been of any vintage between 1825 and 1870) was sumptuous; deep oily garnet in colour, of enormous richness with some of the singular tang of oranges that I had once detected in a Constantia of the same approximate date. It seems likely that this bottle was the work of Macarthur's son, Sir William, who became a respected authority on vines and winemaking, contributed to periodicals (under the pen-name Maro), and whose nursery, as we shall see, supplied plants for new enterprises all over Australia.

THE FIRST NEWSPAPER PUBLISHED IN AUSTRALIA was the Sydney Gazette of March 5th, 1803. That there was a public with ideas beyond Bengali rum is proved by the article on the back page, the first of a series on how to plant a vineyard and make wine. It may well be that the editor's motive was to free his readers from the monopoly of the Rum Corps in getting any drink at all beside their lethal spirit. Unfortunately, although the readers undoubtedly made some sort of wine for a while, any dreams they had of Sydney as a new Bordeaux (or even Douro) were short-lived. They did not know what ailed the vines; it was the humid subtropical climate. Nor, probably, was there anyone among them who could indicate even what kind of wine they should be trying to make. The Britain they had left behind was the land where port reigned supreme: the very idea of light wines was unfamiliar to almost anybody who found himself in Australia. The climate, moreover, if it allowed grape-growing at all, was bound to produce extremely sweet fruit – hence strong wine; the inclination would be to dose it with brandy, both to help it keep and to make it more port-like.

IT MUST HAVE BEEN DISORIENTING TO ARRIVE IN A LAND where not a single creature or plant was familiar. To British settlers without a tradition of vine-growing the only precedent to follow was that of a gardener. Which makes it all the more remarkable that the explorer Gregory Blaxland, hacking a farm out of the bush by the Parramatta river 12 miles inland from Sydney, was far enough advanced in the 1820s to send samples of wine to England, and to be awarded Silver (1822) and Gold (1828) medals by the Royal Society of Art. And more remarkable still that in 1823 one of the first settlers in Tasmania, the off-shore island then called Van Diemen's Land, Bartholomew Broughton, produced a vintage which, according to one taster who compared it with Blaxland's, was "as far superior as fine port to Blackstrap".

Tasmania, 500 miles south, has a very much cooler climate than New South Wales. This is the first recorded hint of a theme that has run right through the story of wine in Australia up to the present time: that the cooler the climate, the finer the wine. It found its first clear expression in a booklet *On Colonial Wines* published in 1867 by Australia's direct successor to the wine-loving priests who had for so long led the way in Europe. The Reverend John Bleasdale was a Lisbon-trained Jesuit who settled in Melbourne. "Whatever the wine is, sweet or dry, one thing is certain", he wrote; "that in hot climates you can never produce wine with the perfume peculiar to those of colder regions. . . . If you are to have the perfumed wine of France – Sauterne or fine Chablis for example – you must also have the other conditions, especially slow, long-continued fermentation at a low temperature". Bleasdale was, of course, begging one question: whether the Australians wanted fine wines or just strong ones. The fact is that from the start they made both more or less haphazardly, but the national taste favoured strength and sweetness above refinement – and so indeed did the popular taste in their export market, Britain: a situation which held back the progress of the industry for 150 years.

MOST FUNDAMENTAL, ALTHOUGH EITHER IGNORED OR JUST MUDDLED by most of the early planters, was what variety of vine to plant. Many of the first introductions were from northern Europe and almost certainly doomed to failure, either as vines or as wine, in the New South Wales climate. Probably most of the first successes were from vines collected en route at Madeira or the Cape (where, for instance, the Macarthurs collected "Black Constantia"), or indeed Rio de Janeiro, where the First Fleet had put in for provisions.

The man who turned his mind to this problem, and who has been labelled the "father of Australian wine" as a result, was a young immigrant from Edinburgh, James Busby, who with notable precociousness and foresight, before leaving for Australia with his parents at the age of 23, made a visit to France to find out what he could about wines and vines. He whiled away the months on the voyage out to Australia by writing *A Treatise on the Culture of the Vine and the Art of Making Wine*, largely culled from Chaptal, with a little from Arthur Young, but also full of such pungently original remarks as, "Constantia has a taste rather than a flavour". "The flavour of Madeira is nothing but that which we know is given by means of bitter almonds"; "the wretched Lisbon wines acquire what little taste they have from oak chips", and, concerning brandy being added to port, "of which the chief fault is that of being too strong already", the result is "fit for hogs only".

Busby's *Treatise* was addressed to the "higher classes" in New South Wales whom he supposed would be interested in wine-growing. Five years later, with experience of the realities of Australia, having managed a curious sort of orphanage which was a farm and sat at the feet of Blaxland and Macarthur, he published a smaller and extremely practical *Manual of Plain Directions* for "the class of smaller settlers" – a book which had a widespread popular influence and must have set many stumbling growers on their feet. (His father, meanwhile, had furnished Sydney with its first regular water supply.)

At the same time, with what seems extraordinary foresight, he struck out 100 miles north of Sydney to the Hunter River Valley and started a farm he called Kirkton after his Edinburgh birthplace, left it to his brother-in-law to manage, and in 1830 set sail again for Europe to deepen his knowledge of winemaking, but above all to collect suitable and correctly identified vines.

The Journal of a Tour through some of the Vineyards of France and Spain, published on his return in 1833, is an exact contemporary of Cyrus Redding's great *History*. It dispenses with literary airs and graces, but loses very little as a result. Its observations could not be more pithy or to the point. Meeting with some soldiers from Algeria, for example, he took the opportunity of quizzing them on wine-growing in a country he conceived to be similar to New South Wales. Little seems to have escaped his attention, from prices to table manners. ("Fine wine" in France he observed was drunk from a wine glass; "wine" from tumblers with water).

As for his vines, collected and labelled at Montpellier and in Paris (also at Malaga and Jerez), he contrived to have them transported free on the convict ship Camden which was on the point of sailing when he arrived in London. No less than 570 varieties arrived in Sydney in good condition. He gave a specimen of each to the Botanic Gardens on Sydney Harbour and planted the remainder at Kirkton.

By the age of 35, therefore, this driven Scotsman had told Australians how to make wine, supplied the plants, and discovered and founded, it seems almost by fluke, its first (and still one of its best) wine-growing regions. His motives were a clear-sighted mixture of business sense and philanthropy. He firmly believed that a supply of good wine would put an end to the drunkenness engendered by spirits. He also saw wine as the ideal return-voyage cargo for the convict-ships. John Bull had been let down in his first attempt at his own vineyard, in South Africa, (or second, if you count Oglethorp's madcap scheme in Georgia), chiefly, said Busby, by the idleness and bad husbandry of the Boers. There was no reason for Australia to fail – and there was the whole Indian empire, besides Britain, as a market.

This quixotic young man – his portrait shows a sensitive, saturnine face – did not stay to see his dreams to fruition, to advise Australia, or even to make wine. He departed for New Zealand in 1833 with the appointment of British Resident. But his legacy was vital.

THE HUNTER VALLEY TURNED OUT TO HAVE A CURIOUS LOCAL CLIMATE that mitigated the heat of the New South Wales sun with a regular afternoon haze; often clouds would roll in from the ocean to form as it were parasol over the baking vines. Port-minded or not, such early settlers as George Wyndham and Adam Roth found themselves making wine they likened to burgundy. One of the early growers, James King, exhibited sparkling wines among others at the Paris Exhibition of 1855 (the same at which the famous classification of Bordeaux was made known) and, no doubt to his astonishment, one of his wines (along with one from Camden Park) was chosen to be served to Napoleon III at the state banquet that closed the exhibition.

The official report of the exhibition judges, quoted by James Halliday in his historical account of "the Hunter", read: "The [Hunter Valley] wines included white wines akin to those of the Rhine; red light wines like those of Burgundy; Mousseux varieties with a bouquet, body and flavour equal to the first Champagnes; Muscats and other sweet wines, rivalling the Montignac of the Cape." "Montignac" seems to have slipped from history, but the verdict is unequivocal. Within 25 years of Busby's Hunter Valley enterprise New South Wales wine had entered European high society. Not surprisingly, a grape-rush filled the valley. In the 1860s and '70s, its acreage multiplied several times. If it did not last (and things went very quiet later in the century) it was because all Australia's large wine companies, even those such as Lindemans and MacWilliams which had grown up in the Hunter Valley, found the taste for table wines was a minority one. The money was to be made from ports, sherries or muscats grown in hotter areas elsewhere.

FORMAL FEDERATION DID NOT COME TO AUSTRALIA until 1901. The different regions of the continent were separately explored and developed. South Australia was started as an independent colony in 1836; Victoria in 1837 as part of New South Wales (becoming a state in its own right in 1851). Both had vines from the moment of their inception and strangely, both received their first plants from the not very significant island of Tasmania off the south coast.

The matter of precedence in any case is unimportant. What matters is that both Adelaide and Melbourne proved excellent vineyard country; cooler and less humid than Sydney, and capable from the first of making extremely good wines.

Perhaps the most auspicious start was made by a Devonshire farmer's son called John Reynell in the "Southern Vales" just south of Adelaide in 1838. He brought cuttings from the Cape and was encouraged by Sir William Macarthur (whose nursery at Camden must have seemed almost as far away). By the time, a dozen years later, he took on another Devonshire immigrant called Tom Hardy as a labourer he had already built the unique cellar which still squats, a half-submerged barn like an enormous grassy burial mound, beside his beautiful verandahed farmhouse. It is typical of Australia's story that Reynella, the most perfectly-preserved of the country's original wineries, is now the headquarters of Thomas Hardy and Sons, descendants of the muscular young Tom.

In the 1840s wine-farms (the drab word winery had not been invented) were springing up all around Adelaide, each with its stirring, or touching, or funny story of another hopeful immigrant, for the most part British, prepared to work every daylight hour for the freedom and satisfaction (and even the money) that winemaking brought. In the hills at Magill overlooking Adelaide from the east the young Dr Christopher Penfold from Sussex started both a general practice and one of Australia's most famous vineyards, with a view out to the distant Saint Vincent gulf. The practice came first: wine-growing was an after-thought, as he discovered how wonderfully his patients cheered up when he prescribed a glass.

THE FAMOUS EXCEPTION TO THE ANGLO-SAXON DOMINATION OF South Australian wine-growing is the Barossa Valley, 30 miles north-east of Adelaide, which was colonised in 1841 by a philanthropic Scot, George Angas, as a profitable means of releasing dissenters from religious persecution. Angas was the chief executive of the South Australian Company, established to assist emigration to the new colony. Hearing that Lutheran dissenters were being persecuted in Silesia, on the borders or Prussia and Poland – not by any means wine country – he chartered three ships and offered passages and land to farmers who would volunteer. Other parts of the Barossa Valley and the hills and vales around were taken in hand by such families as the Smiths of Yalumba (Samuel Smith was an English brewer; his family is still at Yalumba), but the whole cultural tilt of the region was determined by the Lutheran influx. Other more prosperous Germans came too: most notably the Gramps and the Seppelts, who became major forces in the economy of the colony. In the 1900s Seppeltsfield was South Australia's largest and most spectacular winery by far, with avenues of palm-trees reaching for miles (as they still do). Most of the Silesians simply became grape-growers, and multiplied their prim little churches and grape clusters all over the valley. They did not abandon dissenting when they abandoned Silesian rain for Barossa sun. Quite the contrary; during the Second World War their steadfast point of view called for an internment camp in the Barossa valley. It is perhaps fanciful to suggest that there is a direct connection between the valley's German settlers and its affinity with Rhine Riesling. Much the greater part of its production has always been fortified wines and brandy. Nonetheless, soft, strong and baked brown as they may have been, Rieslings have long been a special feature

Dr Christopher Penfold was the first of a long line of Australian medical doctors who have made wine. Penfold's name lives on: the firm, founded in 1844, was family-controlled until 1962 and their Grange Hermitage is recognized as Australia's first-growth.

of "the Barossa". The valley floor is categorically too hot to suit such a northern vine, but the stony uplands around are not, and now produce some of the best Rhine Riesling in Australia.

A MUCH LATER DEVELOPMENT OF SOUTH AUSTRALIAN WINE-GROWING, which gave it the new dimension of an altogether cooler climate, as well as some quite exceptional soil conditions, was the foundation in 1890 of the "Penola Fruit Colony", in the south of the state between Coonawarra and Mount Gambier and not far from the sea. It was a speculative venture by one John Riddoch, a Scotsman who had accumulated well over 100,000 acres of freehold land, besides many square miles of leasehold grazing and scarcely countable sheep. He was advised by another Scot, a gardener from Fife named Wilson, who had served in the army in the (then British) Greek Ionian islands and turned his green fingers to vine-growing, that the red soil of a very small part of his property was priceless. Riddoch advertised 10-acre blocks for sale, and built a wonderful winery building (familiar today on Wynn's labels), the plan being that he would buy all the grapes – as indeed he did. The magnificent venture and the notion of Coonawarra wine, however, died with the man, not to be seriously revived until the 1950s.

What was to become the state of Victoria was settled from two directions at once: from the sea at Melbourne on Port Phillip Bay, and overland from New South Wales in 1837 by William Ryrie, who brought with him both sheep and (Macarthur) vine-cuttings. The two could almost be called the armorial attributes of the infant state. Ryrie settled in the beautiful Yarra valley just north of Melbourne, and it was there, and in Melbourne itself, and at Geelong just along the bay, that the 1840s saw the first successes of Victorian wine.

Of Australia's three first centres of population southern Victoria came much the closest to the cool conditions John Bleasdale had recommended. It also had the fortuitous advantage of a leading citizen, and from 1851 a first Governor, who was a native of a European wine region.

Charles La Trobe had lived at Neuchâtel in Switzerland, where he had prudently married a very well-connected lady. He was so greatly taken with

VINOUS MISNOMERS

Australia's confusion about exactly which grape variety is which has lasted into modern times; if not in the minds of specialists, at least in the minds and on the labels of more rustic winemakers. The most famous misnomer is the "Hunter Riesling", which is really the Sémillon. Sémillon suited New South Wales from the start and was for many years its most-planted high-quality white variety. (Today it is challenged by Chardonnay). What was grown as "Clare Riesling" in the Clare valley in South Australia was assumed to be the same until recently, when it was identified as a much more pedestrian variety, the Crouchen, apparently introduced from Austria. Certainly its Clare wine has nothing to apologize for. But Barossa's Riesling, on the other hand, is the real McCoy. Two warm-climate white varieties that can excel in Australia are Madeira's Verdelho and the Marsanne of the Rhône valley – to say nothing of the Muscat.

Much the most important red-wine grape in Australia from the beginning has been the Syrah (of the Rhône), under its Australian noms de verre of Shiraz or Hermitage. It is ideally suited to hot dry vineyards and will make a passable performance of anything from strong dry rosé to "port". It still makes, in the Barossa valley, Australia's single greatest wine, "Grange Heritage", although fashion has steadily abandoned it in favour of the Cabernet Sauvignon.

Melbourne and the country around that he and his wife's family prevailed on two more Swiss families, the de Castellas and the de Purys, along with two winegrowers called Deschamps, to emigrate and settle in the Yarra valley.

Paul de Castella, a native of Gruyère (which is scarcely the heart of Swiss wine-country) bought the Ryrie property of Yering and soon caught the wine bug. He was not content with Camden cuttings: he acquired 20,000 three-footers from Château Lafite. Trailing him by some years was his brother Hubert, who modestly called his vineyard St Hubert's: by 1875 it covered 200 acres. Baron de Pury's property (where his descendants still live) is called Yeringberg. Together with the more famous Chateau Tahbilk, on the Goulburn River in the heart of Victoria, Yeringberg is a priceless, almost unaltered relic of the highly enjoyable Victorian heyday of a century ago.

The atmosphere of the Yarra valley is very different from the Hunter or the Barossa. All are beautiful in their low-key, soft-contoured Australian way: Lilydale and Coldstream, the villages of the Yarra, particularly so. The Yarra valley has never made the sort of wine that in Australia grows big wineries; it is too cool, and it was (and still is) the fixed intention of its settlers to make the finest table wines they could. They sent them to competitions in Europe, and Europe accepted them without question. Medals from Vienna in 1873, Brussels in 1876, and Bordeaux in 1882 tell the story in gold, silver and bronze.

THE HUMAN FACE OF VICTORIA WAS CHANGED ALMOST OVERNIGHT by the gold-rush of 1851; by a strange coincidence only three years after gold-fever had hit California. It

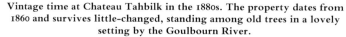

Vintage time at Chateau Tahbilk in the 1880s. The property dates from 1860 and survives little-changed, standing among old trees in a lovely setting by the Goulbourn River.

Tahbilk's current range of wines – white Marsanne, Riesling, Cabernet and Shiraz reds – echoes the wines that made Victoria famous a century ago. Phylloxera, which arrived in this country at about the same time, is still a problem at Chateau Tahbilk.

brought in the manpower and the money to expand wine-growing from the little base around Port Phillip Bay all over the state. Immigrants who poured in in the '50s prospected everywhere: there was no single "mother lode". If they failed to find gold (or when it ran out) they planted vines. The wine-growing map of Victoria can only be explained in these terms: a haphazard scattering of vineyards where the gold was, and some where it wasn't. In the 1870s and '80s the gold-fields of Ballarat, of Bendigo, of Great Western, and up on the Murray River in the north-east round Rutherglen all turned their energies to winemaking – with considerable success, even if more by luck than judgment.

Untutored and uninhibited, they discovered for themselves the sort of wines their soils and climates dictated – and also what the market would buy. Some turned out to be great originals: no dessert muscat in the world since Constantia has had the astonishing honeyed-velvet quality of some from north-east Victoria. On the whole, though, it was the cheap, sweet and strong that would sell – also the fizzy.

The thriving multiplication of vineyards all over Victoria would probably have resulted in its becoming Australia's most viticultural state, but for the arrival of phylloxera on a shipment of vines to Geelong on Port Phillip Bay in 1877. Slowly but inexorably, helped by the prevailing southwest winds, it found its way to almost all the scattered plantings of vines in the state and wiped them out. A few, such as Chateau Tahbilk, were at least partly protected by having sandy soil; others, such as Great Western, by their remoteness (and position slightly up-wind). It took nearly 20 years for the pest to reach Rutherglen in the north east of the state – where it stopped: there were hundreds of miles of vineless grazing land in southern NSW.

The means to combat phylloxera by grafting were available. Unfortunately Australians had already demonstrated their lack of enthusiasm for the delicate table wines of the southern areas that were worst affected. There was no point in replanting while all the demand was for wines that South Australia could so easily provide.

Providentially the pest was never delivered alive to Adelaide, nor do winds from Victoria blow that way. South Australia therefore remained phylloxera-free, with the Victorian market at its feet.

Inland Victoria, warmer and more generous than the Yarra valley, rapidly overtook it in the market. However fine the cool-climate wines were, the time was not ripe, and vineyards gradually gave way again to grazing.

THE OLDEST WINE-FARM STILL IN PRODUCTION in Australia is in none of the regions we have visited, but 2,000 miles nearer "home", as the settlers' ships sailed, on the banks of the Swan River in Western Australia. The vine rooted there in 1829, several years before it was introduced to either South Australia or Victoria. Conditions here are hotter even than in the Barossa valley: the natural produce is very strong wine indeed. It is typical of Australian resourcefulness that in such an area one of the country's classic originals was born. The "White Burgundy", made since the 1920s by Houghton's (founded in 1840, and still in the suburbs of Perth) contrives to be soft yet intense, full of flavour but remarkably refreshing.

The sad part of the story, here as in all of Australia, was that for most of the existence of the industry the overwhelming demand was simply for strong drink, sweet or dry. Coonawarra offered South Australia all the possibilities of a cooler climate in the 1890s. The same thing happened at the same time in Western Australia. Two hundred miles south of Perth the Margaret River was discovered to be an excellent source of grapes for good table wine, cooled by the breezes off the Indian Ocean. Both shared the fate of the Yarra valley: no demand.

Australia is the France of the southern hemisphere: there seems to be no limit to her potential (enormously reinforced by modern technology) for producing ideally-balanced, delicate wine very much in the French style (though with original touches of her own). But potential alone has never been enough. Fine wine has only been made at moments in history when the market has asked for it.

One anecdote, painful as it is to relate, sums up the attitude that held back Australia's potential for a century and a half. The time is the 1930s; the place, London. The sales director of a famous South Australian company is visiting the buyer of an important chain of British stores. Having been kept waiting for two hours he is briefly admitted to the buyer's office for a short and very depressing discussion, uniquely about prices. At the end of the interview he offers his samples, carefully cradled over 12,000 miles. "Samples be damned", was the buyer's answer. "If the wine's no good I'll send it back."

There is a tendency to believe that all Australia's old-style wines, before the advent of modern technology, were crude and boozy. It is sadly misleading. Even in some very hot areas with primitive winemaking conditions and no training but experience, gifted winemakers were at work following their own inclinations with characteristic self-respect and extraordinary effectiveness.

On my first visit to Australia in 1966 I was captivated by deep earthy dry red Hermitage and soft golden "Hocks" that are the anthithesis of currently fashionable taste. They were made without benefit of refrigeration, aged for remarkable periods in old oak casks in cellars that were by no means cool; yet winemakers knew their "material" and some made spectacularly good use of it – which makes it all the more sad that their efforts were ignored except by their grateful neighbours, and a diminutive band of fanatics who followed their every bottling. Indeed Australian wine history has probably been recorded and studied in greater detail than that of any other country. Its sheer originality makes it a richly rewarding subject, and its remaining historical bottles priceless relics.

CHAPTER 35

EAST COAST, WEST COAST

Northerica made its first appearance in our story when Leif Erikson was moved by the great vines clambering and cascading in its forests to call it Vinland. Much the same feature of their new surroundings must have struck the 16th-century seamen who made their landfall much further south. Huguenot refugees from the Wars of Religion in France, building their cabins in Florida near where Jacksonville now stands, must have been nonplussed by the peculiar vines that congested the woods, vines whose huge grapes grew not in tight bunches but spaced apart in clusters and whose tough skins slipped off, leaving the flesh like a slimy marble. Having no others, they tried to make wine of sorts from these grapes, and found it strong, very dry or harsh, but better than no wine at all. And the pattern was repeated, almost everywhere settlers landed along the east coast: there were plenty of grapes, none of them familiar, and nobody much liked their wine.

Looking around among the wonderful woods of this wilderness, coming right down to the shore in many places, countrymen and gardeners among the settlers, wherever they came from in Europe, found themselves half-recognizing many plants. Instead of one kind of oak there were a dozen more or less oak-like trees – none of them the familiar *Quercus robur* that framed their ships. It was the same with vines: the differences in leaf were no greater, perhaps, than between two varieties of *Vitis vinifera*. Not all fruit was as bizarre as the Scuppernong grape of Florida. But its wine was hard to take. Why, therefore, take it? Why not bring cuttings over and plant this fertile virgin soil with the grapes of Burgundy, Bordeaux and the Rhine?

The 17th and 18th centuries are a repetitive saga of wasted effort, trying to do what appeared so simple. Wheat, beans, apples – almost everything else from Europe grew. When it failed there was usually some obvious and visible reason in the shape of a caterpillar or a hurricane, a blistering heat or weeks without a thaw. In the end, when Lord Delaware, Governor Winthrop, Lord Baltimore, William Penn (to name only four of hundreds who invested money, time and effort) had lavished care on their imported vines – Penn planted 200 acres – and their vines had all died, the consensus was – quite rightly – that the extremes of climate of the east coast are unfriendly to the European vine, and that a variety of insect pests were ready to finish off the struggling plant.

THIS WAS THE SITUATION IN THE 1770s when the most famous, and one of the most determined, of America's amateur scientists, gardeners and naturalists joined the fray. Thomas Jefferson not only had a taste for wine, which we have seen him cultivating in France; he was also convinced that lack of wine, except of the expensive imported kind, was driving America to strong drink. He welcomed the legislation which in 1791 put an excise tax on liquor, but exempted American-made wines. "I rejoice", he wrote, "as a moralist, at the prospect of a reduction of the duties on wine by our national legislature. It is an error to view a tax on that liquor as merely a tax on the rich. . . . No nation is drunken where wine is cheap; and none sober, where the dearness of wine substitutes ardent spirits as the common beverage. It is, in truth, the only antidote to the bane of whiskey."

The moral question overrode in his mind considerable reservations he formed in France about wine-growing as an economic form of agriculture. "The culture of the vine", he wrote, "is not desirable in lands capable of growing anything else. . . . It is a resource for a country, the whole of whose good soil is otherwise employed, and which still has some barren spots, and surplus of population to employ on them. There the vine is good, because it is in the place of nothing".

Long before he went to France he experimented on his estate in Virginia, and encouraged friends and neighbours to do likewise. The most ambitious of these projects was the invitation, originally issued by Thomas Adams to a Florentine named Philip Mazzei, to import Tuscan winegrowers and vines from the best vineyards of Europe to give the Virginian wine industry the best possible start.

PHILIP MAZZEI

Mazzei, though a failure as a winegrower, is one of the more intriguing bit-part players in our story. He was born in 1730 into a Tuscan family of merchants and brandy distillers and showed signs of being a free-thinker from an early age. Interested, but not qualified, in medicine he went to Smyrna in Turkey to practise, then to London as an importer and merchant of Mediterranean delicacies. In London he met Benjamin Franklin and Thomas Adams, who must have been attracted by this unusual merchant's ideas; together they formed a project for a 4,000-acre plantation of vines, olive-trees, fruit and mulberry trees in Virginia. London investors were not convinced, though, and he finally sailed from Livorno in 1773 with ten winegrowers and the blessing of the Grand Duke of Tuscany.

When they arrived in Virginia, Thomas Jefferson more or less took them over and settled them on the hill next to Monticello, where Mazzei built a house, which he called Colle. Mazzei and Jefferson became firm friends and he began to move in the loftiest Virginian circles, writing to George Washington that "this country is better calculated than any other I am acquainted with for the produce of wine; but I cannot say the same in regard to oil and lemons" – this last in view of a great frost that should have made it clear that Virginia is no Tuscany. Mazzei, like many others, was overwhelmed by the size and variety of native vines, claiming that his Tuscans had identified "two hundred varieties of wild grape". Their wine "when I pulled the cork three months later – was like the sparkling wine of Champagne" (presumably it was still fermenting). He was, however, no farmer, and became, like all Virginians at the time, more deeply interested in politics than cultivation. The War of Independence saw his interest in Colle evaporate and his winegrowers do likewise. In 1779 he rented the property to a Hessian officer, Baron von Riedesel, who had been serving with the British forces and been made prisoner at Saratoga. Thomas Jefferson's own words can finish the story: "Riedesel's horses in one week destroyed the whole labor of three or four years; and thus ended an experiment which, from every appearance, would in a year or two more have established the practicability of that branch of culture in America".

The dining room at Jefferson's Monticello. A dumb waiter beside the fireplace communicates directly with the cellar, bypassing even the kitchen. Priorities were firmly established.

Mazzei's experiments were frustrated by the events of the War of Independence, and he moved on to Poland and further adventures. One Tuscan, however, Anthony Giannini, stayed on at Monticello and became Jefferson's estate manager, continuing to experiment with vines during Jefferson's three-year absence. The Monticello vineyard has recently been reconstructed, staked out boldly on the steep slope under the garden wall. How dogged these efforts were is shown by the fact that in 1802, almost 30 years after his first essays with European vines, Jefferson was still importing cuttings – and still none of them lived for long.

What finally seems to have altered his view, and reconciled him to the fact that America must make the best of its own vines, was the influence of a surveyor in Georgetown, John Adlum, who had served in the war as a major. In October 1809 Jefferson wrote to Adlum, "I think it would be well to push the culture of that grape [Fox grape] without losing our time and efforts in search of foreign vines, which it will take centuries to adapt to our soil and climate. . . ." He went on to ask for cuttings of this vine, the Alexander, a seedling (possibly a chance hybrid between the American *Vitis labrusca* and a plant of *Vitis vinifera*) found by the eponymous gardener to Governor John Penn (William's son) in Philadelphia. "I have drank of the wine", wrote Jefferson; "It resembles the Comartin Burgundy". Could he have meant Chambertin?

From this time on Jefferson became increasingly reconciled to the strange taste and smell, known as "foxy", of American vines; particularly the hardy and prolific *Vitis labrusca*, which Jancis Robinson describes (and who can contradict her?) as "like an artificial strawberry drink". By 1817 he was convinced that the Scuppernong might be used to make fine wine, even if he was a trifle confused as to exactly how. North Carolina's "Scuppernon wine . . . would be distinguished on the best tables of Europe, for its fine aroma, ('resembling Frontiniac', he says elsewhere) and chrystalline transparence. Unhappily that aroma, in most of the samples I have seen, has been entirely submerged in brandy. This coarse taste and practice is the peculiarity of the Englishmen, and of their apes, Americans. I hope it will be discontinued. . . ." Jefferson, in his seventies, was growing a little tetchy; even perhaps forgetting the taste of French wine.

But Scuppernong wine, it seems, cannot be made without brandy. A report of the North Carolina Agriculture Experimental Station in 1909 describes the process. The grapes are squeezed "in a cider press as soon as they are gathered, when it is put in a clean barrel. In every three quarts of grape juice one quart of brandy is added. . . . Some have tried fermentation but it did not answer." It is, in other words, to use the good old Dutch term, a "stum" wine.

ADLUM, MEANWHILE, HAD HAD A LUCKY FIND OF HIS OWN, a vine growing beside an inn in Maryland, transplanted there from North Carolina in 1802. He took cuttings, was delighted with the resulting wine, and named the vine Tokay. In 1823 he sent a bottle to the octogenarian Jefferson, who found it "truly a fine wine, of high flavour, and as you assure me there was not a drop of brandy or other spirit in it, I may say it is a wine of a good body of its own". Jefferson thus, three years before he died, tasted the first all-American wine that would make his dreams come true. The "Tokay" was soon after renamed by Adlum the Catawba, after the river in North Carolina.

The Catawba was to be not a stop-gap, but a smash-hit, in the hands of America's first big-time commercial winemaker, the diminutive Nicholas Longworth (he stood five foot one) from New Jersey.

THE LONGWORTH STORY STARTED WITH HIS OPENING A LAW PRACTICE IN CINCINNATI, in the brand new state of Ohio, in 1803. He grew rich and bought land. Like Jefferson, he believed in combating the evils of whiskey with wine and in 1823 he began planting vines on the banks of the Ohio river. At first he suffered the time-honoured frustration of watching thousands of European vines die. Then Major Adlum came to his rescue. In 1825 Adlum sent him cuttings of Catawba; by 1842 he was growing 1,200 acres and making America's first sparkling wine.

Allowing for journalistic hyperbole, it seems that not only America but Europe became enamoured of his strange strawberryish liquor. Leon Adams quotes from *The Illustrated London News* of 1858, which described the Still Catawba as " a finer wine of the hock species and flavour than any hock that comes from the Rhine", and allowed that Sparkling Catawba "transcends the Champagne of France".

Henry Longfellow, then Professor of English at Harvard, bestowed literary immortality in his *Ode to Catawba Wine* of 1854 – he was practising for *Hiawatha* (1858) at the time:

VIRGINIA DARE

America's most successful winemaker in the years leading to Prohibition (and just after Repeal) was living proof that Jefferson was right – up to a point. The winemaker was Paul Garrett from North Carolina, and his wine was called Virginia Dare – appropriately, the name of the first child born of English parents in America in the 17th century (which also just happens to sound like a comic-strip heroine). Virginia Dare was a blend of Scuppernong juice, with its strange plummy and musky scent, with typically foxy and strawberryish eastern wines and a good measure of relatively neutral California wine for bulk and strength.

The Temperance movement drove Garrett out of the south in 1913, and he established Virginia Dare wineries in Upper New York State and Cucamonga south of Los Angeles. When Prohibition was repealed Virginia Dare was the first wine to be nationally available.

"Very good in its way
Is the Verzenay,
Or the Sillery soft and creamy;
But Catawba wine
Has a taste more divine,
More dulcet, delicious and dreamy".

IN 1859 OHIO, "THE RHINE OF AMERICA", HAD A THIRD OF ALL THE VINES in the United States and made twice as much wine as California. But Cincinnati's story as America's wine capital ended even more suddenly than it began: fungus diseases caught hold and ravaged the vineyards. Longworth died. The Civil War broke out. By the time it was over so was the idea of America's Rhine – but not the career of the vine in Ohio. Growers moved north and established themselves in the more temperate and breezy conditions of Lake Erie and its islands, where rot and mildew were not a problem. By 1870 America's largest winery was to be found in the unlikely setting of Middle Bass Island, off-shore from Sandusky, which also had huge vineyards. For a while, just after the Civil War, Missouri challenged Ohio as the state with most vines. On Lake Erie the Catawba continued to flourish until the Temperance movement called a temporary halt to operations.

The rural idyll in the Ohio vineyards is contrasted with the smoky paddle-steamers forging westward down the river. The illustration dates from the 1860s, and is taken from an advertising pamphlet issued by Longworth's Ohio wine company, which at the time was producing copious amounts of sparkling wine.

An even greater, and far longer-running, success story than the Catawba was a native *Vitis labrusca* seedling selected by one Ephraim Wales Bull at Concord, near Boston in Massachusetts, in 1849. The Concord, as he named his grape, has all the winemaking faults of *Vitis labrusca* in the highest degree: indeed the wine made from it, unblended with alleviating juice of something less pungent, is almost undrinkable. Alas it is the easiest fruit to grow. As the basis of America's grape-jelly industry it is all too available to winemakers in the north-east and has tainted their wine, and the reputation of their industry, right up until modern times.

NOT SO FAR TO HAVE MADE MENTION OF CALIFORNIA IS NOT AN OVERSIGHT, it is to stress the totally separate origins and evolution of winemaking on the west coast. And yet, curiously, we can start the clock there running in the very year when Thomas Jefferson, in the elegance and comfort of his Virginia plantation, received and planted his first experimental vines. It was in that year, 1769, that the frontiersman Franciscan friar, Father Junipero Serra, set foot for the first time in what is now the United States, at San Diego, California, as part of the process of a combined missionary and military occupation of the west coast.

Why had the Spanish, who had by then occupied Mexico for more than 250 years, left it so long before paying any attention to Upper California? Surely its coastline must have tempted them north. It has good harbours (though not many) and forests and grazing land as fine as any in Texas or New Mexico. The answer seems to be simply that the Spanish were fully occupied in the south where the Indians had showed them that there was silver and gold. As far as anyone knew there was no treasure to be found by going north, so no-one went until, in the second half of the 18th century, the natural question arose: who was eventually to occupy this land? The empire-building British could not be ruled out; settlers from the United States were steadily probing further and further west, and even Russians were building cabins down the coast; fur-trappers from Alaska attracted to this bountiful unclaimed land.

SPARKLING NEW YORK

Vines have been grown in Upper New York State, in the Chautauqua region south of Buffalo, since 1818 and in the Finger Lakes district to the east since the Civil War. Most of the Chautauqua grapes are Concord, used for eating, or juice or jelly rather than winemaking. In the 1860s the Pleasant Valley Wine Company started using the better-quality derivatives of America's native grapes at Hammondsport, the centre of the Finger Lakes region. It took up where Nicholas Longworth had left off and similarly specialised in sparkling wine; even calling it Sparkling Catawba, until in 1870 a judge coined the name Great Western by exclaiming "This'll be the great Champagne of the West!".

To legitimise the Champagne connection the company took the rather unorthodox measure of calling its own post office Rheims.

The Pleasant Valley Company was joined at Hammondsport in 1865 by the Urbana Wine Company, which coined the name Gold Seal for its products, and set out to raise the standard of Finger Lakes Wine to international level. Champagne-makers from Louis Roederer, Moët et Chandon and Veuve Clicquot have all directed its operations.

The third in time, and later the biggest of the Hammondsport wineries, was founded in 1880 by Walter Taylor. These three firms upheld the idea of all-American wine flavours (though modified a little with juice from California) until after Prohibition, when a new race of hardy hybrid grapes gave them more interesting possibilities.

Spanish politics were clear on this point: western America belonged to Spain, so it must be occupied, however symbolically and half-heartedly. Hence the chain of missions that spread relatively quickly up the coast from San Diego: 21 in all, the northernmost just north of San Francisco Bay at Sonoma. To the missions, wine-growing was both incidental and essential. It was also easy. The west coast has two native grape-vines; they make undrinkable wine, but they have no significant specific pests or diseases. The dry climate of Southern California discourages fungi. So nothing invisible and sinister stood in the fathers' way.

They only troubled with a single grape, which presumably had come from Spain centuries before. Its name, the Mission, is little help. In South America it is called the Criolla, which means colonialized European. Certainly it is a variety of *Vitis vinifera*, but of very modest quality: an early-maturing dark-skinned bag of sweet juice; no more.

Nor did the Franciscans share the high-tech aspirations of their Cistercian brothers: the only instruction book we know they possessed was a general agricultural treatise first published in Spain in 1513. An approximate account of their winemaking methods was given years later, by Charles Krug, based on his experience in 1859 investigating the Napa Valley. He had been offered "a tin cup full of elegant claret which was fermented in large cow-hides lassoed between trees, and filled with grapes crushed by Indians. In the lowest place of the hide stuck a little plug and by pulling it out the cup was filled with the glorious drink."

Not surprisingly, a large proportion of the Mission wine was distilled to make a spirit which could at least be kept, and was probably used to fortify and preserve the rest of the wine (not that for the altar, which in theory should have been "pure").

Missions varied in the success and scale of their wine-growing. San Gabriel at Los Angeles was much the biggest (when it was secularised, in the 1830s, it possessed over 160,000 vines, and produced an annual 35,000 gallons, making it the first sizeable winery in California). According to Father Narciso Duran, in charge of winemaking at Santa Barbara and San José, San Gabriel also made the best Mission wine. Only two of the 21 missions made no wine: Santa Cruz and Dolores, in what is now San Francisco, where the climate was too cold and foggy.

The Mexican government secularized the missions in 1833. In the half-century of their existence they had introduced wine-growing to California – without refinement, but as an established fact. By the time they finished their work, or even before, there were others ready to build on what they had begun: most notably around their proven success, San Gabriel. It was Los Angeles where the secular wine industry of California took off; to be precise, exactly where Union Station now stands. Its prime mover was an immigrant from Bordeaux, from the town of Cadillac where the abbé Bellet had kept his painstaking record of grapes that were rotten and grapes that were not. The obvious predestination in his name, Jean-Louis Vignes, had not prevented him from trying his hand at rum-making in Honolulu and the Sandwich Islands, before arriving at Monterey just as Mexico's newly-won independence was sending ripples of uncertainty up the coast.

After a short stay in Monterey and San Diego, Vignes managed to buy 100 acres close to the river and the pueblo of Los Angeles, named it Rancho El Aliso, and set out straight away to plant vines. He appears to have been the first Californian to look beyond the Mission grape: he ordered plants from France (presumably Bordeaux) via Boston and Cape Horn. Members of his family followed (speaking the Gascon dialect, they found it easy to communicate in Spanish). By 1851 he had 40,000 vines producing 1,000 barrels of wine a year (as well as California's first orange groves). He is even said to have shipped barrels of wine to Boston and back, Madeira-style, to age it.

His friend William Heath Davis, who helped him sell his wines, has left us a picture of a well-contented man. "Don Luis [as he was known] was truly one of the most enlightened pioneers of the coast . . . full of history of wine matters . . . and overflowing with brilliant anticipation of the future. . . . His choice old wine could be drunk with impunity. . . . He was generous to the poor; in their distress he helped them with bread, money and wine. . . . It is to be hoped that historians will do justice to his character, his labors and his foresight."

A contrary view of contemporary California wine – admittedly not of Vignes' – was voiced by an English visitor, Sir George Simpson of the Hudson's Bay Company: "with the exception of what we got at the Mission of Santa Barbara, the native wine, that we tasted, was such trash as nothing but politeness could have induced us to swallow".

AT THIS POINT THERE IS A DIRECT COMPARISON TO BE MADE between California and Australia. Australia's first wine regions (the Hunter Valley, southern Victoria, the Adelaide area and the Swan River) were all initiated in the same decade, the 1830s, as the Missions of California were disbanded. If Australia took off more quickly, planting more varied vines in a more enquiring spirit, it was due to two things: the omnipresence of the Mission grape in California as a disincentive to experiment, and the lack of any organizing authority such as Britain was to its colonies. The mother hen, however far away, was constantly bossing and exhorting her chicks (and sending them supplies). California's Spanish start had to be overcome before there could be real progress. Settlers scattered like bird-shot all over the state, and it was to be a long time before Californians came to understand their great empty land; above all its climate, dominated by the cold Pacific alongside.

In Australia (other things being equal) north means hotter; south means cooler. But in much of California you can almost say that east and west take the relative places of north and south: the further you go from the ocean, the hotter the climate. Above all what matters most to any developing enterprise is the market, and here, too, there was a big difference between the two wine-lands. In Australia the gold rush accelerated what was already happening: in California it changed the name, address, and rules of the game.

DON LUIS RETIRED IN 1855, SELLING EL ALISO TO HIS NEPHEW Jean-Louis Sansevain, who had the very reasonable idea that events up north called for champagne. In 1848 gold had been discovered at Sutter's Mill. Suddenly it was San Francisco, Sacramento and the gold country where the market was. Sansevain's "champagne", for some reason, was not the greatest success and he ran into difficulties. But two wily German musicians, Kohler (flute) and Frohling (fiddle) set up an efficient two-ended operation; Frohling making wine in Los Angeles and Kohler selling it in San Francisco. Evidently they had the right formula. By the mid '50s they were desperate for grapes. Their answer was to organize a colony on the Santa Ana river in Orange County, just south of Los Angeles, and offer 20-acre blocks, already irrigated and fenced (nothing grows without irrigation in Los Angeles), to their fellow-countrymen. To make them feel at home they called it Anaheim. By 1862, when Frohling died, they had an agent in New York and were selling Anaheim wine in most of the principal cities of the Union.

Such success brought in investors from far and near. The 1870s saw the climax of Los Angeles winemaking; a scheme to build the world's largest winery at San Gabriel. How little California changes! It was not built; by this time northern California had got into its stride. The climate of Los Angeles limited its possibilities to strong or sweet wines; the north, it seemed, could turn its hand to any style. Providence was particularly unkind to the growers of Anaheim. In 1885 a mysterious disease hit their vines like one of the plagues of Egypt. Today we know that "Anaheim disease" is a bacterial infection. In the 1880s it was simply a message to move north.

THE TINY SONOMA MISSION, THE NORTHERNMOST OF THE CHAIN, had been established for only nine years when in 1833 the order came from Mexico to disestablish it (just as Napoleon, a bare generation before, had sent the monks packing from Kloster Eberbach and Cîteaux). Lieutenant Mariano Vallejo was sent from Mexico to see to it, and in the mission's place to build a barracks and lay out a town. There was unusual urgency in these orders: the Mexican government had noted a distinct look of permanence about what the Russians were doing only a few miles north at Fort Ross. (History does not record what grape variety they planted in their vineyard on that clammy piece of coast.)

Vallejo was only a lieutenant, 26 years old, but he had no senior officer in California. He was, ipso facto, commander in chief of Mexico's California army, with absolute power. Over the next 30 years he was to devote himself to the interests of California and shepherd it safely into American hands – all from Sonoma, the corner of paradise he made his own.

WINE WAS NOT VALLEJO'S FIRST PRIORITY. Already he owned some 44,000 acres of potential grazing land north of Sonoma. Soldiers and cattle between them kept him busy. It took him several seasons to refurbish the already tangled mission vineyard, and he was content to let the Indians tread the grapes in cowhides, mission-style. One subtle refinement was that the first juice to run was distinguished as "white" wine, while the result of further pounding away with Indian feet, and subsequent pressing, was "red".

Sonoma is well blessed with springs; Lachryma Montis ("tear of the mountain") was the name Vallejo gave to one which supplied the pueblo with water: and also the vineyard. Since vines needed irrigation in southern California they were irrigated here too, whether they needed it or not.

Politics must have been Vallejo's main concern. It was not the Russians, it turned out, who were coming: it was the "Yanquis". Two of his sisters married

General Mariano Vallejo, last Spanish governor of California and the first large-scale winegrower at Sonoma.

Agoston Haraszthy left California a legacy of innumerable vine varieties, perhaps including the mysterious Zinfandel.

Americans; there was a steady flow of settlers from the east with energy and ideas – and nothing from Mexico. It seemed increasingly ridiculous for Americans to be obliged to be naturalized Mexican (and baptized, to boot) to get land grants. In 1846 a headstrong group descended on Sonoma, locked up Vallejo as the effective Mexican governor, and hoisted the Bear Flag of the short-lived Republic of California, declaring Sonoma its capital. They had mistaken their man: Vallejo was already more of a Californian than any of them, and continued to lead the development of the new-born state. But the tenor of life changed radically from 1848. Vallejo heard the news of the gold-strike when he wrote to John Sutter to ask if he had a brandy still to sell. The answer came back that he had not, but that he had "made the discovery of a gold mine, which, as far as we have investigated, is extraordinarily rich".

THE PRICE OF GRAPES WENT UP WITH EVERYTHING ELSE. Grape-growers left for the gold-fields; miners brought expensive thirsts. Vallejo felt it was time to move out of the barrack block in Sonoma into a more commodious residence, and take wine-growing seriously. He built his new house, a trim verandahed villa in "carpenter's gothic", beside Lachryma Montis, Sonoma's spring, and it was here, in the early 1850s, that he greeted the man who was to revolutionize California's wine-growing, the Hungarian Agoston Haraszthy.

THERE ARE MANY PARALLELS BETWEEN HARASZTHY and Australia's James Busby. Each is known as the "father of wine-growing" in his respective adopted land. Both introduced many of the vines that were to shape the flavours of the future. Both travelled to Europe to investigate and report, in most readable journals, on the regions that every ambitious winegrower would want to emulate. They were both quixotic men who left schemes half finished because something else caught their fancy. The principal difference is that Busby, the young Scot, set his heart on wine-growing from the start, while Haraszthy, a nobleman (so he claimed) from a part of Hungary which is now in Yugoslavia, was an all-purpose adventurer who happened to pick on wine-growing to absorb the energies of his middle years.

Haraszthy arrives on the scene (and departs from it, too) in an aureole of legend. He was (it says) educated in law, served in the Austrian Imperial Guard at the age of 18 and acquired the rank of colonel, became private secretary to the Viceroy of Hungary under the Austrians, left to grow wine and silkworms on his country estate, married a Polish countess, the beautiful Eleanora de Dedinski, and became embroiled in the Magyar independence movement. Political exile was the reason he gave for suddenly taking ship from Hamburg to New York in 1840, at the age of 28. A young cousin who went with him said it was just wanderlust.

The count – or colonel, he answered to either – made straight for Wisconsin, where he formed a partnership with an Englishman named Bryant to found the town that is now Sauk City. (He called it Town Haraszthy). America was buzzing with such entrepreneurs at the time. They operated steamboats and stores, farms and construction companies. Haraszthy also found time to travel round the States and write a book encouraging his fellow-Hungarians to emigrate to this bountiful land. Indeed he went home and fetched his family and his parents himself.

News of the gold-strike in California was bound to attract Haraszthy. He had been sadly disappointed that wine was not a proposition in icy Wisconsin. The whole family and a number of friends joined the '49ers in the gruelling slog by ox-wagon down the Santa Fe trail, losing only one member, his 15-year-old son Gaza, who decided to enlist with a cavalry unit in New Mexico to see some Indian sport.

Their goal was the new town of San Diego, just developing from the little mission pueblo and with a population of 650. Haraszthy was soon (instantly, rather) speculating in real estate, running a livery stable and even a butcher's shop, and also running for election. In 1850 he became the town's first sherriff. The jailhouse he built fell down, but the gallows did its work. Then in 1854 he tired of San Diego, and went to serve on the state assembly in California's new capital, Sacramento, where he backed a move to divide the state in two. At the same time he bought land between San Francisco and the ocean: 200-odd acres near the old Mission Dolores. Was he about to settle down? If he had enquired about the mission he would have learned that its vineyard was never a success.

Haraszthy nonetheless had a bundle of vines just arived from Hungary, and he planted them. According to his son Arpad, writing years later, they included the first plants of the vine that is inextricably associated with his name: the Zinfandel, and also the Muscat of Alexandria.

There was a brisk market in San Francisco, Haraszthy discovered, for eating grapes. What he could not supply he bought in Los Angeles – the Mission grape was good to eat. Perhaps buying different varieties from "Don Luis" in Los Angeles he realised the possibilities (and the need) for more varieties in much larger numbers in North California. In any case he rapidly abandoned his foggy property and moved down the San Francisco peninsula about 25 miles to Crystal Springs, where by 1856 he had managed to acquire some 1,000 acres. Cattle, fruit trees, strawberries, grain, grapes; he raised them all. He also went into the gold-assaying business which was frantically overstretched by the flow of gold from the mines, and in no time was made the US government's smelter and refiner: the head of the San Francisco mint.

No novelist could have invented Haraszthy. There is a surprise around every corner of his life – and how many lives have had so many corners? After two years of supervising the blazing furnaces of the mint, which ran day and night, he was charged with embezzling $151,000 worth of gold. What had happened, as the jury discovered, was that the rooftops of San Francisco were liberally gilded with the specks of gold that had flown up the overheated chimney.

While the mint was too hot, Crystal Spring, Haraszthy found, was too cold. Even down the peninsula he had a fog problem: his grapes were failing to ripen. In his mind's eye he had an earthly paradise north of the Bay where he had called on General Vallejo. Sitting on the porch of Lachryma Montis, the legend runs, he had sipped his host's wine and delivered the deathless line, "General, this stuff ain't bad!" In January 1857 he bought 560 acres almost next door to Vallejo and set his son Attila to planting cuttings from Crystal Springs, while he projected a sort of Pompeian villa to be called Buena Vista.

This is where his contribution to California's wine-growing really began. In contrast to the General and everyone else, he planted dry slopes with no possibility of irrigation. Most of his vines were still the faithful old Mission, but there was no mistaking the difference in quality that dry-farming made. Furthermore he persuaded a dozen prominent San Franciscans to invest with him in the new experiment. Charles Krug, shortly to become the virtual founder of the Napa Valley wine industry and the deadly rival of Sonoma, was among them.

ZINFANDEL

Haraszthy's son Arpad claimed that his father was the first to import the Zinfandel vine into California. Many doubt the claim, since a grape with the same name was already being offered by the most famous eastern nursery, Prince's of Long Island, New York, in 1830 as "Black Zinfardel [there are several spellings] from Hungary", and many Californians bought trial vines from the east coast.

Whoever introduced it, the Zinfandel is an excellent all-round red grape for California, and has almost (but not quite) done the job that the Shiraz has done in Australia. Zinfandel has a wide range, from "port" to white wine, but never quite the quality of the best Shiraz. In the late 1960s it was identified by Dr Austin Goheen of the University of California as being the same variety as the Primitivo di Gioia, a grape used locally in Apulia, the heel of southern Italy.

The question is how could this grape be sent (to either Prince's or Haraszthy) from Hungary, where it is not grown? One argument put forward by an American scholar, Miles Lambert-Gócs, is that a 19th-century Hungarian nursery might well have had this variety, which is not a native of Apulia either. The Austro-Hungarian Empire then included Dalmatia, the east coast of the Adriatic only 100 miles or so from Apulia. Suppose the unknown origin of the grape is somewhere in the eastern Mediterranean (which is true of most good varieties) there is nothing improbable in its being used at more than one point on the old Venetian trade-route (indeed near Ragusa and Otranto, two old Venetian ports).

Lambert-Gócs explains its name as a misreading or corruption of the Hungarian Zierfandler. Although the Zierfandler is a white grape, "Blauer Zierfandler" is a synonym for the Kékfrankos (a.k.a. Blaufränkisch, Nagyburgundi, and Limberger) used at Sopron in western Hungary. Suppose (which is perfectly possible) Haraszthy did receive it from Hungary – and whether first or not is unimportant – there remains the question of why he did not recognize its name. Two explanations are offered: his own property was far from Sopron, in a region where the Blauer Zierfandler was unheard of, and the label on the moss-wrapped bundle was nearly illegible. He simply thought he read Zinfandel. Doubtless other explanations will turn up as scholars pursue the matter further.

Buena Vista was Haraszthy's grandiloquent answer to his neighbour Vallejo's Lachryma Montis. He planted 300,000 vines here before leaving California. The winery was re-established in 1943, but these buildings are now just a showplace.

For the moment the competition was between Haraszthy and Vallejo. A newspaper reported in 1860 that "there is still an active rivalry (between them) as to who shall have the neatest-looking vine-fields and make the best wine. Dr Faure, a French gentleman, has charge of the General's wine department. His last year's make of white wine is of excellent quality."

Meanwhile Haraszthy, at the request of the Californian State Agricultural Society, wrote a *Report on Grapes and Wines in California*, a manual on planting and winemaking, urging experimentation of all kinds, particularly with different vines on different soils – but also a polemic urging the government to spend money on collecting cuttings in Europe, using the consulate service, and distribute them in California. At Buena Vista he propagated vines by the hundred thousand. And he dug deep tunnels in the hillside to store their produce.

HARASZTHY WAS STILL NOT READY TO PAUSE FOR BREATH. He urged that more research was needed. In 1861 the state governor commissioned him to visit Europe to learn all he could in the best wine areas and to bring back vines. His journey from San Francisco via New York to Southampton took six weeks. From late July to October he stormed round Europe, from Paris to the Rhine, to Switzerland, to Piemonte and Genoa, to the Languedoc, to Bordeaux, round Spain, to Montpellier and Burgundy, and back to Liverpool. Within six months he was back in Sonoma, finishing his book on the whole experience and awaiting the arrival of 100,000 vines of 300 different varieties, which the Wells Fargo Company delivered in January.

Most writers agree that this collection was the Hungarian's most important contribution to Californian viticulture. It (theoretically) made possible all the experiments that were so necessary to match vines with soils and climates. That they were largely frustrated by the legislature, who declined to distribute the cuttings, or even to pay him for them, was partly perhaps due to the Civil War in the distant east (Haraszthy, as you might expect, supported the rebel South), but largely to the stinginess and apathy of civil servants. Nothing (or not greatly) daunted, Haraszthy did his best to distribute them himself.

Just how essential his imports were is shown in the plantings that, even two years later, he and Vallejo had in Sonoma, the most go-ahead district in the state. Both were still planting the Mission massively. Haraszthy had 120,000 Mission vines established, plus 140,000 newly planted, as against 6,000 "foreign" vines established, and 40,000 new-set. Vallejo had 40,000 old Mission and 15,000 new, with 3,000 established foreign vines and 12,000 new.

It was only from the mid 1860s that superior vines were available in any numbers in California, with Sonoma enormously in the lead. The next few years saw the apotheosis of Buena Vista, and its collapse. The final act of Haraszthy's frantic story should be told here, before we survey the rest of the awakening state. In 1868, disillusioned with California, he decided the future lay in Nicaragua, rum and sawmills. In 1869 he fell into a stream where there were alligators.

THE PUBLICITY THAT ALWAYS SURROUNDED HARASZTHY may well exaggerate his importance; it certainly lays too much stress on his uniqueness. He was not the only one importing vines. Tentative efforts were being made, for example, in Santa Clara county, south of San Francisco Bay, and almost the mirror-image of Sonoma, one range back from the sea, while Haraszthy was still a law-officer in San Diego. Santa Clara had a direct line to France. In 1849 a French nurseryman, Antoine Delmas, settled here and was enraptured with the growing conditions. He was soon followed by fellow-countrymen: Prévost, Bontemps, Pellier were all pioneers, on a small scale, with a wide variety of grapes grown mainly for eating.

The man who made the region famous for wine was a Frenchman, too: Charles Lefranc. In 1857 he founded what was to become the hugely successful Almadén vineyards, planting Cabernet, Pinot Noir, Malbec, Sémillon and many of the varieties that Haraszthy later imported to distribute. The difference was that Haraszthy operated in the glare of publicity. Lefranc simply made good wine – and so, in due course, did his son-in-law from Beaune, Paul Masson.

WITH SO MUCH EXCITEMENT GOING ON OVER THE HILLS IN SONOMA, it is slightly surprising that the Napa valley, one range further inland from the ocean, but equally accessible by steamer across the Bay from San Fancisco, should have lagged behind by what, at the speed settlers worked, was a fair margin.

George Yount was the first to settle. He had arrived in California to trap seals for fur with his friend William Wolfskill. Wolfskill was diverted to Los Angeles to become a vineyardist almost on the scale of "Don Luis", but Yount fetched up at General Vallejo's, looking for work. In 1838 he had ridden over the wild Mayacamas mountains to look at the next valley, to find it, the story goes, a sea of golden poppies. Vallejo had no objection to the young man going to live in Indian country, provided he went through the formalities and was baptized Jorge de Concepcion Yount as a proper Mexican. His grant was 1,200 acres, on which he dutifully planted some Mission grapes – though without help cattle-ranching was about all he could handle. That very year small-pox carried off almost all the Napa Indians.

THE NAPA VALLEY REMAINED, INSOFAR AS IT WAS SETTLED AT ALL, STOCK-RAISING and cattle-farming country for almost a generation after Yount's arrival. A description of it by Titus Fey Cronise, though published in 1868, gives some idea of the beauty that still makes visitors gasp. He painted a picture of the ultimate rural idyll: of

Looking across the floor of the Napa valley, with the Inglenook winery
at the foot of the wooded hills and the characteristic clouds atop them.
Inglenook, founded in 1881, survived Prohibition and made classic
Cabernets under John Daniel in the middle of this century.

immaculate mixed farms, airy houses, trim fences, in a majestic natural frame of
wonderfully various trees, shrubs and flowers – with a quail for the pot under every
bush.

By 1868 there were 29 substantial farmers in the valley with vines, led by the
plutocratic Mormon Sam Brannen of San Francisco, who owned most of the
northern end of the valley and the hot springs of Calistoga. The second biggest
grower was Dr Crane, who is credited with building the first redwood tanks and
having the first wine-press in the valley. The third was Charles Krug, who later
chronicled the early years.

In the 1860s the vast majority of Napa's grapes were Missions, although
"foreign" varieties were grown by such enterprising souls as Dr Crane of St Helena
and Mr Osborne of Oak Knoll Farm, Napa (who had bought a standard collection,
mainly of table grapes, that was offered by the nurseries of the east). The most
enterprising cultivator was Hamilton Crabb from Ohio, who arrived in 1865 and
by 1880 had 400 different varieties growing. But to grow exotic grapes was one
thing. To make good wine was another.

"In the next 30 years", according to a later famous winemaker, John Daniel of
Inglenook, "Charles Krug was the outstanding figure in Napa wines, not only
because of his own operations but because of the leadership he provided . . . and the
training which key industry figures, such as Karl Wente, founder of Wente Bros,
Charles Wetmore, founder of Cresta Blanca . . . and Jacob Beringer . . . all received
when working for him". He was an extremely vocal and persuasive man; and an
effective spokesman when necessary for the whole California wine industry.

IT WAS TO A LARGE EXTENT GERMANS WHO SET THE NAPA VALLEY ON ITS FEET. They arrived in large numbers from the 1850s on, many of them Rhineland winegrowers disillusioned with a Germany that was turning more and more to beer, and more seriously, being dominated more and more by Prussia.

Many had put their hope in the liberal revolution at Frankfurt in 1848 – the year when France, Italy, Austria and Hungary also manned the barricades. Its only result was a tightening of the Prussian grip. The coincidence of the California gold strike in the same year must have helped many emigrants to make up their minds.

The calibre of these men is shown by the way they adapted their winemaking to a totally strange world. If the methods of the Rhineland were out of place in northern California, they doggedly found ways to match what they knew with what they found. For years the business of the Napa valley was conducted in German – and of parts of Sonoma too, as the Gundlach family, among others, grew prosperous just along the hill from Lachryma Montis. Fewer of the early settlers of the north coast counties were Italian. The brothers Simi from Piemonte were well ahead of their time in 1876 when they built their positively stately stone winery in the Russian River Valley, north of Sonoma. Of the early winemen it could be said in general that the Germans brought the brains, the Italians the brawn – taking over, in many cases, from the Chinese as craftsmen, stone-masons and labourers.

Down in Santa Clara you would pass the time of day in French; over east of the Bay in the Livermore valley, named by the Englishman Robert Livermore in the 1840s, you would have a choice of French, German, English or Italian, in a district that was proving itself exceptional for table wines from its distinctive gravel soil.

THREE THINGS DETERMINE THE DIRECTION OF A NEW WINE INDUSTRY: its natural conditions; the techniques, traditions and intelligence brought to it by its pioneers; but more even than these, it is the market-place that points the way.

Up to the 1870s California had no mass market for wine. Its chronic problem was a surplus of grapes. Europe and the east cost were effectively almost equally far away. Both had their own wine supplies.

COOLIE POWER

Lack of affordable manpower was the principal problem for anyone in California with a big project on hand. Haraszthy solved it by talking to Ho Po, a Chinese labour contractor in San Francisco, whose business was bringing in skilled hands from Guangdong. The east coast labourers' rate was about $10 a month. In California it was $30. Ho Po charged $8 plus board and lodging for eager and indefatigable workers. The great projects that were to come both in Sonoma and Napa were largely manned by Ho Po's coolies. In the 1880s they provided over 80% of the California wine workforce. But in the 1890s racial prejudice drove them out of the country they had so honourably served. It was largely Italian labour that took their place.

From the opening of the rail link between the coasts in 1869 all this was to change. The conditions that so limited grape-growing in the east were unknown in the west. Californians made much of the fact that their wines never needed the help of added sugar. There were bitter battles as east and west accused each other of malpractice: the Californians of using European labels on their own bad wines; the easterners of putting California labels on bad European wines. In 1872 Arpad Haraszthy, the count's son, wrote "the reputation of California wines in Eastern States is . . . undergoing one of the severest trials . . . that of palming off upon the confiding public spurious, inferior and bare-faced imitations of the same, which never saw the soil of our state, nor resemble wines in any particular. This unscrupulous traffic is carried on openly thoughout the Eastern States. . . ." The situation was made worse by a short but ugly economic slump that hit the nation. Congress tried to protect both east and west from European imports by protective tarrifs – which had the usual effect of provoking retaliation.

Had all the winegrowers known how much worse their problems were to become they might have formed a united front. The Temperance terrorists were stalking them; Kansas became the first "dry" state in 1880. And so was phylloxera; it had already reached Sonoma to begin its slow but deadly work in 1873.

FOR THE MOMENT, THE CREATIVE ENERGY OF NORTHERN CALIFORNIA'S GROWERS was being used in the study and nurture of their precious vines. By the 1880s in the Napa valley, according to Krug himself, "the new plantations were not any more of Mission, the Zinfandel and Malvoisie for clarets, and the Riesling, Chasselas, Burger and Muscatelles for whites. During the last few years the ambitious winemen planted, or rather grafted . . . Cabernet, Petit Sirah, Miller Burgundy, Crabb Burgundy, Malbec, Mondeuse, which elegant varieties will improve the character of our clarets wonderfully . . . and added to the Riesling . . . such as the Sémillon etc, and to produce white wines of the Sauterne character, such varieties as Sauvignon Blanc. . . ." Was this the influence of Haraszthy, taking so long to cross the hills? The answer is that many worked at the same thing at the same time.

It is much more remarkable, this knowledgeable listing of varieties, when you consider that it was only a century since the first methodical study of them was attempted even at Montpellier or Bordeaux. Only a century separates the recognition of Cabernet as the best grape for Bordeaux and the same recognition in the Napa valley.

As always, it was comparing notes that led to progress: as early as 1854 the farmers of Napa had formed an Agricultural Society to exchange their experiences. More help was to come from academic sources. In 1868 the University of California was founded at Berkeley with a Professor of Agriculture; in 1874 it had the good fortune to acquire a German-born soil-scientist of genius, Eugene Waldemar Hilgard, who might be said to have taken on Haraszthy's mantle – or one of them. Hilgard had some powerful things to say about growers who sold their wine under foreign labels "after two trips across the Atlantic, or even perhaps only across the Bay". "The growers need to know," he said, "and that quickly, which of the 2,500 varieties they should choose". His thinking was eventually to lead to the formal analysis of the whole of California into its wayward and elusive climate zones, and the recommendation of which grape varieties are best suited to each. In 1878 Hilgard welcomed a visit from the Reverend John Bleasdale, who came from Melbourne to judge a wine and brandy competition in San Francisco. In Australia Bleasdale had already been preaching the gospel of cool climate for 10 years.

FOG IS A FACT OF LIFE IN CALIFORNIA. It needed no University department to point out that the nearer you got to the ocean, the greater the chance of its towering white fog bank blotting out the sun. Its influence on inland valleys is much more subtle, but it soon began to be felt by grape-growers. One Judge Stanley, who owned land near Napa City, was ready in 1889 to tell the *San Francisco Chronicle*, "I consider that the lower end of the Napa Valley is the most suitable locality for grapes that will yield dry red wine. . . . The district is within the range where sea air permeates the atmosphere. From this sea air the vines extract properties which increase the tannin in their fruit." In a word (though the judge used many) he specifically compared the Carneros district with the Médoc.

It was time to make comparisons with France and see how California was getting on. In that same year, 1889, they did, at the Exposition Universelle in Paris, and had no reason to be ashamed of their results. Of 34 medals or awards given to California entries for wines of various sorts, the Napa Valley won 20. From that date on, justly or unjustly, it can be said to have assumed the lead in prestige, which it never lost through all the troubles that lay ahead.

THERE ARE CERTAIN TIMES AND PLACES IN HISTORY where I would dearly have loved to be. High on the list is northern California in the late 19th century, before the Golden Gate bridge strode across the cold channel which leads into the deep branching Bay; when schooners and steamers clustered at the foot of Market Street and Nob Hill was spawning mansions above a town that uniquely combined the Wild West and the Ritz.

Robert Louis Stevenson's romantic heart was stirred by the very name of the Silverado Trail, winding up the sun-burnt side of the Napa Valley to the silver diggings on Mount St Helena. I confess that mine is too, and climbing the redwood-shaded hill to the white house with its deep porch where he called on Jacob Schram, the barber turned winemaker, I hear ghosts about me everywhere: Schram's guttural exclamations answering the soft Edinburgh intonation of the writer, when the clatter of the day's last waggon has died away. . . .

"One corner of the land after another is tried with one kind of grape after another," wrote the author of *Treasure Island* in his one essay at wine-writing. "So, bit by bit, they grope about for their Clos Vougeot and Lafite." The process he describes is if anything even more topical today than when he noted it. What were Schram's Schramsberg Champagnes like? How good were these proud medal-winners that were all to disappear? To Stevenson they were "bottled poetry" – so nothing has really changed.

CHAPTER 36

THE GOLDEN AGE

The Golden Age of wine-growing in Bordeaux and Burgundy in the 19th century is no fable. It is true that for a while in mid-century the owning of vineyards, especially in Bordeaux, was the most fashionable game in town, that bankers were ready to pay any money for famous properties, that vintage-time in the Médoc was a Champs Elysées of flounces and flirting.

The image of that era has been assiduously cultivated through hard times since. It has stuck, especially in Bordeaux, largely because it took a permanent form in ostentatious architecture – and above all because it gave rise to what could be described as the myth of the "château". But it is only a quarter of the story of the century that finally fixed the properties and the wines in their modern mould. There was much to be learned, much fine-tuning to be done – and several major crises to overcome before the Belle Epoque brought the century to a close.

AT THE END OF THE 18TH CENTURY THE LEADING PROPERTIES of both Bordeaux and Burgundy had reached a fair level of technical competence based on centuries of well-learned lessons. They had almost completed the evolution of the style of wines they would be always be known for: especially among the reds of the Médoc and the Côte de Nuits.

Bordeaux still had some adjustments to make in its choice of grape varieties. The Cabernets Sauvignon and Franc and the Merlot were well-established but by no means universal. Petit Verdot and Malbec still played important roles, besides many minor varieties that have since all but disappeared.

Similarly in the techniques of winemaking there were many fine points to be adjusted and decisions to be taken. The chief concern of the time, though, was marketing; the relative roles of grower and merchant, the definition of a property and its wine – and, the great theme, a classification by quality to help everyone from grower to consumer and oil the wheels of the whole business.

IN BORDEAUX THE END OF NAPOLEON'S WARS brought no immediate relief – except that the customers did at least keep coming. Centuries of habit were not to be broken by even 20 years of fighting. Britain remained interested in only the very best wines; Holland's interest continued, though mainly for cheap white wines and palus reds (or "cargo" wines), while Germany's purchases rose, until altogether she took a third of all Bordeaux's exports. A sad blow was the loss of much of the French colonial market that had been a mainstay of the 18th century. But in its place there began a small but growing interest from both North and South America.

An indication of the low state of the market was that the Bank of Bordeaux, newly opened in 1825, almost failed in 1830 and categorically refused stocks of wine as collateral for loans. The lack of credit gave the ever-watchful merchants of the Quai des Chartrons more opportunities than ever for dictating terms to growers. The lead was taken by the powerful Nathaniel Johnston, backed up by Mr Barton and M. Guestier – both of whom were able to buy themselves magnificent Médoc châteaux in the 1820s. (Guestier was known to growers as "Pierre le Cruel".)

Johnston accused the first growths (Margaux and Haut-Brion in particular) of trading on their names with an 1834 vintage that was "no better than a 3rd or 4th growth". Growers' finances were so tight that in 1844 both Châteaux Margaux and Latour, looking for reassurance, signed 10-year contracts to sell their whole crop, good vintage or bad, at a preset price of 2,100 and 1,750 francs a tonneau respectively – which sounded reasonable until Château Lafite, under its most famous and spirited régisseur, Joseph Goudal, remaining staunchly independent, sold the 1844 crop for 4,500 francs – more than twice as much.

A CONTRACT WITH A NÉGOCIANT WAS MORE THAN A SIMPLE AGREEMENT to sell. Now that, for the first time, it was the merchants who were financing the growers they made strict stipulations about how the estate was to be run, even down to the

Château Margaux's classically memorable façade dates from 1811. At this date the present hierarchy of châteaux, formalized by the 1855 classification, was in place. Margaux, Lafite, Latour and Haut-Brion were clear leaders in price and thus status, and very little has changed.

number of cultivations of the vineyard, the timing of manuring (once every 19 years for a first growth), the rate at which old vines should be replaced, and the Baltic oak that the barrels should be made of – with six hoops.

Goudal would have none of this. Luckily, in the long run, for all estate owners, he had the solid backing of enormously rich proprietors, the Vanlerberghe family (who had been described as "gun-runners" in the wars and conducted operations through a London banker, Sir Samuel Scott). Goudal declared open war on the Quai des Chartrons. He sold his excellent 1841 vintage at a colossal price over their heads – and on the condition that customers took some of the mediocre 1842 as well. Johnston was outraged and circulated his English customers, almost asking them to boycott Lafite. His idea was an orderly market – with the Chartronnais calling the tune. Johnston wanted to go so far as to accept orders only for first, second, third or fourth growth wines – the customer to leave it to his discretion whether he delivered Latour or Lafite; in other words for the Chartronnais to control the entire system and effectively abolish the carefully-nurtured notion of the individual cru, replacing it with an overall classification. (Heaven knows, said the proprietors, what the merchants would have got up to in their cellars.)

That there was a classification in place already there is no doubt. It did not become official until 1855, it covered only the Médoc (and Sauternes), and until the early 19th century it was more of a confidential consensus among the trade than an actual list. But ever since the early 1700s the brokers had been studying form – and it had been remarkably consistent. The first growths were not only first in time; by and large, year after year, they remained first in quality. And the price differentials were enormous: in the 18th century first growths sold for twice as much as seconds, three times as much as thirds and four times the price of fourths. Even granted that

BARON PHILIPPE

The 1855 Classification still stands today officially exactly as it was first published, with one famous exception. In 1973 Mouton-Rothschild was promoted from being first of the second growths to a first growth. The change was entirely the work of Baron Philippe de Rothschild, the greatest promoter of the Médoc in general, and his own properties in particular, of the 20th century.

Mouton was established in the 18th century by the Baron de Brane, who acquired it from the Ségurs (it had formerly been part of Lafite). How de Ségur knew where to draw the line separating the two parcels of ground with such different personalities is one of the mysteries of the Médoc. Brane-Mouton was the name of the property, acknowledged to be among the first growths, and with the added distinction of being among the pioneers of Cabernet Sauvignon in the Médoc. It was sold in 1830 to a M. Thuret, whose stewardship was apparently undistinguished. He sold it at a loss in 1853, while oidium was

plaguing the Médoc, to Baron Nathaniel Rothschild, of the English branch of the family. When the 1855 classification was drawn up two years later, its status over the previous generation did not warrant it being included among the first growths.

It was this wrong that Baron Philippe, inheriting the property in 1922, set out to right. The process took 51 years of dedicated winemaking and relentless propaganda. The quality of the wine was not in question, but Bordeaux feared the can of worms which could open if once the sacred tablet of 1855 was altered. There was also an open rivalry between the Rothschilds of Mouton and their cousins who had bought Lafite 15 years later in 1868 (for much more money). Mouton possessed no dwelling house until the 1870s, when Baron James built a modest weekend residence known as Petit Mouton. Today's beautiful "château", a converted farm-building, was the work of Baron Philippe (who died in 1988) and his American wife Pauline.

millionaires and their money are easily parted the long-term consistency is impressive: such a consensus surviving from one generation to another can hardly all be done with mirrors.

THE PUBLIC FIRST LEARNED OF THE CLASSIFICATION in Jullien's *Topographie*. He was such a confirmed classifier of everything that they may not have realized the special significance of the ranking of Bordeaux. In his first (1816) edition in any case it was very simple, and evidently gleaned from the broker Lawton, who had briefed Thomas Jefferson on the top wines. Jullien distinguished between the "High" and "Low" Médocs, and gave what were to become almost the conventional characterizations of the four first growths (Haut-Brion included). His descriptions still ring remarkably true today. He listed seven second growths (Rauzan and Gorce in Margaux; Léoville and Larose in St-Julien; le Clos de Brane-Mouton and Pichon-Longueville in Pauillac; and Calon in St-Estèphe.) After that he was content to list the communes in order of quality with notes on the characters of their wines. On the quality of the top Médocs in general, though, he wrote both specifically and lyrically: their flavour, he said, reminded him of the smell of the very best sealing wax, "and their bouquet shares the scents of the violet or the raspberry".

Jullien, the Parisian, was rapidly (in 1824) followed by a German Bordeaux négociant, Wilhelm Franck, who pushed the matter far further, naming a total of 408 properties in 41 communes in the Médoc, and setting out four classes, growths or crus. After the four firsts, he listed only four seconds, then eight thirds, then 18 fourths.

Franck in turn was rapidly (in 1828) followed by a broker, M. Paguierre, whose book was published in both French and English (in Edinburgh) at the same time. Paguierre's classification follows Franck almost to the letter. The chief interest in his book lies in his recommendations to growers on how to make the most suitable wine for each foreign market. His formula for red wine making is extraordinary. He proposes making a "mother-vat", a "mère-cuve" in which the very best and ripest grapes are given a month-long maceration in "trois-six", or double-strength brandy, while the rest of the harvest is trodden and fermented in the usual way. The contents of the mère-cuve "having finished fermenting" (in practice they would not ferment at all, being pickled in spirits) should then be added as a small dose to each of the regular barrels. Evidently he was looking for extra strength and colour, but going about it in a most peculiar way.

As for foreign customers, Paguierre's experience tells him that the Dutch want natural wine so that they can mess it about in their own way at home, the Russians and Prussians want two or three year old wine, racked clear of any lees, while the incorrigible British, still hankering after the kick of Port and Spanish wines, are only happy with the traditional "travail" of adding Hermitage, Midi or worse (he does not mention brandy) which makes their claret turn brown and dry with age. Powdered iris root helps the bouquet, he adds – and so does two fingers of "raspberry spirit" in each barrel.

MORE SURPRISING THAN TO FIND THE TOP GROWTHS confidently classified are references, already in the 1820s, to a hierarchy in far greater depth, which is not elaborated on, but which extends downwards from the "crus classés" to "vins bourgeois superieurs", "bons vins bourgeois", "petits vins bourgeois", and even "petits vins de Médoc paysans".

So the brokers had already done their research and grading among what today are usually referred to as petits châteaux. By the fourth (1848) edition of Jullien he was even ready to coin this oft-repeated phrase: "These wines [the crus bourgeois] often acquire in maturity a degree of quality which makes them very difficult to distinguish from the fifth growths".

EVEN THOUGH BUSINESS WAS SLOW IN BORDEAUX one can feel a mounting public interest in this curiously-constructed animal as list after list appeared. There was a consensus gradually coming about which was unique in the world; a sort of perpetual auction in which properties were finding their relative values. The idea of grading the quality of land is logical enough. But in Bordeaux that was not what was happening. What was being classified was property – which inevitably includes the human element.

The book that brought interest to a peak is nowadays reverentially referred to simply as the Bordeaux Bible. It was a joint production by an English professor (and freemason) named Charles Cocks and a Bordeaux bookseller called Michel Féret. In 1846 Cocks alone published *Bordeaux, Its Wines and the Claret Country* in English. It included the most comprehensive classification that had yet appeared, based, he said, on Franck's latest revision of his list, but augmented by his own researches, "price having appeared to me the best test of the quality supposed to exist in each wine".

It would be good to know more about this freemason, whose translations included a book called *Priests, Women and the Family*. He certainly knew his wine. His observation that "a considerable time must elapse before any vintage can finally be pronounced upon" is a nugget of wisdom that is still almost universally ignored. Féret clearly pounced on this authoritative work and its writer, rechecked and slightly modified the list, and in 1850 brought out the first French edition, *Bordeaux et ses Vins, Classés par Ordre de Mérite*. Since then there have been 14 more editions of *Cocks and Féret*, growing ever stouter, until today it lists 7,000 properties.

Cocks must have been very close to the brokers. Had he lived one year longer, to 1855, he would have seen something very like his list appear as the official considered Classement by the Syndicat des Courtiers de Commerce, in response to a demand to the Bordeaux Chamber of Commerce from Napoleon III, as its contribution to the Paris Exposition Universelle of that year.

The document, a fading parchment in cursive writing, survives in the President's office of the Chamber of Commerce, that great Palais de la Bourse which was Intendant de Tourny's first splendid contribution to the glorification of Bordeaux. No single document can ever have done so much to publicize a product, and indeed keep it in the public eye, as a matter for discussion and debate, for over 130 years.

THE KEY WORD WHICH IS MISSING from the Classement of 1855, or at any rate only appears on it five times, is the word "château". Seventy-four of the 79 properties listed (58 red wine producers, 21 white) appear as a simple name (Mouton, for example, or Langoa), followed by the commune and the name of the owner. To refer to the property the word cru or sometimes clos was commonly used, but château apparently only if a major building that justified the term existed (e.g. at Beychevelle) or had once existed (e.g. at Latour). It was the pretentions of proprietors, building themselves imposing residences in the full flush of the coming Golden Age, that brought the term château into common use.

FROM THE 1850S ON THE MÉDOC BEGAN TO ACQUIRE its familiar appearance; that of a series of large, vaguely historical-looking country-houses scattered among rolling parkland in which, instead of oaks and herds of deer, there are vines, vines and more vines.

The feeling of the period is best summed up in such mansions as Pichon-Lalande, Pichon-Longueville and Palmer. Pichon-Lalande was commissioned in 1851 from Bordeaux's most fashionable architect, Burguet, by Albert, the childless last Baron Pichon. He was already 60, and a despondent old legitimist who was shaken by the revolutionary events that shook Europe in 1848. "In hope of better times" is the wistful inscription over the door. Happily he lived until 1864, to see the better times come. Such a success was his "Louis XIII" château that it won Burguet commissions for his nephew's property, Pichon-Longueville, just across the road, and for Palmer in Margaux. The first he designed as an almost Disneyesque pastiche of a château, with pointed witches' hats as exclamation marks. The second, for the Paris banker Isaac Pereire, is one of the Médoc's most charming houses. Basically it is a bourgeois box, but there is a strong hint of the Loire – Azay le Rideau perhaps – in its pretty neo-Renaissance turrets and the steep roof, as sharp and shiny as a blade. Pereire was also investing at the time in the new resort of Arcachon on the coast. The same gay eclecticism and happy harmony of styles turns up at Palmer and the seaside.

The Burguet style and its successors suggest, above all, a man of commerce proud to have become a landowner, and reaching for some worthy symbol of his new identity. Some mercifully had a sense of proportion (even of humour) to guide them. Others did not. But every pocket proprietor did his best to follow suit. The golden years of the '60s and '70s gave the growers deep purses. It was a poor vigneron indeed who could not afford at least one turret tacked onto his farmhouse, to lend credence to the title "château".

Chateau Palmer is a third growth of Margaux which is consistently better than the second growths today, and sometimes challenges the firsts. Its distinctively English name recalls Major General Charles Palmer from Bath, who in the year before Waterloo found himself sitting in a coach for three days travelling from Lyon to Paris with a beautiful young widow. His military heart was touched by her story: she was going to Paris to sell her late husband's estate in the Médoc. Palmer bought it, changed its name from de Gasq to his own, and more by luck than judgement found himself the owner of the immediate neighbour to Château Margaux, with one of the finest vineyards in the Médoc.

According to Captain Gronow, an acquaintance of the general who tells the story, Palmer engaged a Mr Gray, "a man of captivating manners but almost as useless a person as himself", to be his agent. Samples were offered to the Prince Regent, who compared the pure Palmer with the fortified claret offered by his wine-merchant, Carbonell. His advice to Palmer was to try different vines and put some guts in it. Palmer foolishly listened, ruined his estate and went bankrupt.

Cos d'Estournel's *chais* (there is no house) acquired its Oriental excesses,
so one story goes, in an attempt to gain sales in the booming markets of
British India and points East. A good example of the use of the château
concept as marketing ploy.

SO ONCE THEY HAD THEIR TURRETED BUILDINGS, what was the definition of a château to be? The answer is peculiarly un-French. For a nation that prides itself on being categorical it is more like a typically British fudge. A château is rather like the British constitution. It is what it does.

Joseph Goudal had had the wit to point out to his employers, when times were hard for his neighbours, that any land that Lafite bought from them immediately multiplied in value – because it became part of Lafite. They foolishly turned down several opportunities before, in the 1840s and for a considerable sum, buying the next-door patch called Les Carruades. But the principle is exactly correct and adds an almost mystical air to the notion of a "cru classé": it can consist of single block of land, or several blocks, or indeed separate rows of vines all over the commune. So long as it belongs to its own tradition, as it were, all its wine can be labelled with its classed-growth name.

There is one document that finally tried to pin down what a château is – but not until 1942, and then without success: the name château (on a wine label) must be "linked to the existence of a particular 'cru', a specific vineyard that has been known for a very long time by the name in question, in accordance with its meaning and with local, faithful and reliable usage". Little, if any, of this relates to actual practice. The vineyard can even be exchanged for another (so long as that other is also classified – or apparently in some cases whether it is or not). There does not have to be any building on the property at all. The only word that really rings true is "usage": a château is what it does. There is a word that fits it rather neatly: a brand. Though the number of crus classés has remained unaltered in the Médoc and Sauternes since 1855, the number of "châteaux" leapt from a dozen or two in all of Bordeaux, to 700 in 1874, 1,300 in 1893, and today stands at over 4,000.

THE GOLDEN AGE ARRIVED WITH THE CLASSIFICATION. On the face of it, times were not at all auspicious. A potent new fungus disease, oidium or powdery mildew, had appeared in Bordeaux three years before (having already decimated vineyards elsewhere in France) and was crippling or killing vines by the thousand. On the other hand despite poor vintages shortage of wine made prices rise. It was also the very time when the gold-rushes of California and Australia fed a great deal of money into the world economy. And in 1853 the railway was completed between Bordeaux and Paris.

To Bordeaux as a seaport the railway was not quite such a revolutionary release from old constraints as it was in land-locked Burgundy – although steamships were

---

OIDIUM

"Vine disease" was the name given at first to a mysterious malady that appeared in Bordeaux's vineyards in 1851. It was soon identified as a form of powdery mildew called *Oidium Tuckeri*, of English origin, transmitted via Belgium to the vineyards of France. Its fungus spores spread with dreadful swiftness, encouraged by a cool damp summer, so that in two years the whole region was in a panic. A serious vine disease was something it had never had to face before. Countless descriptions, explanations and proposed remedies were forthcoming. It attacked different vine varieties to different degrees in different soils. It killed the young shoots of the vines and halved the crops. A large reward was offered for a remedy, with the usual results: electricity was one of the first helpful suggestions.

The cure, suggested as early as 1852 but not widely believed or welcomed, was to dust the vines with finely powdered sulphur. It is credited to the Comte de la Vegne, whose palus vineyard at Ludon in the southern Médoc was badly affected. He experimented with the best way of reaching all the leaves with the powder, enthusiastically supported by the Comte Duchatel, Finance Minister to Louis-Philippe, whose magnificent property at Lagrange had the biggest vineyard in the Médoc, and the proprietor of Château Giscours in Margaux. Most proprietors were at first frightened of giving their wine a sulphurous taint: but the efficacity of the system (and lack of alternatives) soon convinced them. By 1857 the practice was general throughout Bordeaux and by 1861 the vines had returned to full health – at the expense of a regularly-repeated dusting with sulphur.

Although the crisis was short-lived (and incidentally was at its height in the year of the Classification) some of its side-effects were not. It stimulated a great deal of replanting, tending to favour the Cabernet and Malbec at the expense of the Merlot, and the Sémillon at the expense of the Muscadelle. It also gave the impetus to the planting of vines in France's new colony of Algeria – which was to have important consequences for the future.

---

a revolution in themselves. Where it helped most was in speeding travel to Paris and the northern markets such as Belgium and Germany. It brought Parisians to inspect this famous wine region. Having seen it, they wanted to own a part of it.

An account of the vintage at Beychevelle, the property of the great banker Fould, sets the scene. Fould had married the daughter of a New Orleans cotton-millionaire who had bought the baroque palace from Pierre (le Cruel) Guestier. After a vast lunch and cigars on the terrace the party strolled among the outbuildings to watch the harvesters at their cabbage soup (which was good, the writer noted, and full of bits of meat). Then rides or drives up and down the rows of vines – "à côté de nous passe la calèche de la toute gracieuse baronne Gustave de Rothschild et de son mari . . . la jolie famille de M. Johnston . . . Duchatel . . . comte d'Aguado . . . Prince et Prinesse Murat . . . les Ségur . . . les d'Erlanger . . . c'est le Faubourg St Honoré, ce sont les Champs Elysées prolongés, c'est Paris."

Where was the wine going, from this socially and industrially revolutionized Bordeaux? A very great deal (though not of the best qualities) was crossing the Atlantic. Argentina, the land of beef and wheat, became Bordeaux's biggest single client in the years 1860-90, while the United States picked up the taste for claret (but not its English name) in the 1840s, rising to a peak in the 1850s, when for a whole decade they remained Bordeaux's best customer of all. It was the Civil War that ended this (since long-forgotten) era of American thirst, together with growing Temperance propaganda and the trend towards protectionism in America's trade policies. Later in the century California's growing production took up the slack.

By the 1860s, though, exactly the opposite was happening in Europe. A whole series of reciprocal treaties freeing customs barriers between nations started with the Prussian-inspired German Customs Union, the Zollverein, in the 1830s. Histori-cally most significant for Bordeaux was the Anglo-French trade treaty of 1860. It led directly to the ending of the nearly two centuries old discrimination against French wine that had driven England to port. Suddenly the duty on French table wines entering Britain was one twentieth of what it had been in 1815.

The British gave all the credit to the Chancellor of the Exchequer, William Gladstone. "Gladstone claret" was what they called the wonder of affordable

---

The famous "Gladstone Budget" in Britain in 1860 was followed by a best-selling *Report on the Cheap Wines of France, Italy, Austria, Greece and Hungary* by a wine-loving physician, Dr Robert Druitt.

"I have bought and drunk", says the doctor, "not for gratification of the palate, but for real professional study, specimens of most of the varieties of wine available" – for the first time, that is, to a wide public.

Druitt recommended Bordeaux and Burgundy as an alternative to Spanish and Portuguese wines; claret "particularly for child-ren, for literary persons, and for all those whose occupations are chiefly carried on indoors, and which tax the brain more than the muscles" –

including women who are "lying-in".

The poetry of wine was not lost on the doctor. "We may admire the rosebud and the snowdrop, but there is a place in our affections for something fuller, warmer, rounder, and more voluptuous. As is Aphrodite to a wood-nymph . . . so are thy wines, O Burgundy, to those of thy sister Bordeaux!"

As for his doctor colleagues who prescribe port, he fears that they have no idea how bad bad port can be. "The only questions we need ask ourselves are, not what is the chemical compo-sition [of a wine], but do you like it, and does it agree with you? The stomach is the real test-tube for wine; and if that quarrels with it, no analysis is worth a rush."

Bordeaux. Between 1860 and 1873 the British (who had not by any means forgotten sherry, or anything else potable) multiplied their intake of French wine eight times.

Very few statistics are needed to sketch the progress of the Golden Age. Bordeaux in 1858 (recovering from oidium) made 1.9 million hectolitres of wine; in 1862 3.2 million; in 1869 4.5 million and in 1874 and 1875 over 5 million.

As ever, the Medoc was in the forefront of these events. The story of St-Emilion and its neighbours in the 19th century is roughly parallel, though starting at a more modest level and remaining more closely knit, with less outside influence. Stolid is the word that springs to mind. Respectable Libournais familes stayed put and steadily improved their wines as new ideas came along. Brittany and north-east France, Belgium and Holland, continued to be their best clients. If there was any classification it remained a private matter among brokers and merchants; its possible publicity value did not occur to them – and journalists, it seems, did not spend much of their time in Libourne.

The difficulties of shipment in the Napoleonic wars had taught both the Libournais merchants and the growers a valuable lesson: that their wines improved with age much more than they had previously believed; it was worth investing in stocks to mature as they did in Bordeaux. St-Emilions, they found, would keep for 20 years. "Pomerols", wrote the négociant Beylot in 1829, "do not keep as long, but can be bottled earlier, and some have more bouquet than St-Emilions". He did not mention that St-Emilions were often still being used as a Hermitage-substitute to lend strength to under-powered Médocs.

Whereas in the 18th century the wines of the Fronsac Cotes had been rated higher than Pomerols, in the 19th the situation was reversed. Fronsac suffered as an indirect result of the Revolution. The Richelieu family would never let its Fronsac pasture lands be planted with vines. When they were sold as Biens Nationaux, Libourne's bourgeois snapped them up as perfect virgin palus and made large investments converting them to vineyards. The Canon slopes across the river became unimportant in proportion to these productive fields – particularly as all wine prices in the 1830s and 40s were at a low level. Fronsac's name came to be associated more with ordinary "cargo" wine than anything fine.

Pomerol, in contrast, gained because of a change in farming practice. One of its earliest exponents was the editor of an influential but short-lived (1838-1841) monthly journal for winegrowers called Le Producteur. According to his account the immemorial custom on its plateau – ignored only by a few ambitious proprietors along its boundaries – was to alternate vine-rows with strips of ploughland for growing grain. It was impossible to manure these "joualles" without the vines taking their share of the extra nutrients. "It has to be admitted", wrote Le Producteur, "that the wine loses in quality what it gains in quantity".

It was, ironically, the apparent scourge of powdery mildew that did away with the joualles – and also with Pomerol's once-admired white wine. With vines dying all over France, the price of red wine rose to the point where even Pomerol threw aside tradition. It found itself making much better wine just in time to share in Bordeaux's Golden Age. Up to the 1850s Pomerol boasted one "château"; the very old estate of the de May family that had been known as Certan. In 1858 it became the first Pomerol property to be "médocized" by a Paris banker, Charles de Bousquet. He added the inevitable slate-roofed tower and confirmed the antiquity of its standing by calling it Vieux-Château-Certan. Its wine was rated the finest in the district.

Petrus, the property of the Arnaud family, was cited among the good but not outstanding small estates. Old editions of *Cocks and Féret* illustrate the house with an engraving showing a turreted gateway that suggests an old manor, if not an actual castle. The modest house today shows not the slightest signs of any such thing; so perhaps the tower was a case of a château en Espagne. Petrus remained in the Arnaud family until 1929; its hour of recognition still to come. Its name, however, is an example of what was happening in both Pomerol and St-Emilion: proprietors were looking for something snappier and more saleable than their rustic old handles. The Giraud family farm had the scarcely encouraging name of Trop-Ennuie, which could be rendered as "Too much trouble". Trotanoy, the new version, sold very much better. From this era comes a great deal of confusion as families jockeyed for the best old names, often adding their own names, and occasionally even accusing each other of cheating by adding the emphatic "Vrai" (true or original) to their labels.

Storms in teacups most of these adjustments were. One was considerably more: the breaking up of St-Emilion's only great estate of the 18th century – Figeac. Its inheritor, André de Carle-Trajet, with the great vineyard bequeathed to him from Vital de Carle, was one of few who despaired of wine-growing during Napoleon's wars and the blockades. Others sent their wine the difficult and expensive way north by road. Perhaps possessed by the idea of red-coated armies he quixotically replaced half his vines with the dye-plant madder (a substitute for Mexican cochineal, which was blockaded out). By 1823 he was ruined; he died; his widow had to break up the estate. Figeac still exists, as one of the biggest and certainly of the best St-Emilion properties. But out of some of its very best land, on the very boundary-line of Pomerol, the Ducasse family formed a new estate to which they gave the catchy name of Cheval Blanc. What could be more of a brand name than White Horse? From the 1850s onwards Cheval Blanc was destined to become one of St-Emilion's effective first growths; sharing the honours of the gravelly plateau above the town with Figeac, but in the soft richness of its wine drawing nearer to a Pomerol.

At Petrus the modest house has no tower, but even the current edition of *Cocks and Féret* includes this nineteenth-century edifice.

Ausone, Bel-Air, Canon and their neighbours meanwhile continued to dominate the limestone Côtes around and below the town.

St-Emilion had missed a trick in the Exposition Universelle of 1855, which was the triumph of the Médoc. It did not make the same mistake in the 1867 Paris Exhibition. Thirty seven properties collectively won a gold medal. But the renown of its wines beyond their traditional market, and their adoption as chic enough for Paris, really dates from the 1889 Exhibition, in which 60 of them collectively won the Grand Prix.

NOTHING SO DRAMATIC HAPPENED IN BURGUNDY as the 19th century apotheosis of Bordeaux. But then, you might fairly say, it never does. Big players are few in its slowly evolving story, and now that the church had been removed they were fewer still. In chapter 27 we saw how a banker's money made in the wars held the Clos de Vougeot together for several generations, but the overwhelming tendency was for Burgundy's estates, already relatively small, to be divided and subdivided by a process in which the French laws of inheritance played (and still play) a major part.

The assumption on the death of a parent is that all the children inherit the property equally. Most estates today have formed themselves into business ventures to prevent the inevitable break-up that this entails. The Société Civile de Château Latour was the first such arrangement; set up by the descendants of Alexandre de Ségur. In the 19th century, when some of the best land in Burgundy changed hands, its fragmentation was accelerated by the "jeu des heritages". Very few of the ancient clos, put together with infinite pains, survived intact – though here, as in most things, the Côte de Nuits and the Côte de Beaune evolved in different ways. Where there were more têtes de cuvée more money was involved and there were fewer who could take part.

Most of today's Grands Crus in the Côte de Nuits contain sizeable holdings. But very few are "monopoles" – meaning with only one owner. In the Côte de Beaune, on the other hand, the subdivision of the few Grands Crus has reached such a point that in the 30-acre Batard-Montrachet no single grower owns more than one and a half acres.

Was there not an opportunity here for new capital to start the process again, making new clos out of the broken up mosaic? Certainly the merchant houses of Beaune and Nuits-St-Georges took every opportunity to create themselves estates. But it was too late to make a clean sweep: the best that could be done was a gradual accumulation as pieces of the jig-saw came onto the market. The biggest estate today is the size of an important Médoc château – but parcelled out all over the Côte d'Or; and the average acreage, taking all growers, big and small together, is a mere 10 acres – also scattered.

THE PUBLICATION OF CHAPTAL'S TREATISE had given everybody a standard to work to, including such new or revived ideas as adding sugar to the juice and covering the fermenting vat. It was soon followed by many more detailed works dedicated to local conditions; but besides giving empirical advice and building up confidence they did not alter much. Burgundy especially showed the resistance to change to be expected of an old establishment. The famous Dr Guyot, whose oenological advice

Technology reaches Beaujolais – and its loud report reaches the ears of the vineyard workers – in the nineteenth century in the shape of an anti-hail cannon. This spectacular technique was widely used, and even today rockets are occasionally discharged into threatening clouds in the hope that the hail will fall on someone else.

was sought all over France in mid-century, deplored the "immobilisme" of the Burgundian. Reactionary and secretive, it was said he was not concerned to know how things were done in the next village – but very concerned that the next village did not poke its nose into his cellars.

To Count Haraszthy, hurrying through looking for ideas for California, Burgundy seemed very primitive indeed: "Then, according to the size of the tank, from four to ten men, stripped of all their clothes, step into the vessel, and begin to tread down the floating mass, working it also with their hands. This operation is repeated several times, if the wine does not ferment rapidly enough. The reason for this, in my eyes, rather dirty work, is that the bodily heat of the men aids the wine in its fermentation." That same evening back in Dijon: "We partook of white wine that evening, as the process through which the red wine goes did not serve to increase our longing for the ruby coloured liquid."

If the idea of innovation as sacrilege was powerful among the simple it is not difficult to understand. Their special place in the world as Burgundian vignerons was the only thing special about a grinding life: it had almost mystical value and must not be disturbed.

Where Burgundy did make adjustments, and not always happy ones, was in following too closely the taste of the clientele – doing, precisely, what Bordeaux

The Golden Age was a time of gifts and plenty for the ordinary farmers and peasants of France as well as the great landowners and the merchants. This idealised scene of grape-picking expresses the spirit of the age.

had done for a century. Chambertin had been Napoleon's favourite wine; after Waterloo there was an unprecedented demand for Chambertin – especially from England. English taste notoriously called for strong dark heavy wines; merchants were not too proud to oblige. An enquiry into such practices in 1822 found that "coupage" – blending is a kind word for it – had already become "systematic". Chambertin may have been an exception, but it encouraged others to leave their wines longer in the vat to give them more weight and colour. If, as Chaptal had suggested, they also added sugar, they were forcing the delicate Pinot Noir in just the way that deprives it of its unique perfume and tenderness. They were also making it much easier to imitate. With the grapes of Bordeaux – already themselves a mixture – you can get away with a certain amount of "adjustment". Burgundy is either pure or it is nothing.

By the mid-19th century, the prestigious slopes of the Côtes had become almost a monoculture of Pinot Noir, with perhaps some of its close relation, the Pinot Meunier, and remaining plants and vineyards of Fromenteau and Chardonnay. What was to change, as the tide of prosperity at last (and not for long) reached the growers of less favoured sites, was the acreage of Gamay – a simple indicator of the demand for low-price wine within sales-reach of Burgundy.

Burgundy's Golden Age was above all the era of the little man. It began to dawn with the Canal de Bourgogne, which was opened to traffic from 1832. Paris was now as reachable from Beaune as it had been for a century from Beaujolais. But the moment of daybreak was the railway, which reached Dijon from Paris in 1851 – and for the moment went no further. This was the day that the downtrodden had been dreaming of. For a giddy decade Burgundy became the vineyard of the capital – and the plantations of Gamay spread wide out onto the fertile plain of the Saône, and up into the scrubby Arrières-Côtes behind the Golden slope. At last to be a Burgundian vigneron was to have all France – all Europe, even – at your feet. The Free Trade treaties of the Second Empire opened the German market, the Belgian, the Dutch – even Britain came within range. The fact that Burgundy was growing vin ordinaire did not discourage anybody; for a few brief years there was no competition.

Nor were the fine wines of the Côte d'Or forgotten in the rush. Their market expanded even further than the Gamay's – and much more permanently. In 1859 the Hospices de Beaune inaugurated the public auction of its wines; a totally successful piece of propaganda. In 1861 Dr Lavalle's classification of the Têtes de Cuvée was ready for the Paris Exhibition, the German Zollverein, and indeed the British Empire.

After the harvest, the winemaking, when the whole estate was busy. Railways had opened up markets, cities grew and their thirsts with them. The optimism of the age was to be wistfully recalled in the succeeding decades of disaster.

But there was no reason for the railway to stop at Dijon. The advantage of being at the railhead was a purely temporary piece of luck. Once the tracks reached the Midi, Burgundy and all of France was open to the flood of cheaper (and sometimes riper) wines from the lower Rhône and the Languedoc. And meanwhile, without taking a ticket on any train, the phylloxera beetle was hopping, crawling, and winging its way northwards from where it had made its landing in the south.

VILLAGES AND VINEYARDS

It is easy to tell which of the communes of the Côte d'Or were accustomed to commerce in their wines under their own names and which depended on selling under what was effectively a generic title, such as Beaune. Where the village name stands alone, as at Volnay and Pommard, a market existed for wine under that name. Nobody, on the other hand, called for Aloxe or for Morey; all the renown of these communes was concentrated in its tête de cuvée or Grand Cru.

It was a logical step demanded by Burgundy's Golden Age to make the wines of the villages more saleable in their own right. Not everything in Burgundy, after all, was either Beaune or Chambertin. From the 1860s the villages whose names rang no bells in themselves were permitted to attach the name of their most famous vineyard. Thus Gevrey became Gevrey-Chambertin; Morey, Morey-St-Denis from its tête de cuvée Clos St Denis; Chambolle, Chambolle-Musigny; Vosne, Vosne-Romanée; Nuits, Nuits-St Georges; Aloxe, Aloxe-Corton; Pernand, Pernand-Vergelesses and Auxey, Auxey-Duresses. Both Chassagne and Puligny were able to hyphenate Montrachet to their names, since the tiny vineyard straddles the village boundary. Apparently Santenay, Meursault, Volnay and Pommard were sure enough of their market not to look for extra support. Savigny had the reassurance of being called "lès-Beaune" (meaning "near Beaune"). Monthélie and Blagny, the little villages above Meursault, had no famous vineyards to boast of (and in any case probably sold all their wine under the names of their better-known neighbours). The only district which did not adopt this practice was the Côte Dijonnaise, nearest to Dijon, where Brochon, Fixin, Marsannay and Chenôve were well enough known as Dijon's local wines.

CHAPTER 37

ZOLLVEREIN

With so much that is familiar already in place in our story, with the Médoc firmly classified, Champagne sparkling, and Burgundy parcelled out among many of the families who are still tending it, there are still two nations to be created to fit together the map – and the wine-list – of modern Europe. Napoleon's adventures had sowed the seed. But Germany and Italy existed at the start of the 19th century only in a geographical sense, and even that still far from clearly defined. As nations they were not yet even coherent ideas.

You could say the same of Italian wine – but not of German. If there is one region whose wine cannot have changed radically, even over the almost 2,000 years since its vineyards were first planted, it is the Rhineland; and more specifically its oldest wine-bearing tributary, the Moselle. It can never have made other than light white wines, ranging from thin and acid to ripely juicy. But if Germany's style of wine was settled long ago, its techniques, terminology, and even the regional distinctions that now seem set in stone, padlocked in place in a gothic dungeon of legislation, are all the fruit of the last 200 years – starting with the legendary late harvest at Schloss Johannisberg.

The Congress of Vienna set the scene. What Talleyrand was for France, the diplomat of genius, Clemens von Metternich, a Rhinelander from Koblenz, where Rhine and Moselle meet, was for the Austrian Empire. He presided over the re-establishment of the many little German states into something like their old feudal order as the German Confederation, but within newly distinct spheres of influence. Austria, as ever, was the overlord. But the Prussian cohorts that Prince Wolkonski taunted in Reims, and who saved the Duke of Wellington in the "damned close-run thing" at Waterloo, did not go quietly home to Berlin. Prussia was given a buffer zone along the French frontier, which included the Moselle.

Prussia in the past had always been an eastward-looking nation, seeing her opportunities and threats among her neighbours: Poland, Bohemia, Austria and Russia. Napoleon had drawn her attention to the west. Now suddenly she found herself straddling Germany from the Moselle in the west to Memel on the Polish border. Inevitably her fate was to be the fate of all of Germany. On the new-old map Alsace was retained by France. It was largely Britain's contribution to see that the old monarchy of France did not lose territory on Napoleon's account. The Rheingau and Rheinhessen became part of the Princedom of Hesse; while Franconia and the Palatinate, including the old Princedom of Speyer, its wine-growing heart, remained within the Kingdom of Bavaria.

**BORDER OF THE
GERMAN CONFEDERATION**

Metternich did his best to reestablish the ancien regime. He even made it possible for the Church to recover some of its land: the Cathedral at Trier, for example, and the Bischöfliches Priesterseminar, or Episcopal Seminary. But in one respect it was impossible to put the clock back. Feudal fetters had been cut. The little winegrowers had had a glimpse of freedom such they had not enjoyed since the great days of the Middle Ages. In the wine villages of Germany there was a great upsurge of interest in making better wine. Only Alsace became embittered, her produce regarded as a bargaining counter between France and Germany – excluded by tariff walls even from its best old market, Switzerland.

The Moselle entered a period of unheard-of prosperity. Nature gave her the unprecedented number of six excellent vintages in the decade from 1819. And Prussia cocooned its "own" wine region in a very comfortable arrangement of customs barriers that gave it privileged access down the Rhine, to northern Germany, to Prussia proper, to the Low Countries, and even to Britain. Between 1817 and 1840 the wine-growing population of the Moselle grew by 38%. Vines hugged the steep slopes from the river to the crest as they had never done before.

For a decade or so there was an unlooked-for trickle of British tourists, enchanted by the delicate Moselle they had tasted and agog to see the romantic scenery of its home. With Byron and Beethoven and Goethe and Walter Scott there was enough romance in the air, and along the riverside crags, to make a sensitive young person swoon. It is a wry thought that Karl Marx was born in Trier, in 1818, in this buzzing hive of bourgeois sentiment and endeavour. For as usual it was the bourgeois – or rather burghers – who had spent their savings on buying the best vineyards as soon as they were free of feudal ties.

Their satisfaction was short-lived. The weather is rarely so kind to the Moselle as it was in the 1820s. The '30s and 40s saw a succession of terrible vintages. Equally seriously, Prussia began to put into effect her unconcealed ambition of dominating Germany. She achieved it by economic means. It made little sense to have to pay

The Doctor vineyard, a steep slate slope of Riesling, towers above Bernkastel on the Moselle. The site's stature reached a peak in 1900, when the famous merchant firm of Deinhard bought part of it for 100 gold marks a square metre.

customs duties – the old curse of the wine-trade on the Rhine – simply because goods were transported from one part of Prussia to another via another German state. In 1834 Prussia lowered tarriff barriers by agreement with Bavaria and Württemberg; then with Baden and Hesse in 1835. In 1838 almost the whole of Germany was united in the Zollverein, the Customs Union, from which Austria was conspicuously absent. Germany was on her way to becoming a single country – under Prussian control.

What effect did the Zollverein have on wine-growing? The Moselle was not alone in finding itself open to all-comers. Economic unification – like the coming of the railways not long after – meant that there were winners and losers. To places where meagre wines had been grown for cheap local consumption (Prussia's own old vineyards around Berlin and Dresden came into this category) the Zollverein brought better and cheaper wines from the Rhineland. As the French historian Gaston Roupnel pointed out, historically wine was grown where it was convenient; now it could be grown where it was best.

At this stage we can visit the scene with Cyrus Redding, who was perhaps more immediately impressed with the Germans' capacity than the quality of their wine. They "have found out (the secret of) perpetual motion in their cups", he wrote. He scarcely mentions the Moselle (except by quoting Dr Henderson), so perhaps he did not visit it. Brauneberg, the first vineyard on everyone's Moselle list in that era, was the only one he rated; though he mentioned the famous old Carthusian vineyard of Grünhaus. What really impressed him, and Jullien too when he did his investigation, was the sheer stability of German wines. To Redding they were "generous, dry, finely flavoured, and endure age beyond example". "The completeness of their fermentation" made it difficult to "derange their affinities": they did not turn sour, and only very gradually oxidized over many years.

In 1830 at Hochheim, 1775, 1766 and 1748 were the fine old vintages "commonly offered". Such wines, said Redding, seem to be "possessed of inextinguishable vitality". The secret was partly in the solera-like topping-up system. Better to forget to kiss your wife when you come home, went the Rhineland saying, than to forget to keep your barrel full to the bung.

Touring with André Jullien in the 1840s it is clear that he has changed his mind about German wine since his earlier visits. "I was wrong when, in the first two editions of this book, I indicated that (German wines) all contain an acid which is disagreable to those who are not used to it." He admits that it is only true of bad vintages. But nowhere does he mention the word Spätlese, nor the habit of late harvesting which by this time was gaining ground. Late harvesting and the planting of Riesling went hand in hand. By mid-century Riesling was dominant, if not alone, in most of the best vineyards of the Rhineland, and the lesson of Schloss Johannisberg was steadily being learned.

To Jullien, although the "dry and sharp ('piquant') flavour is generally displeasing to the French when they first encounter it", it is "far from being a coarse and corrosive acid . . ." but "fine and delicate. . . ." Furthermore it "does not attack the nerves nor trouble the reason when one has drunk too much". It is one of the endearing things about Jullien that he evidently studied his subject in depth. As for the bouquet, he found it "very aromatic, very distinct, and very smooth. . . . equalling, if not surpassing, that of our best (French) wines".

Nowhere, though, except in Franconia, does he mention sweet wines – and these are not made by late picking, but as "vins de paille" from half-dried grapes. The potent Steinwein of Würzburg, he cautioned, occasioned violent headaches after too liberal use.

SCHLOSS JOHANNISBERG WAS THE EMPEROR'S PERSONAL REWARD to Prince Metternich for his services at Vienna. The new prince flung down the gauntlet to his Rheingau neighbour the Duke of Nassau, who now possessed the Steinberg and Kloster Eberbach, just as the Benedictines had done to the Cistercians a mere generation before. Metternich even made sure of his winemaking by putting the old cellar-master from Fulda, Pater Arndt, in charge. As for his marketing, he made the shrewdest move of all. He contracted with the new Frankfurt bank of Meyer Rothschild and his farflung sons. Since Nathan Rothschild had made an enormous fortune in London gambling on the result of the Battle of Waterloo the Rothschilds had become known as a unique hot-line to every Chancellery in Europe.

There is a distinct affinity between the selling strategy that Metternich adopted and the Médoc's idea that a first-growth should make several distinct qualities of wine. Schloss Johannisberg was indisputably a first-growth. In Bordeaux it would have offered a Grand Vin and a second wine. But with the introduction of late harvesting a German cellar had a more complex set of alternatives; wines picked earlier or later, with more or less flavour, strength, and even sweetness.

For a diplomat of the ancien régime Metternich behaved with remarkable commercial acumen. He designated the different qualities of his wine by two different labels and several different coloured wax seals. The use of "château" labels was revolutionary; the grading system even more so. It formalized the practice of tasting and choosing the best casks in the cellar and settling on a price. In 1830 Metternich became so modern as to order that "no bottled wine from Johannisberg is to be sold unless the label is signed by the cellar-master". These concepts of grading and of guaranteed authenticity were way ahead of their time; eventually they were to build into a system of legislation covering the whole of Germany.

BY THE START OF THE 19TH CENTURY SCHLOSS JOHANNISBERG and the Steinberg systematically harvested as late as the season allowed. Ordinary growers still had to pick when they were told. It was a grave offence even to be found in a vineyard at all outside set hours announced by the church bells. Grapes are all too easy to pilfer. But the exceptional weather of the Comet vintage, 1811, gave even the humblest vintner a taste of nectar. In 1822 another harvest started to rot and shrivel on the vines while the sun still shone. The burghers could not bear to pick on the appointed date. The mayor of Eltville took their case to the ducal officers of Nassau; permission was given to wait for the rot to develop before starting the general harvest – and for the first time the majority of a vintage had the luxurious quality of a Spätlese.

Above all the Riesling showed its class over the earlier-ripening Sylvaner. Its wines, however sweet, maintained their piquancy, their vital nerve of fruity acidity. In normal harvests, and for ordinary wine, Sylvaner provided a great volume of a

Oestrich-Winkel in the Rheingau. Further along the gentle slope, Schloss Johannisberg stands on its hill above the river. Its princely example in picking late and carefully, selecting the best grapes, was followed by the entire district.

pleasant drink. But once late harvesting became legal, it fell back almost to the position of the Gamay in relation to the Pinot Noir.

Certainly by Metternich's time, probably before, the next logical step was taken. If a general late harvest made more potent wines; a selection of only the rotten bunches, kept apart from the rest, would make more potent wines still. Auslese was the term they coined (it means a picking out, or selection); inspired perhaps by the Austrian word Ausbruch for Tokay. In other parts of Germany the word Ausgelesen began to be heard from the early 19th century on. As the century progressed, more Riesling was planted and more care taken over repeated selections, sorting not only the rotten bunches from the merely ripe, but even the individual rotten grapes from within a bunch. The châteaux of Sauternes seem to have been perfecting the same technique at just the same time. Auslese came to mean selected bunches. Then about mid-century the word Beeren, meaning a single grape, was attached to the next degree of selection: a Beerenauslese. Who coined the term and when it was first used does not seem to be on record. Château Yquem could be said to be a Beerenauslese.

AT THE TIME, AND INDEED UNTIL VERY RECENTLY, THERE WAS LITTLE, if any, uniformity in the way growers (even in the same district, let alone in different states) described their more and more carefully selected wines. Where Schloss Johannisberg and some other big estates initiated a system of good, better and best (with stages in between where necessary) many growers were carried away in their enthusiasm over their individual small casks of specially selected and reselected wines that they treated them almost as their children. It is no exaggeration: when there were only enough Beerenauslese grapes to fill a very small cask a grower has been known to keep it in his bedroom or even his bed; fermentation might stop in the cool of the cellar and never restart.

"Auslese" did not express the beautiful delicacy of this cask or that; so it was called a feine Auslese. But if that is feine, this surely, with its extra hint of honey, must be feinste. And this extraordinary wine, with such a peach-like flavour, is nothing if not Hochfeinste. By the end of the tasting no word would do for the ultimate Auslese but Allerfeinste – finest of all. This was not salesmanship; this was pure parental pride. When it came to distinguishing between one champion cask and another the only practical way in the end was by numbering them. Its Füder or Fass number was the way the buyer pinned down precisely the wine he had found most to his liking.

THERE IS NO DOUBT THAT BY THE MIDDLE OF THE CENTURY the first-growths of the Rheingau had mastered the making of superlative sweet wines. We have the evidence of Count Haraszthy – for once (almost) at a loss for words. He and his son went to Kloster Eberbach (the abbey was then partly a prison) to taste the Duke of Nassau's Steinberger: "To describe the wines would be a work sufficient for Byron, Shakespeare or Schiller, and even those geniuses would not do full justice until they had imbibed a couple of glasses full. As you take a mouthful and let it run drop by drop down your throat, it leaves in your mouth the same aroma as a bouquet of the choicest flowers will offer to your olfactories. . . . A young wine of three or four years has this bouquet in a very great degree; but as it becomes older it loses it, gaining instead a most delicate and penetating taste; it now communicates to the palate slowly but surely its perfume."

At Schloss Johannisberg the wines "must be tasted to know their magnificence, for it is beyond the powers of description. These wines, like those of the Dukes of Nassau, are occasionally sold at public auction, but at such exorbitant prices that we poor republicans would shudder as much to drink such a costly liquid as if it were molten gold."

TO WINEGROWERS NOT IN THE STRATOSPHERE OF THE RHEINGAU the policies of the Prussians made almost as much difference as the weather. To the Palatinate it was the dawn of international (or even national) recognition. Rhine travellers since the Middle Ages had spoken warmly of the wines of Bacharach – variant spellings include Bachrag: all supposed it had some connection with Bacchus – on the Middle Rhine. Most reported that it was the heart of an area of flourishing vineyards. In fact it has few, but was the strategic shipping port of the whole west bank of the Rhine in the possession of the house of Wittelsbach, first as Palatine Counts, then, since 1806, as Kings of Bavaria. Wittelsbach territory included much of today's Rheinhessen,

TROCKENBEERENAUSLESE

Sweet wines were made whenever the grapes ripened to high levels of sugar, whether nobly-rotten or simply raisined by a hot autumn. No distinction was made, and the terminology was more imaginative than precise. When the word Beerenauslese (selected grapes) was not emphatic enough to express the richness and rarity of the ultimate gleanings from the vines, Goldbeere-nauslese and Edelbeerenauslese were available superlatives. Today's only legal term is Trocken-beerenauslese ("trocken" means that the grapes were shrivelled almost dry, either by rot or heat). But even in the 1930 wine law this term had no legal definition.

the region of the Nahe and what since 1838 has been called the Rheinpfalz. Even Rheingau wines, though, were shipped from Bacharach for safety: it lies just below the dangerous rapids of the Binger Loch where the river narrows and turns north around the Rüdesheimer Berg.

Unlike most monarchs, the Palatine counts paid little attention to their winegrowers. Neither Church nor State was directly concerned. It was the country of proud, scattered, and usually disorganized gentry or local nobility without the means to make their voices heard, or their wines individually known. The 30 Years War had decimated the region, and so had Louis XIV. Heidelberg Castle, once the seat of the counts, still lies in ruins as a memento of a French visit in the 17th century. But in the 19th the French made amends. In the words of the great historian of German wine, Dr Bassermann-Jordan, a man of the Palatinate, its winegrowers were "freed and awoken by the French Revolution". The region was even briefly a département of France under the name of Mont-Tonnerre. Fine wines had no local market, but the Zollverein gave them their opportunity, and a fortuitous land-tax survey by the Bavarian State in 1828 their specific identity. From the 1830s onwards the names of Deidesheim, Forst, Ruppertsberg, Wachenheim . . . all the villages of the Mittelhaardt that had grown wine since Roman times without proper credit, found their place in the community of excellence. In 1841 appeared the first Deidesheimer Auslese, and it became clear that the climate and soil of the region, geographically a northern extension of Alsace, are the most suited of all in Germany for the making of Spätlese and Auslese wines.

ALSACE MEANWHILE WAS CAUGHT IN THE CUSTOMS TRAP, excluded from the German market as part of France, which did not want its wine either. It was a painful situation for a region which "needed to export to avoid being drowned in its own wine" – and made worse by the dispirited planting of the heaviest-cropping, lowest-quality vine, the Knipperlé. At the same time Strasbourg became one of Europe's great brewing towns, so the danger of drowning was doubled.

Where once Alsace supplied the Black Forest region of Baden across the Rhine (as well as distant markets both down and up the river), Baden began extending its own vineyards. From 1850 even Switzerland closed its borders to the wine that had for centuries been its staple. For Switzerland this meant a spate of creative and experimental planting, particularly in its oldest, warmest and most fertile region, the Valais, which had had a spell as the French département of Simplon, but had been reunited with its brother cantons in 1815. Such ancient alpine vines as Arvine, Amigne and Humagne were elbowed aside to make way for Gamay, Sylvaner, even Pinot Noir and Riesling – but above all for Chasselas, or "Fendant", which somehow seized the personality of the region to make a uniquely smooth and beguiling drink.

Switzerland's other principal regions on Lakes Geneva and Neuchâtel were already planted solid. We have the ubiquitous Haraszthy's report: "We arrived in Geneva (from Neuchâtel) after travelling eight hours continually among vine-yards. . . . Not a spot as large as an ordinary brick-yard was left uncultivated, with the exception of where the old vines have been cut out to give the ground the necessary three years' rest."

Vines still spread along the lake shore to east and west of Lausanne, facing south
above Lake Geneva. The Swiss vineyards reached their greatest extent (85,000
acres) in 1884: their current size is about a third of that.

When in 1870 France fell ignominiously to the Prussian armies, it seemed that
Alsace would have its reprieve. This shuttlecock region was to be German again
until 1918. But Germany regarded the vineyards of the Vosges rather as France did
the Midi: never asking anything from it but a low price. In 1871 it represented more
than a quarter of all Germany's vineyards and produced (this was the problem) 39%
of German wine – unfortunately little of it of the keeping kind. "Furthermore", as
the Alsatian Joseph Dreyer wrote, "the clash of personalities between the Alsatians
and the Germans was irreconcilable. Each found the others' wine of inferior quality
and did not hesitate to say so – with the difference, however, that the German was
the buyer and the Alsatian the seller."

It remained a sad story, with all but a few ignoring the potential of Alsace for
wine of wonderful quality. Each political set-back seemed to be followed by a
natural one. At the end of the century the market was eager; for once there was a
wine shortage – but unscrupulous merchants took the short cut of adulteration.
Many growers who had done their best gave up in despair. As demand grew, the
vineyards shrank.

WHEN NAPOLEON HAD MARCHED IN, FRANCONIA had still been one of Germany's
biggest wine producers. More than any, though, it was a domain of the church, and
thus the most affected by secularization. Würzburg reached its apotheosis in the age
of the baroque. The "thick wreath of vines" of the Middle Ages still surrounded it;
the Prince-Bishop's great Residenz dominated it; its vineyards supported two
charity hospitals (one religious, one lay), each almost on the scale of the Hospices de
Beaune. Germany's romantic poets, Goethe and Schiller, took issue on the merits of
the famous Stein and Leisten slopes overlooking the town. (Goethe's choice was
Stein.)

Secularization is usually given as the prime cause of its decline – but that was not its effect on the Rheingau. In Würzburg the Bavarian state took over the Prince-Bishop's domaine; those of the Julliusspital (the religious hospital) survive – as do those of the Burgerspital. Wine-growing declined in Franconia (as it did in more eastern parts of Germany that once had smaller, but thriving, vineyards) as a result of competition from other occupations – the Industrial Revolution, in other words – and the Bavarian tide of beer. Adverse weather in the 19th century has also been blamed; even the taste for tea-drinking. A more probable cause is the fact that Franconia had no established export-trade; nor even a wine-trade as such of any kind. In the 18th century to sell wine was actually against police regulations. Fear of running dry was given as the reason. But whatever lowered the morale and profitability of its winegrowers they were in no condition to fight the fungus plagues of oidium, and later mildew, when they arrived. Franconian wine today is an expensive luxury used, as it always was, by its own devoted citizens.

WE LEFT THE MOSEL IN THE 1840S STRUGGLING with the dreadful weather and the end of its protective Prussian cloak. Karl Marx had by this time been to his Trier school, the Friedrich Wilhelm Gymnasium, and at the age of 24 was writing stirring newspaper articles in the *Rheinische Zeitung*. The Prussians, he wrote, have realized that their protectorate needs a little discipline, after living (for all of 16 years) "in a state of unparalleled luxury". It was perhaps true that unaccustomed cash in hand had led unsophisticated farmers to overspend and get into difficulties: there were many bankruptcies and large numbers emigrated to America. The Prussians were unconcerned; even, wrote Marx, when a cask of 150 litres of wine was bartered for two loaves of bread, two pounds of butter and half a pound of onions. He called for intervention, organization, diversification, industry – in vain.

What saved the Moselle was not the Prussians, but its own inherent quality: given decent weather its increased plantations of Riesling made uniquely fine wine. Even in bad vintages Moselle Riesling was excellent material for the rapidly-growing sparkling wine industry modelled on Champagne. By the 1840s steamers had shortened the journey time from Trier to Koblenz from two days to ten hours: the "railway effect", in a sense, came early. The 1850s provided three excellent vintages in a row, leading up, with perfect timing, to Gladstone's budget that lowered British duties on light wines.

Most important of all, for all of Germany but especially for the Moselle, was the introduction of Chaptal's idea of adding sugar, suggested by the German chemist Ludwig Gall. It seems extraordinary that in this coolest of wine regions, with unripe, low-strength wine a regular problem, the idea had not been seized on before. The explanation must be that people were accustomed to thin wine (which in any case they used as an all-purpose drink, cold or hot and sweetened according to the season). Chaptalization – they called it "verbesserung", or "improving" – gave them the possibility of saleable wine every year. It is enormously to the credit of the Germans that, unlike the French, they continued to prefer their wine natural, even if that meant drinking it pretty mean. As soon as a wine law was framed, in 1892, it made it mandatory to say whether a wine was natural (i.e. without added sugar) or not. That is still the basis of the German wine law – whereas the French long ago persuaded themselves that the systematic addition of sugar to raise the strength of their wine is none of the public's concern.

At first, of course, finding this new way to make their wine not only saleable, but exportable, the traders of the Moselle over-encouraged sugaring. Good growers resisted. In the region of the Saar, above Trier, they did not give in until the 1920s. But politics once more turned in favour of the Moselle when the war with France in 1870 reminded the Prussians how strategically important their border region was. German prosperity now meant a national market. Wine-merchants learned that by using sugar containing starch they could give their wine something approximately like the rich texture of an Auslese. In doing so they blotted out the delicate transparency of flavour which makes each good Moselle an individual. This struggle, between a gross commodity, cheap to produce and easy to sell, and what I can only call an intellectual one, with specific aesthetic appeal, in one guise or another has occupied the minds of growers, merchants and legislators ever since.

At this juncture, in the last decades of the 19th century, the temptation to produce volume at the expense of quality could hardly have been greater. Over the previous half-century the country's vineyard area had shrunk by as much as half, while the spending-power of the population, especially in the industrial north, had enormously increased. For the first time, Germany was a net importer of wine.

It seems improbable that the words of the Rheinische Zeitung ever reached Berlin. Yet Prussia reacted almost as though Marx was the Kaiser's favourite reading. Not so much by intervention and diversification, as by training, legislation and example, Prussia showed an admirable determination that quality was to be Germany's destiny. Without at first being precisely clear what it meant by pure wine, it declared itself in favour; then in a second law it allowed sugaring, but made any sort of "falsification" a criminal offence.

Perhaps the government's most effective move was to found a state wine school, still one of the world's most famous, at Geisenheim in the Rheingau in 1872, followed by model wine estates near Trier and on the Nahe. The idea of a model wine from a model cellar is perfectly characteristic of Prussian thinking. It allows us to ask the question: what was the ideal German wine of 1900?

It was a Riesling, certainly completely dry, unless it was a Spätlese. There was no ambition to make the type of fruitily fresh wine which is the fashion today – nor any means of adding and controlling sweetness, such as the 20th century has produced. High natural acidity and forceful flavour (the result of a harvest a fraction of the size a modern vine produces) was tempered by long aging in old oak casks,

MULLER-THURGAU

Geisenheim's most famous production, unfortunately, is not one to be proud of. It was there that an ingenious Dr Müller from Thurgau in Switzerland succeeded in 1882 in crossing the Riesling with the Sylvaner to produce a grape which has the quality of neither, and was rightly ignored until the 20th century was well under way, when it swept Riesling from its rightful place in vineyard after vineyard. Its virtues, such as they are, are early ripening and a big crop, with a strong aroma. The climax of its baleful effect is past, but it remains the most widely-planted vine in Germany, and largely accounts for the tedium of Liebfraumilch.

which also served to stabilize it perfectly. Such a wine would strike us as bold, austere, penetrating; an aristocrat, and an unbending one until it mellowed with age. Like a fine Pinot Noir from the Côte d'Or, its "terroir" would determine its precise flavours; its affinity with apples or peaches, slate or smoke or steel.

A Spätlese on the other hand would keep some natural sweetness, and an Auslese a great deal. The natural yeasts were not capable of finishing the fermentation to complete dryness, so the wine was stabilized with a dose of sulphur and left for time to do its work. After several years in cask the sulphur tang would disappear and the wine be totally stable, its sweetness again not fresh and fruity, but deep and satisfying. Such wines created connoisseurs by the very precision of their distinctions. "Intellectual" is the inevitable word.

To compare Prussia and Austria is the best way to emphasise the direction Germany had taken and the progress it had made in the 19th century. Within the Austrian Empire lay all the vineyards of Hungary, of the eastern Adriatic and the Tyrol. In total acreage of vines the Empire had more than half as much as France, twice as much as the Italian states, and three times as much as Spain. Yet the only wine of first-growth standing it produced was Tokay – and indeed all Vienna's best wines came from Hungary.

The liberal Emperor – "enlightened" is the usual term – Joseph II laid down in 1784 the simplest wine law of all. Growers could only sell their own wine. Vienna's uproarious büschenken and heurigen, the winegrower's cellar and his garden turned into a perpetual party, celebrate it to this day.

Happily we have an expert witness to the wines of the Empire on display. Henry Vizetelly was the official British judge at Vienna's Universal Exhibition in 1873,

Schloss Grafenegg at Krems, home of the Austrian branch of the Metternich family, is today the headquarters of the "Metternich Alliance", a group of princely estates which promote Austria's quality wines.

A nineteenth-century German grape-picker needed to be strong – and pretty athletic – to negotiate his day's work. The horse looks on as one agile worker empties his load into a mobile vat.

which claimed to be the first at which all the wines of the world were to be judged in competition together. Austria did not win many prizes.

"The wines of Austria", wrote Vizetelly "are as diverse as its population. At the extreme south (he is speaking of Dalmatia) they are so dark and fullbodied that when mixed with an equal quantity of water they are quite as deep in colour and as spirituous as the ordinary wines of Bordeaux . . . while in less favourable districts they are excessively poor and so sour as to rasp the tongue like the roughest cider. Many [these will be the Hungarians] have the luscious character of Constantia and the muscat growths of Frontignan and Lunel. Several, on the other hand, are disagreably bitter [Tyroleans, perhaps?], others again are so astringent as to contract the windpipe while swallowing them, whereas a few of the lighter varieties possess the delicacy, if not the fragrance, of certain growths of the Rheingau. [Could these have been the Wachau contingent from the Danube?] It must be confessed, however, that although the specimens were remarkably varied and numerous, the better qualities were extremely rare."

MAGYAR ORSZAG

In the second quarter of the 19th century the vineyards of Hungary were larger than those of Italy or Spain. The little country took full advantage of its near-perfect climate for the vine. Tokay apart, though, its winemaking and storage were still medieval. The best hope for its produce was to be bought as early as possible by a Polish merchant skilled in cellar practice.

Until 1848, when the Hungarians revolted against Austrian rule, progress was slow. The Austrians, with Russian help, crushed the revolution, but were forced to abolish serfdom, which gave Hungary the impetus it needed. The golden age of Hungarian wine started, and ended, only slightly later than that of Bordeaux.

Phylloxera attacked Tokay in the 1880s, but grafting was rapidly organised and totally successful. Furthermore, Hungary possessed the ultimate weapon against phylloxera, its Great Plain, the Alföld, whose soil is pure sand. Once before, after the Turkish retreat, the Hungarians had colonised their little Sahara. In the 1880s, they discovered its potential for wine-growing without grafting.

Around Lake Balaton and on the great Esterhazy estates at Mór sandy soil was exploited, new grape varieties were introduced, and Hungarian wine renewed its ancient reputation with new vigour.

The present status of Hungary as a fringe wine-country of the eastern bloc bears no relation to its great past nor its unique potential.

CHAPTER 38

WHEN SORROWS COME

In March 1862 the Emperor Louis-Napoleon invited France's greatest scientist, Louis Pasteur, to the palace of the Tuileries to consult him on an extremely serious problem. Something was going badly wrong with France's wine, and at a time of unprecedented exports, boosted by the new gospel of Free Trade. An embarrassing number of bottles bought by reputable merchants and delivered to important foreign customers were turning out undrinkable. The good name of France, and of her most famous industry, was at stake. In the name of the Empire, said Louis-Napoleon, could the great savant investigate and report?

Pasteur's fame at the time rested largely on the fact that he had at long last discovered the nature of fermentation. Lavoisier had perfectly described the process (he coined the use of the arabic word alcohol for its product) but no-one had ever understood what caused it. Fermentation was due to the action of yeasts in reproducing. Micro-organisms, Pasteur realized, play an unknown number of undreamed-of parts in the functioning of creation.

In 1862, as business enterprises grew to proportions that the world had never seen before, he organized an exhibition in Paris "on the part played by the infinitely small in nature". Nothing could have been more prophetic.

In the letter that he presented to the Emperor two-and-a-half years later, when he was invited to stay at the palace of Compiègne, Pasteur introduced the subject thus: ". . . thanks to the commercial treaties between France and all civilized nations that daily become more numerous, the wines of France are being carried to all the principal markets of the world . . . wine can become for our country so important an object of commerce that it is difficult today even to imagine its value.

"Unhappily French wines are at risk on long voyages. They are subject to numerous sicknesses: to turning sour . . . ropy or bitter. . . . Once landed, they grow worse; still more so when they are left in less skilled hands, in unsuitable cellars, without the thousand attentions which make the proper treatment of wine a rare skill, even in France."

If it is surprising to read this, when France had been exporting wine without such problems (at least in such acute forms) for so many centuries, we should remember that the wines in question came largely from the 1850s, the period of the

Pasteur's track record in alleviating the ills of France – including the diversion of potential disaster in the silk trade – was crowned by the discovery of the process to be called pasteurization. Among its myriad other benefits it prevented the spoiling of much wine. This commemorative portrait hints at the esteem in which he was held.

oidium crisis. One must suspect (although Pasteur does not refer to it) that the vines weakened by the disease were in turn producing disease-prone wine.

To find out why wines turned sour or vinegary ("pricked" is the old English word) he had been, he told the Emperor, to a part of France where the problem was endemic; his own birthplace, the Jura mountains in the south-east, between Burgundy and the Swiss border. The scene he hints at reads like a pastoral-comical play: the famous scholar visiting his father's house in the country on a secret mission; the little town of Arbois all agog; the great man darting in and out of cellars with his sample bag; the makeshift laboratory above the drapers filled with apparatus from the joiner, the ironmonger and the blacksmith. There was a good deal of banter in the streets, but the drama he followed through his microscope was real enough. On his slides he put samples of healthy wine, and wines with "tourne", "pousse", "graisse" – all the diseases that could make it undrinkable. Each slide was like a different cage in a zoo, peopled with entirely different, easily recognizable, microscopic creatures. It was only a step to identifying which of these bacteria was responsible for which wine-disease. After a while, he said, he could tell by looking at a slide sample of a wine what it would taste like. His breakthrough came when he proved that these bacteria, like all creatures, need oxygen to live and reproduce. Sealed in a test-tube without air, wine remained stable; with air its resident bacteria took over. The commonest, in fact the one which is present in all wine, is the vinegar bacteria. If wine is left exposed to air it will sooner or later turn to vinegar.

His practical answer bears his name: pasteurization. It consisted simply of heating the wine in its bottle in a sort of bain-marie of hot water for long enough to kill the microbes or bacteria. He demonstrated that this could be done without giving the wine a cooked taste or otherwise affecting its ability to mature normally.

The applications of pasteurization to other substances – milk in particular – were obvious. Put together with his discovery of a vaccine for rabies, his introduction of asepsis in surgery and his cure for the pest that was threatening the French silk industry, Pasteur's contributions to the health and prosperity of France made him a national and international hero.

"WHEN SORROWS COME, THEY COME NOT SINGLE SPIES, but in battalions". Not a year had passed since the scientist with the microscope had saved France's wine from spoiling, when a foe appeared that threatened something far more drastic: literally to cut off the nation's wine-supply at the roots. Within a quarter of a century the vineyards of France, and via France Europe; finally, some four-fifths of the vineyards of the world, were to feel like Pharaoh at odds with Moses and his god – for if seven is a biblical number, so is three. Oidium was the first plague. Its cure (or rather control) took only a decade. After oidium came phylloxera, and after phylloxera, mildew. They not only devastated all but a privileged minority of vineyards; they altered fundamentally and permanently the way vines are grown. Wine, you might say, ended its state of innocence with the multiplied catastrophes that followed hard on its Golden Age. For many marginal vineyards it was the end. At the same time it put the strong in a stronger position than ever before. Nothing was to be the same again after the long struggle to protect and re-establish wine-growing in Europe – a process that in some cases took three-quarters of a century.

PASTEUR NEEDED A MICROSCOPE TO SEE THE ORGANISMS that he brought under control. If you have good enough eyesight to see a pin-prick you can see a phylloxera louse without a lens. But it was still the minute size of this overactive animal that allowed it to escape detection. It had already been frustrating would-be winegrowers for centuries. Phylloxera was the culprit for the failure of Jefferson's, and every other eastern American's, imported vines. If they blamed the climate, the soil or more obvious bugs, it was because they never saw the real cause – nor did it ever occur to them that there might be an all-but-invisible pest to which the native vines, by long association, had become immune.

It was the speed of steamships that brought phylloxera to Europe alive. Many must have set off on sailing-ships, snug in carefully-wrapped bundles of American vine-cuttings or on the roots of potted plants being sent to Europe for ornament or experiment. None survived the weeks at sea. By the 1850s black-smoke-belching steamers had brought the passage down to nine or 10 days. At the European port a train was waiting. Suddenly the tiny pest was in a larder that stretched to infinity. For it arrived just where the vines were thickest, at the mouth of the Rhône.

Bordeaux, Burgundy, Champagne and the vineyards of old renown and new money were not alone in enjoying a Golden Age at this time. In terms of sheer scale their expansion was puny in comparison with that of the south of France, and in particular the Languedoc. The Midi lost little by the Revolutionary years, but gained a wider market for its wine and brandy in the countries Napoleon conquered (and the armies he conquered them with). The industrialization of the wine business came early here; the peace of 1815 found the citizens of the Languedoc prosperous, but lacking coal or materials for industry; so they invested in land, planted more vines and mechanized every aspect of their trade. They set their sights on quantity, not quality, developed such vine varieties as the Carignan, and the undistinguished Aramon, that produced spectacular amounts of juice, and prospered.

Between 1825 and 1850 the vineyards of the central département of the Languedoc, the Hérault, doubled in size. They were reacting to a popular taste for red wine that jumped by almost 10 litres a head in each decade from 1848 to the 1870s. Very much to their advantage, too, was the boom, on northern farms that previously had grown vines, of cereals and sugar-beet to feed and gratify the surging urban population. When in the 1850s the Paris-Lyon-Marseille railway reached the Languedoc from the industrial north the crisis of oidium had just passed in a cloud of sulphur dust. There was a gold-rush feeling in the air. Steamers from Sète were distributing tens of thousands of barrels to customers from Russia to America; but above all to the thirsty colonists in France's new acquisition, Algeria.

Inexorably the vineyard swept down from the hills to claim the fertile sweep of the coastal plain. Between 1850 and 1875 France added 500,000 acres to her vineyards; 325,000 of them in the Languedoc. Cereals, olives, vegetables – every other crop was cast aside. Trade was free, money was easy and Nemesis was standing in the wings.

THE PECULIAR REPRODUCTIVE HABITS OF THE PHYLLOXERA need not concern us. They are complicated, but highly effective. A small import soon became a considerable population. Its effect on the vines was first noticed near Arles in Provence in 1863. Patches of vines, gradually spreading outwards from the country at the mouth of the Rhône, both east and west, were described as having "consumptive symptoms". They were acting rather like a patient with tuberculosis; their leaves withering and dropping, their new shoots without vigour, their fruit remaining unripe. Three years after the symptoms appeared the vine was usually dead.

What looked at first like a local but worryingly unknown disease took three years to make its mark. It was ever thus. When Dutch Elm Disease arrived in Europe in the 1960s there was no authoritative account or sufficient survey until the pest (in this case a vector of a fungus disease rather than the killer itself) was out of control and the elm was beyond saving. The habits of the phylloxera, as well as its size, made it a particularly hard villain to track down, because by the time the corpse was dug up for a post mortem, the culprits had moved on to feed from, and in due course kill, another vine.

The most striking aspect of the dead vine, when it was unearthed for inspection, was that its root system had virtually disappeared, and for no apparent reason. By

Even when it was acknowledged that a myriad of microscopic creatures could kill healthy vines by the hundred thousand, the mystery remained, how is it done? The phylloxera louse induces the vine to reject its own roots and hence effectively commit suicide. In feeding from the tender growing roots with its proboscis it injects a substance that causes root galls or swellings which are apparently regarded as alien by the plant. The sap of the vine ceases to circulate through the infected roots. Eventually it is left literally rootless: in some cases a simple tug will bring it clear out of the ground.

Above ground, phylloxera infestation is easy to recognise by patches of congested red swellings on vine leaves. Where a grafted vine has reverted to its American rootstock the leaves are the part which is attacked.

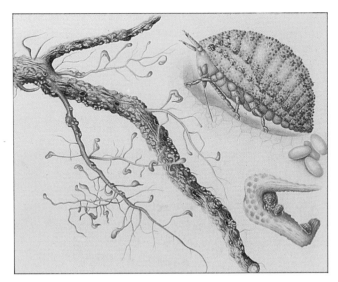

The phylloxera aphid's tiny size and complicated life cycle puzzled scientists for several years. Jules-Emile Planchon discovered that it fatally attacked the roots of the European vine, the vine effectively killing itself by forming root galls which it then discards so that no root is left.

1866 a minority of proprietors in the affected zones (the numbers of the louse were just beginning to become significant) were voicing their concern, which was taken up by the agricultural press. The most active of these proprietors was the Montpellier stockbroker Gaston Bazille, father of the Impressionist painter Frédéric, who had invested heavily in vineyards. Bazille met the professor of pharmacy at Montpellier University, Jules-Emile Planchon, a man of many talents who had studied with the greatest of the Directors of Kew Gardens in London, Sir William Hooker. (Montpellier had the oldest and perhaps most distinguished school of pharmacy in Europe, going back to Arnaldus da Vilanova, and knowledge gleaned from the Moorish university of Cordoba.) One of Planchon's many interests was entomology.

In July 1868 Bazille, Planchon and scientific assistants convened at a wine estate, the Château de Lagoy, near St Rémy, 15 miles from Arles, to get to the root of the mystery. A contemporary print shows them swarming among the vines, magnifying-glass in hand, wearing top hats in the blazing summer sun. There were flourishing, sick and dead vines in the château's vineyard. For the first time they dug up healthy vines as well as obviously affected ones. "From that moment," Planchon wrote in his notebook, "one fact of capital importance was established; namely that an almost invisible insect, developing underground by myriads of individuals, could bring about the destruction of even the most vigorous of vines.

"But what of this insect? From whence did it come? Had it been described? And what were its nearest relatives? These questions . . . could only be answered . . . if all stages of the insect's life-cycle were found."

What they had seen, when they dug up an affected vine, was a seething mass of the tiniest aphids, mere pin-pricks individually but in such numbers that "the roots appeared to be varnished yellow". If this was the louse stage, Planchon realized, the insect must also have a winged phase of life. He soon found it, still needing a magnifying glass to see it: "an elegant little aphid with four flat, transparent wings". As an entomologist he recognised it as being similar to one that causes galls on oak leaves: *Phylloxera quercus.* Looking around at the dead vines, their roots entirely

consumed by the incalculable numbers of the pest, he named it *Phylloxera vastatrix* –
the devastator. At this stage its origin was quite unknown; America was not even
under suspicion – and indeed the majority of opinion was still that something so tiny
could not possibly be the cause of vigorous plants dying wholesale. It was held that
there was something wrong, some degeneration that was weakening the vines,
which then became the prey to this otherwise insignificant little bug.

There were good reasons to worry. By 1867 the unmistakable symptoms had
been spotted hundreds of miles away, in the palus vineyards of Bordeaux. But
nobody in France who was not personally and immediately affected was likely to be
interested in a few dying vines, when the whole nation was moving (as they
thought) into one of its hours of glory. The free-trading, liberal-thinking Empire of
Louis-Napoleon combined glamour and squalor, chic and corruption. Another
Universal Exhibition in Paris in 1868 was to celebrate commercial triumph. In 1869
came the opening of the French-planned Suez Canal, and in 1870, infused with folie
de grandeur, the Emperor decided on a trial of strength with Bismarck's Prussia. It
was France's shortest and most inglorious war. Within weeks Prussia was besieging
Paris, and would withdraw only on payment of 1,460 tons of gold (raised from the
public by government bonds at 6%) and the transfer of long-suffering Alsace and
Lorraine to Germany. No sooner had the Prussians left than the two-month
revolution of the Commune gripped the capital. Lucky the winegrowers of the
south, one might well have said, whose worst problem was some dying vines.

WITH SUCH GENERAL UNCONCERN, THE DEVASTATOR had a flying start. Planchon and a
growing number of associates had been working as an official Commission since
1869; yet in 1872 the Société d'Agriculture of the Gironde put up a prize of a mere
20,000 francs, scarcely enough to buy a second-hand carriage, for an effective
remedy. The list of suggestions makes good light reading. Thousands of useless ideas
came pouring in, ranging from burying a toad under each vine (this was borrowed
from Pliny) to exorcism, to beating the ground mechanically until the pest was
driven into the sea (or over a frontier).

Rewards for brain-waves, of course, were just the reaction of a bureaucracy
wanting to be seen to be doing something. In 1872 the government raised the ante to
300,000 francs (for which the carriage could certainly have had some fine horses).
No-one ever received the reward, although some perfectly justified claims were
eventually made. The sheer number of people involved in finding and applying the
solution made it possible for the government to evade its commitment.

By this time two principal lines of serious research were being followed: one the
elimination of the pest; the other, somehow to find a vine which was immune to its
attack. Under certain circumstances it was found that the bug could be eliminated. If
a vineyard could be completely flooded for a period the aphids would drown.
Unfortunately the few flat vineyards where this was a practical proposition were the
least valuable for the quality of their wine. A vineyard of more or less pure sand was
also apparently immune: the louse could make no headway through its shifting
grains. (Its progress through stony or clay soil is one of the wonders of its vigorous
performance; each clod of earth or pebble is a mountain to a creature so small.) Both
these solutions – the flooding and the sand – were an invitation to plant the flat

coastal strip of the Languedoc. The Salins du Midi, the rich sea salt extraction company which exploits the lagoons at Aigues Mortes, beyond the marshy Camargue, found itself with an extremely profitable second string to its bow as the crisis deepened and more vineyards were destroyed. It planted the enormous and hitherto useless beaches with the Carignan and Aramon. Looking at its giant vineyards (of Grenache, Cabernet, and altogether worthy varieties today), surrounded by fresh-water dikes to keep sea-salt from leaching into the plantations, one is reminded of the miracle of Cana.

In most vineyards the only hope of elimination was by chemical means: fumigating the soil. The chemist Baron Paul Thénard discovered that a substance called carbon bisulphide, made by passing sulphur vapour over red hot charcoal, was extremely toxic to phylloxera and to most other creatures too. Injected into the soil around the vines it left nothing alive. In his early trials he was over-generous with the poison and killed the vines as well. The fumes made workers ill and anyone standing downwind was at risk. It was also so inflammable that an explosion was a strong possibility (although surprisingly few were reported).

FUMIGATION OF ONE KIND OR ANOTHER was widely used from the early 1870s onward, right into this century; indeed until the 1940s there were vineyards in France where phylloxera was kept at bay by soil injection. The standard implement, called a Pal, was rather like a giant hypodermic syringe, with a foot-bar for driving it into the ground and a plunger for injecting the solution, an inexpressibly tedious and terribly expensive operation, made only sightly less so, in vineyards where a horse could traverse the vine-rows, by a later wheeled version which functioned like a plough. The tedium was relieved, in this case, by the blade occasionally striking sparks off stones and setting fire to the apparatus. A sad little procession of a horse, a peculiar plough, a ploughman and a man with a fire-extinguisher was a familiar sight in parts of France for many years.

A more effective alternative was watering the vineyard with a solution of sulphocarbonate of potassium (or sodium), but the gear that was required, pumps, miles of pipes, nozzles and above all a huge amount of water, was either unobtainable or so hugely expensive that only first-growths could afford it. Some did, notwithstanding. Until the First World War a number of great vineyards in the Médoc were paying contractors to disinfect their soil every year, in addition to the sulphuring made necessary by oidium and the equally tedious treatments that became essential when a second form of mildew became rampant in the 1880s.

THE ROUTINE OF GROWING WINE had changed beyond recognition; from a simple, although labour-intensive, matter of pruning, cultivating, weeding, occasionally replanting, and gathering in the harvest, to a seemingly endless round of applying smelly substances to protect the vines from being consumed by insects and fungi. The alternative was to find a vine that resisted all these onslaughts.

The thought had first occurred during the oidium crisis: perhaps American vines might be resistant. Ironically enough, it may well have been the import of vines for oidium trials that introduced the phylloxera. It had simply not occurred to anyone, with the botanic gardens of the world excitedly filling up with exotic plants, that each plant has its pests and that some of them might bring catastrophic consequences in a new environment.

American vines had been tried in France before, in sailing ship days. The foxy flavour of their wine had ruled them out. 1869 was the year when, from several directions at once, they began to look as though they might hold a solution. To accredit the idea, or the work, to any single person is impossible; in the end scores of scientists were involved. But in that year M. Laliman from Bordeaux noted that some imported vines appeared phylloxera-proof. At a congress at Beaune Gaston Bazille suggested grafting: perhaps a French vine-top might "take" on an American root – he did not know then whether American roots would resist the pest or not. The theoretical proposition that they must came from another Montpellier scientist, Gaston Fouex, who was a keen follower of the (in France) still unfashionable Darwinism. He argued that if the phylloxera was a European insect it would long ago have wiped out the European vine; therefore it must be the native of a country where it could live its parasitic life without killing its host.

Planchon was the man who made the discovery that phylloxera is a native of America. In 1869 and 1873 he exchanged visits with Charles Riley, who was already famous for his work on the Colorado beetle. Riley confirmed what he suspected. As Planchon toured America's eastern vineyards, from North Carolina to Ohio, he was even in two minds about the flavour of American wine. He visited the cellars of Mr Werk from Alsace on Middle Bass Island in Lake Erie. His Sparkling Catawba he noted was "très agréable"; his Delaware Blanc light and delicately perfumed, "inclining to Sauternes". About his red Ives Seedling he was a little more reserved. "Fairly full-bodied" was the best that he could say. "American wines," he wrote in summing up, "apart from those that are badly made, or which show the strawberry flavour too blatantly, or which have had too much spirit added to please the Anglo-American taste, do not deserve the bad reputation Europe has given them, based on old prejudices and preserved by ignorance."

As to the aphid, he discovered that it did attack American vines, but by making leaf galls more than eating roots; that some species were fully resistant, others only partly so, and some, including the Catawba, were not resistant at all.

There were many questions to be answered before firm conclusions could be drawn. Assuming that grafting would work, and that French vine-tops could be united with American roots, would the flavour of the wine be affected? Which of the American species would take to the very different soils of Europe? Eastern America generally has acid soil; Europe's best vineyards just the opposite: alkaline soils, rich in lime. And which vines could most easily be propagated in the industrial quantities that would be needed?

Frenchmen in areas already affected would grasp at straws; any American rootstock was worth trying. Others, in regions the phylloxera had not yet reached, were highly sceptical about the whole idea. Chemical methods of control were much preferred by growers who could afford them. In the end they had the benefit of learning from others' mistakes for phylloxera, outside the devastated south of France, was a drama played in slow motion. Ten years passed between it being reported in Bordeaux and reaching the best parts of the Médoc. It was not reported in Burgundy (in Meursault) until 1878. Inevitably a split developed between

Allegory of sickly Europe being saved by vigorous young America amuses our cynical age, but the relief was heartfelt in the phylloxera-devastated 1880s. Phylloxera can cause leaf galls in American plants (left) but the plants survive.

growers of Pinot Noir for fine wines, who dreaded losing their purity of flavour and could afford to fumigate, and Gamay-growers who wanted to graft and get on with it. It was nine years before American roots were allowed by the authorities, under pressure from the prosperous. As a result many American plants were smuggled in, not even to be grafted but to be used as "producteurs directes". Even today it is possible to find a peasant grower in many parts of France who hoards a little supply of his strawberry-flavoured wine that he privately admits to liking.

As for Champagne, it was the last region of all to be attacked; not until 1901 did phylloxera appear along the Marne. But here the argument worked the other way round. The rich, having learned from the rest of France, knew that the best policy was a massive grafting programme. Small growers, who are the backbone of Champagne, saw it all as a plot to gain control of their vineyards.

If a 40-year crisis can have a critical moment it came in the 1880s. The scientists were polarized: chemists against grafters. At the International Phylloxera Conference in Bordeaux in 1881 the "sulphurists" and the "Americanists" presented their opposing points of view in heated debate. Whichever side won (and neither did conclusively) there were enormous physical problems to be overcome.

SURVIVORS OF THE PLAGUE

Here and there among regions whose vines were wiped out by phylloxera there remain small patches which have unaccountably survived. One such is a few rows of vines in the port country, at Quinta do Noval; another, two small blocks of Pinot Noir at Aÿ in Champagne, belonging to the house of Bollinger. The Champagne vines are still propagated by *provignage*, or layering, which became obsolete when all vines theoretically needed grafting. Both the "Nacional" wines made by Noval, and the "Vieilles Vignes Françaises" made by Bollinger exclusively from "pre-phylloxera" vines, have a certain quality and depth of flavour that sets them apart. For port it is highly desirable, but the view of Bollinger's president is that champagne from ungrafted vines (which produce small quantities of highly concentrated juice) is too "fat" for modern tastes. On this evidence, partly by helping to increase the crop, grafted vines seem to have given the wine of the 20th century a lighter and more elegant touch.

A French nursery raising new vines to replace their own devastated plants, having grafted them onto American rootstock. The new plants, though thankfully immune to the louse, were found to be more susceptible to the other twin scourges of the vineyard, oidium and mildew.

George Ordish, the phylloxera historian, has calculated that there were about 11 billion vines in France. American roots for every one would need a length of two million miles of grafting wood, on to which 230,000 tons of French bud-wood would have to be grafted. These figures assume that all the grafts "took", and that all the roots were suitable. In practice many of the early shipments of American vines intensely disliked the soil: it was not until after several years of laborious breeding programmes that truly compatible rootstocks for different sorts of soil, particularly alkaline ones, were created. That in the long run there would be distinct advantages in custom-made roots was too positive a thought for these dark days. For from 1878 the third of the Pharaonic plagues burst upon France with a suddenness and ferocity that eclipsed even phylloxera.

The enormous imports of American vine-wood had brought with them a new and voracious form of mildew, known as "downy" to distinguish it from the "powdery" oidium. Like oidium, it reduced the crop drastically and weakened the resulting wine. It took only four years for the Faculty of Science at Bordeaux to find a preventative: the famous "Bordeaux mixture", a combination of copper-sulphate and lime in liquid form that stains everything it touches brilliant blue. But the decade of the 80s suffered acutely from ruined vintages, from farmers at their wits' ends trying to understand, to master, and to afford new remedies and routines, and, inevitably, from an unstoppable surge of faked and fraudulent wine.

There were rich pickings indeed for the unscrupulous. Chronic shortages (total French wine production fell by almost a half in the 1880s) pushed up the price of real wine inexorably. Wines previously considered fit only for vinegar or distillation now found a ready market, without coming close to making good the deficit. Apart from simply adding water, which cabarets had always done, the readiest answer was to fabricate wine from raisins, imported mainly from Greece and Turkey. Raisin imports before the crisis were only a few thousand tons a year (and were used mainly by patissiers). By the 1880s that figure had reached a million – mainly into such southern ports as Marseilles and Sète. A book published in 1880 in Marseilles was called simply *How to Make Wine from Raisins*. Twelve editions were called for within half as many years.

This is how it was done: take 100 kilos of well broken-up raisins, add to 300 litres of water heated to 30 degrees C, leave to ferment for 12 days. After pressing you

The port of Sète rose, through the wine trade, to become the second most important in Mediterranean France. Sète was a by-word for fraud and fabrication: its "vintners" imported raisins from Greece and mysteriously exported anything from Chambertin to first-growth claret.

have 300 litres of "wine" of 10-11 degrees of alcohol, which after fining and sulphuring can be sent to market as it is, or mixed 50:50 with the cheapest Languedoc red. From 1881 at least two million hectolitres of raisin wine were sold each year: one litre in 15 of France's total wine consumption. In 1890 it reached 4.3 million litres, which was one litre in nine: consumption was climbing again.

THE ALTERNATIVE SIMPLE WAY TO PRODUCE FAKE WINE was with beet sugar. Massive planting in the north of France had brought its price down to a very modest level. Chaptal would have turned in his grave to see the parody of his proposal in a "piquette" made of hot water poured on pressed grape skins and fermented with enough beet sugar to provide its entire alcohol content. This method doubled the amount of wine made from a given quantity of grapes. Figures are not available to tell us what proportion of the Frenchman's daily intake was produced like this.

For Spain, Portugal, Italy; all of France's competitors, the advent of phylloxera seemed at once a threat and an opportunity. In the long run their great gain was the encouragement to challenge France with quality wines. But France was the world's biggest producer and consumer of wine by such a margin that whatever happened to her industry affected everyone. Up to 1870 she had been a net exporter by a proportion of eight to one. By 1880 she was a net importer by three to one and in 1887, at the height of the crisis, imported 12 million hectolitres and exported two.

The immediate gainers by this reversal of France's role were the bulk suppliers of Spain and Italy. Although they too were reached by the aphid (Italy gradually from the early 1870s; Spain progressively from 1878) they went on a planting spree to provide dark blending wine to boost the pallid French production. France, meanwhile, having been attacked first, had discovered the solution, painful though it was. Her neighbours and rivals had the advantage of being prepared. They could begin grafting their vines as soon as falling production demanded it. The Italian government even discouraged treatment, to lower the surplus pouring from its vast new southern vineyards. Germany, with cool efficiency, at first seemed almost successfully to have denied the aphids a visa. In 1900 only 1.5% of German vines had been attacked.

Algeria was the new recruit. At first France had looked on her new colony as a market for wine, not a supplier. In the 1880s this policy was dramatically reversed.

Rather than import her needs from Italy and Spain, France would grow her own wine in North Africa. There were thousands of ruined winegrowers eager to emigrate. Algeria's vineyards (even in pre-French days the Algerians enjoyed their wine) multiplied 10 times in the last 20 years of the 19th century, despite phylloxera, which found its way across in 1885.

It has often been said (and was said very loudly at the time) that wines even from the best vineyards after phylloxera lacked something of the quality they had had before. It would be surprising indeed if nothing had changed. To isolate any one aspect as responsible, particularly grafting onto American roots, is to oversimplify the total revolution brought about by one deadly pest and two recurring diseases all arriving within less than 30 years, and in some places almost simultaneously. Nor were they the only problems; two new parasites, the eudemis and cochylis grubs, added their nuisance value to the problems of every grower.

One natural reaction was to be over-generous with the fertilizer. Even in such austerely-controlled vineyards as the Médoc first-growths, harvests surprisingly increased in the '80s, when the vines were affected by both phylloxera and mildew. The soil-sterilizer sulphocarbonate was itself a fertilizer, but managers experimented with both organic and chemical compounds as never before, trying to keep up the crop and to give vigour to the threatened vines. At Château Latour experiments were made with ground roast leather to put pep into the vines.

The aim of top-quality producers was to fight for the life of each vine and replace them individually as they died. A high proportion of old vines lies at the heart of the idea of a Grand Vin. Once a vine was dead, it could easily be pulled out of the ground with a simple pulley; there were no roots left to resist. Small proprietors took a deep breath and got it over with, uprooting their whole vineyards and replanting with grafted plants as quickly as they could. It is hard to exaggerate, though, how hard the proprietors of great châteaux fought their losing rear-guard action. Again, as in the 1840s, they were obliged to contract for several vintages to the Chartronnais, and the Chartronnais stipulated no grafting on American roots. This was as late as the years up to the First World War. In Burgundy it was not until 1945 that the old ungrafted vines of Romanée-Conti were finally pulled up.

PASTEUR THOU SHOULD'ST HAVE BEEN LIVING AT THIS HOUR. The great man died in 1895. Among his disciples in micro-biology were the scientists who pondered each new problem as it arose. The greatest, perhaps, was Ulysse Gayon, the founding director of Bordeaux's first permanent scientific institute for the study of vines and wine. Even with their help, the first two decades of the 20th century proved to be the worst of all. The recently planted grafted vines were under attack by mildew in any humid weather, needing regular spraying at great expense. Now oidium returned to batten on the struggling young plants. At the same time the results of over-fertilizing inflated the quantity and diluted the quality of the crop. Prices fell, and even first growths were losing serious money.

As if this were not enough, the impudence of the "fraudeurs" knew no bounds. If they were going to offer bogus Bordeaux or Burgundy, why not go the whole way and label it with a first-growth label?

Public reaction was only natural. The clientele for great wines was still essentially British high society. But everyone had heard of the recurring plagues. Almost from the moment when French wines were welcomed back to Britain by lowered duties, one problem after another in the vineyards made the headlines. What might the sulphur and the copper treatments do to the consumer? It is a familiar cry, and it gave the Scotch whisky industry its great opportunity. Suddenly the fashionable drinks were Scotch and mineral water. There was to be no general recovery of the prestige and profitability of wine for over 50 years.

The final score of the half-century that followed the Golden Age in France is not easy to draw up. Most dramatically, it reduced the total area of vines in France by almost one-third: 30% of what was destroyed has never been replaced. Whole regions such as the Meurthe in the north-east where the vine was a marginal crop gave it up altogether.

To counterbalance this the Languedoc replanted to excess. In 1875 it had 17% of France's vines; today it has 27% and most of them on rich farm land which in the graphic local phrase "fait pissèr la vigne". Its decline from the hills to the plain can be plotted in its ever-increasing productivity. One acre of vines produced three times as much wine in 1900 as in 1800 and today produces three times as much again.

The positive good that years of crisis did was to bring science into what was too often the hermetic ignorance of unquestioned tradition, and government into affairs it had generally been content to leave alone.

THE SCOURGE CONTINUES

Far from being a problem that has been solved once and for all, phylloxera is making a comeback in many parts of the world today: particularly in California, Australia and New Zealand. The primary reason is complacency. There has been widespread planting of ungrafted European vines in vineyard areas where no phylloxera has been seen for many years, or virgin areas where they are the first vines. Monterey County in California is a case in point: 30,000 acres of ungrafted vines were planted there, far from any older vineyards. Yet the aphid found them and is munching them to gradual destruction. "The insect", says William Wildman of the University of California, "has an insidious manner of showing up when and where you least expect it."

Today its progress can be monitored by aerial infra-red photography. Once an infestation is clearly visible the vineyard's days are numbered, its length of survival depending largely on the soil. In the Napa valley it might continue producing for a dozen years; in Monterey only eight.

Considerably more alarming is the recent appearance of a new strain of phylloxera which can destroy rootstocks immune to the old strain. Whether this "type B" phylloxera could ever cause total devastation is unknown. There is still no practical and ecologically acceptable insecticide available to eliminate another plague, but a future Planchon would at least have a camera to help him in his task.

CHAPTER 39

RISORGIMENTO

Wine is more central to the identity of Italy even than it is to that of France. The name the Greeks gave to the peninsula was the Land of Wine. It has no single province where the vine is not at ease; and when the moment came, in the 19th century, for Italy at last to become a single nation, it was reforming landowners, men preoccupied with the agriculture of their respective provinces, who like sagacious senators of old brought about the Risorgimento of their country.

To the creators of modern Italy, oidium and the Austrians were both deadly enemies. It was the warrior Garibaldi who persuaded the peasants to save their vines with sulphur. The story of viticultural and political change are warp and woof in the epic of their doings.

THAT MOST IMPARTIAL OF REPORTERS, ANDRÉ JULLIEN, wrote of Italian wine in the early 19th century in terms of disappointment more than condemnation. "The soil of Italy is famous for its fertility. Its climate and the long chain of mountains that stretch from the Alps to the foot of Calabria, offering in their length every variety of soil and situation favourable to the vine, seem to justify the name of Oenotria that the ancients gave it. One could believe that this country produces the best wines of Europe; but while the people of less favoured lands are busy choosing the best vines to suit their intemperate seasons, the Italians, accustomed to seeing the vine grow almost spontaneously, and everywhere give ripe fruit, never even try to maximize their advantages. Being sure of a sufficient crop, they neglect the care of their plants, even in the districts where the quality of their produce invites attention . . . one can find dessert wines of extremely good quality, but those for daily consumption, which might be called "mellow", cannot be compared with their equivalents in France. Most of them are at the same time sweet and sharp, often coarse, and even when they appear to have plenty of body and strength, travel badly and rapidly decline, even without having travelled.

"Their bad quality comes not only from neglect in cultivation, but even more from sheer bad winemaking." Almost all Italian vines, Jullien goes on to say, are grown up trees, forming high curtains of foliage while the farmer plants his grain and beans below – in the words of Jules Guyot, the philosopher-scientist of French wine, "a liberty, equality and vegetable fraternity that destroyed three-quarters of their vigour and fecundity". It is precisely the method described by Pliny, still being faithfully followed at the time of the Napoleonic wars.

"What object has an Italian in labouring to improve that which cannot by improvement turn out of the slightest profit to himself? Trampled by the Austrian military, or by the feet of native tyrants, destitute of adequate capital, and weighed down by a vexatious system of imposts, what has he to hope for . . .?" This, with the utmost sympathy, was Cyrus Redding, despairing over the Italy where the patriot bands of Carbonari were beginning to rise in liberal revolutions.

THAT THE COUNTRY WAS FRAGMENTED was not itself the problem: when had it not been since the fall of Rome? It was partly the very ease with which the ancient land of vines could find its sustenance that held it in a time-warp. Certainly atrocious government and exploitation played their part. But there is also the question of geography to consider: Italy lies surrounded by lands that also grow the vine. Where but in her own cities would her winegrowers find a market? Naples and Rome were her only substantial cities, and they both lacked the prerequisite for a healthy wine trade: a powerful and numerous middle class.

Portugal and Spain had been organized by the needs of northern Europe, as much because they were a convenient market for manufactured goods as for any special winemaking talent they possessed. From this point of view Italy was too distant. Her natural trading links were with her neighbours France and Austria; both had wine supplies greater than Italy's on their own accounts.

To "sit under the shade of his own vine, with his wife and children about him, and the ripe clusters hanging within his reach" was James Busby's definition of happiness. Why should we feel sorry for the Italian contadino, the peasant whose fertile lands supplied all Europe with its romantic images of beauty? Goethe, journeying through Italy 40 years earlier, had part of the answer. "They are completely at the mercy of the merchants, who, in bad years, lend them money to keep them going and then, in good years, buy their wine for a mere song. But life", added the poet philosophically, "is like that everywhere".

Italy did once have an export business. Venice in the 14th century had been one of the centres of the world's wine trade, even creating "Greek-style" wine in the Veronese hills. The Florentine renaissance had seen a ripple, if not a flood, of international interest in flasks of Florence wine. And in the 18th century we have seen an English epicure working his way down the peninsula looking for, and finding, sweet and fragrant wines. If Italy had anything approaching a five-star wine in international eyes, it was Lachryma Christi from Vesuvius.

Italy and the outside world agreed that her wines fell into two categories: those from the tree-clinging vines which formed the great majority, and the staked vines that, just as they had done two thousand years before, marked out the areas of Greek influence. These were the wines, if any, that the world looked for from Italy: wines that were strong and sweet, or at any rate sweet, made in the Greek tradition. Exceptions to this rule were rare. Renaissance Florence undoubtedly drank good wine more or less in the Chianti style – though it was more famous for its strong Vernaccia and sweet Aleatico and vinsanto. We cannot imagine the Medici, or indeed the Borgias, raising jewelled chalices, poisoned or not, of a thin and vinegary drink because it was the best their great estates could produce. The Antinori family is proud to have been selling Florentine wine from the 14th century; the Frescobaldi, too, whom we have met as bankers all over medieval Europe, traded in wine and textiles as a matter of course.

But there is a depressing sameness in the commentaries of 18th-century writers. According to Sir Edward Barry, "Chianti was formerly much esteemed here in England, but entirely lost its character; large quantities of the red Florence are still imported in flasks, but from the disagreeable roughness and other qualities, seldom drunk. They have a freshness and a beautiful deep colour and are probably chiefly

These scenes of Italian vine growing date from the 1950s, but could have been taken at any time since the invention of photography – or indeed for two millennia before that. Vines were (and still are) grown up trees to economize on space, often allowing two crops to be grown in the same field. But the fruit produced by this arrangement is inferior.

consumed in making artificial claret, or Burgundy wines, or in giving more lightness and spirit to heavy vapid port."

On the threshold of her independence Italy had no export market for anything but her sweet wines. Variety she certainly had; there were many hundreds, if not thousands, of local sorts of vines, and local ways of using them. But only rarely, even in the villas and castles of the aristocracy (including the aristocracy of the church) was wine made with any care and knowledge, and it was not at that time the fashion for noblemen to offer their wine for sale at their palace doors.

GOVERNO

What was wrong with the majority of peasant-made wines in Italy was largely unfinished fermentation. Perhaps the natural yeasts did not have the capacity to convert all the sugar in the juice. More probably unclean barrels and slovenly practices stored up a population of micro-organisms that attacked the yeasts and the wine, making it fundamentally unstable; sweet to drink while its sugar remained, but well on its way to vinegar at the same time. Even today the popular Italian taste is for red wine that is distinctly sweet and unpredictably fizzy.

The system known as "Governo" was introduced in Tuscany (and perhaps elsewhere) in about the 14th century, probably to stabilise the wine – although opinions today differ. When fermentation was apparently finished they added a fresh batch of half-dried grapes to liven up the yeasts and make them consume the remaining sugar; sometimes successfully, finishing with a fully dry and stable wine, and sometimes only adding another stage of unfinished fermentation, in which case the wine would not keep, but could be praised for its youthful liveliness.

415

THE TWO SOVEREIGN STATES THAT HELD OUT HOPE for Italy were Tuscany and the Kingdom of Sardinia – a misleading name because its capital, and all its cultural life, were in Piemonte, centred round Turin.

Tuscany was where reform tentatively began, under the Grand Duke Peter Leopold, a Hapsburg by descent and a vassal of Austria in fact, but a worthy successor to the long line of Medici Grand Dukes nonetheless. His 25 years of rule, ended by the armies of the French Revolution, were notable for liberal policies – at least towards trade and the landowning class. At the time when Arthur Young was conducting his one-man survey of the agriculture of France, Tuscany's noble landowners attended their Georgofili Academy to study the products of their soil – including the composition of its wine. Such families as the Capponi, Ridolfi and Firidolfi-Ricasoli were at least in theory the Florentine equivalent of the Townsends and the Cokes who were dedicated to modernizing their great Norfolk estates in England – with the crucial difference of the still-feudal Italian concept of the peasant bound to his plot. If Tuscany's land-holding system had been capable of reform progress might have been made, but the deeply conservative peasants were accustomed to the mezzadria, the system of crop-sharing by which they never gained a greater share of their land. Even if their equally conservative landlords had wanted to change the system the toilers would have thought it was a plot against their ancient tenure of the soil.

Napoleon's wars were over, Metternich had tidied up, and Tuscany was back in Austrian hands, when Baron Bettino Ricasoli inherited Brolio, the heavily indebted estate of his ancient family. To the Ricasolis the Medicis had been parvenues; they were (and are) the true *noblesse d'epée*, tracing their lineage back to Lombard barons of the 11th century. When the baron moved from Florence to his family's neglected estates (some say to put his beautiful young wife at a distance from the temptations of society) the reform of his property and its wine became his ruling passion.

Brolio is the very heart of Chianti Classico; the region of tumbled hills of oaks, olives and vines where Florence and Siena had struggled for mastery four centuries earlier. The magnificent austerity of Brolio Castle prepares you for the character of the man. Portraits of the gaunt short-sighted aristocrat tell half the story. On the attic floor of the great gothic pile he rebuilt, in red brick like the Piazza del Campo in Siena, his study and his bedroom remain just as he left them: bare-floored, minimally furnished; more like a hermitage than a noble's lodgings. Haughty and ascetic, he dedicated himself – along with his wife, his children, his tenantry, and the region's wine – to education and reform.

In his researches he travelled through France and Germany studying every possible way of growing vines. He imported countless varieties, with an almost Haraszthyan hunger to try everything. Chianti Classico emerged from his experiments as the Italian equivalent of de Pontac's "new French claret" – not, however, by adopting new varieties, but by rationalizing the old. He finally narrowed his model down to the three Tuscan grapes that he found harmonized; to make what Pepys would have called a most particular flavour. Ricasoli wrote of his findings that "Chianti wine draws most of its bouquet (which is what I aim for) from Sangioveto; from Canaiolo a sweetness that tempers the harshness of the latter without detracting from its bouquet; whereas Malvasia (which could be used less in wines that are to be aged) tends to accentuate the taste, while at the same time making it fresher and lighter and more suitable for daily use at table." One could say, in Bordeaux terms, that Canaiolo is to Sangioveto what Merlot is to Cabernet – but that the white Malvasia is added to make an easier and a smoother blend. Ricasoli did not admit the Trebbiano, the slightly sharp, otherwise neutral and only too productive grape that farmers like to add (and that modern law allows) because it is so easy to grow.

Alas Ricasoli was denied the satisfaction of seeing his formula accepted as a fine wine by the world. In 1848 (the year of revolutions in Italy as in the rest of Europe) his countess died and his taste for his estates and their reform was swept away in his grief – and perhaps the new calling he found as a politician. In the 1850s oidium, the powdery mildew, struck, and the crop-sharing peasants, the mezzadri, abandoned the land in droves, flocking to cities or to America. The Brolio estate grew by 300 little farms as the mezzadri left their vines untended and their cottages to crumble.

PIEMONTE WAS THE ONE OTHER AREA OF ITALY whose landowners had traditionally, if not consistently, taken their wine production seriously. In the Middle Ages the nearness of Genoa had had its effect. Genoa, like Venice, had little land of its own but lived by and for the sea. Its hinterland, admittedly a stiff climb over the coastal Ligurian Alps, is the sheltered and fertile basin of Piemonte before the main body of the Alps begins; a basin only in a relative sense; its Monferrato hills about the towns of Alba and Asti have steeper slopes and higher ridges than the hills of Tuscany.

Pietro de Crescentius, author of the *Liber Ruralium Commodorum*, lived as a judge at Asti in the 14th century at the time when "Greek" wines were in high demand. The grapes, he wrote, were left to overripen on the vines here with their stalks half-twisted. Because this was impractical in high festoons among the trees the vines of Moscato and Malvasia, newly introduced to make "Greek" wine, began to be short-pruned and staked. For centuries both kinds of vineyards continued side by side, "altinis et spanis"; proof that the growing of strong and aromatic wines was a

Brolio, Ricasoli's brick *castello* in the Tuscan hills is the birthplace of Chianti, where the baron refined the recipe in the 1850s. Chianti's official baptism dates from 1716, when the Grand Duke of Tuscany posted an edict "in the usual and even unwonted places" defining Chianti's borders and laying down severe penalties for its adulteration. The Ricasoli family acquired the castle and its vineyards in 1141.

specialized and more profitable branch of viticulture, practised by owners of land who did not have to subsist on what they grew. It is tempting to equate "spanna", the name for a vine-stake, with the local name given in Novara to the Nebbiolo, the best of their vines.

The Monferrato hills were to the capital of Turin almost what Chianti was to Florence and Siena: the rustic retreat where game and wine were plentiful, and large estates were left in the hands of share-croppers as the easiest way to manage and maintain the land. Not that the court was averse to a little villegiatura, or even to occasional experiments with new kinds of wine. In the 17th century the court jeweller to King Carlo Emanuele, Giovan Battista Croce, set the fashion for a new-style Chiaretto, a pale red wine made from Nebbiolo grapes apparently as carefully handled as Dom Pérignon's Pinot Noir.

References to the Nebbiolo as the grape of choice in Piemont go back to the 13th century. It was to be joined by many others; red Dolcetto in the 16th century, white Cortese and red Barbera in the 17th, yet none of them are favourably mentioned in the early 19th century for anything but sweet wine. Jullien does not even consider the dry reds of the region. The King of Sardinia and his court imported their table wines from France – while much of the crude production of their tree-hung vines went to quench thirsts in neighbouring Milan, the capital of Lombardy and under Austrian control.

How often has the customs officer played the part of Messenger for some significant twist to our story? The Methuen Treaty, the Zollverein and Gladstone's Budget are only three examples. It was the customs officer who blew the whistle for the Risorgimento. In 1833 the Austrian government had lowered duties on Piemontese wines imported into its north Italian Empire of Lombardy, the Veneto and Emilia in the north-east. In 1846, under pressure from its winegrowers, notably the Hungarians, Austria doubled the tariff and cut Piemonte off from its one export market. The following year Count Camillo Cavour, a landowner on the Ricasoli model in the Monferrato hills, who had been to England to study advanced farming methods, founded the newspaper called *Risorgimento*. In the same year King Carlo-Alberti used the Agricultural Congress at Casal Monferrate to denounce the Austrians in terms that smacked of war.

Piemonte went into the war of 1848 alone, fought two battles against the veteran General Radetzky at Custoza and Novara in Lombardy, and lost. Carlo-Alberti abdicated in favour of his son, Vittorio-Emanuele II. Garibaldi, meanwhile, briefly succeeded in establishing a Roman Republic and became the country's hero. Cavour, now Prime Minister in Turin, was forced to turn to France for help as troubles descended. Napoleon III was to be his ally against Austria; French winemaking science his aid as the invasion of oidium decimated the Piemontese vines.

Sulphuring was known to control oidium, as Bordeaux had discovered, but who could persuade the peasantry to spray their vines, which sprawled in the tree-tops? The answer was Giuseppe Garibaldi, a son of Nice (then part of the kingdom of Sardinia) and so not only a national but a local hero. When in 1856 only those growers who had used sulphur had any grapes to pick, Garibaldi's stock as a miracle-worker was at its height.

IN SCARCELY ANY PART OF ITALY is "tradition" so revered, or so often given as the reason for this procedure or that, as in Piemonte. Yet hardly anywhere does tradition mean so short a span of time. Piemonte's wines were reinvented in the Risorgimento years, not by seeking to perfect an old formula, but by hiring professional advice from France. The Marchesa Falletti of Barolo did the recruiting. Louis Oudart was the wine-scientist he found. Cavour, with his own estate at Grinzane in Barolo, became his second client. The Frenchman found the Nebbiolo grapes superb, but could not understand why they were not fermented into a dry red wine. There was no inherent reason but bad winemaking: the fermentation died away but never finished, leaving the wine rather sweet and very unstable. Ripe grapes and a clean cellar were all that was needed. As the 1850s progressed the wine we know today as Barolo emerged: dark, potent, dry and stable, with almost limitless potential to age.

Piemonte had no such thing until Falletti and Cavour commissioned his researches. If it could be done with Nebbiolo there were other possibilities for other grapes. Oudart set up his own establishment at Neive in Barbaresco, and the new king, an eager supporter of Cavour's reforms, dedicated his magificent shooting-lodge and romantic retreat of Fontanafredda in the hills at Serralunga d'Alba, in the heart of the Barolo country, to making the revolutionary new wine.

Political considerations were next on this curiously interwoven agenda. Cavour's reforms included the roads and railways (which greatly helped the distribution of wine), the army, industry and the financial system. In Turin he was

Garibaldi took an enlightened view both of politics and of agriculture. His status as a national hero was cemented by his sensible advice to vine-growers. Fontanafreda (left) in the heart of Barolo at Serralunga, was converted from a royal retreat to a powerhouse of experimental winemaking in the 1870s. The king's son, Conte Emanuele Guerrieri, was the driving force. Today the estate is owned by a bank.

laying the foundation of a workable Italian state. By 1858 he was ready to ally himself with Louis-Napoleon in a second campaign against the Austrians. With two great victories, Marengo and Solferino, Italy seemed secure – too secure for Louis-Napoleon. He deserted his ally at the critical moment, claiming Nice and Savoy from Sardinia as the reward for his intervention. He also lent the reactionary Pope Pius IX a garrison for Rome. It was not part of his plan for Italy to be too easily united. On the contrary he had a plan that involved Tuscany as a separate central Italian state.

The climax of the Risorgimento came in 1860. Ricasoli the winemaker was now virtual dictator of Tuscany – and he was fixed on union with Cavour. In May Garibaldi sailed with his thousand redshirts from Genoa to Sicily, landing on what was virtually British territory at Marsala to put an end to the appalling regime of the Bourbons in Naples; the Kingdom of the Two Sicilies that Nelson had once saved from the French. This time the British navy was on the other side. By June Sicily was in Garibaldi's hands; by September, Naples. The southern half of Italy was now united to the Kingdom of Sardinia; Tuscany had voted for union as Ricasoli had told it to do. At this moment Cavour died; Ricasoli became Prime Minister of the new Italy.

It remained only for Venice and the Papal States to fall for the Risorgimento for it to have achieved its aim. In the end it was the Prussians, defeating Austria in 1866 and France in 1870, who delivered the final pieces of the jigsaw – save for the Alto Adige, or Austria's Südtirol, which was to become Italian, not without mixed feelings, after the First World War.

For a few years in the 1860s, before the fall of Rome, Chianti should have enjoyed its hour of glory. Florence became the capital of Italy. The creator of Chianti was the Prime Minister. Royalty and embassies from all over the world were thronging its cafés and its countryside. Alas, it seems they hardly noticed the local wine. This was the Golden Age of Burgundy and Bordeaux.

THE FACT THAT THERE WAS NOW A UNITED ITALY did not of course mean that there was, or ever would be, a meeting of minds about Italian wine. But the government, pressed with the problem of oidium, followed by scattered outbreaks of phylloxera, and thinking of the possibilities offered by oenology, was not slow to establish

An arbour of vines in the Alto Adige or South Tyrol, the last part of the peninsula to become Italian and a place where wine traditions of both north and south of the Alps meet and merge.

institutes to preach the gospel according to Pasteur and Planchon. Two were founded in Piemonte in 1872, both under the direction of Dr Cerletti. Piemonte was to be the first province to make creative use of the new wine-science on its grapes.

From the Nebbiolo, in the footsteps of Barolo, the districts of Barbaresco and Gattinara created similar dark and powerful, tannic and tremendous wines. Lesser grapes, Barbera, Dolcetto and Grignolino, made distinct, if not distinguished, dry reds. Freisa and Brachetto developed the hedonistic old idea of reds that were sweet and fizzy and stained the table-cloth, while Carlo Gancia, at Canelli, invented a new role for the moscato; not as "Greek" wine, but as the lightest and sweetest imaginable nursery-version of Champagne.

Despite the genial chaos of vineyards here as in every other part of Italy, Piemonte developed a different type of wine for each of its profusion of grape varieties. There appears to have been no calculated blending (as there might well have been, so close to Turin, the capital city of vermouth) to find an equivalent of claret or Chianti. Piemonte was a pioneer in naming wines by the names of grapes – or perhaps it was a throwback to the Middle Ages, when Malmsey was Malmsey, wherever it came from.

DOCTOR CERLETTI OBLIGINGLY LEFT A SUMMING-UP in French of the state of the Italian wine industry in 1889. It was a time of strained relations everywhere. France's gigantic appetite for supplies had provoked the planting of whole new regions where vines had never been grown before, and led to fabrication of bogus wine as much in Italy and Spain as in France itself. Genoa was a principal centre of the trade.

Allowing for his understandable desire to present Italy in a favourable light, Cerletti gives plenty of evidence of the progress made in the generation since the Risorgimento. Phylloxera seldom reached epidemic proportions in Italy's far-from-monocultural landscape. It is easy to exaggerate the problem in the regions it reached once the solution of grafting was known and tried. On balance it may often have been beneficial in making the winegrower look again at his vines, and replant, when he did, with better varieties in better health.

The worst damage phylloxera did to Italy was indirectly, in the 1880s, before it had really taken hold, when it encouraged the notion that any sort of wine was saleable. The time was ripe for technical advance and the selection of the best vines. In most cases the opportunity was thrown away.

Cerletti describes an Italy which is learning to bring down its vines from the treetops and where the acreage of vineyards was increasing almost everywhere. The exception was the north, where only the modernizing Piemonte expanded its acreage. Liguria, Lombardy and the Veneto made less wine – especially the Veneto, whose Austrian market had disappeared. By far the biggest increase was in Sicily and the south, where valleys that had never seen the vine were being planted, financed by foreign capital from France and Austria. In the 20 years from 1870 to 1890, the critical years for France, Italy's production of wine doubled – and most of the increase came from Piemonte and the south.

Of Piemonte Cerletti reports that in the last 30 years, since the Risorgimento, the vines have been abandoned in damp valleys (where they suffered most from mildew) and concentrated on the hilltops, newly cleared of forests. The emphasis, as always, is on reds, and the northern province of Novara, in the foothills of the main body of the Alps, is flourishing with such Nebbiolo wines as Gattinara and Ghemme, and one of Piemonte's rare and more delicate blended wines, Lessona. The sweet Moscato Spumante has become an industry, and vermouth, which he dates back to 1835, is exported all over the world. One of the great advantages of Piemonte, he claims, is the abundance of good cold cellars where wine will stabilize and mature, to be bottled when it is ready to drink – often after 10 or 15 years in barrel. Strong southern wine was at this time entering more and more into the composition of these relatively expensive products, just as Burgundy and Bordeaux borrowed support from the natural potency of the Rhône.

Only two areas of Lombardy have seriously to be considered: the Oltrepò Pavese, near Pavia, whose business was in supplying bulk wine to the merchants and restaurants of Milan (and which had no hesitation in buying southern wines to give them muscle), and the remote and individual Valtellina, which can almost literally be described as the south wall of the Alps. Here was yet another, and much the furthest north, of the pockets of "Greek" winemaking. Its dried-grape speciality, Sforsato or Sfursat, was customarily exported the very short distance to Switzerland.

Of the Veneto the only thriving region was Verona. Oidium and downy mildew were rife in the humid climate to the north of Venice, but Valpolicella and its neighbours Valpantena and Soave had a ready market. All the best wines of the Veneto were made of half-dried grapes in the Greek style; either strong and sweet as Recioto, or fully fermented as Amarone, when a characteristic vein of bitterness joins the formidable alcohol content. These are surely the sort of wines the ancients cut with water; the Venetian version of what they sent galleys to fetch from Chios before the Turks arrived.

Around Vicenza the name of Torcolato refers to the twisting of the grape-stems to concentrate their sugar. Each of the provinces had its approximate equivalent. In Treviso to the north of Venice it was Picolit; in most the umbrella term vinsanto covered such heirloom wines, concentrated and rare; stored, often, in the conditions Pliny recommended, where extremes of temperature would hasten their oxidation. Up under the rooftiles was a favourite place – and still is.

Suddenly this is not history any more, but an account of an ageless Italy. Cerletti is a guide to the Italy of a century ago, yet much of what he says needs little altering. Crossing the plains of the Po with him in Emilia we see the tree-hung vines that now

VERMOUTH

Turin, as an old capital city, has long enjoyed the advantage of well-established commerce and a substantial middle class, frequenters of cafés and leisurely social drinkers. In the 18th century the old alchemy of blending herbs, sweetening and eau-de-vie became a commercial proposition: making the fortune of Signor Carpano (whose recipe took the name of Punt e Mes "point and a half" from the Milan Stock Exchange). Others followed, perhaps the most famous being Messrs Martini and Rossi who, with a third partner, Signor Sola, bought another established company in 1864. The generic name is the French for wormwood, or *Artemisia absinthium*; the bitter principle in the majority of such concoctions. The part of the old kingdom of Sardinia which is now in France, Savoie, shares the tradition with Turin, only making its vermouth (of which Noilly Prat is the most famous brand) drier and more herbal.

produce Italy's most-exported wine: Lambrusco. Who is having the last laugh? Is it the ghost of Pliny we see flitting through the vast Riunite bottling factory?

Over the Appenines in Tuscany our guide of a century ago announces great advances since the Iron Baron's time: the addition of 10-15% of Cabernet or Malbec to Chiantis to be aged. "Wines thus treated", he says, "have a savour and bouquet similar to Bordeaux". Who knows when the Cabernet was introduced to Tuscany? It was the vintages of Carmignano and Artimino, both of which "traditionally" add a measure of Cabernet, that André Jullien had singled out as some of the best of Tuscany half a century before.

CERLETTI WAS WRITING JUST TOO SOON to have heard of the enterprise of Ferruccio Biondi-Santi, a young veteran of Garibaldi's army, who in the warm south of Tuscany at Montalcino was reconstituting his phylloxera-struck vineyards. The traditional Moscadello had suffered badly from oidium and mildew. But Montalcino (like Montepulciano down the road) had its own local form of Sangioveto, known from the colour of its larger grapes as Brunello or Sangioveto Grosso. The young Ferruccio planted pure vineyards of Brunello (though still in the traditional Tuscan mixture with other crops). He took Barolo as his model and looked for stability in a decade of barrel-ageing. 1888 was the first famous vintage of what rapidly became Italy's most sought-after wine.

The Romans, as ever, were the country's thirstiest citizens. To supply their needs parts of the Castelli Romani in the Alban hills were abandoning their tree-hung vines. Frascati and villages around had dug deep cellars for their always-fragile wine. The journey to Rome was usually enough to turn it brown. It was better drunk in the hills than after a hot and bumpy journey and the attentions of a Roman tavern-keeper.

Above all, Cerletti said, it was the Mezzogiorno that had been revolutionized. His book, for French consumption, does not mention that its speedy planting had been largely to supply the deficit caused by disease in France. It was French, German, Austrian and Swiss capital that had turned the olive-groves of Apulia and the corn-lands of Sicily into a monoculture of the vine. These were not wines for drinking, he frankly admits. The heat of summer and their sheer strength makes it difficult to finish their fermentation. "Bulk wines produced by fascinating methods that are always inaccurate" is a contemporary description that rings all too true.

As the raw material for blending they were so dark and strong that winemakers in the north, whether of France or Italy itself, rarely resisted the temptation to add a tincture of this potent brew. In Italy, once France had enough (or too much) of her own (and Algeria's) wine for her blending vats, it was an unforeseen outcome of the Risorgimento that could set back the quality of her northern vineyards indefinitely. It was not in Ricasoli's mind, nor Cavour's, that the old wine areas should face a great invasion from the south of duty-free, incredibly cheap and formidably strong blending wines.

CHAPTER 40

HISPANIC REVIVAL

Travellers in Spain in the last century, and those who drank Spanish wine at home, had very different impressions of Spain's capabilities. Nowhere, not even in Italy, was the distinction between wine for export and wine as daily sustenance so vividly clear. This is the wine the Spaniard drank, in the measured words of Alexander Henderson:

"Throughout the greater part of Spain, the peasantry store the produce of their vintages in skins, which are smeared with pitch; from which the wine is apt to contract a peculiar disagreeable taste called the *olor de bota*, and to become muddy and nauseous. Bottles and casks are rarely met with: and, except in the monasteries and great commercial towns, subterranean wine-cellars are almost unknown. Under such management we cannot be surprised that the common Spanish wines should fall so far short of the excellence that might be anticipated . . . or that the traveller, in the midst of the most luxurious vineyards, should often find the manufactured produce wholly unfit for use."

In defence of the *bota*, or leather bottle, it must be said that a well-used and carefully-tended one, never allowed to dry out or go thirsty (for they live on wine, and die without it) is a friendly and functional receptacle. Its purpose is not the same as that of a crystal goblet, but it perfectly expresses the place of wine in Spanish life, and certainly did not die out with the coming of glass. The real argument is not with the bota, but with the *borracha*, the whole animal-skin, as Richard Ford was at pains to point out (see opposite).

The distinction remained, though, between wines intended for export, and those for local use. One incident stays in my mind to illustrate the standing of the latter. The housekeeper clearing the lunch table at a house near Alicante habitually put the water-jug in the fridge, but poured the remaining red wine down the sink.

OF WINES FOR EXPORT, BY FAR THE MOST IMPORTANT A CENTURY AGO was sherry. In 50 years an industry had grown up that had overtaken port. In the view of many connoisseurs (especially, though not uniquely, in Britain) it was, or could be, the finest white wine on earth. Spain had no red to be compared with it; indeed Spain's only red wine exports were of the inky variety used for blending with one exception: Rioja was just finding its place as the luxury table wine of Spain, directly inspired by Bordeaux.

What had happened to the vaunted wines of Spain's great days of Empire? The elaborate Ordenanzas of the 16th century had not been framed for "muddy and nauseous" wine. But Spain in the 18th century was sadly in decline. The famous vineyards of the Duero that had supplied the capital of Valladolid had sunk into oblivion. Madrid drank the wines of La Mancha, with no distaste, but nor, it seems, with any great discrimination.

It was, as always, a case of the market setting the standards. When Valladolid was capital and Old Castile was the heart of Spain the produce of the Duero basin, of Medina del Campo and Rueda, was proudly produced and proudly drunk. When the court moved to Madrid the great plain of La Mancha to the south became its supplier. Although the old Valladolid vineyards were still closer in distance, the Sierra de Guadarrama raised a formidable mountain barrier to transport. In La Mancha the towns of Valdepeñas and Manzanares won reputations for quality. The stately cellars of the Duke of San Carlos at Manzanares were said to produce "rich and racy" wines, while the best Valdepeñas was frequently compared with Burgundy even, surprisingly enough, by Frenchmen. White Valdepeñas had a less favourable press, being compared with sherry of the second class.

The stumbling-block, as usual in Spain, was that a long journey over the parched plains of La Mancha was essential to appreciate this nectar. It was not to be judged by what taverns could offer in Madrid. "All these wines are normally transported on mule back in skins which impart to them their evil savour. Exceptionally wealthy citizens order them in little barrels. . . ."

WINE-SKINS

"One word on this *Bota*, which is as necessary to the rider as a saddle to his horse. This article, so Asiatic and Spanish, is at once the bottle and the glass of the people of the Peninsula when on the road. A Spanish woman would as soon think of going to church without her fan, or a Spanish man to a fair without his knife, as a traveller without his *bota*. Ours, the faithful, long-tried comforter of many a dry road, and honoured now like a relic, is hung up as a votive offering to the Iberian Bacchus. Its skin, now shrivelled with age and with fruitless longings for wine, is still redolent of the ruby fluid, whether the generous *Valdepenas* or the rich *Vino de Toro*: and refreshing to our nostrils is even an occasional smell at its red-stained orifice. There the racy wine-perfume lingers, and brings water into the mouth, or even into the eye-lid. What a dream of Spanish odours, good, bad, and indifferent, is awakened by its well-known *borracha* . . . !

"The *Bota* is not to be confounded with the *Borracha* or *Cuero*, the wine-skin of Spain, which is the *entire*, and answers the purpose of the barrel elsewhere. The *bota* is the retail receptacle, the *cuero* is the wholesale one. It is genuine pig's skin, the adoration of which disputes in the Peninsula with the cigar, the dollar, and even the worship of the Virgin. The shops of the makers are to be seen in most Spanish towns; in them long lines of the unclean animal's blown-out hides are strung up like sheep carcases in our butchers' shambles. The tanned and manufactured article preserves the form of the pig, feet and all, with the exception of one: the skin is turned inside out, so that the hairy coat lines the interior, which, moreover, is carefully pitched like a ship's bottom, to prevent leaking; hence the peculiar flavour, which partakes of resin and the hide, which is called the *borracha*. This flavour is peculiar to most Spanish wines, sherry excepted, which being made by foreigners, is kept in foreign casks."

It was by this distinction, repeated presumably in every part of Spain, that the scent and flavour of barrels came to be identified unequivocally with the indulgence of the rich. Foreign merchants made use of barrels in Andalusia for their sherry and Malaga, and in Valencia even for their blackstrap Benicarlo on its way to Bordeaux for blending – the appearance of cowhides on the Quai des Chartrons might have been cause for comment. Aristocrats used them for their private supplies. Whatever potential Spanish wine might have would never be explored except around the coasts, in export areas, which were fundamentally two: Andalusia and the adjacent Valencia to the east, and the north-west, from Galicia along the Biscay coast.

Why was it that Catalonia, whose climate is so perfect for the vine, and which has Barcelona as an ideal port, played such a small part in exports until recent times? The answer lies partly in its often-tragic history, caught between Spain and France, but perhaps more in its ominously named *Rabassa morta*, a form of share-cropping very much to the landlord's advantage that held it rigidly in the Middle Ages until well into the 19th century. Catalonia was visible in the statistics, but mainly as a purveyor of eau-de-vie, with a footnote for the sweet and potent Malvasia of Sitges near Barcelona, and (until monasteries were secularized) for the celebrated black Priorato of the Carthusian house of Scala Dei, regarded more as a medicine than a drink. What revolutionized Catalonia's reputation for quality was the genius of the Raventos family who, in the 1870s, made the discovery that its native Parellada grape formed the ideal basis for sparkling wine.

THE RIOJA, THE UPPER EBRO VALLEY BETWEEN LOGROÑO AND MIRANDA DE EBRO, had been mentioned by enthusiasts at intervals since the Romans. Alas, the legions had not left their usual legacy of roads. Only a trickle of Rioja reached the outside world – despite the pilgrim ways to Santiago de Compostella passing through. In the 17th and 18th centuries the Basque provinces expanded their trade and population and tempted the Riojanos to grow more wine. What could be done with ox-carts and borrachas no doubt was done. Miranda de Ebro, nearest to the coast, did relatively well, but Logroño always had more wine than it could sell. One can imagine the stink of wine-skins getting stronger, until what the locals had not drunk had to be thrown away.

The story of Rioja's first attempt to modernize, and how it was frustrated, is a sadly typical tale of Spain in the 18th century. At length plans were laid to build the essential road to Logroño along the Ebro valley. In the 1780s the dean of Burgos and a native of Rioja, Don Manuel Quintano, travelled to Bordeaux to learn how wine could be made to keep.

Don Manuel's introduction to Rioja of Bordeaux methods, but above all of barrels, was an instant success – except with other winemakers. Cellar-aged wines were triumphantly exported to Cuba and Mexico and survived the voyage. But the authorities, instead of embracing the idea, reacted with petty envy by declaring that all Rioja must be sold at the same price. The cost of barrels and of three years' ageing was disallowed – even on appeal to the Council of Castile. One might almost believe that Quintano smiled a sardonic smile when Napoleon's armies poured through the region a few years later and both Bordeaux methods and the new road were forgotten: the road for only 20 years, the barrels for half a century.

The wide upland valley of the river Ebro in northern Spain sits on the cusp of Atlantic and Mediterranean climates, providing ideal conditions for fine wine. The Rio Oja is a little tributary stream.

OIDIUM WAS WHAT WOKE THE NORTH OF SPAIN FROM ITS TORPOR. Galicia on the north-west coast still maintained a moderate overseas trade with its Ribadavia, but the wines of Leon, the Duero and Rioja rarely struggled further than the cities of the north coast. From 1850 the powdery mildew, imported from Portugal on American vines, laid waste the vineyards of the rainier regions. Rioja was affected, but Galicia with its grey skies was devastated. Many of its winegrowers had already emigrated; and in a region where rain falls intermittently all summer long, even sulphur could be only an expensive palliative; never a cure.

What Galicia lost by oidium, Rioja was to gain. Already it was almost the only supplier of the thriving port of Bilbão. It had supplies that France was desperate for. Even in the oidium years, and without a railway, the French came knocking at its doors for wine. In 1864, no sooner had the railway been built linking Logroño with Bilbão, Madrid and the frontier at Irun, than news came of the phylloxera at work in France. Suddenly Rioja could sell the French all the wine it could make, and a fury of planting swept down the valley.

Its growers found that the vigorous Garnacha vine, the French Grenache, needed less spraying against oidium than their delicate Tempranillo (the name means "early one") – the secret of Rioja's fragrance and vitality. For bulk business it did not matter; there were great new warehouses in Bilbão where Rioja was blended in any case with Duero and La Mancha wines before joining the tide of wine heading for France. But there were more far-sighted landowners who looked beyond the sudden boom of an open French market. Either Rioja could become the concubine of France to be forgotten once the French vineyards had recovered, or it could invest its unaccustomed income in offering France a challenge.

The same thought had evidently come to several Spaniards even before the oidium arrived. In Rioja it had a military and patriotic birth. Its sponsor was the Duke of la Victoria, the former General Espartero and briefly Prime Minister of

The founder of Rioja as a region of fine wine was Luciano de Murrieta, later made Marqués, born in Peru, exiled to England and inspired by Bordeaux.

Spain, who had his own private bodega in Logroño, his home town. His aide de camp in the 1840s was the young Colonel Luciano de Murrieta y Garcia-Lemoine, who was born and brought up in Peru, in a family that owned a silver mine. General and colonel had both had been obliged to find exile in London. They were conservatives, Carlists, and on the losing side, in the civil war of succession that plagued Spain at intervals until the 1870s.

Evidently it was in London, where he lived for five years, that Luciano de Murrieta became interested in wine. Was it at dinner with the duke that the idea of modernizing Rioja came to them both? On his way back to Spain he stayed and studied in Bordeaux. In 1850 he was back in Logroño starting experiments with Bordeaux methods in the ducal vineyards and bodega. All the traditional methods had to go. The old Rioja way was treading and fermenting in shallow lagos like the lagars of the Douro. Many of the grapes remained uncrushed, fermenting by degrees in what today is known as "carbonic maceration"; a process that was lengthy, hard to control, and woefully unhygienic. Murrieta's new method was rapidly crushing the grapes into deep vats to ferment; the classic *cuverie* of a Bordeaux château.

Like Quintano's, Murietta's idea was not just to ship the wine in barrels as Bordeaux did, but to age it. There were no barrels to be had in Rioja. Even Bilbão could provide only little casks, much smaller than the Bordeaux models. At first Murrieta made do with quarter-casks to prove his point. Even within a year the hard young wine had smoothed and taken on new flavours that promised well. Rioja in future was to acquire its characteristic taste not just from its fragrant Tempranillo grapes, but from ever longer ageing in oak. Oak, rather than grapes, became the immediately recognizable Rioja scent and even flavour.

The new Rioja, in a word, epitomized the wealthy Spaniard's idea of what good wine, red or white, should taste like: as far from the borracha as possible: limpid and lively, clean, light and clear.

Would it survive a journey? It depended on the ship. Of Murrieta's first vintage, 1850, aged experimentally for only two years, half was sent to Cuba and was rapturously received; half was sent to Mexico and was ship-wrecked on the way.

MURRIETA WAS NOT THE FIRST TO BUILD HIS OWN BODEGA; that credit goes to a man of greater means and rather different ambition. Don Camilo Hurtado de Amezaga, Marqués de Riscal, had fallen in love with Bordeaux. In 1850 he set about building a veritable château, or at least the working parts of one, over the river from Logroño in the province of Alava. Don Camilo must have been in Bordeaux at the same time as Don Luciano, but their ideas were not the same. One set out to perfect Rioja; the other to imitate Bordeaux.

In 1850, while Murrieta was making his wine from the duke's vineyards and in his bodega, Riscal was recruiting quarrymen in Galicia to excavate what Henderson would call his subterranean cellars. This was not like the Médoc, where the wine lives at ground level, but perhaps he was concerned about the summer heat of Spain. Building and planting to his satisfaction took a full 10 years. It is easy to picture him, top-hatted on the train, feeling the excitement in the air as he arrived at Bordeaux station to order his supplies and taste the latest vintage. Oidium was conquered; the Golden Age was opening. His aim was to present Bordeaux with wine it could not distinguish from its own.

Of his 500 acres (no château in Bordeaux had half as many) he planted three-quarters with Rioja's grapes, one quarter with Bordeaux's, and even a little Pinot Noir. He employed a Bordeaux manager, a man called Jean Pineau who had been recruited by the provincial government to encourage other winegrowers with little tangible result. Even before he had made his wine, aged it to his satisfaction, and put it on the market, he was already expanding and modernizing his great stone-built establishment – while in Madrid he was founding a newspaper, *El Dia*.

At last in 1862 his wine was ready. Following the latest fashion in Bordeaux he refused to sell his Grand Vin (*Reserva* is the Spanish term) in barrel, but bottled it in Bordeaux bottles wrapped in wire mesh and sealed; a publicity touch that the Médoc would not have been ashamed of. The moment of truth came in 1865, when he entered his wine in open competition in Bordeaux itself. For the ultimate test, this wine was Tempranillo pure; Cabernet in his eyes would have been less than a fair trial. It won first prize and disbelief that such a wine could come from Spain.

So close in time that precedence is immaterial, the third of what might well be called the original first-growths of Spain took shape, not in Rioja, but in the once-famous region of the Duero. The idea of imitating Bordeaux was clearly in the aristocratic air. But only one stout-hearted landowner had the faith to plant Bordeaux grapes at well over 2,000 feet in country which bakes and freezes in a most un-Médoc manner.

The great estate of Vega Sicilia belonged to Don Eloy Lecanda y Chaves, who made the Bordeaux pilgrimage to buy his vines and his barrels with no encouragement or even curiosity from his neighbouring vintners. He was, and long remained, the only one. If Vega Sicilia has a mystique no other Spanish wine quite shares, it comes partly from its eccentric geography (until recently the nearest comparable bodega was over 100 miles away) but equally from its quite alarming horsepower. In an analogy with Bordeaux and its first-growths you would have to call Riscal the Lafite of Spain: at its best all perfume and silk. Murrieta is perhaps the Mouton; rich and resonant and deep. Vega Sicilia is the Latour; but Latour of a vintage that has raisined the grapes and fried the picking crews.

WHAT THESE THREE GREAT ORIGINALS HAVE IN COMMON, apart from ambition and success, is that all were conceived and operated well before phylloxera had arrived in France, and a decade before it became a crisis in Bordeaux. Rioja's rise to fame is often represented as an exodus of stricken winemakers across the Pyrenees. But that was a later phase of its development. The point by then had already been proved that Spain, after all, could make wine comparable to France's best.

The news was borne to England by the studious Dr Thudicum in 1873. Having roundly condemned "almost all" the wines of Catalonia, Aragon and Valencia as adulterated and fraudulent, he went on "In the Ebro valley, however, much wine is made in the purest possible manner, and it is not unlikely that we may be supplied hereafter with exquisite wine at moderate price from the part called the Rioja".

Rioja's two first growths did not remain alone for long. At some point in the '60s Murrieta moved from the duke's to his own bodega. Curiously the date is unrecorded, but he bought the 600-acre estate of Ygay near Logroño where the company is today about a decade later, in 1872. By this time winegrowers all over Spain were in a state of euphoria. Phylloxera had swept though the Midi and the French were on their knees for wine. Rioja certainly supplied its share of the dark anonymous fluid that most French wine-merchants were looking for. Most of it came from the warmest part of the region, further east down the Ebro valley on the borders of Navarre; the Rioja Baja, where the Garnacha soon became the principal vine.

Yet the bodega builders of this excited time took their lead from Riscal and Murrieta, aiming to sell oak-aged wine and build a market of their own on the proven quality of the region. Its best white grape, the Viura, turned out to be as capable of ageing to splendid distinction as its red. It also had just the freshness that makes the basis of good sparkling wine. All the raw materials were here to make a Bordeaux, a Burgundy and a Champagne for Spain.

By the end of the '80s there were six large bodegas incorporating the new ideas; most of them built with French advice and some of them with French partners. But unlike Riscal they were not imitating anything specifically French, or even, by 1890, aiming at the French market. Spain by itself was market enough. Madrid, Bilbão, and overseas Cuba and Mexico were ready to buy everything they made. Rioja had locked on to a formula of its own, in which ageing in barrel played an ever-increasing part. Perhaps the idea came from Jerez. Certainly it went far beyond anything that Bordeaux ever practised. To keep a wine, even a white wine, in barrel for 20 or 25 years was nothing exceptional – and not because sales were slack. A great vintage was one which could undergo such treatment and still keep the

The sparkling wines of Catalonia, then shamelessly named "champagne", were very much part of the riotous gaiety of the "Naughty Nineties". Today the Cava companies (Cava is a new generic name for Spain's bottle-fermented sparklers) such as Codorniu draw on this rich design tradition in promoting their wines.

Haro, though smaller than nearby Logroño, is the heart of Rioja's wine world. Elaborate architecture, such as this crowning turret to the Lopez de Heredia bodega, speaks of the confident expansion of a century ago, when industrial methods and new markets made Rioja boom.

sweetness of fruit. These wines, like no others, were built to be marathon runners, surviving not (like vintage port) by their heavy build, but by exceptional sinew and vitality.

It is tempting to class as second growths, if not as firsts, two enterprises of the '70s that gave a different shape to Rioja by shifting the centre of gravity west to the higher and more humid Rioja Alta. From now on the little town of Haro was to be the wine-capital of the region. Around its railway sidings the new bodegas clustered with that jaunty air that the 19th century contrived to put even into its industrial architecture. One, strange to tell, was founded by a youth of 20 who was born in Chile; Rafael López de Heredia. The other, the Compania Vinicola do Norte de España, by brothers from Bilbão with a partner from Champagne.

RIOJA WAS TO UNDERGO ANOTHER TECHNICAL REVOLUTION a century later, when a new generation of bodegas with contemporary ideas enlarged its market to a truly worldwide one for the first time. The marvel is that the old guard, a bare half dozen bodegas of the first generation, have remained a living museum of high-Victorian wine technology, with Rioja's special flavour. The legacy of the young Chilean is perhaps, of all the wonderfully varied shrines of Dionysus all over Europe, the most operatically eccentric. Deep below its raffish seaside villa façade on its railway siding, rock-cut stairs lead into a world utterly cut off from time. Wines are kept here in barrels for decades; in bottles for generations. A spring refreshes the caverns where stacked bottles of antique white wines still give off pale lemon gleams as you pass by.

López de Heredia was an inspired showman. His tasting room is a cave so lofty that you are aware only of the centenarian spiders' webs that hang in heavy festoons over the a table that almost fills the room. The walls around are library shelves of bottles going back to Don Rafael's time. Half a century, or half as much again, seems only to emphasise that these wines, red or white, have found that limpid equilibrium which is the quintessence of Rioja.

As for Castillo Ygay, the estate of the founding father, it was only recently that its current vintage of red Reserva moved on from 1934 to 1942, and white from 1962 to 1970. Nothing could be more impractical and less in vogue than making table wines for future generations. Yet those who can (as Bordeaux amply demonstrates) feel driven to push the astonishing potential of their vines as far as nature will allow.

APART FROM THE REMOTE AND ALMOST UNOBTAINABLE VEGA SICILIA, Rioja remained the only quality table wine supplier of Spain for almost a century. Long after the immediate French interest in supplies died away French merchants and wine-growers who had discovered the virtues of the region continued to build its markets in Spain and Spanish America.

Phylloxera reached Rioja in the 1890s, wearing, it must have seemed for some, an air of retribution. Unscrupulous merchants had been using the good name of the region to sell wine fabricated with the very cheapest industrial alcohol from Germany. But Basque investments (above all the bourgeois of Bilbão saw Rioja as their own vineyard) and the continued presence of the French were a secure base. The stability of Rioja came partly from its very lack of exports – Spain was 80% of its market – and partly from its profoundly bourgeois structure. From an early stage small winegrowers found the new barrel-ageing system beyond their resources and contented themselves with simply growing grapes for the big bodegas. The current law only confirms what for a long time had been an established practice: only bodegas with a storage capacity of 750,000 litres, and at least 500 "bordelesas", the Rioja term for the barrel it so profitably borrowed from Bordeaux, may export their wine with the seal of the regulating body, the Consejo Regulador.

Nor did French interest disappear with the recovery of France's vineyards and the arrival of phylloxera (and mildew) in Spain. Bodegas Franco-Españolas and Bodegas Riojanas are two companies that continued to employ French staff up until the years of the Spanish Civil War.

WE LAST CAUGHT SIGHT OF THE WINES OF SPANISH AMERICA almost three centuries before the emergence of Rioja, when the pirate Drake intercepted a galleon carrying wine-skins from the new colony of Chile to the slightly older one of Peru. It had never realistically been within Spain's power to prevent her American colonies from supplying themselves with wine, rather than obediently waiting for vinegary supplies from the mother country. Yet even as late as the Napoleonic wars Madrid was doggedly sending futile orders to uproot vines and buy more wine from Andalusia.

On the other hand, while South America remained in the illiberal grip of Spain, there were no prospects of more than the most modest improvements. When in the second two decades of the 1800s the colonies one after another declared their independence from the decrepit empire it was the high coastal valleys of Peru which produced the most highly-regarded wine in the greatest quantity.

The principal grape of Peru, as of Chile, was the Pais or Criolla, the same pious plant as the Mission of the Franciscans in California. But much preferred, both for sweet wine and as the basis of the local eau de vie, Pisco, was the Muscatel. The poet Byron's grandfather, the Admiral Byron known as "Foulweather Jack", having survived shipwreck on Cape Horn and made his way half the length of Chile to Santiago, gave a glowing account of Chile's muscat, which he found "full as good as

The colourful but orderly procession of modern Chilean grape-pickers. Harvesting early in the morning while the grapes are still cool, the use of shallow trays to prevent crushing and the grapes' rapid transfer to the winery all help to preserve the superb quality of the fruit.

Madeira". It is uncharacteristic of André Jullien that his view of Chilean wines is contrary, to say the least; if not downright jaundiced. "They have the colour", he writes, "of a potion of rhubarb and senna, and their taste, coming from the tarred goatskins in which they are transported, comes close enough to these same drugs."

One could perhaps venture that shipwreck affects the critical faculty when it comes to wine. On the other hand Chile remained content with its traditional vintages for 30 years or more after its independence. It was not until prosperous Chileans started to visit Europe that their own wines began to seem inadequate.

THE PIONEER IN IMPORTING NEW AND BETTER VINE VARIETIES, Don Silvestre Ochagavia Errazuriz, came from a Basque family that had first settled in Brazil. It is pure coincidence, but extraordinary nonetheless, that Chile's wine industry in the modern sense is precisely contemporary with that other Basque creation: Rioja. For it was in 1851, just as young Colonel Murrieta was making his first wines, that Ochagavia employed a French oenologist on his estate just south of Santiago to introduce the vines of Bordeaux. Cabernet, Merlot, Malbec, Sauvignon Blanc and Sémillon were his first choice. Seeing how ideal conditions were, he also wisely tried the Riesling, which showed its adaptability here just as it was doing at the same time in South Australia.

The valleys of central Chile might have been planned for a great wine industry since the earth took shape. With fertile soil, bountiful sunshine, low humidity, and an infinite supply of water for irrigation – the snowmelt from the Andes – their

Phylloxera has managed to find its way to most of the wine-growing regions of the world. Chile so far has entirely escaped. Isolation is usually given as the reason: this remote patch of vines hemmed in between the Cordillera of the Andes and the Pacific Ocean, with great deserts to the north, obviously has that advantage.

New Zealand, on the other hand, is at least as isolated and yet has been infected. Perhaps, like South Australia, Chile has simply been lucky to escape; the insect has never been introduced. It is also perhaps possible that the regular practice of irrigation by flooding the vine-roots has eliminated any incipient epidemic.

vines were untroubled by disease, and from the start their vintages fermented without problems into powerfully fruity, healthy, stable and transportable wines.

The ruling elite of Chile a century ago was largely Basque in origin, mixed with not a little British and Irish blood from the veterans of Napoleon's wars who had gone to South America to see what that secretive continent had to offer. Most of the principal bodegas of Chile were founded in the river valleys around Santiago in the generation following Ochagavia's lead; substantial investments in land and equipment, including imported oak for vats and barrels (Chile has no suitable native timber) – often built with money made from the silver-mines of the north. The peasant grower on his few acres continued to plant the Pais. As in Rioja, fine wine was made by a relatively small number of large bodegas.

If OCHAGAVIA IS CREDITED WITH THE ROLE of a rather less frenzied Haraszthy in the history of Chile, his equivalent across the Andes in Argentina was almost Haraszthyan, at least in vigour and versatility. As a young man Don Tiburcio Benegas distinguished himself as a cool head in an emergency. In 1861 the old colonial city of Mendoza in the Andean foothills was destroyed by an earthquake. Its commercial and financial system seized up. Benegas, at the age of 25, became the city's banker and restored its dislocated finances.

His interest in wine started with his marriage in 1870 to the daughter of a progressive landowner in the remote province. Mendoza is very much nearer to Chile and Santiago than to the centre of population of Argentina. Mendoza and Santiago are only 150 miles apart but the journey between the two is a considerable one. The highest part of the long blade of the Andes, Aconcagua and Tupungato, lies directly between the two cities.

Conditions on the Argentine side are perhaps marginally less perfect for wine-growing than in the valleys of central Chile – the missing element being the ocean to moderate extremes of temperature. Irrigation is essential in both. In Benegas' time a more important missing element was a market. In due course, in the 1880s, he was to bring the railway to Mendoza and to become the Governor of the province. Meanwhile, on his own property of El Trapiche in the neighbouring province of Godoy Cruz (now San Vicente), he experimented with European vines imported both from Chile and directly from Europe. There was no doubt that with access to Buenos Aires the Andean foothills of Argentina could become one of the most prolific sources of good quality wine on earth.

It was the market that would determine its style. Chile developed an idiom based on the ideas of the north of Spain and heavily influenced by France. Without a great domestic market for quality wine it became the principal exporter within South America. Its tendency was to improve as far as possible its already naturally high standards. In Argentina the reverse happened. The great influx of Italian immigrants early in the 20th century pointed the direction for its wine. It was to be rough and ready, sweet and tannic, plentiful and cheap.

PART V

Abstract in stainless steel: an Australian winery of the 1980s

CHAPTER 41

FIFTY YEARS OF CRISIS

The vintages of 1899 and 1900 made, in Bordeaux, one of those famous pairs, like 1982 and 1983, both excellent, each with its own style and character, that offer a glow of reassurance to lovers of wine – not to mention their producers. Nature was bountiful, and even those growers who were still struggling against phylloxera may have felt that the worst was over. Half a century of battling with pests and diseases had not prevented some great vintages from being made. The buoyancy of the Belle Epoque meant that demand for fine wine was high – high enough for fraud to be a flourishing industry and a national scandal.

What Jeremiah would have foretold as the 20th century opened that the wine industry would be on the brink of a depression that would be the longest and most severe in its modern history? The patches of clear sky in the first 50 years of this century were few and fleeting. Poor weather, war, slump and intemperate fanaticism were all to contribute to Dionysus' distress. These were the labour pains of the world of modern wine. Modern standards of winemaking, of authenticity, and even our very habits of appreciation and enjoyment were to emerge from this long-drawn-out travail.

IT IS NOT SURPRISING THAT (AT LEAST IN FRANCE) it was hard for winegrowers to grasp at this moment in history that their problem was simply too much wine. Recent memories were full of the risk, and often the reality, of whole vineyards being snuffed out. One could still taste the miserable fabrications that had been passed off as wine, even under respected names, when the real thing was lacking. The notion of shortage was too deeply ingrained to be quickly supplanted by one of excess, however glaring the evidence. The fact that France had had to import huge quantities of wine was proof enough to a Frenchman that once she was self-sufficient again, all would be well.

Every region, every nation had acted independently on the same instincts. Algeria, once a market for French wine, now possessed vast vineyards whose whole purpose was to supply its old supplier. Sicily and the south of Italy had turned their cornfields and olive groves into vineyards. Spain had extended all its vineyards. Hungary had reclaimed its great sandy plain for the vine. Above all the Languedoc had reacted to phylloxera by becoming a monoculture of the vine – and at the most basic level. Inevitably prices collapsed. In the phylloxera years of the 1880s a hectolitre of wine in the Languedoc had fetched its grower 30 francs. By 1900 the price was down to 10 francs, while the grower's cost was 15.

By being first to suffer, first to discover the remedy of grafting, and first to replant with grafted vines the Languedoc had taken on itself the role of a well of wine for all of France to dip into. Such marginal regions as Paris or Auxerre or Lorraine in the north could tell by a simple calculation that for them replanting could never be worthwhile. For them wine-growing was over.

It came as more of a shock for the Midi to discover that its wine was not wanted. Its growers looked for scapegoats – and in 1907, when the price had fallen to less than half the cost of production, they found a redeemer to lead them, as they thought, out of their misery.

THEIR SINGULAR CHOICE WAS NO RANTING DEMAGOGUE but a middle-aged farmer from Narbonne called Albert Marcellin. His rallying cries picked as the principal cause of their discontent an evil which, though obvious, showed how little he and his followers understood the real situation. They blamed the fabricators of fake wine – whose business had in reality collapsed even faster than their own.

A more realistic plank in their platform was protest against the chaptalization which enabled northern producers to offer them competition. In most of northern France phylloxera was still in full cry: growers were desperate for something to sell. To add sugar and water was, after all, permitted by the great Chaptal . . . and at this very moment the Chamber of Deputies in Paris was debating whether to tax sugar at 15 francs per 100 kilos (the plea of northern deputies – in whose constituencies the sugar beet was also grown) or 60 francs, the demand of the south.

"Vive le vin naturel" and "Down with the poisoners" were the shouts of the crowds who gathered round Marcellin in alarming numbers at regular Sunday demonstrations in the spring of 1907; swelling from 80,000 in Narbonne in early May to over half a million in Montpellier in early June. They chose to ignore (or did not understand) the fact that they themselves were compounding the problem by importing potent Algerian wine to blend with the thin produce of their over-

GOOD YEARS AND BAD

As though in sympathy with the turbulence of the times, the weather in Europe in this century, up to the outbreak of the Second World War, left a trail of poor vintages to add to the wine-grower's problems.

Obviously there were wide variations from region to region, but taking Bordeaux, and more particularly the Médoc, as our sample, the first 40 years of the century produced only 11 vintages that can be described as generally good, of which two, without qualification, were great.

The first 19 years produced two extremely fine vintages: 1900 and 1906. 1920 and 1929 were the great vintages whose wines have reached

pinnacles of perfection. In comparison, the 40 years between 1940 and 1980 were generally successful at least twice as frequently.

One can argue that 23 vintages produced a clear majority of good or very good wines – although again only two vintages (1945 and 1961) can confidently be described in terms of the very highest praise. 1982, which may in time prove to be among the best of the century, falls just outside the 40 years in question.

The record of the '80s, though, with seven good or very good vintages out of nine, serves to stress that our immediate forebears were particularly unlucky.

abundant harvests. While the demonstrations were going on more than half of the local councils of the region resigned en bloc to show their support – a fact that the government in Paris could not ignore.

The Prime Minister, Clemenceau, was not known as "le Tigre" for nothing. He sent troops to Narbonne to arrest the ringleaders. Five protesters were killed in the resulting riot. Marcellin, who had consistently preached non-violence, went to Paris to talk to Clemenceau – walking unannounced, it is said, into the great man's office. He was ridiculed for it; but it worked. By the end of June the government had brought in a law which provided for the first time in history for a census of how much wine was made each year and how much was held in stock. It demanded a statutory "Déclaration de Récolte" from every winegrower in the land. The law provided no control over how much might be made, but at least it gave the government a dipstick for the great sump which held so much potential trouble. Further measures brought in in September required a record of the use of sugar for chaptalization, and most fundamentally of all gave wine for the first time a legal definition, as being made "exclusively from the alcoholic fermentation of fresh grapes or fresh grape juice".

FOR THE MOMENT THE WINEGROWERS OF THE SOUTH WERE CONTENT. The government had listened and acted – although it had done nothing to tackle the overproduction which was the root of the problem. By chance, bad harvests (there were serious recurrences of mildew in 1910 and 1915) raised wine prices in the years leading up to the First World War. Then it was the war itself that, for the time being, boosted the market. In the autumn of 1914 the Languedoc showed a shrewd blend of patriotism and public relations. The harvest had been huge, and the region made a present of 20 million litres to the army. Napoleon's armies had had wine rations; now the War Ministry could scarcely refuse them to the troops. Throughout the war and the 1920s France's wine consumption rose. In 1900 it had been 100 litres a head; in 1926 it was 135. Naturally the growers seized the chance to plant more vines.

Once again euphoria was to be followed by a slump. This time, however, the government grasped the nettle. Algeria had more than doubled its production. The Languedoc was awash. And perhaps of more immediate concern was the post-war crisis that had left France's prestigious exporting wine regions bereft of customers. Not one of the nations that had bought bordeaux, burgundy and champagne with such enthusiasm before the war had any money left to spend on luxuries. The Russian Revolution had removed one of France's most profitable markets – seemingly for ever. Germany, Austria and Hungary were ruined by the war. Belgium would take years to recover. Britain, having bought as heavily as it could of the great mature champagne vintages that had survived the war, made a virtue of necessity by persuading itself that much cheaper cocktails were more fashionable. Only America had money – and America had shot itself in the foot with the 18th Amendment that brought in National Prohibition in 1919.

There were, as we shall see, compensations for the fortunate few in the devastation of the market for fine wines. The immediate problems, though, were to stem the flow of unwanted vin ordinaire, and to protect the great heritage of the regions that made their living by pursuing quality.

THE FIRST WAS ACCOMPLISHED, AT LEAST IN PART, BY DECREES between 1931 and 1936 that banned new planting, ordered the distillation of great quantities of wine, and obliged all départements that had indulged in the recent planting spree to pull up a proportion of their vines. Not only was France's total vineyard reduced by 10 per cent by this measure, but the most popular (because most prolific) of the American-French hybrid vines planted after phylloxera, the Jacquez, the Noah and the Clinton – names not mentioned in polite circles – were banned from the Déclaration de Récolte, which meant that growers might drink their wine if they chose, but they were legally debarred from selling it. On the whole these measures were a success. They certainly amounted to a degree of government intervention in what might be grown where and by whom that would scarcely have appealed to Montesquieu.

But the time was ripe, because running parallel with the heavy political question of trying to balance supply and demand there had been, from the beginning of the century, a much more specific movement building strength. It concerned the right to use the world-famous names of the great wines: a matter which in the past had always been left to local authorities to police.

Phylloxera had brought matters to a head with its subsequent tidal wave of fraud. Growers declared that not a single drop of wine that had passed through a merchant's hands could be reckoned to be authentic. Merchants pointed out that growers themselves were not above temptation. Given the circumstances, it seems remarkable that bottles from the great châteaux (and many lesser ones) from this era have in many cases turned out in the long run to be extremely fine.

The first region to react in self-defence was, logically enough, the one that probably needed authenticating most urgently: Chablis. In 1900, 79 Chablis producers formed a group to guarantee that of all the millions of bottles labelled with the best-known name of all French dry white wines (or indeed all white wines of any sort) only theirs were the real thing. Their move of course made not the slightest impression on Californian, Australian, Spanish or any other producers, who continued to sell whatever wine they liked as Chablis. But a stand had been taken. It meant that any of that minority of consumers who even cared if their wine was authentic or not was being offered a guide.

The Médoc followed, a year later, with a Union Syndicale de Propriétaires des Crus Classés du Médoc; a considerably more influential body which encouraged other regions to follow. The trend was clear enough for the government to back it with legislation. In 1905 it passed the law which was eventually to lead, 30 years later, to the system of appellations controlées. At this stage no definitions were even attempted. It contented itself with a statement of principle against the fraudulent or deceptive use of names and descriptions. As far as it went, its sentiment still holds good. It threatened fines or imprisonment for "whoever would deceive, or try to deceive another party, either as to the nature, the substantial quality, the composition and the content in relevant substances of all merchandise, whether of their kind or of their origin. . . ."

The question now remained to be answered (and indeed to be asked): where do you draw the boundary line around a name? It was left to the local administration to decide what was (or was not) within the limits of Chablis or Champagne. In 1908 a new law more explicitly laid down that delimitations would be made by decree and following "local usage". Over the following years discussion was intense. In Bordeaux it raised the ancient question of the High Country wines. Often in the past they had been sold as Bordeaux when need arose. But now, as in the past, the influence of Bordeaux was greater than that of its scattered country cousins. In 1911 their status was finally decreed. Bordeaux meant the département of the Gironde alone. The High Country, including even Bergerac, was excluded.

Champagne provided the cause célèbre of this administrative dilemma. It was more than a matter of simple delimitation. It awkwardly combined with a situation similar to that in the Languedoc in 1907: real human distress over low prices and miserable living conditions. In 1908 the decree was published drawing the boundaries of Champagne. It included most of the communes of the département of the Marne; some in the neighbouring Aisne (whose wine the Marne growers described as "bean soup") – but none in the southern part of the province, the Aube, around Troyes where the medieval Champagne fairs had been held. Immediately the Aubois were up in arms. Were they not the true Champenois? – Only historically, came the reply from the Marne: the wine that bears the name of Champagne was born in the Marne valley: Aubois wine cannot hold a candle to the great crus immortalized by Dom Pérignon. The government was indecisive, and appeared to favour the argument of the Aube.

MORE SERIOUSLY, THE VINTAGE OF 1910 WAS THE LAST STRAW in a succession of four appalling years for all champagne growers. To the battle with phylloxera, then at its height in Champagne, (15,000 acres of vines died in that year alone), was added a catastrophic year of rain and mildew when many growers made no wine at all. In 1911 the growers of the Marne, privileged or not, took to the streets against the merchants whom they believed not just to be pulling the strings of the administration, but cheating them by buying bulk wine from outside the region altogether. Famous houses, the growers said, had been bringing in wine from Touraine and Anjou, the Midi, and even as far afield as Germany and Spain. Prices were low because they, as well as the customers, were being defrauded.

The violence of their reaction went far beyond anything seen in the Languedoc four years before. Aÿ was the centre of the storm. This was no protest meeting, but a settling of old scores. Several thousand winegrowers set upon the merchant–houses of the little town, broke down their doors, smashed their bottles, opened their barrels and let the wine flow into the streets. The homes of several merchants were similarly ransacked (though all agreed that the house of Bollinger in the centre of the town should be left untouched). Finally they set fire to houses and even vineyards (which were full of straw for frost protection). Firing the vineyards was inexplicable: it suggests that anarchists from outside the region must have been involved.

Champagne, as we have seen, is well accustomed to the sight of troops. This time it was a military police force that descended on it, 40,000 strong, to take up billets in every village of the region. A temporary compromise was reached by which the Aube was accorded the title of "Champagne – second zone", but before the government had had time to settle the issue, it was not friendly troops that were parading though Reims and Epernay, it was Germans.

The Champagne Riots of 1911 saw angry growers sack the cellars of merchants they accused of importing wine from outside the region to pass off as "champagne". Troops restored order – but only after violent scuffles had broken out between bottle-throwing growers and dragoons.

THE MARNE WAS THE SCENE OF TWO OF THE DECISIVE BATTLES of the First World War; in September 1914 when the German advance was checked in 10 days of fighting among the heavy-laden vines, and in September 1918 when the Allies finally pushed the Germans from their positions and went on to victory. In the four years between Reims was continuously in the front line, suffering more than 1,000 days of German shelling beginning with the systematic bombardment and destruction of the cathedral in which the kings of France were crowned.

Reims would have ceased to exist during the war had it not been for its champagne cellars, the great deep chalk-pits that underlie most of the city. They became an underground fortress, linked by tunnels, in which up to 50,000 troops lived. Astonishingly, the champagne industry went on, even in this beleaguered barracks. More astonishingly still, the growers continued to tend their vines even among the trenches that criss-crossed the northern slopes of the "mountain" overlooking the city. They crawled like infantrymen through the white mud of winter to prune, and in the golden days of October they ran out to harvest with their usual songs. 1914, 1915 and 1917 were vintages of exceptional quality: 1914 one of the greatest and longest-lived of the century – due, it is said, to some of the grapes having been picked under-ripe, with extra high acidity, and some overripe and unusually sweet.

Scarcely was the Armistice signed in November 1918 than the government in Paris returned to the question of appellations – so rapidly, in fact, that before the Treaty of Versailles that formally ended the war was ready for signature, the concept of France's appellations controlées was formulated and included as a clause that the Germans were obliged to accept.

At least one lesson had been learned from the pre-war problems: appellations were too delicate a matter to be handled by simple administrative decree. In 1919 the government passed the problem over to the courts of law as a more sensitive instrument – still, however, with no greater ambition than to draw accepted boundary lines. How little these meant on their own was aptly illustrated not by a wine region, but by something even more emotive to the French public: a cheese.

The scandal broke in 1925. Roquefort, that most piquant and creamy of cheeses, had duly been granted a delimited area of production in the mountains of the Aveyron, the southern central highlands of France. The court, however, had said nothing about its most vital characteristic: that it is (or should be) made of ewe's milk, not of cow's. Here was the problem in a nutshell. It was seized upon by Joseph Capus, professor of agriculture at Cadillac and member of the Chamber of Deputies for the Gironde. Capus saw for himself how the appellations of the great vineyards of Bordeaux were being used by unscrupulous (or indeed just stupid) growers for wines made by any methods from any grapes. It was not a question of ewe's milk or cow's but of Cabernet or Noah. In 1927 his influence added another law to the statute book, introducing the element that the Dukes of Burgundy had seen as fundamental four centuries before. The phrase the law employed might almost have been drafted by Philippe the Bold himself: "using grape varieties hallowed by local, loyal and established custom".

Capus was leading in the right direction. Eventually he would be recognized as the godfather of the Appellation laws – "le loi Capus" is a phrase one still occasionally hears. But others were studying their regions in much greater depth; none more so than the owner of Château Fortia, one of the most important estates of Châteauneuf du Pape, Baron Le Roy de Boiseaumarié.

The notion of "terroir", now so emotively used to express the precise ecosystem of each vineyard, could be said to have sprung from this enlightened proprietor's proposals. It was he who in 1923 described the soil best suited to the 13 grape varieties of Châteauneuf in terms of its natural flora of lavender and thyme. But just as important as the terroir were the cultural practices, the pruning, the maximum crop that would make good wine, the ripeness of the grapes and the way they were handled in the cellar. These were the missing links in all the legislation that had gone before. Unless the appellation laws took each of the elements of wine quality as a separate and serious issue, they would be to no avail.

The law that eventually brought these elements together was largely Joseph Capus' work. It established, in 1935, the Comité National des Appellations d'Origine; a perpetual expert body to examine every aspect of each claim by a region for an appellation controlée. In 30 years France had progressed from a simple decree against undefined fraud to a system to define the identity of each distinctive wine. The work was not complete: indeed 1935 was the starting date. But the

LES TROIS GLORIEUSES

Burgundy in the '30s was in a sorry state, with sales so low that many non-resident proprietors, seeing no return on their investments, sold their vines, even in some of the Grands Crus vineyards. It was an opportunity that the working vignerons were never likely to see again, and life-times' savings were shrewdly spent on buying little parcels of the land they had worked for others.

In an effort to promote sales and reawaken public interest two leading citizens of Nuits St Georges, Georges Faiveley and Camille Rodier, had the inspiration of starting the Confrérie des Chevaliers du Tastevin, which was inaugurated at a banquet at the Château de Clos de Vougeot in November 1934, on the eve of the annual auction of the wines of the Hospices de Beaune. The village of Meursault had initiated the "Paulée", a public lunch to celebrate the end of the harvest, in 1925. The three events, the banquet of the Confrérie, the auction and the Paulée de Meursault, taking place every year on the third weekend of November, became known as Les Trois Glorieuses; a promotional event that has stood Burgundy in good stead ever since.

principles were established. The processing of hundreds of appellations could now begin. After the Second World War the Comité became an Institut: the INAO, the governing body of the French world of wine and the model to which almost every nation looks as it struggles with its own version of the same intractable problem: how to legislate for something so variable as wine.

WE HAVE SEEN HOW ADVERSITY HAD CREATED what might still be at the discussion stage without the conditions of the time. Perversity had its part to play as well. It was as the Great War ended, and the prospect of normality was rekindling spirits everywhere, that America produced the black joke of Prohibition. No-one, at least in America, could say they had not been warned. The temperance movement, despite its complicated internal power-struggles, had been gradually gathering strength all the while America itself had been growing and learning to use its power. It was like a cancer in the body of the country built on freedom; a coalition of quite disparate interests, of sincere reformers and power-brokers on the make, that joined in exploiting what they chose to see as a weakness: the freedom of men and women to refresh and restore themselves as their ancestors had done since history began.

This is not the place either to retail the machinations, or even to deplore the obvious consequences of the catastrophe. It is hard to imagine a greater spur to law-breaking even by agents seeking to destroy the nation. Its moral repercussions were horrifying. The systematic hypocrisy it introduced into public life was as bad as the simple slaughter of individuals who were caught in the wrong gang of bootleggers at the wrong time. The best excuse of those who promoted Prohibition is that they had no idea what its consequences would be. Nowhere is this more true than in the world of wine. Its net effect was to add more than half as much again to America's wine consumption. Production averaged over 76 million gallons a year over the 13 years the law was in force, compared with 50 million gallons in the record pre-Prohibition year. Nobody knows how much wine was smuggled in from abroad (although the figure offered by the champagne industry is over 70 million cases during the years in question).

The wine industry did not even have to go underground. Although it was strictly policed (at least 1,000 enforcement officers were found guilty of extortion, conspiracy, perjury and other offences) it was still permitted to make wine for medicinal and sacramental use. Anyone could call himself a rabbi or indeed found a "church". Every drugstore sold medicinal wine, and every doctor would prescribe Paul Masson's excellent "Medicinal Champagne" for any patient suffering from an otherwise incurable thirst.

These legitimate exceptions, though, made up only perhaps 5% of the wine that Americans drank during Prohibition. By far the greatest part was also made more or less legally, but under a gaping loophole in the so-called Volstead Act, the 10,000 word document that put flesh on the bones of the 18th Amendment.

The loop-hole was a sentence in Section 29. It read, in part: "The penalties provided in this Act against the manufacture of liquor without a permit shall not apply to a person for manufacturing nonintoxicating cider and fruit juices exclusively for use in his home. . ." – up to a limit of 200 gallons a year. "Nonintoxicating" apparently was too long a word for the millions of Americans who suddenly became home winemakers. A demand grew almost overnight for grapes in quantities never transported before. It was bad news for the wineries, but a bonanza for grape-growers, and for railroad companies. Within two years the price of grapes in California rose to three times its average before Prohibition as dealers filled every waggon they could find to rush them to the cities of the east. Wine grapes, table grapes and raisin grapes were all just grapes to them – with the proviso that the thicker the skin and the darker the juice the better.

The ideal, and the grape that was planted massively at the expense of better varieties, was the Alicante Bouschet – the red-juiced "teinturier" that M. Bouschet had bred to lend colour to the pallid production of the Languedoc. So dark was its pulp and skin that after it had been pressed a second and even a third batch of "wine" could easily be made by fermenting sugar and water on the remaining "marc". Its thick skin also survived the railway journey better than any other. The New York yards of the Pennsylvania Railroad became the auction room for the grapes as they arrived. "What Wall Street is to the investment business, the Penn yard is to the grape business", as Business Week explained. In 1928 one buyer bought 225 carloads of Alicante Bouschet as a single auction lot: enough to make over two million gallons of "wine". This, of course, was very much the wholesale side of things – the bootlegging business that principally supplied restaurants and speakeasies. On the retail side, although many turned up at the Pennsylvania yard with everything from wheelbarrows to baby buggies, most citizens, having experimented with one sticky bath-full of grapes, were prepared to pay extra for convenience.

Prohibition's repeal captured in allegory by a Spanish artist. All the party-goers were celebrating was a return to easier drinking, not to drinking *per se*. Anyone with money, and quite a few without, was able to circumvent the ban. Several modern drinks companies owe their origins to the successful slaking of illicit American thirsts.

"Grape bricks" of concentrated juice were one solution; each one bearing a warning "Do not add yeast or contents will ferment". A far more imaginative procedure was dreamed up by Paul Garrett, the creator of Virginia Dare: to use federal funds to "save the bankrupt grape industry" by making and marketing juice concentrate. What industry was more in need of President Hoover's farm relief programme? Fruit Industries, Inc, was the name of Garrett's enterprise, uniting his interests in California and grape-growing New York.

In 1930 "Vine-glo" was advertised – in terms which suggest a certain over-confidence, to say the least. Eight varieties were offered to the public: Port, Muscatel, Tokay, Sauterne, Virginia Dare, Riesling, Claret and Burgundy. Not only was the concentrate delivered to your home, but a service man came with it to start the fermentation, and came back again 60 days later to bottle and label the (presumably "nonintoxicating") wine – and more than likely bring another keg.

So audacious a scheme attracted compliments from the highest quarters. Al Capone is reported to have banned Vine-glo from Chicago on pain of death. More seriously, a Kansas City court saw straight through the whole charade. But by this time the end of Prohibition was in sight. The next year, with Roosevelt's election as President, California became the first state to repeal its Prohibition laws, and from December 1933, in the depths of the Depression, the "noble experiment" petered ingloriously out across the nation.

IF THERE WAS REJOICING IN THE VINEYARDS, IT WAS TO BE SHORT-LIVED. By vintage time Repeal had been imminent enough for wineries (most of which had not made wine for years) to wind up for action. They were to discover that the realities of re-starting were less attractive than the idea. Most of the vineyards had been replanted with "shipping" grapes. Much of their equipment and cooperage was unusable. Many were inexperienced or rusty in even the principles of their craft.

Wines made in a hurry, some still fermenting, were rushed to the Christmas market. Bottles that had not turned to vinegar exploded in shop windows. Nothing could have persuaded the public more effectively that it was better off with the home-brew it was used to – on which, besides, there were no taxes to pay.

America had lost not only its wine industry: it had lost its taste for wine – orthodox wine, that is, for drinking with meals at home as part of daily life. Dry wines depend on good grapes and on reasonable skill in winemaking. Tastes vitiated by a dozen years of home-brew were looking for something sweet and strong. This was the way the industry had to go. The historian Leon Adams worked as a journalist in San Francisco through the whole unhappy period. "Most of the people in the industry thought of wine as a skid-row beverage", he recalls. "The bankers regarded wine as one by-product of the grape industry. . . . Some growers, such as John Daniel of Inglenook, tried to secure larger loans to plant premium wine varieties – but grapes were grapes as far as banks were concerned."

In 1934, in the giddy aftermath of Prohibition, 800 wineries had licences, three-quarters of them new, in California. A few years later barely more than 200 were still in business. It was a desperately slow climb back, led by a handful of men whose faith was not to be shaken; true heirs of Jefferson who understood that natural wine stands apart from all other beverages. Among them were the aristocracy who had survived: the firms of Krug, of Inglenook, Beaulieu and Wente, Martini and Paul Masson. Most active in the politics of the business were the Rossi twins, Edmund and Robert, whose Tipo wines from their Italian Swiss Colony winery in Sonoma county never made claims to greatness, but who passionately took up the cause of wine against hard liquor and laid the foundation of today's Wine Institute of California. Quietly getting on with their business of making low-price wine in ever-increasing quantities in the Central Valley were three Italian firms, the future giants of the industry: the Franzias, Louis Petri, and the brothers Gallo.

A VISIONARY JOURNALIST IN THE EAST, MEANWHILE, had germinated an idea that was to revolutionize the way California (and eventually a much wider world) thought and talked about its wines, the grapes it made them from, and the standards by which they could be compared and judged. Frank Schoonmaker asked the most fundamental questions from his suppliers in France, when he started a wine-importing business shortly after Repeal. Few Frenchmen at the time were aware of the vital importance of grape varieties. The law that made them mandatory for appellation wines was only six years older than Repeal. Carrying the thinking of Joseph Capus into his own selection of California wines, he abandoned the convention that borrowed a European name for every kind of wine. What, after all, in California, was the difference between a "Burgundy" and a "claret", a "Chablis" and a "Rhine"? One man's Rhine was another man's Sauterne. Instead, for his Selections made by Almaden, he named the grape variety involved (or dominant). His light-hearted back-labels gave a little vinous education and initiated the revolution to the use of "varietal" names for most quality wines.

The woes of the winegrower in the 1910s, 20s and 30s had one unpredictable result that has since stood him in good stead; the price of the finest wines came down to a level where they could be drunk by a much wider and more inquisitive range of amateurs than the plutocratic few they were designed for. The discussion of wine took on a new dimension as more palates became practised on wines of exceptional quality from different countries and regions. It is notable that the 19th century, for all the extravagance of its menus, produced practically no writing on the subject of wine with food or wine at table. It is clear from the menus of the gross banquets that were the order of the day that little consideration was given to the matching of the wine being served with the flavour of the dish that accompanied it. Nor, probably, was much critical attention given to the wine itself.

In the grandest households wines of every sort were offered at the same time – a footman bringing a glass of whatever wine was asked for. In bourgeois Britain it was routine to start dinner with sherry or madeira, then to drink moselle or hock, white burgundy or white Hermitage, then (always in the middle of the meal) champagne, then claret or burgundy or both, then to finish with port, and sometimes claret again. In France sweet champagne was served with the sweet dishes (and dry champagne not at all).

Certainly there were wine books, both of the business-like and the poetic kind. What was lacking was a voice that was personal and critical; a memoir of good and bad wines tasted, setting them in the context of the writer's (or the reader's) life. Colette wrote magically in this vein at moments. It was an Englishman, though, who is credited with launching the new genre: George Saintsbury, who had been both journalist and Professor of Literature, whose modest jottings, his *Notes on a Cellar Book*, opened the way in 1920 to the new critical and personal school.

Notes on a Cellar Book is charming but slight. Its influence, though (not least on publishers, for it went into several editions), led to a spate of more studied works in this vein which 70 years later shows no sign of abating.

The most prolific and most influential of all writers on wine from that day to this was André Louis Simon, a French ex-patriate in England, agent for Pommery champagne from 1902 (when he was 25) to 1932, who loved printer's ink almost as much as he loved good wine. In 1906–9 he published, in excellent English and at his own expense, the first three volumes of his *History of the Wine Trade in England* – the fruit of research that would have taken many historians half a lifetime. From the '20s on the flow of his books and pamphlets was unending: all pithy, original and practical, yet with the irresistible trace of the Frenchman's oratory.

Around André Simon gathered a group of friends, wine-merchants and men of letters, who in 1931 founded a dining club in honour of George Saintsbury which still meets twice a year. Two years later, still during the Depression, several of the same friends founded the Wine and Food Society to proselytize in the name of "the art of good living": never wanton extravagance or elaborate meals; just what Simon called "honest wines and wholesome fare". The Society's quarterly journal helped to spread his gospel. Today 150 branches of the International Wine and Food Society around the world have many thousands of members.

There is an English clubbiness about the books of Simon's friends that rarely seeks to look beyond the world of "classic" wines. H. Warner Allen, Charles Walter Berry, Ian Campbell and Maurice Healy set the tone; reminiscent, sometimes, of Silas Weir Mitchell's old Madeira Party, or even the table talk of Oliver Wendell Holmes.

Yet Simon himself was acutely aware of the latent potential of the New World's wines. He travelled many times to America (first, as a champagne salesman, to Chile in 1907: the wealth of Chile's nitrate mines gave it the highest consumption of champagne per head of population in the world). On his arrival in New York in 1934 to found new chapters of the Wine and Food Society a newspaper headline proclaimed "Europe's Greatest Eater With Us". The first American chapter was founded in New Orleans in 1935. Even at the age of 87 André Simon was ready to investigate new ground. In 1964 he visited Australia and New Zealand and was so impressed with Australian wine that *The Wines, Vineyards and Vignerons of Australia* was the penultimate book of his score of more than 100.

André Simon (1877–1970) was the prophet of the modern "art of good living".

The essential unpretentiousness that made Simon the ideal interpreter of wine to the world is summed up in his modest definition of a connoisseur: "one who knows good wine from bad, and is able to appreciate the different merits of different wines". Many who have gone further have said too much.

CHAPTER 42

THE NEW WORLD CHALLENGES

Now that the New World's vineyards, Australia and California, New Zealand and even South Africa, are giving us wines comparable to all but the very finest wines of France, it might seem their potential was never in doubt. But that is very far from the way it felt to André Tchelistcheff, a Russian emigré who came via France to the Napa valley in 1937. He had been hired in Burgundy by Georges de Latour, the owner of the Beaulieu estate, to make the wines of his small private company, which had tottered through Prohibition with a sacramental licence.

Tchelistcheff had been working in France during the bleakest period of the '30s, yet his first impression, he recalls, was of the startling crudity of California methods. Sulphur was thrown on the new-picked grapes by the bucketful until they were almost bleached; there was a mere vestige of a laboratory; when a fermenting vat grew dangerously hot (dangerous for the wine, that is) the only remedy was to heave in great blocks of ice to cool it down – a method which was not unknown, it must be admitted, even in Bordeaux. Stranger to him, and certainly less attractive, was the secrecy and suspicion that surrounded every operation. It was unthinkable to show your neighbour how you made your wine.

THE FIRST ''GRANGE''

Australia also had its Tchelistcheff: an original genius working at precisely the same time with very similar ideas, to set a new standard for his whole country, and upset, once and for all, the idea that France had a monopoly of great red wine.

The Australian pioneer was Max Schubert, the winemaker for Penfold's at Magill in the suburbs of Adelaide. In 1950 Schubert visited France for the first time, was introduced to Bordeaux by Christian Cruse of the patrician Chartronnais family, and went home to experiment with the best grapes he could find. These were Shiraz, grown on Dr Penfold's original property, Grange Cottage, and some from Mor-

phett Vale, a few miles to the south (with sometimes a little seasoning of Cabernet).

Like Tchelistcheff, he matured his wine in new small barrels of American oak. Knowing what a revolutionary wine he had made, fruitier and with a more powerful structure than anything Australia had seen, he persuaded Penfolds not to release it until it had matured in bottle for four years. Even then he was so far ahead of his time that critics rejected the new wine, and from 1957 for three years no new barrels were used. Grange Hermitage, as it was called, simply needed more time in bottle. Not until 1960 did it dawn on Australia that Schubert had made the first great Australian red wine.

Thirty years before, Napa had been making wines that regularly won prizes in Europe. The old vineyards of Cabernet that had survived the rush to coarse varieties (there were about 200 acres left) were producing wonderful fruit. But now there was virtually no market for good California wine, and scarcely any equipment to make it with. With a handful of exceptions (nearly all discerning citizens of San Francisco and the surrounding cities) Americans continued to spurn the wines of their own soil. In New York, where fashions were set, it would have been eccentric, to say the least, to serve "domestic" wine. An enormous effort of will, and many years of research, were needed before California wines (and for California you can read Australia throughout this period) were to become, and be acknowledged, challengers on an equal footing to the finest in the world.

TEMPERATURES WERE THE KEY. THERE WAS AN INFINITY OF DISCOVERIES and refinements to be made, but before all else the difference between France and the New World vineyards that hoped to emulate her is the climate. Bleasdale had realized this in Australia, and Hilgard in California, many years before. But to calculate all the implications was another matter.

To a grape-grower, a Mediterranean climate is the recipe for an easy life, but the winemaker has to take a different view. The superiority of French and German wines over all others was based on the matching of grape varieties to a relatively cool growing season, followed (and this was equally important) by the natural air-conditioning of autumn weather with cool nights, followed by winter cold. These thoughts were half-formulated by such as Judge Stanley, who had praised the seaside air of the Carneros vineyards near San Francisco Bay, and by every winemaker who had hired coolies to drive tunnels in his hillside to keep his wine cool as it matured. Clearly, cooler conditions make better wine. But the full implications of this were seized only when the University of California looked in detail at the state's complicated climate, and found affordable means to control the temperature of fermentation without recourse to blocks of ice.

Fitting the grape varieties to the climate was the first great undertaking of the University of California's department of viticulture and oenology, which had moved in the '30s from Berkeley to Davis, inland near Sacramento. As far back as the 1880s Professor Hilgard had made the obvious distinction between the Coastal Ranges, where the ocean has a measurable effect, and the Central Valley where it has little or none. Wasting no time after Repeal, in 1936 Dr Albert Winkler set out the principles of "heat-summation", or totting up the average temperatures of the days in the growing season when the thermometer is above 50°F. This wonderfully simple measure seems to work. At 50°F the vine is active and growing: what heat-summation does is to add up the temperatures of its active hours. It gives a direct means of comparison between vineyards across the world. The Médoc, for example, has about 2,500 "degree-days", or total degrees above 50°F during the growing season; the Napa valley has a range from 2,340-2,610. Cabernet therefore should grow perfectly in the Napa valley – and it does. By 1944 Winkler and his colleague Maynard Amerine had taken countless thermometer readings wherever grapes were, or might be, grown: data that rapidly became the grape-grower's bible – not least because it was so full of surprises.

Little, if anything, is predictable in the choppy Coastal Ranges, where all depends on the cold sea air being vacuumed inland through gullies and over passes by the great hot updraught in the Central Valley. Sometimes a promising valley whose "degree-days" were a perfect match for Pauillac or Beaune turned out to be a funnel for howling gales on summer afternoons. But Winkler and Amerine's work has been text-book material now for over 40 years; the equivalent of centuries in the history of European wine.

When Tchelistcheff arrived in California he was thunderstruck to see that wineries grew grapes for every sort of wine in the same vineyards. At Beaulieu there were 28 different sorts of wine being made. The young Russian was a product of Capus' France: appellations were all the talk. It seemed almost a moral outrage to plant Riesling and grapes for port side by side, and hopelessly optimistic to think that both should produce usable results. "Ecology", he recalls, "was known to us in Europe, but it was an absolutely foreign word here." Little by little that began to change, as winegrowers listened to what Davis (and Tchelistcheff) had to say, and as the merits of specialization were pointed out to them. But the distribution system still demanded a "full range" of wines to make up a brand, and it was not a good moment to tell your salesmen that your philosophy was different.

WITH HINDSIGHT IT SEEMS STRANGE THAT THE OTHER CRUCIAL ASPECT of temperature, that of the fermenting tank, had not been tackled long before. The purpose of the buckets of sulphur was largely to prevent premature and precipitate fermentation, by which the wine lost all the flavour and perfume of the fruit, and rushed headlong towards becoming vinegar. It was certainly known that low temperatures do the same, far more effectively.

How to cool the vat in practice was the problem. Mr Brame in Algeria had bought a brewery cooling-system out of desperation in the 1880s when his fermenting vats had grown so hot that fermentation stopped, leaving him with a volatile mixture that was neither juice nor wine. He seems to have been the first methodically to cool his fermentation – simply in order to finish it at all.

André Tchelistcheff wrote many of California's house rules. His advice continues to point the way today.

From North Africa the idea found its way to Australia – apparently via an Englishman who was brought up in Tunis, studied at Montpellier, and was recommended by the great Gaston Fouex, one of the conquerors of phylloxera, to teach at Roseworthy, South Australia's college of agriculture. Arthur Perkins' first Australian vintage was 1898. He was ready for it with one fermenting vat, fitted with a copper coil to circulate cold water through the must.

He went on to design a more effective system, in which instead the must was pumped through the coil which was itself immersed in water. "The whole arrangement worked very well, and we found that wine passing once through the coil was reduced to 5°F. Not only was it beneficial in cooling the 'must', but the reduction of the cellar temperature was very considerable." So much for the theory. But at this time there were only very few wineries that could afford this expense – or indeed that had the water available.

As far as California was concerned, in the coastal valleys at least, and certainly in stone-built wineries or cellars, the hope was that the atmosphere would be cool enough to prevent disasters – and while vats were small in volume this was probably the case. The advice in the text-books was clear: use a cold room or a cooling coil – or both. Yet in 1938 André Tchelistcheff was still resorting to blocks of ice. When he brought in cooling machinery it was still classified information. As he reported in an interview years later (his Russian accent has never left him): "Refrigeration – coil refrigeration in the tank – was the biggest secrecy, and the refrigeration tanks, with the Frigidaire compressor, which was a very modern machinery then in the industry, was placed above, where nobody can see it." The general use of temperature- (and pressure-) controlled fermentation had to wait another 20 years, until stainless steel and electricity in large amounts became affordable. To most, in the 1950s, they were still a futuristic dream.

A DOZEN CALIFORNIA WINEMAKERS WERE FEELING THEIR WAY TOWARDS QUALITY in the late '40s and early '50s. There had been a handful of hopeful little start-ups: Mayacamas in the mountains between Napa and Sonoma, Buena Vista (restarted in '43 in Haraszthy's old cellars), Martin Ray near Paul Masson in Santa Clara County, south of the Bay, and (an estate that was to become a miniature jewel, a sort of secret first growth for white wines) Stony Hill at St Helena in the Napa valley. Three or four of the old-established Napa wineries knew exactly what they were doing. Cabernet Sauvignons of the Beaulieu, Inglenook, Krug and Martini vineyards of that decade have survived into the 1980s, and have matured into very handsome wines. But (and the but is not intended to be critical) they were wines in the vernacular style. It would have been hard to have mistaken them for French.

As for the white wines of the years after Repeal, and before Renaissance, it was the Riesling that made the most distinguished bottles. Even when it was made strong and dry without cold fermentation the Riesling stood apart – just as it did in Australia. Picked at the right moment it maintained its balancing acidity and aged beautifully. But again, nobody would have mistaken the wine for German.

This observation would not have bothered the winemakers. Louis Martini, an Italian by origin, had a fully justified faith in his way of working with huge redwood tanks, and large old oval barrels. Inglenook had a German winemaker who was very happy with the German-style barrels made of long-aged Baltic oak bought by the firm's Swedish founder. Even André Tchelistcheff, working for the one French-born proprietor among them, and the first to age his Cabernet in small oak barrels, did not flatter himself that he was making wine like Bordeaux. (For one thing he preferred American oak.) All aimed in their different ways at making irresistible wine from Napa Valley grapes; some more tannic, some less, some easy to drink young, some husky and demanding a decade in the bottle, but none in any sort of borrowed finery or modelled on Château Lafite or Château Latour.

THIS IS WHERE THE HANZELL WINERY WAS DIFFERENT. Its founder was the former U.S. ambassador to Italy, James D. Zellerbach, who had returned in 1948 with his wife

Hannah and his fortune to a secluded upland valley just north of the town of Sonoma. During his time in Europe he had drunk much burgundy. Nothing had given him greater pleasure. So his retirement ambition was formed: to make wine as close to burgundy as he could get in California, by faithfully following every step of the Burgundian way of doing things.

He planted 17 acres of Pinot Noir and Chardonnay (then a rare grape in California) on a slope not unlike – except in soil – the Côte d'Or, and built a cottage-sized cuvier and cellar which even bears a passing resemblance to the Château de Clos de Vougeot. He found a young winemaker, Bradford Webb, who was as dedicated to burgundy as himself and who filled a laboratory with costly equipment. He installed temperature and humidity controls to match the atmosphere of a Burgundy cellar, and brought in new oak barrels from the tonnelier in Nuits St Georges, just as his favourite Burgundian proprietors did every year.

The story does not end happily for Mr Zellerbach. His wife (despite her half-share in the name of the winery) did not share his passion for perfection. Not a vintage that he made through the '50s quite measured up to his idea of great burgundy, and he died without knowing that his place in history had been won. Mrs Zellerbach sold his last vintages in barrels at auction – fortunately to one of the most far-sighted and ambitious young men in the Napa valley: Joseph Heitz. It was then, in 1960, that the word got out. Hanzell wines, but especially Hanzell Chardonnay, had the buttery, half-smoked aromas and flavours that up to then had spelt only Meursault, Montrachet and Corton-Charlemagne.

Nothing could have revived the hopes of California more than this unexpected discovery. Proud as her winemakers were of their well-tuned wines, the realization that French flavours were within their grasp changed the morale of the industry almost overnight. In Chardonnay the French oak flavour is something tangible, easy to see, simple to comprehend. Once you had learned to recognize the flavour, it could give the smack of quality, it seemed, to every wine. Heitz became the apostle of French oak, as much for his famous Martha's Vineyard Cabernet as for the Chardonnays and Pinot Noirs he had bought from Mrs Zellerbach. He had the audacity to charge $6 when the going rate was $2.5 or $3. In 1961 he opened his own winery, to add to the mere two dozen that were all the Napa valley had still running. It was the valley's lowest point, with less vineyard and fewer wineries than at any time since Prohibition. But from that moment on what had long seemed a huddle of eccentric craftsmen began once more to look like an industry.

THOSE FIRST YEARS OF THE '60S ARE THE TURNING POINT IN MODERN WINE HISTORY. A radical new idea was born in many places at once: that wine was not an esoteric relic of ancient times that was disappearing even in Europe, nor just a cheap way to get drunk, but an expression of the earth that held potential pleasure and fascination for everyone.

How do we otherwise account for the coincidence (among others) that in 1962 a university group in Seattle, Washington, founded Associated Vintners, and with it an industry in the North West, and that in 1963 Max Lake, a surgeon in Sydney, determined to make great Cabernets in the Hunter Valley, where the idea was deemed so eccentric that he named his little winery Lake's Folly?

This was the era when the term "boutique winery" was coined, as dozens at first, and later hundreds, joined the rush to found their own. By 1970 there were 220 wineries in California; by 1980 more than 500. And the figures for Australia were not very different. Many were ephemeral; others have become landmarks, exploring new ideas and making original contributions of hand-made wines that bigger companies' accountants will not allow them even to try.

TRUE, TANGIBLE AND SPECTACULAR EVIDENCE THAT THE NAPA VALLEY WAS REBORN came in 1966, with the launching of what has been its flagship for the past quarter of a century, the Robert Mondavi winery. Symbolically, Mondavi harked back to the spirit of the missions in the broad adobe arch of its façade. More significantly, when it was built it displayed the full glitter of the new technology: great stainless steel cylinders rearing up in the open air, their temperature monitored and controlled to the last degree by jackets of cooling fluid. It was a highly visible investment to challenge the leaders with technology that was "state of the art" (for once the phrase rings true), interwoven with old lessons learnt from France. Mondavi not only bought hundreds of barrels in France; he tried every different type of oak and barrel-maker in as many combinations as that makes. His philosophy was empiricism to the point of mania. "There is everything to be learnt", he said. He was bursting to experiment and discuss – and he carried California with him.

The vineyard figures tell the story. In 1965 there were 110,000 acres of wine (as opposed to table, or raisin) grapes in the whole of California, most of them of inferior varieties and few in the best cool regions. Ten years later there were three times as many acres, many in the right places, many not; with 24,000 acres of Cabernet Sauvignon – but still only 10,000 of Chardonnay. Ten years later again the figure was only slightly higher, but there was an important shift towards the cooler coastal zones. While the Cabernet acreage had stayed about the same there were over 30,000 acres of Chardonnay. Cool-climate Chardonnay, seasoned with French oak, had become the nation's favourite wine. But far more important, in 1980, for the first time in America's history, the nation drank more wine than liquor.

Robert Mondavi's dramatically confident winery of 1966 has echoes of the Mexican missions and a promise of revolution in the world of California wines.

Wherever we have seen a revolution in taste, it has been the market that has pointed the direction. Specifically it was the long-awaited revival of Bordeaux in the 1950s that gave the signal – not just for Europe, but for the New World too. The '40s had had four very good but small vintages: '43, the famous '45, '47 and '49. 1950 was a very big vintage, and a bargain even by the standards of the

time. The Bordeaux of 1953 was seductive from the start. In 1955 prices were firmer than they had been for many years. Then came a killing frost in '56 and three appalling years that made the baking summer of '59 a talking point, and its wine, in the crass phrase newspapers use, "the vintage of the century".

The tell-tale sign, if one had been reading the entrails, was that the phrase was taken up and repeated in America. The quality of a vintage made a headline; something it could not have done for 40 years. There are many self-evident reasons why Americans, war-veterans of Europe many of them, were ready to turn their interest to wine. The nation was becoming more outward-looking, more interested in its food, its health, and the tastes of other countries. If a certain timidity prevailed for far too long, it was due to the absurd notion, put about by writers of snobbish articles on etiquette, that there was only one "right" wine, right glass, right temperature to serve it at, and smart remark to make to the sommelier.

In California the lead came from the consumers of San Francisco. Leon Adams has pointed out that even in the years of Prohibition the people of northern California were able to make a better bath-tub brew. They could use real wine-grapes, Cabernet and Zinfandel, bought straight from good vineyards without suffering long journeys on a train. As the old Napa wineries had revived, rusty though they may have been, a trickle of good wine became a modest stream, at which a small but fascinated audience of prosperous young professionals in San Francisco and the cities round about had gathered to drink. Some, like the parlementaires of 18th century Bordeaux, did more: they bought land and planted vines.

IN AUSTRALIA THE NEW INTEREST SHOWED ITSELF IN THE QUICKENING PACE at state and national competitions; the way the Australian wine industry has felt its own pulse since the agricultural shows of the Victorian era. Again, the enthusiasm was limited at first to a small group who could (or cared to) remember the interminable "bin numbers" by which most of the better wines of the long-established companies were known – just like the cask numbers that made German wine connoisseurs almost a secret society.

The new technology of wine dispenses with châteaux and even with grape pickers. Stainless steel tanks, cooled to a precise temperature, are the winemaker's key weapon, offering control over wayward fermentation. A picking machine can work fast and work all night, harvesting grapes at optimum temperature and ripeness.

In both California and Australia, though, we must look at the mass market for the steps that made the '60s the industrial, as well as the gastronomic, turning point. 1964 was the year that the Gallo winery at Modesto in the Central Valley, on the point of becoming America's largest, on the basis of such "pop" (i.e. sweetened and flavoured) wines as Thunderbird, launched two landmark natural wines that assumed that Americans in very large numbers would actually like the taste. Chablis Blanc and Hearty Burgundy, although still clinging to borrowed French names, proved more than anything else that America was ready for wine as a clean, fruity, not quite dry, mealtime drink.

Australia's big companies went a slightly different way. By the mid '60s they had the technology (the pressure tanks and coolers) in place to reinvent Australian white wine altogether. In place of the old burnt-out "dry reds" that, with port and sherry (and of course beer) were Australia's staples, they suddenly offered "Moselle", a Riesling- or Traminer-flavoured and distinctly sweet white wine. It was new German technology in the form of superfine filters that made it possible. It had been too risky before to leave unfermented sugar in the wine when it was bottled. But Seitz filters could clinically remove all trace of yeast that could possibly cause trouble. It remained only for Australia to adopt the "bladder pack", the plastic

By far California's biggest winery, and the world's, the Gallo complex at Modesto needs an aircraft to frame a comprehensive view. Over 50 years the Gallo Brothers built an empire and slowly, cautiously but consistently led mass-market taste through "pop" to jug wines and on to varietals and oak-aged Chardonnays.

bag of three litres in a cardboard box with a tap, and all memories of fusty old bottles and corkscrews could be thrown aside. By the mid-'70s the word wine, to most Australians, meant a white fruit-juicy thirst-quencher as an alternative to beer.

What had changed, once for all, regardless of country or culture or latitude, was that the fundamental lessons (among many others) had at last been learned: to choose grape varieties according to the climate; to control the temperature of the fermentation; and – to give wines a taste of luxury – to age them in French oak. Some of this was known in theory back in 1940; by 1975 it was known for certain everywhere.

What could be applied to old wine-country could equally be applied to virgin territory. Now that the ground-rules at last were known, hopeful vintners could survey the globe and calculate their chances on the basis of scientific knowledge. One vital element remained a mystery: the one the French believe lies behind the ultimate quality of their wines: the influence of the soil. Still in 1980, in the hundredth anniversary issue of *California Agriculture*, an issue devoted to viticulture and oenology, not a single reference was made to the land itself, the soil in which the grape-vines have their roots.

CALIFORNIA WAS RANSACKED FOR COOL VALLEYS to grow not just the fashionable favourites, Cabernet and Chardonnay, but the much less easily pleased Pinot Noir. A shrewd eye observed that the Willamette valley in Oregon has a climate closer to that of Beaune than can easily be found in California. In 1965 David Lett began to plant his Eyrie Vineyard and in 1970, with his first vintage, brought Oregon into the roster of quality wine regions. Washington was just a whisker ahead. The university amateurs who called themselves Associated Vintners went commercial in 1967, encouraged by André Tchelistcheff, in retirement from Beaulieu and acting as mentor to countless hopeful wineries. The same year saw the first vintage of Chateau Ste Michelle, which has grown to be the biggest winery in the North West.

The same principles led Australia's vintners not just to re-examine where their grapes were planted, but to realize that their traditionally narrow repertoire of varieties was by no means the best they could grow. If Max Lake was, in theory, going against the rules (though with remarkable success) by planting Cabernet in as warm a region as the Hunter Valley, there was the old Yarra Valley and Geelong vineyards in southern Victoria to be revived, virgin territory in southern South Australia to be planted, and a whole region south of Perth with a sea-cooled climate still unexploited for wine. South was one way to go: the other was uphill. In Pewsey Vale, high above the Barossa valley, Riesling found perfect cool ripening conditions, and even in warm northern Victoria growers have found the necessary cool nights by climbing to 2,500 feet and more. Coolest of all, with brilliant promise for Riesling, Chardonnay and Pinot Noir, was Tasmania. But in 1958, it was a bold man who pioneered Hobart as a vineyard area.

NOTHING COULD HAVE DRAMATIZED THE MILLENNIUM BETTER than a tasting that was organized in Paris in 1976 by an English wine merchant, Steven Spurrier. It was the Bataille de Vins of seven hundred years before replayed – but this time with French judges and an English referee.

He assembled a company of some of the best-respected winegrowers of Bordeaux and Burgundy, restaurateurs from Paris, and even the senior inspector of the Institut National des Appellations d'Origine, and offered them a range of French and California wines in unmarked bottles. California Cabernets were mingled with Médoc crus classés and California Chardonnays with Grand Cru and Premier Cru white burgundies.

In both groups, red and white, a California wine was judged best: in the Cabernet line Stag's Leap 1973 from the Napa Valley, with Château Mouton-Rothschild 1970 as runner-up, and in the Chardonnays, Château Montelena 1973, also from the Napa Valley, with a Meursault Charmes in second place. The other wines jostled closely in a finishing line that proved quite simply that their qualities, in expert French eyes, were approximately equal.

There was much disclaiming of the results (though not by the judges), saying (which is perfectly true) that the best bordeaux and burgundy need longer to reach maturity and – more important to the tasters at the time – that the sheer ripeness of California grapes suggests to the French-trained palate an exceptional vintage. All this is beside the fundamental point. Whether or not the ultimate quality and value of the wines was precisely as they were found to be on that day, the principle was proven: after little more than a decade of experience with French techniques, Californians were able to match the originals they so much admired.

SECOND-HAND WINES

To anyone looking for omens of the future of fine wines, a small but clear signal appeared in London in 1966. The famous fine-art auction house of Christie's bought the small specialist wine auctioneers, W & T Restell, who conducted monthly sales of wines of all sorts in the City of London, with the wine trade as the principal buyers and sellers.

Christie's had in the past held occasional wine sales, starting from the foundation of the firm in the 1760s and ending only during the Second World War. But their resumption in 1966 was both to reflect and greatly to encourage interest in the intrinsic value of fine wine. Their serious intent became clear when they recruited one of Britain's most gifted wine merchants and tasters, Michael Broadbent, from Harvey's of Bristol, to direct operations. He combined knowledge and judgment of wine with the scholarly approach and flair of a fine art dealer. It was to prove a formidable combination.

Far from being a passive auctioneer, he set out to find the finest old wines which had accumulated in the cellars of great houses of the British Isles over, literally, centuries – as they had almost nowhere else. It soon became clear both how eclectic British wine-buying had been, and how often the owner had died leaving some of his finest bottles undrunk. The cellars of a Scottish castle or an English mansion had frequently become a museum of the best wine of the past century of so, which the present owners were reluctant to drink because it seemed almost part of the fabric of their inheritance – and not infrequently because they lacked knowledgeable friends to share and discuss these heirlooms with. A double magnum of pre-phylloxera claret can be a knotty problem for an elderly bachelor.

By making the particular history of each cellar and bottle, and often its owner, a matter of precise research and scholarly presentation, Christie's skilfully stressed that wine can truly be living history in a way that nothing else can. The effect on the price of fine old wines was predictable: they have become collectors' items – which in turn has had an effect on the price of young wines of top quality by giving them the value of realizable investments.

CHAPTER 43

THE OLD WORLD
RESPONDS

The world's most technically advanced big wine estate today is in neither California nor Australia, nor in France, nor on the vast plains of Spain or Argentina. It is in Tuscany, in the land where even the concept of a vineyard, in contrast to a friendly muddle of vines and poplars, olives, beans and corn, is a novelty that sits oddly on the crumpled landscape.

Crowning the highest hill of the estate, where the cypress avenue files in black emphasis, is an ancient Lombard castle built on foundations of Etruscan stones; where wine may have been drunk from jewelled beakers by men and women with an elfin smile even before the Greeks rowed up the coast. In the valley-bottom, half-underground, is five acres of the future: a stainless steel world of humming pumps and winking consoles where wine is made under computer control; where even the immaculate files of casks and vats lead an entirely air-conditioned life.

Castello Banfi is American in ownership and inspiration: Italian in everything else. It is the logical outcome of the newest way of looking at the ancient world of wine: a way that sees technology as the path back to tradition.

For if the New World has successfully reproduced the crown jewels of the old, the classic wines of France, it has set Italy and Spain and the other ancient wine-lands a delicate problem. Should they pursue their own destinies, a complex of traditions that they themselves only partly believe in (or understand), or fall in step behind countries with no traditions to inhibit them? Should they let themselves be led by Americans and Australians in a global race to emulate the same few models?

Pride and patriotism pull one way; the demands of the market the other. The 1980s have seen the puzzle develop, and the beginnings of some possible solutions.

There is nothing new or reprehensible about emulating, even imitating, the best you know. The ancient Greeks made Byblian wine as close as possible to Canaan's best. For centuries the whole Mediterranean world made what it chose to call "Greek" wine, to signify that it was sweet and strong. When pioneers planted in New South Wales or Santa Clara it did not occur to them to speak of their dry white wines as anything but Chablis or their fruity reds as Burgundy. The world was large enough, and the chances of mistaken identity seemed remote (although, one imagines, much to be desired). What could South Africa call its solera wines but sherry – or anybody call anything sparkling but Champagne? A far more vital issue

The face of the future in high-technology winemaking. Banfi Vintners'
cellars near Montalcino in Tuscany achieves total physical control of
every stage from crushing to bottling.

at the time was outright fabrication, which happened much closer to home.

Yet throughout the history of wine the way to recognise a significant step
forward in quality has been the declaration of a new identity. Just as Haut-Brion
signified that Bordeaux had new ambitions, and the careful selecting of Têtes de
Cuvée meant that the Côte d'Or was raising its sights, so each added piece of specific
information has meant potential extra value for any kind of wine. It works at every
level: a vintage champagne (or port) has more value than a non-vintage blend; a
German wine from a specified vineyard more than one from a region or "bereich",
and a late-picked one more than a bottle from the bulk of the crop. Each country,
even each district, puts the emphasis on the aspect of its wine – the soil, the grapes,
the ripeness, the year – that in its own eyes raises its value most.

It was America's good fortune to hit on grape varieties as its distinguishing
marks – at first for lack of anything more specific to say. For centuries certain wines
had indicated their style by referring to the grape. Malmsey and muscatel are grape
varieties: they are also time-honoured categories of wine, wherever they are grown.
In America the inspiration goes back at least to "Sparkling Catawba". Before
Prohibition some vintners used such terms as "Finest Old Cabernet Claret".

From the 1950s on the pattern was set: a premium wine was a "varietal".
Elementary wine literature still repeats the gist of the first explanatory labels; that
Cabernet is "the premier red grape of the Bordeaux area of France", and
Chardonnay "the sole source of the great French white burgundies". By the 1970s,
when for a while wine-tasting threatened to become America's national sport, these
footnotes were redundant. When virtually every winery made them, Cabernet and
Chardonnay had also turned into categories of wine and so, to an only slightly

smaller public, had Sauvignon Blanc, Riesling, Gewürztraminer and Pinot Noir.

The tables were turned on Europe. Bordeaux, which up to then had been publicly vague about the grape varieties it used, suddenly, to Americans, became part of the great international category of Cabernets and was even questioned, with the slightest hint of suspicion, about the percentage of other varieties in its vineyards, as though it was not quite baseball to sully the purity of Cabernet – at least on its home ground.

To the French all this was gain – though some may not have realized it at the time. Far from being apprehensive that they were no longer alone as the purveyors of the most luxurious of tastes, the leaders of France's industry saw that they had been paid the sincerest form of compliment, and what is more, that nobody was in a better position to benefit from it than themselves.

History, authenticity, scarcity, the possession of the "original", quite apart from intrinsic quality, were all on their side, and would always be enough to keep the prices of their first growths, at least, ahead of any followers. But equally important, their reputation would enhance whatever they touched; as Moët & Chandon effortlessly proved, when in 1973 they started to make Napa Valley sparkling wine. Climate and soil, the French are quick to stress, will always prevent wine they make outside France from exactly matching the original. But (philosophically) no two wines ever can be or should be identical: let us enjoy them all for what they are. Besides, to a winemaker, there is fascination in adapting your skills and knowledge to different natural conditions, a different terroir. The collaboration and the free exchange of students and professors between universities, and staff between wineries, has enlarged the total sum of understanding to everybody's benefit. It has also made sure that France has not lagged behind in any new research.

THE POSITION OF THE MEDITERRANEAN WORLD WAS VERY DIFFERENT. Italian vintners who had emigrated had left behind traditions that were only local, without a history of exporting to make their names into an international shorthand for luxury. Instead of taking the finest Sangiovese vines to make a great Chianti in California, they gave

Robert Mondavi, left, and the late Baron Philippe de Rothschild together planned Opus One, a Napa Valley wine with a Médoc inspiration, thereby settling all disputes about the equal status of the best of old world and new.

A radical departure in the Médoc. Conventional chais are rectangular barns half-buried in the ground. In 1988 Château Lafite opened a new circular chai deep under the vineyard.

its name to any cheap, usually sweet and often fizzy, red. Almost without exception the most proficient producers of mass market wines were Italian. The Gallo brothers, Ernest and Julio, personally built up, over 50 years, the largest-volume wine company in the world, making and bottling one bottle in four of all California wine. The names of Martini and Mondavi stand as high as any for the quality of their French-style wines. But where are the Barolos, the Barbarescos and the Brunellos of California? And for that matter where are the Tempranillos or the Parelladas, the logical contributions of Spain? They lacked the cachet of international success, so winegrowers ignored them.

The long gestation period of an accepted name is one of the recurring themes throughout this book. Even more emphatic is the need for an identity that the market can understand. They were brave law-givers who first conceived the idea of national legislation about so variable and elusive a commodity as wine. Until the

BORDEAUX: STILL MOVING FORWARD

Even the apparently unchanging firmament of Bordeaux has acquired a new constellation since the 1950s: the empire (that is the only word) of Jean-Pierre Moueix, a Libourne merchant whose acumen has raised the status of St-Emilion and Pomerol (where he controls Petrus) to equal that of the Médoc for the first time in history.

Moueix realized the potential of Pomerol in particular in the 1930s. He realistically describes its great advantages as being seductive to drink at an early age, and being easier to comprehend than the complex of communes and classifications that mystifies initiates to the Médoc. Starting during the years of the Depression, carrying a bag of samples through their traditional limited market of northern France and Belgium, he and his sons have conquered the principal markets of the world. His company owns, controls or manages a dozen of the best properties in the two regions, and markets a fair proportion of the rest.

20th century it was each region for itself. It was one thing to legislate nationally in broad terms in favour of purity and against fraud, as Germany did in 1901 and France in 1905, but a different matter altogether to try to force local traditions into the framework of the law.

France's Appellations evolved gradually over more than 30 years into a crisply detailed schedule. Germany was slightly ahead in time, but less ambitious in definitions, and its law of 1930 needed constant clarification and revision. Portugal was the other country that in the '30s granted a few historic regions "selos de origen". All that happened in Italy and Spain was that the producers of the best-known wines formed associations to defend and promote their names. In Spain it was Rioja (in 1926) and Jerez (in 1933); in Italy Chianti was the inevitable test case.

The government in Rome would not be drawn into demarcating boundaries, but would agree only to legislate on the "special and constant characteristics" that Chianti should have. The producers of the central zone between Florence and Siena took the matter into their own hands. In 1924 they formed the Consorzio del Vino Chianti Classico, to be followed three years later by their northern neighbours, who formed a rival Consorzio, adopting a cherub, a "putto", as its badge.

Over the rest of Italy anarchy reigned until 1963, when the government began its labours of Hercules, the task of even agreeing the names, let alone framing by-laws, for the country's labyrinth of "traditional" wines. Twenty-five years later it is still not finished and will probably never be. To induce a consensus among neighbouring farmers may take ten years of negotiation; to wrangle with the bureaucracy of Rome another five – and meanwhile events move on. Italy now has more than 220 Denominazioni di Origine Controllati, which specify not only exactly how much wine at what strength, pressed from what weight of which grape varieties in which demarcated zone, may bear the name of the "D.O.C.", but also, something that France's Appellation laws have never attempted, a full-frontal description of what the customer is to expect: the colour, scent and flavour which constitute the "special and constant characteristics" of each wine.

SADLY FOR ITALY IT BEGAN ITS TASK EITHER TOO LATE OR TOO EARLY; in any case at the moment when "tradition" was far from being the first priority of a quickly-changing world. A "D.O.C." presupposes that whatever wines have been made in the recent past constitute the best that a region can produce. It does nothing more than freeze the status quo. Italy's best producers pay lip-service to the law, but make most of their best wines outside it. Why, they argue, follow the small print simply to qualify for the designation of a traditional wine, when there was very little demand or respect for the tradition in the first place? At least half of Italy's best wines today are downgraded to vino da tavola, the humblest designation, by their own makers. At the same time their prices are raised, to make the point that they are better wines than those made in the strait-jacket of a D.O.C.

This was (and is) the quandary for Italy, Spain and Portugal. If they pursue their traditions – even obey their laws and ignore the world's great appetite for grapes whose names it knows, they risk being relegated as producers of esoteric specialities. But an equal risk is to lose their historical identities by trailing after the New World with yet more versions of wines that originated in France.

Italy and Spain can make Chardonnay and Cabernet as good as California's best. Angelo Gaja's Chardonnays from Piemonte, and the resplendent Sassicaia from the Tuscan coast, leave no-one in any doubt. Nor do the wines of Torres, which have revolutionized Catalonia. But what a tragedy it would be if this were all they did, and let all their ancient alternatives, their varieties dating back to colonists from Greece or Phoenicia, fall by the wayside. It is not a thought their best wine-makers can contemplate. What they are doing is walking the tightrope between the old and new. They are keeping their names before the public by competing in international categories with wines that have nothing specifically Italian or Spanish about them. But their long-term goal is to find, propagate and perfect the cream of

At each landmark in history stands an individual. Miguel Torres father and son have revolutionised the quality of Catalan wine since the 1940s.

their countries' native vines. That was how in the last century Murrieta found the unique flavour of Rioja, and Biondi-Santi created Brunello di Montalcino. This is the purpose of Castello Banfi: to make enough of the still-rare Brunello to bring it into the international category of luxury wines.

BOLDNESS IS THE SECRET OF SUCCESS. The future lies with wines of distinct and memorable flavours, whether immediately familiar or not. One of the most individual wines and greatest reputations is in danger today because of a loss of nerve; in this case by politicians. German wine began to fall seriously in public esteem in the 1970s when its clearly-defined character became blurred.

A radical new wine-law in 1971 allowed electoral politics into the control of quality: it lowered the minimum standards of ripeness to suit the convenience and aspirations of farmers. Where Spätleses and Ausleses had been the uncertain reward for perseverance and risk-taking, the currency was devalued to bring them within the reach of every grower. Fatally, Riesling gave ground to Müller-Thurgau as growers looked for easier vines to grow. By abandoning the high ground Germany found a new export market, but at low prices for sweet and watery wine.

NEW ''TRADITIONS''

In the search for wines of popular appeal Portugal and Italy both showed what can be done with freely-interpreted traditions. Mateus Rosé in the 1950s was loosely based on Portugal's vinho verde. To call it a latter-day Ribadavia would be to exaggerate, but the idea of a light, slightly fizzy wine (though not its sweetness) has genuine ethnic roots. The Lambrusco that America loves is scarcely modified from the traditions of the Po valley – except in predictability and quality control. The concept of the cheerfully frothing sweet red wine is entirely Italian.

Happily, German wine-drinkers have no appetite for sugar-water and are demanding their wine as bold and dry as it used to be. To find the old mouth-filling taste, and the old ability to mature which made Rhenish the wonder of our ancestors, the grower must be content with a far smaller crop, but can command a far higher price. Where national wine-laws have failed, local syndicates have gone back to the old self-help model. In the Rheingau, for example, the Charta Association restates the truism that quality cannot be legislated for: it must be self-imposed.

In the end it is the market that decides, and the message that it gives today is unambiguous: the days of the nondescript are numbered. This is most clearly spelt out in the countries, led by Italy and France, where wine has traditionally been the common everyday drink. Quantity is rapidly giving way to quality. The average Frenchman spends twice as much today as he did 20 years ago on little more than half the quantity of wine. He drives a car; this perhaps more than anything has cut down his consumption. But because his wine is better made, and has more flavour, he also needs less of it for satisfaction. The mounting ambition of the Languedoc, and the emergence of excellent wines from its once-abandoned hills, is one of the clearest signals of the change. In supermarkets, anonymous vin ordinaire is steadily being replaced by vins de pays; wines of local character from specific, if obscure, grapes and regions – some of them, perhaps, the Appellations of the future.

The same message is coming from the countries where wine consumption is still relatively small, but has doubled in the past decade or so. They were content to cut their teeth, starting in the 1950s, on bland and repetitive brands; Mateus and Lancers, Yugoslav Riesling or Liebfraumilch. Now these are considered the wines of novices who will move on to better (because more individual) things.

Diners-out today expect to find an infinitely wider choice than ever before – even in Japan, the newest recruit to the wine-drinking community. In the 1980s the Japanese learned to drink neutral blended wines, imported in bulk (and labelled ''made in Japan''). To watch Japanese wine-drinkers' aspirations grow is like watching a film played at fast-forward speed. Today they own châteaux in Bordeaux and wineries in California; tomorrow there will be authentic Japanese Chardonnay competing in the international arena.

THE VITALITY OF THE WORLD OF WINE is the concluding message of this book. Never before has it had so many admirers, critics, friends (or enemies) as in the last decades of the 20th century. From being the daily drink of a handful of Mediterranean nations, and an exotic luxury to the rest of the world, it has become a subject of intense worldwide interest, competition and comparison, an industry comparable in some ways with fashion, with the great difference that for all the style and glamour of its market image, its roots are in the earth.

For no critic should forget, as he dallies with epithets, sipping his oak-fermented Chardonnay, or rates one precious bottle half a point behind another, that wine is one of the miracles of nature, and that its 10,000 years of partnership with man has not removed that element of mystery, that independent life that alone among all our foods has made men think of it as divine.

Farmer and artist, drudge and dreamer, hedonist and masochist, alchemist and accountant – the wine-grower is all these things, and has been since the Flood.

BIBLIOGRAPHY

GENERAL

AMERINE, M.A. & SINGLETON, V.L. *Wine* (1976, Davis)

BARRACLOUGH, G. (ed) *The Times Atlas of World History* (1978, London)

CARTER, E.H. & MEARS, R.A.F *The History of Britain* (1948, Oxford); *Concise Dictionary of National Biography Vol I to 1900* (1903, Oxford)

JOHNSON, H. *Wine Companion* 2nd edn (1987, London); *World Atlas of Wine* 3rd edn (1985, London)

NOUVEAU PETIT LAROUSSE ILLUSTRE 16th edn (1953, Paris)

PALMER, A. *Penguin Dictionary of Modern History 1789-1945* (1981, London)

PEYNAUD, E. *Le Gout du Vin* (1983, Paris)

ROBINSON, J. *Vines, Grapes and Wines* (1986, London)

SCHOONMAKER, F. *Frank Schoonmaker's Encyclopaedia of Wine* (1964, New York)

WAGNER, P. *Grapes into Wine* (1974, New York)

WILLIAMS, E.N. *The Penguin Dictionary of English and European History 1485-1789* (1980, London)

CHAPTER 2

CHARDIN, Sir J. *Travels into Persia and the East Indies through the Black Sea and the Country of Colchis* (1686, London)

CHARPENTIER, L. *Le Mystère du Vin* (1981, Paris)

DRAGADZE, T. *Banqueting in Soviet Georgia* [Private dissertation, St Anthony's College, Oxford]

THE NEW ENCYCLOPAEDIA BRITANNICA 15th ed (1983, Chicago)

ENCYCLOPAEDIA JUDAICA (1972, Jerusalem)

HYAMS, E. *Dionysus: A Social History of the Wine Vine* (1965, London)

LANG, D.M. *Armenia: Cradle of Civilization* (1970, London); *The Georgians* (1966, London)

LAUFER, B. Chinese Contributions to the History of Civilisation in Ancient Iran: the Grape-Vine, in *Sino-Iranica* (1919. Chicago)

LEONARD, W.E. *Gilgamesh: Epic of Old Babylonia* (1934, New York)

MACLEAN, F. *To Caucasus* (1976, London)

MELLAART, J. *The Neolithic of the Near East* (1975, London)

RAMISHVILI, R. New Archaeological Evidence on the History of Viniculture in Georgia, in *Matsne* No.2 (1983, Tbilisi)

VIN ET CIVILISATIONS Centre International de Liaison des Organismes de Propagande en Faveur des Produits de la Vigne (1983, Paris, Turin)

CHAPTER 3

BASS, G.F. Oldest Known Shipwreck Reveals Splendours of the Bronze Age, in *National Geographic* (Dec 1987)

DARBY, W.J. *Food: the Gift of Osiris* (1977, London)

FINET, A. L'Euphrate, Route Commerciale de la Mesopotamie, in *Annales Archéologiques Arabes Syriennes* (1969)

HERODOTUS *The Histories of Herodotus of Halicarnassus* translated by Harry Carter (1962, Oxford)

LESKO, L.H. *King Tut's Wine Cellar* (1977, Berkeley)

LUTZ, H.F. *Viticulture and Brewing in the Ancient Orient* (1922, Leipzig)

MACQUEEN, J.G. *The Hittites and Their Contemporaries in Asia Minor* (1986, London)

MONTET, P. *Les Scènes de la Vie Privée dans les Tombeaux Egyptiens de L'Ancien Empire* (1925, Strasbourg)

POLANYI, K. (ed) *Trade and Market in the Early Empires* (1963, Glencoe)

SMITH, J.M.P. *The Origin and History of Hebrew Law* (1931, Chicago)

YOUNGER *Gods, Men and Wine* (1966, London)

CHAPTER 4

BOARDMAN, J. *The Greeks Overseas* (1980, London)

BILLIARD, R. *La Vigne dans L'Antiquité* (1913, Lyon)

FRASER, P. *Ptolemaic Alexandria* (1972, Oxford)

HAMMOND, N.G.L. & SCULLARD, H.H. (eds) *The Oxford Classical Dictionary* (1979, Oxford)

JOFFROY, R. *La Tombe Princière de Vix* (1983, Chatillon-sur-Seine)

LUCIA, S.P. *A History of Wine as Therapy* (1963, New York)

RENFREW, C. *The Emergence of Civilisation* (1972, London)

SPARKES, B.A. Kottabos, in *Archaeology* (1960)

STANISLAWSKI, D. Dark Age Contributions to the Mediterranean Way of Life, in *Annals of the Association of American Geographers* (1973)

VICKERS, M. *Greek Symposia* (1978, London)

WARNER ALLEN, H. *A History of Wine* (1961, London)

CHAPTER 5

DODDS, E.R. *The Greeks and the Irrational* (1951, Berkeley)

EVANS, A. *The God of Ecstasy: Sex Roles and the Madness of Dionysus* (1988, New York)

FARNELL, L.R. *Cults of the Greek States* (1896-1909, Oxford)

GRAVES, R. *Greek Myths* (1958, London)

HAGENOW, G. *Aus dem Weingarten der Antike* (1982, Mainz)

HAMDORF, F.W. *Dionysos Bacchus* (1986, Munich)

JOHNS, C. *Sex or Symbol: Erotic Images of Greece and Rome* (1982, London)

KERENYI, C. *The Gods of the Greeks* (1958, London); *Dionysus* (1977, London)

LEVI, P. *A History of Greek Literature* (1985, London)

MCDONALD, A.H. Rome and the Italian Federation 200-186 BC, in *Journal of Roman Studies* (1944)

NILSSON, M.P. *The Dionysiac Mysteries of the Hellenistic and Roman Age* (1957, Lund)

PARKE, H.W. *Festivals of the Athenians* (1977, London)

RUCK, C.A.P. The Wild and the Cultivated: Wine in Euripides' Bacchae, in *Journal of Ethno-Pharmacology* (1985)

STANISLAWSKI, D. Dionysus Westward: Early Religion and the Economic Geography of Wine, in *The Geographical Review* (Oct 1975)

CHAPTER 6

ANDRE, J. *L'Alimentation et la Cuisine à Rome* (1981, Paris)

BOULOUMIE, B. Le Vin Etrusque et la Première Hellenisation du Midi de la Gaule, in *Revue Archéologique de l'Est et du Centre-Est* (1981)

CHASTAGNOL, A. A Wine Scandal During the Late Empire, in *Annales ESC* (1970)

CHILVER *Cisalpine Gaul* (1944, Oxford)

DEISS, J. *Herculaneum* (1968, London)

DUNCAN JONES, R. *The Economy of the Roman Empire* (1982, Cambridge)

ETIENNE, R. *La Vie Quotidienne à Pompeii* (1966, Paris)

GALEN *De Antidotis*

LEVICK, B. Domitian and the Provinces, in *Latomus* (1982)

PEYRE, C. *La Cisalpine Gauloise du IIIe au Ier Siècle Avant J-C* (1979, Paris)

PLINY *Natural History Book XIV* translated by H. Rackham (1938, London)

PURCELL, N. Wine and Wealth in Ancient Italy, in *Journal of Roman Studies* (1986)

SCARBOROUGH, J. Galen and the Gladiators, in *Episteme* (Jan-Mar 1971)

TCHERNIA, A. *Le Vin de l'Italie Romaine: Essai d'Histoire Economique d'Après les Amphores* (1986, Rome)

WHITE, K.D. *Roman Farming* (1970, London)

CHAPTER 7

AQUINAS, T. *Summa Theologica, Part 3, Treatise on the Sacraments, Vol 18/19* (1928/1932, London)

CORBLET, J. *Histoire du Sacrament de l'Eucharistie* (1885, Paris)

DROWER, E.S. *Water into Wine* (1956, London)
ENCYCLOPAEDIA JUDAICA (1972, Jerusalem)
JOHNSON, P. *A History of Christianity* (1976, London)
WILKEN, R. *The Christians as the Romans Saw Them* (1984, New Haven)
YERKES, R.K. *Sacrifice in Greek and Roman Religions and Early Judaism* (1953, London)

CHAPTER 8
BARTY-KING, H. *Tradition of English Wine* (1977, Oxford)
DION, R. *Histoire de la Vigne et du Vin en France* (1959, Paris)
ETIENNE, R. *Bordeaux Antique* (1962,Bordeaux); Note à Propos du Vignoble Hispano Romain de Betique, in *Geographie Historique des Vignobles* (ed A. Huetz de Lemps) (1978, Paris)
FORGEOT, P. *Origines du Vignoble Bourguignon* (1972, Paris)
GALTIER, G. La Création du Vignoble Languedocien, in *Cahiers Ligures de Préhistoire et d'Archéologie* (1959)
GADILLE, R. *Le Vignoble de la Côte Bourguignonne* (1967, Paris)
HUETZ DE LEMPS, A. *Vignobles et Vins du Nord-Ouest de l'Espagne* (1967, Bordeaux)
HUTCHINSON, V.J. *Bacchus in Roman Britain* (1986, Oxford)
ISNARD, H. *La Vigne en Algerie* (1955, Gap)
de KERDELAND, J. *Histoire des Vins de France* (1964, Paris)
PEACOCK, D.P.S. The Rhine and the Problem of Gaulish Wine in Roman Britain, in *Roman Shipping and Trade* (ed H. Cleere) (1978, London)
PIGGOTT, S. (ed) *France Before the Romans* (1974, London)
READ, J. *Wines of the Rioja* (1984, London)
ROUPNEL, G. *Histoire de la Campagne Française* (1932, Paris)
SEALEY, P. & DAVIES, G.M. Falernum in Colchester, in *Britannia* (1984)
STANISLAWSKI, D. *Landscapes of Bacchus* (1970, Austin, Texas)
TCHERNIA, A. Italian Wine in Gaul at the End of the Republic, in *Trade in the Ancient Economy* (eds P. Garnsey, C.R. Whittaker & K. Hopkins) (1983, London)
TERNES, C.M. *La Vie Quotidienne en Rhenanie à l'Epoque Romaine, Ier-IVe Siècle* (1972, Paris)
THEVENOT, C. *Histoire de la Bourgogne Ancienne* (1981, Dijon)
TORRES, M. *The Distinctive Wines of Catalonia* (1986, Barcelona)
WILLIAMS, D. A Consideration of the Sub-Fossil Remains of *Vitis-vinifera*, as Evidence for Viticulture in Roman Britain, in *Britannia* (1977)

CHAPTER 9
BOWEN, J.C.E. *Poems from the Persian* (1948, Essex)
CHARDIN, Sir J. *Travels into Persia and the East Indies through the Black Sea and the Country of Colchis* (1686, London)
HAMIDULLAH, M. *Introduction to Islam* (1980, Luton)
HEINE, P. *Weinstudien: Untersuchung zu Anbau, Produktion und Konsum des Weins im Aabisch-Islamischen Mittelalter* (1982, Wiesbaden)
KHAYYAM, O. *Rubaiyat* translated by E. Fitzgerald (1868, London)
THE KORAN translated by N.J. Dawood (1974, London)
LUCIA, S.P. *A History of Wine as Therepy* (1963, New York)
NESTOR THE ANNALIST *The Russian Primary Chronicle* Laurentian text translated by S.H. Cross & O.P. Sherbowitz-Wetzor (1953, Cambridge, Mass)
PLANHOL, X. Une Rencontre de l'Europe et de l'Iran: Le vin de Shiraz, in *Iran* (eds D. Boidanovic & J.L. Bacque-Grammont) (1972, Paris); Le Vin de l'Afghanistan et de l'Himalaya Occidental, in *Revue Géographique de l'Est* (1977); *Le Monde Islamique* (1957, Paris); Notes sur la Géographie des Spiritueux dans l'Islam, in *Eaux-de-Vie et Spiritueux* (eds A. Huetz de Lemps & P. Roudie) (1985, Paris)
RICE, D.S. Deacon or Drink: Some Paintings from Samarra Re-Examined, in *Arabica* (1958)
VOLKOFF, V. *Vladimir the Russian Viking* (1984, London)

WILLIAMS, J.A. *Themes of Islamic Civilisation* (1971, Berkeley)

CHAPTER 10
AMBROSI, H. & BECKER, H. *Der Deutsche Wein* (1978, Munich)
ARNZT, H. *Aus der Geschichte des Deutschen Weinhandels* (1964, Wiesbaden)
BASSERMANN-JORDAN, F. *Geschichte des Weinbaus Unter Besonderer Berucksichtigung der Bayerisches Rheinpfalz* (1907, Frankfurt)
BONAL, F. *Le livre d'Or du Champagne* (1984, Lausanne)
DION, R. *Histoire de la Vigne et du Vin en France* (1959, Paris)
DUBY, G. *L'Economie Rurale et la Vie des Campagnes dans l'Occident Mediéval* (1962, Paris)
FREEDEN, M.H. *Festung Marienberg* (1982, Wurzburg)
HALKIN, J. *Etude Historique sur la Culture de la Vigne en Belgique* (1895, Liége)
HIMLY, F. L'Exportation du Vin Alsacien en Europe au Moyen-Age, in *Revue d'Alsace* (1949)
LACHIVER, M. *Vins, Vignes et Vignerons* (1988, Paris)
LANGENBACH, A. *German Wines and Vines* (1962, London)
RICHE, P. *La Vie Quotidienne dans l'Empire Carolingien* (1973, Paris)
SCHAEFER, A. *Die alte Rheingauer Freiheit* (1973, Wiesbaden)
SCHREIBER, G. *Deutsche Weingeschichte* (1980, Bonn)
SIMON, A.L. *The History of the Wine Trade in England* (1906-9, London)
VANDYKE PRICE, P. *Alsace Wines* (1984, London)
WADDELL, H. *Medieval Latin Lyrics* (1929, London)
WARNER ALLEN, H. *A History of Wine* (1961, London)
WEINHOLD, R. *Vivat Bacchus* (1978, Watford)
WOLFF, C. *Riquewihr: Son Vignoble et Ses Vins à Travers les Ages* (1967, Ingersheim)

CHAPTER 11
de CRESCENTIIS, P. *Liber Ruralium Commodorum* (1471-85)
DION, R. *Histoire de la Vigne et du Vin en France* (1959, Paris)
GRACIA, J.J.E. Rules and Regulations for Drinking Wine in Frances Eiximenis' *Terc del Crestis* (1384), in *Traditio* (1976)
HERON, A. *Oeuvres de Henri d'Andeli* (1881, Rouen)
LACHIVER, M. *Vins, Vignes et Vignerons* (1988, Paris)
LUCIA, S.P. *A History of Wine as Therapy* (1963, New York)
RENOUARD, Y. Le Vin Vieux au Moyen Age, in *Annales du Midi* (1964)
de SERRES, O. *Le Théâtre d'Agriculture et le Mesnage des Champs* (1804 edn, Paris)
SIGERIST, H.E. *The Earliest Printed Book on Wine* (1943)
The History of Wine: Sulphorous Acid - used in wineries for 500 years, in *German Wine Review* No.2 (1986, Neustadt an der Weinstrasse)

CHAPTER 12
AMBROSI, H. *Das Weinkloster Eberbach im Rheingau* (1988, Eltville)
BAZIN, J-F. *Le Clos de Vougeot* (1987, Paris)
BERLOW, R.K. The Disloyal Grape: the Agrarian Crisis of Late 14th-Century Burgundy, in *Agricultural History* (1982)
BOURASSIN, E. *Les Ducs de Bourgogne* (1985, Paris)
DION, R. *Histoire de la Vigne et du Vin en France* (1959, Paris)
DUMAY, R. (ed) *Le Vin de Bourgogne* (1976, Paris)
GADILLE, R. *Le Vignoble de la Côte Bourguignon* (1967, Paris)
LACHIVER, M. *Vin, Vignes et Vignerons* (1988, Paris)
LANDRIEU-LUSIGNY, M-H. *Les Lieux-Dits dans le Vignoble Bourguignon* (1983, Marseille)
LEBEAU, M. *Abrégé Chronologique de l'Histoire de Cîteaux* (1980s, Nuits-Saint-Georges); *Essai sur les Vignes de Cîteaux des Origines à 1789* (1986, Dijon)
PRO-RIESLING: Verein zur Forderung der Riesling-Kultur *Der Riesling und seine Weine* (1986, Trier)
RENOUARD, Y. La Consommation des Grands Vins du Bourbonnais et de Bourgogne à la Cour Pontificale d'Avignon, in *Annales de Bourgogne* (1982)

SCHREIBER, G. *Deutsche Weingeschichte* (1980, Bonn)
SEWARD, D. *Monks and Wine* (1979, London)

CHAPTER 13
BARTY-KING, H. *Tradition of English Wine* (1977, London)
CRAWFORD, A. *A History of the Vintners' Company* (1977, London)
DION, R. *La Création du Vignoble Bordelais* (1952, Anger)
ENJALBERT, H. *Great Bordeaux Wines: St-Emilion, Pomerol and Fronsac* (1985, Paris)
HARDING, V. *The Port of London in the 14th Century: its Topography, Administration and Trade* [PhD thesis] (1983, St Andrews)
HIGOUNET, C. *Cologne et Bordeaux – Marchés du Vin au Moyen Age*, in *Revue Historique de Bordeaux* (1968)
JAMES, M.K. *Studies in the Medieval Wine Trade* (1971, Oxford)
MARQUETTE, J.B. *La Vinification dans les Domaines de l'Archevêquée de Bordeaux à la Fin du Moyen Age*, in *Géographie Historique des Vignobles* (ed A. Huetz de Lemps) (1978)
PENNING-ROWSELL, E. *The Wines of Bordeaux* (1969, London)
PIJASSOU, R. *Un Grand Vignoble de Qualité: Le Médoc* (1980, Paris)
PLATT, C. *Medieval Southampton* (1973, London)
RENOUARD, Y. *Les Conséquences de la Conquête de la Guienne par le Roi de France pour le Commerce des Vins de Gascogne*, in *Etudes d'Histoire Médiévale* (1968)
SIMON, A.L. *The History of the Wine Trade in England* (1906-9, London)

CHAPTER 14
BAYNES, N.H. & MOSS, H. *Byzantium* (1948, Oxford)
BRAUDEL, F. *The Mediterranean and the Mediterranean World in the Age of Philip II* (1972, London); *Civilisation and Capitalism, Vol III, Perspective of the World* (1984, London)
DION, R. *Histoire de la Vigne et du Vin en France* (1959, Paris)
FRANCIS, A.D. *The Wine Trade* (1972, London)
HARDING, V. *The Port of London in the 14th Century: its Topography, Administration and Trade* [PhD thesis] (1983, St Andrews)
NEWETT, M.M. *Canon Pietro Casola's Pilgrimage to Jerusalem in the Year 1494* (1907, Manchester)
PRAWER, J. *Colonisation Activities in the Latin Kingdom of Jerusalem*, in *Revue Belge de Philologie et d'Histoire* (1951)
RICHARD, J. *Croisés, Missionaires et Voyageurs* (1983, London)
SIMON, A.L. *The History of the Wine Trade in England* (1906-9, London)

CHAPTER 15
ADAMS, L.D. *The Wines of America* (1985, New York)
BENNASSAR, B. *Valladolid au Siècle d'Or* (1967, Paris)
BETHELL, L. *Cambridge History of Latin America, Vol I* (1984, Cambridge)
BRAUDEL, F. *The Mediterranean and the Mediterranean World in the Age of Philip II* (1972, London)
CHILDS, W. *Anglo-Castilian Trade in the Later Middle Ages* (1978, Manchester)
CUSHNER, N.P. *Lords of the Land* (1980, Albany NY)
FRANCIS, A.D. *The Wine Trade* (1972, London)
GUERRERO, R. *Notes sur un Vignoble Vieux de Quatre Siècles: le Chili Mediterranéen*, in *Géographie Historique des Vignobles* (ed A. Huetz de Lemps)
HUETZ DE LEMPS, A. *Vignobles et Vins du Nord-Ouest de l'Espagne* (1967, Bordeaux)
LIVERMORE, H.V. *A New History of Portugal* (1976, Cambridge)
LYNCH, J. *Spain Under the Hapsburgs, Vol II, Spain and America 1598-1700* (1981, Oxford)
MACKAY, A. *Spain in the Middle Ages* (1977, London)
O'CALLAGHAN *A History of Medieval Spain* (1975, Ithaca)
READ, J. *Wines of Spain* (1982, London); *Wines of Portugal* (1982, London)
SIMON, A.L. *The History of the Wine Trade in England* (1906-9, London)
STANISLAWSKI, D. *Tabla de las Ordenanzas Nuevas Hechas por Valladolid Contenidas en Este Volumen* Privately translated by Maite Manjon
TORRES, M. *The Distinctive Wine of Catalonia* (1986, Barcelona)
VASSBERG, D. *Land and Society in Golden Age Castile* (1984, Cambridge)

CHAPTER 16
CONNELL SMITH, G. *Forerunners of Drake* (1954, London)
GONZALEZ-GORDON, M.M. *Sherry, the Noble Wine* (1972, London)
JEFFS, J. *Sherry* (1982, London)
SIMON, A.L. *The History of the Wine Trade in England* (1906-9, London)
UDEN, G. *Drake at Cadiz* (1969, London)

CHAPTER 17
BRAUDEL, F. *The Structures of Everyday Life* (1981, London)
BRINDLEY, J.H. *The History and Commerce of Coffee* (1926, London)
DARBY, W.J. *Wine and Medical Wisdom Through the Ages*, in *Wine, Health and Society* (1982, San Francisco)
ELLIS, A. *The Penny Universities* (1956, London)
HARRISON, W. *Description of England* (1586)
MONTAIGNE, *The Complete Works of Montaigne, Essays, Travel Journals, Letters* (translated by D.M. Frame) (1965, London)
REDI, F. *Bacco in Toscana* translated by Leigh Hunt (1825, London)
WILBRAHAM, A. *The Englishman's Food* (1957, London)

CHAPTER 18
CRAWFORD, D. *Journals of Sir John Lauder, Lord Fountainhall* (1900, Edinburgh)
DELAMAIN, R. *Histoire du Cognac* (1935, Paris)
DION, R. *Histoire de la Vigne et du Vin en France* (1959, Paris)
ENJALBERT, H. *Aux Origines du Cognac*, in *Eaux-de-Vie et Spiritueux* (eds A. Huetz de Lemps & P. Roudie) (1985, Paris)
LACHIVER, M. *Vins, Vignes et Vignerons* (1988, Paris)
MCNULTY, R.H. *Common Beverage Bottles, Their Production, Use and Forms in Seventeenth and Eighteenth Century Netherlands*, in *Journal of Glass Studies, XIII* (1971)
PIJASSOU, R. *Un Grand Vignoble de Qualité: Le Médoc* (1980, Paris)
SCHAMA, S. *The Embarrassment of Riches* (1987, London)
ZUMTHOR, P *Daily Life in Rembrandt's Holland* (1962, London)

CHAPTER 19
BARRELET, J. *La Verrerie en France de l'Epoque Gallo-Romaine à Nos Jours* (1954, Paris)
CHARLESTON, R.J. *English Glass and the Glass Used in England Circa 400-1940* (1984, London)
DUMBRELL, R. *Understanding Antique Wine Bottles* (1983, Woodbridge, Suffolk)
GODFREY, E.S. *The Development of English Glassmaking 1560-1640* (1975, Oxford)
HARRISON, W. *Description of England* (1586)
KLEIN, D. & LLOYD, W. *The History of Glass* (1984, London)
MCKEARIN, H. *Notes on Stopping, Bottling and Binning*, in *Journal of Glass Studies* (1971)
MCNULTY, R.H. *Common Beverage Bottles, Their Production, Use and Forms in Seventeenth and Eighteenth Century Netherlands*, in *Journal of Glass Studies, XIII* (1971)
MARIACHER *Italian Blown Glass from Ancient Rome to Venice* (1961, London)
PETERSSON, R.T. *Sir Kenelm Digby: The Ornament of England* (1956, London)
RUGGLES-BRISE, S.M.E. *Sealed Bottles* (1949, London)

CHAPTER 20
DION, R. *Histoire de la Vigne et du Vin en France* (1959, Paris)
ENJALBERT, H. *Comment Naissent les Grands Crus: Bordeaux, Oporto, Cognac*, in *Annales E.S.C.* (1953)
FRANCIS, A.D. *The Wine Trade* (1972, London)
GINESTET, B. *Margaux* (1984, Paris)

HIGOUNET, C. *La Seigneurie et le Vignoble de Château Latour* (1974, Bordeaux); *Histoire de Bordeaux* (1980, Toulouse)

HUETZ DE LEMPS, A. *Géographie du Commerce de Bordeaux à la Fin du Règne de Louis XIV* (1975, Paris); Le Commerce Maritime des Vins d'Aquitaine de 1698 à 1716, in *Revue Historique de Bordeaux* (1965)

LOUGH, J. (ed) *Locke's Travels in France 1675-9* (1953, Cambridge)

MASSE, P. Le Dessèchement des Marais du Bas-Médoc, in *Revue Historique de Bordeaux* (1957)

PIJASSOU, R. *Un Grand Vignoble de Qualite: Le Médoc* (1980, Paris)

ROBERTS, L. *The Merchants' Mappe of Commerce* (1638, Amsterdam)

C H A P T E R 2 1

BONAL, F. *Le Livre d'Or de Champagne* (1984, Lausanne)

DION, R. *Histoire de la Vigne et du Vin en France* (1959, Paris)

DUMAY, R. *La Mort du Vin* (1976, Paris); (ed) *Le Vin de Champagne* (1977, Paris)

FAITH, N. *The Story of Champagne* (1988, London)

FORBES, P. *Champagne* (1967, London)

GANDILHON, R. *Naissance du Champagne* (1968, Paris)

LACHIVER, M. *Vins, Vignes et Vignerons* (1988, Paris)

NOLLEVALLE, J. *Aÿ en Champagne: un Bourg Viticole à la Fin de l'Ancien Régime* (1984, Aÿ)

RHODES, A. *Princes of the Grape* (1975, London)

SIMON, A. *The History of Champagne* (1962, London)

SPALATIN, K. *Saint-Evremond* (1934, Zagreb)

STEVENSON, T. *Champagne* (1986, London)

C H A P T E R 2 2

AMES, R. *The Search After Claret* (1691, London)

BRADFORD, S. *The Story of Port, the Englishman's Wine* (1983, London)

ENJALBERT, H. Comment Naissent les Grand Crus: Bordeaux, Oporto, Cognac, in *Annales E.S.C.* (1953)

FISHER, H.E.S. *The Portugal Trade 1770-1770* (1971, London)

GUICHARD, F. & ROUDIE, P. *Vins, Vignerons et Coopérateurs* (1985, Paris)

MACAULAY, R. *They Came to Portugal* (1946, London)

SIMON, A. *Port* (1934, London)

SMITH, J.A. *Memoirs of the Marquis of Pombal* (1843, London)

C H A P T E R 2 3

GUNYON, R.E.H. *The Wines of Central and South-Eastern Europe* (1971, London)

HALASZ, Z. *The Book of Hungarian Wines* (1981, Budapest)

HENDERSON, A. *The History of Ancient and Modern Wines* (1824, London)

KOMOROCZY, G. *Borkivitelunk Eszak Fele* (1944, Kassa/Kosice)

SZABO, J. & TOROK, S. *Album of the Tokay-Hegyalja* (1867, Tokay)

WELLMANN, I. Communautés de Viticulteurs dans la Hongrie des XVIIe au XVIIIe Siècles, in *La Pensée* (1974)

C H A P T E R 2 4

BURMAN, J. *Wine of Constantia* (1979, Cape Town)

DE JONGH, F. *Encyclopaedia of South African Wine* (1981, Durban)

JULLIEN, A. *Topographie de Tous les Vignobles Connus* (1816, Paris)

KENCH, J., HANDS, P. & HUGHES, D. *The Complete Book of South African Wine* (1983, Cape Town)

LEIPOLDT, C.L. *Three Hundred Years of Cape Wine* (1946, Cape Town)

SIMON, A.L. *Bottlescrew Days* (1926, London)

C H A P T E R 2 5

COSSART, N. *Madeira* (1984, London)

DUNCAN, T.B. *Atlantic Islands: Madeira, the Azores and the Cape Verdes in 17th-Century Commerce and Navigation* (1972, Chicago)

FRANCIS, A.D. *The Wine Trade* (1972, London)

VIZETELLY, H. *Facts About Port and Madeira* (1880, London)

WEIR MITCHELL, S. *A Madeira Party* (1975, reprint Sacramento)

C H A P T E R 2 6

BUTEL, P. & POUSSOU, J.P. *La Vie Quotidienne à Bordeaux au XVIII Siècle* (1980, Paris)

DETHIER, J. (ed.) *Châteaux Bordeaux* (1988, Editions du Centre Georges Pompidou, Paris)

ENJALBERT, H. *Great Bordeaux Wines: St-Emilion, Pomerol and Fronsac* (1985, Paris)

FAITH, N. *The Winemasters* (1978, London)

FORSTER, R. The Noble Wine Producers of the Bordelais in the Eighteenth Century, in *Economic History Review* (1961)

HIGOUNET, C. *Histoire de Bordeaux* (1980, Toulouse)

LACHIVER, M. *Vins, Vignes et Vignerons* (1988, Paris)

OLNEY, R. *Yquem* (1985, Paris)

PIJASSOU, R. *Un Grand Vignoble de Qualite: Le Médoc* (1980, Paris); Les Grands Régisseurs et la Naissance des Vins Fins de Bordeaux, in *Etudes Géographiques Offerts à Louis Papy* (1978, Bordeaux)

REDEUILH Notes sur l'Ancienneté de la Méthode des Vendanges Tardives et des tries' en Sauternais, in *Vins et Vignobles d'Aquitaine; Actes 20e Congres Fédération Historique de Sud-Ouest* (1970, Bordeaux)

de TREVILLE LAWRENCE, R. (ed) *Jefferson and Wine* (1989, Virginia)

YOUNG, Arthur *Travels During the Years 1787, 1788 and 1789* (1792, Bury St Edmunds)

C H A P T E R 2 7

ARNOUX, C. *Dissertation sur la Situation de la Bourgogne* (1728, London); *New and Familiar Phrases and Dialogues in French and English* (1761, London)

BAZIN, J-F. *Le Clos de Vougeot* (1987, Paris)

COURTEPEE, C. & BEGUILLET *Description Générale et Particulière du Duché de Bourgogne* (1775-88, Dijon)

DELISSEY, J. & PERRIAUX, L. Les Courtiers-Gourmets de la Ville de Beaune (XVI-XVIII Siècle), in *Annales de Bourgogne* (1962)

DION, R. *Histoire de la Vigne et du Vin en France* (1959, Paris)

GADILLE, R. *Le Vignoble de la Côte Bourguignonne* (1967, Paris)

LACHIVER, M. *Vins, Vignes et Vignerons* (1988, Paris)

RICHARD, J. *Histoire de la Bourgogne* (1978, Toulouse)

C H A P T E R 2 8

BERGER, A. & MAUREL, F. *La Viticulture et l'Economie du Languedoc du XVIIe Siècle à Nos Jours* (1980, Montpellier)

CHARPENTIER, L. *Le Mystère du Vin* (1981, Paris)

DION, R. *Histoire de la Vigne et du Vin en France* (1959, Paris)

GALTIER, G. *Le Vignoble du Languedoc Mediterranéen et du Roussillon* (1960, Montpellier)

LACHIVER, M. *Vins, Vignes et Vignerons* (1988, Paris)

WOLFF, C. *Riquewihr: Son Vignoble et ses Vins à Travers les Ages* (1967, Ingersheim)

YOUNG, A. *Travels during the Years 1787, 1788 and 1789* (1792, Bury St Edmunds)

C H A P T E R 2 9

ARNZT, H. *Aus der Geschichte des Deutschen Weinhandels* (1964, Wiesbaden)

BUSCH, J. *Der Eberbacher Cabinetkeller 1730-1803* (1981, Wiesbaden)

CHRISTOFFEL, K. *Durch die Zeiten Stromt der Wein* (1957, Hamburg)

de TREVILLE LAWRENCE, R. (ed) *Jefferson and Wine* (1989, Virginia)

EISINGER, J. Lead and Wine: Eberhard Gockel and the Colica Pictonum, in *Medical History* (1982)

KALINKE, K. *Der Rheingau, Weinkulturzentrum Gestern, Heute und Morgen* (1969, Wiesbaden)

PRO-RIESLING: Verein zur Forderung der Riesling-Kultur *Der Riesling und seine Weine* (1986, Trier)

SCHREIBER, G. *Deutsche Weingeschichte* (1980, Bonn)

STAAB, J. *Beitrage zur Geschichte des Rheingauer Weinbaus* (1970, Wiesbaden)

C H A P T E R 3 0

BAKER, C.H.C. *The Life and Circumstances of James Brydges, First Duke of Chandos* (1949, Oxford)

BARTY-KING, H. *Tradition of English Wine* (1977, Oxford)

BUTLER, R. & WALKING, G. *The Book of Wine*

Antiques (1986, Woodbridge, Suffolk)
CARTER, E.H. & MEARS, R.A.F. *The History of England* (1948, Oxford)
HENDERSON, A. *The History of Ancient and Modern Wines* (1824, London)
HERVEY, S.H.A. *The Diary of John Hervey, First Earl of Bristol* (1894)
HUGHES, W. *The Compleat Vineyard* (1670, London)
FRANCIS, A.D. *The Wine Trade* (1972, London)
KAY, B. & MACLEAN, C. *Knee Deep in Claret* (1983, Edinburgh)
MENDELSOHN, O. *Drinking with Pepys* (1963, London)
MURDOCH, T. (ed) *The Quiet Conquest* (1985, London)
PLUMB, J.H. *Sir Robert Walpole* (1956, London); *Men and Places* (1963, London)
SALISBURY ARCHIVES Courtesy of the Marquess of Salisbury
SCOTT THOMPSON, G. *Life in a Noble Household* (1937, London)
SIMON, A.L. *Bottlescrew Days* (1926, London)
WEINREB, B. & HIBBERT, C. *The London Encyclopaedia* (1983, London)
WILBRAHAM, A. *The Englishman's Food* (1957, London)

CHAPTER 31

BARRY, Sir E. *Observations Historical, Critical and Medical on the Wines of the Ancients* (1775, London)
CHAPTAL, J.A. *Traité Théorique et Pratique sur la Culture de la Vigne* (1801, Milan)
FLOURENS, M. *Eloge Historique de Jean-Antoine Chaptal* (1835, Paris)
FRANCIS, A.D. *The Wine Trade* (1972, London)
GABLER, J. *Wine into Words* (1985, Baltimore)
HENDERSON, A. *The History of Ancient and Modern Wines* (1824, London)
JULLIEN, A. *Topographie de Tous les Vignobles Connus* (1816, Paris); *Manual du Sommelier* (1822, Paris)
LACHIVER, M. *Vins, Vignes et Vignerons* (1988, Paris)
LOEB, O.W. & PRITTIE, T. *Moselle* (1972, London)
MACK, SMITH D. *A History of Sicily: Modern Sicily After 1713* (1968, London)
REDDING, C. *A History and Description of Modern Wines* (1833, London)
RHODES, A. *Princes of the Grape* (1975, London)
de SERRES, O. *Le Théâtre d'Agriculture et le Mesnage des Champs* (1804 edn)
WYNNE-THOMAS, R.J.L. Relics of the Marsala Wine Trade, in *The Connoisseur* (1975)
YOUNG, A. *Travels During the Years 1787, 1788 and 1789* (1792, Bury St Edmunds)

CHAPTER 32

BRADFORD, S. *The Story of Port, the Englishman's Wine* (1983, London)
BUSBY, J *Journal of a Tour Through Some of the Vineyards of Spain and France* (1833, Sydney)
CRAWFORD, A. *Bristol and the Wine Trade* (1984, Bristol)
DELAFORCE, J. *The Factory House at Oporto* (1983, London)
FORRESTER, J. *Proceedings at the Meeting Held at Pezo-da-Regoa, 8th October 1844* (1844); *Observations on the Attempts to Reform the Abuses Practised in Portugal in the Making and Treating of Port Wine* (1845, Edinburgh)
FRANCIS, A.D. *The Wine Trade* (1972, London)
GONZALEZ BYASS & CO. LTD. *Old Sherry* (1935, London)
GONZALEZ-GORDON, M.M. *Sherry, the Noble Wine* (1972, London)
JEFFS, J. *Sherry* (1982, London)
JULLIEN, A. *Topographie de Tous les Vignobles Connus* (1816, Paris)
MACAULAY, R. *They Came to Portugal* (1946, London)

CHAPTER 33

BONAL, F. *Le Livre d'Or du Champagne* (1984, Lausanne)
de CHIMAY, J. *The Life and Times of Madame Veuve Clicquot Ponsardin* (1961, Reims)
FORBES, P. *Champagne* (1967, London)
HENDERSON, A. *The History of Ancient and Modern Wines* (1824, London)
JULLIEN, A. *Topographie de Tous les Vignobles Connus* (1816, Paris)
REDDING, C. *A History and Description of Modern Wines* (1833, London)

SUTCLIFFE, S. *A Celebration of Champagne* (1988, London)
VIZETELLY, H. *A History of Champagne* (1882, London)

CHAPTER 34

BENWELL, W.S. *Journey to Wine in Victoria* (1960, Carlton)
BISHOP, G.C. *Australian Wine-Making, the Roseworthy Influence* (1988, Adelaide)
BUSBY, J. *Journal of a Tour etc; Treatise on the Culture of the Vine* (1825, Sydney); *Manual for Vineyards and Making Wine* (1830, Sydney)
HALLIDAY, J. *The Australian Wine Companion* (1985, Sydney)
HUGHES, R. *The Fatal Shore* (1987, London)
HYAMS, E. *Dionysus: A Social History of the Wine Vine* (1965, London)
LAKE, M. *Classic Wines of Australia* (1967, Melbourne)

CHAPTER 3·5

ADAMS, L.D. *The Wines of America* (1985, New York)
CAROSSO, V. *The California Wine Industry 1830-1895* (1951, Berkeley)
de TREVILLE LAWRENCE, R. (ed) *Jefferson and Wine* (1989, Virginia)
FEY CRONISE, T. *The Natural Wealth of California* (1868)
FREDERICKSEN, P. The Authentic Haraszthy Story, in *Wines and Vines* (1947)
HARASZTHY, A. *Grape Culture, Wines and Winemaking* (1862, New York)
JORE, L. Le Bordelais Jean-Louis Vignes: Pionnier de la Viticulture en Californie, in *Revue Historique de Bordeaux* (1959)
LAMBERT-GOCS, M. On the Trail of the Zinfandel, in *Journal of Gastronomy* (1986)
MCKEE, I. Early California Wine Growers, in *California, Magazine of the Pacific* (1947); Early California Wine Commerce, in *Wine Review* (1947); The Beginnings of California Winegrowing, in *Quarterly Historical Society of S. California* (1947); Jean-Louis Vignes, California's Pioneer Winegrower, in *Wine Review* (1948); Vallejo, Pioneer Sonoma Wine Grower, in *California, Magazine of the Pacific* (1948); Early California Wine Dealers, in *Wines and Vines* (1950)
MUSCATINE, D., THOMPSON, B. & AMERINE, M.A. (eds) *Book of California Wine* (1984, Berkeley & London)
SCHOENMAN, T. (ed) *Father of California Wine: Agoston Haraszthy* (1979, Santa Barbara)
TEISER, R. & HARROUN, C. *Wine-Making in California* (1983, New York)
THOMPSON, B. & JOHNSON, H. *The California Wine Book* (1976, New York)

CHAPTER 36

DETHIER, J. (ed.) *CHATEAUX BORDEAUX* (1988, Editions du Centre Georges Pompidou, Paris)
COCKS, C. *Bordeaux: its Wines and the Claret Country* (1846, London)
ENJALBERT, H. *Great Bordeaux Wines: St-Emilion, Pomerol and Fronsac* (1985, Paris)
GADILLE, R. *Le Vignoble de la Côte Bourguignonne* (1967, Paris)
GINESTET, B. *Margaux* (1984, Paris); *Pomerol* (1984, Paris)
HARASZTHY, A. *Grape Culture, Wines and Winemaking* (1862, New York)
HIGOUNET, C. *Histoire de Bordeaux* (1980, Toulouse)
JULLIEN, A. *Topographie de Tous les Vignobles Connus* (1816, Paris)
LACHIVER, M. *Vins, Vignes et Vignerons* (1988, Paris)
LAURENT, R. *Les Vignerons de la Côte d'Or* (1975, Dijon)
LOUBERE, L. *The Red and the White* (1978, New York)
PAGUIERRE, M. *Classification et Description des Vins de Bordeaux* (1829, Edinburgh)
PENNING-ROWSELL, E. *The Wines of Bordeaux* (1969, London)
PIJASSOU, R. *Un Grand Vignoble de Qualité: Le Médoc* (1980, Paris)
ROUDIE, P. *Vignobles et Vignerons du Bordelais 1850-1980* (1988 Paris)
YOXALL, H.W. *The Wines of Burgundy* (1968, London)

C H A P T E R 3 7

AMBROSI, H. & BECKER, H. *Der Deutsche Wein* (1978, Munich)
ARNZT, H. *Aus der Geschichte des Deutschen Weinhandels* (1964, Wiesbaden)
BASSERMANN-JORDAN, F. *Geschichte des Weinbaus Unter Besonderer Berucksichtigung der Bayerisches Rheinpfalz* (1907, Frankfurt)
COUTAZ, G. *Les 450 Vendanges des Vignobles de la Ville de Lausanne* (1987, Lausanne)
GUNYON, R.E.H. *The Wines of Central and South-Eastern Europe* (1971, London)
HALASZ, Z. *The Book of Hungarian Wines* (1981, Budapest)
HALLGARTEN, S.F. & HALLGARTEN, F.L. *Wines and Wine Gardens of Austria* (1979, London)
HARASZTHY, A. *Grape Culture, Wines and Winemaking* (1862, New York)
JULLIEN, A. *Topographie de Tous les Vignobles Connus* (1816, Paris)
LANGENBACH, A. *German Wines and Vines* (1962, London)
LOEB, O.W. & PRITTIE, T. *Moselle* (1972, London)
PIGOTT, S. *Life Beyond Liebfraumilch* (1988, London)
PRO-RIESLING: *Verein zur Forderung der Riesling-Kultur, Der Riesling und seine Weine* (1986, Trier)
REDDING, C. *A History and Description of Modern Wines* (1833, London)
RHODES, A. *Princes of the Grape* (1975, London)
SICHEL, P.M.F. *The Wines of Germany* (1980, New York)
STAAB, J. *Beitrage zur Geschichte des Rheingauer Weinbaus* (1970, Wiesbaden)

C H A P T E R 3 8

BERGER, A. & MAUREL, F. *La Viticulture et l'Economie du Languedoc du XVIIe Siècle à Nos Jours* (1980, Montpellier)
BONAL, F. *Le Livre d'Or du Champagne* (1984, Lausanne)
CUNY, H. *Louis Pasteur* (1965, London)
GALTIER, G. *Le Vignoble du Languedoc Mediterranéen et du Roussillon* (1960, Montpellier)
GRANETT, J., GOHEEN, A.C. & LIDER, L.A. Phylloxera in California, in *California Agriculture* (1987)
ISNARD, H. *La Vigne en Algerie* (1955, Gap)
LACHIVER, M. *Vins, Vignes et Vignerons* (1988, Paris)
LAURENT, R. *Les Vignerons de la Côte d'Or* (1975, Dijon)
LOUBERE, L. *The Red and the White* (1978, New York)
ORDISH, G. *The Great Wine Blight* (1972, London)
PASTEUR, L. *Etude sur le Vin* (1866, Paris)
PIJASSOU, R. *Un Grand Vignoble de Qualite: Le Médoc* (1980, Paris)
PLANCHON, J.E. *Les Vignes Americaines* (1875, Paris)

C H A P T E R 3 9

ANDERSON, B. *Vino: the Wines and Wine-Makers of Italy* (1980, Boston); *Biondi Santi* (1988, Florence)
BELFRAGE, N. *Life Beyond Lambrusco* (1987, London)
CERLETTI, C.B. *Notes sur l'Industrie et le Commerce du Vin en Italie* (1889)
FLOWER, R. *Chianti* (1978 London)
JULLIEN, A. *Topographie de Tous les Vignobles Connus* (1816, Paris)
LOUBERE, L. *The Red and the White* (1978, New York)
PELLUCCI, E. *Il Brunello di Montalcino* (1979, Fiesole)
RATTI, R. *Guida ai Vini del Piemonte* (1977, Turin)

C H A P T E R 4 0

DUIJKER, H. *The Wines of Rioja* (1988, London)
FORD, R. *A Handbook for Travellers in Spain* (1847, London)
HENDERSON, A. *The History of Ancient and Modern Wines* (1824, London)
HUETZ DE LEMPS, A. *Vignobles et Vins du Nord-Ouest de l'Espagne* (1967, Bordeaux)
JULLIEN, A. *Topographie de Tous les Vignobles Connus* (1816, Paris)
LLANO GOROSTIZA, M. *Los Vinos de Rioja* (1974, Bilbao)
LORD, T. *The New Wines of Spain* (1988, London)
READ, J. *Wines of the Rioja* (1984, London); *Wines of Spain* (1982, London); *Chilean Wines* (1988, London)
TORRES, M. *The Distinctive Wine of Catalonia* (1986, Barcelona)

C H A P T E R 4 1

ADAMS, L.D. *The Wines of America* (1985, New York)
ADAMS. L.D. *Revitalizing the California Wine Industry* (An interview conducted by Ruth Teiser) (1974, Berkeley)
BONAL, F. *Le Livre d'Or de Champagne* (1984, Lausanne)
FORBES, P. *Champagne* (1967, London)
Institut National d'Appellation d'Origine *Une Réussite Française: l'Appellation d'Origine Contrôlée* (1985, Paris)
LACHIVER, M. *Vins, Vignes et Vignerons* (1988, Paris)
MUSCATINE, D., THOMPSON, B., AMERINE, M.A., *Book of California Wine* (1984, Berkeley & London)
PIJASSOU, R. *Un Grand Vignoble de Qualité: le Médoc* (1980, Paris)
ROUDIE, P. *Vignobles et Vignerons du Bordelais 1850-1980* (1988, Paris)
SAINTSBURY, G. *Notes on a Cellar Book* (1920, London)
SIMON, A.L. *By Request* (1957, London)

C H A P T E R 4 2

ADAMS, L.D. *The Wines of America* (1985, New York)
AMERINE, M.A. et al *Technology of Winemaking* (1980, Westport)
BISHOP, G.C. *Australian Wine-Making, the Roseworthy Influence* (1988, Adelaide)
COOPER, M. *The Wines and Vineyards of New Zealand* (1985, Auckland)
EVANS, L. et al *Complete book of Australian Wine* (1978, Sydney)
HALLIDAY, J. *The Australian Wine Companion* (1985, Sydney)
MEREDITH, E.J. *The Wines and Wineries of America's Northwest* (1986, Kirkland)
MUSCATINE et al *Book of California Wine* (1984, Berkeley & London)
SCHUBERT, M. et al *The Rewards of Patience* (1980, Adelaide)
TCHELISTCHEFF, A. *Grapes, Wine and Ecology* (An interview conducted by Ruth Teiser and Catherine Harroun) (1983, Berkeley)
THOMPSON, B. *Notes on a California Cellar Book* (1988, New York)
THOMPSON, B. & JOHNSON, H. *The California Wine Book* (1976, New York)

Among those many people whose personal communications have helped me in this work I particularly want to acknowledge and thank Leon Adams, Dr. Hans Ambrosi, Prof. Maynard A. Amerine, Burton Anderson, Marchese Piero Antinori, Prof. Dr. Helmut Arnzt, Nan Ashcroft, David Balls, Paul Bartlet, Anthony Barton, Ghislaine Bavoillot, Dr. Helmut Becker, Alexis Bespaloff, Madame Lalou Bize-Leroy, Christian Bizot, Trudy Bolter, Claude Bouchard, Jean-Michel Boursiquot, Bernhard Breuer, Michael Broadbent, Brian Buckingham, Tucker Catlin, Louis-Marc Chevignard; Sybil, Lady Cholmondeley; Darrell Corti, Frère Jean de la Croix, Brian Croser, Elizabeth David, Jack & Jamie Davies, Georgina Denison, Don José-Ignacio Domecq, Robert Drouhin, Michael Druitt, Hubrecht Duijker, Terry Dunleavy, João Enriques, Len Evans, Charles Eve, Dereck Foster, Marchesi Leonardo de' Frescobaldi, John Gano, Michael Gill, Don Mauricio Gonzales Gordon Diaz, Garry & Marlies Grosvenor, James Halliday, Comte Louis d'Harcourt, Sir James Hardy, Hon. Alan Hare, Heino Heine, Russell Hone, Ian Jamieson, Alois Lageder, Max Lake, Miles Lambert-Gócs, Michel Laroche, Robert Lautel, Daniel Lawton, Prof. Noel Leneuf, The late Alexis Lichine, John Lipitch, Signora Lungarotti, Comte Alexandre de Lur Saluces, Catherine Manac'h, Antonio Mastroberardino, John Mariani, Graf Erwein Matuschka-Greiffenclau, Yvette Maurin, Dr. Franz Werner Michel, Robert Mondavi, Dr. Leonardo Montemiglio, William J. Morris III, Duc & Duchesse de Mouchy, Christian Moueix, Jean-Pierre Moueix, Prof. Kirby Moulton, Dr. Robert Parsons, Pierre Poupon, Eric Purbrick, Alain Querre, Christopher Ralling, Don Manuel Raventos, Jan and Maite Read, Baron Bettino Ricasoli, Riccardo Riccardi, Ezio Rivella, Jancis Robinson, Prof. Philippe Roudié, Baron Eric de Rothschild, Baroness Philippine de Rothschild, The Marquess of Salisbury, Prinz Michael zu Salm, Wolfgang Schleicher, The late Frank Schoonmaker, Peter A. Sichel, Peter M.F. Sichel, The late André L. Simon, Ghislaine Simon, Prof. Vernon Singleton, Dr. Walter Somerville, Quentin Stanham, Shizuo Suzuki, James Symington, Michael Symington, Paul Symington, Pierre Tari, André Tchelistcheff, Bob and Harolyn Thompson, John and Janet Trefethen, Shizuo Tsuji, Peter and Sue Vinding-Diers, Comte Alain de Vogüe, Shimshon Welner, Nina Wemyss, William Wildman, Hiruki Yamagata.